Dan Fox

SAMS Teach Yourself

ADO.NET

in 21 Days

SAMS

201 West 103rd St., Indianapolis, Indiana, 46290 USA

Sams Teach Yourself ADO.NET in 21 Days

Copyright © 2002 by Sams Publishing

International Standard Book Number: 0-67232-386-9

Library of Congress Catalog Card Number: 2001099342

Printed in the United States of America

First Printing: July 2002

05   04   03   02   4   3   2   1

Trademarks

Warning and Disclaimer

EXECUTIVE EDITOR
Michael Stephens

ACQUISITIONS EDITOR
Kim Spilker
Sondra Scott

DEVELOPMENT EDITOR
Shannon Leuma

MANAGING EDITOR
Charlotte Clapp

PROJECT EDITOR
Elizabeth Finney

PRODUCTION EDITOR
Michael Henry

INDEXER
Sandra Henselmeier

PROOFREADER
Abby VanHuss

TECHNICAL EDITOR
Chris Thibodeaux
Doug Ellis

TEAM COORDINATOR
Lynne Williams

MULTIMEDIA DEVELOPER
Dan Scherf

INTERIOR DESIGNER
Gary Adair

COVER DESIGNER
Aren Howell

PAGE LAYOUT
Cheryl Lynch
Michelle Mitchell

Contents at a Glance

Table of Contents

About the Author

Dan Fox is a Technical Director for Quilogy in Overland Park, Kansas. Quilogy (www.quilogy.com) is a leading Microsoft Gold Certified Partner and Solution Provider.

Dan is a Microsoft Certified Solutions Developer, Systems Engineer, and Trainer who has been a consultant, instructor, and managing consultant on a variety of projects. In his role as a Technical Director, Dan provides technical guidance to Quilogy's consultants and customers.

Before joining Quilogy in 1995, Dan worked for Chevron in Houston, Texas, and the National Association of Insurance Commissioners in Kansas City, Missouri. Dan got his B.S. in computer science from Iowa State University in 1991.

Dan has been a columnist for *.NET Magazine* and a frequent contributor to the *Visual Basic Programmer's Journal* and *Visual Studio Magazine* and has written numerous articles for *SQL Server Magazine*, Advisor journals, *MSDN Magazine*, and InformIT.com. He authored the books *Building Distributed Applications with Visual Basic .NET* and *Pure Visual Basic* from Sams and coauthored a book on the Visual Basic 6 Distributed Exam (70-175) for Certification Insider Press. He has spoken at TechEd and several Developer Days conferences and Microsoft events.

Dan, with his ever-patient wife, Beth, and two young daughters, Laura and Anna, lives in Shawnee, Kansas, where as another spring arrives hope is renewed for a Cubs victory in the Fall Classic.

About the Technical Editors

Doug Ellis has worked in the software business for more than 15 years. He graduated from Indiana University with a degree in accounting, and obtained his CPA and MBA while working in various Fortune 500 finance roles. His finance background led him to the accounting software market, where he assisted clients in selecting and implementing various accounting packages. It was through these projects that Doug began to provide custom database programming for multi-user applications. His experience expanded into network implementation for Novell networks and Windows NT, leading him to obtain his Microsoft Certified Professional status including SQL administration. Doug is currently a Technology Manager for Cognos, an international business intelligence software developer focusing on the Fortune 2000 market. He has done extensive work with both Microsoft SQL and SQL Server Analysis Services, Microsoft's OLAP platform.

Chris Thibodeaux, MCSE+I, MCDBA, MCSD, is the Principal Consultant of Empowering Solutions, Inc., a management and technology consultancy in southern California. His primary areas of expertise are in both systems and database architecture. Chris teaches SQL database design, Web database management, and Internet/intranet security at a local community college near his home.

Dedication

To Beth, my best friend, who has (to quote John Adams) "always softened and warmed my heart" and who "shall restore my benevolence as well as my health and tranquility of mind."

Acknowledgments

First, I'd to thank the tag-team editors on this project at Sams, Sondra Scott and Kim Spilker. Both helped to make the project go smoothly from the initial concept right up until publication, and for that I am grateful. And as with the last book I wrote, Development Editor Shannon Leuma did a wonderful job in making sure that the content was consistent, well organized, and that the elements used in the book were the correct ones. I'm also indebted to production editor Mike Henry and the two technical editors, Doug Ellis and Chris Thibodeaux, all of whom made suggestions and corrections that made both the written word and technical content better than I could have produced on my own. Finally, the content of the book was shaped through numerous reviews of the concept before I even signed on to the project. That feedback was instrumental in making sure the book was targeted to the correct audience and covered the proper material.

Although this book, as almost every other, was a team effort, any errors are only mine and so I welcome your e-mail at `dfox@quilogy.com` with corrections and suggestions.

As always, my family deserves most of the credit because they make sacrifices both large and small when I undertake a project like this one. And so to Beth, Laura, and Anna, I can only say thank you and pledge that you won't be the cobbler's family forever.

We Want to Hear from You!

As the reader of this book, *you* are our most important critic and commentator. We value your opinion and want to know what we're doing right, what we could do better, what areas you'd like to see us publish in, and any other words of wisdom you're willing to pass our way.

As an executive editor for Sams Publishing, I welcome your comments. You can email or write me directly to let me know what you did or didn't like about this book—as well as what we can do to make our books better.

Please note that I cannot help you with technical problems related to the *topic* of this book. We do have a User Services group, however, where I will forward specific technical questions related to the book.

When you write, please be sure to include this book's title and author as well as your name, email address, and phone number. I will carefully review your comments and share them with the author and editors who worked on the book.

E-mail: feedback@samspublishing.com

Mail: Michael Stephens
            Executive Editor
            Sams Publishing
            201 West 103rd Street
            Indianapolis, IN 46290 USA

For more information about this book or another Sams Publishing title, visit our Web site at www.samspublishing.com. Type the ISBN (0672323869) or the title of the book in the Search field to find the page you're looking for.

Introduction

It is a capital mistake to theorize before one has data.

—Sherlock Holmes, "Scandal in Bohemia"

Just as in Holmes' chosen field of detection, retrieving and manipulating data is a prerequisite for building modern business applications. This explains why ADO.NET, Microsoft's data access technology for the .NET Framework and Visual Studio .NET, is perhaps the most talked and written about, critiqued, and, I'd venture to say, important aspect of Microsoft's newly released developer suite of tools.

Understanding ADO.NET is critical to successfully developing the full range of .NET applications, from Windows Forms to ASP.NET Web Forms to XML Web Services, and in a nutshell is why this book exists. To put it simply, this book can be used as a guide for understanding not only the architecture and syntax of ADO.NET, but also how it can be used to build modern multi-tier applications.

The Structure of This Book

As with all books in the *Sams Teach Yourself in 21 Days* series, this book consists of three main sections (or weeks) of seven chapters (or days) each, and each week focuses on a different aspect of ADO.NET. During Week 1, you'll first get an overview of ADO.NET and focus on its design goals and its place in the history of data access technologies. You'll then drill down into the first of the two main ADO.NET components—the DataSet. During this week, you'll learn how to manipulate and employ the DataSet using the disconnected programming model that ADO.NET exposes to make building stateless and scalable applications easier.

Week 2 will focus on the members that make up the second major component of ADO.NET: the .NET Data Providers that communicate with data stores such as SQL Server and Oracle. Each day this week you'll focus on a different aspect of .NET Data Providers, and will be given plenty of hints and techniques for getting the most out of each set of objects.

Finally, Week 3 will be centered around using ADO.NET in the context of a multi-tier application. During the early part of the week, you'll learn how ADO.NET fits into each of the layers of a multi-tier application. The week will end with a discussion of performance and a look at the future.

By laying out the book in this way, I hope to provide you with a balance of concrete and theoretical information that enables you to start using ADO.NET immediately and appropriately.

Conventions Used in This Book

As with all books in the *Sams Teach Yourself in 21 Days* series, I've used a few conventions in this book that I hope will make it easier for you to learn about the topics we're discussing.

All the source code I've included in the book will appear in monospace font, and the larger, complete code will be called out in numbered listings. As with other books from Sams, you can download all the listings, as well as other relevant material, on the book's Web site at www.samspublishing.com by searching on my name, the title, or the ISBN. (This is also the place to look for errata that is corrected after publication.)

To call special attention to a topic, I've used the following in-text features:

Note

Notes offer you extra insight into a particular topic. They also indicate where you can go to find additional information about the topic at hand.

Tip

Tips give you special advice about the topic we're discussing.

Caution

Cautions alert you to common mistakes and pitfalls of a subject we're discussing.

Sidebars

Sidebars provide you with more information about a subject related to what we're discussing.

NEW TERM The New Term icon lets you know when I'm introducing a new term in the chapter.

ANALYSIS The Analysis icon (which usually follows a numbered code listing) indicates that I'll be discussing the code at length and offering insights as to how the particular code applies to topics discussed in the chapter.

Each day ends with a Workshop section. This section contains a quiz to help you remember the key concepts discussed during that day, as well as an exercise designed to enable you to try out your newly gained knowledge. I've left the instructions for each lab fairly vague by design so that you'll have to work through your own solution, although I also provide a possible solution. The exercises are designed not to take much time so that you're not bogged down in writing code for my sample scenario, and can instead focus on applying what you learn to your applications. After all, that's why you want to learn ADO.NET, right?

VB or C#?

This book includes code snippets and listings in either Visual Basic .NET (simply referred to as VB) or Visual C# .NET (C#). The tack I've taken is to alternate roughly the language used on each day. I include notes and parenthetical comments throughout the text to indicate differences in the coding practices for each language when the difference is significant enough that I thought it might cause confusion. I believe this approach is effective because it highlights the fact that the syntax that pertains to ADO.NET is for the most part identical between VB and C#. At the same time, it should serve to expose each language's adherents to the other language, and once again confirm that the most important aspects of programming in .NET are understanding how the common language runtime works and understanding the classes of the .NET Framework, such as those that comprise ADO.NET.

The Audience for and Purpose of This Book

I wrote this book primarily for developers who have developed applications using ADO 2.x or other Microsoft data access technologies. In addition, it places non-proportional emphasis on SQL Server (particularly SQL Server 2000) as the data store. This is the case because it's my view that many, if not most, developers who are moving to ADO.NET will at least be using SQL Server in addition to other data stores such as

Oracle. And, of course, my experience working for a Microsoft partner is primarily with SQL Server, so I can certainly speak to its integration with ADO.NET from first-hand knowledge rather than having to rely on third parties as I would have to do with other data stores.

You'll also notice that I make several references to my previous .NET book, *Building Distributed Applications with Visual Basic .NET* in notes and tips. Although I admit there's an aspect of self-promotion in play, that book goes more deeply into topics that are particular to the .NET Framework and common language runtime itself, whereas this book strives to stay focused on data and how to use ADO.NET. As a result, you'll often find more in-depth discussions of threading, delegates, garbage collection, and other issues in that book.

Finally, I wrote this book because I think ADO.NET as a technology is well suited to building modern Web-based and multi-tier applications. Its deep integration with XML, for example, makes it ideally suited for use in the brave new world of XML Web Services. Explicating its virtues in the *Sams Teach Yourself* series offers a unique approach to learning ADO.NET that's more interactive than a simple reference title, and yet isn't a bland tutorial of overly simplistic walkthroughs (my personal pet peeve with so many developer books). In any case, I hope you enjoy the book and I look forward to your feedback.

Dan Fox

Shawnee, Kansas

March 2001

WEEK 1

At a Glance

The goal of this week is to get you familiar with ADO.NET concepts and the ways in which you can use the `DataSet` object in disconnected scenarios. A basic understanding of managed execution and either VB or C# syntax in VS .NET is also recommended, although a short primer about managed code is given on Day 1.

This week is basically split into two sections. Days 1 and 2 provide the introduction and overview of ADO.NET. During these first two days, you'll learn about the history of Microsoft data access technologies and how ADO.NET was designed to further extend those models and to help developers avoid common mistakes. In addition, you'll be exposed to the integration of ADO.NET with VS .NET to get a feel for how VS .NET can be used to assist in the development of your applications.

In Days 3 through 7, you'll dig into the details of the `DataSet` object and explore how you can use it to select, find, view, and otherwise manipulate data. You'll also learn about its internal structure and the objects it contains, how changes to data are tracked, how derived `DataSet` classes can be generated and assist in development, and, finally, the ways in which the `DataSet` is based on and integrates with XML standards. At the end of the week, you should be totally comfortable with using a `DataSet` both graphically and programmatically to utilize the disconnected programming model in your applications.

1

2

3

4

5

6

7

DAY 1

ADO.NET in Perspective

Welcome to *Sams Teach Yourself ADO.NET in 21 Days*! I hope you find this book both informative and applicable as you embark on using .NET technologies to solve real business problems and build the next generation of enterprise applications. Today's goal is to familiarize you with ADO.NET, how it fits into both the history and evolution of data access in the Microsoft platform, and its place in Microsoft's .NET initiative as a whole.

Today you'll learn:

- The history and technologies used to access data
- The design goals of ADO.NET
- ADO.NET's architecture and context in the .NET Framework

Microsoft Data Access Technologies

NEW TERM   If you're a developer who's been working on the Microsoft platform for some time, you're probably painfully aware of the succession of data access technologies that have come down the pike. Although my intent is not to bring up any painful memories regarding conversions or compatibility, I do think it's important to revisit this past to see clearly where we're heading with ADO.NET and why it's important that we do so.

The Long Road to ADO.NET

In many respects, the data access libraries that have been issued from Redmond have followed the architectural trends in software development of the last decade. As the 1990s began, Microsoft released its version of SQL Server (a similar version based on the same code base was released by Sybase), and in doing so, it officially jumped into the world of client/server computing. As a result, Microsoft needed a way for Visual Basic and C developers to make calls to SQL Server and return result sets and other interesting things you can do with a relational database. To fill this gap, a library of code (actually a DLL) referred to as DB-Library was released. Later, the functionality of DB-Library was incorporated into a Visual Basic Custom Control (VBX) called VBSQL that allowed easier access for Visual Basic users.

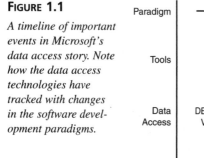

FIGURE 1.1

A timeline of important events in Microsoft's data access story. Note how the data access technologies have tracked with changes in the software development paradigms.

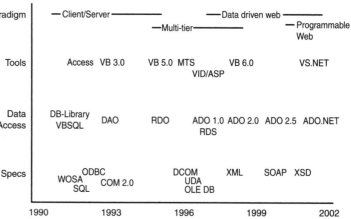

On a parallel track, Microsoft had developed a relational database product, called Access, for desktop and workgroup use. VB developers were clamoring for desktop data access, so in order for VB developers to programmatically manipulate Access databases, an API had to be developed. Data Access Objects (DAO) was released with VB 3.0 in 1993 and proved to be very popular. However, it was designed first and foremost as an API to use with the Access database engine (Jet), so its programming model included objects designed for manipulating Jet tables and queries directly through the `TableDef` and `QueryDef` objects, respectively. Results were returned using a `Recordset` object that could be populated in different ways depending on its initialization.

Data for the Masses

Although DB-Library allowed access to SQL Server and DAO was useful for Jet, the promise of client/server computing relied on interoperability—the ability to develop code that could be easily ported to run against a variety of relational database systems. This meant not having to use a different library and rewrite all your data access code. To address this issue, in the early 1990s, Microsoft was working to create the Open Database Connectivity (ODBC) standard. This standard incorporated Structured Query Language (SQL) and is based on, and is actually a superset of, the Call-Level Interface (CLI) specifications from X/Open and ISO/IEC. In addition, ODBC adheres to Microsoft's Windows Open Services Architecture (WOSA) model, which dictates that the API exposed to developers in a client application be held constant while the function-ality that differs must be abstracted into vendor-specific drivers.

> **Note**   Although sometimes confused as to its name (it's referred to as both Windows Open Systems Architecture and Windows Open Standards Architecture in Microsoft documents), Microsoft has used the WOSA design pattern successfully in a whole host of scenarios including messaging (MAPI), telephony (TAPI), networking (Windows Sockets library), and universal data access (OLE DB).

ODBC obviously became the de facto standard for relational database access and has now gone through several major releases, each adding additional functionality, such as a cursor library supporting scrollable cursors and connection pooling. In addition, ODBC drivers can now be found for scores of data sources. The success of ODBC meant that both Access and DAO gained the ability to connect to ODBC data sources and so, for VB developers, DAO could be used as the common data access API for both Jet and other data sources. Of course, ODBC also exposed its API through DLL functions, so C devel-opers, as well as intrepid VB developers, could use its functionality directly.

Although DAO could be used to access an ODBC data source, doing so often incurred extra overhead that decreased performance. Also, its object model was more complex than necessary for ODBC applications. To address these issues, Microsoft released Remote Data Objects (RDO) with VB 5.0 in 1996. RDO is mostly a lightweight object wrapper around the ODBC APIs. This resulted in increased performance while simplify-ing the object model for developers. In addition, as the name implies, RDO introduced the concept of disconnected or disassociated result sets through the use of its Client Batch Cursor Library. This allowed an `rdoResultset` object to be populated and then disassociated from a connection object so that the client application was free to make changes and then send them to the server at a later time.

Go Connectionless

Even though RDO supported disassociated result sets, up to this point the data access technologies were really built around the paradigm that the application would run in a continuously connected LAN environment and further, that the data access model was two-tier. In other words, the code that implemented the user interface (UI) would be making calls directly to the database and processing the results. This was central to client/server computing architectures using products such as PowerBuilder.

Two developments in the industry upset this apple cart: the adoption of multi-tiered architectures to create distributed applications and the use of the Internet for database-driven applications, both of which had gained popularity by 1995. Together, these events required that a new data access model be developed that was better designed to handle these new architectures.

NEW TERM In response, in 1996, Microsoft introduced its Universal Data Access (UDA) strategy that at its core consists of a series of COM interfaces dubbed OLE DB. These interfaces allow developers to build **data providers** that flexibly represent data that is stored in various formats, and use **service components** to manipulate data through cursor and sorting engines. Although the familiar WOSA concept is utilized, the major difference between OLE DB and ODBC is found in the flexibility of using OLE DB to access more than simply tabular data from relational databases.

For example, Microsoft created OLE DB providers for non-tabular data sources such as Microsoft Index Server, Active Directory Services Interface (ADSI), and Microsoft OLAP Services. In addition, OLE DB can be used to connect to ODBC data sources through a special OLE DB provider called MSDASQL. As with the DLL interface of ODBC, the COM-based OLE DB model is great for C/C++ programmers, but because it requires manipulation of interface pointers, VB programmers can't access it directly. This is where ADO—originally from the term ActiveX Data Objects, which has since been dropped—comes in. ADO was developed as an object interface to OLE DB accessible by automation clients, so ASP and VB developers could use OLE DB through ADO to communicate with data providers.

Because scripting clients could not otherwise use OLE DB, the first release of ADO coincided with the introduction of Visual InterDev (VID) in 1996 for building Web-based applications using Active Server Pages (ASP) on IIS 3.0. ADO consists of a very simple and non-hierarchical object model that provided increased performance and made it easy to build data-driven Web sites with ASP. ADO, through a special OLE DB provider called the Data Shape Provider, also provided rudimentary support for hierarchical data.

1

Middleware to the Rescue

Although ADO allowed simple ASP Web sites to access data, it didn't initially support building multi-tiered distributed applications. At the same time, Microsoft released the first component-oriented middleware product with the unfortunate name of Microsoft Transaction Server (MTS). Simply put, MTS provided an environment complete with interception, activation, and threading support in which COM components could be hosted. It also allowed the components to participate in distributed transactions using resource managers such as ODBC and OLE DB and using a two-phase commit protocol. Utilizing MTS meant that components accessing data could reside in isolated processes and even remote machines. This architecture furthered the need for a good way to move ADO `Recordset` objects between tiers of the application.

The need to move data between physical tiers was addressed with the introduction of the disconnected `Recordset` in ADO 2.0 in 1998. Originally, Microsoft introduced the technology as a part of Active Data Services (ADS), renamed to Remote Data Services (RDS) for use in Internet Explorer (MSIE). The idea was that a `Recordset` could be created on the Web server and downloaded to MSIE, where it was cached and manipulated on the client. The success of this technique was limited because of the obvious problem of moving away from browser independence (the Internet's key strength). In addition, the client had to have the correct versions of the various DLLs. It turned out that the major usefulness for disconnected record sets as implemented in ADO 2.0 was to move data between components residing in MTS (and later COM+) and ASP pages that manipulated the data for display on the page. This enabled data access code to be truly separate from presentation code. In addition, it provided a standard, albeit proprietary, way to move data without resorting to manually parsing the data for insertion in custom data structures or simply using the `GetRows` method of the `Recordset` object to stream the data to a `Variant` array.

As OLE DB and ADO went on to supplant ODBC and RDO as Microsoft's flagship data access technologies, new versions with features such as asynchronous programming, events, a more sophisticated cursor library, advanced searching, and custom control of updates were introduced. Typically, the new releases would ship with new products, such as when ADO 2.0 shipped with VB 6.0 and ADO 2.1 shipped with SQL Server 7.0 and Office 2000.

Note

For more information on ADO and how to use it in various scenarios, see Chapter 14 of my book *Pure Visual Basic,* published by Sams.

At this point, it became apparent that the collection of data access technologies and their various versions had become interdependent and taken on a life of their own. Microsoft responded by creating a separate group and distribution point for the Jet, ODBC, ADO, and OLE DB software (although Jet software and the desktop ODBC drivers were removed starting with MDAC 2.6). All the data access software is now bundled in the Microsoft Data Access Components (MDAC) SDK and can be downloaded in installation packages from www.microsoft.com/data. As of this writing, the current release is version 2.7 and was installed with Windows XP.

Note   As discussed shortly, ADO.NET actually requires MDAC 2.6 or later to be installed because use of both the SQL Server .NET Data Provider and the OLE DB .NET Data Provider require it.

The Web Grows Up

As the Internet protocols TCP/IP, HTTP, and HTML became ubiquitous, the breadth of applications that were targeted for the Web increased. In addition to basic "brochure ware" Web sites, organizations began using the Web for selling products, as typified by high-profile e-commerce sites such as Amazon.com. As bandwidth increased, other organizations soon recognized that business transactions could be conducted over the Web as well. Unfortunately, there were few common data exchange formats and none that spanned more than a single industry. The need for efficiently exchanging data over the Web led to the development of the eXtensible Markup Language (XML) 1.0 specification by the World Wide Web Consortium (W3C) and its release as a recommendation in February 1998. Quickly, vendors—with Microsoft leading the charge—began adopting XML and incorporating it into their products.

Unlike HTML, another markup language derived from SGML, the key feature of XML is, of course, the fact that it's a self-describing, structured document that's strictly parsed and can be validated against a schema to ensure that it's both syntactically and semantically correct.

Note   For a good overview of XML and its related specifications, see the book *Sams Teach Yourself XML in 21 Days, Second Edition* by Devan Shepherd.

Although ADO incorporated some basic support for XML in ADO 2.5 with the ability to save a `Recordset` as XML to a file or COM object that implemented the `IStream` interface, ADO was obviously not designed from the ground up to work with XML. For example, when saving an ADO `Recordset` to XML, it always used the same schema. Developers would have to spend development time (and CPU cycles) coding transformations using eXtensible Stylesheet Language Transformation (XSLT). Clearly, as XML and its related specifications (XSD, XSLT, XPath, among others) became the primary way to describe and exchange data over the Web, Microsoft's data access technologies would have to evolve.

The XML Embrace

It cannot be said strongly enough that Microsoft has gotten the XML religion and has been the clear leader in adopting XML in its products, as well as working with the World Wide Web Consortium (W3C), an industry organization whose over 500 member organizations work to create standard protocols and specifications for use on the Internet, to further define XML-based standards.

First, Microsoft has been active in integrating XML into its products. For example, the XML support added to SQL Server 2000 allows XML documents to be created using a FOR XML statement. In addition, support for querying XML data using XML templates via http is available. XML has found its way into products as wide ranging as Office and BizTalk Server 2000, and even Bill Gates noted at the Microsoft PDC in 2001 that XML is the core technology that Microsoft has rallied around to build the next generation of all its products.

Another primary example, of course, is the Simple Object Access Protocol (SOAP) specification. This specification was originally jointly developed by Microsoft, DevelopMentor, and UserLand Software and subsequently led to collaboration with IBM, Hewlett-Packard, and others. Version 1.1 was submitted to the W3C (www.w3c.org) in May 2000. Visual Studio .NET (VS .NET) and the .NET Framework are testaments to Microsoft's commitment to XML because they are steeped in XML and SOAP 1.1 from their very foundations. Everything from configuration files, to data access, to XML Web Services, to classes used to manipulate XML documents, to the serialization format of objects within the Common Language Runtime (CLR) relies on XML, SOAP 1.1, and an XML specification for describing XML Web Services called Web Service Description Language (WSDL), pronounced "wiz-dull." In addition, Microsoft has recently worked with IBM to develop the next set of SOAP-based standards for adding enterprise features such as reliable messaging, routing, security, and inspection to the protocol under the umbrella term *Global XML Web Service Architecture*.

Finally, Microsoft is embracing XML in its .NET "My Services" initiative designed to unify disparate silos of information and make them securely accessible via Web protocols. Basically, to developers, the interaction with .NET My Services takes the form of sending and receiving XML documents to do things such as send an alert notification to a user that his or her flight is going to be delayed.

Certainly, in all these ways, Microsoft has been ahead of the curve, so it's no surprise that from the ground up, ADO.NET is built around XML.

The final twist in this road is the idea of using the Internet as the platform for application development. This is the thrust of Microsoft's .NET strategy, which was first announced in June 2000. The core of this strategy is to build products and services for a "programmable Web" where information and services are exchanged not just by human interaction through browsers, but also programmatically through software. Because XML's strength is its self-describing nature, it became the obvious technology substrate upon which to build the programmable Web. For developers, the end result is exposing functionality over the Web programmatically through the use of the XML grammar SOAP. Visual Studio .NET and the .NET Framework fully support this new paradigm by providing tools to create and consume XML Web Services. Of course, all these new XML Web Services will need to interoperate with backend data stores. This is where ADO.NET comes in.

So, this is the landscape from which ADO.NET arose. There was a clear need for a data access technology that deeply integrated XML standards and provided the scalability to satisfy an increasing demand for Web-based applications of all kinds, including XML-based data exchange and XML Web Services.

ADO.NET Design Goals

Before digging into how ADO.NET has been architected, let's take a brief look at the design goals, which provides insight into the final implementation. To that end, ADO.NET was designed with five primary goals in mind.

It Efficiently Supports a Multi-Tiered Programming Model

As mentioned earlier, one of the key shifts in software development in the past several years has been to a multi-tier (or n-tier) programming model. In that model, data is read from a data source, disconnected from the source, and moved across tiers. If you think of those tiers as not simply machines within an organization, but as Web sites that span organizations (as with XML Web Services), it becomes immediately apparent that the disconnected record sets of ADO 2.x won't satisfy this model. This is the case because a disconnected Recordset is a COM object and, therefore, you need a COM infrastructure on both ends of the channel. Although the COM/DCOM component model has been extremely successful, it is, for all intents and purposes, wedded to the Windows platform. This means that an organization running a different platform (for example, Sun Solaris) can't exchange data through a Recordset. In fact, even two Microsoft shops will have difficulty doing this because firewall configurations often prevent DCOM communication.

1

To address the disconnected model, the core ADO.NET object is an in-memory XML-based cache called the `DataSet`. Because the `DataSet` is a managed class, it can take advantage of the runtime's ability to serialize and deserialize it to XML, thereby allowing it to pass more easily between tiers in a multi-tiered architecture. Because the `DataSet` is so fundamental, you'll explore it in depth in Days 3, "Working with `DataSet`s," 4, "`DataSet` Internals," and 5, "Changing Data."

It Deeply Integrates XML Standards

If XML is the primary means of exchanging data over the Web, ADO.NET needs to support it in a robust way. This means that not only should you be able to transform data into XML, but also control the schema and read and write data natively as XML. To that end, the `DataSet` is a fully XML-enabled object. Its structure is defined by an XSD schema and its data is represented as XML. Further, ADO.NET integrates the way you work with both relational and XML data. In the past, ADO could be used to manipulate relational data, whereas the MSXML parser could be used to manipulate XML documents. Within the .NET Framework, these two models are fundamentally joined. You'll look at this in more detail on Day 7, "`DataSet`s and XML."

It Leverages Current ADO Knowledge

First and foremost, although there's always a little pain when learning a new data access model, the goal was to allow current ADO developers to move into ADO.NET with their current skill sets intact and therefore minimize the learning curve. As a result, you'll find many familiar concepts in ADO.NET, including connection, command, and parameter objects. You'll look at this side of ADO.NET in depth in Week 2.

This is also important because, as you'll see, ADO.NET isn't a wholesale replacement of ADO and OLE DB, but is rightly thought of as an addition to it. ADO.NET, in its current incarnation, targets only a specific set of application scenarios—that is, Web-based distributed applications—whereas ADO can still be used to build connected applications that rely on features such as server-side cursors.

Why ADO.NET?

Good question. Officially, the acronym ADO no longer stands for ActiveX Data Objects (the term *ActiveX* was coined in 1995 when the term *OLE* had fallen out of favor for describing components based on the COM specification). So, ADO simply refers to a data access technique, and to provide continuity with the past, the term ADO was incorporated into the new name. Originally, ADO.NET was called ADO+ just as ASP.NET was called ASP+.

Even though the name has continuity, keep in mind that the infrastructures upon which ADO and ADO.NET are built are completely different. ADO is built on the COM infrastructure, with its IUnknown interface, registry entries, reference counting, and vtable layouts, whereas ADO.NET is managed code executed by the common language runtime using the Common Type System, assemblies, XML, and garbage collection.

The continuity between ADO and ADO.NET is most clearly seen in the fact that existing OLE DB providers and ODBC drivers can be used in ADO.NET through .NET Data Providers created for that purpose. In this way, ADO.NET can also be thought of as an evolution of ADO. However, because of its deep reliance on XML, as you'll learn on Day 7, perhaps a more appropriate name might be XDO.NET (XML Data Objects).

It Combines Relational and Object-Oriented Paradigms

As you're probably aware, the substrate upon which ADO.NET is built, the .NET Framework (the common language runtime plus the base class libraries), is fully object-oriented to the core. This means that developers now have the opportunity to create OO designs using overloading, inheritance, polymorphism, and encapsulation. This in turn means that developers will want to treat and work with data in terms of objects rather than simply as a collection of columns in a row.

Although there was no mechanism, outside of hand coding, for "objectifying" data in ADO, ADO.NET supports the ability to create strongly typed `DataSets` that provide a natural OO interface to data. You'll take a look at how this works on Day 6, "Building Strongly Typed `DataSet` Classes." In addition, we'll talk about some exciting new features to take this concept one step further on Day 21, "Futures and Wrap-Up."

It Reduces Programming Errors

Even though leveraging ADO knowledge is a good thing, many ADO programmers admit to a certain degree of confusion, especially when working with the interplay of cursor types and locations with a specific OLE DB provider. Alleviating this confusion and reducing common programming errors was another design goal of ADO.NET.

This has been done by simplifying the ways in which data can be accessed. For example, in ADO.NET there are two ways to get data: either you read an entire result set and cache it in a `DataSet`, or you stream through it in a read-only, forward-only manner using a `DataReader` object. There's no option for manipulating server-side cursors, so the issues of seeing changes made by other users, encountering deleted rows, dealing with keyset cursors, and using positioned updates all go away.

1

Although some readers might be alarmed by this loss of functionality, those features were the ones that caused developers the most problems and were the source of performance problems because they were often used incorrectly or inadvertently. We'll discuss ADO.NET futures and how some of this functionality might be restored in future releases on Day 21.

The root of these problems is that ADO tried to be all things to all people. By incorporating a full cursor model into the Recordset, ADO provided a unified programming model at the expense of confusion because each OLE DB provider could choose to implement the features differently or not at all. ADO.NET solves this problem by allowing each .NET Data Provider (roughly the equivalent of an OLE DB provider) to provide its own programmatic interface to handle special functionality. A great example is the fact that the SQL Server .NET Data Provider includes a special method to execute Transact-SQL statements that return XML via the FOR XML statement. This does fracture the programming model slightly, but makes working with any particular data source simpler.

On a second level, the classes (their methods, properties, and events) in ADO.NET have been designed to eliminate the most common programming errors. For example, ASP developers often forgot to include the MoveNext object when coding a loop to display a Recordset on a page. The resulting infinite loop often caused severe problems with the Web server, which then had to be shut down manually and restarted, affecting other sites on the server. Because ADO.NET's DataReader exposes rows as a collection, they are iterated using the For Each syntax, making this sort of error impossible.

And, of course, you'll put all the features used to satisfy these design goals to use on Days 15 through 18.

ADO.NET in .NET

In this section, you'll drill down to look at how ADO.NET is architected to realize the design goals discussed in the previous section. Let's begin with a review of the execution environment in which ADO.NET runs and then move on to the namespaces, classes, and interfaces that make up ADO.NET in the .NET Framework.

Managed Code Review

Although the ins and outs of managed code and the Common Language Runtime are beyond the scope of this book, it's important to have a foundational understanding of how the code you write for ADO.NET is actually executed.

Note

For an in-depth look at the common language runtime, see *Essential .NET Volume I* by Don Box, published by Addison-Wesley. Chapter 1 of my Sams book *Building Distributed Applications with Visual Basic .NET* also provides a more in-depth look at the common language runtime from a Visual Basic perspective.

NEW TERM To begin, all code you write to work with ADO.NET, whether in VB .NET, VC# .NET, or any of the .NET languages, will by executed by the common language runtime and is thus referred to as **managed code**. The common language runtime includes a host of runtime features including a class loader, thread support, exception manager, security engine, garbage collector, code manager, and type checker. In turn, all managed code is first compiled to a machine-independent intermediate language called Microsoft Intermediate Language (MSIL), and subsequently compiled to native instructions for execution in a just-in-time (JIT) manner as the common language runtime's class loader loads code at runtime. This process is outlined in Figure 1.2.

Note

Yes, it is also possible to pre-JIT code at install time. This can be done using a command-line utility that stores the resulting native code (executable or DLL) in a code cache on the machine. When the assembly is to be executed by the common language runtime, it locates the native code and runs it directly instead of using JIT compilation.

FIGURE 1.2

The managed code execution environment. This diagram depicts how managed code is compiled and executed by the common language runtime.

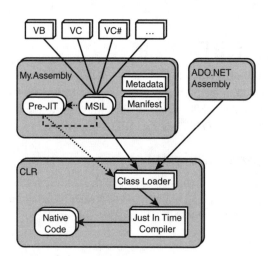

NEW TERM When your code is compiled to MSIL, it is stored in a PE (portable executable) file called a **module**. The module contains the MSIL instruction in addition to

1

metadata that describes the types (classes) in the code you've written, along with the dependencies on other types. The metadata is roughly equivalent to a COM type library. This metadata is heavily relied upon by the common language runtime and other tools in VS .NET to make sure that the appropriate code is loaded and to assist in enabling features such as IntelliSense and debugging. A module can then be incorporated in, or exist independently as, an **assembly**. An assembly is the fundamental unit of packaging, deployment, security, and versioning in .NET and contains a **manifest** (embedded in one of the modules or in its own PE file) that describes the version, an optional public key (called a **strong name**) used for uniquely identifying this assembly from all others, and a list of dependent assemblies and files.

As you'll note from Figure 1.2, ADO.NET is itself an assembly (written in VC# .NET) called System.Data.dll that is a part of, and is installed with, the .NET Framework in the *windowsdir*\Microsoft.NET\Framework*framework_version* directory. As a result, the manifest of your assemblies will reference the ADO.NET assembly and so, at runtime, the common language runtime will be able to make sure that ADO.NET is loaded and JIT compiled.

Note

By running the .NET Framework Configuration Manager from the Administrative Tools group, you can view what is called the Global Assembly Cache (GAC). Simply put, the GAC is a machinewide store for assemblies that have been given a strong name. Putting an assembly in the GAC makes it easy for thecommon language runtime's class loader to find it at runtime. Not surprisingly, the ADO.NET assembly is placed in the GAC when you install VS .NET. You'll also notice that the Configuration Manager depicts assemblies with two different icons. The lion's share of the assemblies in the GAC is placed there after simply being compiled to MSIL. The core assemblies that are used in almost every .NET application such as mscorlib, System, and System.Xml, however, have been pre-JITted to native code for better performance.

The last, and perhaps most important, point to note about the managed code environment of the common language runtime is the existence of the Common Type System (CTS). In the CTS, all data types (simply referred to as *types*) are ultimately derived from a base object called Object (System.Object) and found in the assembly mscorlib.dll. The CTS is key to understanding .NET because it governs how types are represented and dealt with by the common language runtime.

NEW TERM For example, Figure 1.3 shows that all types are classified as **value types** or **reference types**. As the name implies, value types are typically passed by value in applications and are used to represent simple data types such as integers, Boolean, and character. Value types are simply allocated on the stack and therefore are very light-weight. Reference types are allocated on the heap, are addressed by their memory location, and are used to represent classes, interfaces, pointers, strings, and delegates (which you can think of as object-oriented function pointers). Therefore, the high-level objects found in ADO.NET such as the `DataSet` are reference types. This distinction is important because reference types are automatically garbage collected by the common language runtime, although they can also expose a `Dispose` or `Close` method for de-allocation.

FIGURE 1.3

The Common Type System. This diagram shows how the CTS is organized. All types are derived from `System.Object`.

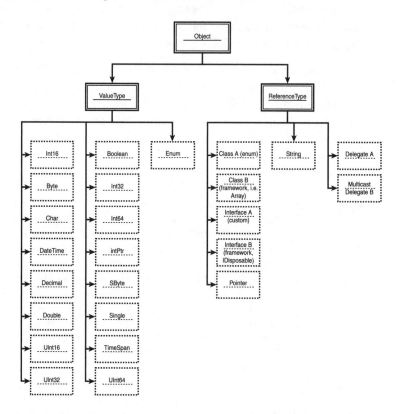

The CTS is what makes cross-language development in .NET a reality. By using the same underlying representation of types as managed by the common language runtime, languages can freely use types created in other .NET languages without having to perform any translation or coercion. This also means that an assembly written in one language can even inherit from a type written in another language. This is fundamental to ADO.NET because the ADO.NET classes were written in VC# .NET, but can be used, for example, as base classes for code written in VB .NET.

The `System.Data` Namespace

Assemblies in .NET contain classes, interfaces, and enumerated types arranged hierarchically in namespaces. Namespaces can cross assembly boundaries and can themselves contain other namespaces. They are simply a convenient way to arrange code and can be navigated using the familiar dot notation. Within the ADO.NET assembly, the primary namespace is, not surprisingly, `System.Data`. Within `System.Data` are four namespaces that implement specific ADO.NET features as shown in Table 1.1.

TABLE 1.1   The `System.Data` namespaces. These namespaces comprise the functionality of ADO.NET.

Namespace	Description
`System.Data`	Contains the heart of the ADO.NET architecture, including more than 45 classes and more than 20 enumerations that comprise the `DataSet` and a dozen or more interfaces that are implemented by .NET Data Providers
`System.Data.Common`	Contains about a dozen classes shared by .NET Data Providers such as the OleDb and SqlClient providers
`System.Data.OleDb`	Contains approximately 20 classes and a few enumerations that make up the OLE DB .NET Data Provider
`System.Data.SqlClient`	Contains approximately 20 classes and a few enumerations that make up the SQL Server .NET Data Provider
`System.Data.SqlTypes`	Contains more than a dozen structures that map to data types exposed by SQL Server in addition to a couple of enumerations and classes used to perform comparisons and handle exceptions

In addition, the ADO.NET assembly contains one class from the `System.Xml` namespace, most of which is defined in the System.Xml.dll assembly. This class, `XmlDataDocument`, is used to bridge the gap between relational and XML data. We'll discuss this on Day 7.

As you can see from Table 1.1, the first two namespaces contain types that are for general use, whereas the last three implement features particular to accessing data through an OLE DB provider or to accessing SQL Server. This highlights the fundamental division of ADO.NET into the `DataSet` and .NET Data Providers, as shown in Figure 1.4.

As mentioned previously, the `DataSet` implements the in-memory cache for disconnected data and as a result is not dependent on any particular data source. The classes exposed by the .NET Data Providers, particularly the `DataAdapter`, are used to populate the `DataSet`. The `DataSet` can then be serialized and passed between tiers of a distributed application using the facilities of the common language runtime. In addition, it can load data from multiple data adapters and represent the data hierarchically through a set of relationships defined by its XSD schema. Finally, changes can be made to the `DataSet` that are tracked by the `DataSet` and it can be passed back to the .NET Data Provider in order to update the underlying data store.

FIGURE 1.4

ADO.NET architecture. This diagram depicts the architecture of ADO.NET and its fundamental division between the `DataSet` and the .NET Data Providers.

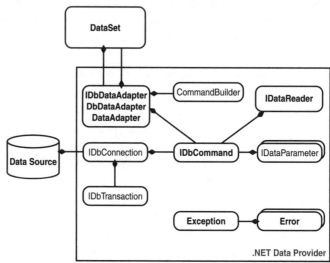

Table 1.1 also shows that ADO.NET ships with two .NET Data Providers: `System.OleDb` and `System.SqlClient`. The role of the providers is to implement classes that use the interface and classes in `System.Data` and `System.Common` to expose the functionality of a particular data store. In other words, the .NET Data Providers are analogous to OLE DB providers and ODBC drivers, with the exception that they expose functionality at the programmatic layer rather than simply as an abstraction. This means that vendors writing .NET Data Providers can expose custom functionality to developers directly as additional classes or methods.

At a functional level, as shown in Figure 1.4, providers will expose functionality based on the interfaces and classes in `System.Data` and `System.Data.Common` to connect to the data store, initiate transactions, communicate with a `DataSet`, handle exceptions, execute commands, handle parameters, and stream through data in a fast-forward read-only fashion. All the interfaces and classes shown in Figure 1.4, with the exception of `CommandBuilder`, `Exception`, and `Error`, are implemented or inherited by an actual provider to provide the programming model for implementing a provider. By convention, the provider also exposes the `CommandBuilder` class to automatically populate a data adapter with commands used to select, insert, update, and delete data from the data

1

source and `Exception` and `Error` classes to handle errors returned from the data source. Finally, access to providers can be controlled through the use of code-access security implemented as permission objects. You'll explore each of these functions in depth during Week 2.

> **Note**   In addition to the two providers that ship with ADO.NET, there is also an ODBC .NET Provider available for download from `msdn.microsoft.com`.

Interface-Based Programming

NEW TERM   As you can see from Figure 1.4, ADO.NET makes use of interfaces (those identifiers prefixed with an `I`, such as `IDbDataAdapter`, `IDbConnection`, and `IDataReader`) to provide the template or contract between a class that uses the interface and the client. By implementing or deriving from an interface in a class, you ensure that the methods, properties, fields, and events that your class exposes follow a particular semantically related pattern. You can also implement several interfaces in the same class to support different sets of functionality. This is called **interface inheritance**. In turn, following a predefined pattern allows client code to be written that can work with any class that implements a particular interface. This is referred to as **polymorphism**, and in ADO.NET can be very useful in writing code that works with multiple .NET Data Providers.

.NET languages based on the common language runtime also support single-implementation inheritance wherein a class can be derived from another class, and in addition to inheriting its member definitions, it also inherits the implementation or code behind those members. You can see from Figure 1.4 that the classes `DbDataAdapter` and `DataAdapter` can be used in this way.

If you're a VB or ASP developer, you've probably not worked with interfaces very much. This is primarily the case because although VB 6.0 supported interfaces through the use of the `Implements` keyword, it was not natural to create interfaces in VB 6.0 and ASP did not support them at all. Secondarily, although the COM programming model relied on interfaces in a very fundamental way, VB did a good job of hiding that fact from developers.

Generic Versus Specific Providers

As is implied by the previous discussion, .NET Data Providers can come in several flavors. The OLE DB and ODBC providers are generic in that they are used to access a variety of data stores and more or less act as a pass through to other software that communicates with the actual data store. On the other hand, the SQL Server provider is an example of a specific provider because it bypasses OLE DB and ODBC and talks to SQL Server directly using SQL Server's native Tabular Data Stream (TDS) protocol. This provides for better performance. This architecture points to the fact that vendors will likely implement specific providers to expose custom functionality and improve performance, while OLE DB and ODBC can still be used through the generic providers. As you'll learn on Day 14, "Working with Other Providers," you can also take advantage of this architecture to build your own generic and specific providers for enterprise applications.

Because .NET Data Providers implement the functionality shown in Figure 1.4, Figure 1.5 shows the same diagram, this time with the specific classes implemented by the SQL Server provider in the System.Data.SqlClient namespace.

FIGURE 1.5

The SqlClient .NET Data Provider. This diagram shows the implementation of the SqlClient provider.

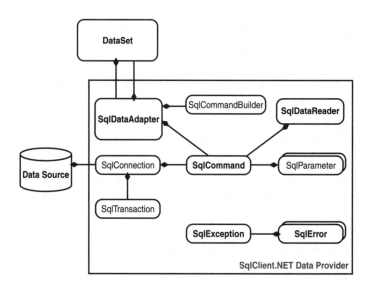

It's also important to keep in mind that ADO.NET, although a fundamental part of the .NET Framework because of its importance for most corporate developers is, in terms of the number of classes it includes, a very small part of the framework as a whole. In its entirety, the .NET Framework encompasses more than 6,500 classes, and includes functionality for everything from building XML Web Services and Windows Forms to building components that can be hosted by Component Services.

A Note About Language Choice

If it wasn't clear from the discussion on managed code, it cannot be overemphasized that one of the fundamental goals of .NET is to provide a language-independent framework for developing modern distributed applications. To that end, it doesn't matter whether you program ADO.NET from VB .NET, VC# .NET, or any of the other languages targeted for the common language runtime. However, because the two primary languages that most developers will use initially are VB and C#, all the examples in this book will use one of those two languages. I'll alternate the language used in the listings and the exercise solutions throughout the book, but of course you're free to implement the exercises in whatever language you choose. I think you'll find it fairly easy to read code written to use ADO.NET in either VB or C#, although I'm certainly aware that there might be concepts in each language that will need further explanation. At those times, look for tips and notes for clarification.

Summary

Today you learned how the data access technologies on the Microsoft platform have developed in the last decade and set the stage for the introduction of ADO.NET in the .NET Framework. In addition, you reviewed the managed code environment in which applications written to use ADO.NET will execute. Finally, you saw the ADO.NET architecture from a high level and learned about the fundamental division of ADO.NET into the DataSet and .NET Data Providers.

Tomorrow, you'll actually start working with ADO.NET both graphically and programmatically to learn how it is exposed in Visual Studio .NET.

Workshop

This workshop will help reinforce the concepts covered in today's lesson.

Quiz

1. What limits ADO 2.x from being used in Web-based distributed applications?

   Although ADO 2.x supports disconnected Recordset objects that can be moved between tiers in a distributed application, those tiers must be based on the COM/DCOM infrastructure. This is the case because DCOM doesn't work well through firewalls, COM is not platform independent, and the record set is not represented in an industry standard way using XML. These factors together make it difficult, if not impossible, to pass ADO record sets between organizations.

2. What is the key technology upon which Microsoft is building its next generation of software?

XML. XML is the industry standard controlled by the W3C. It is the basis for standards such as XSD for capturing the structure of an XML document, XPath for querying XML documents, SOAP for invoking services over the Web, and WSDL for describing the functionality of XML Web Services. There are other specifications in the works that will likely be rolled into future versions of VS .NET to support higher levels of functionality as well.

3. What key design goal will make it easier for ADO programmers to grasp ADO.NET?

The goal of leveraging current ADO knowledge. This is accomplished by using some of the same object types that are found in ADO, including connection, command, and parameter.

4. How does .NET achieve language choice and interoperability for developers?

The common language runtime and the CTS together allow developers to write code in any managed language that can fully interoperate with code from any other language. This includes cross-language inheritance and full fidelity of all types created in any .NET language.

5. What are the two parts of ADO.NET?

ADO.NET is divided into the `DataSet` object for manipulating disconnected data and the .NET Data Providers for communicating with backend data stores and the `DataSet`.

Exercise

Because this book deals with Enterprise ADO.NET, you'll need a server database to work with while going through this book. The exercises in the remainder of the book will work with SQL Server 2000 and Visual Studio .NET Professional, so the only exercise today is to set up the database by running the script provided by downloading the code for this book from `www.samspublishing.com`. When you unzip the code, look for the ComputeBooksDb.bat script in the Day01 directory. Execute this on the machine with SQL Server and it will attach the ComputeBooks database. This database contains a schema that a fictional bookstore might use to inventory books, track customers, and take and fulfill orders. After the database has been created, you're all set for tomorrow.

DAY 2

Getting Started

Yesterday you learned about the history and goals of ADO.NET that hopefully allowed you to put it in proper context. Today you'll begin to use ADO.NET both graphically and programmatically. Today's goal is to familiarize you with the two primary ways of working with ADO.NET in Visual Studio .NET (VS .NET). To that end, you will learn:

- How to connect to and view data through the Server Explorer
- How to use the VS .NET designer to build a simple application to retrieve data and update a database
- How to programmatically instantiate, populate, and invoke ADO.NET objects to retrieve and update data in a simple application

ADO.NET in Visual Studio .NET

Because data access is so central to the design of most corporate enterprise applications, VS .NET includes a wealth of features designed to make using ADO.NET simple. These include the use of the Server Explorer, component designer, and wizards to graphically manipulate the underlying database and write the code to work with the ADO.NET classes.

To begin, let's walk through the construction of a very simple ASP.NET application in C#. This application queries the ComputeBooks product catalog and allows the user to make some modifications to demonstrate the graphical features of VS .NET that can be used with ADO.NET.

First, of course, you need to create an ASP.NET Web site using the New Project dialog accessed by clicking File, New Project or through the New Project button on the VS .NET Start Page. In this case, under Visual C# projects, select ASP.NET Web Application and call it ComputeBooksSimple. When completed, a new virtual directory will have been created on the Web server and the project will contain AssemblyInfo.cs, WebForm1.aspx, Global.asax, and Web.config files.

NEW TERM   Before getting started keep in mind that the application you're walking through today is an example of what I refer to as a **two-tier Web application**. That means that the code used to create the user interface uses ADO.NET objects directly to communicate with a database. Although you can certainly create two-tiered applications effectively with ASP.NET, ADO.NET, and VS .NET, a more robust design pattern for enterprise applications calls for the use of an n-tiered model where the ADO.NET code (referred to as the **data services tier**) is abstracted from the user interface code (the **presentation tier**) and also from reusable business logic (the **business services tier**). Designing applications using this approach allows their constituent parts to be more maintainable, reusable, and scalable at the cost of increased complexity. On Days 15 through 17, you'll explore how an n-tiered pattern can be used with ADO.NET.

Using the Server Explorer

The Server Explorer window is available in all VS .NET projects and can be used for viewing resources such as message queues, event logs, performance counters, services, and databases on a local or remote machine. The purpose of the Server Explorer is to enable graphical interaction with these services and visual designers within the development environment. It can be accessed from the View menu or by typing Ctrl+Alt+S. Like other windows in VS .NET, it will by default auto-hide itself when your cursor is not over it. To pin it to the surface, use the pin icon in the upper-right corner.

Tip

> If you don't like the default way in which the windows behave or are arranged, click on the Start Page and go to My Profile. Here you can choose from seven profiles (or build your own) to customize the look and feel based on your previous experience. In this book, I'll use the default Visual Studio Developer profile, although others for Visual Basic, Visual C++, and Visual InterDev developers are available.

In addition to the server-based resources, the Server Explorer also contains a Data Connections node that can be used to connect to and view a particular data source. If you're familiar with the Visual Studio 6.0 IDE, you'll recognize this as analogous to the Visual Data Tools.

Creating a Connection

To create a connection to a data source, simply right-click on the Data Connections node and click Add Connection. You'll notice that you can create both a SQL Server database and a data connection simultaneously by selecting Create New SQL Server Database.

The resulting dialog, shown in Figure 2.1, is the familiar Data Link Properties dialog. Through this dialog, you can configure the connection. By default, it assumes you're going to connect to SQL Server, although this can be changed by selecting the appropriate OLE DB provider in the Provider tab. In this case we're going to connect to the ComputeBooks database you created during the exercise on Day 1, "ADO.NET in Perspective," on the local server (denoted by using a "." in the server name field), and authenticate using Windows NT integrated security. Obviously, you would change these settings if the location or authentication requirements of your server differed.

FIGURE 2.1

Data Link Properties. This dialog is used to create a data connection in the Server Explorer.

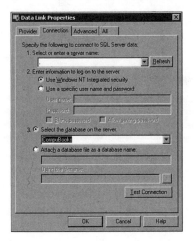

> **Note**
>
> Note that even though we're using SQL Server for our data connection, we're not yet using the SQL Server .NET Data Provider. The connections made through the Server Explorer use the SQL Server OLE DB provider. This is evident by selecting the connection in the Server Explorer window and choosing Properties.

When it's connected, the new connection will appear in the Server Explorer. You can then drill down through it to view the tables, views, and stored procedures. By double-clicking on a table, you can view and edit the data (depending on your permissions as defined by how you authenticated). Figure 2.2 shows the IDE after double-clicking the Titles table and using the Query toolbar to activate all the panes (diagram, grid, SQL, results) available. You can use the panes to modify the query, as was done in this case, to show only some of the data by selecting particular columns or to add a where clause or sorting condition.

FIGURE 2.2

Using a data connection. You can use a data connection to inspect and edit the data in the underlying database.

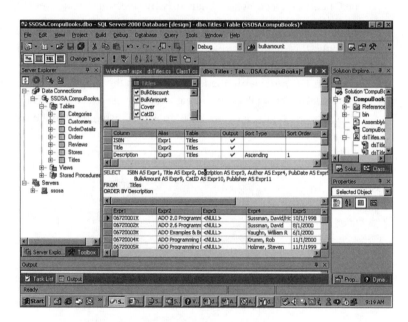

 Tip

> In the Professional edition of VS .NET, you can view and edit data and execute views and stored procedures, but cannot create and alter these objects. These features are enabled in the Enterprise Developer and Enterprise Architect versions of the product. To ensure that all readers will be able to follow along, in this book I'll use the features of the Professional edition.

NEW TERM   You'll also notice that you can inspect the SQL Server databases on the local server by drilling down into the SQL Servers node in the Server Explorer window. Although this provides the same level of functionality as creating your own connection, again depending on your permissions, the database connections are permanent connections and will be loaded each time you start a new instance of VS .NET. The VS .NET documentation distinguishes between these by calling the connection we just created a **database reference**, while referring to connections under the SQL Servers node, **database connections**. The other primary difference is the additional functionality you gain when using a reference if you have the Enterprise versions of VS .NET as noted.

Creating a Data Adapter

When the connection (or reference) has been established to the database, you can use it to incorporate data access code into your project. To do so, simply drag and drop an object from the connection onto a designer in the IDE. For example, to create code to access the Titles table, drag and drop the table onto the WebForm1.aspx designer surface.

A Bit About Designers

One of the interesting features of the .NET Framework and VS .NET is the interaction between classes and designers. The Framework ships with several visual designers, each of which is implemented by a type. The designer's type is then associated with a class through the use of metadata, specifically, the `DesignerAttribute` type. This allows developers to create and associate their own designers with their custom classes, thereby extending the development environment. In our example, to create code to access the Titles table, a table is dragged onto a Web Form and its associated designer. However, you can also create your own components that can be added to the Toolbox and subsequently dragged and dropped on a designer surface by directly or indirectly implementing the `System.ComponentModel.IComponent` interface.

Finally, you can graphically interact with inherently non-visual components by creating a class derived from `System.ComponentModel.Component` because it is associated with the designer implemented by the `System.ComponentModel.Design.ComponentDesigner` type.

As a result of dragging and dropping the table onto the WebForm1.aspx designer surface, two objects, `sqlConnection1` and `sqlDataAdapter1`, will be created and placed at the bottom of the designer surface. By dropping the table, VS .NET assumed you wanted to connect to the database and select, insert, update, and delete data from the table and so it added both objects to the form. You can then inspect and change the default properties it set for the objects by clicking on them and viewing their properties in the Properties window. To provide easier configuration, if the Data Adapter Configuration Wizard does not open automatically, you can invoke it by right-clicking on the `sqlDataAdapter1` object and selecting Configure Data Adapter.

This wizard has several interesting features, including the ability to generate SQL statements and stored procedures to populate the data adapter. To begin, it allows you to choose an existing data connection or create a new one on the fly. After selecting the connection, you are presented with the dialog shown in Figure 2.3.

FIGURE 2.3

Choose a query type. This part of the Data Adapter Configuration Wizard allows you to specify how data from the database is accessed.

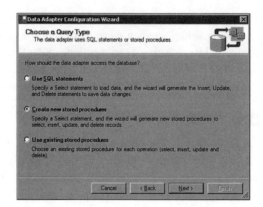

NEW TERM   This dialog is used to specify how the data adapter will communicate with the data store. Because ADO.NET was designed with the goal of flexibility, it's just as easy to use a SQL statement as it is a stored procedure. In most enterprise applications, you'll want to use stored procedures because of the added performance, abstraction, and security they provide. We will discuss this in more detail on Day 10, "Working with Commands."

In this case, you'll choose Create new stored procedures and click Next. From here, you can specify a SQL statement to use as the basis for specifying the data that the data adapter will access, or you can use the query builder to build a SQL statement graphically. By default, a SELECT statement with all the columns will be created. In this case, either use the Query Builder or simply modify the SQL to remove the Cover column from the SELECT clause and sort the result set in ascending order by title. This dialog also contains the Advanced Options button, which controls how the stored procedures are to be written. The three options allow you to specify

- Whether insert, update, and delete statements are generated in addition to a select statement
- Whether optimistic concurrency is used when formulating the WHERE clauses in the update and delete stored procedures
- Whether a SELECT statement will be added to the insert and update stored procedures

NEW TERM   If you unselect the optimistic concurrency option, only the primary key will be used in the WHERE clause. As changes hit the database, they will overwrite existing records that might have been changed by other users since the data was first selected. This increases **concurrency** (the ability to have many users using the database simultaneously) and decreases the chances of an error. Leaving the option checked ensures that the data has remained untouched. However, it means that the stored procedure must be passed both the new and original values, and will obviously increase the likelihood that a change will fail, thereby decreasing concurrency. For this example, turn off the Use Optimistic Concurrency option.

The third option to refresh the DataSet is useful, especially in situations where the table contains server-generated values such as IDENTITY columns and default values in order to make sure they are visible if the modifications are successful. Click OK to close the Advanced Options dialog and click Next to move to the Create the Stored Procedures step shown in Figure 2.4.

FIGURE 2.4

Naming procedures. This step of the Data Adapter Configuration Wizard allows you to pick names for the stored procedures, and optionally review and save the script used to create them.

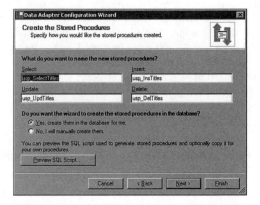

In the step shown in Figure 2.4, you have the option of naming the stored procedures that are about to be created and either allowing the wizard to create the procedures or saving the script and running it at a later time. You should use the latter option when you do not have permissions to create objects in the database or if you want to further modify the script by, for example, adding additional SQL Data Definition Language (DDL) statements to it.

As shown in the figure, you should publish and use a naming convention in your organization for your procedures so that other developers can easily identify them. In this example, we're using the convention where the procedure is prefixed with usp (so as not to be confused with the sp prefix reserved for system stored procedures), followed by Select, Ins, Upd, or Del, depending on the function of the procedure and finally the name of the table affected.

Developer Rights

It's important to remember that in SQL Server 2000 it's not adequate to simply be logged on with an account that's a member of the db_ddladmin or even the db_owner fixed database role. Being a member of the role will certainly allow you to create a stored procedure; however, the procedure will be created under your account and so its fully qualified name will be, for example, ssosa.dfox.usp_SelectTitles. In other words, the object will be owned by your account and not the database owner (dbo), as is preferred. Having the objects owned by dbo allows all accounts access to the objects transparently without having to specify the owner using dot notation.

This situation can be avoided in one of three ways. First, if you're a member of the sysadmin fixed server role, any objects you create will be owned by dbo. Second, if you're a member of the dbcreator fixed server role and create the database in which you are attempting to create objects, they'll be owned by dbo. Finally, the option that is typically used, the server administrator can alias your account as dbo by using the system stored procedure sp_addalias. In this way, any object you create will be owned by dbo. This option gives you the necessary control of the database while not allowing you to administer the server or create other databases. Of course, it goes without saying that developers can be aliased to dbo in development databases, but certainly not in production.

You should then preview the SQL script using the appropriate button to make sure that the script is as you specified. By clicking Next, the wizard presents a final checklist and then creates the procedures and writes the necessary code in the Web Form to instantiate, populate, and invoke the SqlConnection and SqlDataAdapter objects.

In this example, in addition to querying data for the Titles, we also need to query data from the Categories table because there is a foreign key relationship between Titles and Categories (each book belongs to exactly one category). To query the Categories table, simply drag and drop it on the Web Form and once again invoke the Data Adapter Configuration Wizard. This time, however, instead of creating stored procedures, select Use existing stored procedures and select the existing usp_SelectCats stored procedure for the Select command. Because the Categories table will not be modified in this application, you needn't fill in the rest of the commands. You'll notice that the wizard allows you to modify the names of the columns in the data row that map to the parameters that are required by the stored procedure. As you'll learn on Day 12, "Using a Data Adapter," the data adapter contains a mapping collection that is used to map columns in the data source to those in the DataSet. By default, mappings are assumed to use identical names and so you don't need to change the default values.

After finishing the wizard, you will now see two data adapter objects and one SqlConnection in the designer. To make things simpler to read, you can rename

sqlDataAdapter1 to daTitles and sqlDataAdapter2 to daCategories using the
Properties window.

As a final touch, invoke the Table Mappings dialog for the daCategories object by
clicking on the ellipses button next to the TableMappings property in the Properties window. The dialog shown in Figure 2.5 can be used to modify the table mappings discussed
previously. It can also be used to set the name of the table in the DataSet this data
adapter will fill. Change the name from usp_SelectCats to Categories.

FIGURE 2.5

*Table mappings. This
dialog is primarily
used to provide the
mapping layer between
a DataSet and the data
adapter.*

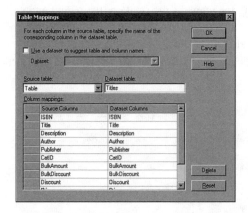

Tip

After the data adapters are configured, you can preview them by choosing
the Preview Data option on their context menus. The resulting dialog simply
allows you to see the data selected by the adapter, and that will be used to
populate a DataSet.

Creating a DataSet

Now that the project contains two data adapters that will provide the communication to
the data source, you must add a DataSet to cache the data for display and modification.
To do so, right-click on the designer near the objects you just created and select Generate
DataSet.

The Generate DataSet dialog presents a list of the data tables it found in the Web Form;
in this case, finding both the Titles and Categories tables from the data adapters. By
selecting both tables, the tool will create a DataSet that contains two distinct tables that
can contain data from different data adapters. The obvious implication is that DataSet
objects can be used to store and combine heterogeneous data easily. You can also change
the name of the DataSet; in this case, change it to dsTitles.

The `DataSet` then will be added to the project (viewable in the Solution Explorer window) as dsTitles.xsd (because the structure of a `DataSet` is represented by the XML Schema Definition [XSD] grammar). By double-clicking on the `DataSet`, the schema editor will be invoked showing the two data tables side by side. As mentioned previously, in the ComputeBooks database, the `Titles` and `Categories` tables have a foreign key relationship. To represent that relationship in the `DataSet`, you need to create a relation by right-clicking on the `CatID` element (column) and selecting Add, New Relation. You can then use the Edit Relation dialog, shown in Figure 2.6, to set the properties of the relationship, including the name of the relation, the parent and child elements, the fields that will participate, and any additional constraints such as mandating cascading deletes or setting the child field to `Null` in the event the parent field is deleted. In this case, the child element should be set to `Titles`, which will automatically change the name as well.

FIGURE 2.6

Editing relations. You can visually edit and define relationships between data tables in a `DataSet` using the Edit Relation dialog.

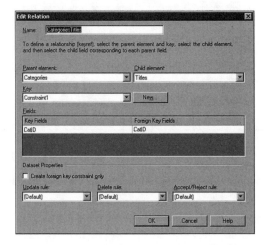

By clicking OK, the relation will be created and depicted with a dotted line.

At this point, you can view the XSD syntax for the `DataSet` by clicking on the XML pane at the bottom of the editor. You'll learn more about the syntax shown here on Day 7, "`DataSets` and XML." You can also get a preview of Day 6, "Building Strongly Typed `DataSet` Classes," by clicking on the Show All Files icon in the Solution Explorer and expanding the dsTitles.xsd node. You'll see that beneath the `DataSet` is a file called dsTitles.cs. This code file contains the programmatic definition of a typed `DataSet` that maps to the schema.

Viewing the Code

One glaring fact should be pointed out before going any further: Up until this point, we've not written a single line of code in order to declare, instantiate, populate, or invoke any of the objects we've manipulated graphically. So, where's the code?

To access the code for the Web Form, right-click on the designer and choose View Code. The code for the form should appear similar to that shown in Listing 2.1.

LISTING 2.1 The generated code. This listing shows the code generated by the various wizards used thus far today.

```
using System;
using System.Collections;
using System.ComponentModel;
using System.Data;
using System.Drawing;
using System.Web;
using System.Web.SessionState;
using System.Web.UI;
using System.Web.UI.WebControls;
using System.Web.UI.HtmlControls;

namespace ComputeBooksSimple
{
        /// <summary>
        /// Summary description for WebForm1.
        /// </summary>
        public class WebForm1 : System.Web.UI.Page
        {
        protected System.Data.SqlClient.SqlDataAdapter daTitles;
        protected System.Data.SqlClient.SqlDataAdapter daCategories;
        protected System.Data.SqlClient.SqlCommand sqlSelectCommand2;
        protected System.Data.SqlClient.SqlCommand sqlSelectCommand1;
        protected System.Data.SqlClient.SqlCommand sqlInsertCommand1;
        protected System.Data.SqlClient.SqlCommand sqlUpdateCommand1;
        protected System.Data.SqlClient.SqlCommand sqlDeleteCommand1;
        protected ComputeBooksSimple.dsTitles dsTitles1;
        protected System.Data.SqlClient.SqlConnection sqlConnection1;

                private void Page_Load(object sender, System.EventArgs e)
                {
                        // Put user code to initialize the page here
                }

                #region Web Form Designer generated code
                #endregion

        }
}
```

ANALYSIS You'll notice that although declarations have been created for the `SqlConnection`, two `SqlDataAdapters`, and several `SqlCommand` objects, no code to manipulate these objects is evident. Because the code was generated by a wizard and can therefore be changed by a wizard, the Web Form Designer places the code in the expandable region after the `Page_Load` method. By expanding the region, you can view the roughly 130 lines of code that were generated, which we'll discuss later today.

Creating the User Interface

The only remaining task to make this application functional is to put a user interface on the Web Form and write some minimal code to get things rolling.

To begin, you'll need to drag and drop a `DataGrid` control, found in the Toolbox on the Web Forms tab, onto the Web Form. As you'll learn on Day 16, "ADO.NET in the User Services Tier," VS .NET ships with a variety of controls that can be bound to a `DataSet`, data reader, or in fact any object whose class implements the `IEnumerable` interface. When the grid is positioned and sized correctly, right-click on it and choose Property Builder to invoke the Properties dialog. From the Properties dialog, you can configure almost all the properties necessary to allow the user to display and edit the information in the product catalog.

Under the General tab, you first must bind the `DataGrid` to the `dsTitles1 DataSet` by choosing it from the drop-down menu. In addition, you must set the `DataMember` property to `Titles` because `dsTitles1` contains two tables and therefore can be used to display both `Titles` and `Categories` data. You can then set the Data key field option to `ISBN` because `ISBN` is the primary key of the `Titles` table, as shown in Figure 2.7.

FIGURE 2.7

The DataGrid Properties dialog. The General tab is used to set up data binding on the DataGrid.

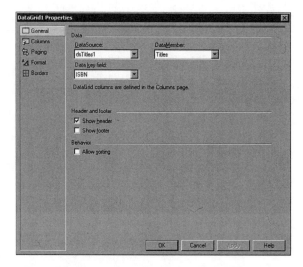

You'll do most of your work under the Columns tab. As you'll notice, the Create columns automatically at run time option is selected by default and will set up the grid for you automatically. In this case, because you want to allow editing of the grid, you should uncheck the box and select (All Fields) from the Available columns list and move it across to the Selected columns list using the arrow button.

As you scroll through the Select columns list, you'll notice that properties, such as the header text, can be set for each column. In this case, because you want the user to be able to edit only certain columns, you can go through the columns and mark ISBN, Title, Author, Publisher, and PubDate as read-only. In addition, because several of the columns (BulkDiscount, Discount, and Price) display currency, change their data formatting expression to "{0:c}" in order to display the amounts correctly.

For the grid to allow the user to shift a particular row into edit mode and subsequently update that row, you must add a Edit, Update, Cancel column to the grid found under the Button Column node in the Available columns list. After selecting it and moving to the Selected columns list, be sure to move it to the top of the list using the arrow button.

The only remaining task in the Columns tab is to transform the editable columns into template columns. Simply put, template columns can be used in a DataGrid control to render data items differently depending on the edit mode. In this case, we want to make sure that each editable column is rendered with a TextBox control to allow the user to change its values. To create the template columns, simply click on each editable column (Description, BulkAmount, BulkDiscount, Discount, and Price) in the Select columns list and click the link found at the bottom of the dialog to convert the column into a template column.

Also, in the Properties dialog, you can set the paging options using the Paging tab to ensure that only a specific number of rows is visible at any particular time. In this case, you might check the Allow paging option and set the page size to 5. Other navigation options are available, although the defaults will suffice in this case. Of course, you might also want to format the grid using the Format tab, for example, to change the font and size of the text that displays for the DataGrid, header, footer, or to even alternate items. After you've set the options you want, click OK and the grid should appear with the bound columns on the Web Form, as shown in Figure 2.8.

Tip

To easily format the grid with a professional appearance, right-click on it in the designer and select Auto Format. The grid shown in Figure 2.8 has been formatted using the Colorful 2 option.

FIGURE 2.8

A formatted DataGrid
control. Note that the
Properties window can
also be used to config-
ure properties such as
data binding for the
grid.

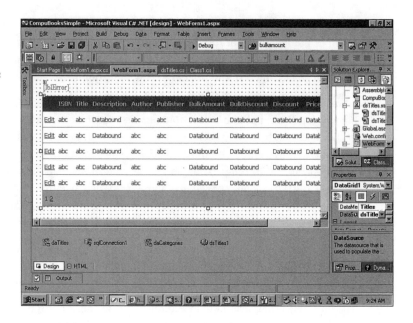

As mentioned previously, in this example we're using template columns to allow users to edit some of the columns when they click on the Edit link for a particular row. To provide specific names for the TextBox controls that are displayed, you can right-click the grid and select Edit Template. You'll see the five templated columns displayed. Click on each one in turn and the grid will show the template editor. Note that a templated column can render the header template, item template (the default view of the column), edit template, and footer template. The EditItemTemplate should already contain a TextBox, so you can simply click on it and change its ID in the Properties dialog. The names you can use might include txtDesc, txtBulkAmount, txtBulkDiscount, txtDiscount, and txtPrice. When you've renamed each of the controls, select End Template Editing from the context menu.

In addition to the grid control, add a Label control from the Web Forms tab of the toolbox to the top of the Web Form. This control will be used for rudimentary error handling, so rename the control lblError. You can place it at the top of the page.

At this point, we need to add code to the page to query the database and bind the data to the grid, to handle the paging of the grid, and to respond to the user clicking on Edit, Update, or Cancel for a particular row. To view the code, again right-click on the designer and select View Code or double-click on the WebForm1.aspx.cs code file in the Solution Explorer.

Retrieving Data

First, in a Web Form, the Load event of the page is called each time the page is first loaded and when the page is posted back to the Web server in response to a user action such as clicking the Edit link. To make the data from the database available to code in the page, you must write code that queries the database, populates the DataSet, and binds it to the DataGrid control. To do so, you can write the code shown in Listing 2.2.

2

> **Note**
>
> One of the great things about ASP.NET is that it provides an event-driven programming model for Web-based applications similar to that familiar to developers who have used Visual Basic in the past. As in this example, you can simply write code that handles events fired (actually posted) as the user manipulates the page. The ASP.NET page framework handles the details of posting the events and calling the correct event handlers on the server side. For more information about the sequence and processing that takes place, see Chapter 11 of my book *Building Distributed Applications with Visual Basic .NET,* published by Sams.

LISTING 2.2   Page Load event. The Load event of the page can be used to populate the DataSet and bind it to controls on the page.

```
private void Page_Load(object sender, System.EventArgs e)
{
  // Fill the dataset
  daCategories.Fill(dsTitles1, "Categories");
  daTitles.Fill(dsTitles1, "Titles");

  if (!Page.IsPostBack)
    {
      // Bind the Data
      DataGrid1.DataBind();
    }
}
```

ANALYSIS   In Listing 2.2, we first use the two data adapters to query the database using their Fill methods. The Fill method invokes the SelectCommand associated with the data adapter, and uses the results to populate the DataSet passed as a parameter. The Fill method is overloaded (that is, it has multiple sets of arguments), and in this case, you can pass the DataSet along with the name of the table within the DataSet that should be populated. Then, to make sure that the data is bound to the grid, you simply call the DataBind method of the control. This snippet also shows wrapping the execution of the DataBind method in a check of the IsPostBack property of the page so that the binding occurs only when the page is first loaded, and not in response to user actions such as putting the grid into edit mode.

Allowing Navigation

Next, you can add code for the PageIndexChanged event raised when the user navigates to a new page. Although the Properties dialog sets up all the required properties, it does not write the code to handle the event, which is shown in Listing 2.3.

LISTING 2.3 Handling navigation. The PageIndexChanged event will fire when the user navigates to a new page within the grid control.

```
private void DataGrid1_PageIndexChanged(object source,
  DataGridPageChangedEventArgs e)
{
  DataGrid1.CurrentPageIndex = e.NewPageIndex;
  DataGrid1.DataBind();
}
```

ANALYSIS As you can see in Listing 2.3, the DataGridPageChanged object contains the number of the page the user is navigating to in its NewPageIndex property. Setting the CurrentPageIndex property of the DataGrid and then calling DataBind displays the appropriate page in the grid.

Handling Editing Events

Finally, the most sophisticated code you need to write handles the three events raised when the user initially selects a row for editing, updates the row, or chooses the cancel option. Keep in mind that these options are available because you added the button column to the grid in the Property Builder dialog.

The three events can be handled using the code shown in Listing 2.4.

LISTING 2.4 Handling editing events. This listing shows how you can handle the events fired when the user edits data in a DataGrid control.

```
private void DataGrid1_EditCommand(object source, DataGridCommandEventArgs e)
{
    DataGrid1.EditItemIndex = e.Item.ItemIndex;
    DataGrid1.DataBind();
}

private void DataGrid1_CancelCommand(object source, DataGridCommandEventArgs e)
{
    DataGrid1.EditItemIndex = -1;
    DataGrid1.DataBind();
```

LISTING 2.4 continued

```csharp
    }

    private void DataGrid1_UpdateCommand(object source, DataGridCommandEventArgs e)
    {
        // Extract the data from the template controls
        TextBox descBox = (TextBox)(e.Item.Cells[1].FindControl("txtDesc"));
        string desc = descBox.Text;

        TextBox baBox = (TextBox)(e.Item.Cells[1].FindControl("txtBulkAmount"));
        string bulkAmount = baBox.Text;

        TextBox bdBox = (TextBox)(e.Item.Cells[1].FindControl("txtBulkDiscount"));
        string bulkDiscount = bdBox.Text;

        TextBox disBox = (TextBox)(e.Item.Cells[1].FindControl("txtDiscount"));
        string discount = disBox.Text;

        TextBox prBox = (TextBox)(e.Item.Cells[1].FindControl("txtPrice"));
        string price = prBox.Text;

        try
        {
            // Update the DataSet
            dsTitles1.Titles[e.Item.DataSetIndex].Description = desc;
            dsTitles1.Titles[e.Item.DataSetIndex].BulkAmount =
                System.Int16.Parse(bulkAmount);
            dsTitles1.Titles[e.Item.DataSetIndex].BulkDiscount =
                System.Decimal.Parse(bulkDiscount);
            dsTitles1.Titles[e.Item.DataSetIndex].Discount =
                System.Decimal.Parse(discount);
            dsTitles1.Titles[e.Item.DataSetIndex].Price =
                System.Decimal.Parse(price);

            // Update the database
            daTitles.Update(dsTitles1.GetChanges());
        }
        catch (Exception ex)
        {
            lblError.Text = "An error occurred:" + ex.Message;
            return;
        }

        // Switch out of edit mode.
        lblError.Text = "";
        DataGrid1.EditItemIndex = -1;
        DataGrid1.DataBind();
    }
```

2

ANALYSIS As you can see from Listing 2.4, two of the events are trivial. The EditCommand and CancelCommand events of the DataGrid are used to simply shift the grid into and out of edit mode. This is done by setting the EditItemIndex property of the DataGrid to 1 and -1, respectively, and calling the DataBind method to bind the data from the dsTitles1 object to the grid.

The code in the UpdateCommand, however, is more complicated because it's responsible for extracting the modified data from the TextBox controls and saving the data to the database. As you can see, the first section of the code extracts the values from the Text property of the TextBox controls by finding the control in the current row using the FindControl method. The Item (row) that is being edited is passed in the DataGridEventArgs object and its cells accessed through the Cells collection.

Next, the DataSet and database updates are wrapped in a try catch block in order to intercept any exceptions that might be thrown and display the message in the lblError control before exiting the method. Exiting the method before changing the EditItemIndex property back to -1 ensures that the grid will remain in edit mode, and gives the users a chance to correct their errors and resubmit the changes. The DataSet needs to be updated because while the columns in the grid are bound to the DataSet for display, they do not automatically update the DataSet. In this case, the DataSetIndex property of the Item can be used to determine which row in the DataSet was changed, and then its properties are set accordingly using the Titles DataTable object exposed by the dsTitles class. Note that the data types of the columns must be honored, so the strings must be converted to short or decimal data types in this case.

> **Note**
>
> As you learned yesterday, the ability to access data both relationally and in an object-oriented syntax was a design goal for ADO.NET. The typed DataSet dsTitles exposes objects such as Titles that make accessing the underlying data much easier.

To actually perform the database update, call the Update method of the daTitles data adapter and pass it a DataSet to update. The GetChanges method of the DataSet simply creates a DataSet with only the modified rows in it. This obviously cuts down on the amount of data being passed to the method, and is particularly effective when passing data between processes or machines in a distributed application. The Update method looks for modified and deleted rows and invokes its UpdateCommand or DeleteCommand, respectively. In this case, the usp_UpdTitles stored procedure that was created previously will be called with the new data.

Tip

When using SQL Server, to see the statements invoked on the server and to aid in debugging, use the Profiler utility found in the Microsoft SQL Server program group.

If no exceptions occur, the EditItemIndex property is set back to –1 to take the grid out of edit mode and the new data is bound to the grid for display.

Binding the Events

The final step is to bind the three methods in Listing 2.4 and the method for the PageIndexChanged event to the events of the grid control. This can be done graphically by clicking on the lightning bolt in the Properties window for the grid and dropping down the appropriate event and selecting the methods you just created. This adds code like that shown in Listing 2.5 to the Web Form Designer generated code in the InitializeComponent method.

LISTING 2.5 Binding the events. This listing shows how you add event handlers for the events of the DataGrid control.

```
this.DataGrid1.PageIndexChanged += new
    System.Web.UI.WebControls.DataGridPageChangedEventHandler(
    this.DataGrid1_PageIndexChanged);
this.DataGrid1.CancelCommand += new
    System.Web.UI.WebControls.DataGridCommandEventHandler(
    this.DataGrid1_CancelCommand);
this.DataGrid1.EditCommand += new
    System.Web.UI.WebControls.DataGridCommandEventHandler(
    this.DataGrid1_EditCommand);
this.DataGrid1.UpdateCommand += new
    System.Web.UI.WebControls.DataGridCommandEventHandler(
    this.DataGrid1_UpdateCommand);
```

 Note

In case you're not familiar with C#, the this operator is used to reference members of the current instance. In other words, this.DataGrid1 refers to the instance of the DataGrid1 object associated with the current page.

You can then run the page in the browser and it should appear as shown in Figure 2.9. Note that in this figure the Edit link for the row has been clicked and the row's data has been edited. The product catalog application can be tested by modifying the values and clicking Update to save the record to the database.

FIGURE 2.9

Running the product catalog. Here the row is in edit mode and its data can be modified.

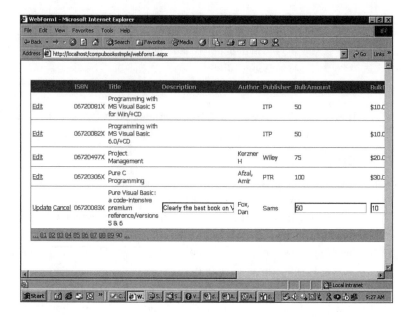

ADO.NET in Code

Although you have completed a functional ADO.NET application, you've only written a handful of lines of code to make it functional. As mentioned previously, this is due to the work of the various wizards, particularly the Data Adapter Configuration Wizard, and the property dialogs. This section will briefly look at selected sections of the ADO.NET code that was written so you can begin to get familiar with what's under the covers in preparation for the days ahead.

All the code that will be discussed was placed in the private `InitializeComponent` method of `WebForm1` class in the WebForm1.aspx.cs file. This method is called in the `OnInit` method of the `WebForm1` class, itself called by ASP.NET the first time the page is loaded when requested by an individual client. You can view the `InitializeComponent` method by expanding the Web Form Designer generated code region.

Making a Connection

First, remember that the data connection we created at the very beginning of this day was used by the Data Adapter Configuration Wizard to place the `sqlConnection1` object on the form designer. The result included two lines of code in addition to the declaration shown in Listing 2.1:

```
this.sqlConnection1 = new System.Data.SqlClient.SqlConnection();

this.sqlConnection1.ConnectionString = "data source=.;" +
  "initial catalog=ComputeBooks;integrated security=SSPI;persist security" +
  " info=False;workstation id=SSOSA;packet size=4096";
```

Obviously, the first line instantiates the new connection object, and the second initializes the string that contains the properties used to create the connection. In this case, you'll notice that the connection string indicates that the data exists on the local server, and integrated security (the identity or Windows account of the process running the code) will be used for authentication. These settings can be changed simply by editing the string here, although a more maintainable approach is to store the connection string separate from the code so that it can be changed without changing and recompiling the code. Several techniques for doing so will be discussed on Day 9, "Using Connections and Transactions."

The other interesting point to note is that the Open and Close methods of the SqlConnection class are never called explicitly. This is the case because the SqlDataAdapter calls them for you as it is used to Fill a DataSet and Update its contents.

Setting Up a Command

For the data adapter to do its work, of course, it must call the stored procedures that were created when you ran the Data Adapter Configuration Wizard. As mentioned yesterday, one of the convenient aspects of ADO.NET is that it integrates support for calling stored procedures to perform all aspects of data manipulation. In addition to creating stored procedures in the ComputeBooks SQL Server database to handle the select, insert, update, and delete actions for the Titles table, it wrote code in the InitializeComponent method to instantiate a SqlCommand object for each object and configure its parameters. For example, the code in Listing 2.6 was written to define the command object used to handle the update action of the user called when the Update method of the data adapter is called in Listing 2.4.

LISTING 2.6 Creating a command. This code written by the wizard configures the update command for the data adapter.

```
this.sqlUpdateCommand1 = new System.Data.SqlClient.SqlCommand();

this.sqlUpdateCommand1.CommandText = "[usp_UpdTitles]";
this.sqlUpdateCommand1.CommandType = System.Data.CommandType.StoredProcedure;
this.sqlUpdateCommand1.Connection = this.sqlConnection1;
```

LISTING 2.6   continued

```
this.sqlUpdateCommand1.Parameters.Add(new
  System.Data.SqlClient.SqlParameter("@RETURN_VALUE",
  System.Data.SqlDbType.Int, 4, System.Data.ParameterDirection.ReturnValue,
  false, ((System.Byte)(0)), ((System.Byte)(0)), "",
 System.Data.DataRowVersion.Current, null));
this.sqlUpdateCommand1.Parameters.Add(new
  System.Data.SqlClient.SqlParameter("@ISBN",
  System.Data.SqlDbType.NVarChar, 10, "ISBN"));
this.sqlUpdateCommand1.Parameters.Add(new
  System.Data.SqlClient.SqlParameter("@Title",
  System.Data.SqlDbType.NVarChar, 100, "Title"));
this.sqlUpdateCommand1.Parameters.Add(new
  System.Data.SqlClient.SqlParameter("@Description",
  System.Data.SqlDbType.NVarChar, 2048, "Description"));
this.sqlUpdateCommand1.Parameters.Add(new
  System.Data.SqlClient.SqlParameter("@Author",
  System.Data.SqlDbType.NVarChar, 250, "Author"));
this.sqlUpdateCommand1.Parameters.Add(new
  System.Data.SqlClient.SqlParameter("@Publisher",
  System.Data.SqlDbType.NVarChar, 50, "Publisher"));
this.sqlUpdateCommand1.Parameters.Add(new
  System.Data.SqlClient.SqlParameter("@CatID",
  System.Data.SqlDbType.UniqueIdentifier, 16, "CatID"));
this.sqlUpdateCommand1.Parameters.Add(new
  System.Data.SqlClient.SqlParameter("@BulkAmount",
  System.Data.SqlDbType.SmallInt, 2, "BulkAmount"));
this.sqlUpdateCommand1.Parameters.Add(new
  System.Data.SqlClient.SqlParameter("@BulkDiscount",
  System.Data.SqlDbType.Money, 8, "BulkDiscount"));
this.sqlUpdateCommand1.Parameters.Add(new
  System.Data.SqlClient.SqlParameter("@Discount",
  System.Data.SqlDbType.Money, 8, "Discount"));
this.sqlUpdateCommand1.Parameters.Add(new
  System.Data.SqlClient.SqlParameter("@Price",
  System.Data.SqlDbType.Money, 8, "Price"));
this.sqlUpdateCommand1.Parameters.Add(new
  System.Data.SqlClient.SqlParameter("@PubDate",
  System.Data.SqlDbType.DateTime, 4, "PubDate"));
this.sqlUpdateCommand1.Parameters.Add(new
  System.Data.SqlClient.SqlParameter("@Original_ISBN",
  System.Data.SqlDbType.NVarChar, 10, System.Data.ParameterDirection.Input,
  false, ((System.Byte)(0)), ((System.Byte)(0)), "ISBN",
  System.Data.DataRowVersion.Original, null));
```

ANALYSIS   As you can see from Listing 2.6, the `sqlUpdateCommand1` object is instantiated first. The command is then configured by setting its `CommandText` property to the name of the stored procedure to execute, and setting the `CommandType` to a value from an enumerated type that specifies what kind of command was placed in the CommandText property. Finally, the connection object that will be used to communicate with the database is set using the Connection property.

In addition to the command shown in Listing 2.6, the wizard also created and configured four other command objects that include the select, insert, and delete commands for the daTitles data adapter and the select command of the daCategories data adapter.

The remainder of Listing 2.6 contains code used to create the parameters used to call the stored procedure. Note that the parameters are added to a collection using the Add method. You'll learn more about parameters on Day 10. For comparison, the actual stored procedure generated and saved to SQL Server by the wizard is shown in Listing 2.7.

LISTING 2.7 The Update stored procedure. This procedure was created by the Data Adapter Configuration Wizard and is used to update a row in the Titles table.

```
CREATE PROCEDURE dbo.usp_UpdTitles
(
        @ISBN nchar(10),
        @Title nvarchar(100),
        @Description nvarchar(2048),
        @Author nvarchar(250),
        @Publisher nvarchar(50),
        @CatID uniqueidentifier,
        @BulkAmount smallint,
        @BulkDiscount money,
        @Discount money,
        @Price money,
        @PubDate smalldatetime,
        @Original_ISBN nchar(10)
)
AS
SET NOCOUNT OFF;

UPDATE Titles SET ISBN = @ISBN, Title = @Title, Description = @Description,
 Author = @Author, Publisher = @Publisher, CatID = @CatID,
 BulkAmount = @BulkAmount, BulkDiscount = @BulkDiscount, Discount = @Discount,
 Price = @Price, PubDate = @PubDate WHERE (ISBN = @Original_ISBN);

SELECT ISBN, Title, Description, Author, Publisher, CatID, BulkAmount,
 BulkDiscount, Discount, Price, PubDate
FROM Titles
WHERE (ISBN = @ISBN) ORDER BY Title
GO
```

Configuring a Data Adapter

Not only did the wizard create the command objects that execute the stored procedures in the database, it also had to configure the data adapters to associate them with the command objects. Data adapters expose `SelectCommand`, `InsertCommand`, `UpdateCommand`, and `DeleteCommand` properties that are populated with commands like those shown in Listing 2.6. In the `InitializeComponent` method, the code looks like the following:

```
this.daTitles.DeleteCommand = this.sqlDeleteCommand1;
this.daTitles.InsertCommand = this.sqlInsertCommand1;
this.daTitles.SelectCommand = this.sqlSelectCommand1;
this.daTitles.UpdateCommand = this.sqlUpdateCommand1;
```

Finally, the wizard configured the `TableMappings` collection as shown in Figure 2.5. The code to do so can be seen in Listing 2.8.

LISTING 2.8   Table mappings. The wizard wrote the following code to add the table and column mappings to the data adapter.

```
this.daTitles.TableMappings.AddRange(
 new System.Data.Common.DataTableMapping[] {
  new System.Data.Common.DataTableMapping("Table", "Titles",
    new System.Data.Common.DataColumnMapping[] {
    new System.Data.Common.DataColumnMapping("ISBN", "ISBN"),
    new System.Data.Common.DataColumnMapping("Title", "Title"),
    new System.Data.Common.DataColumnMapping("Description", "Description"),
    new System.Data.Common.DataColumnMapping("Author", "Author"),
    new System.Data.Common.DataColumnMapping("Publisher", "Publisher"),
    new System.Data.Common.DataColumnMapping("CatID", "CatID"),
    new System.Data.Common.DataColumnMapping("BulkAmount", "BulkAmount"),
    new System.Data.Common.DataColumnMapping("BulkDiscount", "BulkDiscount"),
    new System.Data.Common.DataColumnMapping("Discount", "Discount"),
    new System.Data.Common.DataColumnMapping("Price", "Price"),
    new System.Data.Common.DataColumnMapping("PubDate", "PubDate")}})});
```

ANALYSIS   Basically, this code adds new `DataColumnMapping` objects to a collection associated with the `Titles` table in a `DataSet` that the data adapter will populate using its `Fill` method. The data adapter uses this collection to map the column names from the database (the first argument in the constructor) to the columns in the `DataSet` (the second argument in the constructor). In this case, you'll notice that all the mappings use the same names, so the map needn't have been created.

Summary

Today you learned how to create a simple ASP.NET application using ADO.NET to update the product catalog of the ComputeBooks database. This application demonstrated some of the features of VS .NET and how they work with ADO.NET to generate code and allow graphical creation of even Web applications. In addition, you gained a perspective on how the components of ADO.NET fit together and the rudimentary code needed to make them work.

Tomorrow, you'll start to delve deeply into the DataSet object and how it can be manipulated programmatically.

Workshop

This workshop will help reinforce the concepts covered in today's lesson.

Quiz

1. What is the purpose of the Server Explorer in Visual Studio .NET?

   The purpose of the Server Explorer, along with the visual designers in VS .NET, is to allow rapid application development for server-based and middle-tier components by providing a drag-and-drop interface for manipulating server resources such as databases, message queues, event logs, and performance counters.

2. What three options does the Data Adapter Configuration Wizard provide for defining a query?

   Using SQL statements typed in or built with the Query Builder, creating new stored procedures on the fly, or specifying existing stored procedures. Stored procedures are recommended for accessing a SQL Server database.

3. How can you generate a DataSet from existing data adapters?

   If you have data adapters defined on the designer, you can right-click on the designer and choose Generate DataSet. The resulting dialog allows you to choose which select commands from the data adapters will be used to generate the definition of the data tables in the DataSet.

4. What is the purpose of template columns in a DataGrid control?

   Template columns are used to provide alternative renderings for columns in the DataGrid. For example, you can provide a Label control for default viewing of the column and a DropDownList control for editing.

Exercise

You'll notice that although we added a data adapter to read the Categories table and create a relation in the DataSet to relate the CatID columns in the Titles and Categories table, we didn't actually display a Categories column. In this exercise, modify the WebForm1.aspx page to add a read-only column to display the category description.

Answers for Day 2

Exercise Answer

One simple technique that you can use to add the category description column to the grid is to first create a new template column in the grid. This can be accomplished programmatically by editing the HTML and adding the new Category column after the Price column as follows:

```
<asp:TemplateColumn HeaderText="Category">
 <ItemTemplate>
  <asp:Label id="Label7" runat="server"
    Text='<%# this.GetCategory(DataBinder.Eval(Container,"DataItem.CatId"))%>'>
  </asp:Label>
 </ItemTemplate>
</asp:TemplateColumn>
```

Note that this template column contains only an ItemTemplate tag because the column is not editable. The Text attribute passes the CatId column for the current row to a method on the page called GetCategory. This method should return the Description given the CatId as follows.

```
protected string GetCategory(object CatId)
{
    dsTitles.CategoriesRow dr =
     (dsTitles.CategoriesRow)dsTitles1.Categories.Select(
     "CatID = '" + CatId.ToString() + "'")[0];
    return dr.Description;
}
```

You'll learn more about the Select method used here tomorrow.

WEEK 1

DAY 3

Working with DataSets

Yesterday you walked through an end-to-end example of building an ASP.NET application designed to put the use of ADO.NET in perspective. However, the reliance on code-generating wizards can certainly obscure the breadth of functionality that is at your disposal. For that reason, today and the next four days will be devoted to an in-depth look at all aspects of the `DataSet` object. Unlike yesterday, the format of the next few days will not take you through an application or work with graphical tools, but rather will examine short snippets and code listings that highlight specific features and behaviors of the `DataSet`. Specifically, today you will learn the most common techniques for working with `DataSet` objects, including

- How a `DataSet` compares to an ADO `Recordset`
- How to programmatically populate and traverse a `DataSet`
- How to select and find rows within a table
- How to copy, clone, and merge `DataSet` objects
- How to be notified of events
- The importance and use of a `DataView`

Understanding the ADO.NET DataSet

The DataSet class is a member of the System.Data namespace. It represents the first of the two major components of the ADO.NET architecture you learned about on Day 1, "ADO.NET In Perspective," the other being the .NET Data Providers. Its major attributes include the following:

- It is XML-based.
- It is an in-memory cache of data that is not backed by a file or data store—it is disconnected.
- It is independent of a data store and cannot communicate with one by itself.
- It can store data in multiple tables from multiple data stores that can be related through foreign key relationships.
- It stores multiple versions of the data for each column and for each row in each table.
- It can be serialized with full fidelity to XML for transport between tiers of a distributed application even when those tiers reside on separate physical machines.

As is evident from this list, the DataSet provides the core object for building applications using a disconnected programming model. ADO.NET also supports a connected model for data retrieval through the use of the data readers, as you'll learn on Day 11, "Using a DataReader."

This list should also point to several of the similarities and differences between the DataSet and the Recordset object available in ADO that might be helpful if you are experienced with ADO. Similar to the DataSet, a Recordset could be disconnected from its data store and therefore act as an in-memory cache of data. Of course, it could also be used in a connected model depending on the cursor options that were set. Although the Recordset object stored multiple versions of each column for each of its rows, it was not by nature able to represent multiple tables without the use of the Data Shape Provider. The Recordset was not XML-based and could not be serialized to XML easily or flexibly. Finally, a Recordset was not independent of a data store because it tracked a Connection object and through its methods could send queries to the data source to populate, update, and refresh its data. To that end, the Recordset contained functionality found in the ADO.NET DataSet, data reader, and data adapter objects.

The DataSet class itself is derived from the class System.ComponentModel.MarshalByValueComponent, from which it receives its ability to be serialized, added to the VS .NET toolbox, and visually designed in a designer. Its place in the .NET Framework is shown in Figure 3.1.

FIGURE 3.1

The DataSet *in context within the .NET Framework. Note that all objects are ultimately derived from* System.Object *and that namespaces are denoted with dotted borders.*

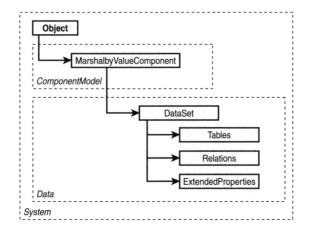

The major properties, methods, and events (collectively referred to as *members*) of the DataSet class can be seen in Table 3.1.

TABLE 3.1   Important DataSet Members

Member	Description
Properties	
CaseSensitive	Property that gets or sets whether string comparisons are case sensitive
DataSetName	Property that gets or sets the name of the DataSet
DefaultViewManager	Property that gets a custom view of data to allow searching, sorting, and filtering
EnforceConstraints	Property that specifies whether constraint rules are followed when updates occur
ExtendedProperties	A collection of custom information that resides with the DataSet
HasErrors	Property that indicates whether there are errors in any rows in any of the tables
Namespace	Property that gets or sets an XML namespace for the DataSet
Prefix	Property that gets or sets an XML prefix for the namespace for the DataSet
Collections	
Relations	A collection of relations housed in a DataRelationCollection object that link tables through foreign keys
Tables	A collection of tables (DataTable objects exposed through a DataTableCollection object) that store the actual data

TABLE 3.1   continued

Member	Description
Methods	
AcceptChanges	Method that commits all changes to the DataSet
Clear	Method that removes all rows from all tables
Clone	Method that copies the structure but no data from the DataSet
Copy	Method that copies both the structure and data of a DataSet
GetChanges	Method that returns a copy of the DataSet with only changed rows or those that match a given DataRowState filter
GetXml	Method that returns an XML representation of the data
GetXmlSchema	Method that returns an XML representation of the structure of the DataSet
HasChanges	Method that returns a value indicating that there are pending changes
InferXmlSchema	Method that infers the structure of the DataSet based on a file or stream
Merge	Method that merges this DataSet with one provided
ReadXml	Method that loads an XML schema and data into a DataSet
ReadXmlSchema	Method that loads an XML schema into a DataSet
RejectChanges	Method that rolls back all changes made to a DataSet (opposite of AcceptChanges)
Reset	Method that reverts the DataSet to its original state
WriteXml	Method that writes XML data and optionally the schema to a file or stream
WriteXmlSchema	Method that writes the XML schema to a file or stream
WriteXmlSchema	Method that writes the XML schema to a file or stream
Events	
MergeFailed	Event that fires when a merge fails due to constraint violations

Throughout the next several days, you'll become very familiar with these members and how they can be used in your applications. Keep in mind that through overloading, many of the methods shown in Table 3.1 can accept different sets of arguments and therefore work in several different ways.

Populating a `DataSet`

As you learned yesterday, a `DataSet` can be populated by a data adapter by calling the data adapter's `Fill` method. The `Fill` method invokes the command object referenced in the data adapter's `SelectCommand` property, and the data is subsequently loaded into the `DataSet` using the mapping found in the `TableMappings` property of the data adapter. This technique is far and away the one that you'll use most frequently to load data into a `DataSet`.

However, because the `DataSet` is a standalone object, it can also be programmatically loaded using its `Tables` collection. For example, the code in Listing 3.1 written in VB .NET creates a `DataSet` and populates it with two stores.

> **Referencing ADO.NET**
>
> Because ADO.NET is so integral to creating applications in .NET, when using VS .NET, new projects in both VC# .NET and VB .NET automatically add a reference to the ADO.NET assembly. However, in VC# .NET, you must include a `using System.Data;` statement in your source code file to avoid having to fully qualify the names of ADO.NET objects as in `System.Data.DataSet`. In VB .NET, the story is a little different because its Project Property dialog includes the Imports page that by default includes the `System.Data` namespace. Therefore, the `Imports System.Data` statement doesn't have to appear in VB .NET source code files (unless you're going to compile them from the command line). The page can be seen and modified to include other namespaces, such as `System.Data.SqlClient` or `System.Data.OleDb`, by right-clicking on the project name in the Solution Explorer when working with a VB .NET project and selecting properties. The Imports page is under Common Properties.

LISTING 3.1 Populating a `DataSet` programmatically. This code populates a `DataSet` with store information.

```vb
Dim stores As New DataSet("NewStores")
Dim storesTable As DataTable
Dim store As DataRow
Dim dcID As DataColumn

stores.CaseSensitive = False
stores.Namespace = "www.compubooks.com/stores"
stores.Prefix = "cbkss"

' Add the new table
storesTable = stores.Tables.Add("Stores")

' Define the columns
```

LISTING 3.1 ` continued

```
With storesTable
  .Columns.Add("StoreID", GetType(System.Guid))
  .Columns.Add("Address", GetType(String))
  .Columns.Add("City", GetType(String))
  .Columns.Add("StateProv", GetType(String))
  .Columns.Add("PostalCode", GetType(String))
End With

' Create a new row
store = storesTable.NewRow
With store
  .Item("Address") = "5676 College Blvd"
  .Item("City") = "Overland Park"
  .Item("StateProv") = "KS"
  .Item("PostalCode") = "66212"
  .Item("StoreID") = System.Guid.NewGuid
End With

' Add it
storesTable.Rows.Add(store)

' Add a second row
Dim newValues() As Object = {System.Guid.NewGuid, _
  "5444 Elm", "Shawnee", "KS", "66218"}
storesTable.Rows.Add(newValues)
```

ANALYSIS You'll notice in Listing 3.1 that the constructor of the DataSet accepts a string that is used to specify the name of the DataSet. This can also be set using the DataSetName property if you use the alternative constructor that accepts no arguments. Properties of the DataSet including the XML Namespace and Prefix are then set to ensure that if it were serialized to XML and transported to a trading partner, for example, the data could be differentiated.

Note

In this example, the CaseSensitive property is set to False to disable case-sensitive searching and filtering on the DataSet. As you'll learn tomorrow, there is also a CaseSensitive property on the DataTable class. As you would expect, setting the property on the table overrides the property on the DataSet, and resetting the property on the DataSet has no effect on tables that have already had their CaseSensitive property set. It should also be noted that the CaseSensitive property affects only string comparisons with data and not the names of columns. In other words, case is not taken into account when accessing column names even if the CaseSensitive property is set to True.

To track store information, a `DataTable` object is created and added to the `Tables` collection of the `DataSet` using the `Add` method of the underlying `DataTableCollection` object. As you'll learn tomorrow, the `DataTable` exposes a collection of the `DataColumn` objects in its `Columns` collection. In Listing 3.1, columns are added to the table using the `Add` method. Although there are several overloaded `Add` methods, the one used here simply accepts the name of the column and its data type. The `StoreID` column is the unique identifier, and so its data type is `System.Guid`, whereas the rest simply map to the VB .NET `String` data type (`System.String` behind the scenes).

After the table's structure is created, the first row is added by first creating the `DataRow` object using the `NewRow` method and then populating each individual column exposed through the `Item` collection. Although the new row was created with the `NewRow` method, it must be added to the table explicitly using the `Add` method of the `DataRowCollection` class exposed through the `Rows` property.

The second row is added using a different technique. In this case, the values for the new row are placed into an array of type `Object` and then simply passed to the overloaded `Add` method of the `DataRowCollection` class. Note that in this case the values must be placed into the array positionally coinciding with the order of the columns in the `DataTable`. In addition, notice that the expression `System.Guid.NewGuid` is added as the first element in the array. This is the case because the first position represents the `StoreID` column, which must be uniquely generated.

Of course, you can also use a combination of the `Fill` method and the programmatic approach to build a `DataSet`. One typical example is when you want the `DataSet` to include both data from a data source and some application-generated data. For example, the rather hard-coded example in Listing 3.2 shows how the `DataSet` can first be filled using the `Fill` method and then modified to add a second table to store the criteria used to populate the other table. The criteria can then subsequently be used to remind the users how the rows they're seeing were found.

> **Tip**
> As you'll learn on Day 7, "DataSets and XML," a `DataSet` can also be loaded from an XML document.

LISTING 3.2   Combining techniques to populate a `DataSet`. This listing uses both the `Fill` method and the programmatic approach to populate a `DataSet`.

```
Dim con As New OleDbConnection( _
    "provider=sqloledb;server=ssosa;database=compubooks;trusted_connection=yes")
Dim da As New OleDbDataAdapter("usp_GetTitles", con)
Dim books As New DataSet("ComputeBooksTitles")
```

LISTING 3.2   continued

```
Dim criteria As DataTable
Dim strISBN As String = "06720001X"

da.SelectCommand.CommandType = CommandType.StoredProcedure
da.SelectCommand.Parameters.Add("@isbn", strISBN)

da.Fill(books, "Titles")

criteria = books.Tables.Add("Criteria")

' Define the columns
With criteria
  .Columns.Add("ISBN", GetType(String))
  .Columns.Add("Title", GetType(String))
  .Columns.Add("Author", GetType(String))
  .Columns.Add("PubDate", GetType(Date))
  .Columns.Add("CatID", GetType(System.Guid))
End With

' Add the row
Dim newValues() As Object = {strISBN, Nothing, Nothing, Nothing, Nothing}
criteria.Rows.Add(newValues)

' Make it permanent
criteria.AcceptChanges()
```

ANALYSIS   A second interesting aspect of Listing 3.2 is that it calls the AcceptChanges
method of the criteria DataTable when the criteria row has been added. This
is done to make sure that the new row has been committed to the DataSet and so if the
DataSet is passed to a data adapter for update, the adapter will not attempt to synchronize the changes with the data store. The code could have alternatively called the
AcceptChanges method of the DataSet, as shown in Table 3.1. This would have had the
effect of committing all changed or new rows in all tables within the DataSet.
Obviously, in this case, it makes sense to call AcceptChanges because the criteria will
never actually be stored in the database. In Listing 3.1, the AcceptChanges method
wasn't called because the new stores may be later inserted into a database using a data
adapter.

Traversing a DataSet

It should come as no surprise that after a DataSet has been populated, both its structure
and data can be traversed programmatically. Listing 3.3 uses the collections of the
DataSet and its children to write out information about each of the tables as well as the
rows in a DataSet populated through the stored procedure usp_GetTitlesLookups.

LISTING 3.3 Traversing a DataSet. This listing populates and traverses both the structure and data in a DataSet.

```
Dim con As New SqlConnection( _
  "server=ssosa;database=compubooks;trusted_connection=yes")
Dim da As New SqlDataAdapter("usp_GetTitlesLookups", con)
Dim dsLookup As New DataSet("LookupData")
Dim dt As DataTable
Dim dc, pk As DataColumn
Dim dr As DataRow

da.SelectCommand.CommandType = CommandType.StoredProcedure

da.MissingSchemaAction = MissingSchemaAction.AddWithKey
da.Fill(dsLookup)

For Each dt In dsLookup.Tables
  ' Table info
  Console.Write(dt.TableName)
  Console.WriteLine(" has " & dt.Rows.Count & " rows")
  Console.Write("Primary Key: ")
  For Each pk In dt.PrimaryKey
    Console.Write(pk.ColumnName)
  Next
  Console.WriteLine()

  ' Column Info
  For Each dc In dt.Columns
    Console.Write(dc.ColumnName & " ")
    Console.Write(dc.DataType.ToString & " ")
    Console.Write(dc.AllowDBNull & " ")
    Console.WriteLine(dc.Unique)
  Next
  Console.WriteLine()

  ' Data
  For Each dr In dt.Rows
    For Each dc In dt.Columns
      Console.Write(dc.ColumnName & ":")
      Console.WriteLine(dr.Item(dc))
    Next
  Next

Next
```

ANALYSIS In Listing 3.3, you'll notice that the DataSet is populated with the Fill method from the stored procedure. The interesting aspect of the usp_GetTitlesLookups stored procedure is that it contains SELECT statements from not just one but three tables, as shown here:

```
Create Procedure usp_GetTitlesLookups
As
Select * From Titles
Order By Title
Select * From Categories
Order by Description
Select * From Publishers
Order by Name
```

As a result, if the data source can stream multiple result sets to the client in a single statement, the Fill method of the data adapter can simply iterate them and create multiple tables within the DataSet. You'll also notice that the MissingSchemaAction property of the data adapter is set to the AddWithKey value from the MissingSchemaAction enumeration. Although covered in more detail tomorrow, this setting ensures that the tables within the DataSet will be loaded with the primary key and other information about the columns.

After filling the DataSet, the code consists of a series of For Each loops used to iterate the various collections. Each loop prints table and column information to the console followed by all the data in the table. A sample of the results printed to the console is shown here:

```
Table has 605 rows
Primary Key: ISBN
ISBN System.String False True
Title System.String False False
Description System.String True False
Author System.String False False
PubDate System.DateTime False False
Price System.Decimal False False
Discount System.Decimal True False
BulkDiscount System.Decimal True False
BulkAmount System.Int16 True False
Cover System.Byte[] True False
CatID System.Guid False False
Publisher System.String True False

ISBN:06720199X
Title:.NET Framework Essentials
Description:Great Books
Author:Thai/Lam..
PubDate:6/1/2001 12:00:00 AM
Price:29.99
Discount:10
BulkDiscount:11
BulkAmount:51
Cover:
CatID:21b60927-5659-4ad4-a036-ab478d73e754
```

```
Publisher:ORly
...
```

Note that unlike in ADO, the number of rows returned for each table can be queried before the data is traversed because the entire result set is first downloaded to the client. In addition, by setting the MissingSchemaAction property, the PrimaryKey property of the DataTable and the AllowDBNull and Unique properties of the DataColumn objects are populated with the correct values corresponding to the primary key constraint, nullability (NULL or NOT NULL) setting, and unique constraint information in SQL Server, respectively.

Finally, the data is traversed by iterating the Rows collection of DataRow objects. In this case, the ColumnName is printed along with the value.

Note

> Note that even though Option Strict is turned on, you don't have to convert the value of each column, dr.Item(dc), to a string using the CType function. This is because the WriteLine method of the Console object actually supports 18 different signatures that accept the data types returned by the Item collection. As a result, the appropriate data type will be chosen at runtime and converted to a String for display. This is an excellent example of an effective way to use overloaded members in a class.

Selecting Data

Although it is more efficient to supply the appropriate row selection criteria to a SELECT statement through a WHERE clause, there are times when you'll need to create a subset of the rows loaded to a DataSet. This can be accomplished through the use of the Select and Find methods of the DataTable and DataRowCollection objects, respectively.

The Select method of the DataTable object is overloaded and can return the entire contents of the table, the contents filtered by an expression, filtered and sorted rows, as well as filtered and sorted rows that match a particular state. For example, building on the code in Listing 3.3, the following code could be written to create an array of DataRow objects containing the books for a particular author:

```
Dim titles As DataTable
Dim foundRows() As DataRow

titles = dsLookup.Tables(0)

foundRows = titles.Select("Author = 'Fox, Dan'")
```

As you can see, the filter expression is similar to a WHERE clause but contains its own set of rules, as shown in Table 3.2. The array of DataRow objects can then be traversed using the For Each syntax shown in Listing 3.3. Of course, if just the rows for this author were required from the database, you should use the following syntax directly in the SelectCommand of the data adapter used to populate the DataSet or in the stored procedure with the author name passed in as a parameter:

```
SELECT * FROM Titles
WHERE Author = 'Fox, Dan'
```

TABLE 3.2 Expression Syntax Rules

Rule	Description
Column Names	You refer to column names using the name defined in the DataSet rather than the name in the underlying data store. Further, if a column name contains a special character, such as ~ ( ) # / \ = > < + - * & % | ^ ' " [ ], the name must be wrapped in brackets.
Literal Values	Strings must be placed in single quotes, dates must be bracketed in # (for example, #11/25/2001#), and numeric expressions can contain decimal points.
Operators	AND, OR, NOT, =, <, >, <=, >=, IN, LIKE, +, -, *, /, % (modulus) operators are supported with optional parentheses; otherwise, normal precedence rules apply. Note that string comparisons are case sensitive based on the CaseSensitive property of the DataSet object.
Wildcard Characters	Both * and % can be used interchangeably in wildcard expressions (for example, LIKE 'Fox*' or LIKE 'Fox%'). If the literal string contains one of these characters, it can be set off in brackets.
Functions	The CONVERT, LEN, ISNULL, IIF, and SUBSTRING functions are supported. They work as you would expect. More information can be found in the online help.
Aggregate Functions	The Sum, Avg, Min, Max, Count, StDev, and Var functions are typically used in conjunction with a reference to parent or child rows.
Parent and Child Relations	Rows associated through relationships can be accessed using dot notation, as in Child.column or Parent.column. If more than one child exists, you can pass the name of the relation using the syntax Child(relation).column.

Note

Table 3.2 lists the rules for creating expressions that are also used with the `Expression` property of the `DataColumn` class, which we'll discuss tomorrow, and the `RowFilter` property of the `DataView` class. However, each of these properties can be used for different purposes, and so although legal, not all the available syntax will make sense when used with a particular property. For example, using a string appropriate for a filter in the `Expression` property of the `DataColumn` will simply evaluate to a Boolean statement that will cause the value of the column to be a 0 (False) or 1 (True).

WHERE Versus Select

So, when should you use the `Select` method versus explicit parameters? The rule of thumb is always to retrieve only the data from the database that you're going to use. This means only the data the user needs to see and perhaps modify. In other words, it should be rare that you'd select the contents of an entire table and load it into a `DataSet`. Most `DataSets` will contain rows already filtered through a `WHERE` clause. They can then be further filtered for a particular use through the `Select` method.

This is the case because in most enterprise databases, the primary tables will contain many more than the approximately 600 rows in the `Titles` table in the sample database. Can you imagine loading the millions of titles tracked by a real bookseller into a `DataSet`? That approach would be terribly slow and consume a tremendous amount of memory on the middle-tier server where the `DataSet` is created. Database products such as SQL Server and Oracle are optimized to select data very quickly based on indexes created by the database administrator. As long as you query data based on these indexes, you're always better off letting the database do the heavy lifting.

In the previous example, if the `DataTable` has a primary key defined on it, as this one does, the rows will be added to the array in the order of the key. If no key is specified, the array will simply be populated in the order the rows were added to the table.

To explicitly control the sort order, you can specify the sort expression in the overloaded `Select` method. For example, to select all the books published by Sams in order of publication date, starting with the most recent, the following code could be used:

```
foundRows = titles.Select("Publisher = 'Sams'", "PubDate DESC")
```

In the previous two examples, the `Select` method filtered and sorted the current rows in the `DataSet`. However, because the `DataSet` stores both original and modified versions of each row, the `Select` method also supports selecting rows based on the state of the row in the table. The states are tracked using the `DataViewRowState` enumeration and can be set to one of eight values (Added, CurrentRows, Deleted, ModifiedCurrent, ModifiedOriginal, None, OriginalRows, and Unchanged). In other words, the previous example is equivalent to

```
foundRows = titles.Select("Publisher = 'Sams'", "PubDate DESC", _
    DataViewRowState.CurrentRows)
```

So, for example, you can use this overloaded signature to select rows that have not yet been modified like so:

```
foundRows = titles.Select("Publisher = 'Sams'", "PubDate DESC", _
    DataViewRowState.Unchanged)
```

You'll learn more about changing data and how it is tracked on Day 5, "Changing Data."

The second technique for selecting data is to use the Find method of the DataRowCollection object (exposed through the Rows collection of the DataTable object) to find one particular DataRow in the table based on the primary key. For example, using the Titles table retrieved in Listing 3.3 once again, the following syntax can be used to find a specific title:

```
Dim isbn As String
Dim foundRow As DataRow

isbn = "06720606X"

foundRow = titles.Rows.Find(isbn)
```

Note that the Find method is overloaded and accepts either a single value of type Object or an array of objects. In this case, a single value is passed because the primary key contains a single column. If the primary key were a composite key consisting of more than one value, an array containing these values in the order they are defined in the key could be passed. In addition, note that although Find accepts arguments of type Object, a String can be passed (even with Option Strict On) because all types in .NET derive from System.Object.

Of course, if no primary key is defined on the DataSet—for example, if the DataSet were not populated using MissingSchemaAction.AddWithKey—the Find method would throw a MissingPrimaryKeyException.

Manipulating Multiple DataSets

After a DataSet has been populated, you often need to use it in conjunction with other DataSet objects. In this section, you'll learn how to create a new DataSet based on an existing one as well as merge it with other DataSet objects.

Copying and Cloning

As you can see from Table 3.1, the `DataSet` object supports both `Copy` and `Clone` instance methods. Neither method is overloaded or accepts any arguments; however, the former copies both the data and structure of the `DataSet` and returns a new `DataSet`, whereas the latter copies only the structure.

As you might imagine, you should use the `Copy` method when you need to maintain the original `DataSet` and pass a copy to a process that may modify it. For example, Listing 3.4 shows an `AddCriteria` method that is passed in a `DataSet` and that then copies the `DataSet` and adds to it a new `DataTable`. The result is that the original `DataSet` remains unaffected, and a new `DataSet` with the new table will be returned from the method.

LISTING 3.4   Copying a `DataSet`. This method copies and then alters the new `DataSet`.

```
Public Function AddCriteria(ByVal ds As DataSet) As DataSet

    Dim criteria As DataTable
    Dim dsCopy As DataSet

    dsCopy = ds.Copy

    criteria = dsCopy.Tables.Add("Criteria")

    ' Define the columns
    With criteria
      .Columns.Add("ISBN", GetType(String))
      .Columns.Add("Title", GetType(String))
      .Columns.Add("Author", GetType(String))
      .Columns.Add("PubDate", GetType(Date))
      .Columns.Add("CatID", GetType(System.Guid))
    End With

    Return dsCopy

End Function
```

The `Clone` method works similarly but copies only the structure of the `DataSet`. You can use it, for example, to create a `DataSet` that will hold similar information but is not yet populated, as shown in the following code snippet:

```
Dim samsTitles As DataSet

samsTitles = titles.Clone()
```

3

In this case, `titles` is assumed to be a `DataSet` that might or might not have been previously populated with titles. However, the new `DataSet` will contain only Sams titles, so its structure can be populated by cloning `titles`.

Although you can use the `Copy` method to copy an entire `DataSet`, it is usually more important to create a new `DataSet` based on a subset of the rows from an existing `DataSet`. This can be easily done using the `GetChanges` method. This overloaded method is exposed by both the `DataSet` and `DataTable` objects. It returns either a new `DataSet` or `DataTable` that includes all the changes made to the object since the last time `AcceptChanges` was invoked, or the set of changes based on one or more of the five values from the `DataRowState` enumeration.

For example, Listing 3.5 is a template that shows how a client application could use the `GetChanges` method to create a new `DataSet` that contains only the rows that have been modified by the user and then send those changes to a data access object.

LISTING 3.5   Filtering rows. This method filters the rows that are sent to the data access object using the `GetChanges` method.

```
Public Sub SaveChanges(ByVal ds As DataSet)

  Dim dsErrors As DataSet

  If ds.HasChanges(DataRowState.Modified) Then

    Try
      Dim bus As New DAObject()

      ' Call the business object
      dsErrors = bus.Update(ds.GetChanges(DataRowState.Modified))

    Catch e As DAException
      ' Handle exception here
    End Try

  End If
End Sub
```

ANALYSIS   Note that in Listing 3.5, the `HasChanges` method of the `DataSet` object is also overloaded and can be passed a value from the `DataRowState` enumeration. In this case, it checks to see whether any rows have been modified and if so, instantiates the data access object and calls its `Update` method. The `Update` method accepts a `DataSet` that is created and populated on the fly with only changed data using the `GetChanges` method. Using this technique increases efficiency because passing only changed rows to the data access object results in less data being copied between tiers in your application. After updating the underlying data source (typically using a data adapter), the data access object may throw its own exception if an error occurs. It may, alternatively, pass back a DataSet object that contains the rows that caused errors or perhaps the original DataSet with values calculated by the data source (for example, primary key values or computed columns). You'll learn more about the GetChanges method and its usefulness on Day 5.

Merging DataSets

In addition to creating subsets of a DataSet, you can also merge the contents of two DataSet objects using the overloaded Merge method. This is particularly useful when you want to retrieve data to the client in smaller chunks or merge updated data returned from a middle-tier object with existing data on the client.

The Merge method can merge an array of DataRow objects, a DataTable object, or an entire DataSet into the current DataSet, defined as the one on which the method is called. Along the way, the method accepts optional arguments that specify whether rows from the merged data overwrite changes made to the current rows (the default) and what action to take if the schema of the merged rows doesn't match that of the current DataSet. To give you a feel for how the Merge method works, consider the code in Listing 3.6.

LISTING 3.6 Merging a DataSet. This code merges several DataSets together using various overloaded signatures.

```
Dim books As DataSet
Dim books1 As DataSet
Dim books2 As DataSet
Dim books3 As DataSet

books = GetTitles("Sams")

books.Tables(0).Rows(0).Item("Description") = "Interesting book"

books1 = GetTitles("Sams")

books.Merge(dsBooks1, True)

books2 = GetTitles("IDG")

books.Merge(dsBooks2.Tables(0).Select("Author = 'Krumm, Rob'"))

books3 = GetTitles("Wrox")
books3.Tables(0).Columns.Add(New DataColumn("Pre-release", _
  GetType(System.Boolean)))

books.Merge(dsBooks3, False, MissingSchemaAction.Add)
```

ANALYSIS Although the code in Listing 3.6 is contrived, it provides a good overview of how the Merge method works. First, assume that the GetTitles method returns a DataSet populated with the titles for the publisher passed in as the argument. In this case, the code first populates the books DataSet with the 44 titles for Sams in the database. The code then modifies the Description column of the first book to a String value in the next statement before retrieving the Sams titles again into a different DataSet called books1. The Merge method of books is then called and is passed both the DataSet to merge with books and an argument that indicates that previous changes to books will be preserved. Because the two DataSets contain the same set of primary keys, the Merge method will compare the key values and overlay the new data from books1 onto the rows in books while preserving any modified data in books. If the second argument were set to False, the rows from dsBooks1 would overwrite the books data completely. The end result is that books (or, more appropriately, the DataTable in books) still contains 44 rows, one of which has been modified.

Tip

In order for the Merge method to be able to compare rows based on the primary key, the key information must be defined for the DataSet. As mentioned previously, this can be done by setting the MissingSchemaAction property of the data adapter used to fill the DataSet to AddWithKey.

The code then retrieves the 22 titles from IDG into books2 and then uses the Select method to merge the returned array of DataRow objects into books. In this case, the author used in the filter expression has authored one book, and so books will now contain 45 rows.

Finally, the 49 Wrox titles are retrieved and placed in books3. In this case, the DataTable that contains the Wrox titles is modified to include a new Boolean column called Pre-release. When the Merge method is called to merge the Wrox titles into books, the third argument specifies the action to take if the Merge method finds that the schemas differ. The default, as is specified here, is to simply add the new column to the existing schema using MissingSchemaAction.Add. In cases where the data being merged comes from a trading partner or other organization, you might want to be alerted to the fact that the schemas do not match. To do so, use the MissingSchemaAction.Error value and a DataException will be thrown.

Handling Merge Errors

Merging data can cause errors to occur in two different ways. First, as you'll learn tomorrow, a DataSet can contain constraints including primary and foreign keys. Just as in a relational database, these constraints can be violated as data is merged into a DataSet that already contains data. For example, if data is loaded into a table that has a foreign key constraint on another table in the DataSet, and one or more rows do not contain valid foreign key values, the constraint will be violated.

During the merge process, the constraints are disabled and then re-enabled at the end of the merge. At that time, if the constraints can't be set due to errors, a ConstraintException will be thrown and the EnforceConstraints property will be reset to False, and the rows that contained errors are marked as such. Of course, if the EnforceConstraints property is set to False before the Merge method is called, the constraints are not re-enabled and so no errors will occur until the property is set to True.

Secondly, because the Merge method uses the primary key information in the tables being merged to match up rows that should be merged, the primary keys must be identical in the tables. If the primary keys differ in the number of columns that make up the key, an ArgumentException will be thrown. However, if the key length is the same but the columns differ, a ConstraintException will be thrown. In both cases, the MergeFailed event shown in Table 3.1 also will be fired. To capture the MergeFailed event, you can use the C# event handling syntax you learned yesterday or dynamic event handling syntax in VB as shown in Listing 3.7.

LISTING 3.7 Adding an event handler. This listing shows how to add a handler for the MergeFailed event.

```
AddHandler dsBooks.MergeFailed, AddressOf HandleMergeErrors

Try
  books.Merge(books1)
Catch e As ArgumentException
  ' Key lengths are different
Catch e1 As ConstraintException
  ' Keys have different columns
End Try


Private Sub HandleMergeErrors(ByVal sender As Object, _
  ByVal e As MergeFailedEventArgs)
  ' Called before Catch block is entered above
  Console.WriteLine(e.Conflict)
  Console.WriteLine(e.Table.TableName)
End Sub
```

ANALYSIS In Listing 3.7, the AddHandler statement in VB .NET is used to hook the MergeFailed event of the books DataSet object to the delegate returned by the

AddressOf operator. The delegate then points to the HandleMergeErrors method that accepts the standard object that produced the error (in this case, the DataSet) and an object of type MergeFailedEventArgs. The MergeFailedEventArgs object exposes the Conflict and Table properties that can then be inspected to return the particular error message and the table in which the error occurred, respectively.

Note

Delegates in .NET can be thought of as object-oriented function pointers and are used as the basis for events in the .NET Framework. In Listing 3.7, the AddressOf statement is actually shorthand for the statement New MergeFailedEventHandler(AddressOf HandleMergeErrors), where MergeFailedEventHandler is a delegate that is used to call methods that handle MergeFailed events. Using VB .NET, you could also declare the DataSet at the class or module level and use the WithEvents and Handles keywords to handle the event.

Using a DataView

The final common technique used to work with a DataSet is to display its data using a DataView. Simply put, a DataView object is a view of a particular DataTable within a DataSet that can expose the data in a particular sort order or can filter the data. In other words, you can use a DataView to create a filtered and sorted view of a DataTable and then bind that view to a Windows or Web Forms control by referencing the DataView in the control's DataSource property. Unlike the Select statement discussed earlier, the DataView doesn't create copies of the rows, but is dynamic in that all changes to the underlying DataTable are immediately reflected in the DataView.

Note

A DataView is different from a relational database view in several respects. First, a DataView always contains the entire set of columns present in the DataTable it references, whereas a relational view is often used to expose a subset of the columns from a table or to add additional computed and aggregated columns. Second, a DataView always refers to a single DataTable and therefore can't be used to display data from multiple tables as is frequently done in a relational view.

The important members of the DataView class are shown in Table 3.3.

TABLE 3.3 Important `DataView` Members

Member	Description
	Properties
AllowDelete	Property that gets or sets whether deletes are allowed
AllowEdit	Property that gets or sets whether modifications are allowed
AllowNew	Property that gets or sets whether new rows are allowed
ApplyDefaultSort	Property that gets or sets whether the default sort should be applied
Count	Property that returns the number of records in the view after the filters have been applied
DataViewManager	Property that gets the `DataViewManager` object associated with this view
Item	Property that returns a column value based on the index or name and an optional `DataRowVersion`
RowFilter	Property that gets or sets the expression used to filter the rows
RowStateFilter	Property that gets or sets the `DataViewRowState` value(s) used to filter the rows
Sort	Property that gets or sets the columns and sort orders to apply
Table	Property that gets the underlying `DataTable` object for this view
	Methods
AddNew	Method that adds a new row to the `DataView`
CopyTo	Method that copies the column values into an array
Delete	Method that deletes the row at the specified index
Find	Method that finds a row based on the current sort index
FindRows	Method that finds rows based on the current sort index
	Events
ListChanged	Event that fires when the underlying `DataTable` is changed

Creating a `DataView`

A `DataView` can be created either by instantiating a new `DataView` object and using its overloaded constructor, or by creating a reference to the view exposed by the `DefaultView` property of the `DataTable` object.

In the first case, the constructor is overloaded to accept the `DataTable` from which to create the view and, optionally, the sort order, row filter, and row state filter used to sort and populate the view. For example, the following code snippet creates a `DataView` that contains all the unchanged titles written by an author, sorted by title:

```
Dim books As DataSet
Dim dt As DataTable

books = GetTitles("Sams")
dt = dsBooks.Tables(0)

Dim dv As New DataView(dt, "Author = 'Fox, Dan'", _
  "Title ASC", DataViewRowState.Unchanged)
```

The last line of code above could also have been rewritten as follows:

```
dv = books.Tables(0).DefaultView

With dv
  .Sort = "Title ASC"
  .RowFilter = "Author = 'Fox, Dan'"
  .RowStateFilter = DataViewRowState.Unchanged
End With
```

In both cases, the resulting `DataView` is now ready to be used.

Sorting and Filtering

As is obvious from the preceding code snippets, the `Sort`, `RowFilter`, and `RowStateFilter` properties control how a `DataView` is sorted and filtered. It should be noted that the `Sort` property is of type `String` and can be set to multiple columns in order to create a multi-level sort. For example, to sort on `Price` and `PubDate`, you could use the following expression:

```
dv.Sort = "Price DESC, PubDate ASC"
```

When the `Sort` property is set, the `DataView` builds an index that is then used to display the data in sorted order. You'll also note from Table 3.3 that the `DataView` object exposes an `ApplyDefaultSort` property. This property can be set to `True` when the `Sort` property is set to an empty string or `Nothing` (null). It will reset the `Sort` property to sort by the value of the primary key if one is defined. Conversely, if the `Sort` property is already set, or a primary key hasn't been defined on the underlying `DataTable`, setting the property has no effect.

The `RowFilter` property is used in much the same way as the `Select` method of the `DataTable` object discussed previously. In fact, the expression syntax shown in Table 3.2 also applies to the `RowFilter` property. The `RowStateFilter` property can accept a bit-wise combination of values from the `DataViewRowState` enumeration also discussed earlier.

Finding Rows

In addition to being able to filter the DataView based on the RowFilter property, you can also more quickly search the DataView using the index built when the Sort property is set using the Find and FindRows methods.

The Find method is overloaded to accept a single Object or array of objects that map to the columns defined in the Sort property. For example, if the Sort property is set as in the previous code snippet, the following code would return the index of the row that has a price of $44.99 and a PubDate of 11/16/2001:

```
Dim row As Integer

row = dv.Find(New Object() {44.99, CType("11/16/2001", Date)})
```

If the row is not found, a –1 is returned.

The FindRows method is analogous to Find in its signatures, but returns a one-element array populated with a DataRowView object in order to expose the row to Windows Forms as a control. You wouldn't typically call the FindRows method yourself.

Capturing Changes

Just as with the DataSet class, the DataView class exposes a single event, in this case, called ListChanged. This event is fired anytime the data or schema of the underlying DataTable changes, including changes in the sort order or filter applied to the view. The ListChangedEventArgs object from the System.ComponentModel namespace passed to the event handling method exposes the ListChangedType, NewIndex, and OldIndex properties, which encapsulate the reason why the event was fired, the new index of the item in the list, and the original index of the modified item, respectively.

As you might expect, the values in the NewIndex and OldIndex properties are populated based on the value of the ListChangedType property. The ListChangedType property returns one of the eight values of the ListChangedType enumeration. For example, if the ItemMoved value is specified, both the NewIndex and OldIndex properties will be populated, whereas if the ItemAdded value is specified, only the NewIndex property is set. The default for both properties when not set is –1.

In addition to standard ItemAdded, ItemDeleted, ItemChanged, and ItemMoved values, the ListChangedType property also includes PropertyDescriptorAdded, PropertyDescriptorChanged, PropertyDescriptorDeleted, and Reset values. The first three values in the preceding list are set when schema additions, changes, and deletions are made to the underlying DataTable. The Reset value is used when the Sort, RowState, or RowStateFilter properties of the DataView are set.

3

Tip

Keep in mind that the way in which the RowStateFilter property is set also influences what the ListChangedType property will be set to. For example, if the RowStateFilter is set to DataViewRowState.Unchanged, a change to an underlying row in the DataTable will generate a value of ItemDeleted rather than ItemChanged because the row will be removed from the view. In the same way, changing the value of a column on which the Sort property is set generates an ItemMoved value rather than ItemChanged because the row must be moved within the DataView's index.

As an example, consider the code in Listing 3.8, which builds on the previous code that created the DataView object referred to as dv.

LISTING 3.8   Detecting changes. This code hooks the ListChanged event and writes the ISBN of the modified row to the Trace object.

```
AddHandler dv.ListChanged, AddressOf TitlesChanged

Private Sub TitlesChanged(ByVal sender As Object, _
  ByVal e As ListChangedEventArgs)

  If e.ListChangedType = ListChangedType.ItemChanged Then
    Dim dv As DataView
    Dim dr As DataRow
    dv = CType(sender, DataView)
    dr = dv.Item(e.NewIndex).Row
    Trace.WriteLine("Changed ISBN: " & dr.Item("ISBN").ToString)
  End If
End Sub
```

ANALYSIS   Note that in Listing 3.8, the AddHandler statement is used to enable the ListChanged event handler using the ListChangedHandler delegate encapsulating the address of the TitlesChanged method. In this case, the TitlesChanged method uses the ListChangedType property to determine whether a row was changed and, if so, uses the sender argument and the NewIndex property to reference the row that was changed. The WriteLine method of the Trace class is then used to log the fact that a change occurred.

Tip

The Trace class is a member of the System.Diagnostics namespace and can be used to instrument or equip your application with tracing code that displays to the Command Window in VS .NET or any target (such as an event log or text file) specified by a class derived from TraceListener. When used with the BooleanSwitch or TraceSwitch classes, you can create applications that selectively log trace information based on settings in the application's XML configuration file.

Managing Multiple Views

Because a DataSet can store data from multiple tables or data sources, it makes sense that you can also control the view settings (sort order and row filters) for each table in the DataSet. This is accomplished through the use of the DataViewManager class. The DataViewManager is primarily useful when you want to bind a DataSet with multiple tables to a control such as a grid to ensure that the grid displays each table correctly. Once again, you can populate the control's DataSource property with the DataViewManager object.

As with the DataView class itself, a DataViewManager object can be created in one of two ways. First, as you'll notice from Table 3.1, the DataSet exposes a DefaultViewManager property that points to a DataViewManager object that exposes a collection of DataViewSetting objects (DataViewSettingCollection) corresponding to each DataTable in the DataSet, as shown in Figure 3.2. By simply referencing the DefaultViewManager property, you are returned a DataViewManager object that contains DataViewSetting objects for each table. Second, you can instantiate your own DataViewManager, passing the DataSet into the constructor or populating its DataSet property.

FIGURE 3.2

The object hierarchy of the DataViewManager *class. The* DataViewManager *object for a* DataSet *can be accessed through the* DefaultViewManager *property.*

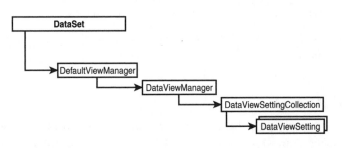

The DataViewSetting object exposes only a subset of the DataView members, including the ApplyDefaultSort, RowStateFilter, RowState, and Sort properties, along with properties that reference the underlying DataViewManager and Table. As a result, the DataViewSetting object is useful for changing the display characteristics of the underlying `DataTable`, but cannot be used to find rows or set the modification behavior. However, if the `RowFilter`, `RowStateFilter`, or `Sort` properties are changed in the `DataViewSetting` object, the corresponding properties in the `DataView` will also be set. This is the case because the `DataViewSetting` object simply reflects the values of the actual `DataView`.

As an example of using multiple views, consider the code snippet below. In this example, the `DataSet` dsOrders contains two tables that contain the `Orders` and `OrderDetails` information from the ComputeBooks database for a particular customer.

```
Dim orderV, orderDetV As DataViewSetting

orderV = orders.DefaultViewManager.DataViewSettings("Orders")
orderDetV = orders.DefaultViewManager.DataViewSettings("OrderDetails")

orderV.RowFilter = "OrderDate > #1/01/2002#"
orderDetV.Sort = "UnitPrice DESC"
```

In this case, the `DefaultViewManager` property of the `DataSet` object is used to access the `DataViewSettingCollection` in order to reference each `DataViewSetting` object. The `DataViewSetting` objects are then used to set the `RowFilter` property on the `Orders` table to display only the current year orders and sort the `OrderDetails` table by `UnitPrice`.

Optionally, the `dvsOrder` and `dvsOrderDet` objects could have been created independently, like so:

```
Dim dvm As New DataViewManager(dsOrders)

orderV = dvm.DataViewSettings("Orders")
orderDetV = dvm.DataViewSettings("OrderDetails")
```

In this case, the new `DataViewManager` object was passed the `DataSet` to create its collection on.

Summary

Today you learned about the basic workings of the `DataSet` and how it can be created, populated, traversed, searched, and viewed. These basic skills will allow you to work with `DataSet` objects programmatically. However, tomorrow you'll delve more deeply into the internals of the `DataSet` and explore the structure of `DataTable` objects as well the constraints that can be placed on data.

Workshop

This workshop will help reinforce the concepts covered in today's lesson.

Quiz

1. What data access programming model does the `DataSet` enable?

   The `DataSet` allows you to build applications that work with data that is entirely disconnected from its data source. It does this by storing the data in an in-memory cache represented as XML and that is serializable for transport across tiers in your application.

2. Can a single `DataSet` be populated using both a data adapter and explicit code?

   Yes. Different tables in a `DataSet` can be populated in different ways. For example, one table could be populated from a data adapter connected to SQL Server, another to a data adapter connected to Oracle, and a third through explicit code that creates new rows manually. This feature is what allows the `DataSet` to store heterogeneous data.

3. How do you combine the contents of two `DataSet` objects?

   You can combine the data in multiple `DataSet` objects using the `Merge` method of the `DataSet` object that will act as the final repository. Keep in mind that errors might result if the schema of the tables differs or if constraints are violated, and that changes in the original `DataSet` will be overridden by default. If the two `DataSet` objects contain different tables, they can simply be merged into a single `DataSet` that contains both tables.

4. What is the primary use for the `DataViewManager`?

   The `DataViewManager` is used to manage the view settings for the collection of tables in a `DataSet`. Basically, it exposes the sorting and filtering properties of the `DataView` objects associated with the tables in the `DataSet`. The `DataViewManager` can then be associated with a control's `DataSource` property to enable custom views during data binding.

Exercise

To try out the concepts discussed today, write a method that retrieves the `Titles`, `Categories`, and `Publishers` information from the ComputeBooks database using the `usp_GetTitlesLookups` stored procedure. After retrieving the data into a `DataSet`, create a `DataViewManager` that shows only the titles with a price greater than $25 and sorts the publishers by `PubCode`.

Answers for Day 3

Exercise Answer

One possible solution to the exercise is as follows:

```
Public Function GetTitlesLookups(ByVal connect As String) As DataViewManager

  Dim con As New SqlConnection(connect)
  Dim da As New SqlDataAdapter("usp_GetTitlesLookups", con)
  Dim dsTitlesLookups As New DataSet("TitlesLookups")

  ' Fill the DataSet
  da.Fill(dsTitlesLookups)

    ' Create the data view manager and set the properties
    Dim dvm As New DataViewManager(dsTitlesLookups)
    dvm.DataViewSettings("Table").RowFilter = "Price > 25"
    dvm.DataViewSettings("Table2").Sort = "PubCode ASC"

    Return dvm

End Function
```

In this method, the dsTitlesLookups DataSet is populated by the SqlDataAdapter da
using the Fill method. The DataSet will contain three tables (Table, Table1, and Table2,
which are the defaults) with the Titles, Categories, and Publishers data. The
DataViewManager can then be created and its individual DataViewSettings accessed
through the collection.

DAY 4

DataSet Internals

As you'll recall, yesterday's goal was to familiarize you with the various ways that you can manipulate DataSet objects when dealing with disconnected data. Today you'll dig deeper into the structure of the DataSet in order to fully exploit its capabilities to maintain data consistency and integrity. In fact, the three key topics in this chapter explore the three children of the DataSet class: Tables, Relations, and ExtendedProperties exposed as properties as shown in Figure 3.1. Much of the functionality of the DataSet is encapsulated in the objects of these three children.

Specifically, today you'll learn the following concepts:

- The classes used to represent tables, relationships, and properties in a DataSet
- How to create expression columns in a DataTable
- How to specify default values and set other properties of columns
- How to define and add unique, foreign, and primary key constraints to a DataTable
- How to generate primary keys on the client to be used in a database
- How to use extended properties

Data Table Structure

Certainly, the primary collection exposed by a DataSet is encapsulated in the DataTableCollection object and exposed through the Tables property. The DataTableCollection object in turn exposes DataTable objects that are used to cache the data within the DataSet. In this section, you'll learn how that data is exposed through rows and columns and how you can customize the properties of the table to assist in maintaining data integrity.

As you might imagine, the DataTable exposes some members that are similar to those found in the DataSet. The reason for this overlap is that the members of the DataSet, such as HasErrors, look at all tables within the DataSet, whereas the DataTable properties are particular to an instance. The major methods, properties, and events of the DataTable class can be seen in Table 4.1. You'll notice from Table 4.1 that the DataTable exposes more events to provide notification for changes to the data.

TABLE 4.1 Important DataTable Members

Member	Description
	Properties
CaseSensitive	Property that gets or sets whether string comparisons are case sensitive
ChildRelations	Property that gets or sets a collection of relationships for the table in a DataRelationCollection object
Columns	Property that gets or sets the collection of DataColumn objects associated with the table in a DataColumnCollection object
Constraints	Property that gets or sets the collection of constraint objects for the table in a ConstraintCollection object
DataSet	Property that gets the DataSet object this table belongs to
DefaultView	Property that gets a custom view of the table to allow searching, sorting, and filtering
DisplayExpression	Property that gets or sets a String used to represent the table in the user interface
ExtendedProperties	A collection of custom information that resides with the DataTable in a PropertyCollection object
HasErrors	Property that indicates whether there are errors in any rows of this table
MinimumCapacity	Property that gets or sets the initial size of the table defaulted to 25 rows; used by the system to efficiently allocate resources

TABLE 4.1 continued

Member	Description
Properties	
Namespace	Property that gets or sets an XML namespace for the DataTable
ParentRelations	Property that gets the collection of parent relationships for this table in a DataRelationCollection object
Prefix	Property that gets or sets an XML prefix for the namespace for the DataTable
PrimaryKey	Property that gets or sets an array of DataColumn objects that represent the primary key of the table
Rows	Property that gets the collection of rows in the table exposed in a DataRowCollection object
TableName	Property that gets or sets the name of the table
Methods	
AcceptChanges	Method that commits all changes to the DataTable
BeginLoadData	Method that turns off all notifications, indexes, and constraints during the loading of data
Clear	Method that removes all rows from this table
Clone	Method that copies the structure but no data from the DataTable
Compute	Method that computes the given expression on the current rows not excluded by filter criteria
Copy	Method that copies both the structure and data of a DataTable
EndLoadData	Method that turns on notifications, indexes, and constraints after loading data
GetChanges	Overloaded method that returns a copy of the DataTable with only changed rows or rows that match a given DataRowState value
ImportRow	Method that copies a given DataRow into the table preserving original and modified values as well as property settings
LoadDataRow	Method that finds and updates a specific row if present, and creates a new one if not; used with BeginLoadData and EndLoadData
NewRow	Method that returns a new DataRow with the same schema as a row in the table
RejectChanges	Method that rolls back all changes made to a DataTable since it was loaded or since AcceptChanges was called (opposite of AcceptChanges)

4

TABLE 4.1 continued

Member	Description
Methods	
Reset	Method that reverts the DataTable to its original state
Select	Overloaded method that returns an array of DataRow objects based on filter criteria or row state
Events	
ColumnChanged	Event fired after a value in a DataColumn changes
ColumnChanging	Event fired when a value in a DataColumn is being changed
RowChanged	Event fired after a DataRow has been successfully changed
RowChanging	Event fired when a DataRow is being changed
RowDeleted	Event fired after a DataRow has been deleted from the table
RowDeleting	Event fired before a row is deleted from the table

As with the DataSet, the DataTable class contains several collections, as shown in
Figure 4.1. These collections are used to represent the columns, rows, constraints, relationships, and extended properties.

FIGURE 4.1

The DataTable *object
and its child collec-
tions. This diagram
highlights the collec-
tions exposed by the*
DataTable *that make
up its structure.*

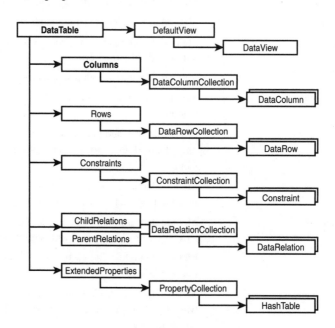

To illustrate the use of several of the methods of the `DataTable` class, consider the `LoadStores` method shown in Listing 4.1. Here, the method accepts a `DataTable` as a parameter and loads it with store information found in a text file.

LISTING 4.1   Loading a `DataTable`. This method loads a table from a text file.

```
Private Sub LoadStores(ByRef stores As DataTable)

  Dim storeFile As FileStream
  Dim reader As StreamReader
  Dim strLine As String
  Dim storeValues() As String
  Dim sep As String = ","

  Try
    storeFile = New FileStream("stores.txt", FileMode.Open)
    reader = New StreamReader(storeFile)
  Catch e As IOException
    ' Handle file errors here
  End Try

  Try
    stores.MinimumCapacity = 125
    stores.BeginLoadData()

    Do While True
      strLine = reader.ReadLine()
      If strLine Is Nothing Then
        Exit Do
      End If

      storeValues = strLine.Split(sep.ToCharArray)

      Dim dr As DataRow
      dr = stores.LoadDataRow(storeValues, False)
      dr.Item("StoreID") = System.Guid.NewGuid
    Loop

    stores.EndLoadData()

  Catch e As DataException
    ' Handle data exception (violated constraints)
  Catch e As IOException
    ' Handle file IO problems
  Catch e As Exception
    ' Handle other exceptions
    Throw e
  Finally
```

4

LISTING 4.1   continued

```
        storeFile.Close()
    End Try

End Sub
```

ANALYSIS Although Listing 3.1 in the previous chapter showed two methods that could be used to populate a `DataSet` programmatically, Listing 4.1 shows how you can also use the `LoadDataRow` method of the `DataTable` object directly. This is especially effective when you want to batch load a significant amount of data, as in this example.

> **Note** This method shows the basic use of the `FileStream` and `StreamReader` objects from the `System.IO` namespace to open and read the text file. As a result, this code would need the `Imports System.IO` statement at the top of the source file.

You'll notice in the second `Try` block that the `MinimumCapacity` property is first set to 125 to allow the common language runtime to preallocate resources for at least 125 rows. Setting this property appropriately can speed up the process of inserting data. The `BeginLoadData` method is then called to disable all notifications and constraints on the table to ensure that the data can be loaded without interruption.

> **Note** The `MinimumCapacity` property defaults to 25 and therefore should be used when you know that the `DataTable` will contain a good deal more than 25 rows because it can optimize performance. That said, worrying about setting this property—to the extent that you incur an extra roundtrip to the data store—doesn't make sense. The cost of the roundtrip will far outweigh the savings in memory allocation for the `DataTable`.

The data is then read from the text file and parsed into an array of strings using the `Split` method of the `String` class. If the array contains valid values for the columns in the `DataTable` that match the positional order of the columns, it can then be loaded with the `LoadDataRow` method. The second argument specifies whether to immediately call `AcceptChanges` on the row, thereby marking the row as having no pending changes in the `DataTable`.

Immediately after loading the row, the StoreID column is populated with a GUID using the NewGuid method of the Guid structure. This ensures that the store has a unique identifier used as the primary key. Note that if BeginLoadData hadn't been previously called, the LoadDataRow method would throw a DataException and not accept the row because the text file contains only an empty string for each StoreID.

After the data has been loaded, the EndLoadData method is called to enable the constraints. At this point, if the data doesn't adhere to the constraints, a DataException is thrown and can be handled in a Catch block. In either case, the input file is closed in the Finally block. Note that the stores object is passed into the method by reference (ByRef), so when the method returns, the calling code will have a fully loaded DataTable that can then be synchronized with a database using a data adapter.

Dealing with Rows

In previous listings and code snippets, you have no doubt noticed that the rows in a DataTable are accessed via the Rows property, which returns a DataRowCollection object that exposes a collection of DataRow objects. Each DataRow exposes its data as a collection of values that adhere to the data types of the columns for the table and are accessible via the Item and ItemArray properties. The members of the DataRow class can be seen in Table 4.2.

TABLE 4.2 Important DataRow Members

Member	Description
	Properties
HasErrors	Property that indicates whether there are errors in any rows of this table
Item	Property that gets or sets the value of a column in the row accessible via the ordinal number or the name (in C#, this property is the indexer and so it doesn't show up in the member list)
ItemArray	Property that gets or sets the entire row of values through an array
RowError	Property that gets or sets the error description for the row
RowState	Property that gets the current DataRowState
Table	Property that gets the DataTable this row belongs to

TABLE 4.2   continued

Member	Description
	Methods
AcceptChanges	Method that commits all changes to the DataRow since the last time AcceptChanges was called
BeginEdit	Method that suspends event notifications so that changes can be made without triggering validation rules—calling on a deleted row throws an exception
CancelEdit	Method that cancels the edit on the current row and reverts to the original values and re-enables event notifications
ClearErrors	Method that clears the errors on the row including the RowError property and errors set with SetError
Delete	Method that deletes this DataRow
EndEdit	Method that ends the edit of the current row—will throw an exception if a constraint was violated or the ReadOnly or AllowDBNull properties of a column are violated
GetChildRows	Overloaded method that returns an array of DataRow object by navigating the relationships between tables and optionally looking at a DataRowVersion
GetColumnError	Overloaded method that returns the error description for a given column on the current row
GetColumnsInError	Method that gets an array of DataColumn objects that contain errors on the current row
GetParentRow, GetParentRows	Overloaded methods that return the parent DataRow or an array of parent DataRow objects for the current row based on the relation and an optional DataRowVersion
HasVersion	Method that returns a Boolean indicating whether the current row contains a given DataRowVersion
IsNull	Overloaded method that returns a Boolean indicating whether the given DataColumn in the current row contains a null value
RejectChanges	Method that rejects all changes on the current row since AcceptChanges was last called
SetColumnError	Overloaded method that sets the error description for the given DataColumn
SetParentRow	Overloaded method that associates a parent DataRow with the current row

As shown in Table 4.2, you can use the members of the DataRow object to access error information in the event that an exception is thrown after calling the EndEdit method. For example, the TraceRowError method shown in Listing 4.2 accepts an array of DataRow objects and an error message, and writes each DataRow's error information to the trace listeners collection using the WriteLine method of the Trace class.

LISTING 4.2 Manipulating row information. This method prints error information to the active trace listeners.

```
Private Sub TraceRowError(ByRef dr() As DataRow, ByVal message As String)

    Dim dc As DataColumn
    Dim strError As String
    Dim strPk As String = "{"
    Dim row As DataRow

    For Each row In dr
      If row.HasErrors Then

        ' Get the primary key
        For Each dc In row.Table.PrimaryKey
          strPk &= ":" & dc.ColumnName & " = " & row.Item(dc).ToString
        Next
        strPk &= "}"

        ' Log the error
        Trace.WriteLine(Now & " " & message & ": DataRow  error occurred " & _
      strPk & row.RowState.ToString & row.RowError)

        ' Log errors for each column
        For Each dc In row.GetColumnsInError
          strError = row.GetColumnError(dc)
          Trace.WriteLine(dc.ColumnName & " = " & strError)
        Next

      End If
    Next

End Sub
```

ANALYSIS In Listing 4.2, the first For loop iterates the array of DataRow objects that presumably contain errors by checking the HasErrors property. Within the loop, the Table property is first used to access the primary key of the table to which the passed-in row belongs. Each primary key column and its value are then concatenated to the strPk String. Next, a timestamp, the custom message, the primary key information, the current state of the row, and the error message are all written to the trace listeners. Finally, the

GetColumnsInError method is used to retrieve an array of DataColumn objects that contain errors, and each column name and its error description are also written to the listeners.

The TraceRowError method can then be called from a Catch block and passed the row that contains the error and any custom message, as in the following code snippet where dtTitles is a DataTable object:

```
TraceRowError(dtTitles.GetErrors(), "Error saving Titles")
```

As evidenced by Table 4.2, in addition to simply finding errors, you can write code that creates error conditions using the SetColumnError and RowError properties. For example, if several columns in a particular row must be correlated, you can inspect their values in the RowChanging event for the DataTable and then set the error appropriately. Listing 4.3 shows the StoresRowChanging method that is used to hook the RowChanging event of a DataTable that encapsulates information about stores. The method uses the DataRowChangeEventArgs object to inspect the reason the event was fired, and if a change occurred, enforces the rule that either the postal code or the city and state must be present.

LISTING 4.3   Creating errors. This event handler creates an error if the row doesn't have the correct columns populated.

```
Private Sub StoresRowChanging(ByVal sender As Object, _
   ByVal e As DataRowChangeEventArgs)
   ' Make sure we have a valid address
   If e.Action = DataRowAction.Change Then
     If e.Row.Item("PostalCode") Is DBNull.Value Then
       If e.Row.Item("StateProv") Is DBNull.Value _
         OrElse e.Row.Item("City") Is DBNull.Value Then
         e.Row.RowError = "Must have a Postal Code or City and State"
       End If
     End If
   End If
End Sub
```

By setting the RowError property to a String value, the HasErrors property of the row, the table, and the DataSet will all be automatically set to True.

Manipulating Columns

Of course, at the base level, the data in a DataTable is represented by a collection of DataColumn objects in a DataColumnCollection object exposed through the Columns property, each of which exposes a set of properties used to define the column, as shown in Table 4.3.

TABLE 4.3 Important DataColumn Members

Member	Description
AllowDBNull	Property that gets or sets a value indicating whether null values are allowed in this column
AutoIncrement	Property that gets or sets a value indicating whether the value for the column is automatically generated by incrementing
AutoIncrementSeed, AutoIncrementStep	Properties that get and set the starting value and increment used when auto-incrementing values
Caption	Property that gets or sets the caption for the column that can be used by controls to which the column is bound
ColumnMapping	Property that gets or sets the MappingType for the column controlling how it's displayed as XML
ColumnName	Property that gets or sets the name of the column as it appears in the DataColumnCollection
DataType	Property that gets or sets the type of data stored in the column
DefaultValue	Property that gets or sets an expression used as default value when new rows are created
Expression	Property that gets or sets an expression used to create a calculation or an aggregate value for the column
ExtendedProperties	Property that gets or sets a collection of custom information in a PropertyCollection object
MaxLength	Property that gets or sets the maximum length for a text column
Namespace	Property that gets or sets the XML namespace used for the column
Ordinal	Property that returns the position of the column in the DataColumnCollection
Prefix	Property that gets or sets the XML prefix used for the Namespace of the column
ReadOnly	Property that gets or sets a value indicating whether changes are allowed to the column once a new row has been added

4

TABLE 4.3   continued

Member	Description
Table	Property that returns the DataTable to which this column belongs
Unique	Property that gets or sets a value indicating that the values within the column must be unique across all rows

In the remainder of this section, you'll learn some common ways the properties of the DataColumn object are used to ensure better data integrity.

Using Column Properties

As you can see from Table 4.3, the properties of the DataColumn class mimic to some degree the kinds of information you'd find when viewing a table definition in a relational database such as SQL Server. Particularly, the AllowDBNull, ColumnName, DataType, and MaxLength properties provide the core information about a column. Typically, all these properties will be populated from the underlying data store when using a data adapter if the MissingSchemaAction property is set to the AddWithKey value of the MissingSchemaAction enumeration. If you don't use AddWithKey, only the ColumnName and DataType will be populated.

Tip

> Even though you might assume that it does, creating a unique constraint or a unique index on a column in a SQL Server 2000 database and using the AddWithKey value does **not** automatically set the Unique property of the DataColumn to True. You must set this yourself if you want to ensure uniqueness.

The DataType property is particularly interesting because it allows data to be stored in the DataColumn based on any type in the Common Type System (CTS), including custom types you create. However, the following base set of simple types from the CTS is implicitly understood by the DataType property, and therefore will be typically used by data adapters when populating a DataSet. For example, the SqlDataAdapter will translate the SQL Server data types nvarchar, smalldatetime, and money to the CTS types String, DateTime, and Decimal, respectively.

CTS types supported by the DataType property are

- Boolean
- Byte

- Char
- DateTime
- Decimal
- Int16, Int32, Int64
- SByte
- Single
- String
- TimeSpan
- UInt16, UInt32, UInt64

The primary reason these types are used is that they can be easily translated to types used in the XML Schema Definition (XSD) upon which the DataSet is based. (You'll learn more about this on Day 7, "DataSets and XML.") The use of common types allows DataSets to be passed to and returned from XML Web Services more easily, as you'll learn on Day 18, "ADO.NET and XML Web Services."

Regardless of which properties are automatically populated, you can then set additional properties to further conform the data. For example, the code in Listing 4.4 sets some of the properties for the columns in a DataTable that caches information from the Titles table.

LISTING 4.4   Setting column properties. This code sets the Caption and other properties of the columns in a table that stores rows from the Titles table.

```
With titles
  .Columns("PubDate").Caption = "Publication Date"
  .Columns("BulkDiscount").Caption = "Bulk Discount"
  .Columns("BulkAmount").Caption = "Bulk Amount"
  .Columns("ISBN").ReadOnly = True
  .Columns("Title").Unique = True
  .Columns("CatID").DefaultValue = _
    New Guid("21B60927-5659-4AD4-A036-AB478D73E754")
End With
```

ANALYSIS   In Listing 4.4, the Caption properties of the PubDate, BulkDiscount, and BulkAmount columns are set because the column names themselves aren't formatted properly for display. In addition, the ISBN column is set to ReadOnly because it's the primary key and therefore shouldn't be changed (assuming this simple structure stores only a single version of each title). The Unique property of the Title column is used to ensure that the same title isn't added twice under different ISBNs. In addition,

the `DefaultValue` property of the `CatID` column is set to a general programming category so that the book can be categorized at a later time.

Using Auto-Incrementing Columns

The other interesting properties exposed by the `DataColumn` class are those that deal with
creating auto-incrementing columns: `AutoIncrement`, `AutoIncrementSeed`, and
`AutoIncrementStep`. Together these properties mark the column as being one whose
value is automatically generated each time a row is added to the `DataTable` and whose
data type is `System.Int32`, the value for the first inserted row (defaulted to `0`), and the
increment to use for each successive row (defaulted to `1`), respectively.

Although you might not expect it, setting the `AutoIncrement` property to `True` on a column not defined as an `Integer` (`Int32`) automatically coerces the column into that data
type. As mentioned previously, setting the value to `True` on a column that has its
`Expression` property set throws an exception.

Typically, you'd use these properties when you want to ensure that you can uniquely
identify a row in the case where a naturally occurring unique value isn't present. This
often occurs with detail rows that track multiple occurrences of similar events, such as
the reviews of books on the ComputeBooks Web site. You would then use the auto-
incrementing column in a relationship to link two data tables in a `DataSet`, as you'll
learn shortly. However, to ensure uniqueness, you'd need to set the `Unique` property of
the column to `True` and the `ReadOnly` property to `True` for good measure so that changes
can't even be attempted. As an example, consider the definition of a `DataTable` that
stores book reviews shown in Listing 4.5.

LISTING 4.5   Auto-incrementing columns. This code defines a table to hold book reviews
using an auto-incrementing column.

```
Dim reviews As New DataTable()

reviews.TableName = "Reviews"

With reviews
  .Columns.Add("ISBN", GetType(String))
  .Columns.Add("ReviewText", GetType(String))
  .Columns.Add("Stars", GetType(Int16))
  .Columns.Add("ReviewNo", GetType(Int32))
  .Columns("ReviewNo").AutoIncrement = True
  .Columns("ReviewNo").AutoIncrementSeed = 1
  .Columns("ReviewNo").AutoIncrementStep = 1
  .Columns("ReviewNo").Unique = True
  .Columns("ReviewNo").ReadOnly = True
  .Columns("ReviewNo").AllowDBNull = False
End With
```

ANALYSIS In Listing 4.5, the ReviewNo column is used to mark each row as unique. As data is inserted into the table, the first row will start with 1 and increment by 1 thereafter. Keep in mind that setting the ReadOnly property to True disallows changes to the column only after a row has been inserted into the table.

To insert a new row into the table programmatically, you can either omit the ReviewNo column altogether by not setting its value using the Item property, or, if loading from an array, you can simply place a null (Nothing) value in its position corresponding to the position of the column in the array. For example, to insert a row into the Reviews table, you could use the following syntax:

```
reviews.Rows.Add(New Object() {"06720043X", "Good book", 3, Nothing})
```

In the special case where the auto-increment column is the last column in the DataTable, you can simply omit the null value when loading with an array and the elements of the array will be mapped to the other columns.

Columns marked with auto-increment also work in conjunction with auto-incrementing columns generated at the database server. For example, SQL Server allows one IDENTITY column to be placed in each table that auto-increments values on the server in exactly the same way as is done in the DataTable. In fact, if you populate a DataTable from SQL Server that contains an IDENTITY column, the SqlDataAdapter object will correctly set the AutoIncrement, AutoIncrementSeed, and AutoIncrementStep properties if the AddWithKey value of the MissingSchemaAction property is set before calling the Fill method. Further, when you then insert new rows into the table, the new values will pick up where the last value left off. You'll learn more about IDENTITY values in SQL Server on Day 13, "Working with SQL Server."

4

Caution

As a rule, you shouldn't attempt to generate keys on both the client and the server because they can get out of sync and lead to data corruption. This can easily happen in the case of SQL Server because IDENTITY values can "get lost" or go unused due to transactions that are rolled back—a fact that the DataTable won't be aware of. Although it's possible to set the AutoIncrementStep property to -1 in order to create negative values that won't conflict with the positive values generated at the database server, it's not recommended. For this reason—and because auto-incrementing columns are much more difficult to use in distributed database scenarios—you should use auto-incrementing columns in a DataTable only when they are transient, such as when used to temporarily link data tables.

Although auto-incrementing columns can be useful, a better solution for generating keys that are persisted to a database, and the one implemented in this book, is to use GUIDs as the system-assigned keys. They have the advantage of being able to be generated on either the client or the server and on multiple databases and still always retaining their uniqueness. The only downside is that you must use explicit code on the client to populate the Guid column using the NewGuid method of the System.Guid structure, as shown in Listing 3.1.

Using Expressions

One of the most powerful properties of the DataColumn is the Expression property. This property can be used to create computed columns based on the current row and child or parent rows as well as to create computed columns based on aggregate values across rows.

In the simplest case, the Expression property is used to calculate a value for a column based on other values in the row. This is typically used for numeric calculations—for example, to compute the purchase price for an item—or to create a more properly formatted string that combines a number of columns to, for example, create a URL that will be used in an ASP.NET Web Form. In both cases, the expression must evaluate to a String that can be cast to the type appropriate for the DataColumn. As an example, if a DataTable were used to represent customer information from the Customers table in the ComputeBooks database, a new column could be created that concatenates the first name and last name columns. This would allow the name to be easily accessible when binding the table to a control such as a grid. To create the column, you can simply use the Add method of the DataColumnCollection class like so:

```
customers.Columns.Add("Name", GetType(String), "FName + ' ' + LName")
```

In this case, the overloaded Add method accepts not only the name of the new column and its data type, but also the expression used to populate the Expression property. Note that the expression syntax follows the same rules as those found in Table 3.2. Another example of using the Expression property on a single row would be to create a column that holds the price of a title for customers ordering the book over the Web using the Discount column of the Titles table as follows:

```
titles.Columns.Add("WebPrice", GetType(Decimal))
titles.Columns("WebPrice").Expression = "Price - ISNULL(Discount,0)"
```

Here, the Expression property is set explicitly using the ISNULL function to ensure that a numeric value rather than a null is returned in the event the Discount column contains a null value (which is allowed in the database).

> **Note**
>
> Exceptions may be thrown either when the `Expression` property is initially set or when it's evaluated during execution. For example, an `ArgumentException` will be thrown immediately if you attempt to set an expression on a column that has its `AutoIncrement` or `Unique` properties set to `True`. Of course, a `SyntaxErrorException` will be thrown if the expression can't be parsed. Exceptions thrown during evaluation typically involve the use of functions. The `CONVERT` function may cause a `FormatException` or `InvalidCastException` to be thrown if the `CONVERT` function doesn't return a `String` that can be cast into the data type of the column, or if the requested cast isn't possible, respectively. In addition, the `SUBSTRING`, `LEN`, and `TRIM` functions can cause an `ArgumentOutOfRangeException` or simply an `Exception` if invalid arguments are passed to them or if they don't return a `String`.

A more sophisticated use of the `Expression` property involves using aggregate functions and navigating the relationships between tables in a `DataSet`. For example, consider the case where a `DataSet` contains `Orders` and `OrderDetails` tables. As you'll see shortly, these tables can be related within the `DataSet` through a foreign key in the same way that they were related within the relational database. In cases like this, it's often useful to summarize data from the child rows into single columns of the parent row. The `Expression` property can be used to do this easily as follows:

```
orders.Columns.Add("ItemCount", GetType(Integer), "COUNT(Child.ISBN)")
```

In this case, assume that `orders` is the `DataTable` that contains `Orders`. This statement then adds a new column to the `DataTable` to reflect the number of `OrderDetails` rows it's the parent for. The `COUNT` aggregate function is used here and is passed a column from the child table denoted with the `Child` identifier. In a slightly more sophisticated example, you could use computed columns to calculate the order total for an entire order by first creating a compute column on the `OrderDetails` table and calculating the item total by multiplying the `Quantity` and the `UnitPrice`. A column on the `Orders` table could then be created to sum the individual item totals and add any shipping costs that are charged as shown in the following snippet.

> **Note**
>
> Keep in mind that the `Integer` data type in Visual Basic .NET maps to the `System.Int32` data type in the CTS. As a result, the `GetType` statement shown earlier could also have been written as `GetType(Int32)`.

```
orders.Columns.Add("OrderTotal", GetType(Decimal))
orderDet.Columns.Add("ItemTotal", GetType(Decimal))

orderDet.Columns("ItemTotal").Expression = "Quantity * UnitPrice"
orders.Columns("OrderTotal").Expression = _
  "SUM(Child.ItemTotal) + ISNULL(Shipping,0)"
```

Although you might think that you could combine the two expressions into a single expression that calculates the aggregate and does the multiplication on the child rows, the syntax for the Expression property doesn't allow it.

However, just as you can use aggregates with relationships, they can also be used on a single table like so:

```
orders.Columns.Add("MaxDate", GetType(DateTime), "MAX(OrderDate)")
```

Here, each row in the DataTable will contain a column called MaxDate with the most recent (maximum) value from the OrderDate column. Although you could create another table in the DataSet with a single row to act as the parent for all rows (using the SetParentRow method), and then use syntax as in the COUNT example above, a far easier way to efficiently calculate single aggregates is to use the Compute method of the DataTable as shown in Table 4.1. The previous snippet could then be rewritten as

```
Dim maxDate As DateTime

maxDate = CType(orders.Compute("MAX(OrderDate)", Nothing), DateTime)
```

Note that the Compute method simply returns a value of type Object that can be cast to the appropriate data type. Also, the second argument to the Compute method, here simply set to Nothing, can be used to specify a filter expression in order to compute the aggregate over only a subset of the rows.

Where to Aggregate?

The use of aggregate functions in the Expression property raises an issue analogous to the use of the Select method of the DataTable class versus the WHERE clause in a SQL statement discussed yesterday.

Using the aggregates functions as shown in this section means that the aggregations are calculated on the client (likely the middle-tier server) where the DataSet is being populated. However, you can also calculate aggregates on the relational database server using the same basic functions (SUM, MIN, MAX, AVG, COUNT) in SQL statements that typically use a GROUP BY clause. As a general rule, performing calculations on the server is more efficient because with the use of the GROUP BY clause, the detail rows needn't be fully retrieved and sent to the client. Therefore, you should use the Expression property and the aggregate syntax shown here only if you already must retrieve all the detail rows and if the aggregate value can't be precalculated on the server.

Constraints

As you're probably aware by now, you can place constraints on tables to ensure that the data in them conforms to certain rules. Among these are unique constraints, primary keys, and foreign keys.

Applying Unique Constraints

As shown in the previous section, you can use the `Unique` property to enforce uniqueness on a `DataColumn` by setting the property to `True`. Conversely, you can remove the constraint simply by setting the `Unique` property to `False`. However, unique constraints can also include more than one column so that the combination of columns will be unique. Because setting each of the column's `Unique` properties to `True` won't enforce the rule that their combination must be unique, you need some way to group the unique columns together. This can be done with a `UniqueConstraint` object. For example, the following code snippet creates a unique constraint on the `OrderID` and `ISBN` columns of the `orderDet DataTable`, which holds `OrderDetails` records:

```
Dim unique As New UniqueConstraint("OrderID_ISBN", _
    New DataColumn() {orderDet.Columns("OrderID"), orderDet.Columns("ISBN")})

orderDet.Constraints.Add(unique)
```

Once the constraint has been created, it must be added to the `Constraints` collection of the `DataTable` using the overloaded `Add` method. The `Constraints` property exposes a `ConstraintCollection` object that can hold any constraint objects derived from the `System.Data.Constraint` class (as is `UniqueConstraint`). The previous code snippet could also have been rewritten in the following way:

```
orderDet.Constraints.Add("OrderID_ISBN", _
    New DataColumn() {orderDet.Columns("OrderID"), _
    orderDet.Columns("ISBN")}, False)
```

The last argument to the `Add` method in this case specifies that the unique constraint shouldn't also be considered a primary key.

Specifying Primary Keys

As the previous code snippet makes clear, primary keys are simply special instances of unique constraints in the `ConstraintCollection` of a `DataTable`. In fact, the `UniqueConstraint` class exposes a read-only `IsPrimaryKey` property that returns `True` when the constraint is acting as the primary key. As with unique constraints, primary keys can span one or more columns. Of course, one of the differences with primary keys is that they can also be set automatically when the `DataSet` is populated from a data adapter when the `MissingSchemaAction` property is set to `AddWithKey`.

4

Primary keys can be programmatically created in two ways: either by using the
PrimaryKey property of the DataTable or by creating a unique constraint through the
Add method of the ConstraintCollection as shown earlier. For example, the former
method is shown in the following code snippet:

```
orderDet.PrimaryKey = New DataColumn() {orderDet.Columns("OrderID"), _
    orderDet.Columns("ISBN")}
```

In this case, the primary key is set to a composite key of the OrderID and ISBN columns.
Simply setting the PrimaryKey property also adds the constraint to the
ConstraintCollection.

Using Foreign Key Constraints and Relations

The final type of constraint that you can place in a DataSet is the foreign key constraint
represented by the ForeignKeyConstraint class derived from Constraint. As in a relational database, a foreign key constraint is simply a pointer to the primary key of another
table and, as a result, lives in the ConstraintCollection of the child table. Also as in a
relational database, a foreign key constraint has two primary functions. First, it makes
sure that if a child row is added to the DataTable, there is a corresponding row in the
parent table. Second, it controls whether changes to the primary key of the parent table
are cascaded to the child table or disallowed.

There are two ways you can add a foreign key to a DataSet: using the DataRelation
object that is also used to allow navigation between tables, and adding a
ForeignKeyConstraint object to the ConstraintCollection directly. In the latter case,
as with unique constraints, the foreign key can be created independently and added to the
collection using the Add method as shown in the following snippet, or created directly in
the Add method using one of its overloaded signatures:

```
Dim fk As New ForeignKeyConstraint("FK_OrderID", _
    orders.Columns("OrderID"), orderDet.Columns("OrderID"))

orderDet.Constraints.Add(fk)
```

Note

In this release, foreign key constraints aren't populated from a data adapter
in SQL Server when its MissingSchemaAction property is set to AddWithKey.
This example also assumes that the dtOrders and dtOrderDet DataTable
objects refer to tables within the same DataSet that contain high-level order
and order detail information, respectively. Note that they are linked by the
OrderID column and the constraint exists in the dtOrderDet table.

As with unique constraints, foreign key constraints can span multiple columns as long as both the parent and child tables include the columns. However, the column names in both tables must have the same data types or an InvalidOperationException will be thrown. Of course, when placing a constraint between tables that already have data, every child row must have a corresponding parent row or an ArgumentException will be thrown. In these cases, if you would like to create a foreign key constraint—or for that matter a unique constraint—even though the data doesn't conform to it, you can first set the EnforceConstraints property of the DataSet to False and then add the constraint. Later, after the data has been cleaned up, you can once again enable constraints by setting the property to True.

Tip

You don't need to first set the primary key of the parent table in order to create a foreign key, as is the case in most relational databases. If the primary key isn't set, a unique constraint is automatically created on the parent column.

The second way to create a foreign key is to create a DataRelation. Simply put, a DataRelation allows navigation between the parent and child tables by allowing the GetChildRows, GetParentRow, and GetParentRows methods shown in Table 4.2 to be called to navigate through the DataSet. Creating a relation has the side effect of creating a foreign key constraint as well. For example, rather than explicitly creating a foreign key constraint, as in the previous code snippet, you could create a DataRelation as follows:

```
orders.Relations.Add(New DataRelation("FK_OrderID", _
    orders.Columns("OrderID"), _
    orderDet.Columns("OrderID")))
```

Note

Note that here the name of the relation can be specified along with the parent and child columns. The DataRelationCollection class's Add method is also overloaded to accept arrays of parent and child columns. The end result is that the DataRelationCollection objects exposed through the Relations property of the dsOrders DataSet, the ChildRelations property of the dtOrders parent DataTable, and the ParentRelations property of the dtOrderDet child DataTable are all populated along with the addition of the foreign key constraint to the ConstraintCollection of the dtOrderDet child table.

After the relation is in place, you can use it to navigate the DataSet. For example, the code in the following snippet traverses each row in the Orders table and prints each row in the OrderDetails table:

```
Dim orderRow As DataRow
Dim detRow As DataRow
Dim detRows() As DataRow

For Each orderRow In orders.Rows
  Console.WriteLine(orderRow.Item("OrderID"))
  Console.WriteLine(orderRow.Item("OrderDate"))
  detRows = orderRow.GetChildRows("FK_OrderID", DataRowVersion.Current)
  For Each detRow In detRows
    Console.WriteLine("  " & detRow.Item("ISBN").ToString)
    Console.WriteLine("  " & detRow.Item("Quantity").ToString)
  Next
Next
```

Note that the GetChildRows method is overloaded and can accept either the name of the DataRelation to use in the navigation or a DataRelation object. The second argument is optional and specifies which versions of the child rows to return in the array of DataRow objects.

Note   Keep in mind that simply creating a foreign key constraint called FK_OrderID won't allow the code in the previous snippet to work. The reason is that although relations automatically create foreign key constraints, the reverse isn't true.

Cascading Changes

After a foreign key constraint has been created, you can set its AcceptRejectRule, UpdateRule, and DeleteRule properties to affect its behavior as data is modified in the parent table.

The AcceptRejectRule property can be set to either the Cascade or None value of the AcceptRejectRule enumeration. When you set the property to Cascade, each time the AcceptChanges or RejectChanges method is called on a parent row, AcceptChanges or RejectChanges is also called on all its child rows. This is convenient because often parent and child rows will be added to the DataSet at the same time and this avoids having to loop through all the child rows to call AcceptChanges. The default value of AcceptRejectRule, however, is None.

The UpdateRule and DeleteRule properties are similar and can be set to one of the four values of the Rule enumeration (Cascade, None [the default], SetDefault, SetNull). As in a relational database, setting either of these properties to Cascade ensures that if the parent row's primary key is changed, or if the parent row is deleted, the foreign key in the child table is likewise changed or deleted. This prevents orphaned rows from collecting in the child table. For example, the foreign key created previously should have both its DeleteRule and UpdateRule set to Cascade as follows:

```
Dim fk As ForeignKeyConstraint

fk = CType(orderDet.Constraints("FK_OrderID"), ForeignKeyConstraint)
fk.DeleteRule = Rule.Cascade
fk.UpdateRule = Rule.Cascade
```

Should I Cascade?

Although cascading deletes is appropriate for some foreign keys, such as an Orders/OrderDetails relationship as discussed in this section, it isn't for others. This is particularly true of lookups where the parent table stores a set of lookup data used for normalization, such as product codes and categories. Cascading a delete in these cases can have disastrous consequences because it would delete vital data. In those cases, SetDefault or SetNull is more appropriate.

Cascading updates aren't typically used because you should strive to keep primary keys immutable, especially in the case of system-assigned keys such as GUIDs. However, there are times when natural keys (those that reflect real entities such as product codes) must be changed, and so cascading an update is called for.

The SetDefault and SetNull values can be used when the primary key needs to be changed or deleted but when the child row must remain. Using SetDefault populates the child column with the expression in its DefaultValue property, whereas SetNull simply sets the column's value to null (Nothing) assuming that the AllowDBNull property is set to True.

Extended Properties

As you might have noticed, each of the DataSet, DataTable, DataColumn, and DataRelation classes exposes a PropertyCollection object through its ExtendedProperties property. The PropertyCollection class is found in the System.Data namespace and is derived from System.Collections.Hashtable. As a result, a PropertyCollection stores a set of key and value pairs that are stored based on the hash value of the key.

You typically use the extended properties collection to store metadata for the object. As an example, for a DataSet, you might store the date and time the data was retrieved from

the data store, or calculate a time at which the data should be refreshed. For a
DataTable, you might store the criteria that were used when retrieving the data, or the
connection string used to connect to the data store. For a DataColumn, you might store
comments or a description of what data is stored in the column. These values can then be
used both for display to a user of the application and for diagnostic purposes in the event
of an exception. For example, Listing 4.6 demonstrates the creation of several properties
for a DataSet used to cache data from the Orders and OrderDetails tables.

LISTING 4.6   Populating extended properties. This method populates the dsOrders
DataSet and populates several extended properties.

```
Public Function GetOrders(ByVal custID As Guid) As DataSet

    Dim con As New SqlConnection(Me.ConnectString)
    Dim da As New SqlDataAdapter("usp_GetOrders", con)
    Dim orders As New DataSet("Orders")

    da.SelectCommand.CommandType = CommandType.StoredProcedure
    da.SelectCommand.Parameters.Add(New SqlParameter("@CustomerID", custID))

    da.Fill(orders)
    orders.Tables(0).TableName = "Orders"
    orders.Tables(1).TableName = "OrderDetails"

    With orders
      .ExtendedProperties.Add("TimeRetrieved", Now)
      .ExtendedProperties.Add("CustomerID", custID)
      .ExtendedProperties.Add("ConnectString", con.ConnectionString)
      .ExtendedProperties.Add("CommandText", da.SelectCommand.CommandText)
    End With

    Return orders
End Function
```

The properties can then be either accessed individually by passing the key value to the
ExtendedProperties collection, or traversed using an enumerator as shown in the following code snippet:

```
Try
    ' Attempt to update the DataSet
    da.Update(orders.GetChanges())

Catch e As Exception
    ' Log the error
    Dim props As IDictionaryEnumerator = orders.ExtendedProperties.GetEnumerator()
```

```
While props.MoveNext
  Trace.WriteLine(props.Key.ToString() & " = " & props.Value.ToString())
End While

' Other error handling here
End Try
```

ANALYSIS In the previous snippet, the code is attempting to update the data store with changed rows from the dOrders DataSet. If an exception occurs, the Catch block is used to first write all the extended properties to the Trace object for logging. To traverse the properties, the GetEnumerator method of the PropertyCollection object is called to return an enumerator that implements the IDictionaryEnumerator interface. This interface exposes a MoveNext method that is then used to traverse the collection in a loop. Because the collection is positioned before the first element, the MoveNext property can be called at the top of the loop as shown here.

Note In addition to the properties shown, the IDictionaryInterface exposes the Current and Entry properties and the Reset method. The properties are used to represent the key and value pair the enumerator current points to, whereas the Reset method moves the pointer back before the first element in the collection.

4

The only downside to using extended properties is that they aren't represented when the DataSet is serialized to XML using the WriteXml method or returned through an XML Web Service. However, they are included when the DataSet is transported using .NET Remoting.

Summary

Today you delved deeply into the structure of a DataSet and examined each of its constituent parts from the perspective of the object model. Understanding the internal structure is the first step in being able to write applications that take advantage of the features of the DataSet.

Tomorrow, you'll briefly review the various ways data in a DataSet can be modified and how those modifications are tracked and stored.

Workshop

This workshop will help reinforce the concepts covered in today's lesson.

Quiz

1. How are system-assigned keys supported in ADO.NET?

   Automatically generated keys are supported in two primary ways. First, the `DataColumn` class exposes `AutoIncrement`, `AutoIncrementStep`, and `AutoIncrementSeed` properties that when set enable ADO.NET to generate incremental numeric values in the `DataColumn`. These values are often used to relate tables through a foreign key constraint or data relation. Second, you can write your own code to assign values to keys as rows are inserted; for example, by using the `NewGuid` method of the Guid structure.

2. In what ways can expressions be used for a `DataColumn`?

   Expressions, through the `Expression` property, can be used to create calculated columns based on a combination of literal values, numeric and string values, and even aggregate functions and scalar functions such as `ISNULL` and `SUBSTRING`. In addition, expressions can be used to refer to both parent and child rows to perform rollups of data.

3. How does a primary key differ from a unique constraint on a `DataTable`?

   A primary key is actually just an instance of a unique constraint and is represented by a `UniqueConstraint` object in the `ConstraintCollection` of the table. The `IsPrimaryKey` property of the `UniqueConstraint` object will be set to `True` when this is the case. The `PrimaryKey` property of the `DataTable` can be used to set the primary key, which automatically creates the unique constraint.

4. What is the relationship between a foreign key constraint and a data relation?

   A foreign key constraint is used to ensure that data in a child table conforms to the primary key value of a parent table. To that end, foreign key constraints are about data integrity. Data relations, on the other hand, enable programmatic navigation of a `DataSet` through methods such as `GetChildRows` and the `ChildRelations` collection. However, these two concepts are related in that creating a data relation automatically creates a foreign key constraint, although the reverse isn't true.

Exercise

To get some practice in working with the structure of a `DataSet`, write some code in a console application similar to that shown in Listing 4.5 to retrieve the `Titles` table and its associated `Reviews` table. Then create a data relation to relate the tables and use it to traverse `Titles` and the child `Reviews`. Also ensure that the primary keys of both tables are set and that no one can change them.

Answers for Day 4

Exercise Answer

One possible solution is as follows:

```
Dim dr, child As DataRow
Dim con As New SqlConnection(connect)
Dim da As New SqlDataAdapter("usp_GetTitlesReviews", con)
da.SelectCommand.CommandType = CommandType.StoredProcedure

Dim ds As New DataSet("TitlesReviews")

' Get the data
da.MissingSchemaAction = MissingSchemaAction.AddWithKey
da.Fill(ds)

Dim reviews As DataTable = ds.Tables(0)
Dim titles As DataTable = ds.Tables(1)

' Make the PKs read only
reviews.Columns("ReviewId").ReadOnly = True
Titles.Columns("ISBN").ReadOnly = True

' Setup the relationship
ds.Relations.Add("FK_ISBN", titles.Columns("ISBN"), reviews.Columns("isbn"))

' Traverse the tables
For Each dr In titles.Rows
  Console.WriteLine(dr.Item("ISBN").ToString())

  Dim children() As DataRow
  children = dr.GetChildRows("FK_ISBN")

  For Each child In children
    Console.WriteLine("  " & child.Item("ReviewText").ToString())
  Next

Next
```

In this code snippet, the usp_GetTitlesReviews stored procedure returns the Reviews as the first result set and the Titles as the second. The MissingSchemaAction property is set to AddWithKey to ensure that the primary key information is returned. For ease of use, the reviews and titles variables are set to refer to the appropriate tables before setting the primary key columns to read-only and creating the DataRelation. With the relationship in place, the code then traverses the titles table and finds the related reviews with the GetChildRows method.

WEEK 1

DAY 5

Changing Data

Over the last two days, you've delved pretty deeply into the `DataSet` in order to understand the various ways you can work with it programmatically and how it is structured. During that time, you've seen several examples of data modifications and how they are represented without being given the big picture. Today, you'll put the pieces together in a shorter lesson to form a complete picture of how and when changes are tracked in a `DataSet`.

Although today's discussion will focus on modifying data, it won't discuss how data is actually synchronized with the underlying data store. That discussion will have to wait for Day 12, "Using Data Adapters," when you learn about data adapters.

However, today you'll learn the following concepts:

- How row states and row versions are tracked
- How the `GetChanges` method is used to filter rows
- What a DiffGram is and how it is used by a `DataSet`
- When and why to call the `AcceptChanges`, `RejectChanges`, and `Reset` methods of the objects within a `DataSet`

Making Modifications

Obviously, to eventually update a data store with information, it must first be changed in the DataSet that a data adapter will use to synchronize with the data store. These changes can occur through explicit programmatic manipulation of the data by adding, modifying, and deleting data in a DataTable, using the Merge method of the DataSet, the ImportRow or LoadDataRow methods of the DataTable, the Add method of the DataRowCollection object, the Item and ItemArray properties, or the Delete method of the DataRow as you learned over the last two days. In addition, changes can be made implicitly through bound controls on Windows Forms or Web Forms. In the case of the former, the data in the DataSet is changed automatically by the control, whereas in the latter, some additional code must be written in the ASP.NET page.

In either case, the key concept you need to keep in mind is that because the DataSet is a truly disconnected data cache (remember, it doesn't keep track of where it got its data), any changes you make to it won't be reflected in the data store until you synchronize using an object such as a data adapter. This behavior is contrary to the way the Recordset object functioned by default in ADO 2.x. In this way, a DataSet is particularly useful for batch update scenarios.

Note

> Modifying data in a DataSet and then using a data adapter isn't the only technique for making changes to a database. You certainly have the option of executing data modification statements (SQL, stored procedures, functions) using a command object provided by a .NET Data Provider such as OleDbCommand. You'll learn more about this approach on Day 10, "Working with Commands."

However, for a data adapter to take the appropriate action when passed a DataSet, it must know which rows were changed and how they were changed in addition to what the values in the rows were changed to and from.

Understanding Row States

To eventually know which rows should be synchronized with the data store, the DataSet must track the state of each row in each DataTable in its DataTableCollection. It does this using the RowState property of the DataRow object, which is always set to one of the values from the DataRowState enumeration, as shown in Table 5.1.

TABLE 5.1 Values of the `DataRowState` Enumeration

Value	Description
Added	The row has been added to the `DataRowCollection` of a `DataTable` and `AcceptChanges` hasn't yet been called.
Deleted	The row has been deleted using the `Delete` method of the `DataRow` object. It can't subsequently be accessed without throwing a `DeletedRowInaccessibleException`.
Detached	The row exists, but isn't part of a `DataRowCollection` either because it was never added to a `DataTable` or was removed using the `Remove` method of the `DataRowCollection`.
Modified	One or more values in the row have been changed and `AcceptChanges` hasn't been called.
Unchanged	The row hasn't been changed since the last time `AcceptChanges` was called.

To illustrate when the row states are set consider the C# `populateBooks` method shown in Listing 5.1.

LISTING 5.1   Illustrating row states. This method populates a `DataSet` and then manipulates rows to show the values of the `DataRowState` enumeration.

```
private void populateBooks(string connect)
  {
    SqlConnection con = new SqlConnection(connect);
    SqlDataAdapter da = new SqlDataAdapter ("usp_GetTitles", con);

    books = new DataSet("ComputeBooksTitles");

    da.SelectCommand.CommandType = CommandType.StoredProcedure;
    da.Fill(books, "Titles");

    DataTable titles = books.Tables["Titles"];

    // All rows are Unchanged

    titles.Rows[0].BeginEdit();
    titles.Rows[0]["Description"] = "This book is too long";
    titles.Rows[0].EndEdit();
    Console.WriteLine(titles.Rows[0].RowState.ToString());   //Modified

    titles.Rows[0].Delete();
    Console.WriteLine(titles.Rows[0].RowState.ToString());   //Deleted

    DataRow title = titles.Rows[1];
    titles.Rows.Remove(title);
```

5

LISTING 5.1   continued

```
        Console.WriteLine(title.RowState.ToString());    //Detached

        DataRow drNewTitle = titles.NewRow();   //Detached
        titles.Rows.Add(drNewTitle);
        Console.WriteLine(drNewTitle.RowState.ToString());    //Added

        titles.AcceptChanges();   //All Unchanged
    }
```

 ANALYSIS   In Listing 5.1, you'll notice that the Titles table of the DataSet is first populated from a data adapter and then referenced as titles. At this point, all the rows
in titles have their RowState property set to Unchanged. The first row (0) is then modified before being deleted, changing its RowState from Unchanged to Modified to
Deleted. Note, however, that if the RowState had been inspected before the call to
EndEdit, it would have been Unchanged because embedding the change in BeginEdit
and EndEdit methods defers the changes to the row until the EndEdit method is called.
The second row is then removed from the DataRowCollection using the Remove method,
causing its RowState to be set to Detached. Finally, a new row is added to titles, causing its RowState to be set to Added. When AcceptChanges is invoked, all the rows that
have a RowState of Modified or Added will be set to Unchanged, and the Deleted and
Detached rows will be permanently removed.

> **Tip**
>
> This listing shows a new row being added to the titles DataTable first
> using the NewRow method to create the row, and then using the Add method
> to add it to the DataTableCollection. However, the Add method will throw
> an exception if any columns in the table have their AllowDBNull property set
> to False and don't have a DefaultValue that can automatically generate a
> value.

As mentioned on Day 3, "Working with DataSets," the HasChanges method of the
DataSet object returns a Boolean that can be used to quickly determine whether there
have been any changes (row states of Modified, Added, and Deleted) made to any rows
in any of its tables. In fact, the HasChanges method is overloaded to filter based on one
or more values from the DataRowState enumeration to check for specific types of
changes. If the following line of code were inserted just above the call to
AcceptChanges, it would return False because no rows with the Modified state would
exist in the DataSet at that time:

```
Console.WriteLine(books.HasChanges(DataRowState.Modified));
```

The previous paragraph implies that detached rows are handled differently from deleted ones, and in fact this is precisely the case. Simply put, a row that is detached doesn't register as a changed row to ADO.NET, and so a data adapter won't look at it when deciding which rows to delete in the data store. Further, the HasChanges and GetChanges methods of the DataSet and DataTable will ignore detached rows returning False if detached rows exist and not returning rows with a state of Detached, respectively.

In addition to their invisibility, detached rows and deleted rows can cause a RowNotInTableException or DeletedRowInaccessibleException to be thrown if you try to manipulate them. For example, calling the AcceptChanges, GetChildRows, GetParentRows, GetParentRow, RejectChanges, or SetParentRow methods of a DataRow that is detached or deleted will throw a RowNotInTableException. Trying to access the Item or ItemArray properties of a deleted row will cause a DeletedRowInaccessibleException. You'll also find that you can't access the columns of a row after it's been detached without causing an exception. However, this isn't the case with a row that's been newly instantiated and not yet added to a DataTable.

Understanding Row Versions

Marking a row as modified, deleted, or added, however, isn't enough to ensure that the data is properly updated in the underlying data store. The DataSet must also track the versions of values within the rows of a DataTable. This is accomplished behind the scenes in the table and tracked with the DataRowVersion enumeration, as shown in Table 5.2. Various versions of a row can then be made accessible using a DataView and its RowStateFilter property or directly through the Item property of the DataRow object.

TABLE 5.2 Values of the DataRowVersion Enumeration

Value	Description
Current	Represents the data that is currently in the row, including both changed data and unmodified data
Default	Represents the data based on the setting of the RowState property of the row
Original	Represents the data that was originally used to populate the row
Proposed	Represents changes made to the data after BeginEdit was called and before EndEdit—can still be undone if CancelEdit is called

One way you can think of the row versions listed in Table 5.2 is as three distinct copies (Current, Original, Proposed) of each row that a table has available to use, but that need not all be used simultaneously. Values within the copies can be manipulated directly by your code, and the DataSet also moves values between the copies as methods such as

EndEdit, AcceptChanges, and RejectChanges are called. Although there are four values in the enumeration, actually only three copies are available because the Default value simply acts as a pointer to one of the three copies—which copy depends on the value of the RowState property.

To illustrate this, consider the sequence of code based on Listing 5.1 shown in Listing 5.2.

LISTING 5.2   Changing row data. This listing corresponds to Figure 5.1 to show how a DataSet tracks row versions.

```
titles.Rows[0]["Description"] = "Too long";

titles.Rows[0].BeginEdit();
titles.Rows[0]["Description"] = "Way too long";

// See Figure 5.1

titles.Rows[0].EndEdit();
titles.AcceptChanges();
```

ANALYSIS   In Listing 5.2, assume that row 0 was just populated in the DataSet by a data adapter and the value of the Description column was the string "A Great Book." As a result, its RowState would be set to Unchanged. At this point, the DataSet will have created an Original version of each row and a Current version of each row and all their values will be the same. The Default version will simply point to the Current version because the RowState is Unchanged. However, after the first line of code executes, the value of the Description column in the Current version will be changed to "Too Long" and the RowState will be set to Modified. The Default version will still point to the Current version because the modified value is in the Current version. When the BeginEdit method is called, a Proposed version of the row is created and is then populated with the value "Way Too Long." This is illustrated in Figure 5.1, which captures the state of the table directly before the EndEdit method is called.

As shown in Figure 5.1, at this point, the Default version points to the Proposed version and the RowState remains set to Modified because accessing the value of the column will bring back the value "Way Too Long," and the row was previously modified.

When the EndEdit method is called, the values from the Proposed version are copied into the Current version and the Proposed version is destroyed. The RowState remains as Modified. As you might expect, calling CancelEdit will simply destroy the Proposed version without making any changes. Finally, when the AcceptChanges method is called, the Current value is copied into the Original value and so they're once again the same. Calling RejectChanges instead would have copied the Original value back into the Current value. Both methods change the RowState back to Unchanged.

FIGURE 5.1

Row versions. This figure illustrates the state of the table at the commented line in Listing 5.2.

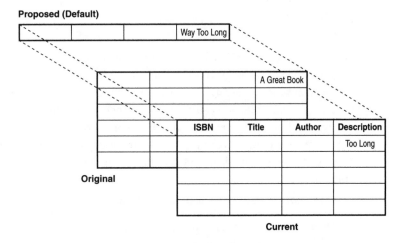

Although not shown in Listing 5.2, it follows that immediately after a row such as drNewTitle in Listing 5.1 is created, it has a Current version but not an Original version because the row wasn't originally retrieved from a data store. When the AcceptChanges method is called, either on the row directly on the table or on the DataSet after the row is added to the DataRowCollection, the Current version is copied to the Original and so both versions are available.

To access the values in the various versions, the Item property of the DataRow is over-loaded to support a second argument that specifies the DataRowVersion to retrieve. For example, between the BeginEdit and EndEdit method calls in Listing 5.2, the following code could be inserted:

```
//returns Great Book
string descO = titles.Rows[0]["Description",DataRowVersion.Original].ToString();
//returns Too Long
string descC = titles.Rows[0]["Description",DataRowVersion.Current].ToString();
//return Way Too Long
string descP = titles.Rows[0]["Description",DataRowVersion.Proposed].ToString();
//return Way Too Long
string descD = titles.Rows[0]["Description",DataRowVersion.Default].ToString();
```

From this snippet, you'll notice that the Default version simply points to the Proposed version as shown in Figure 5.1. It's also important to note the differences in syntax between VB and C# in this context. Because C# supports the concept of an indexer, you needn't reference the Item property explicitly. Simply enclosing the column name in

5

brackets after the row number assumes that you want to access the property denoted as the indexer; in this case, Item. This construct allows access to a property in an array-like syntax. As shown several times yesterday, in VB, you would have to explicitly use the Item property like so:

```
Dim descD As String = titles.Rows(0).Item(
    "Description",DataRowVersion.Default).ToString()
```

Of course, to know which versions of the row are available, you can use the HasVersion method of the DataRow class as shown in Table 4.2. This method accepts a value from the DataRowVersion enumeration and simply returns true if the version has been created for the row. For example, you could use the method to determine whether a row has both Current and Original versions and, if so, compare their primary keys to see whether they have been changed. The method in the following code snippet does just that and returns true or false when passed in the row to inspect and the name of primary key column:

```
private Boolean hasKeyChanged(ref DataRow row, string pk)
{
    if (row.HasVersion(DataRowVersion.Current) &
        row.HasVersion(DataRowVersion.Original))
        {
            if (row[pk,DataRowVersion.Current] != row[pk,DataRowVersion.Original])
                {
                    return true;
                }
                else return false;
        }
        else return false;
}
```

Revisiting DataViews

Obviously, row states and row versions are closely connected because the changing of a row state implies the population of a row version in many cases. This is most clearly seen in the DataView object and its RowStateFilter property. As discussed on Day 3, the DataView object is used to view the rows of a DataTable in different ways. Although Day 3 focused primarily on changing the view based on sorting and filtering the various row versions, the RowStateFilter property actually can be used to see an entire collection of rows from one of the other versions through the DataViewRowState enumeration shown in Table 5.3.

TABLE 5.3   Values of the `DataViewRowState` Enumeration

Value	Description
Added	Allows only new rows (Added state) to be visible—displays their Current version
CurrentRows	Shows the Current version of rows that include rows in the Unchanged, Added, and Modified states
Deleted	Allows rows in the Deleted state to be visible (the Current version)
ModifiedCurrent	Shows rows in the Current row version that are in the Modified row state
ModifiedOriginal	Shows rows in the Original row version that are in the Modified row state
None	No filter will be placed on the view
OriginalRows	Shows all rows in the Original row version including both rows in the Unchanged and Deleted row states
Unchanged	Shows the Current version of rows in the Unchanged state (which would be the same as the Original version)

As you can see from Table 5.3, values of the `DataViewRowState` enumeration encompass aspects of both the `DataRowState` and `DataRowVersion` enumerations to allow you to easily create a consistent view of the data in a `DataTable`. One use of this ability might be to present before-and-after snapshots of the data to a user for inspection before passing the changes to a data adapter for synchronizing with the data store, as in the `showOriginal` method in Listing 5.3.

LISTING 5.3   Viewing row versions. This method binds the original data from a table in a DataSet to a grid using a `DataView`.

```
public DataView showOriginal(ref DataSet ds, String table,
  String sort, ref DataGrid grid)
{
  DataView myView = new DataView(ds.Tables[table],null,
    sort,DataViewRowState.ModifiedOriginal);
  grid.DataSource = myView;
  grid.DataBind();
  return myView;
}
```

ANALYSIS   The `showOriginal` method in the previous code snippet first creates a new `DataView` of the table in the `DataSet` passed into the method. The `DataView` is sorted using the sort string also passed in, and will display only the original rows that have been modified using the ModifiedOriginal value of the DataRowViewState enu-meration. The new DataView is then bound to the ASP.NET DataGrid control and returned from the method.

Retrieving Changes

As you learned on Day 3, the GetChanges method is exposed by both the DataSet and DataTable classes. Both methods are overloaded to accept one or more DataRowState values to return only those rows that match the row state. If no row state is passed, all rows with Modified, Deleted, and Added row states are returned. As you might expect, the return values from the GetChanges method for the DataSet and the DataTable differ in that they return a DataSet and DataTable, respectively.

The primary use of these methods in n-tiered applications is as shown on Day 3; namely, to extract a subset of rows and then pass those rows to a class that can synchronize them with the underlying data store. This technique is useful to minimize the amount of data that must be marshaled between logical tiers (and possibly between machines), and thereby increase performance.

 Tip

As with other methods that accept an enumerated value, such as HasChanges, the GetChanges method can accept multiple values in a logical OR using the VB Or keyword or the C# | operator. So, to create a new DataSet that contains only Detached and Unchanged rows, you could use the VB syntax ds.GetChanges(DataRowState.Detached Or DataRowState.Unchanged) or the C# syntax ds.GetChanges(DataRowState.Detached | DataRowState.Unchanged);.

However, the GetChanges method in conjunction with accessing data in the various row versions can also be used to enumerate all the changes in a table before the AcceptChanges method is called. The code in Listing 5.4 illustrates this concept by showing a WriteXmlChanges method that creates an XML document that encapsulates all the changes to the passed-in DataTable. The method then returns an XmlTextReader that the calling code can use to navigate through the XML using a stream-based approach.

LISTING 5.4 Inspecting a DataTable. This method creates an XML document that describes the changes in a DataTable using the GetChanges method.

```
public XmlTextReader WriteXmlChanges(DataTable dt, String pk)
{
    MemoryStream s = new MemoryStream();
    XmlTextWriter xmlChanges = new XmlTextWriter(s,
```

LISTING 5.4   continued

```
            System.Text.Encoding.Default);

try
{
    xmlChanges.Formatting = Formatting.Indented;
    xmlChanges.Indentation = 4;
    xmlChanges.WriteStartDocument();
    xmlChanges.WriteComment("Changes for the " + dt.TableName + " table");
    xmlChanges.WriteStartElement("diff",dt.TableName + "Diff",
      "http://mycompany.org");
    xmlChanges.WriteAttributeString("primaryKey",pk);

    // Extract Deleted rows
    DataTable del = dt.GetChanges(DataRowState.Deleted);
    if (del  != null)
    {
      xmlChanges.WriteStartElement("Delete");
      foreach (DataRow row in del.Rows)
      {
        xmlChanges.WriteStartElement("row");
        xmlChanges.WriteString(row[pk,DataRowVersion.Original].ToString());
        xmlChanges.WriteEndElement(); //finish the Row tag
       }
       xmlChanges.WriteEndElement(); //finish the Delete tag
    }

    // Extract Modified Rows
    DataTable mod = dt.GetChanges(DataRowState.Modified);
    if (mod  != null)
    {
        xmlChanges.WriteStartElement("Change");
        foreach (DataRow row in mod.Rows)
        {
          xmlChanges.WriteStartElement("row");
          xmlChanges.WriteAttributeString("primaryKey",row[pk,
            DataRowVersion.Original].ToString());
          foreach (DataColumn col in mod.Columns)
          {
            if (row[col.ColumnName, DataRowVersion.Current].ToString()  !=
              row[col.ColumnName, DataRowVersion.Original].ToString())
            {
              xmlChanges.WriteStartElement(col.ColumnName);
              xmlChanges.WriteAttributeString("original",
                row[col.ColumnName,DataRowVersion.Original].ToString());
              xmlChanges.WriteString(row[col.ColumnName,
                DataRowVersion.Current].ToString());
              xmlChanges.WriteEndElement(); //finish column
            }
          }
```

5

LISTING 5.4   continued

```
                    xmlChanges.WriteEndElement(); //finish the Row tag
                }
            xmlChanges.WriteEndElement(); //finish the Change tag
        }

        // Extract Added Rows
        DataTable add = dt.GetChanges(DataRowState.Added);
        if (add  != null)
        {
            xmlChanges.WriteStartElement("Add");
            foreach (DataRow row in add.Rows)
            {
              xmlChanges.WriteStartElement("row");
              foreach (DataColumn col in add.Columns)
                {
                  xmlChanges.WriteElementString(col.ColumnName,
                    row[col.ColumnName, DataRowVersion.Current].ToString());
                }
              xmlChanges.WriteEndElement(); //finish the Row tag
            }
            xmlChanges.WriteEndElement(); //finish the Add tag
        }

        xmlChanges.WriteEndDocument();  //finish the document

        xmlChanges.Flush();
        s.Position = 0;
        return new XmlTextReader(s);
    }
    catch (IOException e)
    {
        logError(e, dt);
        return null;
    }
    catch (XmlException e)
    {
        logError(e, dt);
        return null;
    }
    catch (Exception e)
    {
        logError(e, dt);
        return null;
    }
}
```

ANALYSIS Although Listing 5.4 is fairly long, it can be broken into five distinct sections. The first section instantiates the MemoryStream that will be used to hold the XML document as well as the XmlTextWriter used to write to the MemoryStream. Directly inside the try block, the XmlTextWriter sets up the properties that determine how the document will be formatted as well as writes the root element with an attribute that identifies the primary key and a comment to the stream.

The second section calls the GetChanges method of the DataTable passed to the method to extract only those rows that have been Deleted. If rows are returned, a Delete element is written to the XML document with the WriteStartElement method and each row is written as a Row element inside. The point to note here is that in order to retrieve the values from the deleted row, you must access the Original version of the row. In this case, the primary key column, passed in the pk argument, is the only column written to the XML document because the primary key is all that is required to delete a row.

Note
> The WriteXmlChanges method as shown here would work only with a single-column primary key. It could easily be rewritten to accept an array of strings to represent possible composite keys.

Framework Patterns

This example uses classes from the System.Xml and System.IO namespaces to write out the XML stream and return an object that can be used to stream through the document. The classes in the System.Xml namespace, XmlTextWriter and XmlTextReader, implement a programming model that is different from both the Document Object Model (DOM) and the Simple API for XML (SAX) programming models exposed in the Microsoft XML (MSXML) parser familiar to COM developers. The advantage to using this approach that melds DOM and SAX is twofold. First, like SAX, it doesn't incur the memory overhead of DOM where the entire document is parsed into a tree structure before it's available for inspection. Second, like the DOM, it implements a pull rather than a push model, which allows developers to use a familiar cursor-style looping construct rather than having to respond to events fired from the parser.

As you'll find throughout the .NET Framework classes, the System.Xml classes rely on stream classes from the System.IO namespace to provide the underlying stream of bytes through which to work. In this case, a MemoryStream object is used to represent a stream of bytes stored in memory. Its base class, Stream, also acts as the base class for other stream objects in the Framework, such as FileStream and NetworkStream, that have different backing stores and that can be used polymorphically where a Stream object is called for.

The third section is analogous to the second by retrieving all the modified rows and looping through them, writing a row element for each one. However, inside the loop sits another nested loop that iterates the columns in the row in order to write out both the old and new values to the XML document. Note that the Current and Original versions are used to find the new and old values, respectively, and that only columns that differ between versions in their string representations are written to the stream. In this case, the original value is written as an attribute using the `WriteAttributeString` method.

The fourth section uses `GetChanges` to retrieve the newly inserted rows defined as those with a row state of `Added`. Like the previous section, it loops through all the rows and each column in order to write all the values to the XML stream. Note that, in this case, the `Current` version represents the new values because added rows don't yet have an `Original` version.

Finally, the ending element is written to the document and the `Position` of the stream is reset to the beginning. Because the method returns an `XmlTextReader`, a new object is instantiated and passed the `MemoryStream`. Most of the code is wrapped in a `try catch` block in order to handle any errors. In this case, possible exceptions include `IOException`, `XmlException`, and various exceptions from the `System.Data` namespace that are all caught under the generic `catch (Exception e)` block. In all cases, the exception is simply passed to a method to log the error.

The `WriteXmlChanges` method can then be called like so:

```
XmlTextReader tr = WriteXmlChanges(titles.GetChanges(),"ISBN");
```

Note that the default version of `GetChanges` is used to pass only rows that have been changed to the method. The result is an XML document that can be read from the `XmlTextReader` with the structure shown in Listing 5.5.

LISTING 5.5   XML changes. This listing shows the output from the `WriteXmlChanges` method shown in Listing 5.4.

```xml
<?xml version="1.0" encoding="Windows-1252"?>
<!--Changes for the Titles table-->
<diff:TitlesDiff primaryKey="ISBN" xmlns:diff="http://mycompany.org">
    <Delete>
        <row>06720006X </row>
    </Delete>
    <Change>
        <row primaryKey="06720001X ">
            <Description original="Great Book">Way too long</Description>
        </row>
    </Change>
    <Add>
        <row>
            <ISBN>077802000X</ISBN>
            <Title>Teach Yourself Enterprise ADO.NET in 21 Days</Title>
            <Description />
            <Author>Fox, Dan</Author>
```

LISTING 5.5 continued

```
                <PubDate>4/15/2001 12:00:00 AM</PubDate>
                <Price>31.99</Price>
                <Discount />
                <BulkDiscount />
                <BulkAmount />
                <Cover />
                <CatID />
                <Publisher>Sams</Publisher>
            </row>
        </Add>
</diff:TitlesDiff>
```

ANALYSIS From Listing 5.5, you can see that one row was deleted from the table with the ISBN 06720006X, one row's Description column was modified, and one new row was added.

Obviously, creating an XML document like the one shown in Listing 5.5 isn't something you would do everyday. After all, remember it is the job of the data adapter to look for changed rows much like the code in Listing 5.4 and apply those changes to the data store. However, as you'll learn on Day 14, "Working with Other Providers," there are rare occasions when you might want to write your own .NET Data Provider to work with a proprietary data store or one that's not easily accessible via ODBC or OLE DB. As a result, you might implement an XML message-passing scheme where an XML document is used to notify the data store of changes. In fact, the code shown in Listing 5.4 might be the basis for the Update method of a custom data adapter class that implements the IDataAdapter interface.

In any case, it should come as no surprise that the DataSet already implements functionality similar to that shown in this section.

DiffGrams

NEW TERM It turns out that the DataSet also supports an intrinsic method of creating an XML document to represent the changes in its tables, referred to as a **DiffGram**. DiffGrams were first introduced as a Web update to SQL Server 2000 that extended SQL Server's XML processing capabilities by allowing it to modify tables based on the contents of an XML document that conformed to the DiffGram schema.

To create a DiffGram, you can use the WriteXml method of the DataSet object (which you'll learn more about on Day 7, "DataSets and XML"). Simply put, the WriteXml method writes the contents of the DataSet in XML format to the stream you specify. An overloaded version accepts a value of the XmlWriteMode enumeration as the second argument that specifies what is to be written. By passing the DiffGram value as the second

5

argument, an XML document that shows before-and-after versions of modified rows and new rows is created. The following code is used to generate the DiffGram:

```
MemoryStream s = new MemoryStream();
DataSet dsMod = books.GetChanges();

dsMod.WriteXml(s,XmlWriteMode.DiffGram);
s.Position = 0;
XmlTextReader xmlTr = new XmlTextReader(s);
```

Here, a `MemoryStream` is also used to store the XML document and a new `DataSet` is first created to hold only the changed data. A `DiffGram` is then written to the stream with the `WriteXml` method, and its position is reset to `0` before instantiating the `XmlTextReader` that will be used to read the document. The resulting XML document that incorporates the same changes as the one in Listing 5.4 can be seen in Listing 5.6.

LISTING 5.6   A DiffGram. This listing shows an XML DiffGram produced by the `WriteXml` method.

```
<diffgr:diffgram xmlns:msdata="urn:schemas-microsoft-com:xml-msdata"
  xmlns:diffgr="urn:schemas-microsoft-com:xml-diffgram-v1">
  <ComputeBooksTitles>
    <Titles diffgr:id="Titles1" msdata:rowOrder="0"
      diffgr:hasChanges="modified>
      <ISBN>06720001X </ISBN>
      <Title>ADO 2.0 Programmers Reference</Title>
      <Description>Way too long</Description>
      <Author>Sussman, David/Homer, Alex</Author>
      <PubDate>1998-10-01T00:00:00.0000000-05:00</PubDate>
      <Price>29.99</Price>
      <Discount>9.5687</Discount>
      <BulkDiscount>10</BulkDiscount>
      <BulkAmount>50</BulkAmount>
      <CatID>21b60927-5659-4ad4-a036-ab478d73e754</CatID>
    </Titles>
    <Titles diffgr:id="Titles3" msdata:rowOrder="2"
      diffgr:hasChanges="inserted>
      <ISBN>077802000X</ISBN>
      <Title>Teach Yourself Enterprise ADO.NET in 21 Days</Title>
      <Author>Fox, Dan</Author>
      <PubDate>2001-04-15T00:00:00.0000000-05:00</PubDate>
      <Price>31.99</Price>
      <Publisher>Sams</Publisher>
    </Titles>
  </ComputeBooksTitles>
  <diffgr:before>
    <Titles diffgr:id="Titles1" msdata:rowOrder="0">
      <ISBN>06720001X </ISBN>
      <Title>ADO 2.0 Programmers Reference</Title>
```

LISTING 5.6   continued

```
        <Description>Great Book</Description>
        <Author>Sussman, David/Homer, Alex</Author>
        <PubDate>1998-10-01T00:00:00.0000000-05:00</PubDate>
        <Price>29.99</Price>
        <Discount>9.5687</Discount>
        <BulkDiscount>10</BulkDiscount>
        <BulkAmount>50</BulkAmount>
        <CatID>21b60927-5659-4ad4-a036-ab478d73e754</CatID>
      </Titles>
      <Titles diffgr:id="Titles2" msdata:rowOrder="1">
        <ISBN>06720006X </ISBN>
        <Title>Advanced MS Visual Basic 6/+CD/2nd edition</Title>
        <Author>Mandelbrot Set International Ltd</Author>
        <PubDate>1998-10-01T00:00:00.0000000-05:00</PubDate>
        <Price>59.99</Price>
        <Discount>9.57</Discount>
        <BulkDiscount>20</BulkDiscount>
        <BulkAmount>75</BulkAmount>
        <CatID>21b60927-5659-4ad4-a036-ab478d73e754</CatID>
        <Publisher>Msft </Publisher>
      </Titles>
    </diffgr:before>
</diffgr:diffgram>
```

The key point that should strike you when comparing Listing 5.5 with Listing 5.6 is that the DiffGram schema includes complete representations of the before-and-after states of a modified row and includes the before views in the `diffgr:before` tag and the after views simply inside the root element. Modified rows have their `hasChanges` attribute set to "modified," whereas new rows have theirs set to "inserted." Note also that deleted rows simply appear in the `diffgr:before` element and, as you would expect, have no after representation.

Obviously, you can also capitalize on the DiffGram format if you need to pass XML to update a data store.

Handling Changes

Today's final brief discussion deals with notifying the `DataTable` as to when rows should be "committed" to the table. In other words, at some point you need to know that changed, deleted, and inserted rows can simply be treated as regular rows, most likely because they are now synchronized to the data store.

Using AcceptChanges

The DataSet, DataTable, and DataRow classes all expose AcceptChanges methods that perform the same function although, of course, only in the scopes appropriate for the object. As hinted at previously, when AcceptChanges is called on any of the objects, it performs the following tasks in order:

1. It calls the EndEdit method for any rows where changes are pending, causing Proposed values to be copied to Current values.

2. It changes the rows with the row states of Added and Modified to Unchanged, creating an Original version for added rows and copying the Current version to the Original for modified rows.

3. Rows with the Deleted state or that were detached from the table are removed from the table.

4. It clears out any RowError information and sets the HasErrors property to False.

Of course, as mentioned earlier today, calling AcceptChanges can cause exceptions to be thrown if you call it, for example, on the deleted row. In addition, remember that rows in other tables might be affected by calling AcceptChanges on a row in a parent table when the AcceptRejectRule property of a foreign key constraint (ForeignKeyConstraint) is set to Cascade.

Using RejectChanges

Obviously, the RejectChanges method is exposed on the same objects as AcceptChanges, but has the reverse effects:

1. It calls the CancelEdit method for any rows where changes are pending, causing Proposed values to be destroyed.

2. It changes the rows with the row states of Deleted and Modified to Unchanged, reverting the Original values to the Current values for Modified rows.

3. Rows with the Added state are removed from the table.

4. It clears out any RowError information and sets the HasErrors property to False.

A typical use of RejectChanges is to undo changes if validation errors are placed in the rows as a result of code run in the events of the DataTable such as RowChanging or ColumnChanging, as shown in Table 4.2. For example, the method in Listing 5.7 attempts to resolve a specific error and, if it cannot, calls RejectChanges on the row. After all the rows have been checked, the method calls AcceptChanges on the entire table.

LISTING 5.7 Checking rows. This method checks for a specific error condition and corrects it if possible before calling the RejectChanges or AcceptChanges method.

```
private void checkAddressErrors(ref DataTable dt)
{
  if (dt.HasErrors)
  {
    foreach (DataRow row in dt.GetErrors())
    {
      if (row.RowError == "Must have a Postal Code or City and State")
      {
        row["PostalCode"] = "66218";
        row.RowError = "";    // clear the error, sets HasErrors to false
      }
      else
        row.RejectChanges();
    }
  }
  dt.AcceptChanges();
}
```

ANALYSIS Note in this code snippet that the GetError method of the DataTable is used to retrieve all the rows whose RowError property is set in an array of DataRow objects.

Note

Both the DataSet and DataTable expose Reset methods that simply wipe out all data and columns in the tables, and leave the object in the state it was in directly after it was instantiated. The Reset method would be appropriate to use if you want to clear a DataSet or DataTable and reuse it for a different set of data because neither the data nor structure is preserved.

5

Summary

Hopefully today has clarified in your mind how changes are tracked and applied to the tables in a DataSet using the combination of row states, row versions, GetChanges, AcceptChanges, and RejectChanges. Having a clear picture of how the DataSet operates in this regard is a prerequisite to working with data adapters and design enterprise applications with ADO.NET.

Tomorrow, you'll look at the concept of the strongly typed DataSet and how it can be used to increase programmer productivity and reduce programming errors.

Workshop

This workshop will help reinforce the concepts covered in today's lesson.

Quiz

1. How does a data adapter know which rows have changes?

   A data adapter, or for that matter your code, can inspect the RowState property of the DataRow object to determine the current state of the row. Row states include Added, Deleted, Modified, and Unchanged.

2. How does a DataTable track the old values for a row?

   Each row in the DataTable can have up to three different copies or versions (Current, Original, Proposed) associated with it. The HasVersion method of the DataRow class is used to determine whether a particular version exists by accepting a value from the DataRowVersion enumeration. Various versions can be retrieved using the optional second argument of the Item property (the indexer in C#) of the DataRow.

3. What is the purpose of the GetChanges method?

   The GetChanges method can be used to return a DataTable or DataSet that contains only the rows that have been modified (their row state set to Added, Modified, or Deleted). An overloaded signature also allows only changes from one or more of the row states to be returned.

4. What is the relationship between row states, row versions, and a DataView?

   A DataView, through its RowStateFilter property, can be used to view a collection of rows from a DataTable that have a particular combination of RowState and version. For example, the RowFilter can be set to the ModifiedOriginal value from the DataRowViewState enumeration to show the Original values from rows with a row state of Modified. The DataView can then be bound to a control for display.

Exercise

Today, write a console application that retrieves Reviews from the ComputeBooks database. Then programmatically edit the first row using the BeginEdit and EndEdit methods. Check the RowState property and HasVersion method before and after calling EndEdit to see how the values change. Commit the changes to the row after it has been modified.

Answers for Day 5

Exercise Answer

One possible solution is as follows:

```
static void Main(string[] args)
{
        SqlConnection con = new SqlConnection(
           "server=ssosa;database=compubooks;trusted_connection=yes");
        SqlDataAdapter da = new SqlDataAdapter("usp_GetReviews",con);
        DataTable reviews = new DataTable("Reviews");

        da.SelectCommand.CommandType = CommandType.StoredProcedure;
        da.SelectCommand.Parameters.Add(
           new SqlParameter("@isbn",SqlDbType.NChar,10));
        da.SelectCommand.Parameters[0].Value = "06720083X";

        // Get the data
        try
        {
            da.Fill(reviews);
        }
        catch (SqlException e)
        {
            Console.WriteLine(e.Message);
        }

        // Edit the row
        reviews.Rows[0].BeginEdit();
          reviews.Rows[0]["Stars"] = 4;
          CheckIt(reviews.Rows[0]);
        reviews.Rows[0].EndEdit();
        CheckIt(reviews.Rows[0]);

        // Commit the changes
        reviews.Rows[0].AcceptChanges();
}

static void CheckIt(DataRow r)
{
        Console.WriteLine(r.RowState.ToString());
        Console.WriteLine(r.HasVersion(DataRowVersion.Current).ToString());
        Console.WriteLine(r.HasVersion(DataRowVersion.Default).ToString());
        Console.WriteLine(r.HasVersion(DataRowVersion.Original).ToString());
        Console.WriteLine(r.HasVersion(DataRowVersion.Proposed).ToString());
}
```

In this solution, the Main method of the console application calls the usp_GetReviews stored procedure and passes in an ISBN to retrieve the reviews into a DataTable. The first row of the table is then edited and its RowState and row versions printed by the CheckIt method. The row is then committed using the AcceptChanges method.

5

DAY 6

Building Strongly Typed DataSet Classes

Yesterday you completed a three-day, in-depth look at how a DataSet and its related classes function by examining how the DataSet tracks its changes. At this point, you should have a good understanding of how to work with a DataSet in disconnected scenarios and both its functionality and limitations.

Today's short lesson will focus on extending the base DataSet class using the inheritance features built into the common language runtime in order to create custom DataSet classes. The custom classes are easier for developers to work with because they provide a more object-oriented means to access the data in the DataSet. In addition, they reduce programming errors introduced at design time by providing a strongly typed DataSet class with which to work. Today, we'll also examine techniques for persisting a DataSet to disk and passing it between tiers in a distributed application.

To that end, today you'll learn the following concepts:

- The purpose and goals of a strongly typed DataSet
- How to create a strongly typed DataSet both programmatically and graphically in VS .NET

- How a strongly typed `DataSet` is versioned and can be shared between projects
- How a `DataSet` can be serialized and passed between tiers using .NET Remoting

Strongly Typed `DataSet` Classes Defined

NEW TERM **Implementation inheritance**, or inheriting from a class and extending and reusing the code in its members, is one of the key strengths of the common language runtime and of the languages it supports, as mentioned on Day 1, "ADO.NET in Perspective." Not only does it promote reuse by allowing developers to extend the existing implementation of a class, it also allows you to program polymorphically by creating methods that accept arguments of the base class but that can be used with any of the derived classes. As a result, using implementation inheritance is a natural way to design classes that implement specific behavior but rely on a core set of members that can be coded once in a base class.

Which Inheritance Should I Use?

As mentioned on Day 1, in addition to implementation inheritance, the common language runtime also includes the concept of interface inheritance, both of which promote the writing of polymorphic code. Because both are now available, you need to decide which to use when designing your applications. Basically, implementation inheritance should be used when the derived class follows an "is a" relationship with the base class. For example, an employee "is a" person and so the behavior (implementation of the members) of the person class is probably suitable to be reused in the employee class. The "is a" rule certainly holds for a custom `DataSet` that certainly "is a" `DataSet`.

On the other hand, interface inheritance should be used when multiple classes need to expose the same semantics but implement them in different ways. For example, ADO.NET includes the `IDataAdapter` interface that can be implemented by different .NET Data Providers to provide a consistent set of functionality, but that might be implemented very differently. This is obvious when you consider that one data adapter may communicate with SQL Server in its `Fill` method while the other communicates with a proprietary hierarchical file system.

When you think about it, the `DataSet` fits perfectly into this pattern because an instance of `DataSet` simply reflects a particular set of data that has a particular structure in terms of its table, columns, relationships, and data types. Further, a `DataSet` has core functionality (`GetChanges`, `AcceptChanges`, `Merge`, et al.) that is best written once and called upon in any instance of a `DataSet`.

NEW TERM In this section, you'll learn about the purpose and goals of strongly typed `DataSet` classes, how to create them, and how they can be versioned and shared between projects. Simply put, a **strongly typed DataSet** is a derived DataSet class that exposes the tables, rows, and columns in the DataSet with specific types rather than the standard DataTable, DataRow, and DataColumn types. In addition, a strongly typed DataSet exposes columns contained in a table as properties such as Title, Author, and Price.

Purpose and Goals

Historically, one of the problems that developers have run into again and again is mapping the rows and columns in tables of a relational database or other data store to native data structures (classes, arrays, structures, or user-defined types) exposed by their programming language of choice. In the past, this has entailed writing custom code to read and write the database data to and from the data structures. Not only did this require more coding, but it also brought with it more overhead as additional objects and collections of objects had to be created and managed. In addition, some languages—such as VBScript—used in prior versions of ASP didn't even support the constructs such as classes necessary to create a mapping layer.

> **Note**
>
> The mapping of database data to an object model in VB 6 and prior versions was especially inefficient because scores of COM objects were often created. As a result, different techniques were created to realize the benefits of an object-based approach (as discussed later today), while still maintaining performance. I advocated one technique, the Lightweight Business Object Model (LBOM), in Chapter 15 of my book *Pure Visual Basic*.

Of course, the primary reason developers strive to create a mapping layer in the first place is to be able to work with the data directly rather than through an abstracted construct such as a Recordset. In addition, "objectifying" the data reduces programming errors because the class, structure, or user-defined type directly exposes the column information in a strongly typed field or property rather than as a generic item in a collection. Not only does this reduce runtime and logic errors by giving developers more visibility to the data, when coupled with the IntelliSense feature of the VS .NET IDE, it also makes them more productive by reducing the guesswork involved in determining the names of columns and their data types. For example, the following code snippet from yesterday fills the books DataSet and accesses the Description column of the first row:

```
books = new DataSet("ComputeBooksTitles");

da.Fill(books, "Titles");
DataRow title = books.Tables["Titles"].Rows[0];
```

6

```
title["Description"] = "This book is too long";
```

With a strongly typed `DataSet`, the code snippet could be rewritten as follows:

```
books = new BooksDs();

da.Fill(books);
TitlesRow title = books.Titles.Rows[0];

title.Description = "This book is too long";
```

In ADO.NET, the need to write custom code to populate and synchronize data between a data provider and a class has been alleviated by providing a wizard that can create a strongly typed `DataSet`, like the `BooksDs` object shown in the previous code snippet, based on an XML Schema Definition (XSD). Simply put, XSD is an XML grammar that can be used to define the structure of an XML document. It so happens, as you'll learn tomorrow, that the structure of a `DataSet` is also defined by an XSD. In fact, the XSD can be created graphically from scratch or directly from a database connection in the Server Explorer window.

Note

As mentioned briefly on Day 1, the common language runtime includes a type checker that ensures that variables are accessed only in a type-safe manner, so that the common language runtime can allocate the proper amount of memory for the object and so that a variable can't point to memory it's not supposed to. In that sense, all common language runtime languages are strongly typed. In fact, in the past, VB wasn't particularly strongly typed and frequently coerced types in assignment statements and parameter passing. Even though VB .NET still supports automatic type conversion, it also includes a new level of type safety with the `Option Strict` statement. Turning `Option Strict` on forces VB .NET developers to explicitly do the versions using the `CType` function or the methods of the `Convert` class. VC# .NET is always strongly typed and so casts are required.

Creating and Populating

To use a strongly typed `DataSet`, you first must create it. In this section, we'll look at several techniques you can use to create the `DataSet` and then discuss how it can be populated and manipulated in code.

Note

The examples in this section assume that you have a VC# .NET console application project open if you want to follow along.

Creating the DataSet

The easiest way to create a strongly typed DataSet involves using the graphical designer inherent in VS .NET. To activate the designer, right-click on the project and select Add New Item. The Add New Item dialog then allows you to select from the list of templates grouped into categories that you can explore under the Local Project Items node on the left side of the dialog, as shown in Figure 6.1. You'll find the DataSet under the Data group.

FIGURE 6.1

The Add New Item dialog. This dialog adds a new DataSet to the current project.

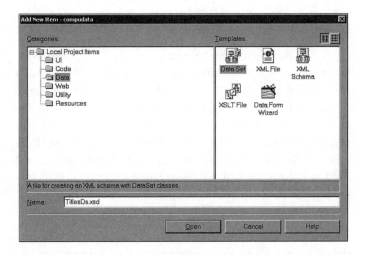

In this case, give the DataSet the name TitlesDs.xsd and click Open. The design surface then appears, ready for you to graphically create the structure of the DataSet. From this point, you can either use the Toolbox to drag and drop building blocks of an XSD schema onto the design surface, or use the Server Explorer to drag and drop database tables onto the designer. Obviously, for most developers, it will be easier to use the latter method because it doesn't require knowledge of XSD. In this way, you can at least jump-start the creation of the XSD and edit it from there.

6

> **Tip**
>
> Alternatively, if you already have an XSD schema that you received from a trading partner or that you built with a third-party tool such as XML Spy, you can import it into VS .NET by selecting Add Existing Item after right-clicking on the project. The schema will then be loaded and graphically displayed in the designer. When you do so, you have the option of adding five annotations (typedName, typedPlural, typedParent, typedChildren, and nullValue) that the code generator will use to customize the names of the classes generated. For more information on these annotations, see the "Using Annotations with a Typed DataSet" topic in the online documentation.

To drag-and-drop tables, you'll need to create a data connection as described on Day 2, "Getting Started." When the data connection to the ComputeBooks database is established, drag and drop the `Titles` and `Reviews` tables onto the designer surface. You'll notice that the tables include all the columns with their correct data types and primary key identified and are mapped to elements in the XSD schema. Not surprisingly, each table will also map to a `DataTable` in the generated `DataSet`. From here, you can edit the list of columns in the `DataSet` in order to change their names or add and remove columns. In this case, we don't need all the columns of the `Titles` table, so you can delete the `Cover`, `CatID`, and `Publisher` columns and add the `CategoryName` and `PubName` columns with a data type of `string`.

Finally, you need to add a relationship between the `Titles` and `Reviews` table by right-clicking on the `Reviews` element and selecting Add, New Relation, just as was done on Day 2. In this case, select `Titles` as the parent element and `Reviews` as the child element. Both the fields should be set to `ISBN`. The properties at the bottom of the dialog should be set to have an update rule of `None`, a delete rule of `Cascade`, and an accept/reject rule of `Cascade`. These properties map directly to the properties discussed on Day 4, "DataSet Internals." As you'll recall from Day 4, creating a `DataRelation` object as we're doing here implies creating a `ForeignKeyConstraint`, but the reverse isn't true. Because we want to be able to traverse the relationship, leave the Create foreign key constraint only checkbox blank.

After the structure of the `DataSet` has been established, you can right-click on it and select Preview DataSet to view the objects that will make up the `DataSet` and their properties. Although you can't edit the properties in this dialog, you can edit some of them (such as `Namespace`, `Prefix`, and `Version`) in the properties window. In this case, change `Namespace` to `http://www.compubooks.com/TitlesDs` and `Version` to "1.0." The end result is the designer shown in Figure 6.2.

 Tip

> To view the XML that makes up the XSD, click on the XML pane attached to the bottom of the design surface. Note that you can also edit the schema directly in this pane, and it even supports IntelliSense to make it easier to code the XML.

You'll notice from Figure 6.2 that the diagram denotes the fact that the relationship is a one-to-many relationship between `Titles` and `Reviews`, where one title may be associated with many reviews. Also, the designer doesn't point to the columns being related (in this case, `ISBN` in both tables) but simply connects the tables as a whole, thereby making it appear as if perhaps `ISBN` was related to `Discount`.

FIGURE 6.2

The TitlesDs DataSet. *This figure shows the designer surface of* TitlesDs *after it has been edited.*

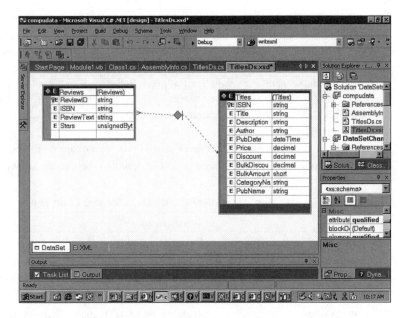

If you right-click on the TitlesDs.xsd file in the Solution Explorer, you'll notice that the Generate DataSet option is checked. This implies that a strongly typed DataSet has already been created and is being constantly updated as changes are made to the graphical representation in the designer. To view the DataSet class, click the Show All Files icon in the toolbar of the Solution Explorer window. Doing so allows you to drill down on the TitlesDs.xsd file to reveal the TitlesDs.cs and TitlesDs.xsx files. The .cs file holds the code generated by the wizard that includes the class derived from DataSet, whereas the .xsx file is an XML document that holds layout information for the components added to the designer surface.

Use the Command Line

Alternatively, you can generate a strongly typed DataSet using the command-line Xml Schemas/DataTypes support utility (XSD.exe). Given an XSD schema, this utility supports the /dataset or /d option to generate a subclassed DataSet. For example, if you already had a schema generated in XML Spy called TitlesDs.xsd, you could create a strongly typed C# DataSet in the TitlesDs.cs file with the following command:

```
XSD.exe TitlesDs.xsd /dataset /1:CS /namespace:Computebooks.Data
```

In this case, the /namespace option instructed the code generator to place the new class in the ComputeBooks.Data namespace. The newly created .cs file can then be added to your project using the Add Existing Item menu option.

6

To run the command-line utilities that ship with VS .NET, open a command window using the Visual Studio .NET Command Prompt icon in the Visual Studio .NET Tools program group under Microsoft Visual Studio .NET.

Both the graphical and command-line tools rely on the `TypedDataSetGenerator` class in the `System.Data` namespace to do their work.

By double-clicking on the TitlesDs.cs file, you can examine the code that was generated. At the highest level, the source code file contains the classes shown in Table 6.1.

TABLE 6.1   Classes Generated in the TitlesDs.cs Source Code File

Class	Description
`TitlesDs`	Derived from `DataSet` and represents the highest-level class.
`ReviewsDataTable`	A child class of `TitlesDs` and derived from `DataTable`. Used to hold the data from the `Reviews` table and exposed as the `Reviews` property of the `TitlesDs` class.
`ReviewsRow`	A child class of `TitlesDs` and derived from `DataRow`. Exposes strongly typed properties for each of the columns in the `Reviews` table along with the `TitlesRow` that is its parent.
`ReviewsRowChangeEvent`	A child class of `TitlesDs` and derived from `EventArgs`. Used to hold event state information such as the `ReviewsRow` the event was fired on and passed to events of the `ReviewsDataTable`.
`TitlesDataTable`	A child class of `TitlesDs` and derived from `DataTable`. Used to hold the data from the `Titles` table and exposed as the `Titles` property of the `TitlesDs` class.
`TitlesRow`	A child class of `TitlesDs` and derived from `DataRow`. Exposes strongly typed properties for each of the columns in the `Titles` table along with a method to retrieve an array of `ReviewsRow` objects that are its children.
`TitlesRowChangeEvent`	A child class of `TitlesDs` and derived from `EventArgs`. Used to hold event state information such as the `TitlesRow` the event was fired on and passed to events of the `TitlesDataTable`.

As you can see from Table 6.1, the generated code implements all aspects of a `DataSet` as you learned on Day 4, but does so using classes derived from the base ADO.NET classes `DataSet`, `DataTable`, and `DataRow` and that reflect the actual table and column information from the database. You can also view the structure of the `TitlesDs` class by switching to the Class View in the Solution Explorer and drilling down on the namespace in which the class exists. By default, the DataSet will exist in the global namespace for the project, although that can be easily changed by editing the namespace declaration in the source file. In this case, we would want to change the namespace to ComputeBooks.Data to reflect the fact that the class is owned by the ComputeBooks organization and falls in the realm of the data for the organization. All the strongly typed DataSet classes and data access classes would likewise be grouped together in this namespace.

Tip

If you want the code you write to conform to the naming and style guidelines that Microsoft used when developing the Services Framework, you should follow the design guidelines included in the online documentation. Search for "design guidelines for class library developers" in the index, and you'll find a whole host of topics from naming conventions to error handling guidelines to common design patterns used in the Framework.

By examining the generated code, you'll notice several key features—four of which we'll discuss here—that make the TitlesDs DataSet a strongly typed DataSet.

First, you'll notice that the TitlesDs class exposes a property for each DataTable, like so:

```
public ReviewsDataTable Reviews {
  get {
     return this.tableReviews;
  }
}

public TitlesDataTable Titles {
   get {
     return this.tableTitles;
   }
}
```

ANALYSIS In both cases, the property is read-only and returns a private instance variable instantiated in the private InitClass method called from the constructor of the class. This is what enables developers using this code to avoid having to manipulate the DataTableCollection directly.

Note

The use of the InitClass method called from the constructor to initialize each class, and use of the InitVars method to ensure that private variables are initialized when the class has been instantiated, are two common features you'll find for the classes generated by the wizard.

6

Second, you'll notice that the ReviewsRow and TitlesRow classes contain properties that return a strongly typed value for each column, as shown in Listing 6.1 for the ReviewsRow class.

LISTING 6.1   The ReviewsRow class. This class exposes the columns of the table as properties that map back to the underlying ReviewsDataTable.

```
public class ReviewsRow : DataRow {

  private ReviewsDataTable tableReviews;

  internal ReviewsRow(DataRowBuilder rb) :
      base(rb) {
    this.tableReviews = ((ReviewsDataTable)(this.Table));
  }

  public System.Guid ReviewID {
    get {
      return ((System.Guid)(this[this.tableReviews.ReviewIDColumn]));
    }
    set {
      this[this.tableReviews.ReviewIDColumn] = value;
    }
  }

  public string ISBN {
    get {
      return ((string)(this[this.tableReviews.ISBNColumn]));
    }
    set {
      this[this.tableReviews.ISBNColumn] = value;
    }
  }

  public string ReviewText {
    get {
      return ((string)(this[this.tableReviews.ReviewTextColumn]));
    }
    set {
      this[this.tableReviews.ReviewTextColumn] = value;
    }
  }

  public System.Byte Stars {
    get {
      return ((System.Byte)(this[this.tableReviews.StarsColumn]));
    }
    set {
      this[this.tableReviews.StarsColumn] = value;
```

LISTING 6.1 continued

```
    }
  }

  public TitlesRow TitlesRow {
    get {
      return ((TitlesRow)(this.GetParentRow(
        this.Table.ParentRelations["TitlesReviews"])));
    }
    set {
      this.SetParentRow(value, this.Table.ParentRelations["TitlesReviews"]);
    }
  }
}
```

ANALYSIS You'll notice from Listing 6.1 that the properties reference strongly typed `DataColumn` objects exposed as properties by the `ReviewsDataTable` class. These properties simply get and set data in the underlying `ReviewsDataTable` object exposed through the `tableReviews` variable. In addition, Listing 6.1 shows that the generated code automatically creates a property that references the parent `TitlesRow` defined by the data relation you created in the graphical designer. By looking at the `TitlesRow` class, you'll also see that it includes a method, `GetReviewsRows`, which returns an array of `ReviewsRow` objects that correspond to its child rows identified in the `DataRelation`.

Third, the generated code includes strongly typed methods that can be used to add rows to the tables. For example, the `ReviewsDataTable` class includes a `NewReviewsRow` method and an overloaded `AddReviewsRow` method that can be used together to create a new row and add it to the `DataTable` as in Listing 6.2.

LISTING 6.2 Adding a new row. These methods can be used to add a new `ReviewsRow` to the `ReviewsDataTable` and show how strongly typed methods are implemented.

```
public ReviewsRow NewReviewsRow() {
  return ((ReviewsRow)(this.NewRow()));
}

public void AddReviewsRow(ReviewsRow row) {
  this.Rows.Add(row);
}

public ReviewsRow AddReviewsRow(System.Guid ReviewID,
    TitlesRow parentTitlesRowByTitlesReviews,
    string ReviewText, System.Byte Stars) {
  ReviewsRow rowReviewsRow =((ReviewsRow)(this.NewRow()));
```

6

LISTING 6.2   continued

```
rowReviewsRow.ItemArray = new object[] {
    ReviewID,
    parentTitlesRowByTitlesReviews[0],
    ReviewText,
    Stars};
this.Rows.Add(rowReviewsRow);
return rowReviewsRow;
}
```

ANALYSIS   In Listing 6.2, the NewReviewsRow method simply creates a new row by calling the base class implementation of NewRow and then casts it to the type ReviewsRow. The first AddReviewsRow method accepts a ReviewsRow object and simply adds it to the collection; the second includes arguments for each of the properties of the row, including the parent TitlesRow.

Finally, each class created for a table, TitlesDataTable and ReviewsDataTable, contains a method that finds a particular row by its primary key column. For example, the ReviewsDataTable contains the FindByReviewID method that uses the Find method of the DataRowCollection class as discussed on Day 3, "Working with DataSets":

```
public ReviewsRow FindByReviewID(System.Guid ReviewID) {
  return ((ReviewsRow)(this.Rows.Find(new object[] {
    ReviewID})));
}
```

The method then returns the found row, casting it to the ReviewsRow type.

Populating the DataSet

Now that the DataSet has been created and added to the project, you can use it either programmatically or graphically. For example, you can drag and drop it on a Web Form or other designer surface as you did on Day 2 and then associate it with a data adapter through the Data Adapter Configuration Wizard.

However, before doing so you need to consider what the code at the database server might be used to populate the DataSet. In the case of TitlesDs, remember that we didn't simply accept the default columns when we dropped the tables onto the design surface. Because we edited the column list of the Titles table, we need to make sure that we write SQL that is true to that list.

As we'll cover in more detail on Day 10, "Working with Commands," when using SQL Server, we would typically use stored procedures because of their performance and security. So, to populate the DataSet, we'll use a stored procedure that includes a SELECT statement to retrieve the data for the Titles table and then one to retrieve the Reviews, as shown in Listing 6.3.

LISTING 6.3 The usp_GetTitlesReviews stored procedure. This SQL Server stored procedure retrieves data from the Titles and Reviews tables.

```sql
CREATE PROCEDURE usp_GetTitlesReviews
@publisher nchar(5) = NULL
AS

IF @publisher IS NULL
BEGIN
  SELECT ISBN, Title, a.Description,
    Author, PubDate, Price,
    Discount, BulkDiscount, BulkAmount,
    b.Description As CategoryName,
    c.Name As PubName
  FROM Titles a JOIN Categories b ON a.CatID = b.CatID
    JOIN Publishers c ON a.Publisher = c.PubCode

  SELECT ReviewID, ISBN, ReviewText, Stars
  FROM Reviews

END
ELSE
BEGIN
  SELECT ISBN, Title, a.Description,
    Author, PubDate, Price,
    Discount, BulkDiscount, BulkAmount,
    b.Description As CategoryName,
    c.Name As PubName
  FROM Titles a JOIN Categories b ON a.CatID = b.CatID
    JOIN Publishers c ON a.Publisher = c.PubCode
  WHERE a.Publisher = @publisher

  SELECT ReviewID, a.ISBN, ReviewText, Stars
  FROM Reviews a JOIN Titles b ON a.ISBN = b.ISBN
  WHERE b.Publisher = @publisher

END
```

ANALYSIS The interesting thing to note in Listing 6.3 is that the publisher parameter is effectively optional because the procedure includes an IF statement to handle the case where the parameter isn't passed or is NULL.

Note

Alert readers will have no doubt noticed that if this stored procedure needed to include several optional parameters in the WHERE clause, the Transact-SQL in Listing 6.3 would grow in complexity. To view a more sophisticated stored procedure that handles multiple arguments, see the usp_GetTitles stored procedure that is installed with the ComputeBooks database and that you used on Day 3.

In addition, you'll see that the SELECT statement that returns data from the Titles table uses JOIN clauses to get the Description column from the Categories table and the Name column from the Publishers table, and aliases them to the CategoryName and PubName columns, respectively, as used in the DataSet. Although the DataSet could have also included tables to hold the Categories and Publishers data separately, it makes more sense to use JOIN clauses to return just the descriptive information if the tables are simply lookup tables. In other words, because the DataSet isn't designed to allow editing of the Categories or Publishers tables, it's less complex and more efficient to directly incorporate the data that you want to include in the TitlesRow through a table join.

It should also be noted that the procedure returns two result sets, one for each table in the DataSet.

The usp_GetTitlesReviews stored procedure can then be used to populate the TitlesDs DataSet. The code in Listing 6.4 populates the DataSet and then manipulates its data using its exposed types.

LISTING 6.4   Populating the TitlesDs DataSet from the usp_GetTitlesReview stored procedure. This listing uses a SqlDataAdapter to populate TitlesDs and access its data.

```
SqlConnection con = new SqlConnection(connect);
SqlDataAdapter da = new SqlDataAdapter ("usp_GetTitlesReviews", con);

da.SelectCommand.CommandType = CommandType.StoredProcedure;

TitlesDs books = new TitlesDs();

books.EnforceConstraints = false;

da.MissingMappingAction = MissingMappingAction.Passthrough;
da.TableMappings.Add("Table","Reviews");
da.TableMappings.Add("Table1","Titles");

da.Fill(books);
books.EnforceConstraints = true;
```

LISTING 6.4   continued

```
TitlesDs.TitlesRow titleRow;
titleRow = books.Titles.FindByISBN("06720002X");

if (titleRow != null)
{
   string bookTitle = titleRow.Title;
   string author = titleRow.Author;

   TitlesDs.ReviewsRow reviewRow = books.Reviews.AddReviewsRow(
      System.Guid.NewGuid(),titleRow,"This was a pretty good book",4);
   reviewRow.AcceptChanges();
}
```

ANALYSIS   The code in Listing 6.4 uses `SqlConnection` and `SqlDataAdapter` objects to connect to the SQL Server and to encapsulate the call to the stored procedure. When the `books` object is instantiated, the constructor of the `TitlesDs` class executes and creates the tables and relation that are exposed through its properties. As a result, before the `Fill` method is even called, the `DataSet` contains two empty tables connected by a data relation with all the columns fully defined. The `EnforceConstraints` property of the `DataSet` is then set to `False` to ensure that the foreign key constraint isn't activated in the event that the `Reviews` table is loaded first.

Tip   Of course, the code in Listing 6.4 would need to be in a source code file with the `using ComputeBooks.Data;` statement at the top and you would need to use the `System.Data` and `System.Data.SqlClient` namespaces.

The next three lines of code dealing with the `MissingMappingAction` and `TableMappings` collection will be discussed in more detail on Day 12, "Using Data Adapters." For now, it suffices to say that the `MissingMappingAction` determines what happens when the columns from the database table encounter columns in an existing `DataTable`. The `TableMappings` are used to map the result sets returned from the stored procedure to the tables in the `DataSet`.

The `DataSet` is then populated with the `Fill` method, which executes the stored procedure. After the data is loaded, the `EnforceConstraints` property is set to `true` to enable the foreign key constraint. At this point, if the `Reviews` table contains any rows that don't match a row in the `Titles` table, a `ConstraintException` will be thrown.

6

To access an individual row in the `TitlesDataTable`, the listing then uses a variable of type `TitlesRow` to return the row from the `FindByISBN` method of the `TitlesDataTable` class. If the row is found, the `Title` and `Author` properties will return the name of the book and its author or authors. Finally, the `AddReviewRows` method of the `ReviewsRow` class is used to add a new review to the title that was found. Note that the primary key of the `Reviews` table is a GUID, so the `NewGuid` method of the `Guid` structure is used to generate the value. The `AcceptChanges` method of the new row is then called to set the row state to `Unchanged`.

Versioning and Sharing

In software development, any time you create an explicit construct to use in favor of an abstracted one in order to increase developer productivity—for example, by making it simpler and less error-prone to access data—you introduce a new dependency that you must manage. This is true of strongly typed classes such as the `DataSet` as well. However, the runtime characteristics of the common language runtime make it relatively easy to share and version a class such as `TitlesDs` both on a single machine and among developers in an organization.

First, because the `TitlesDs` class and any other strongly typed `DataSet` classes you create might be used in multiple projects, you should consider factoring them into their own assembly. As mentioned on Day 1, an assembly is the unit of versioning, deployment, and security in the .NET Framework. By placing all the strongly typed `DataSet` classes and perhaps even data access classes used to populate them in a single assembly, you can version and deploy them as a single unit. To do so, simply open a new Class Library project in VS .NET and add all the source files that define the `DataSet` classes you want to include.

To create a version number for the assembly, edit the `AssemblyVersion` attribute defined in the AssemblyInfo.cs (or .vb) file in the VS .NET project. By default, the attribute will be set to "1.0.*", which will automatically increment the last two parts of the version number referred to as the revision and build numbers each time the project is compiled. As long as the first two parts of the version number—the major and minor build numbers—remain the same, by convention the assembly is said to be compatible with other versions of the same assembly.

NEW TERM As a result you should change only the major and minor versions when changes in types within the assembly will cause errors to be generated in a client application using the assembly. However, absent a binding policy, if you deploy a new version of the assembly to the application directory of a client (referred to as a **private assembly**), the common language runtime's class loader will find it, load it, and attempt to use it. If you've renamed types in the assembly or deleted types that the client is relying on, you might encounter a TypeLoadException or other exception that your client code would have to handle.

> **Tip**
>
> Although beyond the scope of this book, a client application also uses its application configuration file to check for the presence of a binding policy that determines which version of an assembly to load. As a result, an administrator can specify that a certain client application can bind with only a particular version of an assembly. Application configuration files can be built using the Microsoft .NET Framework Configuration icon in the Administrative Tools group.

In the case of strongly typed DataSet classes, you would want to deploy a new version if the data requirements of the application change and you need to add or remove columns from the DataSet. To minimize the amount of rework you would have to do in this event, you should avoid placing custom code in the generated class if possible. That way, you can make your changes in the graphical designer and regenerate the DataSet without having to write any new code. Although it might be tempting to add custom methods to the DataSet class to populate it and synchronize it with a data store, this is the primary reason you should create a separate data access class. Doing so allows you to modify either without touching the code for the other.

As part of the compilation process, you can optionally compile your assembly with a strong name using the AssemblyKeyFile attribute. Adding a strong name enables your assembly to be placed in the Global Assembly Cache (GAC) so that it's accessible machinewide. To ensure that all .NET code (managed code) running on the machine can use the new assembly version if its binding policy allows, you should place it in the assembly cache.

6

> **Note**
>
> In fact, even if a particular client application relies on a specific version of your assembly, you can still accommodate it by adding multiple versions of the assembly to the GAC.

When you compile the project, the resulting DLL will be your assembly, complete with a manifest that describes its types and its dependencies on other types, such as those in the System.Data namespace.

Tip

> If your development team authors classes in multiple languages, for example, by creating one DataSet in VB and another in C#, you can't include both source files in a VS .NET project. However, you can compile them individually into .NET modules using the appropriate command-line compiler and then create a multi-file assembly using the Assembly Linker (AL.exe) command-line utility. See the online help for details.

In addition to deploying DataSet classes in an assembly, you need to consider possible changes to the underlying database from which the DataSet typically receives its data. As you'll learn on Day 12, the MissingMappingAction and MissingSchemaAction properties of the data adapter are used to specify how the data adapter responds when the data from the data store conflicts with the structure of the DataSet. For now, suffice it to say that using the MissingMappingAction.Passthrough value enables new columns added to the result set retrieved by the data adapter to be appended to the existing column list in the DataTable objects. In other words, adding a column to the SELECT statement in a stored procedure doesn't necessarily break the code in Listing 6.4. However, as is obvious, the new column won't be able to be referenced with a strongly typed property but will be accessible via the Columns collection of the DataTable object and the Item and Item array properties of the DataRow object.

DataSet Serialization

On Day 1, you were introduced to the concept of the DataSet by learning that it's the core of the disconnected programming model in ADO.NET. Because it's useful in disconnected scenarios and distributed applications, it must be able to be serialized and deserialized when passed between tiers in an application or persisted to disk. In this final section for today, you'll learn how the DataSet is passed between tiers in a distributed application and how you can persist it to disk in a disconnected applications.

Passing DataSets

By default, an instance of a class in .NET can be passed by value or by reference to, as well as returned from, any method exposed by an object that lives in the same Application Domain. However, in distributed applications, the presentation and data access code may reside on different servers and thus different AppDomains.

What's an AppDomain?

NEW TERM Although not discussed on Day 1, **Application Domains** (AppDomains) are partitions inside a process set up by the common language runtime to provide isolation and fault tolerance. You can think of AppDomains as lightweight processes controlled by the common language runtime that offer better performance than using a technique such as process spawning prevalent in the Unix world. Typically, a client application will have a single AppDomain created by the common language runtime when the application loads. However, you can programmatically create additional AppDomains through the System.AppDomain class. Server applications such as ASP.NET, on the other hand, can and do create multiple AppDomains to service multiple requests or clients and maintain isolation between them.

NEW TERM In order for an object to be referenced or copied across AppDomains, it must be able to be, in .NET parlance, **remotable**. A remotable type is one that derives from System.MarshalByRefObject or System.MarshalByValueComponent, implements the ISerializable interface, or is marked with the Serializable attribute. Deriving from MarshalByRefObject allows an object to be simply referenced from another AppDomain, but it doesn't allow it to be copied. The other three options in the previous list all allow the object to be serialized. Because the DataSet needs to be copied, it's derived from MarshalByValueComponent, implements the ISerializable interface, and is marked with the Serializable attribute. This allows a DataSet created in one AppDomain, perhaps residing in a separate process or on a separate machine, to be passed to a different AppDomain.

Although the presence of the Serializable attribute alone allows a .NET type to be serialized to XML automatically using a generic format, you'll notice that the DataSet implements ISerializable in order to implement a custom algorithm to perform the serialization. This is the case so that the DataSet can fully represent changes made to its data through the DiffGram grammar discussed yesterday. You can get a glimpse of some of the work the DataSet does by examining the code in the TitlesDs class. You'll notice that much of it is devoted to overriding methods of the base class that have to do with serialization. The ShouldSerializeTables, ShouldSerializeRelations, GetSchemaSerializable, ReadXmlSerializable, and especially the protected constructor that accepts an object of type SerializationInfo all work to ensure that the DataSet can be serialized to and from XML. Equivalent code exists in the base DataSet class and so is invisible to developers when working with generic DataSet objects.

NEW TERM Once a type is able to be serialized, it can then be copied between AppDomains using **.NET Remoting**. Briefly, .NET Remoting is the set of .NET Framework components that allow two pieces of managed code (a client and a server) running in

6

separate AppDomains to communicate. The client and the server communicate via an HTTP or TCP channel that is specified in application configuration files or configured directly in code within the application. Remoting allows a client to instantiate a class that lives in the server process (a MarshalByRefObject) in order to call its methods. A method in the server class can then create a DataSet (a MarshalByValueComponent) and pass a copy of it back to the client. The object, such as a DataSet, is then serialized for transport either in an XML format wrapped in a SOAP message or in a compact binary format. Which formatter is used can also be configured in the application configuration files. When the serialized DataSet reaches the client, it's then deserialized into an actual DataSet object. The end result is that a copy of the DataSet now exists on the client and can be manipulated just as any other DataSet. A diagram of this process can be seen in Figure 6.3.

FIGURE 6.3

.NET Remoting. This diagram depicts a DataSet *as it is remoted using .NET Remoting.*

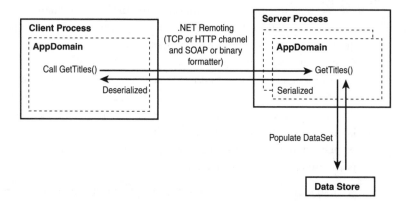

> **Note**
>
> For an overview of .NET Remoting, see Chapter 8 of my book *Building Distributed Applications with Visual Basic .NET*, published by Sams.

A typical scenario for this process includes a managed data access class hosted in a Server Application in Component Services. In this case, the class resides in a separate AppDomain because it's running in a separate process (AppDomains don't cross operating system processes). When the client calls a method of the data access class such as GetTitles, the method communicates with the database to retrieve the results and populate a DataSet. The DataSet is then passed back to the client using .NET Remoting as described earlier.

Note   Another example of where serialization is used is in returning a DataSet from an XML Web Service, as you'll learn on Day 18, "ADO.NET and XML Web Services."

Persisting to Disk

In addition to the scenario where a DataSet is passed between tiers of an application, a common use for serialization is in a truly disconnected application. In these types of applications, the client might need to work with the DataSet offline and then only later reconnect to the network and synchronize its changes with a data store.

Fortunately, the ability of the DataSet to store and track its changes makes it ideal for this type of application. Coupled with the support of classes in the .NET Framework, persisting a DataSet to disk is almost trivial.

To illustrate how this can be done, consider the code in Listing 6.5 that shows methods to save and load a DataSet from the file system.

LISTING 6.5   Saving and loading a DataSet. These methods use the XmlSerializer class to save and load a DataSet using XML.

```
public Boolean SaveDs(DataSet ds, string fileName)
{
  // Open the file for reading
  FileStream fs;
  try
  {
    fs = new FileStream(fileName,FileMode.Create,
      FileAccess.Write,FileShare.Write);
  }
  catch (IOException e)
  {
    throw new Exception("Cannot open  " + fileName , e);
  }

  // Serialize to the file
  try
  {
    XmlSerializer ser = new XmlSerializer(ds.GetType());
    ser.Serialize(fs,ds);
  }
  catch (Exception e)
  {
    throw new Exception("Cannot save " + ds.DataSetName, e);
  }
```

6

LISTING 6.5   continued

```
   finally
   {
     fs.Close();
   }

   return true;
}

public DataSet LoadDs(String fileName, Type dsType)
{
   FileStream fs;
   XmlReader xr;

   // Make sure the file exists
   if (File.Exists(fileName))
   {
     fs = new FileStream(fileName,FileMode.Open,
       FileAccess.Read,FileShare.Read);
     xr = new XmlTextReader(fs);
   }
   else throw new Exception(fileName + " does not exist");

   // Deserialize
   XmlSerializer ser = new XmlSerializer(dsType);
   DataSet ds = new DataSet();

   try
   {
     if (ser.CanDeserialize(xr))
     {
       ds = (DataSet)ser.Deserialize(xr);
     }
   }
   catch (Exception e)
   {
     throw new Exception("Could not load " + fileName,e);
   }

   return ds;
}
```

ANALYSIS   Listing 6.5 contains two methods, SaveDs and LoadDs, which use the
XmlSerializer class from the System.Xml.Serialization namespace. The
XmlSerializer class can be used with any class that includes the Serializable
attribute. As you can see from SaveDs, the DataSet to serialize and the file name
and path are passed to the method. The method then opens the file for reading and

instantiates the XmlSerializer, passing it the type to serialize. If all goes well, the Serialize method can then be called, which serializes the DataSet to the stream passed as the first argument. If you inspect the books.xml file, you'll notice that it contains both the XSD and the complete DiffGram for the DataSet.

You can also see from Listing 6.5 that the SaveDs and LoadDs methods accept and return the generic DataSet class, and so can also be used with any derived DataSet class through polymorphism.

> **Note**
>
> As you'll see tomorrow, this functionality overlaps the functionality of the WriteXml, WriteXmlSchema, InferXmlSchema, ReadXml, and ReadXmlSchema methods of the DataSet class.

The LoadDs method then does the opposite by first making sure that the passed-in file exists and then opening the file for reading. This method also accepts an argument that specifies the type to deserialize to. This is necessary so that you can pass strongly typed DataSet objects into the method and be able to cast them back to their strong type once the method has completed. Because the file will be an XML file, it's passed to the constructor of an XmlTextReader. This is done so that the CanDeserialize can be called to determine whether the document will be able to be deserialized. If so, the Deserialize method is called returning a DataSet object.

The client code to use these methods might look something like the following.

```
TitlesDs books = new DataSet();

// Fill the DataSet

books.ExtendedProperties.Add("SaveTime",DateTime.Now);
SaveDs(books,"books.xml");

// Now shut down the app and return later

DataSet newBooks = new DataSet();
String strTime;

newBooks = (TitlesDs)LoadDs("books.xml",newBooks.GetType());

strTime = "DataSet was saved at " +
  books.ExtendedProperties["SaveTime"].ToString();
```

You'll notice from this snippet that the ExtendedProperties collection was used to store the time the DataSet was saved to disk and can then be read once the DataSet is deserialized.

6

Summary

Today was devoted to the ins and outs of strongly typed DataSet classes. By now you should have a good understanding of how to create them, what the code generator creates for you, how to use them, and some of the issues that arise in terms of deployment and distribution. In summary, strongly typed DataSet classes are extremely useful for providing an object-oriented means for accessing data while preserving the great functionality you get for free with the DataSet.

Although you've been exposed to the XML nature of the DataSet, tomorrow we'll finish out the week by taking a top-to-bottom look at how XML is fundamental to the DataSet.

Workshop

This workshop will help reinforce the concepts covered in today's lesson.

Quiz

1. Do strongly typed DataSet classes rely on the implementation or interface inheritance as supplied by the common language runtime?

   A strongly typed DataSet class is an example of utilizing the implementation inheritance feature of the common language runtime. This means that the derived class inherits not only the method signatures but also their functionality, and can override that functionality as desired.

2. What are four ways you can create a strongly typed DataSet?

   You have the option of designing a strongly typed DataSet from scratch graphically using the designer, by dragging and dropping the database table on the designer from the Server Explorer window, by importing an existing XSD document, or by using the Xml/Schemas DataType Support Utility (XSD.exe).

3. How does the strongly typed DataSet class expose tables in its DataTableCollection object?

   It exposes them as strongly typed properties that refer to child classes that derive from DataTable.

4. Why is a DataSet said to be remotable?

   A DataSet is remotable because it's derived from MarshalByValueComponent and is marked with the Serializable attribute. Together these enable a DataSet object to be passed between tiers in a distributed application across AppDomains. In addition, the DataSet implements the ISerializable interface to perform custom serialization using the DiffGram grammar.

Exercise

Today, create a strongly typed DataSet that includes the Orders and OrderDetails tables. Then write a method that populates the DataSet using the usp_GetOrders stored procedure.

Answers for Day 6

Exercise Answer

First, you must create the strongly typed DataSet by adding a new DataSet to your project and dropping the Orders and OrderDetails onto the designer surface from the Server Explorer. Next, be sure to create the relation between the tables on the OrderId columns because each Order is associated with many OrderDetails rows. Then select Generate DataSet from the menu by right-clicking on the designer surface.

Assuming that the strongly typed DataSet class is called OrdersDs, a method you could possibly use to populate it follows:

```
public virtual OrdersDs GetOrdersByCust(Guid customerId)
{
    SqlConnection con = new SqlConnection(_connect);
    SqlDataAdapter da = new SqlDataAdapter("usp_GetOrders",con);

    // Create the strongly typed instance
    OrdersDs orders = new OrdersDs();

    // Setup the call to the stored procedure
    da.SelectCommand.CommandType = CommandType.StoredProcedure;
    da.SelectCommand.Parameters.Add(
       new SqlParameter("@CustomerID",SqlDbType.UniqueIdentifier));
    da.SelectCommand.Parameters[0].Value = customerId;

    // handle the error
    da.TableMappings.Add("Table","Orders");
    da.TableMappings.Add("Table1","OrderDetails");
    da.MissingSchemaAction = MissingSchemaAction.Error;

    // Get the data
    try
    {
        da.Fill(orders);
        return orders;
    }
    catch (SqlException e)
    {
```

6

```
        // handle the error
        return null;
    }
}
```

The GetOrdersByCust method accepts a Guid to represent the CustomerID and then passes it to the usp_GetOrders stored procedure. For the data to map to the appropriate
tables in the OrdersDs instance (orders), you need to create table mappings for the
default tables. In addition, the MissingSchemaAction property is set to Error to ensure
that the incoming schema is identical to the schema in the strongly typed DataSet.

DAY 7

XML and the DataSet

Today's discussion will bring us to the end of Week 1 and complete our look at the first of the two major components of ADO.NET, the DataSet. Although you've seen glimpses of how the DataSet is based on XML, today you'll go deeper and explore how XML can be read from, defined, loaded to, and synchronized with a DataSet object using its various methods and properties.

Tip

> If you aren't familiar with XML, I recommend you pick up a copy of *Sams Teach Yourself XML in 21 Days,* Second Edition by Devan Shepherd and take a look at the XML tutorials and FAQs at `http://msdn.microsoft.com/xml`. Today's lesson assumes a basic understanding of XML.

As mentioned on Day 1, "ADO.NET in Perspective," the widespread adoption of XML for representing and exchanging data over the Web made it imperative that Microsoft also make it easy for developers to use XML in the .NET Framework. You've seen over the last four days that developers using ADO.NET can work with their data in an object-model paradigm using the DataSet object, and even represent it in a strongly typed fashion by relying on inheritance in the .NET Framework. However, at the same time, a DataSet can be fully represented in terms of its structure and data as XML. The joining of the object model approach with XML into a single coherent programming model is one of the key differentiators between .NET and competing frameworks, such as J2EE, for building enterprise applications.

Today you'll learn the following concepts:

- How to output DataSet contents as XML and to specify the format of the XML
- How an XSD schema maps to the structure of a DataSet and how the structure can be directly loaded from an XSD document
- How to load a DataSet from an XML document
- How to program against a DataSet as if it were XML

Writing Data as XML

As you learned yesterday, a DataSet can be serialized and deserialized to and from XML using the XmlSerializer class of the System.Xml.Serialization namespace. This process occurs when a DataSet is remoted across AppDomains or returned from an XML Web Service.

However, the DataSet also exposes the GetXml and WriteXml methods, which can be called directly to serialize the DataSet to XML. These methods function identically by writing out the contents of the DataSet using the Current row version that includes all modified and added rows and omits all deleted rows. For example, using the TitlesDs strongly typed DataSet defined in yesterday's lesson, the following code can be written to find a particular Sams title and lower its price by 10%:

```
Dim books As TitlesDs
Dim strXml As String
Dim titleRow As TitlesDs.TitlesRow

books = GetTitlesReviews("Sams") ' populate the DataSet
titleRow = books.Titles.FindByISBN("06720083X")
titleRow.Price = titleRow.Price * Convert.ToDecimal(0.90)

strXml = books.GetXml()
```

After the price has been lowered, the DataSet is written to XML and stored in a String variable using the GetXml method. The string can be written to a file or simply returned to the presentation tier. Listing 7.1 shows the relevant parts of the resulting XML.

LISTING 7.1 Writing a `DataSet` as XML. This XML snippet shows the portions affected by the previous code snippet.

```xml
<TitlesDs xmlns="http://www.computebooks.com/TitlesDs">
  <Reviews>
    <ReviewID>9cf97fcc-a6bb-4932-b427-213908427248</ReviewID>
    <ISBN>06720083X </ISBN>
    <ReviewText>Mediocre to the core</ReviewText>
    <Stars>3</Stars>
  </Reviews>
  <Reviews>
    <ReviewID>609a2f74-ec76-4e4e-835c-266f11a32021</ReviewID>
    <ISBN>06720083X </ISBN>
    <ReviewText>Clearly the greatest book ever written</ReviewText>
    <Stars>5</Stars>
  </Reviews>
  <Reviews>
    <ReviewID>5af1077d-77ef-4761-bf1a-6e31b905fa10</ReviewID>
    <ISBN>06720083X </ISBN>
    <ReviewText>It stunk really badly</ReviewText>
    <Stars>0</Stars>
  </Reviews>
  <Titles>
    <ISBN>06720083X </ISBN>
    <Title>Pure Visual Basic: a code-intensive premium
       reference/versions 5 &amp; 6</Title>
    <Description>Great Book</Description>
    <Author>Fox, Dan</Author>
    <PubDate>1999-09-01T00:00:00.0000000-05:00</PubDate>
    <Price>22.491</Price>
    <Discount>9.5647</Dpiscount>
    <BulkDiscount>10</BulkDiscount>
    <BulkAmount>50</BulkAmount>
    <CategoryName>Programming</CategoryName>
    <PubName>Sams Publishing</PubName>
  </Titles>
</TitlesDs>
```

ANALYSIS You'll notice from Listing 7.1 that because this book has reviews associated with it, the reviews are returned first, followed by the data for the book itself. This corresponds to the order in which the tables were added to the strongly typed `DataSet` in its `InitClass` method. The price of the book is now set to $22.49, down from the original price of $24.99. You'll also notice that the XML does not indicate that the price was modified using a DiffGram, even though `AcceptChanges` was not called on the row and it is in the `Modified` row state. You can also see that the namespace associated with the `DataSet` when it was created yesterday is represented in the root element.

7

The end result is that you can use the `GetXml` method when you simply want to quickly return the current contents of the `DataSet` as a `String` and are not concerned with tracking changes.

Although the `WriteXml` method returns the same XML by default, it is much more flexible in that it includes eight overloaded signatures that allow the XML to be written to a stream or its derived classes, the `System.IO.TextWriter`, an `XmlWriter`, or directly to a file specified with its path and name. The other four signatures support a second argument to customize the XML through the `XmlWriteMode` enumeration. The enumeration values include `DiffGram`, which will write the XML using the DiffGram grammar you learned about on Day 5, "Changing Data"; `IgnoreSchema`, which is the default; and `WriteSchema`, which also writes out the XSD for the `DataSet`. For example, to write the DiffGram for a `DataSet` to an in-memory stream, you can use the following code:

```
Dim ms As New MemoryStream()

books.GetChanges.WriteXml(ms, XmlWriteMode.DiffGram)
```

In this case, the `GetChanges` method is first called on the `DataSet` to filter by the modified rows before writing the DiffGram to the `MemoryStream` using the `WriteXml` method.

> **Tip**
>
> Unless you actually want to write the XML to a `String`, using the `WriteXml` method is more efficient. This is because a string doesn't have to be created before the XML is written to a file or memory, as in this case.

Assuming that the same change to the price is still in effect, the resulting XML from the previous code snippet will contain the `Titles` element only, and not the `Reviews` elements, even though the reviews are linked via a `DataRelation`. To write out XML for just one book, you could create a new `DataSet` and copy into it the `Titles` row that was changed along with the related rows from the `Reviews` table. Listing 7.2 shows the code snippet necessary to do so with the strongly typed `TitlesDs` DataSet.

LISTING 7.2   Copying from a `DataSet`. The `WriteTitleXml` function copies a row and its related rows to a new `DataSet` and returns the XML.

```
Public Function WriteTitleXml(ByRef books As TitlesDs, _
 ByRef titleRow As TitlesDs.TitlesRow) As String
   Dim aBook As TitlesDs
   Dim rowVals() As Object
   Dim reviewRows() As TitlesDs.ReviewsRow
```

Listing 7.2 continued

```
' Make a new copy of the DataSet
aBook = CType(books.Clone(), TitlesDs)

' Add the title row
rowVals = titleRow.ItemArray
aBook.Titles.Rows.Add(rowVals)

' Add the reviews rows
reviewRows = titleRow.GetReviewsRows
Dim row As TitlesDs.ReviewsRow
For Each row In reviewRows
  rowVals = row.ItemArray
  aBook.Reviews.Rows.Add(rowVals)
Next

Return aBook.GetXml()
End Function
```

ANALYSIS You'll notice in Listing 7.2 that the original `TitlesDs` `DataSet` and the `TitlesRow` object are both passed into the method. The method then creates a new `DataSet` with the same structure using the `Clone` method. The `ItemArray` property is then used to extract an array of values for the `TitlesRow`, which is then added to the new `DataSet` using the `Add` method of the `DataRowCollection`. To retrieve the related rows from the `Reviews` table, the strongly typed `DataSet` exposes the `GetReviewsRows` method that uses the `DataRelation` to return an array of `ReviewsRow` objects. Each row is then added to the new `DataSet` using the `Add` method of the `DataRowCollection` for the `Reviews` table. Finally, the XML for the new `DataSet` is returned using the `GetXml` method.

Affecting the XML Format

The format of the XML shown in Listing 7.1 is controlled by the XSD generated when the `DataSet` was created in the graphical designer, as you saw yesterday. By default, the data for each `DataTable` appears consecutively, is placed in an element named with the table name, and each column is placed in a sub-element of the table. However, you can override these defaults either programmatically, using the properties of the objects in the `DataSet`, or graphically, in the designer. The former option will, of course, be useful when you are not using a strongly typed `DataSet`.

For example, assume that `books` is an instance of the `TitlesDs` `DataSet`. The following code snippet customizes the XML that will be generated when the `GetXml` or `WriteXml` method is called or when the `DataSet` is serialized to XML:

7

```
books.Titles.Columns("ISBN").ColumnMapping = MappingType.Attribute
books.Reviews.Columns("ReviewID").ColumnMapping = MappingType.Attribute
books.Reviews.Columns("ISBN").ColumnMapping = MappingType.Attribute
books.Relations(0).Nested = True
books.Prefix = "cbks"
```

Here you'll note that the `ColumnMapping` property can be used to specify how a column in the `DataSet` is represented using the `MappingType` enumeration. Other values include `Element` (the default), `Hidden`, and `SimpleContent`. In this case, the primary keys of the two tables, along with the `ISBN` column of the `Reviews` table, will be rendered as attributes.

> **Tip**
>
> The `Hidden` value of the `MappingType` attribute is useful for hiding columns in the table that are used only for relating tables within the `DataSet` and thus are auto-incremented. Basically, you would use `Hidden` with any column that you don't want a client of the `DataSet` to display to a user. However, marking a column as `Hidden` still allows it to be tracked when the `DataSet` is serialized with the `XmlSerializer` object. The hidden column is attached to the XML in a special attribute, called `hiddenColumn`, of the element for each row.

In addition, the `Nested` property of the `DataRelation` used to relate the two tables through their foreign key constraint is set to `True` so that rather than displaying the tables one after the other, the data from the child table (`Reviews`) is rendered as a child element of the particular parent element (`Titles`) to which it belongs. In this case, the ordinal value of the relation is used because there is only one in the collection. Finally, the `Prefix` attribute of the `DataSet` is set in order to associate a prefix with the XML namespace populated when the `DataSet` was created yesterday. The end result is XML like that shown in Listing 7.3.

LISTING 7.3   Reformatted XML. This listing shows the XML of `TitlesDs` after the properties in the previous snippet are applied.

```
<cbks:TitlesDs xmlns:cbks="http://www.computebooks.com/TitlesDs">
  <Titles ISBN="06720083X " xmlns="http://www.computebooks.com/TitlesDs">
    <Title>Pure Visual Basic: a code-intensive premium
       reference/versions 5 &amp;6</Title>
    <Description>Great Book</Description>
    <Author>Fox, Dan</Author>
    <PubDate>1999-09-01T00:00:00.0000000-05:00</PubDate>
    <Price>22.491</Price>
    <Discount>9.5647</Discount>
```

LISTING 7.3   continued

```
        <BulkDiscount>10</BulkDiscount>
        <BulkAmount>50</BulkAmount>
        <CategoryName>Programming</CategoryName>
        <PubName>Sams Publishing</PubName>
        <Reviews ReviewID="9cf97fcc-a6bb-4932-b427-213908427248" ISBN="06720083X">
          <ReviewText>Mediocre to the core</ReviewText>
          <Stars>3</Stars>
        </Reviews>
        <Reviews ReviewID="609a2f74-ec76-4e4e-835c-266f11a32021" ISBN="06720083X">
          <ReviewText>Clearly the greatest book ever written</ReviewText>
          <Stars>5</Stars>
        </Reviews>
        <Reviews ReviewID="5af1077d-77ef-4761-bf1a-6e31b905fa10" ISBN="06720083X">
          <ReviewText>It stunk really badly</ReviewText>
          <Stars>0</Stars>
        </Reviews>
      </Titles>
  </cbks:TitlesDs>
```

Of course, the ColumnMapping property can be set in the graphical designer by dropping down the list next to the column name and selecting A for attribute, for example, rather than leaving it as the default of E (element). Likewise, the Nested property can be set graphically by clicking on the relationship and changing the IsNested property in the properties window to True.

| Tip | If you forget to set the ColumnMapping and Nested properties while designing a strongly typed DataSet, you can re-open the .xsd file by double-clicking on it and then setting the properties. Doing so will regenerate the code for the DataSet, visible by clicking on the Show All Files button on the toolbar. Alternatively, you can edit the generated code and add code like that shown in the previous snippet to the InitClass method of the derived DataSet class. |

Creating the XSD Schema

As you saw yesterday, you can create a strongly typed DataSet using the graphical designer. When you do so, the designer is actually creating an XSD document behind the scenes that is visible by clicking on the XML pane at the bottom of the designer. This is shown in Listing 7.4. In the XML pane, you can edit the XML being produced and even take advantage of IntelliSense.

7

> **Note**
>
> When you right-click on the XML designer and select the Generate DataSet option, the msdata namespace (defined by the URN schemas-microsoft-com:xml-msdata) is added to the definition of the XML document in the root schema element, as is shown in Listing 7.4. Attributes from this namespace are used to add supplementary information to the schema that the DataSet generator will use to write the code for the derived DataSet class. For example, the IsDataSet attribute is added and set to True for the top-level element in the DataSet. In addition, as you'll see shortly, these attributes are maintained internally by the DataSet and can be seen when using the GetXmlSchema, WriteXmlSchema, and WriteXml methods of the DataSet. Essentially, the msdata attributes are what allow an XSD schema to be mapped to a DataSet behind the scenes.

LISTING 7.4   The XSD document. This XSD was produced by the XML Schema Designer for the TitlesDs strongly typed DataSet.

```xml
<?xml version="1.0" encoding="utf-8"?>
<xs:schema id="TitlesDs" targetNamespace="http://www.computebooks.com/TitlesDs"
 elementFormDefault="qualified" attributeFormDefault="qualified"
 xmlns="http://www.computebooks.com/TitlesDs"
 xmlns:mstns="http://www.computebooks.com/TitlesDs"
 xmlns:xs="http://www.w3.org/2001/XMLSchema"
 xmlns:msdata="urn:schemas-microsoft-com:xml-msdata" version="1.0">
    <xs:element name="TitlesDs" msdata:IsDataSet="true">
        <xs:complexType>
            <xs:choice maxOccurs="unbounded">
                <xs:element name="Reviews">
                    <xs:complexType>
                        <xs:sequence>
                            <xs:element name="ReviewID"
                                msdata:DataType="System.Guid, mscorlib,
                                Version=1.0.3300.0, Culture=neutral,
                                PublicKeyToken=b77a5c561934e089"
                                type="xs:string" />
                            <xs:element name="ISBN" type="xs:string" />
                            <xs:element name="ReviewText" type="xs:string" />
                            <xs:element name="Stars" type="xs:unsignedByte" />
                        </xs:sequence>
                    </xs:complexType>
                </xs:element>
                <xs:element name="Titles">
                    <xs:complexType>
                        <xs:sequence>
                            <xs:element name="ISBN" type="xs:string" />
                            <xs:element name="Title" type="xs:string" />
                            <xs:element name="Description" type="xs:string"
```

LISTING 7.4 continued

```
                                    minOccurs="0" />
                    <xs:element name="Author" type="xs:string" />
                    <xs:element name="PubDate" type="xs:dateTime" />
                    <xs:element name="Price" type="xs:decimal" />
                    <xs:element name="Discount" type="xs:decimal"
                      minOccurs="0" />
                    <xs:element name="BulkDiscount" type="xs:decimal"
                      minOccurs="0" />
                    <xs:element name="BulkAmount" type="xs:short"
                      minOccurs="0" />
                    <xs:element name="CategoryName" type="xs:string"
                      minOccurs="0" />
                    <xs:element name="PubName" type="xs:string"
                      minOccurs="0" />
                  </xs:sequence>
                </xs:complexType>
              </xs:element>
            </xs:choice>
          </xs:complexType>
          <xs:unique name="TitlesDsKey2" msdata:PrimaryKey="true">
              <xs:selector xpath=".//mstns:Reviews" />
              <xs:field xpath="mstns:ReviewID" />
          </xs:unique>
          <xs:unique name="TitlesDsKey3" msdata:PrimaryKey="true">
              <xs:selector xpath=".//mstns:Titles" />
              <xs:field xpath="mstns:ISBN" />
          </xs:unique>
          <xs:keyref name="TitlesReviews" refer="TitlesDsKey3"
            msdata:AcceptRejectRule="Cascade" msdata:DeleteRule="Cascade"
            msdata:UpdateRule="None" msdata:IsNested="true">
              <xs:selector xpath=".//mstns:Reviews" />
              <xs:field xpath="mstns:ISBN" />
          </xs:keyref>
      </xs:element>
    </xs:schema>
```

ANALYSIS You'll notice in Listing 7.4 that the XSD is simply an XML document with a root-level schema tag that contains tags such as complexType, element, attribute, and keyref that define the structure of an XML document based on the XSD. You'll also notice that the schema is annotated with attributes from the msdata namespace that control how the schema will map to specific features of the DataSet class.

Although the syntax for XSD documents is beyond the scope of this book, the XML Schema Designer makes it easy to get started writing schemas by providing the XML Schema tab in the Toolbox. The descriptions of the items in the tab found in Table 7.1

7

coupled with the online documentation should be enough to get you started designing your own schema that can be generated as a strongly typed `DataSet` or used simply with XML documents.

TABLE 7.1 XML Schema toolbox items. The icons and their descriptions visible in the XML Schema tab of the Toolbox when designing a `DataSet` (XSD).

Class	Description
E element	Used to declare an element. When dropped on the design surface, it creates an `element` tag with a child complex type that can be filled with other elements or attributes. Used to define the highest-level `DataTable` classes in a `DataSet`.
A attribute	Used to declare an attribute of an element. When dropped independently on the design surface, it creates an attribute for the highest-level element in the document.
AG attributeGroup	Used to group a set of attribute definitions so that they can be used inside a complex type definition. In a `DataSet`, the attributes are simply added to the `DataTable` defined by the complex type. Enables reuse of the attributes.
CT complexType	Used to define the set of elements and attributes defined by one of the following child elements: `simpleContent` (contains a `simpleType` or text with attributes but no elements), `complexContent` (contains only elements or is empty), `group` (contains a reference to a group), `sequence` (contains the specified elements in the given order), `choice` (contains only one of the elements), or `all` (contains any or none of the elements). In a `DataSet`, it is used to represent the `DataTable` structure. Can also be used to define abstract contents used as the basis for derived complex types (analogous to a base class).
ST simpleType	Used to define a type derived from a built-in data type or another simple type. Can be defined with facets such as restrictions for min and max values and length, a list of whitespace-separated values, or an enumeration. The `DataSet` generator maps only restrictions to properties that have equivalents in the `DataColumn`; it does not create enumerations as defined in the XSD.
G group	Used to group a set of element definitions to be used in a complex type. Can be defined by `choice`, `sequence`, or `all`. In a `DataSet`, the elements of the group are simply added to the `DataTable`. Enables reuse of the set of the elements.

TABLE 7.1   continued

Class	Description
any	Used to enable any element to appear from this namespace or any other. Can also specify whether the XML processor should attempt to validate the contents of this element. Not used in a DataSet.
facet	Used inside of a simple type to define the restrictions that can be placed on it. Facets such as maxLength are read by the DataSet generator and used to populate the MaxLength property of the DataColumn object.
anyAttribute	Used to enable any attribute to appear from this namespace in a complex type or attribute group. Can also specify whether the XML processor should attempt to validate the attribute. Not used in a DataSet.
key	Used to define an element or attribute as unique, non-nullable, and always present data for the define scope. When selected, a dialog is displayed where you can define the key. In a DataSet, the key is mapped to the primary key of the DataTable using the PrimaryKey attribute of the msdata namespace. Primary keys can also be defined using the unique element.
Relation	Used to define the data relation and invokes the dialog shown in Figure 2.6 of Day 2, "Getting Started." In the XSD, a keyref element is created that refers to the key or unique element from the parent. Its attributes from the msdata namespace control the rules for cascading updates and deletes and automatically accepting changes.

As a rule, keep in mind that each time you define a complex type, you are defining a DataTable, and that the elements and attributes within the complex type will be represented as columns in that table. To nest complex types, you have two options. First, you could create them separately and then create relations between them with the IsNested property set to True. In that way, the XML generated from the DataSet will be nested. However, this has the downside of not actually being represented in the XSD because setting the IsNested property simply adds the IsNested attribute from the msdata namespace to the keyref element in the XSD.

Alternatively, you have the option of defining a nested complex type directly by choosing the Unnamed complexType option from the Type drop-down when defining the element. Then you can name and create the elements and attributes of the child type. In this case, the DataSet generator will automatically create a hidden column (MappingType.Hidden)

7

and a `DataRelation` in the child `DataTable` that refers to the primary key column of the parent type and whose `Nested` property is set to `True`. Creating the `Reviews` complex type for the `TitlesDs` `DataSet` using this technique would look like the diagram in Figure 7.1 (contrasted with Figure 6.2).

FIGURE 7.1

Nested complex types. This is a screenshot of the XML Schema Designer when the Reviews *element is created as a child element of* Titles.

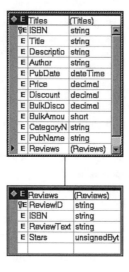

Although the diagram in Figure 7.1 doesn't show it, the relationship between the two complex types is, of course, predicated on the ISBN element of each.

Creating the Schema Dynamically

Although creating a schema to serve as the basis for a strongly typed `DataSet` at design time using the schema designer is recommended and ensures a correct schema, there are scenarios in which this is not practical. For example, consider the situation in which you want to dynamically create schemas based on database tables in order to send those schemas to a trading partner. Or when you receive a schema, or simply an XML document, from a trading partner and want to create a `DataSet` to handle the incoming data. In these scenarios, you can use the `FillSchema` method of a data adapter, or the `ReadXmlSchema` and `InferXmlSchema` methods of the `DataSet` class.

Note   Although the methods discussed in this section also work with the XML Data Reduced (XDR) grammar that Microsoft introduced before XSD became a World Wide Web Consortium (www.w3c.org) recommendation, you should use XSD whenever possible because it's the standard and because support for XDR is not guaranteed in future releases of the .NET Framework.

Filling from a Database

When you want to dynamically create schemas based on database tables in order to send those schemas to a trading partner, you could create a method that writes the XSD schema to a file based on the result set returned from a SQL Server stored procedure, as shown in Listing 7.5.

LISTING 7.5   Creating the schema from a database. The WriteSqlSchema method populates the structure of a DataSet using the FillSchema method of the data adapter.

```
Public Sub WriteSqlSchema(ByVal storedProc As String, _
 ByVal filePath As String, ByVal tableNames() As String)

  Dim con As New SqlConnection(_connect)
  Dim da As New SqlDataAdapter(storedProc, con)
  Dim ds As New DataSet()

  da.SelectCommand.CommandType = CommandType.StoredProcedure

  Try
    If Not tableNames Is Nothing Then
      ' Add the table mappings
      Dim t, dsTab As String
      Dim i As Integer
      For Each t In tableNames
        If i = 0 Then
          dsTab = "Table"
        Else
          dsTab = "Table" & i.ToString
        End If
        da.TableMappings.Add(dsTab, t)
        i += 1
      Next
    End If

    ' Fill the DataSet
    da.FillSchema(ds, SchemaType.Mapped)
    ds.WriteXmlSchema(filePath)
```

7

LISTING 7.5   continued

```
 Catch e As SqlException
    ' Handle SQL Server errors
 Catch e As Exception
    ' Handle other errors here (IO)
 End Try
End Sub
```

ANALYSIS   The `WriteSqlSchema` method in Listing 7.5 first creates the connection and data adapter that will be used to communicate with the data store; in this case, with SQL Server. In addition to being passed the name of the stored procedure to execute and the path of the file to write to, the method accepts an array of table names that will be used to map the tables returned from the database to `DataTable` objects created in the `DataSet`. As you can see, the array of table names is traversed and each is added to the `TableMappings` collection of the data adapter using the `Add` method. The `dsTab` variable denotes the default name in the `DataSet` that each table will be given by the data adapter, whereas `t` denotes the new name. By adding new table mappings, you override the default behavior in which the data adapter creates tables named Table, Table1, and so on for each result set returned from the `SelectCommand` of the data adapter.

The `FillSchema` method is then called and passed both a `DataSet` object to fill and a value from the `SchemaType` enumeration. `FillSchema` automatically opens and closes the database connection, and is also overloaded to accept a single `DataTable` as well as an entire `DataSet` along with a specific table mapping to use. In this case, `SchemaType.Mapped` instructs the `FillSchema` method to use any existing table mappings and schema for the `DataSet` rather than ignoring them, as can be done by passing the `SchemaType.Source` value to the method.

 Note   Although not used in Listing 7.4, the `FillSchema` method also returns either a single `DataTable` object or an array of `DataTable` objects depending on whether the `SelectCommand` of the data adapter returns one or more than one result set.

When `FillSchema` executes, it populates the `AllowDBNull`, `AutoIncrement`, `MaxLength`, `ReadOnly`, and `Unique` properties of the `DataColumn` objects from data provided by the data source while not returning any data. In SQL Server, this is accomplished by the data adapter executing the `SET NO_BROWSETABLE ON` statement before executing the command and turning it off afterward. If a primary key is present, it creates a unique element in the XSD to represent it. In the case where a primary key is not present, it looks for unique constraints and uses their combination as the primary key as long as none of them allows nulls. Columns that are not named are simply named Column1, Column2, and so forth as you might expect.

Tip

> Unfortunately, the OleDbDataAdapter creates a DataTable object for only the first result set returned, while SqlDataAdapter can handle multiple result sets. However, if you must use OLE DB, you can use the Fill method of the OleDbDataAdapter and make sure that the MissingSchemaAction property is set to AddWithKey.

As you probably would have guessed, the FillSchema method cannot create relationships between tables even if more than one result set is returned by the SelectCommand and the base tables have a foreign key relationship. This is because it does not retrieve foreign key constraints from the database.

Finally, the XSD is written to the file using the WriteXmlSchema method, which we'll explore in more detail shortly.

Loading from a Schema

Of course, in addition to programmatically constructing the schema from a database, you could also create it directly from an existing XSD using the ReadXmlSchema method of the DataSet class. This technique might come in handy if you need to dynamically create DataSet objects that correspond to schemas that cannot be specified at design time. It can also be used in derived DataSet classes to maximize flexibility and maintainability in your application.

For example, rather than create a strongly typed DataSet using the XML Schema Designer and the DataSet generator, you might want to create your own class that inherits from DataSet and then, in its constructor, call the ReadXmlSchema method to load a schema from the file system, as shown in Listing 7.6.

LISTING 7.6   A weakly typed DataSet. This complete DataSet class loads its structure at runtime when the constructor is called.

```
<Serializable()> _
Public Class OrdersDs : Inherits DataSet

    Public Sub New()
      MyBase.New()
      initclass()
    End Sub
```

7

LISTING 7.6 continued

```
Public Sub New(ByVal info As SerializationInfo, _
 ByVal context As StreamingContext)
  MyBase.New()
  InitClass()
  Me.GetSerializationData(info, context)
End Sub

Private Sub InitClass()
  ' Read in the schema
  Try
    Me.ReadXmlSchema("OrdersDs.xsd")
  Catch e As Exception
    Throw New TypeInitializationException("Cannot load OrdersDs.xsd", e)
  End Try
End Sub

End Class
```

 In Listing 7.6, the OrdersDs DataSet is derived from DataSet and includes the private InitClass method that attempts to load the schema using the ReadXmlSchema method. Note that the file is hard-coded here, but that ReadXmlSchema is overloaded to accept an XmlReader, stream, or TextReader as well. If the file can't be loaded because it can't be found or is an invalid schema, an exception will be thrown and the exception will be caught and encapsulated as the InnerException of the standard TypeInitializationException. Although in this example the file passed to ReadXmlSchema ostensibly contains only the XSD, ReadXmlSchema can also read an in-line schema (one that is present along with the data) from an XML document.

> **Note**
>
> The Serializable attribute and the constructor that accepts the SerializationInfo and StreamingContext objects from the System.Runtime.Serialization namespace must be present in the event the DataSet is passed between AppDomains.

If the DataSet already contained a schema, it would have been augmented by the ReadXmlSchema method by adding new tables and columns where appropriate. If, however, the data type of an existing column conflicts with the new schema information, an exception will be thrown. Data types will conflict if, for example, the XSD type in the new schema maps to a different .NET type, as shown in Table 7.2.

TABLE 7.2 XSD to .NET types. This table shows the XSD type and .NET equivalent.

XSD Type	.NET Type
anyURI	System.Uri
base64Binary, hexBinary	System.Byte()
Boolean	System.Boolean
Byte	System.SByte
Date, dateTime, gDay, gMonthDay, gYear, gYearMonth, month, time, timePeriod	System.DateTime
decimal, integer, negativeInteger, nonNegativeInteger, nonPositiveInteger, positiveInteger	System.Decimal
Double	System.Double
duration	System.TimeSpan
ENTITIES, IDREFS, NMTOKENS	System.String()
ENTITY, ID, IDREF, language, Name, NCName, NMTOKEN, normalizedString, notation, string, token	System.String
Float	System.Single
int	System.Int32
long	System.Int64
QName	System.Xml.XmlQualifiedName
short	System.Int16
unsignedShort	System.UInt16
unsignedInt	System.UInt32
unsignedLong	System.UInt64

Although all the rules for how an XSD maps to a DataSet are beyond the scope of this book and can be found in the online documentation, the following general rules apply:

- A DataTable is created for each complexType element. Each element and attribute of the complexType are mapped to columns.
- If one complexType is nested inside another, a foreign key constraint, data relation, and hidden column are created on the child table.
- Data types in the schema map to the .NET types as shown in Table 7.2.

7

- unique elements are mapped to unique constraints in the `DataTable` and the `AllowDBNull` property of the column is set to `True`.

- key elements are mapped to unique constraints and the `AllowDBNull` property of the column is set to `False`.

- keyref elements are mapped to a foreign key constraint and a corresponding data relation.

- The `maxLength` restriction on a `simpleType` maps to the `MaxLength` property of the `DataColumn`.

Even though these rules are a good start, they obviously don't contain all the information that can be specified in a `DataSet`. As a result, you can also add to the XSD the attributes from the `msdata` namespace mentioned previously before you read it in using the `ReadXmlSchema`. This can be done either by editing the document directly, using a tool such as XML Spy or VS .NET, or programmatically, using the classes of the `System.Xml` namespace. For example, you can either stream through the XML using the `XmlTextReader` and `XmlTextWriter` or use the Document Object Model as exposed through the `XmlDocument` class. To give you an idea for how this would be accomplished, the `AddPk` method shown in Listing 7.7 adds the `IsPrimaryKey` attribute to a key element of the XSD document passed into the method. I'll leave it to you to explore the `XmlDocument` class and its members.

Tip

> Alert readers will notice that the `msdata` namespace declaration is added to the key element directly rather than to the top-level schema element as is done by the XML Schema Designer. The code could easily be modified to add the namespace declaration first and then add the primary key attribute.

LISTING 7.7   Modifying the XSD. This method marks one of the key elements of the XSD as the primary key prior to reading it into a `DataSet`.

```
Public Function AddPk(ByVal keyElement As String, _
 ByVal xsdFile As String) As Boolean

  Dim xml As New XmlDocument()
  Dim key As XmlNode
  Dim keys As XmlNodeList
  Dim att As XmlAttribute

  Try
    xml.Load(xsdFile)
    att = xml.CreateAttribute("msdata", "IsPrimaryKey", _
      "urn:schemas-microsoft-com:xml-msdata")
    att.Value = "true"
```

LISTING 7.7   continued

```
      keys = xml.GetElementsByTagName("xs:key")
      For Each key In keys
        If key.Attributes("name").Value = keyElement Then
          key.Attributes.Append(att)
          xml.Save(xsdFile)
          Return True
        End If
      Next

      Return False  ' The keyelement was not found
    Catch e As XmlException
      ' Handle XML errors
    Catch e As Exception
      ' Others
    End Try

  End Function
```

Loading from a Document

In the event the `ReadXmlSchema` method is not passed an XSD or an XML document with an in-line schema, it will automatically attempt to infer the schema from the document. This also can be accomplished directly by calling either the `InferXmlSchema` or the `ReadXml` method whose overloads accept an XML document through an `XmlReader`, file path, stream, or `TextReader`.

Regardless of the method used to infer the schema from a document, the framework uses certain inference rules, the most important of which are as follows:

- Elements that have attributes or child elements map to tables. The attributes and child elements are mapped to columns.

- Elements with multiple occurrences are mapped to a single table.

- Attributes, and elements that have no attributes or child elements and that do not repeat, are mapped as columns.

- If the root element of the document has no attributes and no child elements that map to columns, it is mapped to a `DataSet`. Otherwise, it is mapped to a table.

- If a nested or child element is inferred as a table, a `DataRelation` and `ForeignKeyConstraint` are created between the child and parent table, and primary key columns are created in both tables.

- If an element is mapped to a table and has a text value but no child elements, a column called *tablename*_Text is created for the text of the element. However, if the element has text and also has child elements, the text is ignored.

7

Something that might not be immediately obvious from these rules is that the process of inferring the schema is non-deterministic. By that, I mean that two XML documents created from the same schema will not necessarily create identically structured DataSet objects due to the presence or absence of data. This is the case because schemas can define optional elements and might or might not contain repeating elements. This is a good reason to use schemas wherever possible and resort to inference only where necessary.

To see these rules applied, consider the XML document shown in Listing 7.8, which represents sales information for ComputeBooks titles.

LISTING 7.8 Sales data. The XML shown here represents sales figures by time period and title for ComputeBooks stores.

```
<Sales>
 <Title ISBN="06720001X">
  <TimePeriod Date="1/2002">
   <Store id="31B32710-C58A-4483-BB84-4D12865C7772">
    <Units>16</Units>
    <BulkUnits>56</BulkUnits>
    <Revenue>456.50</Revenue>
   </Store>
  </TimePeriod>
  <TimePeriod Date="2/2002">
   <Store>
    <Units>31</Units>
    <BulkUnits>75</BulkUnits>
    <Revenue>789.77</Revenue>
   </Store>
  </TimePeriod>
 </Title>
 <Title ISBN="06720002X">
  <TimePeriod Date="1/2002">
   <Store id="31B32710-C58A-4483-BB84-4D12865C7772">
    <Units>321</Units>
    <BulkUnits>50</BulkUnits>
    <Revenue>6789</Revenue>
   </Store>
   <Store id="57E088EF-3929-41A6-B35F-79048B965489">
    <Units>33</Units>
    <BulkUnits>0</BulkUnits>
    <Revenue>612.67</Revenue>
   </Store>
  </TimePeriod>
 </Title>
</Sales>
```

The following code snippet could then be used to infer the schema from this document:

```
Dim sales As New DataSet()

sales.InferXmlSchema("sales.xml", Nothing)
```

The end result is a DataSet with no data and the following structure:

DataSet: TableName = Sales

Tables (3):

> Title (Title_Id, ISBN)
>
> TimePeriod (TimePeriod_Id, Date, Title_Id)
>
> Store (Units, BulkUnits, Revenue, id, TimePeriod_Id)

Relations (2):

> TimePeriod_Store (ForeignKeyConstraint that relates TimePeriod_Id columns in Store and TimePeriod)
>
> Title_TimePeriod (ForeignKeyConstraint that relates Title_Id columns in TimePeriod and Title)

You'll notice from the preceding description that when the DataSet is inferred, the Sales element (the root element) is mapped to the DataSet rather than being mapped to a table. This is because it has no attributes and its child elements are mapped to tables. Three tables are then created because the Title, TimePeriod, and Store elements all have both attributes and child elements that were mapped as columns. Because the Store element was nested inside the TimePeriod element and the TimePeriod inside the Title, two ForeignKeyConstraint objects were created and added to the DataRelationCollection. In addition, primary keys for each of the parent tables (Title_Id and TimePeriod_Id) were created as auto-incrementing integer columns. Within the DataTable objects, the columns each have their ColumnMapping property set appropriately. For example, the ISBN column is set to MappingType.Attribute, whereas the Title_Id column is set to MappingType.Hidden.

Note

Obviously, the inferred DataSet in this case accurately represents the data, but it does so with the added baggage of columns that needn't have been created and data types that might not be preferred. The ISBN column of the Title table, the Date column of the TimePeriod table, and the id column of the Store table could just as well have served as primary keys. However, without being able to define them as such in a schema, the framework

7

> doesn't have any way of knowing which column is the key. In addition, columns that you would probably like to be numeric are mapped to the System.String data type because the inference process must assume the widest possible interpretation. These are also reasons to use schemas where possible rather than relying on inference.

You'll also notice from the code snippet following Listing 7.8 that the InferXmlSchema method accepts a second argument, which in this case was set to Nothing. The argument can contain an array of namespaces that are to be ignored during the creation of the DataSet. This allows you to read in a document and ignore namespaces that contain data meant for other purposes.

As mentioned previously, the InferXmlSchema method simply creates the schema and does not load any data. To both infer the schema and load the data, you can use the ReadXml method. This overloaded method accepts the same input (XmlReader, TextReader, stream, and filename) as InferXmlSchema, but also accepts an optional second argument that specifies how the XML data is read into the DataSet through the XmlReadMode enumeration, as shown in Table 7.3.

TABLE 7.3 XmlReadMode enumeration. This enumeration is used to specify how the ReadXml method processes the XML it is given.

Value	Description
Auto	The default. When set to Auto, the ReadXml method will automatically set the XmlReadMode appropriately, depending on the contents of the XML. It will use DiffGram when it detects a DiffGram, ReadSchema if the DataSet already has a schema or the document has an in-line schema, and InferSchema otherwise.
DiffGram	Reads the DiffGram and applies its changes to the DataSet using the same semantics as the Merge method. The DiffGram schema must match the schema of the DataSet or an exception will be thrown.
Fragment	Reads XML documents generated by the FOR XML statement in SQL Server 2000 using the default namespace as the in-line schema.
IgnoreSchema	Ignores an in-line schema if one exists. Data that does not match the existing DataSet schema is discarded (new schema information is not inferred).
InferSchema	Ignores an in-line schema if one exists and instead infers the schema and loads the data. If the DataSet contains a schema, it is extended and exceptions are thrown when existing tables or columns conflict.
ReadSchema	Reads an in-line schema if one exists and infers and loads the data, extending the schema of the DataSet. Unlike InferSchema, an exception is thrown if the DataSet already contains any of the tables from the in-line schema.

Obviously, the XmlReadMode argument makes the ReadXml method the most flexible in terms of loading a DataSet from an XML document with or without an in-line schema. For example, you can use the ReadSchema value when you simply want to load additional tables to an existing DataSet or the IgnoreSchema when you want to load only data that matches the existing DataSet structure. The following snippet loads the sales data using the InferSchema value, which would be automatically set because the document doesn't contain an in-line schema and the DataSet doesn't contain a schema:

```
Dim sales As New DataSet()

sales.ReadXml("sales.xml", XmlReadMode.InferSchema)
```

Note

All the overloaded signatures of the ReadXml method return the XmlReadMode used during its processing. This is useful if you don't use the second argument or pass it Auto. In that way, you can tell from which read mode was used, and what the document and DataSet contained.

The DiffGram and Fragment values are particularly interesting because they can be used with XML generated in different ways. For example, the DiffGram value can be used to make changes to a DataSet by applying it through the ReadXml method. This would be useful if your application serializes the DiffGram to a file and then later needs to merge the DiffGram with new data retrieved from a data store. The Fragment value allows you to load partial XML documents like those produced by the FOR XML statement in SQL Server, which you'll learn more about on Day 10, "Using Commands."

Using a DataSet as XML

The final section for today deals with how you can simultaneously manipulate a DataSet both using the objects internal to the DataSet and as XML using the Document Object Model (DOM). It is appropriate that we finish today's lesson with this dual programming model because it represents perhaps the highest point of integration between the DataSet and XML.

The class that provides the integration between the DataSet and the DOM is the XmlDataDocument, found in the System.Xml namespace. The XmlDataDocument is derived from the XmlDocument class and as such contains the methods and properties used to represent an XML document in memory using the DOM.

7

> **Note**   See the online documentation for more information on the members of the
> XmlDocument class.

The purpose of the XmlDataDocument is to provide developers with the option of manipulating DataSet data as if it were simply XML parsed into the node-based hierarchical structure of the DOM. This enables developers familiar with the Microsoft XML Parser (MSXML) to manipulate DataSet data in a familiar way. In addition, as you'll see, using the XmlDataDocument allows you to do things not possible with the DataSet alone.

The XmlDataDocument can be used in two different ways. First, you can pass a populated DataSet to its constructor and it will create the hierarchical node structure on the fly from the data in the DataSet. You can then use the methods of the XmlDataDocument to manipulate the data. For example, the code in Listing 7.9 loads an XmlDataDocument from the sales DataSet created in the previous section. The code then iterates through each Title element and prints the time period recorded for each.

> **Caution**   When an XmlDataDocument is instantiated, it is a fully separate object managed by the runtime that may contain a complete copy of the data from the DataSet. The two objects are kept in sync using events, so keep in mind that if the DataSet contains a large amount of data, so too might the XmlDataDocument. The determination of whether data is copied from one to another relates to the complexity of the XML document. Although the rules for this are complex, in general, the more complex the XML data, the more data will be copied to the DataSet.

LISTING 7.9   Manipulating a DataSet as XML. This listing shows how you can use the XmlDataDocument class to work with a DataSet as XML data.

```
Dim salesXml As New XmlDataDocument(sales)
Dim titles, timePeriods As XmlNodeList
Dim title, timeP As XmlNode
Dim dr As DataRow

titles = salesXml.GetElementsByTagName("Title")

For Each title In titles
   Console.WriteLine(title.Attributes("ISBN").Value)
   timePeriods = title.SelectNodes("TimePeriod")

   For Each timeP In timePeriods
     Console.WriteLine(timeP.Attributes("Date").Value)
```

LISTING 7.9 continued

```
        dr = salesXml.GetRowFromElement(CType(timeP, XmlElement))
        Console.WriteLine(dr.Item("TimePeriod_Id").ToString)
      Next
    Next
```

ANALYSIS As you can see from Listing 7.9 , the GetElementsByTagName method is used to retrieve all the Title elements from the document into an XmlNodeList. The list is then iterated and the ISBN is retrieved from the Attributes collection. The SelectNodes method of the XmlDataDocument is then used to retrieve another list of nodes using an XPath query that in this case simply retrieves the TimePeriod elements. In a similar way, the Date for each time period is printed along with the hidden TimePeriod_Id column accessible through the GetRowFromElement method. Note that this column can be accessed only by referencing the DataSet; it isn't represented in the XML because it is hidden. The XmlDataDocument also exposes the reverse GetElementFromRow method that accepts a DataRow and returns the XmlElement that it represents in the XML.

 Tip Although the DataSet and XmlDataDocument are kept in sync using events, if new nodes are added to the XmlDataDocument that do not correspond to columns in the DataSet, the nodes will be added but will not be synchronized with the DataSet. However, if you attempt to add or remove columns to a table in the DataSet after it has been mapped to an XmlDataDocument, you'll receive an InvalidOperationException.

The second way to use the XmlDataDocument is to load the XML by using its Load method after inferring the schema using the exposed DataSet property as shown here.

```
Dim sales As New DataSet()
Dim salesXml As New XmlDataDocument()
Dim xmlData As New FileStream("royalty.xml", FileMode.Open)

salesXml.DataSet.InferXmlSchema(xmlData, Nothing)
xmlData.Position = 0
salesXml.Load(xmlData)

sales = salesXml.DataSet
```

In this case, a FileStream object is created to read the XML document. The schema for the underlying DataSet is then created using the InferXmlSchema method. This must be done first, otherwise, as noted previously, the new nodes in the XmlDataDocument will

7

not map to anything in the DataSet. After the stream is repositioned to the beginning, the Load method of the XmlDataDocument is used to load the XML. Of course, an alternative technique that could be used in this example is to simply call the ReadXml method and allow it to infer the schema.

Finally, the XmlDataDocument is most powerful when using functionality that is not available when simply using the DataSet. For example, the TransformDs method in Listing 7.10 uses the XmlDataDocument to transform the contents of a DataSet using an XSL stylesheet and save it to a file. This technique could be very useful, for example, if ComputeBooks wanted to create static HTML pages from its catalog in a nightly process.

LISTING 7.10   Transforming a DataSet. This method transforms a DataSet with an XSL stylesheet using the XmlDataDocument and classes from the System.Xml and related namespaces.

```
Public Sub TransformDs(ByRef ds As DataSet, ByVal xslFile As String, _
  ByVal destFile As String)

  Dim xmlData As XmlDataDocument
  Dim xslTrans As New XslTransform()
  Dim xmlWriter As XmlTextWriter

  Try
    ' Load the stylesheet and transform
    xslTrans.Load(xslFile)
  Catch e As Exception
    Throw New Exception("Could not load file " & xslFile, e)
    Return
  End Try

  Try
    ' Create an XmlTextWriter to write to the file
    xmlWriter = New XmlTextWriter(destFile, Nothing)

    ' Populate the XmlDataDocument and do the transform
    xmlData = New XmlDataDocument(ds)
    xslTrans.Transform(xmlData.DocumentElement, Nothing, xmlWriter)
  Catch e As Exception
    Throw New Exception("Could not write to " & destFile, e)
  Finally
    xmlWriter.Close()
  End Try

End Sub
```

ANALYSIS   Although the ins and outs of XSL and transformations are better left to other books, notice in Listing 7.10 that the XslTransform object xslTrans first loads the stylesheet passed in as an argument using the Load method. After opening the destination file using an XmlTextWriter object, the XmlDataDocument object is populated by passing the DataSet as an argument to the constructor. The root node of the XmlDataDocument, in this case xmlData.DocumentElement, is then passed to the Transform method along with the XmlWriter used to output the results of the transformation. The Transform method navigates through an XML document using a cursor model, applying the stylesheet rules found in the XSL document.

Summary

Today you explored the depths of XML integration with the DataSet. This integration extends from its schema represented as XSD to actually manipulating DataSet as XML using the XmlDataDocument object. Today's discussion completes the in-depth look at the DataSet class you started on Day 3, "Working with DataSets." As a result, you should now have a good understanding of how the DataSet can be used in disconnected scenarios in your applications. Next week, we'll delve in the other major component of ADO.NET, the .NET Data Providers.

Workshop

This workshop will help reinforce the concepts covered in today's lesson.

Quiz

1. What is the difference between the GetXml and WriteXml methods of the DataSet class?

   GetXml simply returns a string containing the XML representation of the data in a DataSet, whereas WriteXml is overloaded to support writing to streams, files, the XmlReader, and TextReader objects. For performance reasons, the WriteXml method is usually preferred.

2. When mapping a schema to a DataSet, what element in the XSD maps to tables in the DataSet?

   The complexType element of the XSD maps to DataTable objects in the DataSet.

3. What is the process of inference and how is it used by the DataSet?

   Inference refers to the process of inferring the XSD from an existing XML document. Inference is used when the InferXmlSchema and ReadXml methods are called and passed XML documents that are schemas or that contain in-line schemas. The

7

process uses specific rules to determine which elements map to tables and which to columns, but the process is non-deterministic in that two documents created from the schema may produce different `DataSet` structures. The inference process is also not necessarily lossless, particularly when elements contain both text and child elements.

4. What is the purpose of the `XmlDataDocument`?

The `XmlDataDocument` class is used to provide a DOM view of a `DataSet` that is synchronized with the `DataSet` using events behind the scenes. The `XmlDataDocument` class enables developers to work with the data as if it were an XML document and can then utilize the features of XML documents such as XPath queries and XSL transformation.

Exercise

Write a method that reads the provided sales.xml file into a `DataSet`. Then change its XML representation by changing the `id` attribute of the `Store` element to an element and then writing the new schema and data to a file.

Answers for Day 7

Exercise Answer

One possible solution is shown in the following listing. Note that because of the inference rules, the `Store` element is actually represented in the third of the three `DataTable` objects created.

```
Dim dsSales As New DataSet()

' Read in the file
dsSales.ReadXml("sales.xml", XmlReadMode.InferSchema)

' Change the mapping to element
dsSales.Tables(2).Columns("id").ColumnMapping = MappingType.Element

' Write out the schema and data
dsSales.WriteXml("sales2.xml", XmlWriteMode.WriteSchema)
```

Week 1

In Review

I hope you've enjoyed your first week of *Sams Teach Yourself ADO.NET in 21 Days*! Days 1 and 2 should have given you a good introduction to ADO.NET and helped you to understand the history and thought process that went into its design and implementation. As you can tell by now, ADO.NET wasn't designed to solve every problem, but really focuses on the two most common programming models used in today's distributed Web-based applications: accessing data in a disconnected fashion and streaming through data on the server.

The rest of the week focused on the first of the two programming models and should have forced you to look into almost every nook and cranny of the `DataSet` object. By now, you should feel very comfortable manipulating `DataSet` objects both graphically and programmatically.

So kick back and take a break (although not a long one) and get ready for next week, when you'll dig into the second major component of ADO.NET, its .NET Data Providers.

1

2

3

4

5

6

7

WEEK 2

At a Glance

The focus of this week is on the .NET Data Providers that ship with VS .NET and provide access to a variety of data stores. Throughout the week you'll learn about different aspects of the providers, culminating in a discussion of actually developing your own custom provider!

This week begins with Day 8's general and gentle introduction to .NET Data Providers. This day details the objects that compose the .NET Data Providers along with their responsibilities.

The remainder of the week discusses each of these components in turn by focusing on connections and transactions, command objects, data readers, data adapters, accessing SQL Server data, working with other providers such as the ODBC .NET Data Provider, and building your own custom .NET Data Provider. These lessons detail not only how to use the components, but also recommend specific techniques when dealing with issues that surround them, such as connection pooling, output parameters, and both local and distributed transactions.

By the end of the week, you should be able to access data on a variety of data stores using the appropriate provider and the appropriate objects for your particular scenarios.

WEEK 2

DAY 8

Understanding .NET Data Providers

NEW TERM Today you begin a new week devoted to learning about the architecture and functionality of .NET Data Providers (referred to simply as **providers** from here on out). Providers are the second major component of ADO.NET (the `DataSet` being the first) and serve as the mechanism to communicate with various data stores. Although you had intermittent contact with providers last week, this week you'll explore all facets of providers, not only learning how a provider is architected, but also drilling down into each individual component of a provider and walking through its functionality in detail.

Today's discussion will focus on the classes and interfaces provided by ADO.NET that serve as the blueprint that Microsoft and other vendors can use for building providers. Specifically, today you will learn the following concepts:

- The classification and responsibilities of providers and the classes they contain
- The classes and interfaces in ADO.NET and their key members

Provider Architecture

As mentioned on Day 1, "ADO.NET In Perspective," a provider's main responsibilities include connecting and disconnecting with a data store, performing transaction management, handling exceptions, executing parameterized queries and commands, and then either processing the results directly or interacting with the DataSet object. To that end, ADO.NET provides classes and interfaces in the System.Data and System.Data.Common namespaces that are used as a template for developers building providers to work with specific data stores.

> **Note**
>
> As you look at these common interfaces, you might be wondering why, for the most part, the interfaces such as IDataReader are in the System.Data namespace, but the classes such as DbDataAdapter are in System.Data.Common. The reason is that the classes in System.Data.Common are meant to be used only by developers implementing providers, whereas the interfaces are used both by developers of providers and users wanting to write polymorphic code against multiple providers.

NEW TERM As you're well aware by now, Microsoft ships the SQL Server provider in the System.Data.SqlClient namespace (referred to simply as SqlClient) and the OLE DB provider in the System.Data.OleDb namespace (referred to as OleDb). In addition, the ODBC provider is available as a download from the MSDN Web site. The SqlClient provider is an example of a **specific provider** (sometimes referred to as a **native** or **targeted provider**) that communicates with a single data store (SQL Server 7.0 or later) and exposes functionality particular to that data store. Both the OleDb are ODBC providers are examples of **generic providers** (sometimes referred to as **bridge** or **broad providers**) that act as a managed interface to data that is accessed through an OLE DB provider or ODBC driver, respectively. As such, these generic providers don't offer any functionality not already exposed by the OLE DB provider or ODBC driver. Obviously, specific providers offer not only the opportunity for exposing functionality available to the data store, such as returning XML directly from SQL Server, but also offer performance improvements because the extra layer of abstraction is eliminated. For example, SqlClient talks to SQL Server directly using the Tabular Data Stream (TDS) protocol.

> **Note**
>
> Microsoft is also working on additional providers. For example, beta 1 of the Oracle .NET Data Provider was released on MSDN in early May of 2002, and it is rumored that a DB2 provider is not far behind.

The provision of the classes and interfaces for building providers not only promotes a common programming model but also actually allows you to write code polymorphically to mask the provider being used. (We'll discuss one technique for doing so on Day 17, "ADO.NET in the Data Services Tier.") In addition to implementing the standard classes and interfaces, providers typically implement additional classes that provide error handling and other services, as shown in Figure 8.1 and explained in Table 8.1.

Note   As I'll mention on Day 21, "Futures and Wrap-Up," look for features in future releases of ADO.NET that make it easier to write provider-independent code.

FIGURE 8.1

Provider architecture. This diagram highlights the objects typically exposed by a provider. The highlighted objects have classes or interfaces provided by ADO.NET.

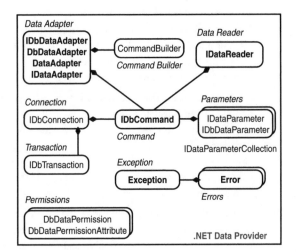

TABLE 8.1   Provider components. This table details each of the primary components of a provider and what each is used for.

Component	Description
Data Adapter	Implemented using the `IDbDataAdapter` or `IDataAdapter` interfaces of the `System.Data` namespace and/or the `DbDataAdapter` and `DataAdapter` classes of the `System.Data.Common` namespace. The data adapter is used to populate a `DataSet` from a connection to a data store and synchronize changes made to the `DataSet` with the data store.
Connection	Implemented using the `IDbConnection` interface of the `System.Data` namespace and used as the means to send queries and commands to the data store. Connection objects control the transactional behavior of the data store and typically raise events and exceptions when the connection state changes or when errors are encountered.

TABLE 8.1   continued

Component	Description
Transaction	Implemented using the IDbTransaction interface of the System.Data namespace. Associated with a connection object and used to initiate, commit, and roll back logical units of works in the data store.
Permissions	Implemented using the DbDataPermission and DbDataPermissionAttribute classes of the System.Data.Common namespace. These classes are used with the code access security system in .NET and, in fact, are derived from classes in the System.Security namespace. They are used to ensure that a user has a security level adequate to access data through the provider. Providers derive classes from these so that both imperative and declarative security checks can be specified directly in the code and made by the runtime when the code is loaded or executed.
Command Builder	Not implemented by all providers; as a result, there is no corresponding class or interface for developers to use. The primary purpose is to automatically build the insert, update, and delete commands used by the data adapter to populate and synchronize data between a DataSet and a data store.
Command	Implemented using the IDbCommand interface of the System.Data namespace and used to encapsulate a command, typically some variant of SQL, that may be executed through a connection object. Commands may be associated with one or more parameters passed to the data store. For relational data stores, commands can typically be either dynamic (containing SQL SELECT, INSERT, UPDATE, and DELETE statements) or refer to procedures or packages stored on the server.
Data Reader	Implemented using the IDataReader and IDataRecord interfaces of the System.Data namespace and used to stream through data returned from a command object in a forward-only, read-only manner. Data readers expose the second major programming model in ADO.NET using a streamed and connected approach as opposed to a cached and disconnected approach exposed through the DataSet.
Parameter	Implemented using the IDataParameter, IDbDataParameter, and IDataParameterCollection interfaces of the System.Data namespace. The first two interfaces listed are used to implement actual parameter classes that map to a name-value pair of a specific data type passed to a command object. The third interface is used to create classes that hold collections of parameters that can be associated with a command object.

TABLE 8.1 continued

Component	Description
Error	Not implemented by all providers; as a result, there are no classes or interfaces in the System.Data namespace to use as templates. Providers implement custom error classes to expose individual errors generated by the data store. In that way, errors can be exposed with properties consistent for the data store. Providers also implement classes used to hold a collection of errors so that if the data store throws more than one error they can all be encapsulated in a single object.
Exception	Not implemented by all providers and so ADO.NET does not contain a generic Exception class. Providers derive their own exception from System.Exception and use it to point to the collection of errors generated by the data store. By using a custom exception class, clients can more easily construct structured exception handling blocks to deal with errors generated by the provider.

For the remainder of today, you'll walk through each of the items in Table 8.1 and explore it in more detail.

Note

> The items shown in Table 8.1 and Figure 8.1 are the primary classes and interfaces. Of course, supplementary classes and interfaces are used within each of the primary items shown here.

As a final note, as mentioned on Day 1, the idea of having different providers to access different data stores at the programmatic level is a departure from the architecture used by Microsoft in DAO, RDO, and ADO. In all those programming models, the idea was that code specific to the data store was abstracted at a lower level into the OLE DB provider or ODBC provider so that the code written by developers differed only slightly, even when accessing different data stores. These small differences included things such as connection strings, the variant of SQL used, and the names of objects such as stored procedures.

Although relying on common interfaces provided by ADO.NET goes some way toward allowing provider-independent code to be written, ADO.NET does not provide the uniform programming model of ADO. This is intentional. The reason is that the cost of building a programming model like ADO—where the Recordset object provided both streamed, batch, and immediate access to the underlying data—is confusion on the part of developers, which results in inefficient code. A good deal of the confusion is related to the fact that OLE DB providers and ODBC drivers don't expose the same set of functionality, so ADO would reset properties based on the functionality available. A typical example is when the ADO developer wants to use a dynamic cursor in order to see changes to the database as they occur, only to find out that the CursorType property of the Recordset object was reset from adOpenDynamic to adOpenStatic, resulting in all the records being downloaded to the client or middle tier, thereby expending extra resources.

Provider Functionality

In this section, we'll explore each of the provider components shown in Table 8.1 and look at their functionality at a high level by detailing the methods, properties, and events that are typically exposed by a provider.

Data Adapter

The data adapter is the bridge between the DataSet and the data store and, as such, is the most important component for providers that want to implement the disconnected programming model for which ADO.NET was primarily built. In fact, vendors who want to create the simplest provider possible can simply implement (inherit from) the IDataAdapter interface or derive from the DataAdapter class.

You'll notice that several different base classes and interfaces are shown in Figure 8.1. DataAdapter is an abstract class that implements the IDataAdapter interface and provides the basic functionality that all providers inherit from. The DbDataAdapter class is also abstract and is derived from DataAdapter to provide the basis for data adapters that work with relational databases. The IDbDataAdapter interface implements IDataAdapter with the addition of properties to refer to select, insert, update, and delete the commands. The result is that providers such as SqlClient and OleDb create their data adapters by inheriting from DbDataAdapter, implementing the IDbDataAdapter interface, and adding custom and overloaded members to implement their own functionality and provide strongly typed access. For example, the SqlDataAdapter class adds its own constructors that accept SqlConnection objects and a strongly typed implementation of the select, insert, update, and delete command properties. Table 8.2 lists the primary members for a data adapter.

TABLE 8.2   Data adapter members. These are primary members implemented by providers.

Member	Description
Properties	
AcceptChangesDuringFill	Property inherited from DataAdapter that specifies whether AcceptChanges is called on a row after it is added to a table.
ContinueUpdateOnError	Property inherited from DataAdapter that specifies whether to generate an exception when an error occurs during the Update method or whether to add error information to the row and continue.
SelectCommand, DeleteCommand, InsertCommand, UpdateCommand	Properties that reference strongly typed command objects used by the data adapter to manipulate data in the data store.
MissingMappingAction	Property inherited from DataAdapter that specifies the action to take when incoming data does not have a matching table or column in the DataSet during the Fill method.
MissingSchemaAction	Property inherited from DataAdapter that specifies the action to take when the schema of the DataSet used in the Fill method does not match the incoming data.
TableMappings	Property inherited from DataAdapter that references a DataTableMappingCollection object that stores the mappings between the incoming data and a DataSet.
Methods	
Fill	Overloaded and overridden method from DataAdapter and DbDataAdapter that populates a DataSet with data from the data store based on SelectCommand.
FillSchema	Overloaded method inherited from DbDataAdapter that adds a table to a DataSet and configures the schema to match the data store.
GetFillParameters	Overridden method inherited from the DbDataAdapter class that returns an array of parameters set by the user in the SelectCommand object.
Update	Overloaded method inherited from DbDataAdapter that calls the insert, update, and delete commands appropriately to modify the data store based on row states in the DataSet, DataTable, or DataRow passed to the method.

8

TABLE 8.2   continued

Member	Description
Events	
FillError	Event implemented by DbDataAdapter that is raised when an error occurs in the Fill method.
RowUpdated	Event raised during the Update method after an update command has been executed.
RowUpdating	Event raised during the Update method before an update command is executed.

Connection

Providers implement connection classes by implementing the IDbConnection interface and then adding their own custom members that provide provider-specific functionality, such as specifying additional attributes that affect the way the connection operates or implementing events that are fired in order to communicate back from the data store. Table 8.3 lists the members of the IDbConnection interface.

TABLE 8.3   Connection members. These are primary members implemented by providers from the IDbConnection interface.

Member	Description
Properties	
ConnectionString	Property that gets or sets the string used to open a connection.
ConnectionTimeout	Property that specifies how long to wait while trying to open a connection before raising an exception.
Database	Property that specifies the name of the current database that the connection will use.
State	Property that gets the current state of the database using the ConnectionState enumeration.
Methods	
BeginTransaction	Overloaded method that begins a new transaction on the connection for the data source. Providers return a strongly typed transaction object.
ChangeDatabase	Method that changes the current database for an open connection.
Close	Method that closes the connection to the database.
CreateCommand	Method that creates and returns a command object associated with the connection.
Open	Method that opens a connection using the attributes of the ConnectionString property.

As mentioned, in addition to the fundamental members shown in Table 8.3, providers implement specific members as well. For example, the OleDbConnection class includes additional Provider, DataSource, and ServerVersion properties that specify the OLE DB provider in use, the location and filename of the data source, and the version of the database server that is being used, respectively. In addition to those, the SqlConnection class adds PacketSize and WorkstationId to get the size of the network packets being exchanged between the client and SQL Server and the name of the client machine. Both providers also implement the InfoMessage and StateChange events in order to receive messages from the database and be alerted when the state of the connection changes.

Transaction

The transaction class implements the transaction semantics for a particular instance of a connection object. In other words, if the connection object's BeginTransaction method is called, a new transaction object is created that controls how the transaction behaves and when it is committed or rolled back. Providers implement the transaction class by inheriting from IDbTransaction, whose members are shown in Table 8.4.

TABLE 8.4 Transaction members. These are primary members implemented by providers from the IDbTransaction interface.

Member	Description
	Properties
Connection	Property that references the connection object that created the transaction. Providers implement a strongly typed version.
IsolationLevel	Property that specifies the locking behavior for the transaction using the IsolationLevel enumerated type.
	Methods
Commit	Method that commits the database transaction. Should throw an exception if the transaction has already been committed or rolled back.
Rollback	Method that rolls back or un-does a transaction after BeginTransaction has been called. Should throw an exception if the transaction has already been committed or rolled back.

You should notice from Table 8.4 that the programming model for transactions in ADO.NET implies an unchained model where, unless the BeginTransaction method is called, each individual command that is executed against a database is an implicit transaction. Commands can then be aggregated into their own logical unit of work explicitly using the BeginTransaction, Commit, and Rollback methods.

Permissions

Providers have the option of creating specific permission classes that work with .NET's Code Access Security (CAS) to enable administrators and developers to control access to the data store. Although a complete discussion of CAS is beyond the scope of this book, the basic idea is that CAS controls access to protected resources such as databases, the file system, the system registry, printing, and others by providing the following:

- Permissions and sets of predefined permissions (FullTrust, Internet, and Nothing, among others) that represent high-level and granular access to various system resources

- **New Term** The capability of users and administrators to set policies in one of three levels (Enterprise, Machine, User) that define the code groups (**code groups** are logical groupings that contain permission sets and into which code is placed at runtime based on a membership condition) and permission sets

- The capability for code (developers) to request permissions (both declaratively and imperatively) it requires, would be nice to have, or does not require to run

- The capability of the common language runtime to determine, based on evidence, whether the code has the required permissions by their inclusion in a code group

---

A Quick CAS Overview

.NET's Code Access Security model relies on the concept of evidence to determine whether code has the required permissions for execution. Evidence includes the Authenticode signer of the code, the URL from where the code was downloaded, the strong name, the zone (such as the Internet Zone), and the application directory, in addition to optional custom attributes.

At load time, the common language runtime uses the evidence to determine which code groups at each policy level the assembly belongs to. After the common language runtime determines which code groups the code belongs to, it combines the permissions defined for each policy level. Finally, the common language runtime intersects the permissions from each policy level so that the resulting permission set contains only the permissions that all policy levels have in common. The set of permissions that has been calculated is compared to attributes defined in the code when it is loaded or executed, depending on where the permission is used, to determine which permissions are actually granted. If permissions that the code requires have not been granted, a SecurityException is thrown.

As an example, CAS allows administrators to edit the machine policy for a Web server to make sure that only code with specific evidence (for example, an assembly with a particular strong name or code signed with a digital signature) can access SQL Server by adding the SQL Server permission to the permission set used by the appropriate code group. This provides a much higher level of security than simply securing resources based on the identity of the account running the code.

Administrators modify policies, code groups, and permission sets through the Microsoft .NET Framework Configuration MMC snap-in found in the Administrative Tools group. Figure 8.2 shows a screenshot of the utility with a dialog showing the editing of the `SqlClient` permission for the permission set.

Note

By default, all code on the local machine runs under the `FullTrust` permission set, which allows unrestricted access to SQL Server. In other words, under the `FullTrust` permission set, all managed code can attempt to connect to a SQL Server by using the `SqlConnection` object. Of course, in order to actually gain access to the database server, the code must also supply the proper credentials.

FIGURE 8.2

Editing a permission. This dialog can be used to edit the SqlClient permission for a particular permission set.

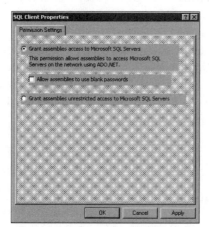

Vendors implementing providers can create both declarative and imperative classes that can be used at the assembly, class, and method levels to make sure that the code has the appropriate permissions before accessing the data store. The abstract `DbDataPermission` class is used as the base class for imperative permission, whereas the `DbDataPermissionAttribute` class is the abstract base class for imperative permissions. The classes themselves are derived from `CodeAccessPermission` and

CodeAccessSecurityAttribute of the System.Security namespace, respectively. The only member that DbDataPermission and DbDataPermissionAttribute add to the base classes is the AllowBlankPassword property. Setting this property to True allows the connection string to omit the password, whereas setting it to False makes sure that a password is used to connect to the data store.

To use CAS security declaratively, you can use attributes at the assembly, class, and method levels. For example, the declaration of a data access class that works against SQL Server might look like the following code snippet:

```
<SqlClientPermissionAttribute(Security.Permissions.SecurityAction.Demand, _
AllowBlankPassword:=False)> _
Public Class ComputeBooksData : Inherits ComputeBooksDABase
   ' members
End Class
```

In this snippet, the SqlClientPermissionAttribute is placed at the class level with its Action property set to Demand and AllowBlankPassword set to False. Setting Action to Demand simply means that code in this class (and any code higher in the call stack) needs to have permission to use SqlClient. Alternatively, the declaration could have used the SecurityAction.Assert value to indicate that only the ComputeBooksData class needs to be granted the permission. This is convenient because calling code won't necessarily be granted permission to access SQL Server. The SecurityAction enumeration also includes additional values to request permissions at the assembly level, deny a permission, and deal with permissions for derived classes.

| Tip | Although using Assert sounds great (and unsecure), there is a catch. To assert permissions, the code (in this case, the assembly that ComputeBooksData is in) must have the assertion security permission (defined using the SecurityPermissionAttribute). Assertion is included by default in the FullTrust, LocalIntranet, and Everything permission sets.

When a method contains a declarative demand for the SqlClientPermission and its assembly has not been granted the permission, the SecurityException is raised only if the method contains one of the objects from the SqlClient namespace, such as SqlDataAdapter or SqlConnection. |

Permissions can also be used imperatively within a method like as shown in Listing 8.1.

LISTING 8.1 Using imperative security. This method uses imperative security to demand the `SqlClientPermission`.

```
Public Function GetTitles() as DataSet
    Dim perm As New SqlClientPermission( _
     PermissionState.Unrestricted, False)

    Try
      perm.Demand()
      ' Go on to execute queries

    Catch e As SecurityException
      ' Handle security errors
    Catch e As Exception
      ' Handle other errors
    End Try

End Function
```

ANALYSIS In Listing 8.1, the permission object is explicitly created and its `Demand` method is called at the appropriate time. The constructor of the `SqlClientPermission` class accepts either the `None` or `Unrestricted` values from the `PermissionState` enumeration. Using `None` specifies that no access to the resource is required, whereas using `Unrestricted` means that the method requires full access to the resource. The second argument to the constructor populates the `AllowBlankPassword` property, so, in this example, blank passwords aren't allowed.

It's a good practice to at least declaratively mark your assemblies that contain data access code with the appropriate permission class so that any security exceptions can be found at load time rather than waiting until the method is called and finding that the assembly doesn't have the appropriate permissions. To do so, you can place the following line of code in the AssemblyInfo.vb (or .cs) file:

```
<Assembly: SqlClientPermission(SecurityAction.RequestMinimum)>
```

 Note When declaring attributes, the Attribute suffix is not required.

Command

The command object encapsulates a query or data modification to execute against a data store through a connection object. Command objects are also referenced in the `SelectCommand`, `InsertCommand`, `UpdateCommand`, and `DeleteCommand` properties of the data adapter used to fill a `DataSet` and synchronize it with the data store. If you've worked with ADO 2.x, the command objects exposed in ADO.NET will no doubt seem familiar because the Command object in ADO exposed many of the same properties.

Vendors implement command classes in a provider by inheriting from the IDbCommand interface and then adding custom members to expose specific functionality of the provider. The most common members of a command class are shown in Table 8.5.

TABLE 8.5 Command members. These are primary members implemented by providers from the IDbCommand interface.

Member	Description
Properties	
CommandText	Property that specifies the text of the command to run against the data store.
CommandTimeout	Property that specifies how long to wait before terminating the execution of a command.
CommandType	Property that specifies how the CommandText property is interpreted using a value from the CommandType enumeration.
Connection	Property that references the strongly typed connection object through which this command will be executed.
Parameters	Property that references a collection of strongly typed parameter objects associated with the command.
Transaction	Property that references the strongly typed transaction object the statement executed by this command will participate in.
UpdatedRowSource	Property that specifies how results from a command are applied to a row being updated using a value from the UpdateRowSource enumeration.
Methods	
Cancel	Method that attempts to cancel the execution of the command.
CreateParameter	Method that creates a new instance of a strongly typed parameter object. Does not automatically add the new parameter to the collection for the command.
ExecuteNonQuery	Method that executes the command against the data store and returns the number of rows affected, but not the rows themselves.
ExecuteReader	Method that executes the command against the data store and returns a strongly typed data reader that can be traversed.
ExecuteScalar	Method that executes the command against the data store and returns only the first column of the first row of the result set, regardless of how many rows and columns are specified by the CommandText.

TABLE 8.5 continued

Member	Description
Methods	
Prepare	Method that creates a compiled version of the query on the data store. This method is not a member of IDbCommand.
ResetCommandTimeout	Method that resets the CommandTimeout property to its default value.

As noted in Table 8.5, of the members listed, only the Prepare method isn't exposed by the IDbCommand interface, although it's implemented by both the SqlClient and OleDb providers. In addition, the SqlClient provider implements an ExecuteXmlReader method used to process results from queries that contain the FOR XML Transact-SQL keyword introduced in SQL Server 2000.

As with other provider-specific classes, members of the command object, including Connection, Transaction, Parameters, CreateParameter, and ExecuteReader, all return strongly typed objects rather than simply the interfaces in the System.Data namespace. For example, the declaration of the CreateParameter method of the OleDbCommand class looks like

```
Public Function CreateParameter() As OleDbParameter
```

rather than like this:

```
Public Function CreateParameter() As IDbParameter
```

In this way, the members are said to be strongly typed and so clients using the classes can always work with the types directly rather than only through the interfaces.

 Note Command builders are closely related to commands. We'll discuss them on Day 10, "Using Commands."

One of the other interesting members in Table 8.5 is the UpdatedRowSource property. This property can be set to one of the values of the UpdateRowSource enumeration (Both, FirstReturnedRow, None, or OutputParameters) to control how results from a command are mapped to a row in a DataSet. Both is the default and specifies that both output parameters and the first returned row are mapped to the changed row. In other words, when a data adapter executes the command referenced in its UpdateCommand property in order to update a row in a database, it will look for the values of output parameters (with the appropriate SourceColumn property set) and columns in a result set, if one is returned that can be placed back into the changed row. This allows the data store to resynchronize data generated on the server with data in the DataSet. The result is that the original row in the DataTable will have its RowState set to Unchanged if the update succeeds.

Data Reader

Data readers are used to expose the second major programming model in ADO.NET: streamed access to one or more result sets returned from a command object. Clients use a data reader by iterating over it in a loop using its Read method. In sharp contrast to the in-memory cache of a DataSet, data readers provide a forward-only read-only model where a row can be accessed only once and no navigation within the result set is possible. After the data reader has been exhausted, it can't be replayed using a second loop.

 Note

> Developers familiar with ADO 2.x will note that the data reader and the DataSet together provide most of the functionality of the Recordset object in ADO 2.x. In ADO 2.x, the Recordset could be used both to stream through data by using a forward-only, read-only cursor (cursor type of adOpenForwardOnly, lock type of adLockReadOnly) and cache data using a disconnected Recordset (cursor location of adUseClient, cursor type of adOpenStatic, lock type of adLockReadOnly).

A provider implements a data reader by creating a class that inherits from both the IDataReader and IDataRecord interfaces. The IDataReader interface provides the members used to provide information about the result set and iterate its rows. The IDataRecord interface provides the members used to read data from the current row in the result set.

Client code never actually creates a data reader (in fact, it can't because the constructor of the data reader is marked as private), but uses instances returned from the ExecuteReader method of the command object. The behavior of a data reader in terms of how rows are streamed to the client is totally dependent on the data store and provider. However, in most cases, as with SqlClient, the data is static after the command that creates the reader has executed, so changes made by other users are not visible.

The members typically implemented in a data reader are shown in Table 8.6 and are drawn from both the IDataReader and IDataRecord interfaces.

8

TABLE 8.6 Data reader members. These are primary members implemented by providers from the `IDataReader` and `IDataRecord` interfaces.

Member	Description
Properties	
Depth	Property from `IDataReader` that returns the nesting level of the current result set. Always zero for SqlClient but depends on the capability of the provider.
FieldCount	Property from `IDataRecord` that gets the number of columns in the current row.
IsClosed	Property from `IDataReader` that indicates whether the data reader is closed.
Item	Overloaded property from `IDataRecord` that gets the value of a column based on name or ordinal value in its native data type. In C#, this is the indexer to the data reader.
RecordsAffected	Property from `IDataReader` that returns the number of rows modified, inserted, or deleted by the command execution.
Methods	
Close	Method from `IDataReader` that closes the data reader.
GetByte, GetBytes	Methods from `IDataRecord` that get the value of the column as a `Byte` or a stream of bytes to be placed in an array based on the ordinal.
GetChar, GetChars	Methods from `IDataRecord` that get the value of the column based on the ordinal as a character or as stream characters to be placed in an array based on an offset.
GetDataTypeName	Method from `IDataRecord` that returns the name of the data type for the column specified by the ordinal.
GetBoolean, GetDateTime, GetDecimal, GetDouble, GetFloat, GetGuid, GetInt16, GetInt32, GetInt64, GetString, GetTimeSpan	Methods from `IDataRecord` that return the value of the column as the appropriate .NET data type based on the ordinal.
GetFieldType	Method from `IDataRecord` that returns the `Type` of the field based on the ordinal value.
GetName	Method from `IDataRecord` that returns the name of the column based on the ordinal.
GetOrdinal	Method from `IDataRecord` that returns the ordinal of the column based on the name.

TABLE 8.6　continued

Member	Description
Methods	
GetSchemaTable	Method from `IDataReader` that returns a `DataTable` that mimics the structure of the current result set.
GetValue	Method from `IDataRecord` that returns the value of the column at the given ordinal.
GetValues	Method from `IDataRecord` that returns an array of objects for the columns in the current row in their native format.
IsDbNull	Method from `IDataRecord` that determines whether the column specified by the ordinal is equivalent to `DBNull`.
NextResult	Method from `IDataReader` that moves the data reader to the next result set returned from the execution of the command object.
Read	Method from `IDataReader` that advances the data reader to the next record in the result set.

As you can see from Table 8.6, the data reader provides strongly typed access to a result set by exposing the Get methods of the `IDataRecord` interface. These methods can be used both to retrieve the value of a single field (that is, `GetString`, `GetInt32`, `GetValue`, and so on) or the values of the entire record using the `GetValues` method. Of course, specific providers such as `SqlClient` can augment this ability to return data in types that are particular to the data store. In fact, as mentioned on Day 1, ADO.NET contains the `System.Data.SqlTypes` namespace that includes classes that represent each of the native types in SQL Server. The `SqlDataReader` class then uses those types by exposing equivalent Get methods that return the types. For example, the `SqlTypes` namespace includes the types `SqlBinary`, `SqlBoolean`, `SqlGuid`, and `SqlMoney`, among others. The `SqlDataReader` class exposes `GetSqlBinary`, `GetSqlBoolean`, `GetSqlGuid`, and `GetSqlMoney` methods accordingly.

What Happened to `GetRows`?

If you have developed in ADO 2.x in the past, you'll note that the data reader does not expose a method analogous to the `GetRows` method of the `Recordset` object. The `GetRows` method of the `Recordset` object reads the entire result set (or a specific number of rows) and creates a multi-dimensional `Variant` array before closing the `Recordset`. Developers used `GetRows` as an alternative to disconnected `Recordsets` to improve performance and eliminate COM marshalling and registration issues when passing data between tiers in a distributed application. However, because the `DataSet` provides the same functionality without the performance hit, the `GetRows` method is no longer needed. The bottom line is this: If you need to cache the data, use a `DataSet`.

8

The ability of data readers to work with multiple result sets is, of course, entirely dependent on the provider and the data store. In most cases, multiple result sets can be returned simply by concatenating SELECT statements in the CommandText property of the command object or in the stored procedure referenced by the CommandText property. You'll learn some specific techniques on Day 11, "Using Data Readers."

Parameter

Parameters are used to represent arguments passed to a command object and ultimately to a data store. Parameters are also used to map columns from a result set, return values, and output parameters back to columns within a DataSet. Providers typically implement strongly typed parameters by creating a class that inherits from both the IDataParameter and IDbDataParameter interfaces.

 Note

> Although most of the properties come from IDataParameter, the IDbDataParameter interface is used by the VB .NET Data Designers to indicate their precision, scale, and size.

To expose a strongly typed collection of parameters, the command object will then expose a collection object that inherits from the IDataParameterCollection interface. For example, the OleDb provider implements the OleDbParameter class that implements the IDataParameter and IDbDataParameter interfaces. A collection of OleDbParameter objects are then contained in an OleDbParameterCollection object exposed through the Parameters property of the OleDbCommand object.

The parameter objects themselves typically support the members shown in Table 8.7.

TABLE 8.7   Parameter members. These are primary members implemented by providers from the IDataParameter and IDbDataParameter interfaces.

Member	Description
DbType	Property from IDataParameter that specifies the data type of the parameter using the DbType enumeration.
Direction	Property from IDataParameter that specifies whether the parameter is input-only, output-only, bi-directional, or a return value using the ParameterDirection enumerated type.
IsNullable	Property from IDataParameter that specifies whether the parameter accepts null values.
ParameterName	Property from IDataParameter that specifies the name of the parameter.

TABLE 8.7   continued

Member	Description
Precision	Property from `IDbDataParameter` that specifies the precision (the maximum number of digits used to represent the value) of numeric parameters.
Scale	Property from `IDbDataParameter` that specifies the scale (the number of decimal places the value is resolved to) of numeric parameters.
Size	Property from `IDbDataParameter` that specifies the size in bytes of numeric parameters.
SourceColumn	Property from `IDataParameter` that specifies the name of the column in the `DataSet` the value of the parameter will be mapped to.
SourceVersion	Property from `IDataParameter` that specifies the `DataRowVersion` to use when populating the value of the parameter.
Value	Property from `IDataParameter` that specifies the value of the parameter.

In addition to the members shown in Table 8.7, the SqlClient and OleDb providers expose properties that return a value from the `System.Data.SqlDbType` and `System.Data.OleDb.OleDbType` enumerations, respectively. In both cases, the provider-specific types are linked to the `DbType` enumeration, so changing one of the properties for a particular parameter changes them both.

 Note   A table of this linkage and how `DbType` maps to the .NET Framework types can be found in the online documentation by searching for the keywords "parameters, DataAdapter" in the index.

Parameters can be created using the `CreateParameter` method of the command object or directly using the `New` (new in C#) keyword with its overloaded constructor. In both cases, the parameters must be added to the parameter collection using the `Add` method of the derived `IDataParameterCollection` object. The order in which parameters are added to the collection might also be important depending on the provider. Provider-specific characteristics also determine which values from the `ParameterDirection` enumeration (`Input`, `InputOutput`, `Output`, or `ReturnValue`) are valid to use with the `Direction` property.

The `SourceColumn` and `SourceVersion` properties are particularly interesting because they determine how the parameter maps to a `DataSet` and which version of the data is updated. For example, the `SourceColumn` property can be used to map a parameter that returns a new primary key value from a database server to the primary key column of a `DataSet`. This technique is often used with `IDENTITY` columns in SQL Server, as will be shown on Day 13, "Working with SQL Server." The `SourceVersion` property allows the `UpdateCommand` of a `DataSet` to use a value other than the `Current` value when performing an update. This can come in handy when you want to make sure that the `Original` value for a particular column is passed back to the data store.

Error and Exception

As noted in Table 8.1, ADO.NET does not provide templates for exposing errors and exceptions, and so each provider is free to implement them as it sees fit. However, the Microsoft providers handle errors in a similar fashion. When an error occurs in SQL Server or the data source that an OLE DB provider is communicating with, both providers create a strongly typed object that exposes properties that identify the error. In the case of SQL Server, the `SqlError` class exposes the properties shown in Table 8.8, whereas for OleDb, the properties of its `OleDbError` class are shown in Table 8.9.

TABLE 8.8 `SqlError` properties. Properties of the `SqlError` object that provide error information specific to SQL Server.

Property	Description
Class	Returns the severity level from SQL Server (1 to 25) with a default of 0. Levels above 20 are severe and usually close the `SqlConnection` object automatically.
LineNumber	Returns the line number in the Transact-SQL stored procedure or command batch that caused the error.
Message	Returns the text describing the error.
Number	Returns the SQL Server error number.
Procedure	Returns the name of the stored procedure or remote procedure call (RPC) that generated the error.
Server	Returns the name of the instance of SQL Server from where the error was generated.
Source	Returns the name of the provider that generated the error.
State	Returns a `Byte` value that corresponds to an error, warning, or no data found.

TABLE 8.9 OleDbError properties. Properties of the OleDbError class that provide information about the error that was found.

Property	Description
Message	Returns a text description of the error.
NativeError	Returns a database-specific error code.
Source	Returns the name of the provider that generated the error.
SQLState	Returns the five-character ANSI standard code representing the state of the database.

As you can see from Tables 8.8 and 8.9, there is virtually no overlap between the properties exposed by SqlError and OleDbError. This is the case because SqlError can expose very specific information from SQL Server, such as the LineNumber in the Transact-SQL command batch or stored procedure that caused the error or the name (Procedure) of the remote procedure call (RPC) or stored procedure that produced the error. The OleDbError object, on the other hand, exposes generic information such as the five-character ANSI code that represents the state of the database (SQLState) and data store–specific information in the NativeError property.

Both providers are capable of generating more than one error, so both implement collection classes to hold a collection of errors. The SqlErrorCollection and OleDbErrorCollection both inherit from the ICollection and IEnumerable interfaces and hold error objects of the appropriate type.

So, when an error occurs, the providers create an error object for each error returned from the data store and place it in the error collection object. The collection is then referenced through the Errors property of the SqlException or OleDbException object, which is then thrown by the provider. As a result, the errors collection will always be populated with at least one error object. As you might expect, the exception objects are derived from SystemException. In addition, the exception objects expose some of the same properties as the error objects, most of which are then populated with data from the first error in the errors collection. For example, the SqlException object exposes the Class, LineNumber, Number, Procedure, Server, Source, and State properties, all of which simply wrap the same property in the first SqlError object in the SqlErrorCollection. However, the Message property of both the SqlException and OleDbException classes automatically concatenates the Message properties from all the errors separated by carriage-return line-feeds.

To fully report the errors generated by the provider, you might use a method like that shown in Listing 8.2.

LISTING 8.2 Logging error information. This method logs the errors reported through a
`SqlException` to the `Trace` object.

8

```
Public Sub LogSqlErrors(ByVal myException As SqlException)
  Dim sqlE As SqlError
  Dim strMsg As String

  ' Write the header and stack dump
  Trace.WriteLine("SqlException occurred at " & _
   Now.ToLongTimeString & " in " & myException.TargetSite.Name)
  Trace.WriteLine(myException.StackTrace)

  ' Walk through all of the errors
  For Each sqlE In myException.Errors
    strMsg = "Source: " & sqlE.Source & ControlChars.Cr & _
        "Number: " & sqlE.Number.ToString() & ControlChars.Cr & _
        "State: " & sqlE.State.ToString() & ControlChars.Cr & _
        "Class: " & sqlE.Class.ToString() & ControlChars.Cr & _
        "Server: " & sqlE.Server & ControlChars.Cr & _
        "Message: " & sqlE.Message & ControlChars.Cr & _
        "Procedure: " & sqlE.Procedure & ControlChars.Cr & _
        "LineNumber: " & sqlE.LineNumber.ToString()
    Trace.WriteLine(strMsg)
  Next
  Trace.WriteLine("End of SqlException")

End Sub
```

ANALYSIS You'll notice from Listing 8.2 that the `LogSqlErrors` method accepts a
`SqlException` object as a parameter and so would be called from the `Catch`
block of a `Try Catch` statement. The method then writes information using the `Trace`
class of the `System.Diagnostics` namespace. The interesting aspect of the `Trace` class is
that your application can create listeners that can capture the trace output to a file, the
console, or even a Windows event log. The `SqlErrorCollection` is then iterated using a
`For Each` loop and the error properties written to the trace output.

Summary

Today, you learned how .NET Data Providers are architected and you walked through
each of the components that make up a provider. This background information will come
in very handy in the coming week as you explore each of the major components and use
providers in a variety of ways. Tomorrow, you'll begin by digging into connections and
transactions.

Workshop

This workshop will help reinforce the concepts covered in today's lesson.

Quiz

1. What is the difference between a generic and a specific .NET Data Provider?

   A generic provider can be used with more than one data store, whereas a specific provider is implemented to communicate with a single data store. The OleDb and ODBC providers from Microsoft are examples of generic providers, and the SqlClient and future Oracle providers are examples of specific providers. Typically, specific providers will outperform generic providers at the cost of flexibility.

2. Which components of a .NET Data Provider are not provided as templates by ADO.NET?

   As shown in Figure 8.1, the command builder, error, and exception objects are all implemented independently by each provider because there are no classes or interfaces to inherit from in the `System.Data` or `System.Data.Common` namespaces.

3. How can a provider allow for secured access to the underlying data store?

   Providers have the option of implementing custom permission classes inherited from `DbDataPermission` and `DbDataPermissionAttribute`. These classes allow both imperative and declarative security checks to be placed in code so that the common language runtime can verify that a particular assembly has been granted the permission. Permissions can be created at virtually any granularity.

4. What is the visibility of data returned through a data reader?

   That depends on the provider and data store in question. Typically, data returned from a data reader is static data and so changes made by other users will not be visible. However, because a data reader remains connected to a data store while it is being traversed, providers can reflect changes to rows and new rows if needed.

Exercise

Write a custom error handling routine similar to that shown in Listing 8.2 to report errors when an `OleDbException` is raised.

Answers for Day 8

Exercise Answer

One possible solution to the exercise is as follows:

```
Public Sub LogOleDbErrors(ByVal myException As OleDbException)
  Dim oleDbE As OleDbError
  Dim strMsg As String

  ' Write the header and stack dump
  Trace.WriteLine("OleDbException occurred at " & _
  Now.ToLongTimeString & " in " & myException.TargetSite.Name)
  Trace.WriteLine(myException.StackTrace)

  ' Walk through all of the errors
  For Each E In myException.Errors
    strMsg = "Source: " & oleDbE.Source & ControlChars.Cr & _
        "NativeError: " & oleDbE.NativeError.ToString() & ControlChars.Cr & _
        "State: " & oleDbE.SQLState.ToString() & ControlChars.Cr & _
        "Message: " & oleDbE.Message
    Trace.WriteLine(strMsg)
  Next
  Trace.WriteLine("End of OleDbException")

End Sub
```

8

DAY 9

Using Connections and Transactions

Yesterday you learned about the various components that make up a .NET Data Provider and how those components rely on base classes and interfaces provided by ADO.NET. Two of the most important of those components are the connection and transaction objects that handle the communication between a provider and a data store and allow multiple statements to be executed as a logical unit of work against the data store, respectively. The command and transaction objects are presented first because they are the first objects you would naturally use when writing code to access a data store.

Specifically, today you'll learn the following concepts:

- How to open and close connections to a data store and how to handle events

- How to specify connection strings and abstract them for different types of applications

- How connection pooling is exposed and can be used with connection objects in the SqlClient and OleDb providers
- How to create and manage transactions in local and distributed environments

Opening Connections and Handling Events

Yesterday you saw how the IDbConnection interface could be used by a .NET Data Provider to implement a class that is used to communicate with a data store. As such, the connection classes are responsible for all communication between the client and the data store, including the execution of queries and commands and the processing of any messages sent back from the data store.

Note

> Because the connection class is responsible for communication, it's also implicitly responsible for providing credentials to the data store in order to be authenticated and authorized to access the data protected by the data store. As you can imagine, the credentials are provided through the ConnectionString property, so handling the connection string with care is an issue you must address. We'll discuss this later today.

Opening Connections

To open the connection to the data store, you must, of course, call the Open method of an instance of the connection class and pass it the connection string. The connection object will then attempt to open the connection and wait as long as specified in the ConnectionTimeout property, whose default for both SqlConnection and OleDbConnection is 15 seconds. This property is read-only and can be set as an attribute of the connection string.

Depending on the results of the Open method, the State property of the connection object will change accordingly to one of the values of the ConnectionState enumeration. Although the ConnectionState enumeration includes six values (Broken, Closed, Connecting, Executing, Fetching, and Open), only Closed and Open are implemented in this release of VS .NET. The code in the following code snippet connects to a SQL Server database:

```
SqlConnection con = new SqlConnection(_connect);

try
{
  con.Open();
```

```
  // Success con.State = ConnectionState.Open
}
catch (SqlException e)
{
  // Failed con.State = ConnectionState.Closed
}
```

You'll notice in the previous snippet that the `ConnectionString` property is populated in the constructor with a `String` variable called _connect, although it could also have been set directly using the `ConnectionString` property. If the `ConnectionString` is not initialized before the `Open` method is called, an `InvalidOperationException` is thrown. If the connection is opened successfully, its `State` will be set to `Open`. If an exception occurs, it will still be `Closed`.

 Tip

> After a connection is open, you can't change the `ConnectionString` property. To reset the connection, you must call its `Close` method first, change the `ConnectionString`, and then re-open the connection using the `Open` method.

Of course, after the connection is open, it can be used to execute command objects. Even though you can open the connection explicitly, the connection can also be opened and closed implicitly by the data adapter when its `Update` method is called.

To break the connection, you can call the `Close` method. Note that if the connection is not open, the `Close` method simply returns.

Handling Events

As you learned yesterday, both the SqlClient and OleDb providers also implement two connection-based events: `StateChange` and `InfoMessage`. The `StateChange` event is fired any time the `State` property of the connection object changes, which, in the initial release, is when the connection is opened or closed. The `InfoMessage` event is fired when the data store generates a message for the client and is useful for retrieving warning messages and other supplementary information. Keep in mind that if a severe error actually occurs, an exception will be thrown rather than informational messages. However, it's up to the provider to determine when that threshold is reached. For example, in SQL Server, if an error is generated with a severity greater than 10, a `SqlException` will be thrown rather than generating an informational message.

To illustrate how and why you would want to catch these events, consider the code in Listing 9.1 where the three methods execute a simple command against SQL Server and catch the resulting events.

Listing 9.1 Connection events. The three methods in this listing show how to handle the StateChange and InfoMessage events.

```
public void PrintEvents()
{
   string _connect =
     "server=ssosa;database=computebooks;trusted_connection=yes";
   SqlConnection con = new SqlConnection(_connect);

    con.StateChange += new StateChangeEventHandler(this.conStateChanged);
    con.InfoMessage += new SqlInfoMessageEventHandler(this.conInfoMessage);

    try
    {
        con.Open();
        SqlCommand com = new SqlCommand(
            "PRINT 'Hello From ' +  @@SERVERNAME",con);
        com.ExecuteNonQuery();
    }
    catch (SqlException e)
    {
        Console.WriteLine(e.Message);
    }
    finally
    {
        con.Close();
    }
}

 // Handle the StateChange event
private void conStateChanged(object sender,  StateChangeEventArgs e)
{
    if (e.CurrentState == ConnectionState.Closed)
    {
        Trace.WriteLine(((SqlConnection)sender).ConnectionString +
          " closed at " + DateTime.Now.ToLongTimeString());
    }
}

// Handle the InfoMessage event
private void conInfoMessage(object sender,  SqlInfoMessageEventArgs e)
{
    Trace.Write(DateTime.Now.ToLongTimeString() + ":");
    foreach (SqlError err in e.Errors)
    {
        Trace.WriteLine("The " + err.Source + " has received a severity " +
            err.Class + " state " + err.State + " error number " + err.Number +
            " on line " + err.LineNumber + " of procedure " + err.Procedure +
            " on server " + err.Server +  "\n" + err.Message);
    }
}
```

As you can see from Listing 9.1, the PrintEvents method simply creates a new SqlConnection object and initializes it with a connection string passed into the constructor. The StateChange and InfoMessage events are then mapped to the conStateChanged and conInfoMessage private methods using the appropriate delegates. The instances of the StateChangeEventHandler and SqlInfoMessageEventHandler are both delegates that simply point to the methods they are passed and are then attached to the events using the += operator.

> **Note**
>
> Delegates in .NET are type-safe function pointers that are used as the basis for events and asynchronous programming in .NET.

In VB, you could dynamically associate the events to their handler using the AddHandler and RemoveHandler statements or statically using the Handles statement in the declaration of the method used to handle the event.

The event handlers themselves take specific types as their second argument; in this case, the StateChangeEventArgs and SqlInfoMessageEventArgs classes. The StateChangeEventArgs class simply exposes the CurrentState and OriginalState properties that map to the ConnectionState enumeration. The SqlInfoMessageEventArgs class exposes a subset of the information as the SqlException class, which includes a collection of SqlError objects. You'll notice in the conInfoMessage method that multiple messages may be returned and can be traversed using a foreach loop. The PrintEvents message simply uses the Transact-SQL PRINT statement to output a string message of severity 0.

Both event handlers write their output to the Trace object through the WriteLine method. This is an interesting use of these events because it allows your application to capture the trace output using a custom listener. Of course, you could always look for specific messages by inspecting the Class, State, or Number properties of the SqlError object. In the same way, the OleDbInfoMessageEventArgs class exposes a subset of the properties of the OleDbException class.

Specifying Connection Strings

As mentioned previously, the connection string contains attributes. The attributes are specified in a semicolon-delimited list of name-value pairs that are used to identify all aspects of a connection, including the security information, the context (location of the data store and the particular database within the data store, if appropriate), and even information that specifies how the connection should behave in particular situations. The particular attributes are dependent on the provider. This section is a discussion of the attributes you can use with the SqlClient and OleDb providers.

Regardless of the provider, the values in a connection string may be delimited either with single or double quotation marks. You need to use quotation marks only if the value contains a space. Any spaces in the string will be ignored, the string is not case-sensitive, and the string is parsed immediately when the property is set, so you should be prepared to handle exceptions if you're building the string programmatically.

 Tip

> If you do build a connection string programmatically, make sure that users can't add their own attributes to the connection by appending a semicolon followed by the name-value pair in the user ID or password text boxes. In other words, parse the connection string before opening the connection to make sure that it contains only the attributes that you require to make your connection.

Specifying Connection Strings with SqlClient

The ConnectionString property of the SqlConnection object supports a number of attributes, many of which are mapped to read-only properties after the connection string is set. In most cases, the attribute has several aliases that also can be used. Table 9.1 shows the primary attributes. There is also a set of attributes used with connection pooling, which we'll address later today.

TABLE 9.1   SqlClient connection attributes. This table lists the attributes you can use in the connection string when using the SqlConnection object.

Attribute	Description
Application Name	The name of the application connecting to the server or .Net SqlClient Data Provider if not set. Can be used to identify the application using the SQL Profiler utility.
AttachDBFileName	Aliased to Initial File Name and used to specify the primary file of an attachable database.
Connect Timeout	Aliased to Connection Timeout; defaults to 15 seconds and maps to the read-only property ConnectionTimeout.
Current Language	The SQL Server Language to be used.
Data Source	Aliased to Server, Address, Addr, and Network Address. Specifies the name or network address of the SQL Server. Can use "(local)" or "." to specify the default instance of SQL Server on the same machine. Maps to the read-only DataSource property.

TABLE 9.1   continued

Attribute	Description
Enlist	Defaults to true and automatically enlists the connection in the current thread's transaction context. Useful in distributed transaction scenarios.
Initial Catalog	Aliased to Database and specifies the name of the database. Maps to the read-only property `Database`. If the catalog isn't specified, the current database will be the default database assigned to the login.
Integrated Security	Aliased to Trusted_Connection and defaults to false. When true, it attempts to use the current thread's identity to authenticate against SQL Server. Valid values are SSPI, true, and yes. Supported on all network libraries.
Network Library	Aliased to Net and defaults to dbmssocn. Specifies the network library to use when connecting to SQL Server. You change this from the default of TCP/IP to a different library, such as IPX/SPX (dbmsspxn), Apple Talk (dbmsadsn), Named Pipes (dbnmpntw), Multiprotocol (dbmsrpcn), or Shared Memory (dbmsipcn), if the application is running on a non-TCP/IP network or must support special features such as encryption.
Packet Size	Mapped to the read-only property `PacketSize` and used to specify the size in bytes of the network packets used to communicate with the server. Defaults to 8192.
Password	Aliased to Pwd and specifies the password for the SQL Server login account to use. Not needed when using integrated security.
Persist Security Info	Defaults to false; when set to true, removes security information from the connection string when it is returned through the `ConnectionString` property if the connection has been successfully opened.
Use Procedure For Prepare	Determines whether SQL Server creates temporary stored procedures when `SqlCommand` objects are prepared using the `Prepare` property. Defaults to 1 (true).
User ID	The SQL Server login account to use. It doesn't need to be set when using integrated security.
Workstation ID	Defaults to the local computer name and can be viewed in the SQL Profiler to assist in debugging and tracing. Maps to the read-only `WorkstationId` property.

9

Using the attributes shown in Table 9.1, a typical connection string for SQL Server might look like the following:

```
String _connect = "server=ssosa;Initial Catalog=ComputeBooks;Enlist=false;"
_connect += "Integrated Security=yes;Application Name='ComputeBooks Web';"
```

In this case, the database server is identified as the server called ssosa and the database to use is called ComputeBooks. Enlist has been set to false as a small performance enhancement because, in this case, the connection string won't be used for connections that participate in distributed transactions (transactions across data sources). The connection will use integrated security, which means that SQL Server will try to match the identity information for the current thread with Windows accounts (users and groups) defined as valid SQL Server logins. Figure 9.1 shows a screenshot of the SQL Profiler after a stored procedure has been executed with this connection.

FIGURE 9.1

SQL Profiler. This utility is useful for debugging code written with the SqlClient provider.

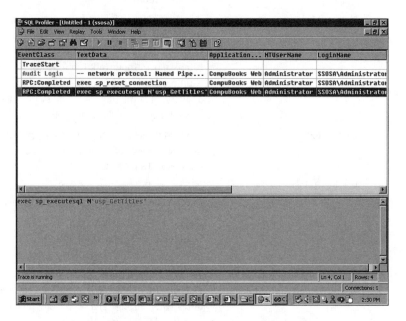

You'll notice in Figure 9.1 that the connection was made using the Named Pipes network library and then the sp_reset_connection followed by the usp_GetTitles stored procedures were executed. Even though TCP/IP is the default network library, in this instance, the server supported connections only over Named Pipes, so SqlClient used Named Pipes. Note also that the Application Name is viewable in the Profiler as is the LoginName that in this case maps to a Windows account.

Note Even if the Network Library attribute is set explicitly, the SqlClient provider can still connect using one of the other network libraries if the server isn't listening using the one specified.

Note that if standard SQL Server security were used, the User Id and Password attributes (unless the password was blank) would have had to be specified in the connection string. In addition, by default the Password wouldn't have been returned in the ConnectionString property after the connection had been successfully opened. Setting the Persist Security Info property to true would persist the Password in the connection string.

Specifying Connection Strings with OleDb

The connection string used with the OleDb provider is similar in many respects, although only the Provider attribute is required (unless a UDL file is used, as I'll discuss later). This attribute points to the OLE DB provider that will be used to connect to the data store.

Note In this initial release, the provider doesn't support OLE DB 2.5 interfaces. Unfortunately, this means that OLE DB providers such as the Microsoft Exchange provider (ExOLEDB) can't be used with the OLE DB .NET Data Provider. However, you can use any OLE DB provider that doesn't use those interfaces that you have installed on your system with the exception of the OLE DB Provider for ODBC drivers (MSDASQL). To connect to ODBC drivers, you must use the ODBC .NET Data Provider that is downloadable from MSDN. The provider also requires MDAC 2.6 or higher, which is installed along with Visual Studio .NET.

If the provider attribute is not set, an ArgumentException will be thrown immediately after setting the ConnectionString property as it is parsed. All other attributes are determined by the provider itself.

Tip You can, of course, determine what attributes a particular provider needs by creating a new data connection using the server explorer. As you learned on Day 2, "Getting Started," a dialog will be presented, allowing you to fill in the properties. You can then inspect the completed ConnectString property by clicking on the connection and viewing the Properties window.

So, for example, the following code snippet would successfully open a connection against SQL Server using the SQL Server OLE DB provider (SQLOLEDB):

```
OleDbConnection con = new OleDbConnection(
"Provider=sqloledb;server=ssosa;database=computebooks;trusted_connection=yes");
con.Open();
```

Typically, providers at least support the Data Source property, so connection strings like the following shown in the online documentation could be used to connect to a Jet or Oracle database:

```
Provider=MSDAORA; Data Source=ORACLE8i7; User ID=scott; Password=tiger
Provider=Microsoft.Jet.OLEDB.4.0; Data Source=c:\bin\LocalAccess40.mdb
```

As with SqlClient, you could also use the Persist Security Info attribute (initially set to false) to persist the password in the `ConnectionString` property. And as with SqlClient, the `ConnectionTimeout`, `Database`, `DataSource`, and `Provider` properties are all read-only properties that can be initially set in the connection string.

Finally, the `ConnectionString` property can alternatively point to a Microsoft Data Link file, also called a UDL file because of its .udl extension. Simply put, a UDL file is set up like an INI file that contains the connection string. UDL files can be easily created by creating a file with a .udl extension and then double-clicking it to invoke the Data Link Properties dialog. After it is built, the file can be referenced simply with the File Name attribute like so:

```
OleDbConnection con = new OleDbConnection(
  "File Name=c:\bin\myconnection.udl");
```

Unfortunately, when you use a UDL file like this, the file must be accessed and parsed each time the connection is opened, resulting in less than optimal performance. As a result, although UDL files provide an easy means of managing connection strings, they aren't recommended.

Storing Connection Strings

After the connection string is specified, it should be securely stored somewhere rather than hard-coded directly in the application. Obviously, storing the connection string enables you to more easily change it as you move from development to test to production. Although there are obviously plenty of options, the second part of this section focuses on the two most common scenarios where connection strings may be stored.

Storing Connection Strings for Serviced Components

 As you'll learn about in more detail on Day 17, "ADO.NET in the Data Services Tier," a **serviced component** is one that is derived from the `ServicedComponent` class of the `System.EnterpriseServices` namespace. As a result, a serviced component can access the run-time services provided by COM+ (Component Services) such as just-in-time (JIT) activation, distributed transactions, object pooling, loosely coupled events, and queued components, among others.

> **Note**
>
> See Chapter 9 of my book *Building Distributed Applications with Visual Basic .NET*, published by Sams, for more information on serviced components and Component Services and .NET.

Related to connection strings, the most interesting aspect of COM+ is its object construction feature. In a nutshell, object construction is analogous to specifying command-line parameters for a COM+ component. In other words, you can declaratively specify a string that will be passed into the component when it's instantiated by COM+. The way this works is that the COM+ runtime tests for the presence of an interface called `IObjectConstruct` when the component is instantiated. If the interface is found, it calls its `Construct` method and passes in the string. The `IObjectConstruct` interface is a COM interface and is implemented by the `ServicedComponent` class, which then exposes its `Construct` method as a protected virtual (`Overridable` in VB .NET) method. This allows classes derived from `ServicedComponent` to simply override the method to catch the construction string. Listing 9.2 shows an example of a serviced component class that contains the bare minimum to use object construction.

LISTING 9.2   Using object construction. This class uses object construction by overriding the `Construct` method and enabling it through the `ConstructionEnabled` attribute.

```
using System.EnterpriseServices;

namespace ComputeBooks.Data
{
    [ConstructionEnabled(
     Default="server=ssosa;Initial
Catalog=computebooks;trusted_connection=yes")]
    public class ComputeBooksStore : ServicedComponent
    {
        private string _connect;
```

LISTING 9.2   continued

```
public string ConstructString
{ //returns the connection string
    get
    {
        return _connect;
    }
}

protected  override void Construct(string s)
{
    // called each time an instance of this class is created
    _connect = s;
}

// other methods here
    }
}
```

 You'll notice in Listing 9.2 that the `ComputeBooksStore` class is derived from
`ServicedComponent` and that it contains a private string called `_connect`. This
private variable is assigned the string passed into the overridden `Construct` method. The
connection string is then made available to descendant classes or clients through the public read-only `ConstructString` property.

You'll also notice that the class is decorated with the `ConstructionEnabled` attribute.
The presence of this attribute enables object construction when the serviced component
is registered in a COM+ application. The `Default` property specifies the default construction string that will be used if it's not overridden in the Component Services administrative user interface. Of course, both enabling construction and setting the construction
string can be performed administratively by right-clicking on the component in the
Component Services snap-in (found in the Administrative Tools group) and selecting
Properties. The construction settings can be found on the Activation tab.

> **Note**   Object construction applies to an entire component (that is, a class in .NET).
> This implies that all methods in the class will use the same connection
> string—a point you'll need to consider when designing your classes.

Because object construction is a service that you might want to implement in many serviced component classes, it makes sense to include it in a base class. On Day 17, you'll
take a look at an abstract base class that abstracts features such as object construction
and pooling for serviced components.

COM+ 1.5 and Aliasing

NEW TERM At first, it might seem as if object construction is limiting because all instances of the component, regardless of the process from which they are constructed, will receive exactly the same connection string. This might not be ideal if you'd like different applications to use the same component but interact with different databases by using different connection strings. Although this can't be done in Windows 2000, Windows .NET Server COM+ 1.5 implements a feature called **component aliasing**. Basically, this feature allows a single implementation of a component to be referenced by more than one name in the same or a different COM+ application. By simply aliasing the component into a different application, you can enable construction for the component on the Activation tab, thereby passing in a unique connection string when the component is instantiated.

Storing Connection Strings for ASP.NET Applications

Of course, object construction is an option only if your components are serviced components running in COM+. In many cases, your components that use providers will be accessed directly from ASP.NET pages or from classes instantiated by ASP.NET pages. In these cases, it makes sense to place the connection string with the other configuration information for the application.

Each ASP.NET application includes a file called Web.config in its virtual directory. This file is a simple XML file that contains settings that allow the ASP.NET runtime to make decisions about how the request is to be processed. Basically, it extends the default processing instructions stored in the Machine.config file found in the .NET Framework installation directory. Examples of the information included in Web.config include the authorization and impersonation scheme to use, which class (referred to as an HTTP Handler) will handle the request, and whether the request should be processed by an HTTP module.

In addition to the processing instructions, the Web.config file can contain an element called appSettings into which you can place application-specific information in name-value pairs using an add element, as shown in Listing 9.3.

LISTING 9.3   Storing a connection string. This Web.config file uses the appSettings element to store the connection string.

```
<?xml version="1.0" encoding="utf-8" ?>
<configuration>
  <appSettings>
    <add key="SQLConnect" value="data source=ssosa;
    initial catalog=ComputeBooks;user id=user;pooling=true" />
  </appSettings>
</configuration>
```

In Listing 9.3, the appSettings collection contains one element, called SQLConnect, which contains the connection string. A class in your application can then access this value using the static (Shared in VB .NET) AppSettings property of the ConfigurationSettings class like so:

```
using System.Configuration;

protected void cmdLogin_Click(System.Object sender, _
  System.EventArgs e);
{
   ComputeBooksStore store = new ComputeBooksStore(
     ConfigurationSettings.AppSettings["SQLConnect"].ToString());
}
```

In this case, you'll notice from the using statement that the ConfigurationSettings class can be found in the System.Configuration namespace. The particular name-value pair is then accessed by passing the key value (or the index) to the AppSettings property, which exposes a NameValueCollection object that stores the data as a sorted collection of strings. The ComputeBooksStore class then accepts the connection string through its constructor as shown in Listing 9.4.

LISTING 9.4   Accepting a connection string. This class accepts the connection string in its constructor.

```
public class ComputeBooksStore
{
    private string _connect;

    public string ConnectString
    { //returns the connection string
       get
       {
           return _connect;
         }
    }

    public ComputeBooksStores(string connect)
    {
        _connect = connect;
    }

    // other methods here
}
```

> **Tip** Although it might seem attractive to do so, you can't use a constructor that accepts connection strings with serviced components. Because COM+ doesn't support parameterized construction, serviced components must expose an empty (default) constructor.

To more generically retrieve configuration information, you can use the static `GetConfig` method of either the `ConfigurationSettings` class or the `HttpContext` class as exposed through the `Context` property of the ASP.NET `Page` class like so:

```
System.Object o = Context.GetConfig("appSettings");
ComputeBooksStore store = new ComputeBooksStore(o["SQLConnect"].ToString());
```

> **Note** Because configuration files are encoded as XML, they are case sensitive. In the previous example, passing the value of `"AppSettings"` rather than `"appSettings"` would result in an unhandled exception.

Although each directory in an ASP.NET application can contain its own Web.config file, the files are processed hierarchically. Therefore, as long as the Web.config file in the root directory of the site contains the `appSettings` element, code in any subdirectories of the site will be able to access it.

This configuration system is, of course, also available to other .NET applications, such as Windows Forms applications. These applications can include their own configuration file, named *appname*.exe.config, in the application directory. The runtime will refer to it when the application is loaded. It can contain the same `appSettings` element in the root `configuration` element, as shown previously.

Pooling Connections

In enterprise applications, it is particularly important to pay attention to issues that influence the scalability of your application. One of the primary issues involved is the handling of connections. This is because connections are generally a limited resource that consumes overhead on the data store. For some time, the idea of connection pooling has been used to achieve scalability by allowing an application thread to free a connection as soon as it is done using it and returning it to a pool of connections that other threads in the same or a different process may use. The overall result is that fewer connections need to be maintained by the data store. In other words, the ratio of connections to users is less than 1 to 1.

Note

In classic ADO, pooling database connections was handled either through the session pooling mechanism of OLE DB or by the connection pooling code implemented by the ODBC Driver manager when using the MSDASQL provider.

In this section, you'll learn how the SqlClient and OleDb providers handle pooling connections to allow applications to scale without consuming precious server resources.

Connection Pooling with SqlClient

Because the SqlClient provider communicates directly with SQL Server, it can't take advantage of OLE DB's connection pooling scheme. Therefore, SqlClient must implement its own connection pooling. It does this by relying on Component Services. As previously mentioned, Component Services supports object pooling. This mechanism allows a predefined number of instantiated object instances to be hosted in a COM+-managed pool. If an object instance is available, one is handed out to a client application when it requests a new instance, and subsequently returned to the pool when dereferenced for use by another client. This scheme allows clients to reuse objects that are expensive to create, thereby reducing the resources required on the server. SqlConnection is therefore a good candidate for a pooled component.

To support creating and configuring a connection pool, several additional attributes are included in the ConnectionString for SqlConnection, as shown in Table 9.2.

TABLE 9.2 SqlClient connection pooling attributes. This table lists the attributes you can use in the connection string when using connection pooling.

Attribute	Description
Connection Lifetime	Checked when a connection is returned to the pool and its creation time is compared to the current time. If the difference exceeds this value, the connection is destroyed. Used to force connections to be recycled periodically. Defaults to 0, which keeps the connection alive until the process ends.
Connection Reset	Defaults to true and specifies whether the connection's state is reset before it's pulled from the pool. Incurs an extra roundtrip to the server, but could be dangerous when set to false.
Max Pool Size	The maximum number of connections allowed in the pool. Defaults to 100.

TABLE 9.2 continued

Attribute	Description
Min Pool Size	The minimum number of connections allowed in the pool. The documentation states that the default is 0; however, tests indicate that two connections are created for each pool by default.
Pooling	Determines whether pooling is enabled. Defaults to true.

As you can see from Table 9.2, the Pooling attribute is by default set to true, so connections will be pooled automatically. In addition, the Connection Reset attribute is also set to true, which results in the `sp_reset_connection` stored procedure being executed on the connection before it is used by subsequent clients. As you might expect, a small performance benefit will be realized if you set Connection Reset to false because it removes the extra roundtrip to the server. However, the state of the connection won't be reset, so database context changes and other SET statements executed by a previous client would still be enforced for a new client, possibly leading to corrupted data. A typical connection string that utilizes pooling might then look like the following:

```
Server=ssosa;Initial Catalog=ComputeBooks;Pooling=true;
 Connection Reset=false;Enlist=true;Min Pool Size=5;trusted_connection=yes;
```

Of course, in order for connections to be pooled, they must be the same. In fact, the connections are pooled per application domain based on the distinct text of the connection string. In other words, any difference at all (including spacing and capitalization) will result in two different pools being created. Obviously, the ideal situation is to pull the connection strings from a central source, as discussed previously, in order to ensure that they are added to the pool. Connections are also pooled based on their transaction context if the Enlist attribute is set to true. This allows components running in the same distributed transaction to pull connections from the pool that have access to the transaction.

Each time a new connection is opened with the Pooling attribute set to true, a new pool is created that contains the connection. If the Min Pool Size attribute is also specified, the appropriate number of additional connections are created and added to the pool.

> **Note**
>
> SqlClient also exposes five performance counters that you can view using the Performance Monitor utility found in the Administrative Tools group. These enable you to view both the current number of connections SqlClient has initiated and the current number pooled.

A second issue to consider is the security context of the pooled connections. Because these connections will be shared by more than one thread, which will likely map to more than one user, as in the case of ASP.NET applications, you'll want to make sure that the connections are made with a shared security context. When using SQL Server standard security, this means creating an account that has the appropriate permissions to the database or databases accessed by the components. When using a trusted connection, this means giving permissions to the Windows account under which the thread is running.

New Term   In the case of ASP.NET applications that use trusted connections, you would, of course, want all the threads doing work on behalf of users to be authenticated to SQL Server using the same account. This can be accomplished by using **impersonation** in ASP.NET. Simply put, impersonation allows the ASP.NET worker threads to run under the identity of an account specified in the Web.config file's identity element like so:

```
<identity impersonate="true" />
```

If a name and password are provided, they will be used in preference to the token passed to ASP.NET from IIS. In this way, you can specify any Windows account and give that account permissions in SQL Server.

As you might be aware, IIS will pass either the IUSR_*machinename* token when using anonymous authentication or the token for the account specified by the client when using basic, digest, or Windows authentication. So, when using basic, digest, or Windows authentication, you want to make sure that you are impersonating a different account and not simply setting the impersonate attribute to true. Otherwise, each user would attempt to log on to SQL Server using the authenticated account as passed from IIS.

By default, however, impersonation is set to false, which means that ASP.NET code will run under the SYSTEM account used by the ASP.NET runtime process (aspnet_wp.exe). It's also possible to change the account under which aspnet_wp.exe executes for all ASP.NET applications on the server by changing the processModel element in the system.Web section of Machine.config as follows:

```
<system.web>
  <processModel enable="true" username="domain\user" password="pwd"/>
</system.web>
```

 Note   The username attribute can also be set to SYSTEM (the default) or MACHINE, which causes the ASP.NET runtime process to run under a special account called ASPNET, which is created when ASP.NET is installed on the server. In both cases, the password must be set to AutoGenerate.

In the case of serviced components, using a trusted connection means that the identity of the thread executing the component will be used to create the connection. In serviced components whose COM+ application is marked as Library (using the administrative interface or the `ApplicationActivation` attribute), this will be the thread that created the component. However, for COM+ applications marked as Server, you can configure the account used to run the components in the application in a separate DLLHOST.exe process.

As you probably guessed, because SqlClient is handling the pooling, the client code simply needs to call the `Close` method of the `SqlConnection` object in order to return the connection to the pool. The programming pattern then is one where the method opens and closes a connection with each invocation, rather than having the class hold on to an open connection. Of course, behind the scenes, the connection will be pulled from the pool and returned to it, thereby increasing performance and reducing the number of connections required.

> **Tip**
>
> Remember that the `SqlDataAdapter` implicitly opens and closes connections and so works well in this context.

To programmatically remove a connection from the pool, you simply need to call the `SqlConnection` object's `Dispose` method. Finally, by default, the pooled `SqlConnection` objects are not destroyed until the process that created them ends or the connection is somehow broken (noticed by the pooler when the connection is actually used).

Connection Pooling with OleDb

 The scheme for pooling connections is different when using OleDb than when using SqlClient in that the support for pooling is provided by the OLE DB infrastructure (introduced in OLE DB 2.0), and is then made available to all OLE DB providers. This feature is referred to as OLE DB **session pooling** (or sometimes as **resource pooling**).

The idea in session pooling is that, if enabled, OLE DB creates separate pools for each distinct set of connection attributes and transactions contexts used by the process. This creates less contention during the process of locking and finding connections to assign. In addition, an index is maintained on the pools in each process and makes finding the correct pool more efficient (rather than having to traverse each pool). In session pooling, if a connection in the pool hasn't been used for 60 seconds, it will be closed and

removed from the pool. This value is configurable by modifying the registry, although
OleDb has no connection string attribute equivalent to the Connection Lifetime attribute
of SqlClient to enable connection recycling. Also, in the event a connection becomes
unresponsive, OLE DB will requery the data source at intervals of 5, 10, and 50 seconds
before giving up and destroying the connection.

To enable session pooling for a particular OLE DB provider on a machine-wide basis,
you must edit the system registry. To enable session pooling, you must add a DWORD value
of OLEDB_SERVICES to the HKEY_CLASSES_ROOT\CLSID*provider* key, in which
provider is the COM class identifier for the OLE DB provider, such as SQLOLEDB or
MSDAORA. By setting this value to 0xffffffff, all OLE DB services will be enabled,
one of which is session pooling. Session pooling can be disabled by setting this value to
0xfffffffe, and all services except session pooling and automatic transaction enlistment
can be disabled by using 0xfffffffc.

You can also enable or disable session pooling on a per-connection basis by adding OLE
DB SERVICES=-1 to enable all service, OLE DB SERVICES=-2 to disable pooling, or
OLE_DB_SERVICES=-4 to disable pooling and automatic transaction enlistment in the connect string. The latter is the equivalent of setting the Pooling and Enlist attributes to false
in a SqlClient connection string. The result might be a connection code like the following:

```
OleDbConnection con = new OleDbConnection(
  "Provider=MSDAORA;OLE_DB_SERVICES=-4;Data Source=ORACLE8i7;
 User ID=scott;Password=tiger");
con.Open();
```

In this case, pooling and transaction enlistment will be disabled.

Using Transactions

As shown in Figure 8.1, providers can support transactions that implement the
IDbTransaction interface and that are associated to the connection class. Both the
SqlClient and OleDb providers include transaction objects that are created using the
BeginTransaction method of the appropriate connection class. Transactions are obviously very useful for making sure that multiple commands (statements) executed against
a single data store are treated as a logical unit of work. In that way, if one of the statements fails, all of them can be rolled back (undone). Likewise, if all of them succeed,
they will all be committed (made permanent) on the data store.

9

Note

As you'll see momentarily, using transactions necessarily implies that the data store needs to lock data while the transaction is active. As a result, you'll want to make sure that your transactions are short-lived, always are either committed or rolled back, and lock only the data they need to. Failing to complete a transaction will cause the locks to remain and possibly prevent other users from accessing the data.

In general, if no transaction has been created, commands executed against a data store operate as a series of implicit transactions. In other words, the scope of the transaction is limited to single statements that make up the command. An example is an `OleDbCommand` object that executes a stored procedure using the `ExecuteNonQuery` method that both inserts a row and then deletes a different row from a table. Without any explicit transaction control, each statement (even if it is contained in a stored procedure) is treated as an implicit transaction. If the insert succeeds and the delete fails, the insert is still persisted to the data store. Of course, stored procedures and other database objects could contain specific transactional statements that control how the transaction occurs. The use of a transaction object in ADO.NET ensures that you can use explicit transactions to control how and when commits and rollbacks occur.

Note

As you'll learn on Day 12, transactions can also be used with data adapters to ensure that either all the changes to a `DataSet` are successfully synchronized with the data store or are rolled back. However, note that each of the command objects associated with the data adapter (`SelectCommand`, `InsertCommand`, `UpdateCommand`, and `DeleteCommand`) must have its `Transaction` property set to the instance of the transaction created with the `BeginTransaction`.

Transactions with SqlClient

To use explicit transactions with SQL Server, you can call the `BeginTransaction` method of the `SqlConnection` class. This method creates the `SqlTransaction` object, which can then be manipulated using its methods. The `BeginTransaction` method is overloaded to accept various combinations of the isolation level and transaction name (a string used to refer to the transaction). However, the `BeginTransaction` method can't be called unless the connection has been opened. This is because it immediately sets the isolation level and issues a Transact-SQL `BEGIN TRANSACTION` statement against the server. Calling `BeginTransaction` on a closed connection results in an

InvalidOperationException. In addition, closing a connection with a pending transaction will automatically issue a ROLLBACK TRANSACTION statement. As a result, the typical pattern for using transactions is shown in Listing 9.5.

LISTING 9.5   Using transactions. This partial method shows how transactions are typically used.

```
SqlConnection con = new SqlConnection(_connect);
SqlTransaction trans;

try
{
    con.Open();
    trans = con.BeginTransaction();
    try
    {
        // do other work here
        // all is well
        trans.Commit();
    }
    catch (SqlException e)
    {
        // log the error
        trans.Rollback();
    }
}
catch (SqlException e)
{
    // connection failed
    // log error
    return;
}
finally
{
    con.Close();
}
```

ANALYSIS   In this snippet, the connection is instantiated with a connection string and the transaction object is declared but not created. After the connection is open, the BeginTransaction method is called. Note that this work is placed in its own try catch block to ensure that the transaction can be initiated once the connection is opened. In the nested try catch block, the actual work would be performed and the transaction's Commit method called if it succeeded. The catch block is used to handle any SQL Server errors and call the Rollback method if one is encountered. As you might imagine, the Commit method executes the Transact-SQL COMMIT TRANSACTION statement while the Rollback method executes the ROLLBACK TRANSACTION method.

As noted previously, the `BeginTransaction` method accepts an argument in its constructor that specifies the isolation level in which the transaction should run using the `IsolationLevel` enumeration. By default, SQL Server operates in `ReadCommitted` mode, which means that the transaction can read only data that has been committed on the server. In addition, share locks are placed on the data only while it is being read. This ensures that transactions are isolated and not able to read data that could in fact end up being rolled back.

However, it doesn't ensure that if the transaction attempts to read the same data twice, that it will receive the same results. As a result, `ReadCommitted` is a compromise between transactions that lock the range of rows they read or modify (`Serializable`) and those that don't lock anything (`ReadUncommitted`). There are obviously scenarios where each of the options makes sense. Generally, the higher the isolation level, the less concurrency your application will support. This is the case because a higher isolation level necessarily means that more locks will be placed on the data, thereby increasing lock contention and allowing fewer users to read or write to the database at one time. To use an isolation level other than the default, you could, for example, use a statement like the following:

```
trans = con.BeginTransaction(IsolationLevel.ReadUncommitted);
```

Tip

> Using `ReadUncommitted` is particularly effective for applications that simply need to build quick reports (sometimes referred to as *flash reports*) on the status of a database that is used for an OLTP application. Reading the data without applying any locks is both very fast and won't interfere with the locking that the OLTP application has to do.

NEW TERM Transactions in SQL Server also support the concept of **save points**. Basically, a save point is a marker or point in the transaction that can be rolled back to. In other words, if you use a save point, you can roll back only to the save point and not the entire transaction. `SqlTransaction` supports save points by exposing a `Save` method that accepts the name of the save point to create. The `Save` method issues a `SAVE TRANSACTION` statement against the server. At some point later, you can execute the transaction's `Rollback` method and pass it the name of the save point. This results in all the work from the save point to the point at which `Rollback` was called to be undone. Although this is handy, keep in mind that any locks created after the save point will still be held until the entire transaction is either committed or rolled back.

Finally, SQL Server supports the idea of nested transactions. Although you can't nest transactions by calling the `BeginTransaction` method on the same connection more than once, you can execute commands or call stored procedures that issue their own `BEGIN`,

COMMIT, SAVE, and ROLLBACK TRANSACTION Transact-SQL statements after you have
called BeginTransaction. SQL Server allows this to occur; however, the actual work of
the transaction and any of its nested transactions is not actually committed until the outermost transaction is committed when you call the Commit method of the
SqlTransaction object. If an inner transaction is rolled back, all the nested transactions
and the outermost transaction are rolled back. This feature of SQL Server is present primarily to support calling stored procedures that contain their own transaction statements.

Note

> Experienced developers might be wondering why the programming model
> for transaction seems a little strange. For example, why doesn't the
> SqlConnection class simply expose begin, commit, save, and rollback meth-
> ods instead of using a second object? The reason is that this model can be
> used to support the parallel transaction feature of the next release of SQL
> Server. In parallel transactions, a connection could spawn multiple transac-
> tions and so the BeginTransaction method could be called more than once.

Transactions with OleDb

Just as in the SqlClient provider, the OleDb provider includes an OleDbTransaction
class that represents a transaction on the data store communicated with by the
OleDbConnection class. The programming model is identical: New transactions are created by calling the BeginTransaction method and are then committed or rolled back
using the methods of OleDbTransaction. The only method that SqlTransaction supports that OleDbTransaction does not is the Save method. This is because most
providers don't support the concept of save points.

Transactions in Serviced Components

NEW TERM   The use of the BeginTransaction method with the connection object is a means
           of using explicit local transactions directly in ADO.NET. A **local transaction** is
one whose scope is restricted to a single database server. However, the classes you write
in .NET can also participate in distributed transactions by using the services provided by
COM+ (Component Services). A **distributed transaction** is one that spans multiple data
sources and even sources of different types. For example, a distributed transaction can
coordinate modifications to an Oracle database, a SQL Server database, and a Microsoft
Message Queue (MSMQ) server and ensure that if all the modifications succeed, all will
be committed. However, if one of the changes fails, all will be rolled back. This is done
using a two-phase commit protocol and the Microsoft Distributed Transaction
Coordinator (MSDTC) service that runs on Windows servers. The MSDTC serviced is a
Transaction Processing (TP) monitor. Typically, distributed transactions are used in
enterprise-scale applications that work with multiple data stores.

Code written with both the SqlClient and OleDb providers can participate in distributed transactions; however, their respective transaction classes aren't used. Instead, as mentioned previously, your .NET class that will participate in the transaction must be a serviced component. A serviced component is a class that is derived from `System.EnterpriseServices.ServicedComponent`, which allows the class to utilize the services of COM+, one of which is distributed transactions. After you have derived from `ServicedComponent`, you use attributes to indicate that your class supports or requires transactions. Finally, the methods in your class must then indicate when the transaction is complete or needs to be rolled back. The `ComputeBooksStore` serviced component from Listing 9.2 has been modified to use distributed transactions as shown in Listing 9.6.

9

 Note

In order for the OleDb .NET Data Provider to participate in transactions, the data store you are connecting to must support the X/Open transaction-processing model. In other words, the underlying OLE DB provider must understand certain commands from the MSDTC service.

LISTING 9.6 Using distributed transactions. This serviced component requires transactions.

```
namespace ComputeBooks.Data
{
    [ConstructionEnabled(
      Default="server=ssosa;Initial Catalog=compubooks;trusted_security=yes"),
    Transactions(TransactionOption.Required)]
    public class ComputeBooksStores : ServicedComponent
    {
        private string _connect;

        public string ConstructString
        { //returns the connection string
            get
            {
                return _connect;
            }
        }

        protected  override void Construct(string s)
        {
            // called each time an instance of this class is created
            _connect = s;
        }

        public ComputeBooksStores(string connect)
        {
```

LISTING 9.6   continued

```
            _connect = connect;
        }

        // other methods here
        public void SaveStore(Object parms[])
        {
            try
            {
                // open a connection
                // use the parms to execute a command with ExecuteNonQuery
                ContextUtil.SetComplete();
            }
            catch (Exception e)
            {
                ContextUtil.SetAbort();
                // throw an exception
            }

        }
    }
}
```

 ANALYSIS   In Listing 9.6, you'll notice that the class has now been decorated with the
TransactionAttribute and, in this case, set to the Required value of the
TransactionOption enumeration. By setting this attribute, you ensure that when any
method of the class is called, a distributed transaction (either an existing one or a new
one) will be created. Other values of TransactionOption include Disabled,
NotSupported, Supports, and RequiresNew. As you can imagine, using Disabled or
NotSupported will in no circumstances allow this class to participate in a distributed
transaction. Using Supports indicates that if a transaction already exists, the methods of
this class will participate. However, a new transaction will not be created. Using
RequiresNew will always create a new transaction for this class.

Note

As you can see, this model supports the idea that individual classes needn't
know nor be concerned with the transactional behavior of other classes. This
means that transactional components can be loosely coupled, which increases the maintainability and extensibility of your applications.

The second aspect of Listing 9.6 to notice is the SaveStore method. This method includes calls to the SetComplete and SetAbort static methods of the ContextUtil class. The ContextUtil class is found in System.EnterpriseServices and exposes methods and properties that serviced components can use to control how they interact with the COM+ runtime. In this case, calling SetComplete when the method is successful indicates that the component's vote in the transaction is to commit. Calling SetAbort indicates that the transaction should be aborted. If all other components participating in the transaction also vote to commit, the MSDTC service will commit them. If any one of the components votes to abort, all will be rolled back. In addition to voting on the transaction, SetComplete and SetAbort also tell the COM+ runtime to deactivate the object instance after the method has returned. If you do not want to deactivate the object, you could alternatively call EnableCommit and DisableCommit.

Rather than having to call the SetComplete and SetAbort methods directly, you can alternatively decorate each method with AutoCompleteAttribute. This attribute indicates that if the method terminates normally, SetComplete will be called automatically. Conversely, if an exception is thrown, SetAbort will be called.

As indicated previously, connections are associated with a particular transaction context. If pooling is enabled when the SaveStore method calls the Open method of the connection, a connection is pulled from the pool with the appropriate transaction context.

Summary

Today you learned how to create and manage connections and transactions using both the SqlClient and OleDb providers. Along the way, you learned how to handle connection events, specify and store connection strings, and manage both local and distributed transactions.

Now that you're intimately familiar with connections and transactions, you can begin to use the connections to execute commands against a data store. Tomorrow you'll take a look at how the command objects work, particularly how to specify and execute commands.

Workshop

This workshop will help reinforce the concepts covered in today's lesson.

Quiz

1. When would you want to catch the InfoMessage event of a connection object?

   The InfoMessage event is fired when the data store returns non–result set information. Typically, this includes warnings, row counts, and other supplementary information. You use InfoMessage if you need to catch this information; for example, when a SQL Server stored procedure returns information using a PRINT statement.

2. Where might you store connection strings and why?

   Because connection strings often change and because they may contain security information, they should be stored in a safe place that can be modified without recompiling your application. For ASP.NET applications, a good place is in the Web.config file in the appSettings element. From there it can be programmatically read. Other .NET applications can use the same strategy in their own configuration files. For serviced components, you can take advantage of object construction and store the connection string in the Component Services snap-in.

3. How can you ensure that your application uses connection pooling?

   First, make sure that Pooling is set to true when using SqlClient or that OLE DB session pooling is enabled when using OleDb. Second, make sure that the connection strings used by the application are identical in every way. Finally, make sure that the security context used by the connection strings is the same; for example, when you're using trusted connections with SQL Server.

4. How can you make sure that two command objects participate in the same logical unit of work?

   Both command objects must have their Transaction property set to the same transaction object. In addition, the transaction must have been created using the BeginTransaction method of the connection objects they will both use.

Exercise

Today write a method that executes two statements against the ComputeBooks database that participate in the same transaction.

Answers for Day 9

Exercise Answer

One possible solution to today's exercise is the following method, which deletes a particular order from both the OrderDetails and Orders tables:

```csharp
virtual void DeleteOrder(String orderId)
{
    SqlConnection con = new SqlConnection(_connect);
    SqlTransaction trans;

    try
    {
        con.Open();
        trans = con.BeginTransaction();
        try
        {
            SqlCommand s1 = new SqlCommand(
                "DELETE FROM OrderDetails WHERE OrderID ='" + orderId + "'",
                con,trans);
            SqlCommand s2 = new SqlCommand(
                "DELETE FROM Orders WHERE OrderID ='" + orderId + "'",
                con,trans);

            s1.ExecuteNonQuery();
            s2.ExecuteNonQuery();
            // all is well
            trans.Commit();
        }
        catch (SqlException e)
        {
            // log the error
            trans.Rollback();
        }
    }
    catch (SqlException e)
    {
        // connection failed
        // log error
        return;
    }
    finally
    {
        con.Close();
    }
}
```

9

DAY **10**

Using Commands

The command object, which inherits from the IDbCommand interface, is perhaps the heart of a .NET data provider. Command objects encapsulate the SQL– or data store–specific syntax that is executed through a connection object. In ADO.NET, command objects are used to feed data readers, populate and synchronize DataSet objects, and execute commands that don't return result sets to the client. Commands can also be populated with parameters to enable dynamic execution.

Today you'll learn about all aspects of command objects and how they work in both the SqlClient and OleDb providers. Specifically, we'll cover the following concepts:

- How to call stored procedures and inline SQL using commands
- How to use the various execute methods to return different types of results through a command
- How to modify data using commands
- How to pass input parameters to a command and return output parameters and return values

Using Command Objects

To use a command object, you must first instantiate it. The constructor of command objects is generally overloaded and can accept the statement to execute (`CommandText`), the connection through which the command should be executed (`Connection`), and the transaction to associate with the connection (`Transaction`). Keep in mind that, as you learned yesterday, if the connection object has had its `BeginTransaction` method called, you must populate the `Transaction` property of the command or an `InvalidOperationException` will be thrown. For example, a command will typically be instantiated as follows:

```
Dim con As New OleDbConnection( _
  "Provider=Microsoft.Jet.OLEDB.4.0; Data Source=nwind.mdb")
Dim com As New OleDbCommand("Products", con)
com.CommandType = CommandType.TableDirect
```

In this case, the `OleDbCommand` object's constructor is passed the name of a table in the database as well as the `OleDbConnection` object to use.

When you populate the `CommandText` property, it can be set to any valid command syntax supported by the provider or data store. Examples include SQL statements, names of stored procedures, names of tables, or simply executable commands in the language of the data store. Typically, of course, the commands take the form of stored procedures, SQL statements, or table names. The type of command is specified using the `CommandType` property and enumeration and can be set to the value `StoredProcedure`, `Text`, or `TableDirect`. Obviously, `StoredProcedure` is used when the data store supports procedures or functions on the server, as in SQL Server when `CommandText` is set to the name of a stored procedure or in Access (Jet) when it's set to the name of a query. The `Text` value of the `CommandType` enumeration is used when the command is simply a SQL statement or a data store–specific command. For example, you would use `Text` when the `CommandText` is populated with the text `SELECT * FROM Titles` or when it contains the Transact-SQL command `SET DEADLOCK PRIORITY`. In both cases, it's the responsibility of the data store or provider to parse the command. As shown in the previous code snippet, `CommandType` can also be set to `TableDirect`. This works when using the `OleDbCommand` object and instructs the provider to retrieve all the rows from the table. However, the `SqlCommand` object will throw an exception if a command is executed with the `CommandType` set to `TableDirect`.

Using Stored Procedures Versus Dynamic SQL

As you might have noticed, most of the examples in this book have relied on stored procedures to encapsulate the SQL used to insert, update, and delete data from the

ComputeBooks database. The reason for this is simple. Stored procedures offer abstraction, better performance, and increased security over using dynamic or inline SQL in the command object. For any data store that supports it, stored procedures are typically the recommended approach. The benefits of using stored procedures are outlined in the following list:

- **Abstraction.** By using stored procedures, you can abstract the SQL from the applications that consume it. This reduces complexity in the application and offers reusability across applications. In addition, developers more familiar with the workings of the particular data store can specialize in writing procedures that are optimized by making sure that they use proper indexes, for example. Simply put, stored procedures can be thought of as the data access API to your data store.

- **NEW TERM** **Performance.** In SQL Server 7.0 and 2000, stored procedures offer certain reuse of cached execution plans on the server. When a procedure or any statement is executed on the server, an execution plan is created and placed into the cache. For stored procedures, this execution plan will be reused with each invocation of the procedure until the SQL Server is restarted. Although the execution plans are also cached for dynamic SQL statements, the server must use a matching algorithm to attempt to match each incoming statement with a cached execution plan. This process, referred to as **auto-parameterization**, is efficient but not foolproof depending on how arguments are passed to the procedure. Therefore, it is recommended that you use sp_executesql on dynamically generated SQL statements if you must use them to ensure that the parameters can be discovered. In addition, stored procedures reduce network traffic because hundreds of bytes in a complicated SQL statement needn't be sent over the wire.

- **Security.** Because stored procedures offer a modular programming model, users can be granted permission to use them and denied permission to access the underlying tables and views. This allows administrators to ensure that the application can execute only the stored procedures it should be executing.

Of course, there are data stores that don't support stored procedures and cases in which it makes sense to write dynamic SQL. For example, if you're developing a packaged application that must work against several data stores that your clients might use, dynamic SQL makes sense. In these cases, you can certainly use dynamic SQL, even with parameters, as you'll learn later today.

10

Note However, even in this case, to access the data most efficiently, you'll want to explore ways of adding a layer of abstraction in order to use procedures where it makes sense. On Day 17, "ADO.NET in the Data Services Tier," you'll learn about the concept of *data factories* and how they can be used to abstract the SQL and the providers used for an application.

Retrieving Data

Command objects generally support two methods for retrieving data from the data store that are implemented in the IDbCommand interface: ExecuteReader and ExecuteScalar. In addition, providers such as SqlClient extend the functionality by including additional execute methods such as ExecuteXmlReader.

ExecuteReader

The ExecuteReader method is used to return an object that implements the IDataReader interface in order to provide streamed access to the data store. As you'll recall from Day 1, "ADO.NET in Perspective," streamed access is the second programming model, in addition to disconnected or cached access using the DataSet, that ADO.NET supports. After a data reader has been opened, its data is exposed as read-only and accessed in a loop as shown in Listing 10.1 (assuming that com is the command object shown in the previous snippet).

LISTING 10.1   Executing a data reader. This listing uses a command object to execute and traverse a data reader.

```
Dim rowData() As Object
Dim dr As OleDbDataReader

Try
  dr = com.ExecuteReader()

  Do While dr.Read
    dr.GetValues(rowData)
    ProcessRow(rowData)
  Loop

Catch e As OleDbException
  ' handle error
Finally
  If Not dr Is Nothing AndAlso Not dr.IsClosed Then dr.Close()
  con.Close()
End Try
```

ANALYSIS Although not shown in Listing 10.1, the connection associated with the command must have been opened before the `ExecuteReader` method is called; otherwise, an `InvalidOperationException` will result. (Only when using a data adapter is the connection opened and closed implicitly.) You'll notice in this snippet that the `OleDbDataReader` is actually instantiated by the `ExecuteReader` method and so doesn't need to be instantiated with the `New` operator. Once open, the data reader is traversed using the `Read` method, as you'll learn about in more detail tomorrow. After the data has been traversed, the `Finally` block ensures that the data reader is closed and then closes the connection.

Note
> The `Finally` block uses the new VB .NET short-circuited `AndAlso` operator. It's useful in this case because if dr is `Nothing`, the expression `Not dr.IsClosed` would throw an exception. This way, the expression after the `AndAlso` won't be evaluated if the data reader hasn't been created.

10

The `ExecuteReader` method is also overloaded to accept an argument from the `CommandBehavior` enumeration. This argument influences how the data reader behaves and gives hints as to how the provider might optimize the execution of the command. The enumeration includes the values shown in Table 10.1.

TABLE 10.1 Command behaviors. The `CommandBehavior` enumeration is used to allow the provider to optimize the command.

Value	Description
`CloseConnection`	Closes the connection object associated with the data reader when the data reader is closed.
`Default`	Same as not using a command behavior. Typically indicates that the data reader can return multiple result sets.
`KeyInfo`	The query returns column and primary key information and doesn't lock any rows on the data store.
`SchemaOnly`	The query returns column information only.
`SequentialAccess`	Allows large columns of binary data to be read as a stream using the `GetBytes` or `GetChars` method.
`SingleResult`	The query will return a single result set.
`SingleRow`	The query will return a single row for each result set.

As you can see, the command behaviors affect both how the result sets are processed by the provider and what information is returned from the data store. For example, the

SingleResult and SingleRow values typically have no effect on the data store but can be used by the provider to optimize the way in which the results are processed, thereby increasing performance. In fact, when using SingleRow, the OleDb provider binds to the result using the OLE DB IRow interface rather than the IRowset interface and exposes only a single row in the data reader. KeyInfo, SchemaOnly, and SequentialAccess, on the other hand, affect what information is returned by the data store and how that information is returned. Using SchemaOnly with the ExecuteReader method of the SqlCommand object prefixes the statement with the SET FMTONLY ON statement, which returns only column information and no rows. Using KeyInfo prefixes the SET NO_BROWSETABLE ON statement in order to return primary key information. We'll discuss the SequentialAccess value in more detail tomorrow because it affects how data is read using a data reader. You can also use more than one behavior in a bitwise combination because the enumeration supports the FlagsAttribute, as illustrated here:

```
dr = com.ExecuteReader(CommandBehavior.SingleResult Or CommandBehavior.KeyInfo)
```

Perhaps the most interesting of the values shown in Table 10.1 is CloseConnection. This behavior is particularly effective when you create methods that return data readers. This is the case because it allows the calling code to simply close the data reader, and the underlying connection will be closed automatically. Without this behavior, the calling code wouldn't have access to the connection object because it isn't exposed by the data reader. This is the key to writing data access and data factory classes that use data readers. This concept is illustrated in the following code snippets:

```
Public Function ReadTitles() As SqlDataReader
  ' create the connection and command
  return com.ExecuteReader(CommandBehavior.CloseConnection)
End Function
```

The client code can then simply close the data reader when finished, like so:

```
Try
  dr = ReadTitles()
  ' process the rows
Catch e As SqlException
  ' handle error
Finally
  If Not dr Is Nothing AndAlso Not dr.IsClosed Then dr.Close()
End Try
```

Note that unlike in the snippet shown previously, the Close method of the connection object isn't called because this code has no access to it. However, the connection will be closed and thereby released to the connection pool if pooling is enabled when the data reader is closed.

ExecuteScalar

As shown in Table 10.1, the `ExecuteReader` method can be passed the combination of the `SingleRow` and `SingleResult` behaviors in order to return only the first column of the first row from the result set. Command objects provide an easier way to do this using the `ExecuteScalar` method.

`ExecuteScalar` is effective for returning the results of a SQL statement that uses an aggregate, such as the `SUM`, `AVG`, `MIN`, `MAX`, and `COUNT` functions. For example, Listing 10.2 shows how `ExecuteScalar` could be used to return the average price of all titles in the ComputeBooks `Titles` table:

 Tip

> Although you can specify SQL statements or execute stored procedures that return multiple rows with `ExecuteScalar`, you wouldn't want to. Doing so increases the burden on the server when you're only going to use the first column of the first row. As a rule of thumb, your stored procedures or `SELECT` statements should ask only for data that the application will use.

10

LISTING 10.2   Using `ExecuteScalar`. This listing returns data from an aggregate function using the `ExecuteScalar` method.

```
Dim avgSql As String = "SELECT AVG(Price) FROM Titles"
Dim avgPrice As Decimal
Dim com As New SqlCommand(avgSql, con)

com.CommandType = CommandType.Text
Try
  con.Open()
  avgPrice = CType(com.ExecuteScalar, Decimal)
Catch e As SqlException
Finally
  con.Close()
End Try
```

ANALYSIS In this case, you'll notice that dynamic SQL is used to specify the `SELECT` statement. Just as with `ExecuteReader`, the connection must be opened before `ExecuteScalar` is called and must be explicitly closed in the `Finally` block. The `ExecuteScalar` method isn't overloaded and returns the value as a `System.Object`, so the `CType` function is used to cast the value to the appropriate type.

There are occasions when you might want to execute a command that returns multiple single-value, single-column results. Unfortunately, the `ExecuteScalar` method doesn't support this, so you would need to use a data reader as shown in Listing 10.3.

Listing 10.3 Returning multiple result sets. This listing shows how you would return more than one single-value, single-column result set using a data reader.

```
Dim sql As String
Dim avgPrice As Decimal
Dim orders As Integer
Dim dr As SqlDataReader

sql = "SELECT AVG(Price) FROM Titles;SELECT COUNT(*) FROM Orders"

Dim com As New SqlCommand(avgSql, con)
com.CommandType = CommandType.Text

dr = com.ExecuteReader()
dr.Read()
avgPrice = dr.GetDecimal(0)

If dr.NextResult() Then
  dr.Read()
  orders = dr.GetInteger(0)
End If
```

 Caution Although the documentation says otherwise, you can't use the `SingleRow` command behavior in this case against SQL Server using either SqlClient or OleDb. Doing so prevents the second result set from being read.

ExecuteXmlReader

The command object is an excellent place for providers to add their own functionality by extending the class to include custom execute functions that return data in a specific way. The SqlClient provider does this by including the `ExecuteXmlReader` function to return XML produced by the `FOR XML` statement that was introduced in SQL Server 2000.

Although a complete discussion of the `FOR XML` syntax is beyond the scope of this book, to use the statement, you simply append the `FOR XML` clause to a `SELECT` statement. SQL Server returns the results formatted as XML, based on the mode, which can be `RAW`, `AUTO`, or `EXPLICIT`. The syntax for a `SELECT` statement with a `FOR XML` clause looks like this:

```
SELECT ...
FROM ...
[WHERE]
FOR XML RAW | AUTO | EXPLICIT [,XMLDATA] [,ELEMENTS] [,BINARY Base64]
```

As you might expect, with FOR XML, you can easily transform a result set into XML. However, you can use the clause only in statements that return data directly to a client and therefore can be processed using the ExecuteXmlReader method. For example, you can't use FOR XML in view- or user-defined function (UDF) definitions, nested SELECT statements, stored procedures that manipulate the result set, INSERT statements, or statements that use a COMPUTE BY clause.

Using FOR XML

To give you a brief overview, the three modes of the FOR XML statement are

- **XML RAW**. XML RAW produces nonhierarchical, generic XML by generating one XML row element for each row that the query returns and mapping each returned column as an XML attribute. XML RAW is most useful when you have generic client code that expects flat XML documents and looks for row elements. Unlike XML AUTO, XML RAW supports the GROUP BY clause and aggregates. All the XML modes let you return the schema by using the XMLDATA argument after the FOR XML clause.

- **XML AUTO**. XML AUTO produces a hierarchical document by transforming into an element each table that the SELECT clause references. By default, XML AUTO transforms each column into an attribute unless you use the ELEMENTS argument to create sub-elements. Keep in mind that XML AUTO doesn't support the GROUP BY clause; the column order in the SELECT statement determines the attributes' nesting order. XML AUTO lets you use table or column aliases as element or attribute names; however, this mode's default is to use the table or view name as the element or attribute name. You can use the BINARY Base64 argument to return image and binary data in binary base64-encoded format. If you don't use BINARY Base64, XML AUTO returns a URL that you can query to return binary data.

- **XML EXPLICIT**. XML EXPLICIT is the most sophisticated and most powerful XML mode. As the name implies, with EXPLICIT mode, you explicitly define the schema for the returned XML by creating a virtual table that SQL Server translates into XML. Because this mode is so flexible, it's particularly good for creating hierarchical documents. EXPLICIT mode enables you to define each column as an attribute or element and even create elements not represented in your database. When you use this mode, you must prefix the result set with two columns, Tag and Parent, which create the hierarchical structure of the resulting XML. As with the other modes, you also must specify the element and attribute names within the SELECT clause.

10

To get an idea for how the ExecuteXmlReader method can be used consider the code in Listing 10.4.

LISTING 10.4   Using `ExecuteXmlReader`. This listing uses `ExecuteXmlReader` to return
results from a `FOR XML` statement in SQL Server 2000.

```
Dim xlr As XmlReader
Dim xmlSql As String
xmlSql = "SELECT isbn, title, price FROM Titles
xmlSql &= "WHERE Author = 'Fox, Dan' FOR XML AUTO, ELEMENTS"

Dim com As New SqlCommand(xmlSql, con)
com.CommandType = CommandType.Text

xlr = com.ExecuteXmlReader()
xlr.MoveToContent()
Do While xlr.Read
  ' parse the XML
Loop
```

ANALYSIS   In Listing 10.4, the `xmlSql` string contains the `SELECT` statements, which includes
the `FOR XML` clause. Here the `AUTO, ELEMENTS` arguments are used to transform
each table and column in the `SELECT` statement into an element as shown in the following
code snippet. After the method has executed, the resulting `XmlReader` from the
`System.Xml` namespace can be used to navigate the document using its `Read` method. The
resulting XML is shown in Listing 10.5.

LISTING 10.5   XML output. This listing shows the XML fragment output from the `FOR`
`XML` statement in Listing 10.4.

```
<Titles>
  <ISBN>06720083X</ISBN>
  <Title>Pure Visual Basic: a code-intensive
    premium reference/versions 5 &amp; 6</Title>
  <Price>24.9900</Price>
</Titles>
<Titles>
  <ISBN>06720072X</ISBN>
  <Title>Building Distributed Applications with Visual Basic .NET</Title>
  <Price>44.9900</Price>
</Titles>
```

You'll notice that the XML produced is actually an XML fragment because it doesn't
have a root element.

Note   The XmlReader is analogous to the data reader and is used to provide streamed access to XML. The System.Xml namespace also provides the XmlDocument class, analogous to the DataSet, to provide cached access to XML documents.

Although you can certainly parse the XML in this fashion, the real power of using FOR XML is to transform the XML generated on the server into HTML or other formats using XML Stylesheet Language (XSL) transformations. The classes that enable you to do programmatic transformations can be found in the System.Xml.Xsl and System.Xml.XPath namespaces. This technique can be used to efficiently generate HTML on the Web server in an ASP.NET application without using server controls or manually looping through a data reader. For example, the CreateCatalog method in Listing 10.6 accepts an XmlReader as an argument and transforms the XML it contains into a stream using the titles.xsl XSL stylesheet.

LISTING 10.6   Transforming XML. This method transforms the incoming XmlReader like that produced by the ExecuteXmlReader method and produces a stream that contains HTML.

```
Private Function CreateCatalog(ByRef xlr As XmlReader) As Stream

    Dim oXsl As New XslTransform()
    Dim s As New MemoryStream()
    Dim oDoc As XPathDocument

    Try
      ' Get an IXPathNavigable interface
      oDoc = New XPathDocument(xlr)
      ' Load the XSL stylesheet
      oXsl.Load("titles.xsl")
      ' Perform the transformation
      oXsl.Transform(oDoc, Nothing, s)

      s.Position = 0
      Return s

    Catch e As Exception
      Throw New Exception("Could not create catalog", e)
    End Try

End Function
```

You'll notice in this method the `XmlReader` passed in as `xlr` is first used in the constructor of the `XPathDocument` object. This must be done to create a cache for reading the input when the transformation is applied. The stylesheet is then loaded using the `Load` method and the transformation performed with the overloaded `Transform` method. The results of the transformation can be sent to a `TextWriter`, `Stream`, or `XmlWriter`. In this case, the method takes advantage of polymorphism to place the output into a `MemoryStream` that is then returned to the caller.

> **Note**
>
> The `Position` property of the `MemoryStream` is reset to 0 before the stream is passed back to the caller because the transformation will leave the pointer at the end of the stream.

The titles.xsl stylesheet that could be used with the output shown in Listing 10.5 is shown in Listing 10.7. This simple stylesheet creates an HTML document that contains a simple table including the ISBN, title, and price.

LISTING 10.7   Simple XSL. This simple stylesheet creates an HTML document from the XML returned from SQL Server.

```xml
<?xml version="1.0"?>
<xsl:stylesheet version="1.0"
xmlns:xsl="http://www.w3.org/1999/XSL/Transform">
<xsl:output method="html" />
<xsl:template match="/">
<HTML><BODY>
<TABLE>
  <xsl:for-each select="Titles">
    <TR>
     <TD><xsl:value-of select="ISBN" /></TD>
     <TD><xsl:value-of select="Title" /></TD>
     <TD><xsl:value-of select="Price" /></TD>
    </TR>
  </xsl:for-each>
</TABLE>
</BODY></HTML>
</xsl:template>
</xsl:stylesheet>
```

After the transformation is applied, the results are as shown in Listing 10.8.

LISTING 10.8   XSL output. This is the HMTL output from the XSL document shown in Listing 10.7.

```
<HTML>
  <BODY>
    <TABLE>
      <TR>
        <TD>06720083X </TD>
        <TD>Pure Visual Basic: a code-intensive
              premium reference/versions 5 &amp; 6</TD>
        <TD>24.9900</TD>
      </TR>
      <TR>
        <TD>06720606X </TD>
        <TD>Building Distributed Application with Visual Basic .NET</TD>
        <TD>44.9900</TD>
      </TR>
    </TABLE>
  </BODY>
</HTML>
```

10

Of course, in an ASP.NET application, the MemoryStream could then be sent to the client's browser through the HttpResponse object.

Modifying Data

In addition to being used to retrieve data, the command object can also be used to execute statements that don't return results to the client. Typically, these statements perform some data modification and are executed using the ExecuteNonQuery method. Because ADO.NET does not provide any way to modify the schema of a database, the ExecuteNonQuery method can also be used to execute statements such as CREATE and ALTER TABLE.

Although a result set isn't returned from ExecuteNonQuery, any output parameters or return values are populated, as you'll learn in the next section. The method does, however, attempt to return the number of rows affected by the statement. As with the other execute methods of the command object, an InvalidOperationException will be thrown if the connection associated with the command isn't open or if the transaction property isn't set and a transaction is in progress.

Because ExecuteNonQuery is most often used for data modification, it's frequently used with parameters. The DeleteTitle method in Listing 10.9 shows a simple example of using ExecuteNonQuery.

LISTING 10.9 Making a modification. This method deletes a single row in the `Titles` table using a stored procedure.

```
Public Function DeleteTitle(ByVal isbn As String) As Boolean

    Dim con As New SqlConnection(_connect)
    Dim com As New SqlCommand("usp_DeleteTitle", con)
    com.CommandType = CommandType.StoredProcedure

    ' Add the parameter
    com.Parameters.Add(new SqlParameter("@isbn",isbn))

    Try
      con.Open()
      If com.ExecuteNonQuery() = 1 Then
        Return True
      Else
        Return False
      End If
    Catch e As SqlException
    Finally
      con.Close()
    End Try

End Function
```

ANALYSIS In this listing, the usp_DeleteTitle stored procedure is passed to the constructor of the command along with the connection object. The isbn parameter is then created and added to the parameters collection of the command. Within the Try Catch block, the connection is opened and the command is executed. If the delete succeeds, the ExecuteNonQuery method should return 1 and True will be returned. If the row isn't found, ExecuteNonQuery will return 0 and False will be returned from the method. The DeleteTitle method implies that isbn is the primary key or is unique in the table. This is because ExecuteNonQuery would return a number higher than 1 if the table contained more than one row with the given ISBN. A SqlException will be thrown only if the connection doesn't have permissions to access the procedure or if an error is encountered, such as the violation of a foreign key constraint in the event that another table references the row.

Of course, command objects are also used by data adapters to insert, update, and delete rows in the data store based on changes in a DataSet. As you'll learn in detail on Day 12, "Using Data Adapters," data adapters execute a command for each row that has been inserted, updated, or deleted in the tables of a DataSet. When a DataRow is updated, the data adapter also has the ability to read the first row returned (if there is one) from the command as well as the output parameters, and to use them to update the DataRow. This is controlled by the UpdatedRowSource property of the command object, as was discussed on Day 8, "Understanding .NET Data Providers."

Note The UpdatedRowSource property will be set to None if the command is generated by a command builder such as SqlCommandBuilder.

Controlling the Command

In addition to the methods and properties already discussed, the command object exposes several members that enable you to control its behavior, including the timeout interval, cancellation, and preparing commands.

First, command objects expose CommandTimeout properties. This property controls how long the command will wait to attempt to execute before throwing an exception. Both SqlClient and OleDb default this property to 30 seconds, which you might consider reducing because users often abandon an application if it appears that nothing is happening for more than 15 seconds or so. You might experience a timeout if the rows on the server that you're attempting to read or write have been locked while a transaction is in process. This is the primary reason you want to make sure that any transactions you start will be finished as quickly as possible by either calling the Rollback or Commit methods of the transaction object.

Caution Keep in mind that a command might not time out until after the execute method returns and when the data is being read. For example, when using a data reader, the command might appear to execute, but when the rows are being retrieved, it might run into one that is locked by another user. In that case, processing would stop and wait for the interval specified in the CommandTimeout property before throwing an exception. As a result, you'll need to trap for exceptions when reading data.

In some cases, you'll also be able to cancel the execution of a command against a data store by calling its Cancel method. For example, if you open a SqlDataReader using the ExecuteReader method of the SqlCommand object, you can subsequently call the Cancel method before the command has finished streaming the rows to the client. When this occurs, an exception will be thrown with the message Operation cancelled by user. In both the SqlClient and OleDb providers, if the command isn't currently executing or the request to cancel fails, no exception is thrown.

Finally, command objects expose the Prepare method. This method instructs the data store or provider to create a prepared or compiled version of the command so that it can be reused without incurring the overhead of recompiling it. For example, by invoking the Prepare method before executing a SqlCommand, the SqlClient provider will call the sp_prepexec system stored procedure to create a compiled version of the command. In that way, on subsequent executions, the compiled statement can be referenced directly, thereby increasing performance in the same way that precompiled stored procedures do. When the command is closed, the sp_unprepared stored procedure is executed to remove the compiled statement.

 Note
Even though the OleDbCommand object supports this property, all providers might not. As a result, calling Prepare might not have any effect. Keep in mind as well that because Prepare is a method, it should be called after the command's properties, such as CommandType, have been fully configured.

Handling Parameters

As you've seen many times throughout this book, command objects use parameters to provide arguments to the command being executed against the data store. You can either create parameters for the particular provider directly by using the New operator or by using the CreateParameter method of the command object. In the case of the former, the constructor is overloaded and can be used to populate almost all the properties shown in Table 8.7. In the case of the latter, the CreateParameter method simply returns a new instance of the parameter and doesn't allow you to provide any of the default values for the property. In both cases, the parameter must be explicitly added to the parameters collection (exposed through a class that implements IDataParameterCollection interface) of the command object using its Add method.

Parameters can be used to both send data into a command and to return data to the client. We'll explore both aspects in the following sections.

Handling Input Parameters

Perhaps the most common use of parameters is to pass values into a stored procedure executed through a command. Listing 10.10 shows a typical example where the SaveTitles method accepts a DataSet and uses a data adapter to synchronize insertions and updates with the ComputeBooks database.

LISTING 10.10   Using parameters. This method creates and populates the parameters collection of a `SqlCommand` object for use in a data adapter.

```
Public Function SaveTitles(ByVal dsTitles As DataSet) As DataSet

  If dsTitles Is Nothing OrElse dsTitles.HasChanges = False Then
    Return Nothing
  End If

  Dim cmSave As New SqlCommand("usp_SaveTitle", _sqlCon)
  Dim da As New SqlDataAdapter()

  da.UpdateCommand = cmSave
  da.UpdateCommand.CommandType = CommandType.StoredProcedure
  da.InsertCommand = da.UpdateCommand

  With cmSave
    .Parameters.Add(New SqlParameter("@isbn", SqlDbType.NVarChar, 10, "isbn"))
    .Parameters.Add(New SqlParameter( _
      "@description", SqlDbType.NVarChar, 2048, "Description"))
    .Parameters.Add(New SqlParameter( _
      "@title", SqlDbType.NVarChar, 100, "Title"))
    .Parameters.Add(New SqlParameter( _
      "@author", SqlDbType.NVarChar, 250, "Author"))
    .Parameters.Add(New SqlParameter("@price", SqlDbType.Money, 4, "Price"))
    .Parameters.Add(New SqlParameter( _
      "@pubDate", SqlDbType.DateTime, 4, "PubDate"))
    .Parameters.Add(New SqlParameter( _
      "@publisher", SqlDbType.NChar, 5, "Publisher"))
    .Parameters.Add(New SqlParameter( _
      "@catId", SqlDbType.UniqueIdentifier, 8, "CatId"))
  End With

  Try
    da.Update(dsTitles)
  Catch e As SqlException
    ' Check for errors
    If dsTitles.HasErrors Then
      Return dsTitles.GetChanges(DataRowState.Modified)
    Else
      _throwcompubookexception("SaveTitles error", e)
      Return Nothing
    End If
  Finally
    If Not _sqlCon Is Nothing Then _sqlCon.Close()
  End Try

End Function
```

10

ANALYSIS What you should notice about the SaveTitles method is that parameters are created using the New operator and added to the collection in a single statement. Because these parameters are of type SqlParameter, the second argument to the constructor uses the appropriate SqlDbType, which maps to the DbType enumerated type as we discussed on Day 7. If you use one of the constructors that doesn't specify the type, DbType.String will be the default. The Direction property of each parameter isn't set because in this case all are input parameters (ParameterDirection.Input), which is the default. In this case, the Value property of each parameter will be set by the data adapter when the command is executed for a DataRow that has been inserted or updated.

One of the other interesting things to note about using parameters with the SqlClient provider is that when the provider creates the Transact-SQL statement to execute against the server, it uses named rather than positional arguments, the opposite of what was done in early versions of ADO 2.x. In others words, the Transact-SQL that would be generated in the case of the usp_DeleteTitle stored procedure shown earlier would be equivalent to

```
exec usp_DeleteTitle @isbn='006720034X'
```

If the procedure accepted additional arguments, they would be appended in a comma-delimited list. Using named arguments means that you can create stored procedures in SQL Server whose parameters are defaulted to NULL, as shown in Listing 10.11.

LISTING 10.11 Optional parameters. Because SqlCommand supports positional arguments, your stored procedures can accept NULL values so that you don't have to create the SqlParameter objects.

```
CREATE PROCEDURE usp_GetTitles
        @ISBN      [nvarchar](10) = NULL,
        @Author    [nvarchar](250) = NULL,
        @Publisher [nchar](5) = NULL

AS
declare @where nvarchar(250)
declare @author_w nvarchar(100)
declare @Publisher_w nvarchar(100)
declare @sql nvarchar(500)

set @author_w = ''
set @Publisher_w = ''

set @where = 'WHERE'
if @isbn is not null set @where = @where +
 ' isbn = ''' + @isbn + '''' + ' and '
if @author is not null set @author_w = ' author like ''%'
```

LISTING 10.11 continued

```
  + @author + '%''' + ' and '
if @publisher is not null set @publisher_w = ' Publisher = '''
  + @publisher + '''' + ' and '

set @sql = 'SELECT * FROM Titles ' + @where + @author_w + @publisher_w
set @sql = substring(@sql,1, LEN(@sql)-4)
exec sp_executesql @sql
GO
```

In this way, your code can be made more efficient because the SqlCommand object needn't contain any parameters if you don't plan on passing a value into these arguments. In this case, the usp_GetTitles stored procedure executes queries with different WHERE clauses, depending on which arguments are passed in.

10

Tip

Whether the OleDbCommand object uses positional or named arguments is dependant on the OLE DB provider. For example, when using the SQLOLEDB provider with OleDbCommand, positional arguments are used rather than named arguments. This implies that you must add all the parameters to the parameters collection.

Input parameters can also be used with dynamic SQL by simply inserting the parameter into the SQL statement and then adding it to the parameters collection, as shown in the following code snippet:

```
Dim com As New SqlCommand("SELECT * FROM Titles WHERE ISBN = @isbn", con)
com.CommandType = CommandType.Text
com.Parameters.Add(New SqlParameter("@isbn", "06720001X"))
```

As with positional and named arguments, the syntax you can use to specify the parameters and how they can be named is dependent on the OLE DB provider.

Handling Output Parameters and Return Values

The Direction property of parameter objects can also be set to InputOutput, Output, or ReturnValue. Each of these three options enables you to read information returned from the data store. As implied by the name, InputOutput enables you to both pass a value into the command and retrieve a (possibly) new value assigned by the command. Output can be used to return new parameters. ReturnValue can, for example, catch the value returned from a stored procedure.

To illustrate the use of output parameters, consider the stored procedure shown here:

```
CREATE PROCEDURE usp_RevByBook
@isbn nchar(10),
@revenue money OUTPUT,
@units integer OUTPUT
AS

SELECT @units = SUM(Quantity), @revenue = SUM(Quantity * UnitPrice)
FROM OrderDetails
WHERE ISBN = @isbn
GO
```

In this case, the procedure calculates the number of units of a particular ISBN that have sold and how much revenue has resulted. Rather than return the results in a result set, you can write code that retrieves the output parameters. For simple results like this, using output parameters is more efficient because a result set needn't be created on the server and the code on the client to retrieve the values is simpler, as shown in Listing 10.12.

LISTING 10.12   Using output parameters. This code calls a stored procedure that returns data through output parameters.

```
Dim com As New SqlCommand("usp_RevByBook", con)

With com
  .CommandType = CommandType.StoredProcedure
  .Parameters.Add(New SqlParameter("@isbn", "06720222X"))
  .Parameters.Add(New SqlParameter("@revenue", SqlDbType.Money))
  .Parameters("@revenue").Direction = ParameterDirection.Output
  .Parameters.Add(New SqlParameter("@units", SqlDbType.Int))
  .Parameters("@units").Direction = ParameterDirection.Output
End With

con.Open()
com.ExecuteNonQuery()
rev = CType(com.Parameters("@revenue").Value, Decimal)
units = CType(com.Parameters("@units").Value, Integer)
con.Close()
```

Note that after the parameters have been created, their Direction property is set to Output. After the command has been executed using ExecuteNonQuery, the values can then be read using the Value property.

Return values are typically used with stored procedures and are ideal for returning a value that indicates the success or failure of the stored procedure. For example, it's very common to use the return value from a SQL Server stored procedure to return the new value inserted into the identity column for a table. You'll learn more about identity columns on Day 13, "Working with SQL Server."

Note

In SQL Server, if no value is specified for the return value using a RETURN statement, 0 will be returned. Also, SQL Server always returns an integer value from a stored procedure.

As with output parameters, the only requirement to using return values is that you add the parameters to the collection and set its `Direction` property to `ReturnValue`.

Summary

Commands are integral to ADO.NET because they are used both by data adapters and data readers to retrieve and modify data. Today you learned about command objects and how they can be used to retrieve and modify data. You also learned how parameters are created and added to the parameters collection of the command. During the next two days, you'll learn more about the data readers and data adapters that use command objects.

Workshop

This workshop will help reinforce the concepts covered in today's lesson.

Quiz

1. Why would you use stored procedures rather than dynamic or inline SQL?

   If stored procedures are supported by your data store, you should consider using them because they can be used to implement a layer of abstraction for your applications, as well as increase both performance and security. However, you might want to use inline SQL if your application needs to supports multiple data stores.

2. Which execute method might you use when executing a SQL statement that uses an aggregate function?

   Typically, SELECT statements that use aggregate functions such as SUM, MIN, MAX, COUNT, and AVG can be easily executed using the ExecuteScalar method. This method returns the first column of the first row of the result set so that you needn't use a data reader.

3. When would you use the `ExecuteXmlReader` method of the `SqlCommand` object?

   This method returns an `XmlReader` from a command that uses the SQL Server 2000 FOR XML statement. This comes in handy if you want to return data from SQL Server as XML in order to send it to a trading partner or transform it for use on a Web site.

4. In what situations would you use output parameters?

   Output parameters are particularly effective when you need to return only one or a few values from a stored procedure. Using output parameters reduces the cost of execution on the server because a result set doesn't need to be created and makes the code you have to write simpler on the client.

Exercise

Write a method and stored procedure that selects all orders based on a given date range and returns a `SqlDataReader`.

Answers for Day 10

Exercise Answer

One possible solution might be the following:

Stored Procedure:

```
CREATE PROCEDURE usp_OrdersByDate
@startdate smalldatetime,
@enddate smalldatetime,
@revenue money OUTPUT
AS

SELECT * FROM Orders
WHERE OrderDate BETWEEN @startdate AND @enddate
ORDER BY OrderDate

GO
```

Method:

```
Public Function GetOrder(ByVal connect As SqlConnection, _
  ByVal startDate As Date, ByVal endDate As Date) As SqlDataReader

  Dim com As New SqlCommand("usp_OrdersByDate", connect)
  Dim dr As SqlDataReader
```

```
  If connect.State = ConnectionState.Closed Then
    Throw New Exception("Must have an open connection")
  End If

  With com
    .CommandType = CommandType.StoredProcedure
    .Parameters.Add(New SqlParameter("@startdate", SqlDbType.SmallDateTime))
    .Parameters.Add(New SqlParameter("@enddate", SqlDbType.SmallDateTime))
    .Parameters("@startdate").Value = startDate
    .Parameters("@enddate").Value = endDate
  End With

  Try
    dr = com.ExecuteReader(CommandBehavior.CloseConnection)
    Return dr
  Catch e As SqlException
    Throw e
  End Try

End Function
```

10

DAY 11

Using Data Readers

As you learned yesterday, data readers are created using the `ExecuteReader` method of the command object. The data reader object that is returned implements the `IDataReader` and, typically, the `IDataRecord` interfaces to allow access to the data in a forward-only, read-only cursor-style object. As a result, data readers are ideal for scenarios in which you don't need to hold on to or cache the data and simply need to read through it quickly. In this way, data readers also reduce the overhead required because more than one row is never held in memory at any one time.

In today's short lesson, you'll look at the various ways you can work with data readers and how you can use them in your applications. Specifically, you'll focus on

- The appropriate uses for data readers and how they differ from the `DataSet`
- How to traverse a data reader and extract its values
- How to use a data reader polymorphically in client code
- How to handle multiple result sets returned from a data store

Data Reader Characteristics

As mentioned yesterday, data readers represent one of the two programming models exposed in ADO.NET that work with data (the other being the `DataSet`, which works with disconnected results). As a developer, you need to choose which programming model you're going to use for a particular scenario. To help you understand the differences and when a data reader might be appropriate, consider the following characteristics:

- **Connectedness**. Because the data reader exposes a connected and streamed model, unlike the `DataSet`, its uses are relegated to situations in which your application can maintain the connection to the data store while the data is being traversed. If you know, for example, that the data must be used offline, using a `DataSet` makes more sense because it can be persisted to a disk and doesn't require a continuous connection to the data store. That having been said, ideally, you should open a data reader and traverse it immediately to minimize the amount of time the connection is in use.

- **Remoting**. Unlike a `DataSet`, a data reader is derived from `System.MarshalByRefObject` rather than `MarshalByValueComponent`. This means that when using .NET Remoting, a data reader can't be passed between application domains by value but must be passed by reference. As a result, a data reader isn't serialized and passed between application domains. Instead, calls to the data reader are passed between domains. If a data reader is used in a remote application data reader and will result in cross-application domain communication each time a method or property of the data reader is accessed. Obviously, this is a situation you want to avoid in physically distributed applications. This architecture makes sense for data readers because the data reader holds on to a connection to a data store. Therefore, if you pass a data reader by value, you would also need to pass the connection object it is using, which would be problematic to say the leastdomain, the domain in which it was created will always host the. Figure 11.1 highlights this architecture by showing how a client application domain would access a data reader created in a separate application domain.

  Although data readers can be accessed by remote application domains, as shown in Figure 11.1, because of the number of calls this would generate between those domains, it's recommended that you use data readers only from within the domain in which they were created. In other words, code that creates a data reader should live in the same application domains (and therefore the same operating system process) as the code that consumes it.

FIGURE 11.1

Data reader architecture. In this diagram, the data reader (dr) is created on the server. When a method such as Read is called, the method is executed on the server and the results are passed to the client.

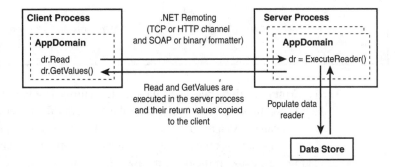

- **Data Sources**. Data readers get their data from a connection object and so, typically, return data from only a single data store. In other words, you can't access data from both a SQL Server database and an Oracle database from the same data reader object. This can be done, however, with a DataSet, whose DataTable objects can contain data from anywhere because the DataSet neither tracks nor cares about the source of its data. For this reason, with respect to data sources, the DataSet is said to be heterogeneous, whereas the data reader is homogenous.

- **Updateability**. The nature of a data reader is that it provides forward-only, read-only, streamed access data. This means that the data isn't updateable. If you wanted to update data retrieved with a data reader, you would need to store it yourself in variables, for example, and later update the data store, perhaps using a command object and the ExecuteNonQuery method. A DataSet provides updateability by tracking the changes made to rows within its tables.

- **Strong-Typing**. As you learned on Day 6, "Building Strongly Typed DataSet Classes," a DataSet object can be strongly typed using the code generator utility accessible through VS .NET or the XSD.exe command-line utility. A strongly typed DataSet allows access to the data in an easier fashion because it derives from DataSet and exposes specific properties that map to the tables, rows, and columns of the DataSet. A data reader has no such equivalent, so you always access columns in a DataSet using a collection syntax with the name of the column or its ordinal.

But Are They Strongly Typed?

Unfortunately, Microsoft chose the term *strongly typed* to refer to a derived DataSet that exposes specific properties. As you'll see, the data reader also allows access to data in a strongly typed fashion in the normal sense of the term, meaning that the actual data is returned as the type it maps to in the database rather than as a generic type such as System.Object. Perhaps a better term for a strongly typed DataSet would be *derived DataSet* or *mapped DataSet*.

11

However, this text uses the Microsoft term to avoid any confusion when you read the online documentation.

- **Data Manipulation**. Because a data reader returns data in a streamed fashion, there is no opportunity to sort or filter the data after the ExecuteReader method has been called. As a result, you need to make sure that the statement that executes on the data store uses the appropriate ORDER BY and WHERE clauses (in the case of a relational database) if the order the rows are returned is important. However, using a DataView, the tables of a DataSet can be filtered and sorted in different ways at different times without having to execute another statement against the data store.

- **Performance**. Because a data reader accesses only a single row at a time, it's very efficient in terms of the memory consumed on the client. This results in the best performance possible for accessing data. However, it should be noted that internally a data adapter will use a data reader to populate a DataSet when its Fill method is called, so the cost of using a DataSet from the server's perspective isn't any greater than using a data reader. The difference lies in the fact that when a DataSet is used, the DataSet must first be populated before the data is accessed, so you don't get direct access to the data as with a data reader. A second consideration is that if a multi-user application such as an ASP.NET Web site uses DataSets, the users will be consuming more resources than they might if data readers were employed. This incremental cost, when totaled over hundreds or thousands of users, can put an extra burden on the Web server. However, because of the disconnected nature of DataSet objects, they can be cached unlike data readers, thereby reducing the number of times the data store needs to be accessed.

Table 11.1 summarizes the differences between the DataSet and data readers.

TABLE 11.1 Data readers versus DataSet. This table summarizes the differences you should consider when deciding which programming model to use.

DataSet	Data Reader
Can be used without a connection	Requires a continuous connection to the data store
Serializable across application domains	Used by reference across application domains
Stores heterogeneous data	Provides access to data from a single source
Is updateable and uses a data adapter for updates	Read-only; must roll your own method to update

TABLE 11.1 continued

DataSet	*Data Reader*
Can be strongly typed	No property access to columns returned
Can be sorted and filtered	Rows can't be retrieved in an arbitrary order or filtered
Performs well but consumes resources on the middle tier	No resource consumption on the middle tier

Traversing a Data Reader

As mentioned yesterday in discussing the command object, the `ExecuteReader` method is used to create a data reader object that can then be traversed. Before calling the method, the command must be associated with a connection object and the connection opened using its `Open` method.

After the data reader has been opened, it can be traversed using its `Read` method. The `Read` method positions the data reader at the next available row and so must be called prior to reading data from the first row. In the process, the `Read` method returns `True` if more rows are available and `False` after all the rows have been read. When the data reader is exhausted, the `Close` method of the data reader and the connection should be called to ensure that the connection is destroyed or released to the pool. The typical pattern for using a data reader is shown in Listing 11.1, assuming that con is a valid connection object:

LISTING 11.1 Opening a data reader. This listing opens and traverses a data reader.

```
Dim dr As SqlDataReader

Try
   con.Open()
   dr = com.ExecuteReader()
   Do While dr.Read()
      '  Process the row
   Loop
Catch e As Exception
   '  Handle the error
Finally
   dr.Close()
   con.Close()
End Try
```

11

Of course, you can alternatively pass the `CloseConnection` command behavior to the `ExecuteReader` method to automatically close the connection when the data reader is closed. As you learned on Day 1, "ADO.NET in Perspective," the fact that developers don't have to check an `EOF` or `BOF` property (as in an ADO `Recordset`) to determine when the result set is exhausted reduces programming errors. This is because the `Read` method must be placed at the top of the loop and therefore can't be forgotten as the `MoveNext` method sometimes was.

Tip

> If you attempt to use the pattern shown in Listing 11.1 in C#, you'll notice that you get the compiler error `Use of unassigned local variable dr` referring to the `Finally` block. To avoid this, you need to initialize `dr` to null in the declaration.

While the data reader is open, the associated connection object will be busy, so it can't be used to execute other statements. Attempting to execute a second command on the connection results in an exception.

Note

> It should be stressed that this is even the case with the SqlClient provider because this behavior is different from what you might have experienced in the past working with SQL Server. Previously, it was possible for ADO to generate multiple connections automatically when the original connection was busy handling results for a fire-hose cursor.

While in the loop, you can use any of the methods exposed in the `IDataRecord` interface or those custom implemented by the data reader class to access the data.

Retrieving Single Values

To retrieve single values from each column returned, you can use any of the 15 methods shown in Table 8.6 that return strongly typed data and accept the ordinal value of the column. For example, to retrieve the values from the `usp_GetTitles` stored procedure, you would use the code in Listing 11.2.

LISTING 11.2   Retrieving values. This listing shows the use of the various methods of the data reader to retrieve strongly typed values.

```
Dim isbn, title, desc, author, publisher As String
Dim price, discount, bulkDiscount As Decimal
Dim pubDate As Date
```

LISTING 11.2   continued

```
Dim bulkAmount As Short
Dim catId As Guid

dr = com.ExecuteReader()

  Do While dr.Read()
    isbn = dr.GetString(0)  'nchar(10)
    title = dr.GetString(1)  'nvarchar(100)
    If Not dr.IsDBNull(2) Then desc = dr.GetString(2)  'nvarchar(2048)
    author = dr.GetString(3)  'nvarchar(250)
    pubDate = dr.GetDateTime(4)  'smalldatetime
    price = dr.GetDecimal(5)  'money
    If Not dr.IsDBNull(6) Then discount = dr.GetDecimal(6)  'money
    If Not dr.IsDBNull(7) Then bulkDiscount = dr.GetDecimal(7)  'money
    If Not dr.IsDBNull(8) Then bulkAmount = dr.GetInt16(8)  'smallint
    catId = dr.GetGuid(10)  'uniqueidentifier
    If Not dr.IsDBNull(11) Then publisher = dr.GetString(11)  'nchar(5)
  Loop
```

ANALYSIS   When a specific method is called, such as GetDecimal, the data returned must be of the correct type or an exception will result because no conversion is attempted. This implies that null values returned from the data store will cause exceptions. You can check for this using the IsDBNull method and passing in the ordinal of the column to check. In this case, only those columns that can accept null values in SQL Server need to be checked for nulls.

Notice that the SQL Server data types are shown in the comment at the end of each line. As mentioned on Day 8, "Understanding .NET Data Providers," the data types for the data store will map to types in the DbType enumeration, which in turn map to types in the Common Type System (CTS). Behind-the-scenes conversions will be done to convert from the SQL Server types to the appropriate DbType value.

Note   You can find definitions of each of the DbType enumeration values in the online documentation.

Data providers can also include their own set of types to provide the mappings, as is done for both the SqlClient and the OleDb providers through the SqlDbType and OleDbType enumerations. In addition, the SqlDataReader class exposes a set of methods that return data from a data reader using the types from the System.Data.SqlTypes namespace. As a result, you could rewrite Listing 11.2 as shown in Listing 11.3.

LISTING 11.3 Using provider types. This listing shows the use of SqlClient-specific types.

```
Dim isbn, title, desc, author, publisher As SqlTypes.SqlString
Dim price, discount, bulkDiscount As SqlTypes.SqlMoney
Dim pubDate As SqlTypes.SqlDateTime
Dim bulkAmount As SqlTypes.SqlInt16
Dim catId As SqlTypes.SqlGuid

dr = com.ExecuteReader

  Do While dr.Read()
        isbn = dr.GetSqlString(0)
        title = dr.GetSqlString(1)
        If Not dr.IsDBNull(2) Then desc = dr.GetSqlString(2)
        author = dr.GetSqlString(3)
        pubDate = dr.GetSqlDateTime(4)
        price = dr.GetSqlMoney(5)
        If Not dr.IsDBNull(6) Then discount = dr.GetSqlMoney(6)
        If Not dr.IsDBNull(7) Then bulkDiscount = dr.GetSqlMoney(7)
        If Not dr.IsDBNull(8) Then bulkAmount = dr.GetSqlInt16(8)
        catId = dr.GetSqlGuid(10)
        If Not dr.IsDBNull(11) Then publisher = dr.GetSqlString(11)
  Loop
```

Using these provider-specific types is both faster and prevents loss of precision. This is because the conversion that is done when calling the generic methods such as GetDecimal isn't performed, and the data returned from SQL Server can be mapped directly to the types in the SqlTypes namespace. In addition, the SqlClient types handle null values as you would expect for SQL Server, which makes coding with them simpler. As you might have guessed, the OleDb provider provides no other types because it's a generic provider.

To retrieve the data without strong-typing, you can use the GetValue method, which places the value in an Object that later can be cast to the proper type. Because the field values are also placed in a collection, they can be alternatively accessed using the Item collection either through the Item property (in VB only because Item is the indexer) or the shortcut syntax. In other words, the following three lines of code are identical in their results:

```
o = dr.GetValue(1)
```

```
o = dr.Item(1)
```

```
o = dr(1)
```

The advantage, however, of using either of the second two techniques is that the Item property is overloaded to accept either the ordinal or the name of the column.

As a result, if you're using the strongly typed methods rather than use the ordinal values, you can instead call the GetOrdinal method, which accepts the name of the column and returns the ordinal like so:

```
Dim ordIsbn, ordTitle As Integer

ordIsbn = dr.GetOrdinal(îISBNî)
ordTitle = dr.GetOrdinal(îTitleî)
isbn = dr.GetString(ordIsbn)
title = dr.GetString(ordTitle)
```

Obviously, the first two statements should be executed before the loop so as not to incur the overhead of looking up the ordinal value with each iteration. In addition, GetOrdinal first performs a case-sensitive search, so using the proper case for the column names will also increase performance.

Although it wasn't shown in the previous code snippets, you can also retrieve binary data from a data reader in several ways. If the amount of data is small, you can simply read the contents directly into an array of bytes as follows:

```
Dim buff() As Byte

' Open the data reader and call Read

buff = CType(dr.Item(4), Byte())
```

ANALYSIS In this case, the cover column from the Titles table in the ComputeBooks database is retrieved as ordinal 4 and its data is placed directly into the Byte array. As in this example, this technique is good for data that you know will be of a small size, such as the cover image of a book. Of course, for providers that support it, you can also use the specific types; in this case, SqlBinary in conjunction with the GetSqlBinary method.

When the data grows larger, however, you might want to read the data in smaller chunks and buffer it in a MemoryStream object before working with it. This can be accomplished using the GetBytes or GetChars methods of the IDataRecord interface. These methods enable you to populate a Byte array using an offset read from the data reader. As implied by the names, GetBytes reads the data as individual bytes, whereas GetChars reads the data as characters. To illustrate the concept, consider the ReadBinaryData method in Listing 11.4.

11

LISTING 11.4   Reading binary data. This method is used to read data from a column in a data reader that stores binary data.

```
Private Function ReadBinaryData(ByRef dr As IDataRecord, _
   ByVal ordinal As Integer) As MemoryStream

   Dim len, offset As Long
   Dim buff(4095) As Byte
   ' Memory stream to hold the result
   Dim memoryBuffer As New MemoryStream()

   Do
      ' Get the next 4096 bytes
      len = dr.GetBytes(4, offset, buff, 0, 4096)
      ' Write the data to the memory stream
      memoryBuffer.Write(buff, 0, CInt(len))
      ' Increment the offset
      offset = offset + len
   Loop Until len < 4096

   ' Reset the position to the beginning
   memoryBuffer.Position = 0
   Return memoryBuffer

End Function
```

ANALYSIS   As you can see in Listing 11.4, the method is passed in a reference to an object, such as SqlDataReader or OleDbDataReader, that implements the IDataRecord interface along with the ordinal of the column that contains the binary data. Using the interface rather than the actual type is an example of polymorphism, which allows your code to be more flexible in working with any object that implements the IDataRecord interface. After instantiating the MemoryStream to hold the result, the GetBytes method is called in a loop to read each 4KB chunk of data and write it to the MemoryStream using the Write method. The offset is then incremented to make sure that data is read starting with the appropriate location the next time through the loop. After all the data is read, the Position property of the MemoryStream is used to place the pointer back to the beginning of the stream before returning the stream to the client.

The calling code would then look as follows:

```
Dim memoryBuffer As New MemoryStream()
' Execute the data reader

Do While dr.Read()
    ' Read other columns
    memoryBuffer = ReadBinaryData(CType(dr, IDataRecord), 4)
    ' Process the memoryBuffer perhaps writing it to a file
Loop
```

As mentioned yesterday, the SequentialAccess command behavior can also be used to ensure that the data from the data reader is only accessed sequentially. In other words, you can read from the columns only in their ordinal sequence (although columns can be skipped). In addition, you must read the data within a column in order as well. Violating either of these rules causes an InvalidOperationException to be generated that contains an error message detailing the violation. Using SequentialAccess allows the data reader to retrieve large binary columns on demand, as streams, rather than retrieving the entire column at once.

Retrieving Multiple Values

The second way to retrieve data from a data reader is to use the methods that return all the column values as an array. The IDataRecord interface supports only one such method, GetValues, which populates an array of type System.Object passed to it with the values of the columns. The method then returns the number of elements in the array. Because the returned values are in an array of type System.Object, the elements of the array can later be cast to the appropriate types in order to work with them in the application. For example, the code in Listing 11.5 could be used to retrieve all the customers from the ComputeBooks database who have valid addresses for creating a text file for use in an application.

LISTING 11.5 Reading multiple values. This listing reads all of the items in each row of the data reader using the GetValues method.

```
Dim values(6) As Object
Dim fs As New FileStream("customers.txt", FileMode.OpenOrCreate)
Dim outputFile As New StreamWriter(fs)

con.Open()
dr = ins.ExecuteReader(CommandBehavior.CloseConnection)

Do While dr.Read()
  dr.GetValues(values)
  WriteCustomer(values, outputFile)
Loop

dr.Close()
fs.Close()
```

ANALYSIS You'll notice in Listing 11.5 that the customers.txt file is opened or created and a StreamWriter from the System.IO namespace is used to write data to the file. After the connection and data reader are opened, the GetValues method retrieves the values on the current row and passes them along with the StreamWriter to the WriteCustomer method shown in Listing 11.6.

In actuality, the array passed to the GetValues method can either have fewer or more elements than the number of fields returned from the data reader. If fewer elements are in the array, the GetValues method will simply populate as many as it can. Likewise, if the array is larger, the extra elements won't be populated. Although this behavior is ultimately flexible, it can lead to problems if you don't make sure that you're getting all the values you need. In addition, passing an array that contains fewer elements than the number of fields returned from the data reader wastes server resources. You should always ask only for the data you need.

If you want to size the array correctly, you can first inspect the value of the FieldCount property of the data reader and then initialize the array accordingly, like so:

```
Dim values(dr.FieldCount - 1) As Object
```

Of course, this statement must follow the call to ExecuteReader. Alternatively, VB developers could use the ReDim statement after first declaring the array without the rank, as in

```
Dim values() As Object
ReDim values(dr.FieldCount - 1)
```

C# developers, on the other hand, would simply do the following:

```
Object[] values;
values = new Object[dr.FieldCount];
```

 Tip
> In VB, the array declaration denotes the upper bound of the array, whereas in C#, the declaration contains the number of elements in the array. Because both are zero-based, in VB you need to subtract 1 from the FieldCount because the first element is 0.

LISTING 11.6 Writing the array. This method accepts the values from the GetValues method and uses it to write data as a StreamWriter.

```
Private Sub WriteCustomer(ByVal custValues() As Object, _
  ByRef tw As StreamWriter)

    Dim fName, lName, city, stateProv, postalCode As String
    Dim name, location As String

    ' Extract the data
    fName = Trim(custValues(1).ToString)
    lName = Trim(custValues(2).ToString)
    city = Trim(custValues(3).ToString)
    stateProv = Trim(custValues(5).ToString)
```

LISTING 11.6 continued

```
        postalCode = Trim(custValues(6).ToString)

        ' Concatenate
        name = lName & ", " & fName
        location = city & ", " & stateProv & " " & postalCode

        ' Write Address
        tw.WriteLine()
        tw.WriteLine(name)
        tw.WriteLine(custValues(4).ToString)
        tw.WriteLine(location)

    End Sub
```

ANALYSIS In Listing 11.6, it happens that each of the elements of the custValues array is ultimately of type String, so the ToString method can be called to create strings for each of the data elements. One of the interesting side effects of this technique is that you don't need to check the IsDBNull method we discussed earlier. This is because the ToString method simply returns an empty string ("") rather than Nothing (null in C#). If the CType function were used to cast the data to a String, an exception would have been thrown because a String can't contain a null value. An empty string is also returned from the ToString method of the Convert class. Of course, if you use this technique, you need to be sure that you can live with empty strings in your data.

After the data has been retrieved, it's manipulated to create a crude address label and then written to the file using the WriteLine method of the StreamWriter object.

In addition to the GetValues method that all data readers will expose, data readers can also expose their own GetValues method to return the data in the types appropriate for the data store. SqlClient does this by exposing a GetSqlValues method that populates an array of type System.Object with data in the native SQL Server data types from the SqlTypes namespace.

Note
> As you learned on Day 8, data readers don't support functionality like the GetRows method found in ADO 2.x because there is no reason for it. If you want to read all the data and cache it, you should simply use the DataSet instead.

11

Advanced Features

In addition to simply retrieving data using a data reader, you can also use it to view schema information, pass result sets between tiers in a multi-tier application, and read multiple result sets generated by the command object.

Retrieving the Schema

In addition to the actual data from the result set, a data reader can also be used to retrieve the schema for the data using the `GetSchemaTable` method. This method is exposed by the `IDataReader` interface and is implemented by both the SqlClient and OleDb data readers. You can call this method anytime after the `ExecuteReader` method has been invoked, even after its data has been read using the `Read` method. You might use this method if you want to dynamically create SQL DDL statements or XSD documents based on the data from the data reader.

Tip

> Although you could use `GetSchemaTable` to do things such as create an XSD document, it would be far simpler to use the technique we discussed on Day 7, "XML and the `DataSet`." In that technique, you can load the schema into a `DataSet` using the `FillSchema` method of a data adapter and then extract the schema using the `WriteXmlSchema` or `GetXmlSchema` methods.

The `GetSchemaTable` method returns a `DataTable` populated with provider-specific column information. For example, the SqlClient provider creates a table with 22 columns that provide everything from the name of the column to the CTS data type it maps to. The OleDb provider returns a table with 18 columns that contain data from the `GetColumnsRowset` method of the OLE DB `IColumnsRowset` interface.

Note

> You can find the columns for both providers and their definitions in the online documentation under the `GetSchemaTable` method for each provider.

Which of the columns are populated depends on the behaviors passed to the `ExecuteDataReader` method. Typically, the minimum amount of information is returned, including the column names, their data types, and sizes. However, you can usually retrieve additional information by using the `KeyInfo` value of the `CommandBehavior` enumeration. This enables you to determine which columns are unique and the names of the underlying tables in the data store. When you couple this behavior with `SchemaOnly` only, you can retrieve only the metadata for the data reader, like so:

```
dr = ins.ExecuteReader(CommandBehavior.KeyInfo Or _
 CommandBehavior.SchemaOnly or CommandBehavior.CloseConnection)
Dim dt As New DataTable()
dt = dr.GetSchemaTable()
dr.Close()
```

Using a Data Reader Polymorphically

As we briefly touched on yesterday, the `CloseConnection` behavior passed to the
`ExecuteReader` method enables you to return a data reader from a method and still
ensure that its connection is closed or returned to the pool promptly when the data reader
is closed. This idea, coupled with the fact that all data readers implement the
`IDataReader` interface, enables you to take advantage of polymorphism to write code
that works with any provider. For example, the `WriteXml` method shown in Listing 11.7
writes the data from the passed-in data reader to an XML file using the `XmlTextWriter`
class from the `System.Xml` namespace.

LISTING 11.7 Using polymorphism. This method can be used to write the data in any
data reader to a simple XML file because all data readers inherit from the `IDataReader`
interface.

```
Private Sub WriteXml(ByVal dr As IDataReader, _
  ByVal fileName As String, ByVal root As String)

   ' Check the arguments
   If dr Is Nothing OrElse dr.IsClosed Then Return

   Dim xtr As New XmlTextWriter(fileName, System.Text.Encoding.Default)
   Dim i As Integer
   Dim fields As Integer = dr.FieldCount

   xtr.WriteStartDocument()
   xtr.WriteComment("Produced " & Now)
   xtr.WriteStartElement(root)

   Do While dr.Read()
     xtr.WriteStartElement("row")
     For i = 0 To dr.FieldCount - 1
         xtr.WriteElementString(dr.GetName(i), Trim(dr.Item(i).ToString))
     Next
     xtr.WriteEndElement()
   Loop

   xtr.WriteEndElement()

   ' Close the data reader and connection
   dr.Close()
```

11

LISTING 11.7   continued

```
    xtr.Close()

End Sub
```

ANALYSIS You'll notice that in Listing 11.7, all the properties and methods of the IDataReader interface can be called, such as FieldCount, Read, GetName, and Close. As a result, the calling code can pass in a SqlDataReader, OleDbDataReader, or other class that implements the IDataReader interface.

Of course, this technique can't be used when you need to call methods that are exposed only by a specific data reader, such as the GetSqlValues method of the SqlDataReader class.

Returning Multiple Result Sets

As you learned on Day 8, one of the interesting things you can do with a data reader is read multiple result sets. Typically, multiple result sets are generated by creating commands that include multiple SELECT statements in a batch. When the first result set is exhausted, the NextResult method can be called and will return True and position the data reader at the next result set if one exists. The next result set can then be traversed using the Read method. Returning multiple result sets in this way enables you to create stored procedures that encapsulate multiple SELECT statements and therefore centralize the logic on both the client and the server.

As an example, consider the generic method shown in Listing 11.8 that reads multiple result sets from a stored procedure and populates ArrayList objects with the results. The array lists can then be bound to controls such as the ComboBox on a Windows Form.

LISTING 11.8   Retrieving multiple result sets. This method extracts all the result sets from a data reader and places them in an ArrayList of ArrayList objects that contain the structure LookupData.

```
Private Function ExtractLookups(ByVal dr As IDataReader) As Array

    ' Make sure the data reader is not closed
    If dr Is Nothing OrElse dr.IsClosed Then Return Nothing

    Dim results As New ArrayList()
    Dim moreResults As Boolean = True

    Try
        ' Keep looping while there are more results
        Do While moreResults
```

LISTING 11.8   continued

```
        Dim res As New ArrayList()
        results.Add(res)
        Do While dr.Read
          res.Add(New LookupData(dr.Item(0), dr.Item(1)))
        Loop
        ' Check to see if there are more results
        moreResults = dr.NextResult()
      Loop

      Return results.ToArray()
    Catch e As Exception
      Throw e
    Finally
      dr.Close()
    End Try

End Function

Private Structure LookupData
  Public key As Object
  Public value As Object
  Sub New(ByVal newKey As Object, ByVal newValue As Object)
    key = newKey
    value = newValue
  End Sub
End Structure
```

11

ANALYSIS As you can see in Listing 11.8, the ExtractLookups method accepts a data reader using the IDataReader interface and returns an Array object. In the Try block, the method loops while there are more result sets to read. Each time through the loop, the method creates a new ArrayList object called res and adds it to the results ArrayList used to temporarily hold the results until the method returns. Each row from the data reader is then read into a structure called LookupData that simply exposes key and value fields. The structure is then placed into the inner ArrayList.

 Note

> This method assumes that each result set contains at least two columns, the first being the primary key value and the second a description that would be displayed to the user.

After all the data has been read, the NextResult method is called to determine whether another result set is present. If so, the loop will be executed again and a new ArrayList will be added the results ArrayList. After all the results have been extracted, the results ArrayList is converted into an Array of type System.Object using the ToArray method.

> An alternative and simpler technique is simply to read both result sets into the tables of a DataSet and then bind them to the controls.

A client could then call the ExtractLookups method like so:

```
Dim results As Array

results = ExtractLookups(bus.GetLookups())

results(0) = cbPublishers.DataSource
cbPublishers.ValueMember = "Key"
cbPublishers.DisplayMember = "Value"
results(1) = cbCategories.DataSource
cbCategories.ValueMember = "Key"
cbCategories.DisplayMember = "Value"
```

ANALYSIS In this case, the bus variable represents a business object whose GetLookups method executes a stored procedure. This stored procedure returns a SqlDataReader containing data from the Publishers and Categories tables in the ComputeBooks database. The data reader is passed to the ExtractLookups method, which returns an array in the results variable. Because the array contains ArrayList objects, they can be used to populate the DataSource property of the cbPublishers and cbCategories ComboBox controls (System.Windows.Forms.ComboBox). The fields from the LookupData structure can then be used to populate the ValueMember and DisplayMember properties of the control so that the proper data will be displayed. This works because controls such as ComboBox that derive from System.Windows.Forms.ListControl can bind to any class that implements the IList interface like an ArrayList.

> For this code to work efficiently, the GetLookups method would need to use the CloseConnection command behavior when opening the data reader.

Although the controls in the System.Windows.Forms namespace can't bind directly to a data reader, the controls in the System.Web.UI.WebControls, such as the DataGrid, DataList, DropDownList, and CheckBoxList, can because they can bind to any object that supports the IEnumerable interface, which the SqlDataReader and

OleDbDataReader do. This makes for a highly efficient way to read static data and bind it to controls on a Web Form.

In addition to returning multiple result sets serially, the OleDb provider can be used to return hierarchical result sets using the Microsoft Data Shape (MSDataShape) OLE DB provider. Although largely superceded by the DataSet, the basic idea is that a nested result set (or *chapter*, as it's called in OLE DB) is accessible through a column in the data reader. The column can then be cast to an OleDbDataReader object and traversed. A simple example adapted from the online documentation is shown in Listing 11.9.

LISTING 11.9 Using the MSDataShape provider. This code uses the data shape provider to read through the Orders and OrderDetails tables in the ComputeBooks database.

```
Dim con As OleDbConnection = New OleDbConnection( _
 "Provider=MSDataShape;Data Provider=SQLOLEDB;" & _
 "Data Source=localhost;Integrated Security=SSPI;Initial Catalog=ComputeBooks")

Dim com As OleDbCommand = New OleDbCommand( _
 "SHAPE {SELECT OrderID, OrderDate FROM Orders} " & _
 " APPEND ({SELECT OrderID, ISBN, Quantity FROM OrderDetails} AS Details " & _
 " RELATE OrderId TO OrderId)", con)

Dim orders, details As OleDbDataReader

con.Open()
orders = com.ExecuteReader()

Do While orders.Read()
  ' Read the order data
  details = CType(orders.GetValue(2), OleDbDataReader)
  Do While details.Read()
    ' Read the details rows
  Loop
  details.Close()
Loop

orders.Close()
con.Close()
```

ANALYSIS In Listing 11.9, the OleDbConnection and OleDbCommand objects are instantiated and populated with the appropriate ConnectionString and CommandText arguments in their constructors. Although the syntax of the MSDataShape provider is beyond the scope of this book, it should be noted that rather than using inline SELECT statements to retrieve the Orders and OrderDetails tables, you can, with SQL Server, call stored procedures in their place. After the connection and data reader are open, the Orders

11

result set can be traversed as normal. However, the third column (ordinal 2) will be appended to the result set and consist of a chapter that contains the related OrderDetails rows. This column is already of type OleDbDataReader, so you can simply cast it to the appropriate type using the CType function. After the inner results are exhausted, the details data reader is closed. Finally, the orders data reader is closed along with the connection object.

Note

> You shouldn't use the CloseConnection command behavior when opening the data reader. Doing so causes the connection to be closed when the details data reader is closed within the outer loop.

As you can imagine, while in their respective loops, the Depth property of the orders data reader will return 0, whereas the Depth property of the details data reader will return 1.

Although using the data shape provider might come in handy if you have existing code that uses it, keep in mind that you get the same result by filling a DataSet with tables that contain the Orders and OrderDetails rows and then creating a relationship between the tables, as you learned during the first week.

Data Modification Statements

Although I'm reluctant to mention it, the command used to call the ExecuteReader method on can also execute other statements that don't return results. For example, the CommandText property for a SqlCommand object might look as follows:

```
SELECT PubCode, Name FROM Publishers;UPDATE PubStats SET Access = Access + 1
```

Of course, alternatively, and more appropriately, a stored procedure would be used to encapsulate both these statements. In this case, the database would not only retrieve the Publishers but would update the PubStats table as well. Although mixing SELECTs and other statements isn't recommended, the UPDATE statement will execute on the data store as soon as the ExecuteReader method is called and before the Read method is called, even though it appears after the SELECT statement. After the data reader is closed, its RecordsAffected property will be set to the number of rows inserted, updated, or deleted by the UPDATE statement. In the event that more than one data modification statement is included in the batch or stored procedure, the sum of all the inserted, updated, and deleted rows will be placed in the RecordsAffected property.

Note
> If the command simply returns rows, the RecordsAffected property will be set to –1.

One note of caution and a reason you should avoid mixing data retrieval and modification statements is that your ability to determine whether the data modification statements failed is dependent on the order of the statements in the stored procedure or batch. For example, if the statements shown earlier were executed and the UPDATE statement caused an error because the PubStats table didn't exist, the data reader would appear to execute normally and you could read its values with the Read method. However, the RecordsAffected property would be set to –1. Also, depending on the provider, you might not be able to even see the error message if it's not returned in the InfoMessage event of the connection (as it's not when using the SqlClient provider). If the statements were reversed, however, a SqlException would be thrown before the SELECT statement was executed and so you could catch it with a Try Catch block. The situation is further complicated if you have more than one data modification statement, in which case everything up to the statement that failed would execute and everything after it would not.

Because of the inherent indeterminacy in mixing retrieval and modification statements, you should stay away from such designs in your applications and segregate the statements that retrieve data from those that modify data in separate stored procedures.

11

 Note
> In future versions of the SqlClient providers, look for InfoMessage events to be fired for each data modification statement.

Summary

Data readers provide an efficient means to access data from a data store using a streamed programming model. The various methods provided by the data reader enable you to get the data one column at a time or as an array. Some providers even implement provider-specific type information to make the access more efficient. You can also use a data reader polymorphically in order to promote code reuse and separation of the tiers in a multi-tiered application. Data readers also expose some advanced functionality such as retrieving schema information, mixing retrieval and data modification statements, and working with OLE DB hierarchical result sets.

Now that you're fully familiar with the streamed programming model, tomorrow we'll once again explore the cached model by showing the techniques used to work with data adapters.

Workshop

This workshop will help reinforce the concepts covered in today's lesson.

Quiz

1. Why can't you pass a data reader by value between application domains?

   Data reader classes are derived from `MarshalByRefObject`, which can be referenced from remote application domains but not serialized and copied between them. As a result, you can pass a data reader by reference but not by value. However, passing it by reference means that each time a method or property of the data reader is accessed from the remote domain, a call to the hosting domain must be made and the results returned. This results in unnecessary overhead.

2. When would you use `GetValues` instead of methods such as `GetString`, `GetInt32`, and `GetByte`?

   The `GetValues` method retrieves all the columns in the row and places them in an array of type `System.Object`. This is more efficient than reading each column individually, although to use the data with a strong type, you then need to access the element of the array and cast it to the appropriate type.

3. How can I retrieve a large binary value with a data reader?

   For large binary values, you would typically want to call the `GetBytes` method on the column repeatedly, each time retrieving a specific amount of data and placing it in a buffer (an array of bytes).

4. Why would you declare a parameter as `IDataReader` rather than as `SqlDataReader` or `OleDbDataReader`?

   Creating methods that accept parameters or variables declared as the `IDataReader` interface rather than a derived type allows your code to work with any .NET Data Provider. Two specific examples include writing code in an ASP.NET page that casts the data reader returned from a data access class into `IDataReader` and then binds the data reader to a `DataGrid`, and writing methods that manipulate any object that implements the `IDataReader` interface.

Exercise

Write a method that uses a `SqlDataReader` to save the cover images of all titles for which images exist in the database. (Note that the images are JPEG and are all the same cover.)

Answers for Day 11

Exercise Answer

One possible solution might be

```
Private Sub SavePhotos(ByVal connect As String)

    Dim con As New SqlConnection(connect)
    Dim com As New SqlCommand( _
      "SELECT ISBN, cover FROM Titles WHERE cover IS NOT NULL", con)
    Dim dr As SqlDataReader
    Dim isbn As String
    Dim cover() As Byte

    Try
      con.Open()
      dr = com.ExecuteReader(CommandBehavior.CloseConnection)

      Do While dr.Read
        isbn = Trim(dr.GetString(0))
        cover = CType(dr.GetValue(1), Byte())

        ' Now write out the file
        Dim fs As New FileStream(isbn & ".jpg", FileMode.OpenOrCreate)
        Dim br As New BinaryWriter(fs)
        br.Write(cover)
        br.Close()
        fs.Close()
      Loop

    Catch e As Exception
      ' Handle the error
      Console.WriteLine(e.Message)
    Finally
      dr.Close()
    End Try

End Sub
```

11

DAY 12

Using Data Adapters

On Day 1, "ADO.NET in Perspective," you learned how ADO.NET was designed with modern distributed applications in mind. One of the primary architectures used in these types of applications entails the use of disconnected data. In this book, we've spent a great deal of time discussing the DataSet class and how it can be used to store and work with disconnected data. However, in enterprise applications, the most common source for, and the destination of, that data is a persistent store such as SQL Server or Oracle. The data adapter is the component of the .NET Data Provider that moves data into and out of the DataSet. Data adapters are classes implemented by the provider that typically derive from DbDataAdapter and inherit the IDbDataAdapter interface.

Although you've run across data adapters in the previous days, today you'll explore data adapters in detail. Specifically, you'll focus on the following concepts:

- How the data adapter fills a DataSet and what rules it follows when doing so
- How to control the amount of data read into a DataSet

- How data adapters synchronize the contents of a `DataSet` with a data store
- How to handle issues of concurrency and isolation with data adapters

Retrieving Data

The first method that most developers will invoke when using a data adapter is the `Fill` method. The `Fill` method is typically overloaded to support a variety of arguments that are used to populate data either in a `DataTable` or in one or more `DataTable` objects contained in a `DataSet`. For example, the `Fill` method of `OleDbDataAdapter` contains six public signatures that enable you to populate a `DataTable`, a `DataSet`, a `DataTable` with a specific mapping name, a specific range of rows in table in a `DataSet`, and even a `DataTable` or `DataSet` with data from an ADO `Recordset` object.

 Note

> In addition, `OleDbDataAdapter` supports four protected signatures for the `Fill` method that are inherited from `DbDataAdapter` but can't be accessed because `OleDbDataAdapter` is a sealed class (`NotInheritable` in VB). This implies that developers writing their own .NET Data Providers can inherit their data adapter from `DbDataAdapter` and override these methods to provide custom functionality.

The `SqlDataAdapter` provides the same set of signatures with the exception of not being able to read from an ADO `Recordset`.

When the `Fill` method executes, it actually executes the command object referenced by its `SelectCommand` property. Typically, the `SelectCommand` is populated using the constructor either by passing in a string that equates to the `CommandText` property of the command object or the instantiated command object itself. If only the command text is passed, the connection object must also be passed in order for the `Fill` method to know which data store to execute the `SelectCommand` against. As a result, the typical pattern is shown in Listing 12.1.

LISTING 12.1   Using a data adapter. This listing shows the typical pattern used to populate a `DataSet` with a data adapter.

```
SqlConnection con = new SqlConnection(_connect);
SqlCommand com = new SqlCommand("usp_GetTitles",con);
com.CommandType = CommandType.StoredProcedure;

SqlDataAdapter da = new SqlDataAdapter(com);
DataSet ds = new DataSet();
```

LISTING 12.1 continued

```
try
{
  da.Fill(ds);
}
  catch (SqlException e)
{
  // Handle error
}
```

As you can see from Listing 12.1, the connection object is first instantiated and passed to the constructor of the `SqlCommand` object, which is in turn passed to the constructor of the `SqlDataAdapter`. Note that the `DataSet` must be instantiated before passing it to the `Fill` method. Not doing so results in an exception.

> **Tip**
>
> As you learned on Day 9, "Using Connections and Transactions," an exception might be raised in the constructor of the connection object if the connection string is invalid. As a result, if you allow the connection string to be built dynamically, you should wrap the instantiation of the `SqlConnection` object in a `try catch` block.

One of the things you should notice in this code snippet is that the connection needn't be opened before calling the `Fill` method. If the connection associated with the `SelectCommand` isn't open already, the data adapter will open and close it as needed. Behind the scenes, the data adapter opens a data reader using the command object and uses it to populate both the schema and the rows of the `DataTable` or `DataSet` passed to the method.

The general rules that the `Fill` method uses are as follows:

- Tables and columns are created only if they don't already exist.

- Column types are created based on a mapping of the Common Types System (CTS) types to the types for a particular provider. You can find the complete list in the online documentation under the topic "Mapping .Net Data Provider Data Types to .NET Framework Data Types."

- By default, the `Fill` method maps the result sets returned from the command to data tables named Table, Table1, and so on. It then attempts to map the column names returned from the data store to the columns of a `DataTable`. This can be specified using table and column mappings.

12

- If tables and columns already exist, the existing schema is used and the value of the MissingSchemaAction property is used to determine the course to take.
- As you learned on Day 4, "DataSet Internals," primary keys aren't created unless they exist in the data store and the MissingSchemaAction property is set to AddWithKey.
- When populating the rows, if the Fill method finds a matching primary key, the data from the data store will be used to overwrite the data in the DataTable.
- If no primary key is found, the rows returned from the data store are simply appended to the DataTable.

In the remainder of this section, we'll take a look at how the schema is generated when filling a DataSet and how table mappings work. We'll also discuss a couple of advanced techniques for populating data using a data adapter.

Schema Generation

As shown in the bulleted rules earlier, ultimately, the Fill method will populate either one or more DataTable objects that are currently empty or that already contain schemas. We'll discuss exactly how this determination happens in detail in the next section. However, in either case, the generation of the schema information for an individual DataTable is controlled through the MissingSchemaAction property of the data adapter. This property can be set to any of the values in the MissingSchemaAction enumeration, as shown in Table 12.1.

TABLE 12.1 Schema generation. The MissingSchemaAction enumeration controls the behavior of the data adapter during the schema generation process.

Value	Description
Add	The default. Adds any columns necessary to complete the schema.
AddWithKey	Adds any columns and primary key information necessary to complete the schema.
Error	Throws an InvalidOperationException if the incoming schema doesn't map exactly to the existing schema of the DataTable.
Ignore	Ignores any extra columns from the data store that don't map to columns in the DataTable.

Obviously, the choice of the MissingSchemaAction value can have a major impact on the resulting data. It can also affect where you look for exceptions. Both the first and second values won't throw exceptions and will add any columns from the data store to the already existing columns in the DataTable. As you learned on Day 4, the AddWithKey option might also populate the AllowDBNull, MaxLength, AutoIncrement, AutoIncrementSeed, and AutoIncrementStep properties of the DataColumn objects as well as the PrimaryKey property of the DataTable, depending on the provider.

Tip

> When using any of these options, the DataTable can contain additional columns not populated by the Fill method. You can then populate these programmatically, through user input, or even through calculated values using the Expression property.

The Error value is the strictest of the MissingSchemaAction values and can be used to make sure that the incoming data maps exactly to the schema of the DataTable. This might be the case when you're using a strongly typed DataSet, as we discussed on Day 6, "Building Strongly Typed DataSet Classes." Note that an exception will be thrown even if the DataTable doesn't contain any columns. The Ignore value won't cause an exception and is useful when you might be populating a DataTable from multiple commands that return variant numbers of columns. It is also useful if you want to protect yourself against changes made to a stored procedure. Generally, of course, using Ignore isn't recommended. This is because you don't want to get into the habit of requesting more columns from the data store than you'll use, thereby increasing the workload of the data store unnecessarily.

Table Mappings

When passed a DataSet, the Fill method must first determine whether an existing DataTable exists into which to place the rows returned from the SelectCommand. It does this by looking at both the names of the existing tables and any table and column mappings that the data adapter has. By default, if no tables exist in the DataSet or none are named Table, a new table with the name Table is created. Its columns are created using the names and data types returned from the data store. As an alternative, the name of a table can be passed as the second argument to the Fill method and it'll be used to map the result set. If the command returns multiple result sets, additional tables are created with the names Table1, Table2, and so on. If the DataSet already contains tables, they'll be used as long as there are either table mappings or their names are Table, Table1, and so on.

12

Note   If the `Fill` method encounters duplicate column names, they'll be named `columnname1`, `columnname2`, and so on. Unnamed columns (such as those resulting from an aggregate function) will be named Column1, Column2, and so on. As a result, you'll want to make sure to avoid these names (as you should anyway) and always use explicit names for your columns.

When using the overloaded signature and when passed a `DataTable`, the `Fill` method first looks for a table mapping. If one isn't found, it simply fills the table regardless of its name, as you might expect. Both the `MissingSchemaAction` and `MissingMappingAction` properties influence this process.

The end result is that these defaults ensure that the data can be added to the `DataSet` or `DataTable` without any table or column mappings and regardless of what tables or columns already exist.

Although this process allows all the data to be mapped to the `DataSet` or `DataTable`, there are times when you want to make sure that the data is mapped to particular tables and columns. This might be the case if you're populating a table in a strongly typed `DataSet` that contains column names that aren't the same as those in the data store. In addition, this might be the case when the `DataSet` was created using an XSD schema supplied by a trading partner so that its data can be written to XML and sent to the partner. In these cases, you can create custom table and column mappings by adding items the `DataTableMappingCollection` object exposed by the `TableMappings` property of the data adapter. As an example, consider the following snippet:

```
da.TableMappings.Add("Titles","myTitles");
da.TableMappings[0].ColumnMappings.Add("Description","Desc");
da.TableMappings[0].ColumnMappings.Add("Title","BookTitle");
da.TableMappings[0].ColumnMappings.Add("Price","RetailPrice");

da.Fill(ds,"Titles");
```

ANALYSIS   In this example, a new table mapping is added to the data adapter with the source name of Titles and the data table name of myTitles. Within the table mapping, the `DataColumnMapping` is populated by passing the column name in the data store along with the column name in the `DataTable`. The overloaded `Fill` method is then called in order to use the table mapping. If the `DataSet` ds doesn't already contain a `DataTable` named myTitles, a new table named myTitles will be created with all the columns returned from the result set. However, the three columns added to the column mappings will be named accordingly rather than as they were named in the data store. If the table already exists, it will contain any existing columns, new columns from the data store that aren't in the column mappings collection, and the three columns in the collection. This is the case because the default for the `MissingMappingAction` property is `Passthrough`.

> **Note**
>
> Passing the name of a table mapping to the `Fill` method as shown in the previous code snippet is at first confusing to many developers. This is likely the case because you can either pass in the name of the table mapping (the first argument to the `Add` method of the `DataTableMappingCollection` object) or the name of the table to create if no table mappings have been defined for the data adapter.

As you can imagine, if you create a table mapping, like so

```
da.TableMappings.Add("Table","myTitles");
```

you don't need to pass the source name (Table in this case) to the `Fill` method. This default table mapping (as reflected by the `DefaultSourceTableName` field of the data adapter) will be used and the name of the new table will be set to myTitles. You can also create default mappings for Table1, Table2, and so on, in the event that the `SelectCommand` of the data adapter returns multiple result sets.

As just mentioned, the `MissingMappingAction` property influences the runtime behavior when table and column mappings are involved, and can be set to one of the values of the `MissingMappingAction` enumeration, as shown in Table 12.2.

TABLE 12.2 Mapping tables and columns. The `MissingMappingAction` enumeration controls the behavior of the data adapter when mappings are being applied.

Value	Description
Error	Throws an `InvalidOperationException` if either the table mapping or an individual column mapping is missing when the `Fill` method attempts to populate a `DataTable`.
Ignore	Any table or column that doesn't have a defined mapping is ignored.
Passthrough	The default. The table and columns are added to the `DataSet` and if a mapping exists, it's used as well.

As you can see from Table 12.2, the `Error` value is the strictest value and ensures that you must have mappings and that those mappings consider all the result sets and columns returned from the `SelectCommand`. As with the `MissingSchemaAction`, the `Ignore` value can be used to ignore any tables or columns that aren't a part of the mapping. `Passthrough` is the default and allows new table and columns to be integrated with those defined in the mapping.

12

Of course, the `MissingSchemaAction` property works in combination so that, for example, by using the `Error` value, you can ensure that the columns defined in the column mappings already exist in the `DataTable`. Likewise, if the `MissingSchemaAction` property is set to `Add`, the columns needn't already have been created in the `DataTable`.

To give you an example of the strictest case where you want to make sure the result set is fully mapped to a `DataTable` with a custom set of columns, consider the code in Listing 12.2.

LISTING 12.2   Using mappings. This code snippet creates table and column mappings for use by the `Fill` method of the data adapter.

```
SqlConnection con = new SqlConnection(_connect);
SqlCommand com = new SqlCommand("usp_GetTitles",con);
com.CommandType = CommandType.StoredProcedure;
com.Parameters.Add(new SqlParameter("@author",author));

SqlDataAdapter da = new SqlDataAdapter(com);
DataSet ds = new DataSet();
ds.ReadXmlSchema(schemaStream);

try
{
  da.MissingSchemaAction = MissingSchemaAction.AddWithKey;
  da.MissingMappingAction = MissingMappingAction.Error;

  da.TableMappings.Add("Table","Titles");
  da.TableMappings[0].ColumnMappings.Add("ISBN","ISBN");
  da.TableMappings[0].ColumnMappings.Add("Author","Author");
  da.TableMappings[0].ColumnMappings.Add("Description","Desc");
  da.TableMappings[0].ColumnMappings.Add("Title","BookTitle");
  da.TableMappings[0].ColumnMappings.Add("Price","RetailPrice");
  da.TableMappings[0].ColumnMappings.Add("Discount","Discount");
  da.TableMappings[0].ColumnMappings.Add("BulkAmount","BulkQualify");
  da.TableMappings[0].ColumnMappings.Add("BulkDiscount","Bulk");
  da.TableMappings[0].ColumnMappings.Add("Publisher","Publisher");
  da.TableMappings[0].ColumnMappings.Add("PubDate","PublicationDate");
  da.TableMappings[0].ColumnMappings.Add("CatID","CategoryId");
  da.TableMappings[0].ColumnMappings.Add("Cover","CoverImage");

  da.Fill(ds);
}
catch (InvalidOperationException e)
{
  // Handle mapping errors
}
catch (SqlException e)
{
  // Handle error
}
```

In Listing 12.2, the same usp_GetTitles stored procedure is used, but in this case it is passed a parameter populated with the variable author. The DataSet ds that is used to hold the results has its schema loaded from a stream variable called schemaStream. Both the MissingSchemaAction and MissingMappingAction properties are set to Error to ensure that the schema from the result set matches exactly with that in the DataSet and that the table and column mappings fully map to the result set. A default mapping is then created that maps all the columns from the Titles table in the ComputeBooks database to columns in the XSD schema loaded from the stream.

> **Note** The source and destination column names in the column mappings don't need to have different names. In the case of ISBN, Author, and Discount, the names are the same.

The Fill method is then called, which uses the default mapping to load the result set into the table named "Titles" in the DataSet. Note that when the schema was loaded, it must then have created a table named "Titles" in order for an exception not to be thrown. The two catch blocks handle errors resulting from the schema and mapping operations and any SQL Server exceptions that are thrown, respectively.

Advanced Retrieval

The techniques shown thus far illustrate the most common ways that a DataSet can be populated. There are, however, additional techniques that you can use to add information to the DataSet and to retrieve data incrementally.

Adding Metadata for SQL Server

As you learned during Week 1, the DataColumn, DataTable, and DataSet objects all expose a set of properties that you can manipulate to make sure that the data in the data store is accurately represented in the DataSet. For example, the DataColumn class exposes the AllowDBNull, MaxLength, Unique, DefaultValue, Caption, and other properties that affect how the data can be manipulated. Although *some* of these properties are populated automatically when you use the AddWithKey value of the MissingSchemaAction enumeration, not all of them are. For example, the Caption and DefaultValue properties aren't populated. It turns out that SQL Server provides extended properties that enable you to easily store and retrieve user-defined metadata directly in the database. You can use extended properties to store information such as the caption and default value, and then read that information dynamically into the DataSet.

12

In SQL Server 2000, extended properties can be placed on various database objects
including tables, views, stored procedures, rules, defaults, and functions. Using the
sp_addextendedproperty stored procedure, you can add any user-defined name-value
pair to the extended properties collection for an object. These values (stored as a
sql_variant of less than 7,500 bytes) can then be read using the fn_listextended-
property function. For example, to specify the captions and default values that applications can use, you could execute the following statements against a SQL Server 2000
database:

```
EXEC  sp_addextendedproperty 'caption', 'Bulk Discount', 'user',
  dbo, 'table', Titles, 'column', BulkDiscount
GO
EXEC  sp_addextendedproperty 'caption', 'Bulk Amount', 'user',
  dbo, 'table', Titles, 'column', BulkAmount
GO
EXEC  sp_addextendedproperty 'defaultvalue',0, 'user',
  dbo, 'table', Titles, 'column', BulkAmount
GO
```

Note See the SQL Server Books Online for more information on the meaning of
the parameters passed to the sp_addextendedproperty stored procedure.

In this example, two caption properties are added for the BulkDiscount and BulkAmount
columns of the Titles table. It should be noted that the selection of the property names
caption and defaultvalue is arbitrary—you can create your own property names as you
see fit. You can also add extended properties through a dialog box by right-clicking on
the object in the Query Analyzer.

Note Microsoft adds an extended property with the name MS_Description for a
column when the description is populated in the table design window in
SQL Server Enterprise Manager.

After the properties are in place, you can create a stored procedure to retrieve all the column properties for a particular table, as shown in the following code snippet:

```
CREATE PROCEDURE usp_GetColumnProperties
@table nvarchar(40)
AS
SELECT *
FROM ::fn_listextendedproperty(null,'user','dbo',
                'table',@table,'column',null)
```

In the `fn_listextendedproperty` function, the values that can vary are passed as null, so the procedure will return all the properties on the given table that are associated with columns. Within your .NET code, it then becomes relatively simple to create a method that can be used to populate the appropriate `DataColumn` properties, as shown in Listing 12.3.

LISTING 12.3 Retrieving extended properties. This method retrieves the caption and default value extended properties and associates them with a `DataColumn` in a `DataTable`.

```
private virtual void GetColumnProperties(String tableName, DataTable dt)
{
    SqlConnection con = new SqlConnection(_connect);
    SqlDataReader dr;

    // Setup the call to the stored procedure
    SqlCommand com = new SqlCommand("usp_GetColumnProperties", con);
    com.CommandType = CommandType.StoredProcedure;
    com.Parameters.Add(new SqlParameter("@table",tableName));

    con.Open();
    dr = com.ExecuteReader(CommandBehavior.CloseConnection);
    while (dr.Read())
    {
        switch (dr["name"].ToString())
        {
            // Handle captions and default values
            case "caption":
                dt.Columns[dr["objname"].ToString()].Caption =
                    dr["value"].ToString();
                break;
            case "defaultvalue":
                dt.Columns[dr["objname"].ToString()].DefaultValue = dr["value"];
                break;
        }
        dr.Close();
    }
}
```

12

ANALYSIS In Listing 12.3, the `GetColumnProperties` method accepts the name of the SQL Server table to query for and the name of the `DataTable` that contains the columns that map to that table. It then calls the stored procedure shown in the previous code snippet and loops through the results. Within the loop, it uses a `switch` statement to look for the appropriate property names before using the value to set the `Caption` and `DefaultValue` properties. Note that this method assumes that the names of the columns in the DataTable are the same as those in the database table. If you used column mappings to fill the DataSet, you would obviously have to query the mappings to determine which column in the DataTable to manipulate. This would make the code slightly more complex.

A client could then call this method after a DataSet or DataTable has been populated, like so:

```
da.Fill(ds);
GetColumnProperties("Titles",ds.Tables[0]);
```

This technique also assumes that the caller of the GetColumnProperties knows which table in the database maps to which table in the DataSet. The obvious benefit of retrieving metadata in this way is that it can be specified once at the database server and not re-specified in each application that accesses the database. However, the cost is that you incur an extra roundtrip to the server to retrieve the properties. As a result, you should use this technique only when the additional metadata you retrieve will be used by the application.

Tip

As you learned on Day 4, each of these classes also exposes an ExtendedProperties property that can hold a collection of custom properties. Given the name of the object in SQL Server, it would be trivial to write a method that retrieves the extended properties for any SQL Server object and adds them to the ExtendedProperties collection.

Retrieving Partial Result Sets

If you are a developer who has built applications that require data access, you'll no doubt have encountered a situation in which you want to incrementally retrieve results from a database. This might be the case, for example, when the potential number of rows a user would like to see is very large, but you would like to avoid having to initially retrieve them all. In ADO.NET, you can use two primary techniques to address this scenario.

First, as discussed previously, the Fill method of data adapter classes is overloaded. One of the overloaded signatures enables you to pass in the row to start with (that is, the row in the result set returned by the SelectCommand to start with) and the maximum number of rows to use to populate the DataTable. For example, to populate the DataTable with the first 50 rows returned in the result set, you would use the following syntax:

```
da.Fill(ds,0,50,"Titles");
```

Note that this signature requires a DataSet to be passed to the Fill method along with a table mapping. Just as we discussed previously, in the event that a table mapping doesn't exist, you can pass in the name of the new DataTable. Of course, rather than hard-coding the starting row and the number of rows to add to the table, it's trivial to make a calculation in order to incrementally add rows to the DataSet using variables as the user requests more data. By passing 0 into the max records parameter (the third argument), all the rows after the starting row will be added to the table. As you might expect, the starting and max records arguments apply to only the first result set in the event that the SelectCommand returns multiple results. Finally, if the table already exists, the data will be appended to it based on the rules discussed at the beginning of today's lesson.

> **Note**
>
> Although the documentation states that the names of tables in a DataSet are case-sensitive, they are in fact not. In other words, adding a table named titles to a DataSet and then using the Fill method to populate a table named îTitlesî in the same DataSet won't result in the creation of two tables.

The downside of this method—and its fatal flaw in all but the simplest applications—is that the query encapsulated in the SelectCommand will be executed in its entirety even though ultimately only a subset of the rows returned will be used. This wastes resources on the server and violates the cardinal rule that you ask the data store for only data that you're going to use. As a result, this technique isn't recommended.

An alternative and more efficient technique you can use to incrementally populate a DataSet is to pass arguments to the SelectCommand, which selects only the specific rows. Typically, this requires that you pass to the command arguments that specify a range of rows. For example, consider the GetOrdersByDate method shown in Listing 12.4 and that calls the stored procedure shown in Listing 12.5.

12

LISTING 12.4 Incrementally retrieving data. This method calls the usp_OrdersByDate stored procedure to incrementally populate a DataSet based on the date range.

```
private virtual void GetOrdersByDate(DataSet ds,
  DateTime startDate, DateTime endDate)
{
    SqlConnection con = new SqlConnection(_connect);
    SqlCommand com = new SqlCommand("usp_OrdersByDate",con);
    SqlDataAdapter da = new SqlDataAdapter(com);
    da.MissingSchemaAction = MissingSchemaAction.AddWithKey;
```

LISTING 12.4   continued

```
// Setup the parameters
com.CommandType = CommandType.StoredProcedure;
com.Parameters.Add(new SqlParameter("@startdate", SqlDbType.SmallDateTime));
com.Parameters[0].Value = startDate;
com.Parameters.Add(new SqlParameter("@enddate", SqlDbType.SmallDateTime));
com.Parameters[1].Value = endDate;

try
{
    da.Fill(ds);
}
catch (SqlException e)
{
    // Handle Exception
}
}
```

LISTING 12.5   Selecting data incrementally. This stored procedure is called by the method in Listing 12.4 to retrieve a range of rows from the `Orders` and `OrderDetails` tables.

```
CREATE PROCEDURE usp_OrdersByDate
@startdate smalldatetime = null,
@enddate smalldatetime = null
AS

IF @startdate IS NULL
 SET @startdate = convert(smalldatetime,'1/1/1900')

IF @enddate IS NULL
 SET @enddate = convert(smalldatetime,'1/1/2079')

SELECT * FROM Orders
WHERE OrderDate BETWEEN @startdate AND @enddate
ORDER By OrderDate DESC

SELECT a.* FROM OrderDetails a JOIN Orders b on a.OrderID = b.OrderID
WHERE b.OrderDate BETWEEN @startdate AND @enddate
GO
```

ANALYSIS   In Listing 12.4, the method accepts a `DataSet` and parameters that specify both the start and end dates to query on. The stored procedure `usp_OrdersByDate` in Listing 12.5 is then called and passed the parameters. Because the `DataSet` is passed into the method, the client can call this method repeatedly and vary the arguments each time to retrieve a subset of the data with each invocation. For example, to retrieve all the orders from January 1, 2000, to the present, the client could make the following two calls:

```
DataSet ds = new DataSet();

GetOrdersByDate(ds,new DateTime(2002,1,1),DateTime.Now);
GetOrdersByDate(ds, new DateTime(2000,1,1), new DateTime(2001,12,31));
```

In the first call, the orders from January 1, 2002, to the present are retrieved. When the DataSet is passed back to the method, the orders from January 1, 2000, to December 31, 2001, are then appended to the two DataTable objects in the DataSet. In this way, the client can incrementally add rows by varying the arguments. Note that this technique also allows the client to skip rows wherever they deem necessary. The AddWithKey value is used for the MissingSchemaAction property to ensure that if the method is called more than once with overlapping date ranges, the Fill method will match the rows based on the existing primary key rather than adding multiple copies of the same row.

Updating a Data Store

After the data has been retrieved and modified by your application, you need to resynchronize it with the data store. Keep in mind that because we're dealing with the disconnected model here, the data adapter handles updates in a batch fashion. In other words, when its overloaded Update method is called, it looks for all changed rows in the given DataSet, DataTable, or array of DataRow objects, and attempts to run the InsertCommand, UpdateCommand, or DeleteCommand associated with the data adapter as appropriate. Of course, as you learned on Day 5, "Changing Data," the data adapter makes the determination about how a row was changed by looking at the value of its RowState property. It hardly needs to be said that for a data adapter to synchronize the data in a DataSet or DataTable with a data store, the AcceptChanges method shouldn't have been called because doing so resets the RowState property to Unchanged.

In the remainder of today's lesson, you'll learn how the Update method accomplishes this and how you can customize its behavior for your particular scenarios.

The Update Process

As you just learned, the data adapter exposes the InsertCommand, UpdateCommand, and DeleteCommand properties that reference command objects called by the Update method as it traverses the changed rows. Behind the scenes, the parameters exposed by the command object are populated with values from the row being inspected. These values are then passed to the command that is executed. It's important to remember that this process is row oriented, so if you change 15 rows in a DataTable and then pass it to the Update method of a data adapter, 15 commands will be executed against the data store, one for each row.

> **Tip**
>
> This process implies that if you wanted to make the same change to multiple rows, you shouldn't retrieve them into a `DataTable` and then make the change to each row and call the `Update` method. It's far more efficient to change multiple rows in a single statement with the appropriate `WHERE` clause using the `ExecuteNonQuery` method.

The interesting aspect of this architecture is that it's flexible by giving you complete control over how the modifications are actually applied. This is the case because the command object can simply reference a statement or stored procedure that actually does the work. This enables you to write commands that can modify multiple tables in the data store based on the data in a single `DataTable`. In addition, you can create multi-function stored procedures that, for example, can be referenced by both the `UpdateCommand` and `InsertCommand`. This can be done by allowing the stored procedure to determine whether the row is already in the table so that you can write a single stored procedure to handle the insert or update of a row in the `Titles` table, as shown in Listing 12.6.

LISTING 12.6 Multi-function stored procedures. This SQL Server stored procedure can be used both to insert and update a row in the `Titles` table.

```
CREATE  PROCEDURE usp_SaveTitle
        @ISBN           [nvarchar](10) = null,
        @Description    [nvarchar](2048) = null,
        @Title          [nvarchar](100) = null,
        @Author         [nvarchar](250) = null,
        @Price          [money] = null,
        @PubDate        [smalldatetime] = null,
        @Publisher      [nchar](5) = null,
        @CatID          [uniqueidentifier] = null
AS

IF EXISTS (SELECT * FROM Titles WHERE ISBN = @ISBN)
BEGIN
  UPDATE Titles
    SET Description = @Description,
    Title = @Title,
    Author = @Author,
    Price = @Price,
    PubDate = @PubDate,
    Publisher = @Publisher,
    CatID = @CatID
```

LISTING 12.6 continued

```
  WHERE ISBN = @ISBN

  RETURN 1

END
ELSE
BEGIN
  INSERT INTO Titles (ISBN, Description, Title,
  Author, Price, PubDate, Publisher, CatID)
    VALUES (
    @ISBN,
    @Description,
    @Title,
    @Author,
    @Price,
    @PubDate,
    @Publisher,
    @CatID
    )
  RETURN 0
End

GO
```

ANALYSIS The procedure in Listing 12.6 uses the Transact-SQL EXISTS clause to determine whether the row already exists based on the primary key column (ISBN). If so, an UPDATE statement is performed; if not, an INSERT is performed. Note that the procedure returns 1 if the row was updated and 0 if the row was inserted.

From within your .NET code, you can then reference the procedure once and associate it with both command objects as shown in Listing 12.7.

12

LISTING 12.7 Modifying data. This code sets up the data adapter to insert, update, and delete rows from the database based on the DataSet.

```
SqlCommand cmSave = new SqlCommand("usp_SaveTitle", con);
cmSave.CommandType = CommandType.StoredProcedure;

SqlCommand cmDelete = new SqlCommand("usp_DeleteTitle", con);
cmDelete.CommandType = CommandType.StoredProcedure;

SqlDataAdapter da = new SqlDataAdapter();
da.UpdateCommand = cmSave;
da.InsertCommand = cmSave;
da.DeleteCommand = cmDelete;
```

LISTING 12.7   continued

```
// Configure save parameters
cmSave.Parameters.Add(new SqlParameter(
  "@isbn", SqlDbType.NVarChar, 10, "isbn"));
cmSave.Parameters.Add(new SqlParameter(
  "@description", SqlDbType.NVarChar, 2048, "Description"));
cmSave.Parameters.Add(new SqlParameter(
  "@title", SqlDbType.NVarChar, 100, "Title"));
cmSave.Parameters.Add(new SqlParameter(
  "@author", SqlDbType.NVarChar, 250, "Author"));
cmSave.Parameters.Add(new SqlParameter(
  "@price", SqlDbType.Money, 4, "Price"));
cmSave.Parameters.Add(new SqlParameter(
  "@pubDate", SqlDbType.DateTime, 4, "PubDate"));
cmSave.Parameters.Add(new SqlParameter(
  "@publisher", SqlDbType.NChar, 5, "Publisher"));
cmSave.Parameters.Add(new SqlParameter(
  "@catId", SqlDbType.UniqueIdentifier, 8, "CatId"));

// Configure delete parameters
cmDelete.Parameters.Add(new SqlParameter(
  "@isbn", SqlDbType.NVarChar, 10, "isbn"));

// Synchronize the data
da.Update(dsTitles);
```

 You'll notice in Listing 12.7 that the cmSave SqlCommand object is instantiated and configured and then used to populate both the UpdateCommand and InsertCommand properties of the SqlDataAdapter. Because the structure of the stored procedure used to delete a row is so different from that used to insert or update a row, a separate command object is used. You'll also notice that in this case, the empty constructor of the SqlDataAdapter is used because the SelectCommand needn't be populated. This is because only the Update method is called in this listing. When the Update method is called, one of the two stored procedures will be executed for each modified, inserted, or deleted row.

> **Note** If the DataSet contains multiple tables, you should specify the source table mapping that the update method should use. If none is specified, it will use the default table mapping and subsequently update the first table in the DataSet. Of course, as we discussed earlier, you can also simply pass the name of the DataTable to process if no table mapping exists for it.

One of the other key points to notice in Listing 12.7 is the last argument passed to the constructor of the SqlParameter objects. This parameter specifies the SourceColumn property that identifies the column in the row from which to populate the parameter. This is what allows the data adapter to associate the data in the row being updated with the parameters of the command object. In addition, an overloaded version of the constructor enables you to pass in the SourceVersion as well. This property maps to a value from the DataRowVersion enumeration discussed on Day 5 and specifies which version (Current, Default, Original, or Proposed) to use for the column. You would use the Original version of the column, for example, to ensure that the WHERE clause in an UPDATE statement modifies the same row that was returned from the data store.

You can also control when exceptions are thrown by this process. By default, the ContinueUpdateOnError property of the data adapter is set to False, so the first command that results in an error will throw the SqlException or OleDbException, as appropriate. This means that not all the rows that were modified, inserted, or deleted might have been processed by the Update method. Setting the property to True won't throw an exception, but will simply update the RowError and RowState properties of the DataRow object. This allows all the changes to be attempted against the data store. As you'll see in the next section, this means that you must programmatically determine whether errors have occurred.

Finally, you can control which rows are processed by the Update method, and in which order, by using the GetChanges method. For example, to make sure that the inserts are processed before the updates and deletes, you could use code like this:

```
da.Update(dsTitles.GetChanges(DataRowState.Added));
da.Update(dsTitles.GetChanges(DataRowState.Modified));
da.Update(dsTitles.GetChanges(DataRowState.Deleted));
```

Keep in mind that you can also pass combinations of DataRowState values to the Update method to send different subsets of the rows.

Handling Events

During the process of updating a data store, the data adapter throws the RowUpdating and RowUpdated events. The former fires immediately before the appropriate command is executed for a row, whereas the latter fires immediately after the command has been executed. The event handlers receive different event argument types derived from the RowUpdatingEventArgs and RowUpdatedEventArgs classes from the System.Data.Common namespace. For example, the event handler for the RowUpdating event for an OleDbDataAdapter receives an OleDbRowUpdatingEventArgs object, whereas the handler for the RowUpdated event receives an OleDbRowUpdatedEventArgs object. Tables 12.3 and 12.4 show the primary properties exposed by each.

12

TABLE 12.3   Row updating event argument properties. These are the properties inherited by the event argument types passed into the event handler for the RowUpdating event.

Property	Description
Command	Gets or sets a reference to the command used to perform the update.
Errors	Returns the exception generated when the command executes.
Row	Returns the DataRow sent to the update statement.
StatementType	Returns a value from the StatementType enumeration that identifies which type of statement is being processed (Select, Insert, Update, Delete).
Status	Gets or sets a value from the UpdateStatus enumeration that indicates how the command will behave. Can be set to Continue, ErrorsOccurred, SkipAllRemainingRows, or SkipCurrentRow.
TableMapping	Returns the DataTableMapping used by the command.

TABLE 12.4   Row updated event argument properties. These are the properties inherited by the event argument types passed into the event handler for the RowUpdated event.

Property	Description
Command	Returns a reference to the command used to perform the update.
Errors	Returns the exception generated when the command executes.
RecordsAffected	Returns the number of rows modified by the command.
Row	Returns the DataRow sent to the update statement.
StatementType	Returns a value from the StatementType enumeration that identifies which type of statement is being processed (Select, Insert, Update, Delete).
Status	Gets or sets a value from the UpdateStatus enumeration that indicates how the command will behave. Can be set to Continue, ErrorsOccurred, SkipAllRemainingRows, or SkipCurrentRow.
TableMapping	Returns the DataTableMapping used by the command.

As you can see from Tables 12.3 and 12.4, you can view all the information that will be used to update a row before it's processed and, in the RowUpdating event handler, even change the command to be used on the fly. In addition, using the Status property is especially interesting because you can affect the behavior of the rest of the Update method by skipping the current row or all remaining rows. In the RowUpdated event, you can also view the exception generated by the command even if the ContinueUpdateOnError property is set to True.

Although not used frequently, the RowUpdated event handler, for example, can be used to log all the changes made to the data for tracking purposes or to manually cascade changes in other `DataSet` objects. Like other events, the technique used to capture them is to create a method to act as the event handler and then add the handler to the invocation list for the event, as shown in the following code snippet:

```
// Handle the RowUpdated event
private void TitleChanged(object sender, OleDbRowUpdatedEventArgs e)
{
    Trace.WriteLine("Primary key " + e.Row.Item(0).ToString()
    + " was " & e.StatementType.ToString() + " on "
    + DateTime.Now.ToLongTimeString());
}

da.RowUpdated += new OleDbRowUpdatedEventHandler(this.TitleChanged);
```

Using a Disconnected Update Model

Now that you've learned the basic way in which updates are processed by the data adapter, it's time to apply this knowledge to a programming pattern that you can use in applications that work with disconnected data.

The basic idea in this disconnected model, of course, is that your application will retrieve rows from the data store and cache them in the `DataSet`. The `DataSet` will then be modified by the presentation code over time and will eventually be re-synchronized using a data adapter. As you'll learn in more detail next week, in multi-tier applications, the synchronization process would eventually occur in a method of the data access tier that accepts the modified `DataSet`. This method is responsible for creating the appropriate data adapter, passing the `DataSet` to the `Update` method, and returning rows that caused errors. As a result, the basic pattern that a method in the data access tier could implement is shown in Listing 12.8.

LISTING 12.8 Implementing the disconnected update. This method shows the skeleton of a method that would be used to synchronize a `DataSet` with the data store.

```
public virtual DataSet SaveMyData(DataSet ds)
{
    //Make sure the DataSet has some changed data
    if (ds == null || ds.HasChanges() == false)
    {
        // Can simply return null
        return null;
    }

    // Create the connection object
    // Create the data adapter (da)
    // Create the data adapter commands and configure their parameters
    //  making sure to map their SourceColumns and SourceVersions
    // Associate the commands with the data adapter
```

LISTING 12.8   continued

```
    // Set the ContineUpdateOnError property to true

    try
    {
        // Call the Update method passing in results of the GetChanges method
        da.Update(ds);

        // Check for errors and return rows that were in error
        if (ds.HasErrors)
        {
            DataSet dsErrors;
            dsErrors = ds.GetChanges(DataRowState.Modified ||
              DataRowState.Deleted);
            return dsErrors;
        }
        return null;
    }
    catch (Exception e)
    {
        // An exception occurred, probably in the connection
        // Wrap and throw a specific exception
    }
}
```

ANALYSIS   What you'll first notice in Listing 12.8 is that the SaveMyData method checks to make sure that the DataSet is instantiated and has changes that can be processed. If there are changes, the method proceeds to create the connection, command, and data adapter objects that will be needed, much as is shown in Listing 12.7. Note that in this model, the method sets the ContinueUpdateOnError property to True to make sure that all the changed rows actually get a chance to be synchronized with the data store. Within the try block, the DataSet is then passed to the Update method.

Note

It's important at this point to pass in the entire DataSet rather than simply the results of the GetChanges method. This is the case because the Update method will modify the properties of the DataTable and DataRow objects in the DataSet, and we need to be able to read those changes when the method returns. If you call the GetChanges method directly in the Update method, copies will be created and the caller won't be able to retrieve the changes.

Because the ContinueUpdateOnError property is set to True, no exception will be thrown when the Update method is called unless the implicit opening of the connection object fails. As a result, the catch block need only wrap the exception that was generated and throw it back to the caller. Once the Update method returns, the data adapter will have successfully synchronized the rows that it could, setting their RowState properties to Unchanged. Each row that failed will have its RowState set either set to Modified (for modified rows that failed) or Deleted (for rows that couldn't be deleted from the data store). Both of these types of rows are then returned from the method in the dsErrors DataSet using the GetChanges method.

Note

> The algorithm shown here is generic and assumes that you'll be updating the lone DataTable in the DataSet. Of course, you could augment this method to accept the name of the table you want to update and even create multiple data adapters to update each of the tables in turn. As we'll discuss shortly, this method also assumes that each row is treated individually and not within the context of a transaction.

The caller can use the SaveMyData method like so:

```
DataSet myErrors;

myErrors = SaveMyData(ds.GetChanges());
foreach (DataRow r in dsErrors.Tables[0].GetErrors())
{
    // Inspect the r.RowError and r.RowState properties
}
```

Notice that the caller passes into the SaveMyData only the changed rows in order to save resources, and then catches any errors in the myErrors DataSet. The tables in the myErrors DataSet can then be traversed and each row inspected using the RowState and RowError properties, which will be set to the original RowState and contain the error message from the data store, respectively.

The client could also, of course, bind the myErrors DataSet to a grid in order to visually present the rows that caused errors to the user. The user could then make additional changes or decide not to reprocess the row. Those rows that are changed a second time could then be sent back to the SaveMyData method, and the others could be merged with the original DataSet using the Merge method.

12

Isolation and Concurrency

In the previous section, you learned how the data adapter processes updates and how you might write data access methods to handle changes in a DataSet. However, the discussion fails to address the issues of isolation and concurrency for those updates.

Isolating Changes

For example, as noted in the previous section, the algorithm shown in Listing 12.8 assumes that each row will succeed or fail individually. As you learned on Day 9, "Using Connections and Transactions," the data adapter can isolate and treat all the changed rows it encounters as a logical unit of work using transactions. If you want to make sure that either all the changes succeed or all of them fail, you would change the algorithm in Listing 12.8 as shown in Listing 12.9.

LISTING 12.9   Implementing the disconnected update. This method shows the skeleton of a method that would be used to synchronize a DataSet with the data store.

```
public virtual void SaveMyData(DataSet ds)
{
    //Make sure the DataSet has some changed data
    if (ds == null || ds.HasChanges() == false)
    {
        // Can simply return
        return;
    }

    // Create the connection object (con)
    // Create the data adapter (da)
    // Create the data adapter commands and configure their parameters
    // Associate the commands with the data adapter
    // Set the ContineUpdateOnError property to false

    try
    {
        con.Open();
        SqlTransaction trans = con.BeginTransaction();
        // Set the Transaction property of the command objects

        try
        {
            // Call the Update method, passing in the DataSet
            da.Update(ds);
            // Commit the changes
            trans.Commit();
            return;
        }
        catch (Exception e)
```

LISTING 12.9 continued

```
        {
            // Rollback the transaction
            trans.Rollback();
            // Wrap and throw the exception
        }
    }
    catch (Exception e)
    {
        // Could not open the connection or start the transaction
        // Wrap and throw the Exception
    }
    finally
    {
        con.Close();
    }
}
```

 ANALYSIS In Listing 12.9, the SaveMyData method is marked as void rather than returning a DataSet that contains the rows that had errors. This is because when the first error is encountered, the method will throw an exception and roll back the transaction. Notice that the connection must be opened explicitly and the BeginTransaction method must be called to initiate the local transaction. You must then set the Transaction property of each of the command objects associated with the data adapter accordingly. Within the nested try block, the Update method is called and if it succeeds without throwing an exception, the transaction is committed. If an exception occurs, the transaction can be rolled back and the exception wrapped and thrown back to the caller.

> **Tip**
>
> When you throw the exception after rolling back the transaction, you should embed the primary key value or row number that caused the error in the message. This will allow the client to more easily process the error.

The outer try block contains a finally block that closes the connection either in the event the connection or transaction had problems or the Update method throws an exception. Note that this algorithm relies on the fact that the ContinueUpdateOnError property is set to False. Doing so throws an exception when the first error is encountered and places the error returned from the data store in the Message property of the exception object.

Handling Concurrency Issues

The previous example dealt with isolating the changes but didn't address the issue of concurrency or how changes from multiple users are handled. In a nutshell, concurrency isn't handled directly by the data adapter, so it must be handled either through local transactions or the commands you use with the data adapter to apply changes to the data store.

NEW TERM In general, concurrency falls into two camps: optimistic concurrency and pessimistic concurrency. The difference between the two is that **optimistic concurrency** strives to allow as many users to simultaneously work with the data as possible, whereas **pessimistic concurrency** tries to ensure that when a user updates a row, the row is in exactly the same state as when it was first read. The tradeoff is that optimistic concurrency creates fewer conflicts at the cost of potentially losing changes made by other clients because it employs a last-in-wins strategy. Pessimistic concurrency, on the other hand, ensures that each client's changes won't be summarily overwritten at the cost of causing more conflicts to occur.

Typically, the disconnected model implies that you use a form of optimistic concurrency because it isn't realistic (and would cause a lot of conflicts) to assume that a row remains totally unchanged while the data is cached on a client somewhere. To use optimistic concurrency, the WHERE clause of the statement that executes as a result of the UpdateCommand should contain only the primary key columns. This is the case in Listings 12.6 and 12.7 where the UPDATE statement in the usp_SaveTitle stored procedure considers only the ISBN in the WHERE clause and where only the values from the current row version are passed to the stored procedure.

> **Note** The implicit assumption made in Listing 12.6 as well as Listing 12.10 (discussed shortly) is that the ISBN is immutable. In other words, once the title is added to the table, the ISBN can't be changed. This can be enforced on SQL Server using a trigger and within the DataSet by setting the ReadOnly property of the DataColumn to True.

That having been said, you can use two techniques to implement pessimistic concurrency with a data adapter. The first is to rely on a local transaction with an isolation level that restricts other users from changing the data while it's locked. In other words, you would start a transaction with an isolation level such as RepeatableRead before invoking the Fill method. You would then make your changes and use the same connection and transaction with the data adapter when calling the Update method. This technique puts the burden of locking the rows on the data store. Although this ensures that the rows remain locked and can't be changed by other clients, it violates the cardinal design rule of transaction usage: Never allow user input in the middle of a transaction. In other words, always make transactions as short as possible so as not to lock out other clients. It also, of course, isn't very useful in applications in which you don't hold continuous connections to the data store, such as ASP.NET applications that use ADO.NET. Because of these reasons, this technique is recommended for only a few specialized scenarios.

The second form of pessimistic concurrency relies on the configuration of the WHERE clause in the UpdateCommand of the data adapter. By including all the columns in the WHERE clause and passing the values that were originally retrieved from the data store to the command, the command can ensure that the row is in exactly the same state as when it was retrieved. For example, if you wanted to create a stored procedure in SQL Server that uses pessimistic concurrency to update a row in the Titles table, the procedure might look like the one in Listing 12.10.

LISTING 12.10   Pessimistic concurrency. This stored procedure could be used to update a row in the Titles table and ensure that the updated row is the same as when it was retrieved.

```
CREATE   PROCEDURE usp_UpdTitle
         @ISBN      [nvarchar](10),
         @Description     [nvarchar](2048) = null,
         @Title     [nvarchar](100) = null,
         @Author    [nvarchar](250) = null,
         @Price     [money] = null,
         @PubDate     [smalldatetime] = null,
         @Publisher     [nchar](5) = null,
         @CatID     [uniqueidentifier] = null,
         @original_Description  [nvarchar](2048) = null,
         @original_Title     [nvarchar](100) = null,
         @original_Author     [nvarchar](250) = null,
         @original_Price     [money] = null,
         @original_PubDate     [smalldatetime] = null,
         @original_Publisher     [nchar](5) = null,
         @original_CatID     [uniqueidentifier] = null
  AS

IF EXISTS (SELECT * FROM Titles WHERE ISBN = @ISBN)
BEGIN

  UPDATE Titles
    SET Description = @Description,
    Title = @Title,
    Author = @Author,
    Price = @Price,
```

12

LISTING 12.10   continued

```
      PubDate = @PubDate,
      Publisher = @Publisher,
      CatID = @CatID
    WHERE ISBN = @ISBN
    AND Title = @original_Title
    AND Author = @original_Author
    AND Price = @original_Price
    AND PubDate = @original_PubDate
    AND Publisher = @original_Publisher
    AND CatID = @original_CatID

    IF @@rowcount = 0
      RAISERROR('The row has been changed',14,1)
  END
  ELSE
    RAISERROR('That ISBN no longer exists',14,1)

  GO
```

ANALYSIS You'll remember from Day 2, "Getting Started," that the Data Adapter Configuration Wizard contains options that enable you to specify the concurrency level. By choosing pessimistic, the wizard will create a procedure very much like that shown in Listing 12.10. In this case, the procedure simply checks to make sure that the ISBN exists and, if so, updates it with the parameters passed to the procedure. The WHERE clause contains all the original values passed in to the procedure. If the row can't be found (that is, it has been deleted) the RAISERROR statement is issued, which will result in a row error in the data adapter. Likewise, if the row can't be updated because one of the columns doesn't match, an error is raised.

The ADO.NET code that configures the data adapter would then have to change to include both the current values that are used in the SET statement and the original values used in the WHERE clause, as shown in Listing 12.11.

LISTING 12.11   Configuring pessimistic concurrency. This code snippet shows how you would add parameters to the command used to update the Titles table using pessimistic concurrency.

```
SqlCommand cmSave = new SqlCommand("usp_UpdTitle", con);
cmSave.CommandType = CommandType.StoredProcedure;

cmSave.Parameters.Add(new SqlParameter(
  "@isbn", SqlDbType.NVarChar, 10, "isbn"));
cmSave.Parameters.Add(new SqlParameter(
  "@description", SqlDbType.NVarChar, 2048, "Description"));
```

LISTING 12.11   continued

```
cmSave.Parameters.Add(new SqlParameter(
  "@title", SqlDbType.NVarChar, 100, "Title"));
cmSave.Parameters.Add(new SqlParameter(
  "@author", SqlDbType.NVarChar, 250, "Author"));
cmSave.Parameters.Add(new SqlParameter(
  "@price", SqlDbType.Money, 4, "Price"));
cmSave.Parameters.Add(new SqlParameter(
  "@pubDate", SqlDbType.DateTime, 4, "PubDate"));
cmSave.Parameters.Add(new SqlParameter(
  "@publisher", SqlDbType.NChar, 5, "Publisher"));
cmSave.Parameters.Add(new SqlParameter(
  "@catId", SqlDbType.UniqueIdentifier, 8, "CatId"));

cmSave.Parameters.Add(new SqlParameter(
  "@original_description", SqlDbType.NVarChar, 2048, "Description"));
cmSave.Parameters["@original_description"].SourceVersion =
  DataRowVersion.Original;
cmSave.Parameters.Add(new SqlParameter(
  "@original_title", SqlDbType.NVarChar, 100, "Title"));
cmSave.Parameters["@original_title"].SourceVersion =
  DataRowVersion.Original;
cmSave.Parameters.Add(new SqlParameter(
  "@original_author", SqlDbType.NVarChar, 250, "Author"));
cmSave.Parameters["@original_author"].SourceVersion =
  DataRowVersion.Original;
cmSave.Parameters.Add(new SqlParameter(
  "@original_price", SqlDbType.Money, 4, "Price"));
cmSave.Parameters["@original_price"].SourceVersion =
  DataRowVersion.Original;
cmSave.Parameters.Add(new SqlParameter(
  "@original_pubDate", SqlDbType.DateTime, 4, "PubDate"));
cmSave.Parameters["@original_pubDate"].SourceVersion =
  DataRowVersion.Original;
cmSave.Parameters.Add(new SqlParameter(
  "@original_publisher", SqlDbType.NChar, 5, "Publisher"));
cmSave.Parameters["@original_publisher"].SourceVersion =
  DataRowVersion.Original;
cmSave.Parameters.Add(new SqlParameter(
  "@original_catId", SqlDbType.UniqueIdentifier, 8, "CatId"));
cmSave.Parameters["@original_catId"].SourceVersion =
  DataRowVersion.Original;
```

12

ANALYSIS As you can see from Listing 12.11, each parameter must be added to the collection. Because the SourceVersion property defaults to Current, the property needn't be set for the parameters that represent the new values to be updated. However, all the original values need to have their SourceVersion property set to Original.

> **Note**
>
> Although one of the signatures for the overloaded constructor of the `SqlParameter` object enables you to specify the `SourceVersion` (so you could avoid coding two statements for each parameter), it also requires several other arguments that are easier to allow to be defaulted.

The obvious downside to using this form of pessimistic concurrency is that both the statement that performs the update against the data store and the ADO.NET code used to configure the data adapter become longer and more complex. Some data stores, however, provide a quicker means of determining whether the row has changed since it was retrieved. In SQL Server, for example, you can add a column with the `timestamp` data type to a table. This column is automatically updated to a unique binary value each time a row is inserted or updated in the table. The result is that you can select this column when the `DataSet` is populated and then pass it back to the `UpdateCommand` of the data adapter. The stored procedure or inline SQL can then compare the value you originally retrieved with the value in the database. If they don't match, the row has been changed. Using a `timestamp` or other equivalent saves you from having to pass two parameters for each column and configuring the `UpdateCommand` with all those parameters.

> **Note**
>
> **NEW TERM** Although the data type is called `timestamp`, it has no correlation with a time or date and isn't human readable. A better way to think of `timestamp` columns is with the term **row version**. In fact, SQL Server 2000 includes a `rowversion` synonym for the `timestamp` data type, which is preferred because it will eventually replace `timestamp` in future versions of SQL Server. You should also specify the same column name for the `timestamp` (`rowversion`) column in all your tables for consistency; for example, calling it `rowVersion`. As you would expect, you can have only one `timestamp` column per table.

Using the `rowversion` column, the `UPDATE` statement in the `usp_UpdTitle` stored procedure would be rewritten as follows:

```
UPDATE Titles
  SET Description = @Description,
  Title = @Title,
  Author = @Author,
  Price = @Price,
  PubDate = @PubDate,
  Publisher = @Publisher,
  CatID = @CatID
WHERE ISBN = @ISBN AND rowVersion = @rowVersion
```

When you configure the data adapter, you would then only need to add the current parameters and the `rowVersion` parameter like so:

```
cmSave.Parameters.Add(new SqlParameter("@rowVersion",
 SqlDbType.Timestamp, 8, "rowVersion"));
```

Refreshing Rows

The final issue that needs to be addressed in this context is re-retrieving data from the data store when an update succeeds or fails. As we discussed previously, the `UpdatedRowSource` property of a command object controls how result sets or output parameters are processed from the `UpdateCommand` as rows in a `DataTable` are updated by a data adapter. This property can be set to one of the values from the `UpdateRowSource` enumeration, as shown in Table 12.5.

TABLE 12.5   Values of the `UpdateRowSource` enumeration. These values determine how a row is refreshed in the event that the command returns data.

Value	Description
Both	Both output parameters and the first returned row are mapped to the row being processed.
FirstReturnedRecord	The first row in the result set is mapped to the row being processed.
None	Result sets and output parameters are ignored.
OutputParameters	Output parameters are mapped to the row being processed.

The default is `Both`, so if the command returns a result set, it will be mapped to the `DataRow` that was updated. This can be useful in pessimistic concurrency situations where if the row has changed, you'd want to refresh the row in the `DataTable` so that the client is aware of the changes. To add this capability to the procedure shown in Listing 12.8, you would simply set the `UpdatedRowSource` property of the command object to either `Both` or `FirstReturnedRecord` and then modify the `IF` statement that checks to see whether the row was successfully updated, like so:

```
IF @@rowcount = 0
BEGIN
    SELECT * FROM Titles WHERE ISBN = @ISBN
    RAISERROR('The row has been changed',14,1)
END
```

This capability can also be useful in conjunction with the `InsertCommand` in the event the data store assigns default or auto-incrementing values to one or more columns in the table. This is the case, for example, with SQL Server `IDENTITY` columns. In this way, the server-generated data will be placed into the row.

12

Command Builders

Some providers (SqlClient and OleDb included) also implement command builder classes that can be used to automatically generate insert, update, and delete commands that work against a single table in the data store. This is typically accomplished by the command builder object examining the SelectCommand and then asking the data store for additional information.

To use a command builder, you can simply instantiate it and pass it the data adapter that will be used, as follows:

```
OleDbDataAdapter da = new OleDbDataAdapter(sqlStatement, con);
OleDbCommandBuilder builder = new OleDbCommandBuilder(da);
```

At this point, nothing occurs. However, the command builder sets up an event handler, so when the Update method of the data adapter is called, it will contact the data store and build the commands that will be referenced by the InsertCommand, UpdateCommand, and DeleteCommand properties of the data adapter. After the initial Update, these commands are associated with the data adapter and won't have to be re-created.

The commands can also be inspected using the GetInsertCommand, GetDeleteCommand, and GetUpdateCommand methods of the command builder. You might do this, for example, to modify the default properties set for the command. If the SelectCommand changes after the commands are built, you need to call the RefreshSchema method to rebuild the commands based on the new SelectCommand.

As you might expect, there are three main drawbacks to using this approach:

1. The commands that are generated use inline SQL and therefore don't take advantage of the performance of database constructs such as stored procedures.

2. For the command builder to build the statements, it must retrieve additional schema information from the data store. This entails an additional roundtrip to the data store, which should be avoided at all costs (another cardinal rule: Minimize round trips to the data store), especially in the multi-user Web applications for which ADO.NET was designed.

3. Command builders work only when the SelectCommand encapsulates a relatively simple statement that it can parse to determine which table to create the commands for. Command builders wouldn't be effective, for example, if the SelectCommand executed a stored procedure that included a JOIN statement.

For all these reasons, you should avoid command builders in most situations.

Summary

Data adapters act as the liaison between the data store and the `DataSet`. As such, they are responsible for filling `DataTable` objects with data and then synchronizing the changes made in your application with the data store. Today you learned how the data adapter accomplishes this by creating or matching a schema and through table and column mappings. In addition, you looked at the various optimistic and pessimistic concurrency techniques you can use to synchronize the data.

As we approach the end of this week, we'll look at specific functionality of providers including tomorrow's look at the SqlClient provider.

Workshop

This workshop will help reinforce the concepts covered in today's lesson.

Quiz

1. When would you set the `MissingSchemaAction` property to `Error`?

    Setting the `MissingSchemaAction` property to `Error` will cause the `Fill` method to throw an exception if the incoming schema (the one from the data store) doesn't exactly match that in the existing `DataTable`. You can use this to ensure that the `DataTable` you're reading into is correct for the data store.

2. What is the purpose of table and column mappings?

    Table and column mappings are used by the data adapter to map the incoming table and column names with `DataTable` and `DataColumn` names to be populated. They can be used both to match an existing schema and to specify what the new schema will look like depending on the value of the `MissingSchemaAction` property.

3. What property controls if the data adapter throws an exception during the `Update` method?

    When the `ContinueUpdateOnError` property is set to `False`, the data adapter will throw an exception when the first error is encountered. Any rows after that row won't be processed.

4. What is the advantage to using optimistic concurrency?

    By using optimistic concurrency and looking only at the primary key value, clients will ultimately encounter fewer conflicts when attempting to update rows. This is the case because optimistic concurrency entails a last-in-wins strategy in which the last client to submit its changes will overwrite other changes previously made, even if the first client wasn't aware they had been made.

12

Exercise

Using the pattern shown in Listing 12.8, write a method that could be used to synchronize data in the Reviews table using optimistic concurrency.

Answers for Day 12

Exercise Answer

One possible solution might be the following:

```
public virtual DataSet SaveReview(DataSet ds)
{
    //Make sure the DataSet has some changed data
    if (ds == null || ds.HasChanges() == false)
    {
        // Can simply return null
        return null;
    }

    // Create the connection object
    SqlConnection con = new SqlConnection(_connect);
    // Create the data adapter (da)
    SqlDataAdapter da = new SqlDataAdapter("usp_GetReviews",con);
    // Create the data adapter commands and configure their parameters
    SqlCommand cmUpd = new SqlCommand("usp_UpdReview",con);
    SqlCommand cmIns = new SqlCommand("usp_InsReview",con);
    SqlCommand cmDel = new SqlCommand("usp_DelReview",con);
    // Associate the commands with the data adapter
    da.InsertCommand = cmIns;
    da.UpdateCommand = cmUpd;
    da.DeleteCommand = cmDel;
    //Select
    da.SelectCommand.Parameters.Add(new SqlParameter(
    "@reviewId",SqlDbType.UniqueIdentifier,16,"ReviewID"));
    //Update
    da.UpdateCommand.Parameters.Add(new SqlParameter(
      "@reviewId",SqlDbType.UniqueIdentifier,16,"ReviewID"));
    da.UpdateCommand.Parameters.Add(new SqlParameter(
      "@isbn",SqlDbType.NChar,10,"isbn"));
    da.UpdateCommand.Parameters.Add(new SqlParameter(
      "@reviewText",SqlDbType.NChar,0,"ReviewText"));
    da.UpdateCommand.Parameters.Add(new SqlParameter(
      "@stars",SqlDbType.TinyInt,2,"Stars"));
    //Insert
    da.InsertCommand.Parameters.Add(new SqlParameter(
      "@reviewId",SqlDbType.UniqueIdentifier,16,"ReviewID"));
    da.InsertCommand.Parameters.Add(new SqlParameter(
      "@isbn",SqlDbType.NChar,10,"isbn"));
```

```csharp
da.InsertCommand.Parameters.Add(new SqlParameter(
  "@reviewText",SqlDbType.NChar,0,"ReviewText"));
da.InsertCommand.Parameters.Add(new SqlParameter(
  "@stars",SqlDbType.TinyInt,2,"Stars"));
//Delete
da.DeleteCommand.Parameters.Add(new SqlParameter(
  "@reviewId",SqlDbType.UniqueIdentifier,16,"ReviewID"));
// Set the ContineUpdateOnError property to true
da.ContinueUpdateOnError = true;

try
{
    // Call the Update method passing in results of the GetChanges method
    da.Update(ds);

    // Check for errors and return rows that were in error
    if (ds.HasErrors)
    {
        DataSet dsErrors;
        dsErrors = ds.GetChanges(DataRowState.Modified &
          DataRowState.Deleted);
        return dsErrors;
    }
    return null;
}
catch (Exception e)
{
    // An exception occurred, probably in the connection
    // Wrap and throw a specific exception
    throw (new Exception("Could not update Review",e));
}
}
```

12

DAY 13

Working with SQL Server

Because the ComputeBooks database is a SQL Server 2000 database, most of the code you've seen in this book has accessed SQL Server through the SqlClient provider. As a result, you've seen some of the ways in which you can take advantage of the features of SQL Server 2000 in your .NET applications. Today's lesson is designed to go a step further than what you've seen and address issues that are particular to SQL Server when building enterprise applications. To that end, the lesson is split into two parts. The first part deals with database design issues, whereas the second part deals with additional considerations for accessing data. Consequently, if you're not designing for SQL Server or already have a good grasp on the fundamental issues involved in designing databases for SQL Server, you'll probably already have a good grasp on much of the material in this lesson.

Specifically, today's lesson will focus on the following concepts:

- How the SqlClient provider communicates with SQL Server
- How to use SQL Server features to create a good database design
- Some alternatives to using the SqlClient provider for accessing SQL Server

SqlClient Internals

The SqlClient .NET Data Provider is what I've termed a *specific* or *targeted provider* because it's able to communicate with only a single data store; in this case, only SQL Server version 7.0, 2000, and later versions such as the release code-named Yukon. As you learned on Day 8, "Understanding .NET Data Providers," the reason you would use specific providers is that they offer two main advantages over the general providers such as OleDb and the ODBC provider.

First, specific providers can expose classes, methods, properties, fields, and events that aren't found in the base provider architecture. These additional constructs enable developers to work with the database server more closely because they expose features that are difficult or impossible to access using a generic provider. One example of this is the ExecuteXmlReader method we discussed on Day 10, "Using Commands."

 Note

> **NEW TERM** Both the ODBC and OLE DB architectures rely on a fundamental software development design pattern known as the **adapter pattern**. Simply put, the adapter pattern allows clients to work with multiple disparate pieces of software by abstracting their functionality into a well-known interface that the clients understand. In this pattern, the differences were abstracted to a lower level (the ODBC driver or OLE DB provider), resulting in wider access to data. The cost, of course, is performance as well as access to features that are very specialized.

Second, a specific provider eliminates a layer of abstraction sitting between the client code and the data store. When this extra layer is eliminated, performance naturally increases. Although much of this week has been devoted to showing the programmatic differences between SqlClient and OleDb, the differences in the underlying communication haven't been addressed. This section will explore the second of these benefits of a specific provider.

Using Tabular Data Stream

Under the covers, every client that communicates with SQL Server does so using the Tabular Data Stream (TDS) wire protocol through a SQL Server client Net-Library. Figure 13.1 depicts this architecture.

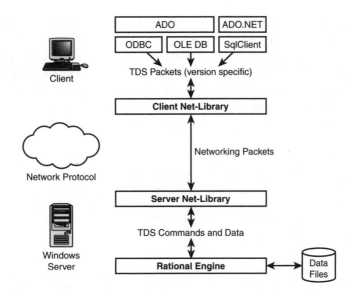

FIGURE 13.1

SQL Server client architecture. This diagram depicts the communication path from a client to a SQL Server.

The definition of the components shown in Figure 13.1 is as follows:

- **TDS**. TDS is the application-level protocol specific to SQL Server. It is a low-level protocol that specifies both commands and data in a specific arrangement. A TDS packet encapsulates the protocol and is configurable on the client. By default, the packet size is set to 4KB and should typically be left alone.

- **Net-Library**. This piece of software (unmanaged DLL) on the client machine receives TDS packets and encapsulates them into packets suitable for the network protocol being used. As a result, there are seven different Net-Library DLLs that install with MDAC 2.7, including Named Pipes, TCP/IP, Multiprotocol, NWLink IPX/SPX, AppleTalk, Banyan Vines, and VIA. They can be configured using the SQL Server Client Network Utility. On the server, the TDS packets are received by an analogous Net-Library (which ones the server listens on can also be configured).

- **Relational Database Engine**. This is the piece of software that does all the work you think of related to a database. The TDS packets are received from the server Net-Library and parsed, executed (including access to the data files), and the results are formulated as TDS packets. The return trip follows the same path in reverse with the server Net-Library encapsulating the TDS packets for transport to the client, where they are unpacked and processed.

13

In the past, on the client side, the ODBC driver and SQLOLEDB OLE DB provider were responsible for creating TDS packets. The SqlClient provider, however, now assumes that role by creating TDS packets directly in managed code and passing them off to the appropriate Net-Library. As you can see from Figure 13.1, different clients use different versions of TDS. This is the reason the SqlClient provider can't support all versions of the SQL Server; namely, it can create packets only for TDS 7.0 or higher, which older versions of SQL Server couldn't understand.

Note   As you no doubt will notice, the communication between SqlClient and SQL Server can be heavily influenced by the connection attributes we discussed on Day 9, "Using Connections and Transactions"—particularly the Network Library and Packet Size attributes.

Because SqlClient creates TDS packets directly, performance is increased. In fact, Microsoft's internal tests have indicated that using the SqlClient provider in .NET applications is even faster than writing a managed Visual C++ application that accesses the SQLOLEDB OLE DB provider directly using COM. In addition, Microsoft's tests indicate that when you scale up and move from a single-processor server to a quad-processor server, performance increases by a factor of three. Rest assured, performance using SqlClient isn't an issue when developing .NET applications.

Database Design

Even if you develop a complete understanding of ADO.NET, the applications you write might still suffer performance, security, and data integrity lapses if the database on which the data resides isn't designed optimally. In many organizations, the initial database design falls on the development team (the architect and developers) and only later is reviewed by a database administrator (DBA). In other organizations, developers are expected to do all the database design, sometimes without the proper background. In either case, if the database design isn't done well, by the time it is realized, it's usually too late or very costly to make the fundamental changes that are necessary.

To that end, this section explores several key areas that you need to consider when designing a database in SQL Server.

Note Where appropriate, I'll point out which features or constructs are available only in SQL Server 2000 because the SqlClient provider can access both SQL Server 2000 and SQL Server 7.0.

Schema Design

New Term Typically, the first step a designer takes when designing a relational database is to create a logical model of the data to be represented before actually creating the physical database. Modeling at the logical or conceptual level enables designers to leave implementation details to later stages and to concentrate on what data needs to be represented and how it's related to other data. Traditionally, many designers have chosen to use a **database modeling** methodology referred to as **entity-relationship (ER) modeling** to graphically produce logical and physical designs represented through an **entity relationship diagram (ERD)**. Even though all the ins and outs of database modeling are beyond the scope of this book, a few key points to help you understand the methodology are in order.

New Term An ERD consists of entities and attributes arranged in the diagram. An **entity** is simply a thing or object that has significance in the problem domain such as a Title or Customer. An **attribute** is information about the entity that describes, identifies, classifies, or quantifies the entity. The attribute or set of attributes that uniquely identifies an entity is referred to as the **identifier**.

New Term Multiple entities are then connected through **relationships**. The relationships indicate how the entities relate to each other and specifically provide the **cardinality**. The cardinality indicates the numerical relationship between entities as in each Title is related to zero or more Reviews or each Order is related to one or more Order Details. These relationships are signified by a specific set of symbols. Although there are several different sets of symbols and notations that can be used—including Bachman, Chen ERD, Martin ERD, and Express-G—one of the most common simply uses the IDEF1X symbol set for the entities with the Information Engineering notation's crow's feet notation for the relationships. Figure 13.2 presents the ERD for the ComputeBooks database using this notation.

13

In Figure 13.2 you'll notice, for example, that the relationship between the Publishers and Titles entities indicates that a publisher can be related to zero or more titles (indicated by the circle and the crow's feet), whereas a title is related to one and only one publisher (indicated by the double barred line).

FIGURE 13.2

*ComputeBooks ERD.
This is the entity rela-
tionship diagram for
the ComputeBooks
database.*

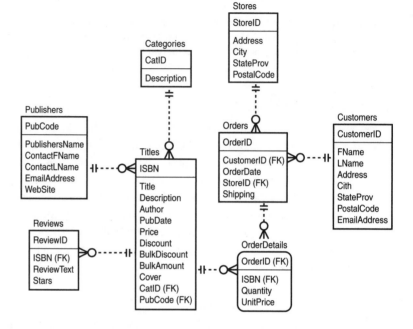

NEW TERM   A variety of software packages, such as Erwin and Visio 2000
(from which Figure 13.2 was created), provide the tools necessary to create logical data models and even reverse-engineer the physical
database from a variety of sources into a logical diagram. This makes viewing the structure of an already existing database easy for documentation or
rework. Most of these tools then enable you to change the model and
update the database (referred to as **round-tripping**).

NEW TERM   Although understanding ER modeling and the notations used isn't difficult,
Microsoft has recently invested much effort in developing a conceptual modeling
approach referred to as **Object Role Modeling** (ORM). Simply put, ORM seeks to make
the relational design process simpler by using a natural language approach through intu-
itive diagrams in which you can place sample data, and by distilling the model into a
series of elementary facts. ORM makes relational database design more approachable for
developers and others not formally trained in database design. As a result, Microsoft is
making ORM available in Microsoft Visio for Enterprise Architects and the VS .NET
Enterprise Architect release.

> **Note**
>
> For more information on ORM, see the article "Object Role Modeling: An Overview" by Microsoft's Terry Halprin on MSDN at `http://msdn.microsoft.com/library/default.asp?url=/library/en-us/dnvs700/html/vsea_ormoverview.asp`.

 Regardless of which techniques you use to create the logical model, eventually, the physical database objects (collectively referred to as the **schema**) must be created. The schema consists chiefly of tables, views, columns, and constraints. A few of the most important aspects of the schema design you should look for follow.

Normalizing the Schema

NEW TERM One of the most powerful concepts in relational database theory is **normalization**. Normalization can be thought of as the process of removing ambiguous and repetitive information from the schema by creating related tables. The sign of a normalized database is that it contains well-focused tables with a reasonable number of columns that are related through foreign keys, rather than one or several tables that contain a large number of columns. By designing a normalized database in SQL Server, you'll maximize the performance of sorting, index creation, and data modifications as well as minimize the storage required.

NEW TERM As you're probably aware, various forms of normalization have been codified in relational theory. These forms specify an increasing and more restrictive level of normalization from First to Fifth Normal Form (and including Boyce-Codd Normal Form). Typically, designers don't attempt to implement anything higher than **Third Normal Form** (**3NF**), the rules for which follow.

A schema is in 3NF if

- Each table (entity) must contain a primary key (identifier) that uniquely identifies a row in the table. In some instances, picking the primary key is simple because one column or a combination of the columns will naturally lend itself to uniqueness, such as PubCode in the Publishers entity or ISBN in the Titles entity in Figure 13.2. In other cases, you'll need the help of the database to assign a system-generated key to ensure uniqueness. All the other entities in Figure 13.2 use system-assigned keys defined with the uniqueidentifier (GUID) data type in SQL Server. As you might expect, the primary key isn't allowed to contain null values. In SQL Server, you'll use a primary key constraint in the CREATE TABLE statement to define the primary key.

13

- Each column in each table is atomic, meaning that it stores one piece of information. In the ComputeBooks model in Figure 13.2, for example, the customer name is split into two columns because it consists of two pieces of information. A good rule of thumb is to avoid storing data in a column that will have to be parsed when it is retrieved.

- Each nonkey column in each table is functionally dependent on the primary key. In other words, all the columns must directly describe the primary key. This is sometimes difficult to see but, for example, if the Reviews table in Figure 13.2 also contained the title of the book, it would violate this rule because the title really describes the ISBN and not the review. Another way to think of this rule is that your tables shouldn't contain repeated data that could be placed in its own table. A symptom of not following this rule is that a change to a single piece of data requires changes to scores of rows because the data is repeated a number of times. It follows, then, that all columns that aren't dependent on the primary key should be placed in their own tables. This rule is fairly strict and would require, for example, that in Figure 13.2 a separate table be created to hold the City and StateProv columns for each store because these columns are actually dependent on PostalCode and not on StoreID. However, reading or designing a model with this rule in mind can help you reduce redundant data.

> **Tip**
>
> As you learned on Day 4, "DataSet Internals," SQL Server also supports IDENTITY columns as a means of creating system-assigned keys. Each table can have one column marked as the IDENTITY column and it will be populated automatically in auto-incrementing fashion based on the seed and increment it's created with. The downside of the IDENTITY values is that they're database dependent and so aren't recommended for distributed database scenarios. However, it's relatively simple to create a stored procedure that inserts a row into a table and returns the new IDENTITY value using the @@IDENTITY global variable. You can then create a SqlParameter object to catch the return value with its SourceColumn property set appropriately in order to populate the new key back into the DataTable.

NEW TERM   Although these rules make a great deal of sense conceptually, in practice, designers choose a level of normalization to fit the needs of the situation. For example, in the ComputeBooks model in Figure 13.2, the Author column of the Titles table is used to store multiple author names in a comma-delimited list. This violates the second rule because the column isn't atomic. A more normalized design would mean that an Authors entity should be created and each author stored there with a primary key that is referenced by the Titles entity. In fact, this design would call for a **many to many relationship** because authors can write many books and books can be written by many authors. This would result in the creation of an additional table to hold the relationship. This design would be more complicated and result in more joins between tables in my queries. I decided not to normalize this column because of the added complexity and because there is no other information I'm storing about authors. In other words, the increased complexity of normalization wasn't justified based on how the data is used.

Note

> However, keep in mind that this design isn't as flexible, so if data about authors needed to be collected in the future, the changes needed would greatly impact the schema. By normalizing early, you typically avoid major changes to the schema down the road.

In general, designers don't fully normalize a schema because doing so would hurt performance. In SQL Server, you should strive for designs in which you aren't regularly joining more than four tables. For example, if one of your most frequent queries must join six tables to retrieve the required information, you should think about denormalizing the schema so that fewer joins are required. In some cases, this might mean keeping your original tables intact but duplicating data in a table that's easier to query. Behind the scenes, you can then write triggers that keep the data in sync. Of course, this approach optimizes query performance at the cost of performance during an insert, update, or delete.

That having been said, not normalizing at all results in very wide tables (tables with many columns) that are difficult to maintain because of repeating data and that perform very poorly when queried.

Choosing Names and Data Types

A second aspect of schema design involves choosing appropriate table and column names as well as data types. As you can see in Figure 13.2, the names in your schema should use a simple naming convention that is human readable, if possible. In this case, each table name is the plural version of the data it stores and each column name is a human-readable identifier of less than 20 characters. In my designs, I prefer to avoid using underscores in favor of capitalizing each word in a compound name and to avoid embedding any data type information in the column name. Some designers will also insist that each column have a unique name in the schema. Even though I follow this dictate for primary keys (rather than simply calling each one ID), if the column names actually have the same meaning (such as Description), there is no problem with using the same name because they can be fully qualified in SQL statements using the table name.

13

A more important issue, however, is the data types you choose. In SQL Server, there are more than 25 data types that you can use in your tables. In many cases, SQL Server supports several versions of the same basic data type; for example, `datetime` and `small-datetime`. The rule of thumb is that you should pay attention to the ranges of data that the data type supports and then pick the smallest data type that spans the entire range of data you expect. This makes sense because you want to minimize the amount of storage for each table, which, more than simply conserving disk space, speeds up queries, index creation, and modifications on the table because less data needs to be considered.

In particular, you can use Table 13.1 as your guide.

TABLE 13.1   SQL Server data types. This table pairs the most common data type decisions designers have to make when creating tables in SQL Server.

Comparison	Choice
`datetime` and `smalldatetime`	`datetime` (8 bytes) can store data from 1753 to 9999 with an accuracy of one three-hundredth of a second, whereas `smalldatetime` (4 bytes) ranges from 1900 to 2079 with an accuracy to the minute. `datetime` is appropriate for historical dates and those recording the specific time of a transaction. `smalldatetime` is useful for recording current dates.
`tinyint` and `bit`	`tinyint` ranges from 0 to 255, whereas `bit` is only 0 or 1. `bit` is useful for Boolean representations, whereas `tinyint` is more appropriate for values fixed in a natural range, such as number of children.
`float` and `real`	Both `float` and `real` are used to store floating point numeric data, but `float` can specify the precision and thus the storage size up to 53. `real` is defined as `float(24)` and uses 4 bytes, whereas `float` uses 8 bytes with a mantissa above 24.
`money` and `smallmoney`	Both `money` and `smallmoney` have the same accuracy, but `smallmoney` only ranges from +/- approximately 214,750 and uses 4 bytes instead of 8. You should take into account the currency when deciding which to use.
`decimal` and `numeric`	`decimal` and `numeric` are equivalent and can be used to represent numbers with a fixed but configurable precision and scale. The data can take from 5 to 17 bytes, depending on the precision specified.

TABLE 13.1 continued

Comparison	Choice
char, varchar and nchar, nvarchar	char and nchar store fixed-length strings, whereas varchar and nvarchar store variable-length strings. char and varchar use non-Unicode characters, whereas nchar and nvarchar use Unicode. All can store up to 8,000 bytes, so nchar strings, for example, can only be of length 4,000. Use char and nchar when the data will be consistently the same length because they perform better. Use varchar and nvarchar for longer strings that vary greatly in order to conserve space. Use nchar and nvarchar when you need to store text from multiple languages in the same database.
varchar, nvarchar and text, ntext	text and ntext can support sizes of more than 2 billion bytes, whereas varchar and nvarchar are restricted to 8,000 bytes. text and ntext aren't stored with the row, so queries are slower. Use text and ntext when storing entire documents in the database.
binary and varbinary	binary can store fixed-length binary data from 1 to 8,000 bytes, whereas varbinary can store a variable amount of data up to 8,000 bytes. Use binary when the amount of data is fixed and the same for each row.
varbinary and image	varbinary can only store up to 8,000 bytes of data, whereas image is like text and can store more than 2 billion bytes in a data structure that is separate from the row. You can use image to store not just graphics, but any binary data that is large and variable, such as Word or Excel documents.
timestamp and uniqueidentifier	timestamp stores an automatically generated database-wide unique 8-byte binary value when a row changes or is inserted. You shouldn't use it as a primary key because it changes. You can use this value to determine whether the row has changed. uniqueidentifier stores a 16-byte globally unique identifier (GUID) typically generated with NEWID function. You can use it as a system-assigned primary key.

13

Of course, as you have already learned, each of the SQL Server data types is represented in the System.Data.SqlTypes namespace and in the System.Data.SqlClient. SqlDbType enumeration. These can be used to read data directly from SQL Server using a SqlDataReader and to specify the data type for SqlParameter objects, respectively.

For SQL Server in particular, you should also try to minimize the number of columns that are nullable in the table. Tables with many nullable columns don't perform as well when queried. They are also more difficult to work with for developers who then need to check for the presence of null values using the IsDBNull method of the data reader, for example. One strategy you can use to avoid a lot of nullable columns is to factor them into their own table that has a one-to-one relationship with the table from which they came. In that way, this optional data can be queried only when it's needed.

User-Defined Data Types

NEW TERM One additional construct that you should consider when designing a database in SQL Server is the **user-defined data type (UDT).** Simply put, a UDT is a database-wide identifier that you create and that maps to one of the intrinsic SQL Server data types. You can use UDTs to standardize the way that certain pieces of information are stored and then reuse the UDTs across tables.

For example, if you want to make sure that e-mail addresses are always represented as nvarchar(200) in your database, you can create a UDT called EmailAddress using the system stored procedure sp_addtype like so:

```
EXEC sp_addtype EmailAddress, 'nvarchar(200)', 'NULL'
```

Now that the EmailAddress UDT exists, you can use it in a CREATE TABLE statement in place of nvarchar(200). If all your tables, such as Publishers and Customers, use the UDT consistently, you'll be assured that e-mail addresses are always stored in the same way.

You can also use UDTs to abstract the definitions one step further. For example, e-mail addresses and Web site addresses store the same kinds of information, so you could create a more general URI (uniform resource identifier) UDT that both the EmailAddress and WebSite columns will use.

UDTs also have the advantage of allowing rules (which we'll discuss later) to be bound to them so that the same rule can apply to multiple tables.

Tip

> The downside to UDTs is that you must define them before you start creating tables, and they apply only to the database you create them in. However, if you create UDTs in the model system database, they'll be copied to any new databases you create on the server.

Using Constraints and Triggers

After you've created a schema with the proper level of normalization and chosen the data types for your columns carefully, you can begin to apply additional constructs to enhance data integrity to the schema. These include foreign keys, defaults, checks, and triggers.

> **Note**
>
> For this entire discussion, constraints can be applied directly in the CREATE TABLE statement or with the ADD CONSTRAINT clause of the ALTER TABLE statement. For more information on the specific syntax, see the SQL Server books online documentation.

Foreign Key Constraints

 NEW TERM Foreign key constraints (also referred to as **declarative referential integrity**, or DRI) enforce the relationships between tables by ensuring that each row in the child table matches to a row in the parent table and that by default, you can't delete a row from the parent table that has child rows related to it. These simple rules go a long way toward ensuring the data integrity of the data that is captured. In SQL Server, foreign key constraints work the same way as the constraints you can add to a DataSet, as you learned on Day 4. In other words, the foreign key constraint between Titles and Publishers ensures that each title (the child) is related to a publisher (the parent) and that a publisher can't be deleted if there are titles associated with it.

Just as with foreign key constraints in a DataSet, you can create cascade rules in SQL Server 2000 (although not in SQL Sever 7.0, in which you have to use triggers to get the same effect) using the ON DELETE and ON UPDATE clauses. For example, when the constraint is defined, you can specify that if the parent row is deleted, the child rows are deleted as well, and if the primary key of the parent table is updated, the foreign key column in the child table is updated as well. This ability comes in handy for relationships in which the child table is fully dependent on the parent. In ER modeling, this is often seen when the foreign key attribute is either a part of or the entire primary key, as is the case with the OrderDetails entity in Figure 13.2 (the rounded corners of the OrderDetails entity also denote this fact). In this case, an OrderDetails row means nothing without an Order row, so you should cascade the delete of the Order row to the OrderDetails row.

13

> **Tip**
>
> Foreign key constraints, along with all sorts of other changes, can be made graphically using a database diagram in the SQL Server Enterprise Manager.

A good schema design dictates that you create foreign key constraints for all your relationships. In most designs, almost every table will be related to at least one other through a foreign key constraint.

Default Constraints

Default constraints can be attached to a column in a table and automatically populate that column with a value when a row is inserted into the table. This is analogous to the DefaultValue property of the DataColumn, although it's more powerful because it isn't restricted to literal values. Default constraints come in very handy for populating non-nullable columns that have standard values and then perhaps change at a later time. For example, the BulkAmount column of the Titles table could have a default constraint placed on it of 50 because the bulk rate typically kicks in at 30. Used in this way, default constraints free the client from having to know the amount, which is better placed closer to the data. Coupled with using optional parameters in stored procedures, the client can create a new row without specifying all the columns.

Note   Remember that you learned on Day 10 that when using SqlClient, you don't have to define all the SqlParameter objects for a SqlCommand object that references a stored procedure if the procedure defaults their values to NULL in the declaration.

Default constraints can be specified using literal values such as numbers or strings (as in the case just specified) or using Transact-SQL functions or values that return a single value. A typical example is to place two non-nullable columns on each table, called CreateDate and CreateUser, whose default constraints are set to the functions GETDATE() and USER, respectively. In this way, the date and time the row was created and the user who created it are captured automatically when each row is added. These columns are very useful for troubleshooting and analysis.

Another good use for defaults—and one that is used heavily in the ComputeBooks database—is to use a default constraint to assign a new uniqueidentifier to inserted rows. The primary keys of all the tables except Publishers and Titles are defined as uniqueidentifier with a default constraint of NEWID(). This ensures that if the client doesn't generate a GUID, one will be created on the server.

Default constraints can be added to a table using the CREATE TABLE or ALTER TABLE statements as well as graphically in the table editor or database diagram with the SQL Server Enterprise Manager.

Note

> SQL Server also supports default objects for backward compatibility because default constraints weren't supported before SQL Server 7.0. Default objects are created with the CREATE DEFAULT statement, and then can be bound to columns or user-defined data types using the sp_bindefault system stored procedure. Default objects aren't recommended because they don't perform as well as default constraints.

Check Constraints

Both check constraints and rules are used to restrict the range of values (the domain) in a column or set of columns during both an insert and an update. Basically, check constraints were introduced in SQL Server 7.0 and offer better performance, whereas rules (like default objects) are a backward-compatibility feature and offer a little added flexibility.

Typically, check constraints are used to check for boundary conditions on columns to make sure that data integrity is maintained. For example, the Price, BulkDiscount, BulkAmount, and Discount columns in the Titles table could also have individual (or column-level) check constraints placed on them so that negative values are rejected. Even though these types of checks are done on the client, it's always desirable to place them on the server as well. This is because multiple applications might be using the data, and the server is the final gatekeeper of the data and is therefore ultimately responsible for data integrity issues.

NEW TERM However, check constraints (and rules) can also apply to more than one column (referred to as **table-level constraints**) in order to make sure that the data in the columns is synchronized. This is similar to using the RowUpdating and RowUpdated events of the data adapter to ensure that column values are compatible. This might be necessary, for example, to make sure that the BulkDiscount falls within a certain percentage of the Price when a title is updated or inserted. As with defaults, check constraints maintain data integrity and should be used in addition to checking down on the client.

13

Note

> Although they don't perform as well as check constraints, rules have the advantage of being able to be created once and then applied to multiple tables or user-defined data types. They're created with the CREATE RULE statement and bound to a table or UDT using the system stored procedure sp_bindrule. Check constraints must be created separately on each column or table.

Triggers

Although not a constraint by definition, a trigger is the most flexible way to maintain data integrity because it's basically an event-driven stored procedure that has access to the data that is being inserted, updated, or deleted before the change is committed. In other words, triggers fire during a transaction (either implicit or explicit), whereas constraints are checked before the transaction begins. This allows triggers to make dynamic decisions but decreases performance. In fact, poorly designed triggers can bring a SQL Server database to its knees. For that reason, you should use constraints whenever possible and resort to triggers for added or special functionality.

 Note

SQL Server 2000 introduced the concept of INSTEAD OF triggers, which can be used to explicitly perform the modification. This gives you complete control over how the modification is made and to which tables it applies.

As an example of a trigger, suppose you want to maintain in a table a column called UpdateUser that tracks the last user to modify the row. Although you can place a default constraint on the column to populate the column when the row is created, the constraint won't update the column when the row is modified. To allow the server to handle this automatically, you could create a trigger on the update event as shown in Listing 13.1.

LISTING 13.1   Using triggers. This simple trigger updates the UpdateUser column with the current user when a row in the Titles table is updated.

```
CREATE TRIGGER upd_Titles
ON dbo.Titles
FOR UPDATE AS

UPDATE Titles
SET UpdateUser = USER
FROM inserted b JOIN Titles ON b.ISBN = Titles.ISBN

GO
```

ANALYSIS   In Listing 13.1, you can see that the trigger is defined with a name, the table it operates on, and the events (UPDATE in this case, but they can fire for more than one) it will fire for. When it fires, it issues a correlated UPDATE statement against the internal inserted table and changes the UpdateUser value for those rows updated by the UPDATE statement. The inserted table is a logical table of the same structure as the table on which the trigger is firing which holds the values that are about to be used to update the row. There is also a `deleted` logical table that holds the old values.

> **Note**
> One of the trickiest aspects of using triggers is that they fire only once even if the statement that caused them results in multiple rows being inserted, updated, or deleted. In other words, the logical inserted and deleted tables can contain more than one row. Any statements you write in the trigger need to take this into account and not assume that only one row is being processed. In Listing 13.1 this is done by using a JOIN within the UPDATE statement.

Although there are several rules for triggers that you should consult in the online documentation before using them, the rule of thumb is to perform the minimum amount of work necessary and then get out. This is the case because the trigger fires in the middle of the transaction, so any work you do in the trigger will delay the statement completion and thus the transaction completion. You should keep in mind that, by default, triggers can also be recursive and nested so that if a trigger on table A updates table B, the triggers on table B will fire, and so on up to 32 levels. Nested triggers can be turned off at the database level as well. Recursive triggers can also be turned off and, as the name implies, allow triggers to perform update statements either directly or indirectly (through other triggers) on the table that started the process. Triggers should also not return result sets because the client program won't be expecting it.

Another typical use for triggers is to maintain denormalized data. For example, if I regularly performed queries that counted the total number of books sold and revenue for each title, I might denormalize the `Titles` table by adding these columns and then use a trigger to update them.

> **Note**
> Because triggers fire in the middle of a transaction, they can also cause the implicit or explicit transaction to be rolled back by issuing a ROLLBACK TRANSACTION statement. When this occurs, the trigger should also issue a RAISERROR statement to ensure that the client is notified that the transaction was rolled back.

13

Finally, one of the other advantages of triggers is that they can reference objects outside the database in which they are defined. Using DRI, you can reference only tables inside the current database; with triggers, you can ensure that data in a separate database on the same or a remote server is synchronized. However, keep in mind that referencing objects outside the current database slows performance—particularly if you're going to reference remote objects.

Note   Remote server can be referenced using linked server through SQL Server Enterprise Manager or the `sp_addlinkedserver` system stored procedure.

Because triggers are so flexible, they can also be used to implement business rules as an alternative to placing the rules in a .NET class. The decision of whether to use triggers in this way is chiefly based on whether the business rule is directly related to the data, and whether it's application specific (in addition, of course, to the portability needs of the application). For example, assume the ComputeBooks has a business rule that states that when a customer's orders total a certain amount, they are entitled to an enhanced status. A trigger could be used to check for this when a new order is inserted in the OrderDetails table and then another table updated with the CustomerID. Although this isn't the only way to accomplish the business rule (for example you could use a stored procedure called from the procedure that inserts the order), it's an example of one that's directly related to the data and applies for the entire organization.

Of course, the alternative is to place business rules in a .NET class in the business services tier of a multi-tiered application. Typically, these business classes rely on the façade design pattern to control an entire process, such as the placing of an order. However, allowing SQL Server to implement relatively simple data-related business rules allows the business classes to concentrate on more complex rules (actually processes) that are application specific and that perhaps span more than just SQL Server.

Stored Procedure Layer Design

After the schema itself has been created, and all the appropriate constraints and triggers have also been created, you can concentrate on the database objects that the code you write in ADO.NET will access directly. In SQL Server, this means creating a stored procedure layer that ADO.NET code will access. The stored procedures are used primarily for data access, but can also implement business rules and processes as well.

There are several reasons why you would want all your clients to use stored procedures rather than inline SQL:

- **Abstraction**. By allowing access only through stored procedures, you abstract the schema from the clients that are accessing it. As a result, you can change the underlying schema (perhaps to denormalize) without affecting the clients as long as the interface for the stored procedure (its name and parameters) remains the same. In this way, you can think of your stored procedures as application programming interface (API) to the data. As a side benefit, they also force you to think about clients that will be accessing the data.

- **Simplification**. By creating an API that developers can use to access the database, you also simplify the process of working with the database. This is the case because the stored procedures can do the complex work of joining the appropriate tables and can simply return result sets with the appropriate columns based on the parameters passed into the procedure. At the same time, stored procedures that perform the updates can provide a consistent API that developers can use to maintain the data.

- **Performance**. In SQL Server, the procedures are certain to take advantage of cached execution plans whereas inline (or batch) SQL statements must attempt to be matched to an existing execution plan each time they're called. Not only is the actual execution faster, but network traffic is also reduced because large amounts of SQL aren't encoded in TDS packets and sent to the server. Finally, using stored procedures as the "official" way of executing SELECT statements makes it simpler to apply the appropriate indexes to speed up queries. This is because the statements that are ultimately executed are restricted.

- **Security**. Accounts in SQL Server can be given permissions to execute views but denied permissions to access the underlying tables directly. This ensures that developers must use the stored procedures rather than writing inline SQL. This only works, however, if the stored procedure or view is owned by the same account that owns the table.

What About Views and Functions?

NEW TERM — **Views** (basically SELECT statements with names that can act like tables) also have some of the same benefits of stored procedures, mainly simplification and security. However, views don't enable you to pass parameters to them and don't provide a significant increase in performance. Views are useful, however, as building blocks in stored procedures that make it easier to code the stored procedure.

NEW TERM — **Functions** were introduced in SQL Server 2000 and come in several flavors, including inline and table functions. Inline functions are equivalent to views that accept parameters (parameterized views), whereas table functions are more flexible and can return

13

any type of data. However, functions must be called in the context of a SELECT statement and so aren't fully encapsulated as are stored procedures. Like views, functions should be considered as building blocks for stored procedures.

When creating the stored procedure layer, you should take the approach of designing the procedures for the specific application you have in mind. In other words, the stored procedures should be application specific. By following this approach, you'll create stored procedures that streamline the coding process in .NET and make the database very approachable. At the same time, you'll likely see that the way in which one application needs to work with the data is very similar to others. As a result, there will be significant reuse of the procedures.

 Tip

As with any abstraction, procedures introduce additional maintenance, so versioning of the procedures in a source code control system such as Microsoft Visual SourceSafe is recommended.

When you create the procedures, you should do so with a naming convention in mind. The convention that you'll see most often will prefix the procedure with usp_ for *user stored procedure* followed by the name of the procedure without underscore and each word capitalized.

As an example of this approach, consider the usp_GetTitles stored procedure in Listing 13.2.

LISTING 13.2   Application-specific stored procedure. This procedure retrieves titles based on optional parameters.

```
CREATE  PROCEDURE usp_GetTitles
        @ISBN         [nvarchar](10) = NULL,
        @Title        [nvarchar](100) = NULL,
        @Author       [nvarchar](250) = NULL,
        @PubDate      [smalldatetime] = NULL,
        @CatID        [uniqueidentifier] = NULL,
        @Publisher    [nchar](5) = NULL

AS

DECLARE @where nvarchar(250)
declare @title_w nvarchar(100)
DECLARE @author_w nvarchar(100)
```

LISTING 13.2 continued

```sql
DECLARE @pubdate_w nvarchar(100)
DECLARE @CatID_w nvarchar(100)
DECLARE @Publisher_w nvarchar(100)
DECLARE @sql nvarchar(500)

SET @title_w = ''
SET @author_w = ''
SET @pubdate_w = ''
SET @CatID_w = ''
SET @Publisher_w = ''

SET @where = 'WHERE'
IF @isbn IS NOT NULL SET @where = @where + ' isbn = ''' +
  @isbn + '''' + ' and '
IF @title IS NOT NULL SET @title_w = ' title like ''%' +
  @title + '%''' + ' and '
IF @author IS NOT NULL SET @author_w = ' author like ''%' +
  @author + '%''' + ' and '
IF @pubdate IS NOT NULL SET @pubdate_w = ' pubdate > ''' +
  convert(nchar(10), @pubdate, 101) + ''' and '
IF @catid IS NOT NULL SET @catid_w = ' CatID = ' +
  convert(nchar(40), @catid) + '''' + ' and '
IF @publisher IS NOT NULL SET @publisher_w = ' Publisher = ''' +
  @publisher + '''' + ' and '

SET @sql = 'SELECT * FROM Titles ' + @where + @title_w + @author_w +
  @pubdate_w + @catid_w + @publisher_w
SET @sql = substring(@sql,1, LEN(@sql)-4)
EXEC sp_executesql @sql
GO
```

ANALYSIS The usp_GetTitles stored procedure in Listing 13.2 is a more complex procedure that's used to retrieve rows from the Titles table based on the parameters passed into it. You'll notice that all the parameters have default values of NULL. As a result, the SqlParameter objects needn't be created if they aren't used because the SqlCommand object uses named rather than positional arguments. The rest of the procedure then builds clauses that can be added to the WHERE clause to retrieve the appropriate rows. The entire SELECT statement is then finally executed using the sp_executesql system stored procedure.

This procedure abstracts, simplifies access to, and secures access to the Titles table. The key benefit, however, is that on the client side, the ADO.NET code is simplified because it can simply call a single procedure and create the parameters as needed, as shown in Listing 13.3.

13

LISTING 13.3   Calling the `usp_GetTitles` stored procedure. This code calls the procedure and adds the parameters as appropriate.

```
Private Function _getTitles(ByVal author As String, ByVal title As String, _
   ByVal isbn As String, ByVal lowPubDate As Date, _
   ByVal catID As Guid) As DataSet

   Dim da As New SqlDataAdapter("usp_GetTitles", MyBase.SqlCon)
   Dim titleDs As New DataSet()

   da.SelectCommand.CommandType = CommandType.StoredProcedure
   Try
     If Not isbn Is Nothing AndAlso isbn.Length > 0 Then
       da.SelectCommand.Parameters.Add(New SqlParameter( _
         "@isbn", SqlDbType.NVarChar, 10))
       da.SelectCommand.Parameters(0).Value = isbn
     Else
       If Not title Is Nothing AndAlso title.Length > 0 Then
         da.SelectCommand.Parameters.Add(New SqlParameter( _
           "@title", SqlDbType.NVarChar, 100))
         da.SelectCommand.Parameters(0).Value = title
       End If
       If Not author Is Nothing AndAlso author.Length > 0 Then
         da.SelectCommand.Parameters.Add(New SqlParameter( _
           "@author", SqlDbType.NVarChar, 250))
         da.SelectCommand.Parameters(0).Value = author
       End If
       If lowPubDate.Equals(Nothing) Then
         da.SelectCommand.Parameters.Add(New SqlParameter( _
           "@pubDate", SqlDbType.DateTime))
         da.SelectCommand.Parameters(0).Value = lowPubDate
       End If
       If Not catID.Equals(Guid.Empty) Then
         da.SelectCommand.Parameters.Add(New SqlParameter( _
           "@catId", SqlDbType.UniqueIdentifier))
         da.SelectCommand.Parameters(0).Value = catID
       End If
     End If

     da.Fill(titleDs)
     Return titleDs
   Catch e As SqlException
     da = Nothing
     titleDs = Nothing
     Call _throwComputeBookException("GetTitles Failed, passed in " & isbn, e)
   End Try
End Function
```

ANALYSIS   As you can see in Listing 13.3, the method is used to call the stored procedure based on the arguments passed into it. The method checks each one and, if it has an invalid value, the `SqlParameter` isn't created. In this way, this one method in .NET can query based on several parameters. As you'll see on Day 17, "ADO.NET in the Data Services Tier," this method can then be called by overloaded public methods that clients can use to retrieve titles.

Index Design

Even if you apply all the design techniques and concepts discussed today, your applications will still perform badly if the server can't get the data fast enough. As the amount of data grows, the issue of indexes on the tables becomes the most important aspect of an application that is to perform well. At the most basic level, whenever SQL Server executes a query, the query optimizer analyzes the query and assigns costs to the various methods it can use to satisfy the query. By building indexes, you allow SQL Server to consider a new way of accessing the data so that it won't fall back to a table scan, which reads the table row by row until the query is satisfied.

Although indexes are a complicated subject and should be applied on enterprise databases by someone with experience, the following are some guidelines to consider:

- **NEW TERM** **What you should index**. You should consider indexing columns used in WHERE clauses and those that are specified in JOIN clauses. These are the columns that define which rows are accessed in the table and can be used most effectively by the optimizer. In addition, if all the columns requested in a SELECT statement are in an index (referred to as a **covered query**), the data can be read directly from the index, which will increase performance.

- **What you shouldn't index**. You shouldn't index columns that aren't used in WHERE clauses or JOIN clauses. The more indexes there are on a table, the slower INSERT, UPDATE, and DELETE statements will execute. In addition, creating indexes on small tables, such as simple lookup tables, might actually decrease performance. This is because a table scan will be faster and SQL Server will waste time considering and possibly using the index.

- **NEW TERM** **What kinds of indexes there are**. Basically, you can create clustered and nonclustered indexes. **Clustered indexes** actually rearrange the data on the disk in the order of the index. As a result, you can have only one clustered index per table. Clustered indexes are useful when the columns indexed will be queried in a range (as with a BETWEEN clause) or frequently sorted by with a SORT clause. **Nonclustered indexes** create the index in a separate data structure and therefore multiple nonclustered indexes can be created per table. Within these,

13

the indexes can be unique. A unique index is like a primary key (in fact, creating a primary key creates an index automatically) in that duplicate values within the index aren't allowed. Indexes can also be composite and contain multiple columns. The order of the columns is important, so you should place more frequently queried column at the front of the index.

- **Whether your indexes are correct.** SQL Server provides the Index Tuning Wizard, accessible from SQL Server Enterprise Manager. This utility can analyze traffic captured by the SQL Profiler and suggest indexes based on the queries it is seeing. You can use this during testing to make sure that you've created the appropriate indexes for your application.

The bottom line is that there is no formula you can apply to decide which indexes you create. The determination comes from the combination of your application, the workload, the amount of data, and the tradeoff you're willing to make between query and modification performance.

Security

To ease the administration of permissions for the objects in the database, you need to apply a sound security design. In SQL Server, the simplest way to accomplish this is to make sure that all your objects are owned by the database owner (dbo) account. This is the built-in SQL Server account that the owner of the database automatically uses when accessing the database. This simplifies your applications in two ways.

First, if all the objects are owned by dbo, you needn't reference the owner in SQL statements. For example, the statement

```
SELECT * FROM Titles
```

will actually default to

```
SELECT * FROM dbo.Titles
```

This is the case because the owner wasn't specified and the account that's currently being used to execute the statement ostensibly doesn't have a table of its own named Titles.

Second, having all objects owned by the same account means that the ownership chain will be unbroken; for example, when a stored procedure or view accesses a table. This is important so that permissions can be revoked from the underlying table while allowing particular accounts to access the stored procedure or view. Developers needing to create objects can do so as an alias, as mentioned on Day 2, "Getting Started."

In addition to having dbo own the objects, you also need to assign permissions to the objects for particular accounts. In a typical Web application, the application will use a single account (either a Windows account or a standard account) that all users will share so that connection pooling will occur. This account, then, can be assigned to particular database roles such as db_denydatareader or assigned permissions directly using the GRANT and REVOKE statements. For example, to revoke permissions to the Titles table and grant permissions to the usp_GetTitles stored procedure, you would invoke the following statements:

```
REVOKE ALL ON Titles to publicsite
GRANT EXECUTE ON usp_GetTitles to publicsite
```

where publicsite is a standard account that the ComputeBooks public ASP.NET Web site uses to log in to SQL Server.

Alternative Data Access Techniques

The final (and much shorter) section of today's lesson focuses on some alternative methods you can use to access data from SQL Server. These technique supplement accessing data using the cached and streamed models available in ADO.NET.

 Note Although the information presented in this section isn't about ADO.NET per se, I think it's important to at least be aware of alternatives when you're designing and implementing your applications. As is often said, "When all you have is a hammer, everything looks like a nail."

Server-Side Cursors

Developers familiar with SQL Server will know that in ADO it was possible to execute queries in which the data remained on the server and rows were pulled down as needed. Although this technique results in more roundtrips to the server, which are typically to be avoided, there might be times when you need to see data as it's changed by other users, or perform positioned updates as you scroll through the result set locking the rows as they're traversed.

13

SQL Server Goes .NET

Microsoft made a design decision with ADO.NET not to support server cursors directly in order to focus on the disconnected and streamed models available through the DataSet and data reader. However, Microsoft is working on a server-side model that will first be released on the Web and incorporated into SqlClient and then, later in 2003, incorporated into the next release of SQL Server code named Yukon. This server model will likely expose a System.Data.SqlServer namespace, a `SqlResultSet` class, and an `ExecuteResultSet` method on the `SqlCommand` object, among others, that will enable you to access server cursors.

Although having access to server cursors from the client will be nice, the real productivity will be gained by embedding the CLR into SQL Server. When this happens, you'll be able to write stored procedures using VB and C# code rather than Transact-SQL. Along with a more productive language, you'll get the benefits of IntelliSense and integrated debugging. You'll also see performance improvements for complex procedures because the managed code will be compiled and not interpreted.

We'll discuss these new and exciting features more fully on Day 21, "Futures and Wrap Up."

NEW TERM One of the means SQL Server uses to do just these sorts of operations is **server cursors**. To create a server cursor, you use a specific Transact-SQL statement, as shown in Listing 13.4. This example shows how you might traverse all the rows in the `Titles` table and perform positioned updates if the row meets certain criteria.

LISTING 13.4   A server cursor. This cursor scrolls through the `Titles` table and performs a positioned update on a row if it is in the *Sams Teach Yourself* series.

```
DECLARE @ISBN nchar(10)
DECLARE @Title nvarchar(100)

DECLARE Titles_Cursor CURSOR DYNAMIC SCROLL_LOCKS FOR
SELECT ISBN, Title
FROM Titles
FOR UPDATE

OPEN Titles_Cursor

FETCH NEXT FROM Titles_Cursor INTO @ISBN, @Title
IF @Title LIKE 'Teach Yourself%'
 UPDATE Titles SET Publisher = 'Sams'
 WHERE CURRENT OF Titles_Cursor

WHILE @@FETCH_STATUS = 0
BEGIN
    FETCH NEXT FROM Titles_Cursor INTO @ISBN, @Title
    IF @Title LIKE 'Teach Yourself%'
      UPDATE Titles SET Publisher = 'Sams'
      WHERE CURRENT OF Titles_Cursor
END

CLOSE Titles_Cursor
DEALLOCATE Titles_Cursor
```

Although you can attempt to wrap each of these statements in a `SqlCommand` object and
execute them using the `ExecuteNonQuery` method, a better approach is to wrap the cursor
in a stored procedure and then simply call it with a `SqlCommand`.

SQLXML

On Day 10, you learned how the SqlClient provider exposes the `ExecuteXmlReader`
method to execute and return the XML generated by a query that uses the `FOR XML`
clause on a `SELECT` statement. The ability to work with SQL Server 2000 data as XML,
however, isn't limited to just `FOR XML`. The group of technologies that integrates XML
and SQL Server is, not surprisingly, referred to as SQLXML. Microsoft has created three
releases of this technology and has made them available on the Web through MSDN. In a
nutshell, the major functionalities include

- **XML Views**. **XML Views** (also referred to as **mapping schemas**) are [NEW TERM] simply XSD documents that map an XML schema to a relational
  schema using attributes. By defining a schema and annotating it (much as you
  would when creating a strongly typed `DataSet`), the SQLXML query processor can
  write SQL statements to access data. The Views can then be queried using XPath
  or XQuery syntax. This allows complete abstraction from the database schema
  because it's mapped to the XSD. An example of a simple XML View is shown in
  Listing 13.5.

LISTING 13.5   An XML View. This document maps the `Customers` and `Orders` table to an
XSD schema.

```
<xsd:schema   xmlns:xsd="http://www.w3.org/2001/XMLSchema"
       xmlns:msdata="urn:schemas-microsoft-com:mapping-schema">
  <xsd:element name="Customer" msdata:relation="Customers">
    <xsd:complexType>
      <xsd:sequence>
        <xsd:element name="Order" msdata:relation="Orders">
          <xsd:annotation><xsd:appinfo>
              <msdata:relationship
                parent="Customers" parent-key="CustomerID"
                    child="Orders" child-key="CustomerID" />
          </xsd:appinfo></xsd:annotation>
          <xsd:complexType>
             <xsd:attribute name="OrderDate" type="xsd:dateTime"/>
          </xsd:complexType>
          </xsd:element>
      </xsd:sequence>
      <xsd:attribute name="CustomerID" />
      <xsd:attribute name="StateProv" type="xsd:string" />
    </xsd:complexType>
  </xsd:element>
</xsd:schema>
```

13

ANALYSIS   Note that in Listing 13.5, the schema looks remarkably like the `DataSet` schema
shown on Day 7, "XML and the `DataSet`." This is the case because both are
XSD documents and use annotations from the `msdata` namespace. In this case, the
schema defines the relationship between the `Customers` and `Orders` tables and exposes
the `CustomerID`, `StateProv`, and `OrderDate` columns. The SQLXML query processor
can then use this information to formulate a `SELECT` statement to join these tables. Note
that if the names of the XML elements defined in the schema are the same as the column
names in SQL Server, no further annotations are required.

- **HTTP Access via a URL.** Using IIS, you can set up a virtual directory through
  which you can query data in SQL Server. You can specify your query directly within the query string, through an XML View, or using an XML Template. An XML
  Template is simply an XML document that encapsulates the SQL statement, XPath
  or XQuery syntax. A sample XML Template is shown in Listing 13.6.

LISTING 13.6   An XML template. This document defines a parameterized XPath query
that accesses the XML View in Listing 13.5.

```
<root xmlns:sql="urn:schemas-microsoft-com:xml-sql"
      sql:xsl="path to XSLT file" >
 <sql:header>
    <sql:param name="state">KS</sql:param>
 </sql:header>


 <sql:xpath-query mapping-schema="customers.xsd">
    /Customers[@StateProv=$state]
 </sql:xpath-query>
</root>
```

ANALYSIS   You'll notice in Listing 13.6 that the document contains the definition of a parameter that can be passed to it, or in this case, hardcoded in the header element.
The Template then contains an XPath query that references the XML View and that
selects all the customers whose `StateProv` matches the parameter. When this template is
processed, the appropriate `WHERE` clause will be appended to the `SELECT` statement that is
produced.

- NEW TERM **XML UpdateGrams**. An **UpdateGram** is an XML document that
  records the before and after state of rows correlated with an XML
  View. The SQLXML query processor then writes `INSERT`, `UPDATE`, and `DELETE`
  statements when the document is processed. UpdateGrams can be used to send
  XML directly to the server rather than it having to go through stored procedures.

- **XML Bulkload**. This feature enables you to bulk load XML data directly into SQL Server using an XML View. This is useful when, for example, you're receiving data from a trading partner that's already in an XML document. Using the XML View, you can create annotations to map the data into your SQL Server database. As you might expect, the performance of XML Bulkload is about 75 percent that of the traditional technique.

- **.NET Access through managed classes.** In addition to accessing SQLXML features via HTTP, a set of managed classes are available. This allows you to work with XML Views and templates directly in your .NET code. A simple example of using these classes is shown in Listing 13.7.

LISTING 13.7   SQLXML managed classes. This short example executes an XPath query against the XML View in Listing 13.5.

```
Dim cmd As New SqlXmlCommand(ConnStr)

cmd.CommandType = SqlXmlCommandType.XPath
cmd.CommandText = "/Customer[@StateProv='KS']"
cmd.SchemaPath = "customers.xml"
cmd.RootTag = "ROOT"

Dim r As XmlReader

r = cmd.ExecuteXmlReader();
'
 Loop through the data

' OR Fill a DataSet

Dim ds As New DataSet()
Dim ad As New SqlXmlAdapter(cmd)
ad.Fill(ds)
' Do some work here
ad.Update(ds)
```

13

ANALYSIS   In Listing 13.7, several of the classes that SQLXML exposes are used, including `SqlXmlCommand` and `SqlXmlAdapter`. These classes are analogous to the `SqlCommand` and `SqlDataAdapter` classes in the SqlClient provider but are used to execute commands that are processed by the SQLXML query processor. In this case, the listing shows how you might execute an XPath query against the XML View in Listing 13.5 and then return the data either through an XmlReader or in a `DataSet`.

- **SOAP for SQL Server.** In the latest Web release (3.0), SOAP support was added to enable you to expose stored procedures or XML Templates as methods in an XML Web Service using SOAP. There's a graphical tool that you can use to pick which procedures and templates to expose.

Summary

Understanding the components of ADO.NET is only part of the picture when designing and implementing applications for SQL Server. It's also important to use good design techniques when building your schema and deciding how your ADO.NET application will communicate with SQL Server.

Today you learned how SqlClient communicates with SQL Server, how to apply some basic relational modeling techniques to your schema, and how SQL Server objects such as constraints can be used to increase data integrity. In addition, you should keep in mind the short discussion about alternatives because they might be more applicable than SqlClient for certain scenarios.

Tomorrow we'll finish the week by looking briefly at the ODBC .NET Data Provider as well as how and why you might build your own provider.

Workshop

This workshop will help reinforce the concepts covered in today's lesson.

Quiz

1. What is the significance of SqlClient formulating TDS packets?

   The SqlClient provider creates TDS packets and hands them off to the Net-Library responsible for building network packets and sending them to the server. The significance of this is that SqlClient is directly using the application protocol that SQL Server listens for and so is much faster than first going through an OLE DB provider or ODBC driver. In fact, SqlClient is the fastest way to access SQL Server.

2. What are some of the benefits of normalization?

   A normalized database eliminates redundant data and therefore reduces the storage required. It also makes the data more maintainable because a single change needn't result in changing rows throughout the table. Normalized schemas also tend to be more flexible with regard to changes.

3. Why would you use a stored procedure layer in your application design?

By requiring that all data access be performed through stored procedures, you can abstract the schema from the clients that use it, simplify the API for client developers, increase performance by taking advantage of compilation and reduced network traffic, and increase security by revoking permissions from the underlying tables and views.

4. Why might you use SQLXML instead of SqlClient to access SQL Server?

Because SQLXML deals with how SQL Server data is exposed through XML, SQLXML might be a good candidate anytime you need to represent your SQL Server data in a particular schema. For example, if you're working with a trading partner and need to create XML documents from your SQL Server database that conform to an XSD schema they've given you, you can create an XML View with the proper annotations and use it to create the XML document for the partner. Further, you can then allow the partner to query for the documents directly by exposing an XML Template that uses the view through SOAP.

Exercise

Because you didn't work with any ADO.NET code today, there is no exercise.

13

DAY **14**

Working with Other Providers

This week you've learned the ins and outs of .NET Data Providers and how you can use them to connect to a data store, execute commands, retrieve rows using a data reader, and use data adapters to synchronize data. Today, we'll round out the subject of providers with a short discussion of the ODBC .NET Data Provider and a look at how and why you might implement your own provider.

To that end, in today's lesson you'll learn

- How the ODBC .NET Data Provider is architected and its key differences from the other providers we've discussed
- Why you might want to create your own .NET Data Provider
- What techniques you can use to create a .NET Data Provider
- How a lightweight provider can be implemented

Accessing ODBC Data Sources

Just as with the OleDb provider that ships with VS .NET, the Odbc provider is an example of a generic provider that can used to access a variety of data sources. As we discussed on Day 1, "ADO.NET in Perspective," ODBC was a major advance in data access technologies because it standardized the way that clients access data by abstracting the data store specifics into an ODBC driver. Clients could then program against the ODBC API and rely on the ODBC Driver Manager to load the appropriate drivers on behalf of the application, pass queries to the driver, and manage aspects of the communication such as pooling connections. As a result, when using the Odbc provider, your application architecture appears as shown in Figure 14.1.

FIGURE 14.1

ODBC architecture. This diagram depicts the architecture of a .NET application using the Odbc provider.

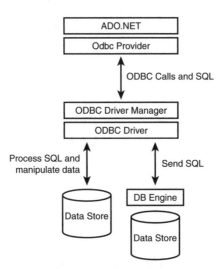

Come and Get It

Although not included in the release of VS .NET, the ODBC .NET Data Provider is available for download from Microsoft on the MSDN site (msdn.microsoft.com). You can find it by going to the MSDN site and typing "ODBC .NET Data Provider" in the Search For box. When you navigate to the page, you can download the installation package by clicking on the Download link. To install, simply execute the odbc_net.msi file that you download and follow the instructions. Note that you must have MDAC 2.7 or higher installed on your machine, which is the same version that installs with VS .NET.

After it is installed, the Odbc provider assembly (Microsoft.Data.Odbc.dll) will be installed in the Global Assembly Cache (GAC), so you can reference it in your projects through the Add Reference dialog.

You should also keep in mind that Microsoft notes in its documentation that the provider supports only the Microsoft SQL Server ODBC Driver, the Microsoft ODBC Driver for Oracle, and the Microsoft Access ODBC Driver. As a result, your mileage might vary when using other drivers. To keep up to date on how other drivers are or are not working, consult the `microsoft.public.dotnet.framework.odbcnet` newsgroup. For example, this newsgroup contains some good information on using the MySQL ODBC driver and the ODBC driver from Oracle.

As you can infer from Figure 14.1, the cost of using the abstraction that ODBC provides is that you must traverse layers of software, which typically slows performance. However, because so many ODBC drivers exist, using the Odbc provider extends the reach of your .NET applications. In addition, you'll notice that there are several kinds of ODBC drivers. Some drivers process both the ODBC calls and the SQL directly, whereas others process the ODBC calls and pass on the SQL to the data store. The former is typical of file-based data stores that have no active database engine, such as Excel and dBASE, whereas the latter is used with enterprise data stores such as Oracle and SQL Server.

Note

Keep in mind that you can't use the OLE DB Provider for ODBC Drivers (MSDASQL) with the OLE DB .NET Data Provider. Using the Odbc provider is your only option for accessing data available only through ODBC.

After you add a reference to the Odbc provider assembly in your project, you can use its types by importing (or using in C#) the `Microsoft.Data.Odbc` namespace. The classes shown in Figure 14.2 are analogous to those in the other providers, as you might expect.

In addition to the classes shown in Figure 14.2, the namespace contains an `OdbcType` enumeration analogous to the `SqlDbType` and `OleDbType` enumerations. This enumeration is used to specify the type when creating `OdbcParameter` objects.

Note

To view the mappings of the enumeration to the Common Type System (CTS) types, see the ODBC .NET Data Provider documentation and navigate to the OdbcType enumeration topic.

14

In the remainder of this section, you'll learn how connection strings and commands are specified and how connection pooling occurs, and you'll look at a simple example of using the Odbc provider to create Excel spreadsheets.

FIGURE 14.2

*Odbc provider archi-
tecture. Just as with
the other providers, the
Odbc provider includes
the standard provider
classes.*

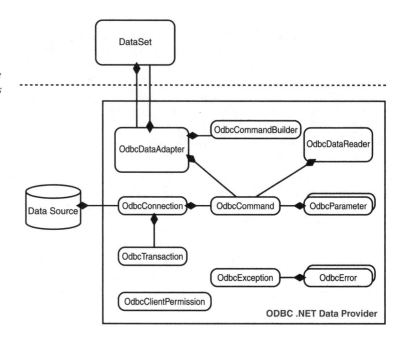

Opening Connections

Perhaps the most difficult part of using the Odbc provider is determining how to formulate a connection string. Just as with ODBC in other environments, you can use either a
user or system DSN, a File DSN, or a DSN-less connection. The DSN and File DSN
connections can be configured in the ODBC Data Source Administrator found in the
Administrative Tools group. An example of each of these three options is shown in the
following code snippet:

```
// User or System DSN
OdbcConnection con = new OdbcConnection("DSN=ComputeBooks");
//File DSN
OdbcConnection con = new OdbcConnection("FileDSN=ComputeBooks.dsn");
// DSN-less
OdbcConnection con = new OdbcConnection(
"Driver={SQL
Server};Server=ssosa;trusted_connection=yes;Database=ComputeBooks");
```

As you can see, when using the DSN-less connection, the attributes of the connection
string outside of the `Driver` are those specified by the driver itself. In this case, the
`Server`, `trusted_connection`, and `Database` attributes are particular to SQL Server. Just
as with the other ADO.NET connection objects, some of the attributes correspond to
read-only properties of the `OdbcConnection` object, such as `Database`, `DataSource`, and

Driver. It should also be noted that the OdbcConnection object doesn't support the Persist Security Info attribute. However, it acts as if it were set to false, so if you do embed the password in the connection string, it won't be accessible after the connection has been opened.

> **Note**
>
> If the ConnectionString property of the OdbcConnection object doesn't include the Driver, FileDSN, or DSN attributes, an OleDbException won't be thrown until the Open method is called. This is unlike OleDbConnection, where the connection string is parsed at the time it is populated (through the constructor or independently).

Although you can use any of the three options to formulate a connection string, the DSN-less connection is preferred because it doesn't incur the overhead of an extra file or registry access. However, because connection strings support only 1024 characters, you must use a DSN or File DSN if you need to set a lot of attributes that would extend the connection string beyond 1024 characters.

Connection Pooling

If you're going to use the Odbc provider for enterprise applications, you need to take connection pooling into consideration because it reduces the load on the data store by allowing clients to reuse connections. The ODBC implementation is analogous to the connection pooling used by the SqlClient provider and the session pooling used by the OleDb provider.

ODBC connection pooling is enabled by the ODBC Driver Manager in version 3.5 (the version installed with MDAC 2.7), and is turned on by default for all ODBC drivers. In a nutshell, ODBC will create up to n pools, where n is the number of processors in the server, for each process (application) on the server that connects using ODBC. Creating multiple pools helps alleviate lock conflicts when multiple threads are running within the application. The pools for each process contain all the connections that have been initiated from the process. When the process initiates a new connection, the ODBC Driver Manager locks and traverses the pools, looking for connections that were created with the same attributes. If a connection is found, it is assigned from the pool and the pool is unlocked. As a result, and as with the other providers, the connection string you use must be identical in order for the connection to be retrieved from the pool.

When you're finished with the OleDbConnection object, you can call its Close method to release it back to the pool. In addition, after all the connections initiated by the application have been closed, you can call the shared ReleaseObjectPool method to release

14

the ODBC environment handle. Calling `ReleaseObjectPool` when connections are active has no effect. As a result, you'd call `ReleaseObjectPool` only if the application has closed its connections and will no longer use any ODBC connections.

ODBC connection pooling works only with 32-bit drivers that are thread safe and (under ODBC 3.5) have the string value `CPTimeout` in the Registry under HKEY_LOCAL_MACHINE\Software\ODBC\ODBCINST.INI*driver*. The `CPTimeout` is used to configure how long a connection remains in the pool before it's destroyed. The default value is 60 seconds, but can be changed so that connections remain in the pool for different periods (under ODBC 3.0, connection pooling couldn't be disabled or configured).

If you begin to encounter errors (which could indicate that the driver isn't thread safe), you can disable connection pooling on a per-driver basis in ODBC 3.5 by removing the `CPTimeout` value in the Registry key. Other than setting `CPTimeout`, you have no way to configure how many connections remain in the pool or to preallocate connections before they're initiated by a process (something you could do with the `Min` and `Max Pool Size` attributes of SqlClient).

The ODBC Driver Manager also uses a retry wait time of 120 seconds that can be changed in the ODBC Data Source Administrator utility. Basically, this setting is used to tell ODBC to wait for 120 seconds before attempting to reconnect if it determines that a data source is unavailable.

Creating Commands

After your connection has been established, you need to create `OdbcCommand` objects to encapsulate the statement or procedure you want to execute. Although working with the `OdbcCommand` and `OdbcParameter` objects is very similar to the command and parameter objects described on Day 10, "Using Commands," there a couple of differences you'll need to be aware of.

First, the `OdbcCommand` objectsupports only positional (rather than named) arguments when using both inline SQL and a procedure. In addition, it uses a question mark as the placeholder for a parameter. In other words, if you're using inline SQL (`CommandType` set to `Text`), you should specify your SQL statement like so:

```
SELECT * FROM Titles WHERE ISBN = ? AND Title = ?
```

Then, when you create your `OdbcCommand` object, you would add the parameters to the command positionally as follows:

```
OdbcCommand com = new OdbcCommand(
  "SELECT * FROM Titles WHERE ISBN = ? AND Title = ?", con);
```

```
com.Parameters.Add(new OdbcParameter("isbn", OdbcType.Text));
com.Parameters.Add(new OdbcParameter("title", OdbcType.Text));
```

Note that it doesn't matter what names you give the parameters; only their position in the parameters collection matters. When the command is executed, the parameters will be plugged into the SELECT statement going left to right, so the parameter at position 0 will be used to specify the ISBN and the one at position 1 will be used to specify the Title.

When calling a procedure (CommandType set to StoredProcedure), you must use positional arguments in addition to the ODBC calling syntax using the call keyword as follows:

```
{[?=]call procedure-name[([parameter][,[parameter]]...)]}
```

Simply populating the CommandText property with the name of the procedure is not sufficient. Notice that to capture the return value from a procedure, you would then need to specify it as the first parameter in the collection. To illustrate this syntax, the following code snippet calls the usp_GetTitles stored procedure:

```
OdbcCommand ocom = new OdbcCommand("{call usp_GetTitles(?, ?)}",ocon);
ocom.CommandType = CommandType.StoredProcedure;
ocom.Parameters.Add(new OdbcParameter("@isbn",OdbcType.NText));
ocom.Parameters.Add(new OdbcParameter("@title",OdbcType.NText));
```

Note that although the usp_GetTitles stored procedure actually accepts six parameters, you needn't specify them if you're not going to use them because they are defaulted to NULL in SQL Server. If you want to specify that a default value is to be used, most ODBC drivers support using the null keyword in place of the question mark.

Using the Odbc Provider

Of course, one of the primary benefits of using the Odbc provider is that it gives you access to a variety of data stores that would otherwise be difficult to read to and write from. To illustrate this point, Listing 14.1 shows a method called CreateActivityReport. This method is used to create an Excel workbook that contains the total units sold and the revenue generated for each book from a given publisher within a given date range.

LISTING 14.1 Creating an Excel workbook. This method creates a workbook and populates it with data from SQL Server.

```
virtual void CreateActivityReport(string fileName, string publisher,
    DateTime startDate, DateTime endDate)
{
    // Kill the file if it exists
    if (File.Exists(fileName))
```

14

LISTING 14.1   continued

```
{
    File.Delete(fileName);
}

// Access SQL Server to get the data
SqlConnection con = new SqlConnection(_connect);
SqlCommand com = new SqlCommand("usp_ActivityReport",con);

// Configure the SqlCommand
com.CommandType = CommandType.StoredProcedure;
com.Parameters.Add(new SqlParameter("@publisher",publisher));
com.Parameters.Add(new SqlParameter("@startDate",startDate));
com.Parameters.Add(new SqlParameter("@endDate",endDate));

// Create the Excel ConnectionString
StringBuilder excelConnect = new StringBuilder();
excelConnect.Append("Driver={Microsoft Excel Driver (*.xls)};");
excelConnect.Append("FirstRowHasNames=1;ReadOnly=False;");
excelConnect.Append("Create_DB=" + fileName + ";DBQ=" + fileName);

OdbcConnection oCon = new OdbcConnection(excelConnect.ToString());

try
{
    // Create the worksheet
    oCon.Open();
    OdbcCommand createWS = new OdbcCommand(
      "CREATE TABLE ActivityReport (ISBN TEXT,Title TEXT, Author TEXT, " +
      "TotalUnits NUMBER, Revenue CURRENCY)",oCon);

    createWS.ExecuteNonQuery();

    // Build the INSERT statement
    StringBuilder ins = new StringBuilder();
    ins.Append("INSERT INTO ActivityReport (");
    ins.Append("ISBN, Title, Author, TotalUnits, Revenue) ");
    ins.Append("VALUES (?, ?, ?, ?, ?)");

    // Build the Insert command
    OdbcCommand  insCom= new OdbcCommand(ins.ToString(),oCon);
    insCom.Parameters.Add(new OdbcParameter("isbn",OdbcType.Text));
    insCom.Parameters.Add(new OdbcParameter("title",OdbcType.Text));
    insCom.Parameters.Add(new OdbcParameter("author",OdbcType.Text));
    insCom.Parameters.Add(new OdbcParameter("units",OdbcType.Int));
    insCom.Parameters.Add(new OdbcParameter("revenue",OdbcType.Double));

    // Get the data from SQL Server
    con.Open();
```

LISTING 14.1 continued

```
            SqlDataReader dr = com.ExecuteReader();
            while (dr.Read())
            {
              insCom.Parameters["isbn"].Value = dr["ISBN"].ToString();
              insCom.Parameters["title"].Value = dr["Title"].ToString();
              insCom.Parameters["author"].Value = dr["Author"].ToString();
              insCom.Parameters["units"].Value = Convert.ToInt32(dr["TotalUnits"]);
              insCom.Parameters["revenue"].Value = dr["Revenue"];
              insCom.ExecuteNonQuery();
            }
            dr.Close();
      }
      catch (SqlException e)
      {
          // SQL Server error occurred
      }
      catch (OdbcException e)
      {
          // ODBC error occurred
      }
      catch (Exception e)
      {
          // Other error occurred
      }
      finally
      {
          con.Close();
          // Close the spreadsheet
          oCon.Close();
      }
  }
```

ANALYSIS

You'll notice in Listing 14.1 that the data for the report comes from the usp_ActivityReport stored procedure in the ComputeBooks database encapsulated in the SqlCommand com. This procedure accepts the publisher and start and end dates as parameters passed into the method.

After the SQL Server objects are instantiated and configured, the method uses a StringBuilder to build the ConnectionString property of the OdbcConnection object. In this case, the Microsoft Excel ODBC Driver is specified. This driver is shipped with the Microsoft ODBC Desktop Database Drivers (which also include drivers for Access, dBASE, Paradox, and Text) and is a Jet-based driver.

14

> **Note**
>
> There are other ways to access Excel from .NET. Options include using COM-based automation through the interoperation services in .NET to program against the Excel object model, and using the Jet OLE DB provider, which is also capable of opening Excel workbooks. Using automation, for example, gives you more control over the output because you can programmatically change fonts, colors, and cell sizes. The technique shown here is meant to show only how you could use the Odbc provider to move data from one data source to another.

In the connection string, the `Driver` attribute specifies the ODBC driver, and the driver-specific attributes `FirstRowHasNames`, `ReadOnly`, and `Create_DB` are used to specify that the first row of the worksheet will contain the column names, that the worksheet is not read-only, and that the file specified in the `DBQ` attribute is to be created when the connection is opened, respectively.

Within the `try` block, the `OdbcConnection` is opened, which creates the Excel workbook. The worksheet is then created by executing the `createWS OdbcCommand` object, whose `CommandText` property is set to a `CREATE TABLE` statement. A second `OdbcCommand` object is then created to encapsulate the `INSERT` statement that will be used to insert the individual rows. Next, the SQL Server data is retrieved using the `ExecuteReader` method and is traversed. Within the `while` loop, the `insCom` command's parameters are populated with the data from data reader, and the command is executed to insert the new row into the Excel worksheet. Each row is inserted by executing the `insCom OdbcCommand`.

You'll notice that the various `catch` blocks can be used to differentiate between errors generated by the Odbc provider and those generated by the SqlClient provider. The `finally` block closes both the connection to SQL Server and the workbook by closing the `OdbcConnection` object.

A client could then call the method like so:

```
CreateActivityReport("sams.xls","Sams",
  new DateTime(2000,1,1), new DateTime(2002,12,31));
```

Building a .NET Data Provider

The .NET Data Providers you have learned about in this book were all built using the classes and interfaces in the `System.Data` and `System.Data.Common` namespaces, as discussed on Day 8, "Understanding .NET Data Providers." The existence of the classes and interfaces provides a pattern or template that developers can use when implementing providers. Not surprisingly, you can also build your own .NET Data Provider. This section will discuss why you might want to embark on this task, some alternatives, and the different forms the provider might take. The section ends with a discussion and a code sample of a simple provider that the ComputeBooks organization might implement to more easily expose and work with XML documents in a file system.

Deciding to Implement a Provider

Before deciding to implement a provider, you should be clear about why you would want to. There are several scenarios to consider in making this decision, including the following:

- **Proprietary Data Store**. If your organization has developed its own proprietary data store, you might consider implementing a provider to interact with that data store. This is analogous to a database vendor building its own provider and is therefore a specific or targeted provider. For example, assume that your organization builds packaged medical software, and that the data storage format and query language for your suite of applications is one that your organization developed in-house. Many organizations have done just this, and have in the past exposed their proprietary data store as functions in a set of DLLs or in COM-based wrappers. By implementing a provider, you can expose the functionality of your data store to managed code in a way that is consistent with what .NET developers will be familiar with. In this way, developers internal to your organization can easily use the data store when building Windows Forms, Web Forms, and XML Web Services applications. In addition, a provider would enable your customers to query and possibly even update the data store in conjunction with other data they are working with. For example, customers could use your provider to fill a table in a `DataSet` and then populate a second table with data from their SQL Server database for display in their Intranet portal.

- **Data Aggregation**. You might also implement a provider to centralize access to organizational data. By abstracting the location and formats for data within your organization and exposing them simply through a provider, you can make the process of creating managed applications simpler for your developers. In this way, developers within your organization can work with the data through a single provider rather than having to figure out how to access the various data stores your applications require. This type of provider is more analogous to the generic providers such as OleDb and Odbc, although it is implemented at the organizational rather than the data store level.

In both cases, the end result is that you allow managed access to data through standard interfaces, thereby making the programming model easier for developers. In addition, the use of standard interfaces such as `IDataReader` and `IDbCommand` enables your developers

14

to take advantage of polymorphism by programming to the interfaces rather than the concrete classes that implement them. In this way, your developers can also write code in the presentation or business services tiers of their applications which works with any provider—true reusability.

> **Note**
>
> In fact, creating a provider that uses the ADO.NET interfaces allows it to be plugged into generic factory classes that abstract all the provider specifics from developers. We'll look at an example of just such a class on Day 18, "Building a Data Factory."

At the same time, however, the fact that you're developing your own classes gives you the opportunity to expose functionality specific to your organization or data store through your provider. For example, if you created a specific provider for a proprietary data store, you could expose additional (overloaded) signatures for the Fill method of your data adapter class that uses the industry standard format that you want the data returned in.

Exploring Alternatives to Implementing a Provider

That having been said, there are also several scenarios in which you might want to consider alternatives to developing a provider.

First, if you're considering implementing a provider for a proprietary data store, you need to consider which clients need access to the data store. Implementing a provider will allow only managed (.NET) clients to access the data store; therefore, it can't be used from other environments such as Win32 applications implemented with MFC or ASP Web sites implemented with VBScript and COM components. If your requirements dictate that you support other types of clients, you should consider implementing an OLE DB provider (or, less likely, an ODBC driver) instead. Implementing an OLE DB provider makes the data store accessible to managed clients through the OleDb provider as well as other data access interfaces such as ADO.

> **Note**
>
> For more information to get you started in implementing an OLE DB provider, see the article "OLE DB Minimum Levels of Consumer and Provider Functionality" and the OmniProv 1.0 sample OLE DB provider, both of which can be found on the MSDN Web site. Probably the easiest way is to use the OLE DB provider ActiveX Template Library (ATL) templates in Visual C++.

Second, you need to consider whether you need the core concepts exposed by the provider. In other words, does your scenario require the use of connections, transactions, data readers, and data adapters, or do you simply need to expose data to clients? If you simply need to expose data and don't want or need to provide the ADO.NET programming model, you might consider creating classes that expose the data as XML using the `System.Xml` namespace classes.

Choosing an Approach to Implementing a Provider

When implementing a provider, there are basically two approaches you can take depending on the needs of your organization:

- **Full Provider**. This type of provider would implement *all* the provider objects (all the interfaces in `System.Data` and `System.Data.Common`) we discussed on Day 8, and provide complete transaction, data reader, and connection support. A full provider could be easily plugged into a data factory (like the one we'll discuss on Day 18) because the factory will be ensured that it supports the full range of provider functionality.

- **Lightweight Provider**. This type of provider would probably implement a *subset* of the provider objects we discussed on Day 8. For example, a lightweight provider would implement a data adapter for filling and synchronizing a `DataSet`, but not necessarily parameters, data readers, transactions, or perhaps even connections. This type of provider would be useful for disconnected scenarios, for example, where you wanted to be able to use your provider to return data from an XML Web Service. The ComputeBooks provider discussed in the next section is just such a provider.

For both types of providers, the available interfaces and their uses are shown in Table 14.1. Obviously, a full provider would implement all the interfaces, whereas a lightweight provider would implement only some of them. Note that, in addition, a full provider might implement command builder, exception, error, and permissions classes as well.

TABLE 14.1 Provider interfaces. Providers implement some of (lightweight) or all (full) these interfaces.

Interface	Use
IDataAdapter	Populates and synchronizes `DataSet` objects with the data store.
IDataParameter	Represents a parameter passed to a command.
IDataParameterCollection	Represents the collection of parameters passed to a command.
IDataReader	Streams through a result set returned from a command.

14

TABLE 14.1 continued

Interface	Use
IDbCommand	Represents a query or command executed against the data store.
IDbConnection	Represents a unique session with the data store usually corresponding to a network connection.
IDbDataAdapter	Represents a data adapter that works with relational databases to support various commands to insert, update, and delete data from the data store. Implements the IDataAdapter interface.
IDbDataParameter	Represents a database parameter with Precision, Scale and Size passed to a command. Implements the IDataParameter interface.
IDbTransaction	Represents a local transaction to group commands into logical units of work.

Implementing a Provider: The ComputeBooks Provider

To illustrate generally how you would implement a provider, this section walks through the implementation of a provider for ComputeBooks. This provider is quite simple in that it simply abstracts access to XML documents stored in a location on the file system.

 Note

Obviously, there are other ways to access XML documents, including using the System.Xml classes directly or abstracting the access in a custom class. The code shown in this example is used only for simplicity and to illustrate the concepts and code required to implement a provider. Most providers will be quite complex and will therefore run into thousands of lines of code.

As discussed previously, the ComputeBooks provider is something of a lightweight provider because it doesn't implement all the interfaces shown in Table 14.1. In particular, there's no need for IDbTransaction or IDataReader because there's no concept of transacted access to the file system and data will always be returned in a DataSet, respectively. The provider also doesn't support command builders, code access permissions classes, or individual error objects. The architecture of the ComputeBooks provider is shown in Figure 14.3.

As you can see from Figure 14.3, each of the classes uses the standard naming convention of prefixing with a three- or four-letter abbreviation for the provider; in this case, Cbks to denote ComputeBooks. In addition, all the classes and enumerated types used by the provider should be placed in the same namespace. The convention, of course, is that the highest-level namespace is that of the organization and the lowest-level namespace is the name of the provider. So, in this case, all the classes are contained in the `ComputeBooks.Data.Cbks` namespace and compiled into a single assembly so that it can be versioned, secured, and deployed to other developers within ComputeBooks.

FIGURE 14.3

ComputeBooks provider architecture. This diagram contains the classes implemented by the ComputeBooks .NET Data Provider.

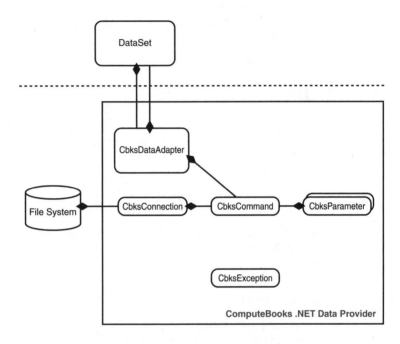

> **Note**
>
> Although the previous code you've seen today was written in C#, the ComputeBooks provider shown in the following sections is written in VB, whereas the client code to access it is written in C#. This is done to illustrate the fact that it doesn't matter what managed language the provider is implemented in.

The Connection Class

The first class that you need to implement when building a provider is the connection class; in this case, `CbksConnection`. Although they aren't strictly required, connection classes are typically relied on by the command class to provide it with the avenue through which to execute. Some of the responsibilities of the connection class are to capture and verify the connection string and open and close the connection. Because `CbksConnection` is the first class we'll discuss, its complete code is shown in Listing 14.2. In later sections, you'll see only portions of each class.

14

LISTING 14.2 Implementing a connection. This listing shows the complete code for the CbksConnection class.

```
Public NotInheritable Class CbksConnection : Implements IDbConnection
  Private _state As ConnectionState
  Private _connect As String
  Private _locationPath As String
  Private _database As String

  ' The default constructor.
  Public Sub New()
    MyBase.New()
    Me.InitClass()
  End Sub

  ' Constructor that takes a connection string.
  Public Sub New(ByVal connect As String)
    MyBase.New()
    Me.InitClass()
    Me.ConnectionString = connect
  End Sub

  Private Sub InitClass()
    _state = ConnectionState.Closed
  End Sub

  Public Property ConnectionString() As String _
    Implements IDbConnection.ConnectionString
    Get
      ' Always return exactly what the user set.
      ' Security-sensitive information may be removed.
      Return _connect
    End Get
    Set(ByVal Value As String)
      ' Parse the connection string for syntax, not content
      Dim h As Hashtable = _parseConnectionString(Value)
      If Not h.ContainsKey("Location") Then
        Throw New CbksException("Must include Location attribute")
      Else
        _locationPath = h.Item("Location").ToString()
      End If
      ' Can look for other specific attributes here
      _connect = Value
    End Set
  End Property

  Private Function _parseConnectionString(ByVal s As String) As Hashtable
    Dim pairs(), a As String
    Dim h As New Hashtable()
```

LISTING 14.2   continued

```
    ' Split into an array of each name-value pair
    pairs = s.Split(CType(";", Char))

    For Each a In pairs
      ' Look for the name and value
      Dim i As Integer = a.IndexOf(CType("=", Char))
      If i = 0 Then
        Throw New CbksException("Connection string is improperly formatted")
      Else
        ' Place them in a hashtable
        h.Add(a.Substring(0, i), a.Substring(i + 1))
      End If
    Next

    Return h
  End Function

  Public ReadOnly Property ConnectionTimeout() As Integer _
    Implements IDbConnection.ConnectionTimeout
    Get
      ' Returns the connection time-out value set in the connection
      ' string. Zero indicates an indefinite time-out period.
      Return 0
    End Get
  End Property

  Public ReadOnly Property Database() As String _
    Implements IDbConnection.Database
    Get
      ' Returns an initial database as set in the connection string.
      ' An empty string indicates not set - do not return a null reference.
      Return _database
    End Get
  End Property

  Public ReadOnly Property State() As ConnectionState _
    Implements IDbConnection.State
    Get
      Return _state
      End Get
  End Property

  Overloads Sub Dispose() Implements IDisposable.Dispose
    ' Make sure all managed and unmanaged resources are cleaned up
    ' In this case there are no unmanaged resources
  End Sub

  Public Overloads Function BeginTransaction() As IDbTransaction _
    Implements IDbConnection.BeginTransaction
```

14

LISTING 14.2 continued

```vb
        Throw New NotSupportedException("Transactions not supported")
    End Function

    Public Overloads Function BeginTransaction(ByVal level As IsolationLevel) _
      As IDbTransaction Implements IDbConnection.BeginTransaction
        Throw New NotSupportedException("Transactions not supported")
    End Function

    Public Sub ChangeDatabase(ByVal name As String) _
      Implements IDbConnection.ChangeDatabase
        ' Change the database setting on the back-end. Note that it is a method
        ' and not a property because the operation requires an expensive
        ' round trip.

        ' Change the path
        Try
          Dim dir As New DirectoryInfo(name)
          _locationPath = name
          _database = dir.FullName
        Catch e As Exception
          Throw New CbksException("Cannot change database", e)
        End Try

    End Sub

    Public Sub Open() Implements IDbConnection.Open
        ' If the underlying connection to the server is
        ' expensive to obtain, the implementation should provide
        ' implicit pooling of that connection.

        ' If the provider also supports automatic enlistment in
        ' distributed transactions, it should enlist during Open().

        ' Make sure the path exists
        Try
          Dim dir As New DirectoryInfo(_locationPath)
          _database = dir.FullName
        Catch e As Exception
          Throw New CbksException("Cannot open connection", e)
        End Try
        _state = ConnectionState.Open
    End Sub

    Public Sub Close() Implements IDbConnection.Close
        ' If the underlying connection to the server is
        ' being pooled, Close() will release it back to the pool.

        _database = ""  ' Reset the read-only properties
        _state = ConnectionState.Closed
```

LISTING 14.2 continued

```
    End Sub

    Public Function CreateCommand() As CbksCommand
        ' Return a new instance of a command object.
        Return New CbksCommand()
    End Function
    Private Function _createCommand() As IDbCommand _
        Implements IDbConnection.CreateCommand
        ' Return a new instance of a command object.
        Return Me.CreateCommand()
    End Function

        ' Your custom properties / methods.
    End Class
```

NEW TERM

ANALYSIS

The first thing you should notice in Listing 14.2 is that the CbksConnection class implements the IDbConnection interface. As a result, all the members of IDbConnection must be implemented by the class. In VB, this is done with the Implements keyword. You'll also notice that although all the methods of the interface are implemented, not all must be supported. To indicate that you don't support a method, simply throw the System.NotSupportedException, as is done in the overloaded BeginTransaction methods. You would use this technique when the client expects some specific behavior to occur when the method is called. If the client wouldn't necessarily expect anything to happen, you can simply leave the body of the method empty, as is done with the Dispose method. This is referred to as a **no-op**, or no operation. For a property that isn't used, you can similarly return the default value in the Get block and throw a NotSupportedException in the Set block.

The primary functionality in the CbksConnection class is to validate the ConnectionString property when it is set, either through the constructor or directly, and then to open the connection.

As you can see from the Set block in the ConnectionString property, the string is passed to the private _parseConnectionString method, which parses a connection string into a Hashtable by first splitting the string into attributes by looking for semicolons (;) and then placing the individual name-value pairs into the Hashtable based on the presence of an equal sign (=). Note that if one of the attributes doesn't contain an equal sign, an exception is thrown. When the Hashtable is returned, the property looks for the Location attribute and raises an exception if it isn't found. If it is found, the location path is stored in a private variable along with the entire connection string. You can use a technique like this to parse your connection string and look for specific attributes.

14

The Open method then simply determines whether the location found in the connection string is valid by using a DirectoryInfo object. If the location exists, the full path is placed in the _database private variable returned through the read-only Database property. Of course, the Open method should then set the State property to the Open value of the ConnectionState enumeration. Conversely, the Close method simply sets the state to Closed and resets the read-only Database property to an empty string.

A client can use the CbksConnection object as follows:

```
CbksConnection con = new CbksConnection("Location=.");
con.Open();
Console.WriteLine(con.Database); //prints the full path of the current directory
con.Close();
```

The Command Class

The command class is responsible for managing the text and type of a command along with its parameters, as well as actually using the connection object to execute the command. Listing 14.3 contains all the implemented code for the CbksCommand. It doesn't include the members that are no-ops and those that will throw a NotSupportedException.

 Tip

> When you're developing classes that contain several members that won't be implemented, you can easily segregate them in VS .NET in a #Region statement and then collapse the region so that you can concentrate on the code you're actually implementing.

LISTING 14.3 Implementing a command. This listing shows the simple CbksCommand class. It implements only the ExecuteNonQuery method and the ability to retrieve data from XML documents.

```
Public NotInheritable Class CbksCommand : Implements IDbCommand

    Private _cmdText As String
    Private _params As CbksParameterCollection
    Private _con As CbksConnection

    ' Default constructor
    Public Sub New()
        _InitClass()
    End Sub

    ' Overloaded constructor
    Public Sub New(ByVal cmdText As String)
        Me.CommandText = cmdText
```

LISTING 14.3   continued

```
  _InitClass()
End Sub


' Overloaded constructor
Public Sub New(ByVal cmdText As String, ByVal connection As CbksConnection)
  Me.CommandText = cmdText
  Me.Connection = connection
  _InitClass()
End Sub


Private Sub _InitClass()        .
  _params = New CbksParameterCollection()
End Sub


' Strongly typed and interface implementations
Public Property Connection() As CbksConnection
  Get
    Return _con
  End Get
  Set(ByVal Value As CbksConnection)
    _con = Value
  End Set
End Property
Private Property _connection() As IDbConnection _
  Implements IDbCommand.Connection
  Get
    Return Me.Connection
  End Get
  Set(ByVal Value As IDbConnection)
    Me.Connection = CType(Value, CbksConnection)
  End Set
End Property


' Strongly typed and interface implementations
Public ReadOnly Property Parameters() As CbksParameterCollection
  Get
    Return _params
  End Get
End Property
Private ReadOnly Property _parameters() As IDataParameterCollection _
  Implements IDbCommand.Parameters
  Get
    Return Me.Parameters
  End Get
End Property


Public Property CommandText() As String Implements IDbCommand.CommandText
  Get
    Return _cmdText
```

14

LISTING **14.3**   continued

```
      End Get
      Set(ByVal Value As String)
        ' Usually commands are not validated until executed so simply set it here
        _cmdText = Value
      End Set
    End Property


    ' Strongly typed and interface implementations
    Public Function CreateParameter() As CbksParameter
      ' Return a new parameter
      Return New CbksParameter()
    End Function
    Private Function _createParameter() As IDbDataParameter _
      Implements IDbCommand.CreateParameter
      ' Return a new parameter
      Return Me.CreateParameter()
    End Function


    Public Function ExecuteNonQuery() As Integer _
      Implements IDbCommand.ExecuteNonQuery

      ' Check for a connection
      If _con.State = ConnectionState.Closed Then
        Throw New CbksException("Connection must be open")
      End If

      ' Go get the files based on the parameters
      Dim files() As String = _validateParms()
      Dim s As String

      Select Case Me.CommandText
        Case "Delete"
          ' Delete each file
          For Each s In files
            Try
              File.Delete(s)
            Catch e As Exception
              Throw New CbksException("Error in command execution", e)
            End Try
          Next
          ' Case other commands to execute here
        Case Else
          Throw New CbksException("Command is not a non query command")
      End Select

    End Function
```

LISTING 14.3   continued

```vb
Friend Function GetData() As XmlReader()
  ' Go get the data based on the command and return XmlReaders
  ' for each document

  Dim readers As New ArrayList()

  If Me.CommandText = "Get" Then
    Dim files() As String = _validateParms()
    Dim s As String
    For Each s In files
      Dim xlr As New XmlTextReader(s)
      readers.Add(xlr)
    Next
    ' Return the array of readers
    Return CType(readers.ToArray(GetType(XmlReader)), XmlReader())
  Else
    Throw New CbksException("Invalid command")
  End If

End Function

Private Function _validateParms() As String()
  ' Translate the parms into an array of files to work with
  Dim filePath As String

  ' Build the filter
  If _params.Contains("Vendor") Then
    filePath = CType(_params.Item("Vendor"), CbksParameter).Value.ToString()
  Else
    filePath = ""
  End If

  ' Build the filter
  If _params.Contains("YearMonth") Then
    filePath &= CType( _
    _params.Item("YearMonth"), CbksParameter).Value.ToString & ".xml"
  Else
    filePath &= "*.xml"
  End If

  Return Directory.GetFiles(Me.Connection.Database, filePath)

End Function
End Class
```

14

ANALYSIS   You'll notice in Listing 14.3 that the CbksCommand object stores the
CommandText, a parameter collection (discussed in the next section), and a reference to a CbksConnection object as private variables in the class. As with all classes in

the provider, you're free to implement whatever constructors you see fit, although following the patterns found in the SqlClient and OleDb providers will make your provider more usable. For example, the CbksCommand object includes three constructors: an empty or default constructor, one that accepts just the CommandText, and one that accepts both the CommandText and the CbksConnection. The fourth constructor implemented by SqlCommand, however, is not implemented because it accepts a transaction and this provider doesn't use transactions. These constructors are used to populate the private variables.

One interesting aspect of Listing 14.3 is the dual implementations of the Connection and Parameters properties and the CreateParameter method. Because the IDbCommand interface dictates that these members be implemented, you must create methods to implement them. However, when you do this, the type of the property or the return type of the method must be the same as that found in the interface. In other words, the Connection property would simply accept and return variables of type IDbConnection rather than the strongly typed (and preferred) CbksConnection. To deal with this situation, you can expose your own strongly typed public member and then make the interface's implementation private. This way, you ensure that clients use only the strongly typed classes as you would expect, while also being able to cast to the interface if the clients want to use polymorphism. This is illustrated by the following code snippet:

```
CbksCommand com = new CbksCommand("Get");
// Calls the publicly exposed property
com.Connection = new CbksConnection("Location=.");
// Calls the private interface implementation
IDbCommand icom = com
Console.WriteLine(icom.Connection.ConnectiongString);
```

You'll notice that when using the property directly, the public implementation is called, whereas after casting to the interface, the private interface implementation is called. This technique works exactly the same way when used with methods as well. Of course, this design means that you need to write two methods, but you should write the code for the methods only once in the public implementation, and then have the private implementation call it, as is done in both the Connection property and the CreateParameter method.

You can create the same design in C# by implementing a public member that uses the strong type and a second whose name includes the interface name and returns the type from the interface. For example, in C#, the private implementation of the Connection property would look like so:

```
IDbConnection IDbCommand.Connection
{
    get
```

```
    {
        return this.Connection;
    }
    set
    {
        this.Connection = (CbksConnection)value;
    }
}
```

The other point to note about `CbksCommand` is that the commands supported include just Get and Delete. These commands simply retrieve and delete a file or files based on the parameters associated with the command. Determining the granularity of the commands you'll support is the biggest issue you'll face when building a provider. For example, in a provider that is used for data aggregation, the commands you support might be less granular and simply point to a type of data and an action such as "get sales" or "get products." However, in a provider used to access a proprietary data store, the commands would need to be granular enough to access individual tables or sets of data analogous to SQL. Generally speaking, the `CommandText` should point to the action you want to take, coupled with the data elements you want, whereas the parameters define the filter to use.

In the case of `CbksCommand`, the `ExecuteNonQuery` method is implemented to be able to delete files, whereas the `GetData` method is used to retrieve file data. Note that, in both cases, the list of files to operate on is determined by the private `_validateParms` function, which returns an array of files. The `GetData` method is marked as `Friend` (internal in C#) because it will be used by the `CbksDataAdapter` when filling a `DataSet` but shouldn't be publicly available. This method illustrates a key design point: When implementing the command object, encapsulate all the behavior of the command within itself. This includes the parsing of the command text and parameters as well as the actual execution of the command. This seems straightforward, but it's tempting, for example, to write code in the `Fill` method of the data adapter that actually performs the query rather than allowing the command object to do it. By allowing each class to do its own work, the provider will be easier to maintain and extend.

The Parameters Classes

Although not required for lightweight providers, by implementing parameter and parameter collection classes, you can allow your commands to vary based on the parameters. By not implementing parameters, you're forced to allow the `CommandText` to contain more information. However, as with other providers, you have the option of allowing both parameterized commands and commands that hard code all the information. In the ComputeBooks provider, it's assumed that unless parameters are provided, the Get and Delete commands will retrieve and delete all the files at the location specified by the `CbksConnection` object.

14

For most implementations, the parameter and parameter collection classes will be the most generic because they simply support the ability to create parameters and put them in a collection. In fact, most of the code in the following listings is based on the sample provider implementation you'll find in the online documentation. The implementation of the CbksParameter and CbksParameterCollection classes (once again, without their not supported and no-op members) is shown in Listing 14.4.

LISTING 14.4   Implementing parameters. This is the code for the CbksParameter and CbksParameterCollection classes used to associate parameters with commands in the ComputeBooks provider.

```
Public NotInheritable Class CbksParameter : Implements IDbDataParameter
  Private _dbType As DbType = DbType.Object
  Private _nullable As Boolean = False
  Private _paramName As String
  Private _sourceVersion As DataRowVersion = DataRowVersion.Current
  Private _value As Object

  ' Default constructor
  Public Sub New()
  End Sub

  ' Specify the type
  Public Sub New(ByVal parameterName As String, ByVal type As DbType)
    _paramName = parameterName
    _dbType = type
  End Sub

  ' Specify the type and value
  Public Sub New(ByVal parameterName As String, ByVal value As Object)
    _paramName = parameterName
    Me.Value = value
    ' Setting the value also infers the type.
  End Sub

  Public Property DbType() As DbType Implements IDataParameter.DbType
    Get
      Return _dbType
    End Get
    Set(ByVal Value As DbType)
      _dbType = Value
    End Set
  End Property

  Public ReadOnly Property IsNullable() As _
    Boolean Implements IDataParameter.IsNullable
    Get
      Return _nullable
```

LISTING 14.4   continued

```
      End Get
    End Property

    Public Property ParameterName() As String _
      Implements IDataParameter.ParameterName
      Get
        Return _paramName
      End Get
      Set(ByVal Value As String)
        _paramName = Value
      End Set
    End Property

    Public Property SourceVersion() As DataRowVersion _
      Implements IDataParameter.SourceVersion
      Get
        Return _sourceVersion
      End Get
      Set(ByVal Value As DataRowVersion)
        _sourceVersion = Value
      End Set
    End Property

    Public Property Value() As Object Implements IDataParameter.Value
      Get
        Return _value
      End Get
      Set(ByVal Value As Object)
        _value = Value
        _dbType = _inferType(Value)
      End Set
    End Property

    Private Function _inferType(ByVal value As Object) As DbType
      Select Case (Type.GetTypeCode(value.GetType()))
        Case TypeCode.Object
          Return DbType.Object
        Case TypeCode.Boolean
          Return DbType.Boolean
        Case TypeCode.Int16
          Return DbType.Int16
        Case TypeCode.Int32
          Return DbType.Int32
        Case TypeCode.Int64
          Return DbType.Int64
        Case TypeCode.Single
          Return DbType.Single
        Case TypeCode.Double
          Return DbType.Double
```

14

LISTING 14.4   continued

```
        Case TypeCode.Decimal
          Return DbType.Decimal
        Case TypeCode.DateTime
          Return DbType.DateTime
        Case TypeCode.String
          Return DbType.String
        Case Else
          Throw New CbksException("Value is of unsupported data type")
      End Select
    End Function
End Class


Public NotInheritable Class CbksParameterCollection : Inherits ArrayList
    Implements IDataParameterCollection

  Friend Sub New()
    ' So that it is not publicly creatable, must go through CbksCommand
  End Sub

  Default Public Overloads Property Item( _
    ByVal parameterName As String) As Object _
    Implements IDataParameterCollection.Item
    Get
      Return Me(IndexOf(parameterName))
    End Get
    Set(ByVal Value As Object)
      Me(IndexOf(parameterName)) = Value
    End Set
  End Property

  Public Overloads Function Contains(ByVal parameterName As String) As Boolean _
      Implements IDataParameterCollection.Contains
      Return (-1 <> IndexOf(parameterName))
  End Function

  Public Overloads Function IndexOf(ByVal parameterName As String) As Integer _
      Implements IDataParameterCollection.IndexOf
      Dim index As Integer = 0
      Dim item As CbksParameter

      For Each item In Me
        If 0 = _cultureAwareCompare(item.ParameterName, parameterName) Then
          Return index
        End If
        index = index + 1
      Next
      Return -1
  End Function
```

LISTING 14.4 continued

```
    Public Overloads Sub RemoveAt(ByVal parameterName As String) _
      Implements IDataParameterCollection.RemoveAt
      RemoveAt(IndexOf(parameterName))
    End Sub

    ' Overloaded Add methods
    Public Shadows Function Add(ByVal value As CbksParameter) As Integer
      Return MyBase.Add(value)
    End Function

    Public Shadows Function Add(ByVal parameterName As String, _
      ByVal type As DbType) As Integer
      Return Add(New CbksParameter(parameterName, type))
    End Function

    Public Shadows Function Add(ByVal parameterName As String, _
      ByVal value As Object) As Integer
      Return Add(New CbksParameter(parameterName, value))
    End Function

    Private Function _cultureAwareCompare(ByVal strA As String, _
      ByVal strB As String) As Integer
      Return CultureInfo.CurrentCulture.CompareInfo.Compare(strA, strB, _
        CompareOptions.IgnoreKanaType Or CompareOptions.IgnoreWidth Or _
        CompareOptions.IgnoreCase)
    End Function
End Class
```

ANALYSIS As you can see from Listing 14.4, the only really interesting aspect of the CbksParameter class is in determining the type of the value. This is necessary because the Value property is of type System.Object. The private _inferType method is called from the Set block of the Value property. The case statement in the method can be used to check for all the types that your provider supports, and will simply throw an exception if the type isn't supported. Although not implemented in the ComputeBooks provider, this is also where you might implement provider-specific types (as in SqlClient) and additionally map the value of the parameter to your specific types.

In the CbksParameterCollection class, you'll notice that it inherits from ArrayList (where it gains much of its functionality) and implements the IDataParameterCollection interface. This class is used to hold the collection of parameters and isn't publicly creatable, as evidenced by its constructor being marked as Friend. This means that an instance of the class is available only through the CbksCommand object. One of its interesting aspects is that the overloaded Item property is

14

marked as `Default`. This allows the property to be accessed directly and by its parameter name, rather than only through the index as implemented in the `ArrayList` base class. Likewise, the properties `Contains`, `IndexOf`, and `RemoveAt` simply provide additional overloads to the methods in `ArrayList` in order to allow access by parameter name. Finally, the `Add` method is overloaded to allow a parameter to be added in various ways. The use of the `Shadows` keyword in VB hides the base class version of the `Add` method that accepts an argument of type Object.

A client would then use the `CbksCommand` and `CbksParameter` objects like so:

```
CbksCommand com = new CbksCommand("Get",con);
com.Parameters.Add("Vendor", "Sams");
com.Parameters.Add("YearMonth", 200203);

Console.WriteLine(com.Parameters[0].DbType.ToString()); //String
Console.WriteLine(com.Parameters[1].DbType.ToString()); //Integer
```

The Data Adapter Class

When you implement a data adapter, you have several options. In fact, there are two abstract classes, `DataAdapter` and `DbDataAdapter`, that you can inherit from in addition to two interfaces, `IDataAdapter` and `IdbDataAdapter`, that you can implement. As you would expect, the `DataAdapter` class implements the `IDataAdapter` interface and the `DbDataAdapter` class inherits from `DataAdapter`. This arrangement can be seen in Figure 14.4.

FIGURE 14.4

Data adapter classes and interfaces. This diagram shows the relationships between the classes and interfaces for building a data adapter.

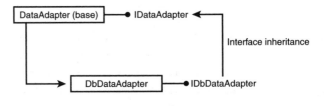

As a result, you basically have two options:

1. If you've implemented a full provider complete with a data reader (discussed in the next section), you can simply inherit from `DbDataAdapter` and override the `OnRowUpdating`, `CreateRowUpdatingEvent`, `CreateRowUpdatedEvent`, and `OnRowUpdated` protected methods to initialize and raise the appropriate events as the data adapter is updated.

2. You can implement the `IDbDataAdapter` interface, which defines the four command properties used by the data adapter to select, insert, update, and delete data.

After you've completed these steps, your work is done. The Fill, FillSchema, and Update methods, along with the properties, are all implemented by the base class for you!

The reason this works is that the overloaded Fill method DbDataAdapter class calls the ExecuteReader method of the command object (passing it a command behavior of Sequential), and uses the returned data reader to populate the DataSet or DataTable objects passed to the method. Likewise, the FillSchema method calls the ExecuteReader method with the command behavior set to the combination of KeyInfo and SchemaOnly to build the schema only.

If you don't implement a full provider, you can alternatively implement either of the interfaces and code the methods yourself.

 Note   Implementing IDbDataAdapter brings IDataAdapter along as well because the former implements the latter.

The CbksDataAdapter class shown in Listing 14.5 takes this approach because the provider doesn't implement a data reader.

LISTING 14.5   Implementing a data adapter. This listing shows the CbksDataAdapter class. It implements only interfaces, so the methods must be coded.

```
Public NotInheritable Class CbksDataAdapter
  Implements IDbDataAdapter

  Private _selCommand As CbksCommand

  ' Default Constructor
  Public Sub New()
  End Sub

  Public Sub New(ByVal selectCommand As CbksCommand)
    ' Assign the command
    _selCommand = selectCommand
  End Sub

  Public Sub New(ByVal selectCommand As String, ByVal connection As String)
    ' Create the connection and command
    Dim con As New CbksConnection(connection)
    _selCommand = New CbksCommand(selectCommand, con)
  End Sub
```

14

LISTING 14.5   continued

```
Public Sub New(ByVal selectCommand As String, _
  ByVal connection As CbksConnection)
  ' Create the new command
  _selCommand = New CbksCommand(selectCommand, connection)
End Sub


' Implements only a SelectCommand
Public Property SelectCommand() As CbksCommand
  Get
    Return _selCommand
  End Get
  Set(ByVal Value As CbksCommand)
    _selCommand = Value
  End Set
End Property
Private Property _selectCommand() As IDbCommand _
  Implements IDbDataAdapter.SelectCommand
  Get
    Return Me.SelectCommand
  End Get
  Set(ByVal Value As IDbCommand)
    _selCommand = CType(Value, CbksCommand)
  End Set
End Property

Public Function Fill(ByVal dataSet As DataSet) As Integer _
  Implements IDataAdapter.Fill
  ' Adds to or loads data into the dataset based on the parameters
  Dim xlr() As XmlReader
  Dim opened As Boolean = False

  ' Make sure the connection is open
  If Me.SelectCommand.Connection.State = ConnectionState.Closed Then
    Me.SelectCommand.Connection.Open()
    opened = True
  End If

  Try
    ' Execute the command and get the xml readers
    xlr = Me.SelectCommand.GetData()
    Dim r As XmlReader

    For Each r In xlr
      ' Add each file to the DataSet
      dataSet.ReadXml(r, XmlReadMode.Auto)
      r.Close()
    Next
```

LISTING 14.5   continued

```
      Return -1
    Catch e As Exception
      Throw New CbksException("Could not fill DataSet", e)
    Finally
      If opened Then Me.SelectCommand.Connection.Close()
    End Try

End Function

Public Function FillSchema(ByVal dataSet As DataSet, _
    ByVal schemaType As SchemaType) As DataTable() _
    Implements IDataAdapter.FillSchema

    ' Fill the schema of the DataSet and return the array of tables
    ' Note we're ignoring the schemaType
    Dim t As DataTable
    Dim i As Integer
    Dim xlr() As XmlReader
    Dim opened As Boolean = False

    ' Make sure the connection is open
    If Me.SelectCommand.Connection.State = ConnectionState.Closed Then
      Me.SelectCommand.Connection.Open()
      opened = True
    End If

    ' Empty the DataSet
    For Each t In dataSet.Tables
      dataSet.Tables.Remove(t)
    Next

    Try
      ' Execute the command and get the xml readers
      xlr = Me.SelectCommand.GetData()

      Dim r As XmlReader
      For Each r In xlr
        ' Add each file to the DataSet
        dataSet.ReadXml(r, XmlReadMode.Auto)
        r.Close()
      Next

      ' Clear out the data
      dataSet.Clear()

      Dim tables(dataSet.Tables.Count - 1) As DataTable
      For i = 0 To dataSet.Tables.Count - 1
        tables(i) = dataSet.Tables(i)
      Next
```

14

LISTING 14.5   continued

```
        Return tables

    Catch e As Exception
      Throw New CbksException("Could not fill the schema", e)
    Finally
      If opened Then Me.SelectCommand.Connection.Close()
    End Try

  End Function

End Class
```

ANALYSIS   As with the other classes, you should follow the conventions and implement four constructors for your data adapter class that accept different combinations of the command used for selecting data and the connection if only the `CommandText` is specified.

You'll notice that `CbksDataAdapter` implements the `IDbDataAdapter` interface, but provides a strongly typed implementation only for the `SelectCommand` because the data adapter can only be used in a read-only mode. The only methods that are supported are `Fill` and `FillSchema`, although you certainly have the option of implementing additional overloaded `Fill` methods to populate a `DataTable`, as is done in `DbDataAdapter`.

In this case, the `Fill` method first makes sure that the connection object associated with the `SelectCommand` is open and, if not, opens it. The `Finally` block is used to `Close` the connection if it was opened within the `Fill` method (that is, implicitly). Then the `GetData` method of the `CbksCommand` class exposed as `Friend` is called to retrieve the array of `XmlReader` objects that will be used to read the XML documents. Each `XmlReader` is then read in to the `DataSet` using the `ReadXml` method with the `XmlReadMode` set to `Auto`. This will have the effect of augmenting any existing schema in the `DataSet` using a schema either inferred from the XML data or provided inline in the `XmlReader`. However, if the schema is incompatible, an exception will be thrown. Note that if all the schemas for the `XmlReader` objects are identical, the end result will be to append the XML data to the same tables within the `DataSet`.

The `FillSchema` method is very similar to `Fill`, although it first deletes all the tables from the passed-in `DataSet` and additionally returns an array of `DataTable` objects. In both cases, of course, the method needs to delete all the data using the `Clear` method because only the schema should be returned.

Finally, a client can then use the entire provider as shown in the following code snippet:

```
CbksConnection con = new CbksConnection("Location=.");
CbksDataAdapter da = new CbksDataAdapter("Get", con);

da.SelectCommand.Parameters.Add("Vendor", "Sams");

DataSet ds = new DataSet();
da.FillSchema(ds);
```

The Exception Class

All the classes in the ComputeBooks provider throw a CbksException when they encounter exceptions they can't handle. Creating custom exception classes is quite simple because you need only inherit from System.ApplicationException. The ApplicationException class inherits from System.SystemException, and simply provides a means of determining whether an exception was raised by custom code or the common language runtime itself. Of course, you can also extend your exception by adding custom members to provide additional information, just as the SqlException and OleDbException objects do.

In this case, the CbksException class shown in Listing 14.6 simply implements the constructors that call the constructors of ApplicationException. The second constructor is used to embed an inner exception, and is useful when the provider classes catch an exception so that the client is able to inspect it. You'll notice that the class is marked with the Serializable attribute to enable the common language runtime to copy it between application domains in the event the exception is thrown from a remote domain. This might occur, for example, if you use .NET remoting to call your provider across the network hosted in IIS.

LISTING 14.6 Implementing an exception. This class implements the CbksException object for the ComputeBooks provider.

```
<Serializable()> _
Public NotInheritable Class CbksException : Inherits ApplicationException

  Public Sub New(ByVal message As String)
    MyBase.New(message)
  End Sub

  Public Sub New(ByVal message As String, ByVal originalException As Exception)
    MyBase.New(message, originalException)
  End Sub

End Class
```

14

Summary

As you begin to develop in ADO.NET, you'll likely need to use providers not shipped with VS .NET. Microsoft and other vendors might build some of these, such as the Odbc, Oracle, and DB2 providers, or you might need to build your own within your organization. The programming pattern exposed in the `System.Data` and `System.Data.Common` namespaces makes both using new providers and building providers relatively straightforward.

Today you learned how the Odbc provider from Microsoft works, along with a few of its differences from SqlClient and OleDb. You also should now be familiar with the reasons you might build your own provider and what a lightweight implementation might look like.

Today's lesson ends Week 2 and the discussion of .NET Data Providers. From here on out, you'll learn how to apply everything discussed in the previous weeks and look to the future.

Workshop

This workshop will help reinforce the concepts covered in today's lesson.

Quiz

1. How can you obtain the ODBC .NET Data Provider?

   The Odbc provider doesn't ship with VS .NET, so you must go to `msdn.microsoft.com` and download it. After it is downloaded, it will install into the Global Assembly Cache (GAC) and can be referenced in your projects using the Add References dialog.

2. What kinds of connections can you use with the Odbc provider?

   Just as traditionally done, you can use either a user or system DSN specified by the `DSN` attribute, a file DSN specified with the `FileDSN` attribute, or a DSN-less connection string that specifies the driver and any driver-specific attributes.

3. What is the advantage to implementing a data reader class in your provider?

   If you implement both a command and a data reader class (that implements the `IDataReader` interface), you can also implement a data adapter class with virtually no work at all. This is possible because you can derive from the `DbDataAdapter` class, which calls the `ExecuteReader` method behind the scenes.

4. What is the primary reason to implement a .NET Data Provider?

The most common reason to implement a provider is to provide managed access to a proprietary data store. This makes a great deal of sense for organizations that produce packaged software and want to start developing .NET applications.

Exercise

To illustrate the side-by-side use of providers, write a method that uses the SqlClient provider to populate a DataSet with Titles and use the Odbc provider to populate a second table in the same DataSet with Publishers.

Answers for Day 14

Exercise Answer

One possible solution to the exercise follows:

```
public virtual DataSet PopulateTitles(string connect)
{
    SqlConnection scon = new SqlConnection(connect);
    SqlDataAdapter sda = new SqlDataAdapter("SELECT * FROM Titles",scon);

    OdbcConnection ocon = new OdbcConnection("Driver={SQL Server};" + connect);
    OdbcDataAdapter oda = new OdbcDataAdapter("SELECT * FROM Publishers",ocon);

    DataSet ds = new DataSet();

    // Fill from SqlClient
    sda.MissingSchemaAction = MissingSchemaAction.AddWithKey;
    sda.Fill(ds);

    // Fill from Odbc
    oda.MissingSchemaAction = MissingSchemaAction.AddWithKey;
    oda.Fill(ds);

    // Add a relationship
    ds.Relations.Add(ds.Tables[1].Columns["PubCode"],
      ds.Tables[1].Columns["Publisher"]);

    return ds;
}
```

Note that a DSN-less ODBC connection string can be built simply by prefixing the one used for SqlClient.

14

WEEK 2

In Review

This week you learned about the various objects that make up the second major component of ADO.NET, the .NET Data Providers. Along the way, I hope you picked up some techniques for using the objects in various situations. In addition, one of the key insights you should have gained is that providers come in two basic flavors, narrow and specific, and that both are based on the common base classes and interfaces in the System.Data namespace.

You started the week by learning about the responsibilities of the various objects typically included in a .NET Data Provider. You then proceeded to go in-depth with each object in turn. This included learning about connections and transactions and how to use connection pooling and connection strings, command objects and the various methods they expose, data readers and their differences from DataSet objects, data adapters and how DataSet objects are filled and updated, various aspects of accessing SQL Server, and techniques for using the ODBC .NET Data Provider as well as building your own provider.

You should now be quite familiar with using the objects in the .NET Data Providers and also be ready to apply them in the design and implementation of a modern multi-tier application, as you'll learn about next week. So, take a short break to prepare your mind for a week of implementation and futures.

WEEK 3

At a Glance

15

After learning about the two major components of ADO.NET during the last two weeks, you should now be ready to apply what you've learned in the context of multi-tier application development during this final week.

16

The first five days of this week focus on the design and implementation of multi-tier applications using ADO.NET. The week begins with a short introduction and overview of multi-tier development, and moves on to discuss techniques that you can apply in the presentation, business, and data services tiers on Days 16 and 17. On Day 18, the focus shifts slightly to the implementation of a data factory class that can be used internally in the data services tier to provide both .NET Data Provider and database independence. Day 19 presents a discussion of using ADO.NET in conjunction with XML Web Services.

17

18

19

Day 20 provides some performance and scalability tips in addition to techniques for interoperating with ADO 2.x `Recordset` objects. The week and this book conclude with a discussion of some future directions that ADO.NET and data access will likely take.

20

21

DAY 15

Using ADO.NET in a Multi-Tier Application

Today, the start of Week 3, you begin the home stretch on your journey through ADO.NET. In the past two weeks, you learned in detail about the two major components of ADO.NET, the `DataSet` and .NET Data Providers. This week, you will apply the knowledge you've gained to design and implement applications using ADO.NET.

The basic design approach that we'll discuss today, a multi-tier (or n-tier) approach, is one that is probably either explicitly or implicitly familiar to you. As you learned on Day 1, "ADO.NET in Perspective," this approach has been widely adopted in the industry because it provides a maintainable and extensible architecture for distributed enterprise applications.

Today's short lesson will focus on the multi-tier architecture in depth to make sure that you understand where ADO.NET fits in and how it can be used. Specifically, you'll learn

- The reasons you might design applications with a multi-tier architecture
- How a multi-tier architecture relates to distributed applications
- Where ADO.NET fits into the tiers of a multi-tier application

The Multi-Tiered Architecture

On Day 1, you learned that one of the design goals of ADO.NET was to efficiently support a multi-tiered programming model. However, before we discuss how you can take advantage of the features of ADO.NET in an application that uses the multi-tier architecture, we need to define it.

> **Note**
>
> There are a variety of terms used in the industry for the approach described in this section. Two of most prevalent are *multi-tier* and *n-tier*, so, as I mentioned earlier, these are the two I will use interchangeably in this discussion. In addition, the terms *design*, *approach*, *architecture*, and *programming model* are all used to convey the same idea: the way that multi-tier applications are put together.

At the most basic level, multi-tier simply means *multiple layers*, so a multi-tier architecture is one in which the code you write is divided into layers that interface with each other and that have specific responsibilities. In most discussions of this approach, you'll see three layers or tiers, as shown in Figure 15.1.

FIGURE 15.1

*Multi-tier architecture.
This diagram shows
the three primary tiers
of a multi-tier design.*

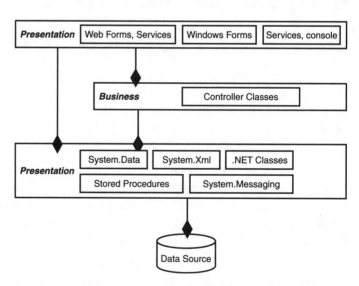

Each of the three layers has certain responsibilities:

- **Presentation Services Tier**. The primary responsibility of the presentation services tier is to provide the interaction with the client, either graphically or programmatically. For example, the presentation services are responsible for how the data is displayed and how the user can interact with the data, but not for actually retrieving or saving the data. As shown in Figure 15.1, the presentation services of a .NET application are written using the classes of the .NET Framework to create Web Forms, Windows Forms, XML Web Services, Windows Services, and Console Applications. In addition, the presentation services layer is responsible for adapting the presentation interface to variations in the client device's capabilities. In VS .NET, this is made much easier by the concept of ASP.NET server controls, which can render HTML for both up- and down-level browsers, and the Microsoft Mobile Internet Toolkit (MMIT), which enables you to build Web Forms that render markup language for different devices by, for example, outputting HTML for Pocket PCs and WML (Wireless Markup Language) for Web-enabled phones.

> **Note**
>
> The MMIT is available for download from msdn.microsoft.com by searching for Mobile Internet Toolkit. After it is installed in the Global Assembly Cache (GAC), the assembly can be referenced in your ASP.NET projects and used to build mobile forms using a suite of mobile controls.

- **NEW TERM** **Business Services Tier**. The primary responsibility of the business services tier is to ensure that business processes are able to be carried out by the presentation services tier. The business services classes, sometimes referred to as *controller classes*, are typically designed with very coarse-grained methods that encompass an entire process and map to a logical unit of work (transaction). For example, a business services class might contain a `PlaceOrder` method that accepts customer, order, and order detail data. This is then used to update one or more backend data stores (message queues, relational databases, and XML documents) using classes in the data services tier, all within the scope of a single transaction. If distributed transactions are required, controller classes can be run under Component Services by inheriting from the `System.EntepriseServices.ServicedComponent` class. Because the business services tier is used to provide a standard interface to coordinate or control the activities of other classes, it follows the **façade design pattern**. As a result, you'll sometimes see this tier described as a *business façade*.

- **Data Services Tier**. Finally, the data services tier is responsible for retrieving, manipulating, and updating data in the underlying data stores and making it available to the business and presentation services. There are several approaches to doing this, as shown in Figure 15.1. For example, the data services tier could expose the data through ADO.NET `DataSet` objects that are then passed between the presentation and business services tiers and finally synchronized again with the data store. Alternatively, it could expose the data through the classes of the `System.Xml` namespace such as the `XmlDocument` or `XmlReader`, work with message queues, or expose data through an object layer created with custom classes. In addition, as you'll learn at a high level later today and in detail on Day 17, "ADO.NET in the Data Services Tier," and Day 18, "Building a Data Factory," the data services tier can itself contain multiple layers of code in order to abstract the provider used and take advantage of implementation inheritance. In addition, because I recommend using a stored procedure layer for communication to the data store, the data services tier includes the stored procedures as well.

Perhaps one of the biggest stumbling points for developers when first considering the multi-tier architecture is their natural tendency to want to follow it rigidly. For example, developers might assume that the presentation services tier should always and only communicate with the business services tier. Although this would provide the greatest abstraction and therefore allow the data services tier to be changed independently of the presentation services tier, it can increase complexity and the cost of maintenance for simpler scenarios.

You'll notice that, as depicted in Figure 15.1, the presentation services tier can communicate directly with the data services tier. This makes good sense because not all the behavior of an application needs to be abstracted. Doing so often results in lots of methods in the business services tier that do nothing more than act as wrappers around methods in the data services tier. This is both more complex and wasteful of resources. Where appropriate, I advocate invoking the data services directly, although that implies that the data services tier must expose a set of meaningful methods.

What About Web Services?

You'll notice in Figure 15.1 that XML Web Services are placed in the presentation services layer of the model. This might seem strange because you generally think of Web services as a means of interacting with data, so you might think they should be placed in the data services tier. However, in many scenarios, Web services simply provide an additional SOAP-based programmatic interface to the data accessible through the firewall, and therefore will call the same business and data services code behind the scenes that a Web Form might rely on.

Having said that, you can certainly create a design in which all your data access flows through Web services that are published internally within your organization. In this design, the Web service layer becomes the external API for the data services tier. In fact, Windows .NET Server will ship with a UDDI (Universal Description, Discovery, and Integration) server that you can use to publish Web services within your organization. However, such a design incurs a performance hit because of the extra processing required to build and parse the SOAP messages. As a result, this approach will be most useful in large and distributed organizations. Generally, within the firewall, the most efficient way to access your data is to use a set of data access classes, in the data services tier, that use specific .NET Data Providers.

Relation to Physical Tiers

15

NEW TERM It is important to keep in mind that the multi-tiered approach discussed in the previous section is a logical construct that doesn't require you to physically distribute the tiers on separate machines. In other words, when you create a data services tier, it doesn't have to be isolated on a separate server or farm of servers. In fact, many Web-based multi-tier applications will locate all their code on a single Web server. However, the design decisions you make when coding your data services tier will influence scalability if you decide to distribute the tiers on multiple servers. For example, the use of the streamed programming model with data readers in ADO.NET is optimal when the data services code runs in the same process as the presentation and business services, but it can cause performance problems when used across machines due to the number of roundtrips that would be incurred. Generally, the goal with a multi-tier architecture is to be able to physically distribute the application at a later time if scalability becomes an issue. This is referred to as the **scale-out** approach because it attempts to amortize the processing of the application across multiple machines. This is contrasted with **scale-up**, which focuses on increasing the resources available on a single server.

> **Note**
>
> Although scalability and performance are related, they can be thought of as two different concepts. For example, an application can perform very well (have high throughput) when serving 100 clients, but can slow to a crawl when serving 1,000 clients. In this case, the application performed well for its normal workload, but wasn't scalable because its increase in throughput did not track linearly with the number of clients. Making an application scalable means keeping the throughput high even as a greater number of clients use the system. Although this can be done to some extent by designing your application to use resources (memory, CPU, network bandwidth) efficiently, at some point, any application will overwhelm the resources of a single server. Scaling-out seeks to increase by scalability by isolating either tasks or clients or both on dedicated servers.

In that respect, there are several different physical architectures for scale-out that you might employ. A typical one is shown in Figure 15.2.

NEW TERM You'll notice from Figure 15.2 that one approach might be to isolate all the presentation services code on a cluster or farm of identical Web servers using the **Network Load Balancing (NLB)** clustering feature of Windows 2000 Advanced and Datacenter Server. NLB distributes incoming IP traffic across a cluster of up to 32 servers that appear to the client as a single IP address. Traffic is processed by the servers based on priority and other configurable settings. When you use this approach, it's important that the presentation services code be as stateless as possible so that subsequent requests from a particular client needn't be handled by the same server (**server affinity**). Although NLB supports server affinity (or "sticky IP"), doing so compromises scalability and fault tolerance because the cluster needs to maintain the mapping of clients to servers, and losing a server might wipe out the client's state information (or session state). The risk of losing a client's session state is mitigated by the fact that ASP.NET allows session information to be stored directly within SQL Server or using a separate Windows Service configured through the Web.config file for the ASP.NET Web site. NLB can be configured both independently and as a part of Application Center 2000 to ease the administration of the cluster.

FIGURE 15.2

Physically distributing an application. This diagram shows how the logical tiers might be distributed across machines.

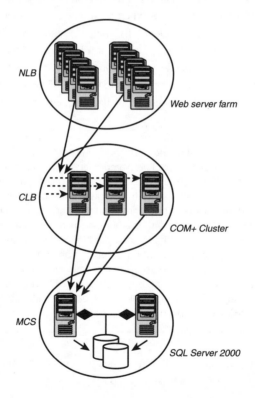

Tip

NLB is a software-based approach used on Windows server. Two other means of building Web farms include using round-robin domain name system (RRDNS) at the network layer, and using load-balancing switches such as the Cisco LocalDirector at the hardware layer.

15

Figure 15.2 also indicates that the business and data services code might utilize the component load balancing (CLB) feature of Microsoft Application Center 2000. Simply put, CLB allows for the creation of a cluster of servers used to load balance requests to components configured in Component Services. As a result, CLB is useful only for business and data services classes that use Component Services by inheriting from the `System.EnterpriseServices.ServicedComponent` class. These classes can also be decorated with the `LoadBalancingSupportedAttribute` to indicate that they support CLB if installed.

However, not all business and data services classes will utilize Component Services, so for many applications, scaling-out simply means running all three tiers on a farm of servers, perhaps using NLB. For those applications, it might be more efficient because the extra latency and complexity introduced by isolating the services on their own servers will wipe out any benefits. Alternatively, as mentioned previously, you can also expose your data services tier through XML Web Services, and then use NLB to create a cluster of servers that expose the Web services for the presentation services tier to use.

You'll also notice that if the business and data services are to be isolated on their own cluster of servers, the issue of server affinity also comes into play. In other words, you want to design your business and data services to be stateless so that any client from the presentation tier can access any of the servers in the CLB cluster. A stateless design is one in which the methods are given everything they need to do their work and do not store any private data between calls. This design also pays dividends even on a single server where the business and data services components can be pooled and reused by Component Services if they are stateless.

Finally, the data store itself can be isolated in a separate fault-tolerant cluster of database server machines. For example, Windows 2000 Advanced and Datacenter Servers support the Microsoft Cluster Service (MCS) that SQL Server 2000 Enterprise Edition can utilize. With MCS, you can create a failover cluster in SQL Server that allows one of the two server machines in the cluster to provide fault tolerance by taking on the workload of the other server if it goes down. As indicated in Figure 15.2, this works by the two servers utilizing a shared disk subsystem and a "heartbeat" that allows the passive machine in the cluster to determine whether the active machine is still functioning. Although SQL Server 2000 can support a fully distributed database scenario using distributed partitioned views (DPV), for all but the largest applications, it's typically more cost effective to scale-up the servers in an MCS cluster rather than designing and maintaining a distributed database.

Which physical configuration you use is, of course, totally dependent on your particular application and its requirements.

Benefits of a Multi-Tier Approach

In addition to the benefit of being able to scale-out the application, there are several other advantages to using a multi-tier approach:

- **Maintainability**. By separating the responsibilities of the application into separate layers, it will be easier in the long run to isolate problems to a specific layer and fix them while not affecting the other layers. Although this isn't always the case, and occasionally a change ripples through all the layers, by paying attention to design ideas such as loose coupling, encapsulation, and well-thought-out and defined interfaces, you can isolate changes to a specific layer and avoid introducing bugs in other layers.

- **Reusability**. Because the layers will be isolated, they should also be able to be reused in different applications. This is particularly true of the business and data services tiers, which might need to be repackaged and reused by a different user interface. For example, the same business and data services might be used both by an ASP.NET application targeted to desktop browsers and one built with MMIT targeted for mobile devices. A second example of reusability is the opportunity to take advantage of implementation inheritance in the .NET Framework to, for example, create base classes that can be used in the data services tier of multiple applications.

- **Extensibility**. As an offshoot of maintainability, the introduction of new requirements should be able to be handled more easily because the tiers are separated. Once again, in conjunction with the use of good object-oriented design patterns, the code in one tier can be extended while not affecting the others.

- **Specialization**. Because not everybody can know everything, splitting the responsibilities of the application into separate layers provides the opportunity for developers to specialize in the techniques and issues inherent in developing for a particular tier. For example, a presentation services specialist might be well versed in writing ASP.NET server controls and the ins and outs of Dynamic HTML, whereas a data services specialist thoroughly understands connection pooling and how to write stored procedures in SQL Server.

- **Rapid Development**. Although not generally thought of as a benefit for multi-tier applications, I submit that multi-tier applications are in fact faster to develop because they clearly delineate the responsibilities of various parts of the application and provide a mental map that makes it simpler for developers to write appropriate code. In many ways, this is the same issue as maintainability because in every software development project, the requirements aren't fully known when development begins, so following an approach that allows for abstraction will typically result in less rewritten and reworked code.

Note   For a good introductory discussion on object-oriented design patterns, see *Design Patterns Explained: A New Perspective on Object-Oriented Design* by Shalloway and Trott, published by Addison-Wesley. ISBN: 0-201-71594-5.

ADO.NET in Context

Obviously, ADO.NET will be used primarily in the data services tier. However, in the context of an entire multi-tier application, you can think of where you'll write ADO.NET code from both the external and internal view with respect to the data services tier. Choosing an approach to take from each of these two views will lead you well on your path to designing the data services tier of a multi-tier application.

The External View

In the external view, you can think of the data services tier as a black box that exposes methods to which you make requests and from which results are returned. As mentioned previously, the code making the requests may be located in either the presentation or business services tiers, as shown in Figure 15.3.

FIGURE 15.3

External view of data services. This diagram depicts how code external to the data services tier will interact with it.

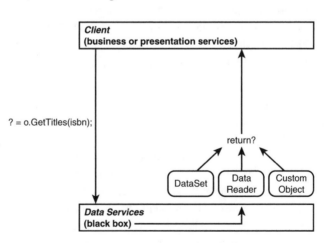

From the external view, the factor that determines whether ADO.NET components are used directly is the mechanism used to return the data. As you see from Figure 15.3, there are three basic approaches that the data services can take.

- **Exposing `DataSet` Objects**. The data services tier may expose all its data in one or more `DataSet` objects. These objects have the benefit of being able to be automatically serialized for transport between tiers, and can be strongly typed to expose specific properties to represent the data. Using this approach, the external code will use ADO.NET to instantiate `DataSet` objects and work with its associated `DataTable`, `DataRow`, and `DataColumn` objects. The external code will then pass the modified `DataSet` to a method in the data services tier to perform the update. This approach has the benefit of allowing data binding in all .NET applications and built-in means of performing disconnected updates using the data adapter.

- **Exposing Data Readers**. For performance reasons and perhaps because the application uses mostly read-only data, the data services tier may expose all its data through data readers. If this is the case, the tiers will likely reside on the same machine. Using this approach, the external code will use ADO.NET to capture a data reader and traverse it using its `Read` method, whereas updates will be performed by invoking methods in the data services tier and passing data as parameters. In this situation, the external code should also strive to use only the `IDataReader` interface to avoid being tied down to using a particular .NET Data Provider.

- **Exposing Custom Objects**. Using this approach, the data services tier will return data through custom objects that expose properties and fields that contain the data. From the external point of view, no ADO.NET code will be required, so the `System.Data` namespace needn't even be referenced in the project. This approach has the benefit of allowing the other tiers to work with the data naturally through objects. The downside is that it requires more work on the part of the data services tier to populate and synchronize the objects.

In all three approaches just cited, the external code should strive to be loosely coupled from the data services. For example, the external code should never have to instantiate or work with command, parameter, connection, local transaction, command builder, or exception objects that are particular to a data provider. The data services tier should completely abstract these concepts and should simply expose the data itself as directly as possible. It's the responsibility of the data services tier to work with the provider, not the external code. For example, the data services tier shouldn't contain methods that return connection objects or expect command objects to be passed to them in parameters. In other words, the external code should work only with `DataSet` or data reader objects and no others from the `System.Data` namespace.

Note Of course, the data services may also expose methods that return simple data types such as System.Int32, System.Boolean, or System.String. This might be the case, for example, for a GetRevenue method that simply returns the total amount of revenue generated for a particular book over a certain time period.

The Internal View

From the view inside the data services tier, ADO.NET and all its features will be leveraged wherever possible. However, once again, there are three options for how you design your data services tier, as depicted in Figure 15.4.

FIGURE 15.4

Data services tier design. This diagram depicts the various approaches to the internal design of the data services tier.

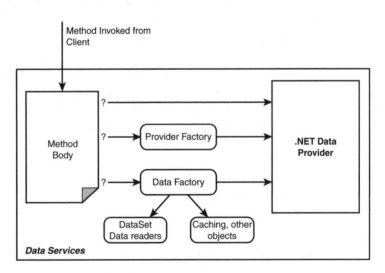

Generally, these three approaches address the use of .NET Data Providers in the data services tier. The approaches are as follows:

- **Direct Approach**. Thus far in this book you've seen examples of using a direct approach to work with the various providers we've discussed. By *direct approach*, I mean instantiating the concrete provider-specific SqlConnection, SqlCommand, and SqlDataAdapter and other classes directly in your code and using them. Within the data services tier, this means, for example, exposing a GetTitles method that uses the SqlDataAdapter directly to fill a DataSet object and return it to the presentation or business tier. This is the fastest approach in terms of development time and performance, although it requires code to be rewritten in the event the provider must be changed in the future. It also offers the least reusability because common operations such as creating parameters are usually done in each method.

- **NEW TERM** **Abstracted Providers**. By relying on the key interfaces we discussed yesterday, a second approach is for the methods that make up the public interface of the data services tier to internally use a specially designed helper class I refer to as a **provider factory** to instantiate the actual provider used. This is a common object-oriented design pattern called the **abstract factory pattern** that can be used whenever your code needs to instantiate a related set of objects such as those from a particular provider (such as OleDbConnection, OleDbCommand, and so on). This approach allows the data access classes to be generic in terms of the provider, making it easier to switch providers down the road if necessary. We'll discuss this approach in detail on Day 17.

- **Internal Data Factory**. A third approach is to not only abstract the provider internally in the data services tier, but also to abstract the most common algorithms performed. For example, many methods in the public interface of the data services tier need to create a connection object, create a data adapter and pass it the stored procedure, create parameter objects, populate the parameters and associate them with the command, and finally fill a DataSet using the data adapter. All this can be abstracted into an internal data factory class, relieving the burden from the developer. In addition, an internal data factory gives you the opportunity to add additional features, such as the caching of command objects when they are built. We'll discuss this approach in detail on Day 18.

As mentioned previously, regardless of which approach you take to build your data services tier, you can take advantage of implementation inheritance and build one or more base classes that take care of some of the common infrastructure-type work that any class in the data services tier might need, such as connection management and logging.

Summary

Building enterprise applications requires a structured approach that allows you to isolate code that you write into distinct services so that your application is maintainable, flexible, and scalable in the face of new requirements and increased workloads. Using a multi-tier architecture gives you a mental map of how to accomplish this and therefore provides a ready-made foundation for building applications.

ADO.NET will be used primarily in the data services tier of a multi-tier application, although there are several design decisions you can make that affect how the other tiers interact with the data services tier. These include the external perspective that relates to how the data will be exposed and the internal perspective as to how you work with providers.

Workshop

This workshop will help reinforce the concepts covered in today's lesson.

Quiz

1. What are the layers in a multi-tier architecture?

   A multi-tier architecture can be divided into the presentation services tier, the business services tier, and the data services tier. Each tier or layer has its own set of responsibilities that tend to provide well-defined boundaries between the tiers or layers.

2. What is relationship between the multi-tier architecture and physical machines?

   Strictly speaking, there is none. The multi-tier architecture is a logical model that speaks to how the application is designed, but not to how it is deployed. At the same time, a multi-tier application can naturally be deployed across multiple servers at the boundaries between the tiers.

3. What are some techniques you can use to increase scalability?

   On the Windows platform, there are several tools you can use to scale-out your application in order to increase scalability. Among these are network load balancing (NLB), component load balancing (CLB), and Microsoft Cluster Service (MCS). Your application can also take steps to increase scalability by, for example, not storing user state on the Web server and taking advantage of ASP.NET services such as caching.

4. What factors influence the design of the data services tier?

   When designing the data services tier, you need to determine how the classes will expose data—for example, using `DataSet` objects, data readers, or custom objects—and how the classes will deal with the issue of providers. After these design decisions are made, the design of the methods themselves is fairly straightforward. In addition, you should strive to make your business and data services tiers stateless so that they can be scaled-out efficiently.

Exercise

Because today's lesson was primarily conceptual, there is no exercise.

DAY **16**

ADO.NET in the Presentation Services Tier

As you learned yesterday, how you design your data services tier has an effect on how the presentation services tier will work with the data in your application. Today, you'll explore those differences in the context of both Windows Forms and Web Forms user interfaces.

Today's discussion will concentrate on how to display and work with data exposed by the objects associated with a `DataSet` and data reader because the majority of user interfaces will use these classes directly. However, we'll also discuss the architecture of data binding, for example, so that you understand how classes you build can also take advantage of the features of controls.

Today, you'll learn the following concepts:

- How to use both simple and complex binding in Windows Forms applications
- How to validate data in Windows Forms applications
- How to use both single-value and multi-record binding in Web Forms applications

- How to store state in Web Forms applications
- How to validate data in Web Forms applications

Windows Forms Applications

The user interface for a Windows-based application is built using the set of classes in the `System.Windows.Forms` namespace, collectively referred to as *Windows Forms*. These types are found in the `System.Windows.Forms.dll` assembly and take full advantage of the user interface features of the Windows operating system. You can create a Windows Forms application by selecting the Windows Application project template in the New Project dialog.

From within a user interface built with Windows Forms, there are two primary concerns when using ADO.NET:

- How you bind data in a `DataSet`, `DataTable`, `DataView`, or `DataViewManager` object to controls
- How you validate the contents of those controls

In this section, you'll learn how to do both.

Using Data Binding

When your data services tier returns data to the user interface, the main requirement, of course, is to display that data so that the user can view and/or edit it. Rather than having to write loops that traverse, for example, the rows and columns of a `DataTable` and place the data in the properties of controls, it is more efficient and productive to take advantage of the data-binding features provided by Windows Forms.

To act as a provider (or data source) to Windows Forms data binding, however, a class must implement particular interfaces. At the most basic level, the `System.Collections.IList` interface (itself derived from `ICollection`) that is the basis for all lists in the framework must be implemented. This interface is implemented by more than 40 classes in the .NET Framework, including `Array` and `ArrayList`, in addition to the `CollectionBase` class that provides the abstract base class for strongly typed collections. In other words, Windows Forms controls can be bound not just to ADO.NET objects, but also to other objects such as arrays and custom collections that implement the `IList` interface. As a result, you can also use data binding with collections of objects you create, as you'll see tomorrow.

Note

Technically, the `DataSet` and `DataTable` classes implement the `IListSource` interface. This interface contains a method called `GetList` and a property called `ContainListCollection` that return an `IList` that can be bound and that specify whether the collection is a collection of `IList` objects or other objects, respectively. The `IListSource` interface is useful because the object might not implement the `IList` interface directly, as in this case.

16

At a slightly higher level, a data source can implement the `IBindingList` interface, which itself implements the `IList` interface. The `IBindingList` interface adds additional methods and properties used to enable editing, sorting, and notification of changes to the list by raising the `ListChanged` event. The `DataView` class in ADO.NET implements this interface.

Finally, the data source can implement the `IEditableObject` interface as the `DataRowView` does to add commit and rollback functionality to the object.

After you have an object capable of acting as a data source, controls or even properties on the Windows Form can act as consumers. The consumer architecture is shown in Figure 16.1.

FIGURE 16.1

Windows Forms consumer architecture. This diagram shows the data-binding architecture used on a Windows Form.

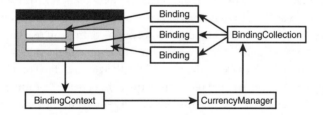

Basically, when you use data binding, the Windows Form will contain instances of the `CurrencyManager` and `PropertyManager` classes for each data source that is used on the form, both of which inherit from the abstract `BindingManagerBase` class. The `PropertyManager` class will be used when the data source returns only a single object, whereas the `CurrencyManager` is used when the data source exposes a collection of objects. The `CurrencyManager` keeps track of the position of the bound object through its `Position` property. This architecture is interesting because it implies that the data source object itself doesn't have any notion of a position, so a single data source can be bound to multiple controls and be navigated independently. Both classes then expose a collection of data bindings (`Binding` objects) through a `BindingCollection` object. The `Binding` object is what actually maps the data source to the property of the control that is being bound. In terms of the control acting as the consumer, the bindings are accessed through the DataBindings property, which returns an instance of the ControlBindingsCollection object.

The form (or actually any class that inherits from Control) then exposes a BindingContext object that manages the descendants of BindingManagerBase.

Tip

> Although you'll typically just use the BindingContext object exposed at the form level, you can create a BindingContext object for a container control such as a Panel or GroupBox. You might want to do this to make your code simpler to write because it eliminates a level in the dot notation you must use.

In the remainder of this section, you'll see how you can use both simple and complex binding to bind data from a data source to controls.

Simple Binding

NEW TERM **Simple binding** refers to the process of binding the property of a control that contains a single value to a data source. In other words, controls such as the TextBox and Label will be simple-bound because their Text properties return a single value, whereas the ListBox control can use complex binding because it returns multiple objects through its Items property. However, a control can use both complex and simple binding because some of its properties might return single values whereas others might return multiple values (as in the case of the MonthCalendar control). In addition, simple binding can be used to bind other properties of controls (or forms) to the data source, like those used to change the display, such as Font, ForeColor, Left, Right, and Top.

Simple binding can be performed both graphically at design time and programmatically at run time. With ADO.NET, you would typically use design-time binding when you have previously dragged and dropped a strongly typed DataSet or DataView onto the form's designer. In other words, to use the graphical interface, the DataSet or DataView must be accessible at the form level by declaring them with the Friend (internal in C#), Protected (protected), or Public (public) keywords in VB. They must also contain tables and strongly typed columns.

When this is the case, it is a simple exercise to navigate to the DataBindings property in the property window and either enter the binding expression in the appropriate sub-property (such as Tag or Text) or click on the ellipsis next to the Advanced property to open the Advanced Data Binding dialog. The Advanced dialog allows you to bind to many of the other properties on the control, as shown in Figure 16.2.

FIGURE 16.2

Using simple binding. This screen shows the Properties window and Advanced Data Binding dialog used to graphically bind a property to a data source.

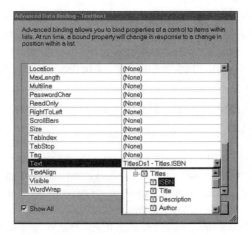

16

However, if you're not using strongly typed `DataSet` objects, you'll need to set up binding programmatically. This can be accomplished by creating a private method within your Windows Form, for example, and creating the `Binding` objects directly. Listing 16.1 shows an example of programmatic data binding.

LISTING 16.1 Programmatic data binding. This method binds the columns of a `DataSet` to controls on a Windows Form.

```
Private Sub _setupBinding()
  ' Set up the DataView
  dv = New DataView(dsTitles.Tables(0))

  ' Set up bindings
  txtISBN.DataBindings.Add("Text", dv, "ISBN")
  txtTitle.DataBindings.Add("Text", dv, "Title")
  txtDesc.DataBindings.Add("Text", dv, "Description")
  txtPrice.DataBindings.Add("Text", dv, "Price")
  txtPub.DataBindings.Add("Text", dv, "Publisher")
  txtAuthor.DataBindings.Add("Text", dv, "Author")
  txtPubDate.DataBindings.Add("Text", dv, "PubDate")
End Sub
```

ANALYSIS You'll notice in Listing 16.1 that the `DataView` (also a form-level object like `dsTitles`) was created from the first table in the `dsTitles` `DataTable` collection. You might want to do this if you need to sort and filter the view of the data that the user will see. The `Add` method of the `DataBindings` collection for each control was then invoked and passed the property to bind to, the data source (in this case, the `DataView`), and the member within the data source to get the data from. Alternatively, the `Add` method can accept a separately instantiated `Binding` object.

One of the interesting points to note is that the second and third arguments of the Add method may overlap, and that the precise syntax you use has an effect on how many CurrencyManager objects are created within the BindingContext. For example, consider what would happen if the method in Listing 16.1 had contained the following two statements:

```
txtISBN.DataBindings.Add("Text", dsTitles.Tables(0), "ISBN")

txtTitle.DataBindings.Add("Text", dv, "Title")
```

Although both would bind to the DataView correctly, because the second argument doesn't refer to exactly the same data source, the BindingContext of the form will see these as two separate data sources and thus create two CurrencyManager objects. The result is that the Text properties of the two controls won't be synchronized as the data is navigated through. This is important because if you create bindings graphically and then want to add a Binding programmatically that uses the same CurrencyManager, you need to specify only the top-level data source object in the second argument and defer the rest to the third argument. For example, the following two statements both bind the ISBN column, but the second specifies the table name in the third argument rather than the second:

```
txtISBN.DataBindings.Add("Text", dsTitles.Tables("Table"), "ISBN")

txtISBN.DataBindings.Add("Text", dsTitles, "Table.ISBN")
```

Note also that in the third argument, you would use the actual name of the table—in this case, the default "Table"--as specified in the TableName property.

Note

> You can also use this behavior when binding to strongly typed DataSet objects. In this case, you don't have to fully qualify the DataSet and table name in the second argument and defer the table name to the third argument using dot notation.

Although this behavior might be useful if you need to display two different rows on the same form, generally, you'll want all the bindings to exist under the same CurrencyManager for a particular data source.

Navigation

Of course, when using simple binding, you'll also need to implement navigation. This is easily done by manipulating the CurrencyManager object's Position property and noting the current position using its PositionChanged event.

For example, to create an event handler for a button that moves the position of the `CurrencyManager` created in Listing 16.1, you could use the following code:

```
Private Sub btnNext_Click(ByVal sender As System.Object, _
   ByVal e As System.EventArgs) Handles btnNext.Click
   Me.BindingContext(dv).Position += 1
End Sub
```

Notice that the default property for the `BindingContext` property returns a `BindingManagerBase` object when passed the data source object for the binding. In this case, a `CurrencyManager` object is returned and its `Position` property is incremented.

 Note

> Manipulating the `Position` property of the `BindingManagerBase` object when it is instantiated as a `PropertyManager` object has no effect.

In the event that the end of the `CurrencyManager` is reached, no exception will be thrown and its position will remain at the end of the cursor. However, if you want to be notified when the beginning or end occurs, you can catch the `PositionChanged` event and test the current position as shown in Listing 16.2.

LISTING 16.2   Position notification. This event handler can be used to catch the invocation of the `PositionChanged` event for a `CurrencyManager`.

```
Protected Sub titles_PositionChanged(ByVal sender As _
   Object, ByVal e As EventArgs)
   If Me.BindingContext(dv).Position = Me.BindingContext(dv).Count - 1 Then
      btnNext.Enabled = False
   Else
      btnNext.Enabled = True
   End If
   If Me.BindingContext(dv).Position = 1 Then
      btnPrev.Enabled = False
   Else
      btnPrev.Enabled = True
   End If
End Sub
```

You might want to do this to change the user interface, as in this case, where the `btnNext` and `btnPrev` buttons are enabled and disabled. Note that the `CurrencyManager` also fires a `CurrentChanged` method when the current row in its list changes. The difference is that the `CurrentChanged` method passes into the handler an instance of `ItemChangedEventArgs`, which includes the `Index` property to enable you to determine the locus of the navigation.

In order for the event to be called, you must also set up a handler for it by using the AddHandler statement in VB or by adding to the invocation list of the delegate in C#. In VB, you might use code like the following in the _setupBinding method shown in Listing 16.1:

```
AddHandler Me.BindingContext(dv).PositionChanged, _
    AddressOf Me.titles_PositionChanged
```

Formatting

When you use simple binding, you also typically need to format the value of the property as it is bound to the control and then parse the value before it's used to update the data source. Fortunately, the Format and Parse events of the Binding object can be used to do this.

The Format event fires as the data from the data source is pushed to the control and again after it has been changed and pushed back to the control. A typical use for the Format event is to format decimal values into currency formats for display in a TextBox. For example, the Price column of the DataView in Listing 16.1 is bound to the txtPrice TextBox control. For the price to display as currency, the event handler in Listing 16.3 could be written.

LISTING 16.3 Formatting data. This event handler handles the Format event of a Binding object to format currency for display in a TextBox.

```
Private Sub _formatCurrency(ByVal sender As Object, ByVal e As ConvertEventArgs)
    If e.DesiredType Is GetType(String) Then
        e.Value = Format(e.Value, "currency")
    End If
End Sub
```

ANALYSIS Note that this method accepts the ConvertEventArgs object as the second argument, which exposes the DesiredType and Value properties. The DesiredType indicates the type of data that the control is expecting (in this case, String) when the value from the data source is formatted. The Value property contains the value from the data source. Here, the DesiredType is checked to ensure that the method is being called only when the property of the control expects a String because the Format method returns a String. By changing the Value, you can explicitly determine how the data will be converted. If you don't handle this event, the data will be automatically cast to the appropriate type. Because this event fires after a user has changed the data in the control, it effectively reformats the data for display when the user moves off the control. This has a nice effect because the users can immediately see their changes properly formatted as they navigate the form. If the data can't be formatted correctly, no exception will occur and the old value will be displayed.

 Note Although the documentation states that the Format event will fire the first time the property is bound, that doesn't appear to be the case. To make sure that the Format event fires, you can set the Position property of the CurrencyManager object to 1 immediately after you set up the bindings; for example, in the _setupBinding method.

16

Of course, for the _formatCurrency event to fire, you need to add an event handler like so:

```
AddHandler txtPrice.DataBindings(0).Format, AddressOf Me._formatCurrency
```

To perform more sophisticated operations, you can also choose to handle the Parse event, which will fire immediately before the data source is updated and before the Format event. The Parse event is useful when the user can enter a more sophisticated string that can't be converted directly to the data type of the data source. For example, if you allow users to enter ISBNs with hyphens (as in 0-6722-1236-5), the parse event could be used to strip the hyphens before the data is sent to the data source. The Parse event also populates an instance of ConvertEventArgs that you can use.

Tip Although it is beyond the scope of this book, the Parse event is a good place to use regular expressions, as found in the System.Text.RegularExpressions namespace. As a simple example, the RegEx class exposes a Replace method that can be used to replace all occurrences of one pattern with another in a string. The string can then be converted to the appropriate type within the Parse event. See the online documentation for more details.

Complex Binding

 NEW TERM Some controls support the ability to bind to an entire collection of items exposed by the data source, referred to as a **complex binding**. Of course, when using ADO.NET this means binding directly to the rows of DataTable objects or indirectly using a DataSet or DataView object. These controls, such as the ListBox, CheckedListBox, ComboBox, and DataGrid, expose their bindings for display through the

DataSource property. Those controls that display only a single value for each item, such as ListBox, CheckedListBox, and ComboBox, expose DisplayMember and ValueMember properties that are set to the member (column) to display and the member to update in the data source, respectively. The DataGrid, on the other hand, can display multiple values for each item, so additional properties aren't required. However, the DataGrid does expose a DataMember property that references the actual object (table) within the data source that provides the items to bind to.

 Note   Just as in simple binding, you have the option of creating the bindings graphically or programmatically. Once again, the graphical approach works particularly well for strongly typed DataSet objects.

Programmatically, this means that when using a ComboBox to display a pickable list of publishers, for example, you could use the following code:

```
cbPub.DataSource = ds.Tables(0)
cbPub.DisplayMember = "Description"
cbPub.ValueMember = "PubCode"
```

In this case, cbPub is the ComboBox and you'll notice that the DataSource property can be set to either a DataTable or a DataView. In addition, the DisplayMember property indicates that the Description column from the table will be shown to the user and will be available through the SelectedText property. The PubCode column will be available through the SelectedValue property.

In order to then bind the SelectedValue property to the DataView shown in Listing 16.1, you can simply add a Binding object programmatically as follows:

```
cbPub.DataBindings.Add("SelectedValue", dv, "PubCode")
```

This ensures that as the CurrencyManager for the DataView is positioned, the correct value in the ComboBox is selected. It also ensures that if the user selects a different value from cbPub, the underlying PubCode column in the DataView will be updated.

For a DataGrid, the DataSource property can be set to either a DataSet or a particular DataTable or DataView. If a DataSet is specified, the DataMember property can also be set to indicate which table is to be displayed. If a table isn't specified in the DataMember property, the grid will display all the table names and the users will have to drill down into the table they want to view. This can be confusing to the user, so you should generally choose one of the tables to display by default.

The most interesting behavior of the DataGrid when bound to a DataSet, however, is that if the DataSet contains relationships, the grid provides a drill-down capability to filter the child rows accordingly. For example, if the dsTitles DataSet contains tables that hold both the Titles and Reviews, by drilling down into each Title, the Reviews for that book will be shown. This is depicted in Figure 16.3.

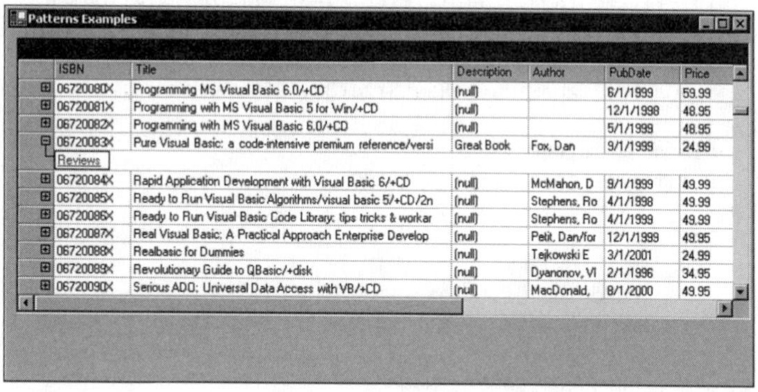

FIGURE 16.3

Navigating relationships. The DataGrid *automatically navigates the relationships when bound to a* DataSet.

16

	ISBN	Title	Description	Author	PubDate	Price
⊞	067200800X	Programming MS Visual Basic 6.0/+CD	(null)		6/1/1999	59.99
⊞	067200801X	Programming with MS Visual Basic 5 for Win/+CD	(null)		12/1/1998	48.95
⊞	067200802X	Programming with MS Visual Basic 6.0/+CD	(null)		5/1/1999	48.95
⊟	067200803X	Pure Visual Basic: a code-intensive premium reference/versi	Great Book	Fox, Dan	9/1/1999	24.99
	Reviews					
⊞	067200804X	Rapid Application Development with Visual Basic 6/+CD	(null)	McMahon, D	9/1/1999	49.99
⊞	067200805X	Ready to Run Visual Basic Algorithms/visual basic 5/+CD/2n	(null)	Stephens, Ro	4/1/1998	49.99
⊞	067200806X	Ready to Run Visual Basic Code Library: tips tricks & workar	(null)	Stephens, Ro	4/1/1999	49.99
⊞	067200807X	Real Visual Basic: A Practical Approach Enterprise Develop	(null)	Petit, Dan/for	12/1/1999	49.95
⊞	067200808X	Realbasic for Dummies	(null)	Tejkowski E	3/1/2001	24.99
⊞	067200809X	Revolutionary Guide to QBasic/+disk	(null)	Dyanonov, VI	2/1/1996	34.95
⊞	067200900X	Serious ADO: Universal Data Access with VB/+CD	(null)	MacDonald,	8/1/2000	49.95

You should also keep in mind that relations can be useful when combining simple and complex binding. For example, assume that a form contains simple bound controls that display the information for a book. In addition to the columns of the Titles table, you might also want to display the number of stars for each review submitted for the book in a ListBox control. This can be done by binding both the simple controls to the dsTitles DataSet and then binding the ListBox through the relation. For example, the following code displays the Stars column in the ListBox:

```
txtISBN.DataBindings.Add("Text", dsTitles, "Table.ISBN")
' Other simple controls
lbReviews.DataSource = dsTitles
lbReviews.DisplayMember = "Table.TitlesReviews.Stars"
```

Here, the simple controls would need to be bound to the DataSet directly and then their columns specified in the third argument to the Add method. The DisplayMember property of the ListBox can then be set to the fully qualified name of the column as navigated to through the view. In this case, the name of the relation is TitlesReviews.

Manual Binding

Although you might think that data readers would be bindable to Windows Forms controls, they aren't because they don't expose the IList or the other interfaces discussed previously. However, data readers can be useful for populating controls that don't support complex data binding, and are typically used for read-only data such as the TreeView and ListView, as shown in Listing 16.4.

LISTING 16.4   Manual binding. This listing shows how you might manually bind a data reader to a `ListView` control.

```
Private Sub _bindLvTitles(ByVal dr As IDataReader)

  ' Setup the ListView
  lvTitles.Columns.Add("ISBN", 250, HorizontalAlignment.Left)
  lvTitles.Columns.Add("Title", 750, HorizontalAlignment.Left)
  lvTitles.Columns.Add("Author", 500, HorizontalAlignment.Left)
  lvTitles.LargeImageList = imgCover
  imgCover.ImageSize = New Size(35, 50)

  Dim n As Integer
  Dim titleItem As ListViewItem

  Try
    Do While dr.Read
      ' Load the ListView
      Dim bytebuffer() As Byte

      ' Read the Cover image
      bytebuffer = CType(dr("Cover"), Byte())
      Dim ms As New MemoryStream(bytebuffer)
      ms.Position = 0

      ' Load the image to the list
      Dim i As New Bitmap(ms)
      imgCover.Images.Add(i)
      n += 1   'index into the ImageList

      ' Add the items to the ListView
      titleItem = lvTitles.Items.Add(dr("ISBN").ToString(), n)
      titleItem.SubItems.Add(dr("Title").ToString())
      titleItem.SubItems.Add(dr("Author").ToString())
    Loop
  Catch ex As Exception
    ' Handle Exception
  Finally
    dr.Close()
  End Try

End Sub
```

ANALYSIS   You'll notice in Listing 16.4 that the `_bindLvTitles` method uses the `lvTitles` `ListView` control to display information about the `Titles`. To allow the method to work with any provider, it simply accepts an open data reader specified using the `IDataReader` interface.

Within the method, the columns of the `lvTitles` `ListView` control are created along with associating an `ImageList` control with the `LargeImageList` property of the control. This allows images to be displayed when the `ListView` control's `View` property is set to `LargeIcon`.

Within the `Do` loop, the `Cover` image of the book is read into the `byteBuffer` `Byte` array and then read into a `MemoryStream`. The `MemoryStream` is then used to create a `Bitmap` object that can be placed into the `ImageList`.

Finally, a new `ListViewItem` is created for each row using the `ISBN` column and is associated with the proper index in the `ImageList` control. `SubItem` objects are then created to display the additional columns; in this case, `Title` and `Author`.

Validating Controls

The final issue you need to consider when using data binding on Windows Forms is validation. Although validation is not dependent on data binding or vice versa, it is almost always used in conjunction with it.

Of course, the most efficient way to validate the contents of controls is to not validate them at all, but rather restrict the user from entering invalid data in the first place. This can be accomplished by using controls appropriate to the data type you are binding to. For example, if you need to display a date, you should use the `DateTimePicker` or `MonthCalendar` controls. Likewise, if you need to bind to a `Boolean`, you should use the `CheckBox`. If you're binding to a small numeric value, use the `NumericUpDown` control, and so on.

Aside from using the appropriate control, you can handle two sets of events to validate data. The first set is the `DataTable` events `ColumnChanged`, `ColumnChanging`, `RowChanged`, `RowChanging`, `RowDeleted`, and `RowDeleting` (which we discussed on Day 4, "DataSet Internals"). The second set is composed of events associated with the control itself and includes

- `Enter`
- `GotFocus`
- `Leave`
- `Validating`
- `Validated`
- `LostFocus`

These events are fired in the order shown here. Of particular interest are the `Validating` and `Validated` events. As in VB 6.0, these events fire only when the `CausesValidation` property of the control that is navigated to (not the control to be validated) is set to True. Typically, all the controls on the form except Help buttons would have their CausesValidation property set to True in order to validate controls as the user navigates the form. The Validating event is also used in conjunction with the ErrorProvider control to avoid having to use message boxes or custom labels on the form.

> **Note** Another alternative is to handle the ItemChanged event of the CurrencyManager object, which is fired immediately before a row becomes current.

To illustrate a simple validation scenario, assume that the txtISBN TextBox on a form must be validated to ensure that it contains exactly 10 characters. To do so, you can handle its Validating and Validated events as shown in Listing 16.5.

LISTING 16.5 Simple validation. This listing shows how you would handle the Validating and Validated events for a control to restrict the contents of a TextBox.

```
Private Sub txtISBN_Validating(sender As Object, _
    e As System.ComponentModel.CancelEventArgs) Handles txtISBN.Validating

  If txtISBN.Text.Length <> 10 Then
    ' Cancel the event and select the text to be corrected
    e.Cancel = True
    txtISBN.Select(0, txtISBN.Text.Length)

    ' Set the ErrorProvider error with the text to display.
    titlesError.SetError(txtISBN, "Must be 10 characters")
  End If

End Sub

Private Sub txtISBN_Validated(sender As Object, _
    e As System.EventArgs) Handles txtISBN.Validated

  ' Clear the error provider of errors
  titlesError.SetError(txtISBN, "")

End Sub
```

ANALYSIS As shown in Listing 16.5, the CancelEventArgs object passed into the Validating event can be used to cancel the navigation and keep the focus on the control by setting its Cancel property to True. In addition, the great aspect of using the

ErrorProvider control is that by calling the SetError method, it automatically pops up a red icon next to the control passed to it and makes the error message available in a ToolTip window. The Validated event is called only if the validation succeeds, and can be used to clear the error provider of the error.

> **Tip**
>
> The Validating event is another great place to use regular expressions to perform more sophisticated validation.

16

Web Forms Applications

One of the great things about ADO.NET is that is can be used efficiently in the presentation services tier of both Windows Forms and Web Forms (ASP.NET) applications even though the two programming models differ greatly behind the scenes. You've probably already gotten an understanding of this fact if you followed the discussion on Day 2, "Getting Started."

In this section, you'll learn how data binding works in Web Forms applications and both how to manage the state of your data and validate it. You can find the controls and other types discussed in this section in the System.Web.UI namespace.

Using Data Binding

Right from the start, it should be noted that data binding in Web Forms applications is much different than in Windows Forms applications because it relies on two key assumptions not present in Windows Forms applications:

- Most data is read-only.
- Web applications are stateless.

From these two assumptions, everything else flows. First, the read-only assumption means that in Web Forms data binding, the value from the data source is pulled into the control as the page is built, but it isn't automatically pushed back to the data source when the page is submitted back to the server. Although you can certainly update a data source from a bound control, Web Forms data binding won't do it for you. Because Web Forms data binding is read-only, it also makes sense to use not only DataSet and DataView objects for binding, but also data readers.

Second, the stateless nature of HTTP and thus Web applications means that Web Forms data binding has no concept of BindingContext and CurrencyManager objects that automatically track the state of the bound controls and the position within the data source.

Once again, this information is available, but you have to manually position the controls, as shown in Listing 2.3 on Day 2. As you'll see, this also has implications for balancing the number of roundtrips to the data store your application will incur against the overhead of storing this state information. The stateless architecture of the Web also fits nicely with the disconnected nature of ADO.NET. As we discussed on Day 4, this was one of its design goals.

To act as a provider for data binding to a collection of objects, a class simply needs to implement the IEnumerable interface, which supports a simple iteration over a collection of objects. This interface is itself implemented by the IList interface, so approximately 100 classes in the framework can all be bound to Web Forms controls. These classes include collection classes such as Array, ArrayList, SortedList, Queue, and Hashtable, as well as the ADO.NET DataSet, DataTable (once again through the IListSource interface), and DataView, and data readers such as OleDbDataReader.

Of course, as in Windows Forms, in addition to the standard properties of controls such as Text, any property or field of the controls or the page itself can consume data from a data source both graphically at design time and programmatically at run time.

In the following sections, you'll learn how to use simple binding (referred to as single-value binding) and complex binding (referred to as multi-record binding) in Web Forms applications.

Single-Value Binding

NEW TERM   **Single-value binding** enables you to bind any property of any control to an expression. This can be done by using the DataBindings dialog in VS .NET, by editing the HTML directly, or using the DataBinding event exposed by each control (inherited from System.Web.UI.Control) and the page (System.Web.UI.Page) itself.

In the simplest case, you can drag and drop a Web Forms control from the toolbox on a Web Form and then open the DataBindings dialog shown in Figure 16.4 by clicking on the ellipsis in the Properties window. This technique comes in handy when you're using strongly typed DataSet objects because they'll appear in the box under the Simple Binding radio button. It's a simple matter to drill down into the DataSet and select the column to bind to. This is shown in Figure 16.4 where the Address column of a strongly typed DataSet called CustomersDs1 is being bound to a TextBox control.

One of the things you'll notice in Figure 16.4 is that as you drill down into the DataSet and underlying DataView, you're automatically specifying a row (in this case, the first row) to bind to. This is the case because the Web Form doesn't have any concept of a CurrencyManager, so you need to explicitly bind to a row.

FIGURE 16.4

Data binding in a Web Form. You can use this dialog to specify single-value binding in a Web Form.

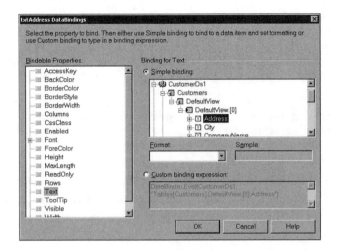

16

> **Note**
>
> When a property is bound with an expression, it will appear with a yellow barrel icon in the Properties window and in the DataBindings dialog.

NEW TERM You'll also notice that the box under the Custom Binding Expression radio button is automatically populated. This denotes the actual syntax that is placed within a **data binding expression** in the HTML page (which you can also edit directly by clicking on the HTML tab in the designer). So, for Figure 16.4, the tag for the `TextBox` would look as follows:

```
<asp:textbox id=txtAddress runat="server"
  Text='<%# DataBinder.Eval(CustomerDs1,
  "Tables[Customers].DefaultView.[0].Address") %>'>
</asp:textbox>
```

The data binding expression is wrapped in the `<%# %>` tags and is evaluated during the page processing on the server. In this case, given a data source, the shared `Eval` method of the `DataBinder` class is used to evaluate the data binding expression and optionally format the results as a `String`. For example, you can use the overloaded version of the `Eval` method to format the `Price` column into currency using a format string like so:

```
<%# DataBinder.Eval(CustomerDs1,
  "Tables[Titles].DefaultView.[0].Price", "{0:c}") %>
```

Although the `DataBinder` class makes formatting simpler, it does so at a cost because it uses late binding. A more efficient technique when using single-value binding is simply to bind directly to the data item and convert it yourself, as in this snippet, where `dr` is a page-level variable that references the current `DataRow` to bind to:

```
<%# Format(dr("Price"),"currency") %>
```

Alternatively, you can do the binding programmatically by handling the DataBinding event at either the control or the page level. For example, the following event handler can be added to the page to handle the DataBinding event for the TextBox that displays the Price:

```
Private Sub txtPrice_DataBinding(ByVal sender As Object, _
  ByVal e As System.EventArgs) Handles txtPrice.DataBinding
   txtPrice.Text = Format(dr("Price"),"currency")
End Sub
```

To set up the binding for the entire page, you can also handle the DataBinding event at the Page level. When the page is processed by ASP.NET, if it encounters a call to the DataBind method of a control, the page will evaluate any data binding expression for the control and any child controls in the HTML page, and fire the DataBinding event for the control and its children. Because the Page class is derived from Control, this applies to the page as a whole as well. In other words, in Web Forms data binding, you must explicitly call the DataBind method of individual controls or the page in order to instruct it to evaluate the data-binding expressions and fire the DataBinding events. Simply calling DataBind on the page will cascade the binding throughout the page.

> **Tip**
> Typically, using the DataBinding events is easier than editing the HTML or using the DataBindings dialog because the syntax is simpler and you have full access to IntelliSense.

Typically, you would call the DataBind event in the Load event of the page, as shown in Listing 2.2 on Day 2.

Multi-Record Binding

New Term   **Multi-record binding** is very similar to the complex binding in Windows Forms in that controls that can bind to multiple records expose DataSource and DataMember properties that can be used to bind to a DataSet, DataTable, or DataView. These controls include DropDownList, ListBox, DataGrid, DataList, Repeater, CheckBoxList, and RadioButtonList. Of those controls, only the DataGrid and DataList also expose the DataKeyField property that can be used to specify the primary key field and populate the DataKeys collection so that the key field needn't be displayed in the control.

In addition, the ListBox, DropDownList, RadioButtonList, and CheckBoxList controls all expose DataValueField, DataTextField and DataTextFormat properties.

16

DataValueField and DataTextField are analogous to the ValueMember and DisplayMember properties of Windows Forms controls, and DataTextFormat is used to apply formatting to the value that is displayed.

Because we looked at binding to the more sophisticated DataGrid control on Day 2, we won't look at more examples here. However, suffice it to say that the DataGrid, along with the DataList and Repeater controls, is a template-based control. A template-based control contains collection templates, each of which can contain child controls that display data in different sections of the control or when the control is in various states. On Day 2, you saw how the EditItemTemplate could be used to display controls when a row in the DataGrid is in edit mode. The template-based controls also expose differing sets of templates, some of which have the same name but are used differently by each control.

Basically, the DataGrid displays the data in a tabular format, whereas the DataList can be used for more flexible formats. The Repeater is like the DataList in that it is flexible but offers no design-time capabilities. Refer to the online documentation for additional examples of using these controls.

 Note

> Data binding expressions inside templated controls use the Container object as a generic way to refer to the data source and row that is being evaluated. Within the Container, they use the DataItem property to reference the column in the row. This is often used in conjunction with the DataBinder.Eval method, as in DataBinder.Eval(Container.DataItem, "Name").

Another typical use of multi-record data binding in a Web Form is to display lookup data in a DropDownList control, as shown in Listing 16.6.

LISTING 16.6 Multi-record binding. This listing shows a method used on an ASP.NET page to bind a data reader to a DropDownList control.

```
Private Sub _loadControls()

  ' Load the Publishers drop down
  Dim dr As IDataReader

  Try
    dr = compData.GetPublishersReader()

    With dlPublishers
      .DataSource = dr
```

LISTING 16.6   continued

```
      .DataTextField = "Name"
      .DataValueField = "PubCode"
      .DataBind()
   End With

 Catch ex As Exception
   Throw New Exception("Could not get publisher data", ex)
 Finally
   dr.Close()
 End Try

End Sub
```

ANALYSIS   As you can see in Listing 16.6, the private _loadControls method is called from the Load event of the page and is responsible for getting a data reader and binding it to the dlPublishers DropDownList control. The method executes the GetPublishersReader method of a data access class referenced by the compData variable to return a data reader that is bound to the control using the DataSource, DataTextField, and DataValueField properties. When the DataBind method is called, the rows are retrieved from the data reader and are rendered by the control.

The interesting aspect of Listing 16.6 is that the dr variable is of type IDataReader, so it can be used with data readers from various providers. Additionally, the data reader returned is ostensibly opened using the CloseConnection command behavior so that when the data reader is closed in the Finally block, the underlying database connection is also closed or returned to the connection pool.

You might be thinking that the technique shown in Listing 16.6 would be a perfect place to use the capability of data readers to return multiple result sets. By doing so, you could encapsulate all the SELECT statements that return read-only data into a single SQL Server stored procedure and then use the NextResult method between the With blocks to bind each control to a result set. Although this does work, unfortunately, it can't be used in conjunction with the CloseConnection command behavior. Specifying this behavior causes the connection to be closed after the first control's DataBind method is called, and therefore results in an exception when the NextResult method is executed. This behavior is particular to SQL Server using both the SqlClient and OleDb providers. As a result, you would need to explicitly create the connection and command objects in the presentation services code or expose a method in the data access class to close the connection.

Mobile Control Binding

If you download and install the Microsoft Mobile Internet Toolkit (MMIT) from MSDN, you can also build Mobile Forms that are targeted for a wide variety of mobile devices such as Web-enabled phones (WAP phones) and Pocket PCs. Interestingly, MMIT includes its own set of Mobile Controls, some of which also support data binding. For example, it includes the List control, which is a template-based control that takes the place of the DataList and Repeater controls; the ObjectList control, which is also templated and used in place of the DataGrid; and the SelectionList control, which takes the place of the CheckBoxList, DropDownList, ListBox, and RadioButtonList by setting its SelectType property accordingly.

The ability to create multiple user interfaces targeted to different devices in the presentation services tier makes it all the more important to abstract the data and business services into separate tiers to get the maximum reuse possible.

16

Storing Object State

Because the nature of the Web—and thus the programming model exposed in a Web Form—is stateless, any page-level objects (such as a DataSet, DataTable, or DataView) you create will be destroyed with each new request to the Web server. As you saw on Day 2, when using ADO.NET, this necessitates reretrieving and rebinding the data, as well as perhaps repositioning list-based controls such as the DataGrid and DataList. This is done in the Load event of the page and obviously incurs a roundtrip to the data store each time the page is posted (even when using custom paging), which in Web Forms might be frequent, especially if you handle lots of events on the server.

To minimize the roundtrips to the server, there are two strategies you can use to store the object used as the data source for binding on the Web server. These include using the Session object and using view state.

 Note

The two techniques discussed here are useful if you need to store data particular to a user. However, some read-only data might be able to be used by multiple users. In these scenarios, you could cache the data in the HttpApplicationState object (exposed through the Application property of the HttpContext object) or by using the Cache object. The advantage to the Cache object is that the items placed in the cache can have an associated absolute or sliding expiration policy so that you can be notified and refresh the data accordingly.

Session State

Just as in ASP, ASP.NET applications can take advantage of the ability to store data between browser requests in name-value pairs within an object managed by the Web server. In ASP.NET, this is an `HttpSessionState` object referenced through the `Session` property of the `Page` itself and through the `HttpContext` object.

> **Note**
>
> The `HttpContext` object is an object that flows throughout a request in ASP.NET and encapsulates all the HTTP-specific information about the request, including references to the `Server`, `Request`, and `Response` objects, in addition to the `Session`, `Application`, and other objects the runtime uses to implement features such as tracing and caching. The `HttpContext` object is accessible through the `Context` property of the `Page` class, and thus the `HttpSessionState` can also be referenced through `Context` as in `Me.Context.Session`. See Chapter 10 of my book *Building Distributed Applications with Visual Basic .NET* (published by Sams) for more information on the ASP.NET runtime and processing model.

> **Note**
>
> As in ASP, the Global.asax file in ASP.NET includes `Session_OnStart` and `Session_OnEnd` methods to intercept the `Start` and `End` events associated with a user's session. You can use the `OnStart` event to preload and cache some information that you know a user will need.

This mechanism enables you to place `DataSet` objects, for example, in session state rather than having to repopulate them from a data store. For example, using session state, the `Load` event of a page that populates two tables in `DataSet` might look like that shown in Listing 16.7.

LISTING 16.7 Using session state. This listing shows the `Load` event of a page using session state information.

```
Private Sub Page_Load(ByVal sender As System.Object, _
  ByVal e As System.EventArgs) Handles MyBase.Load

  If Not Page.IsPostBack Then
    ' Fill the DataSet with titles from a particular publisher
    dsTitles = compData.GetTitles(Me.Request.Form("PubCode"))
    Me.Session("dsTitles") = dsTitles
  Else
    dsTitles = CType(Me.Session("dsTitles"), DataSet)
  End If
```

LISTING 16.7   continued

```
' Bind the Data
DataGrid1.DataSource = dsTitles
DataGrid1.DataBind()
End Sub
```

 In Listing 16.7, you'll notice that if the page has been reposted to the server, the data will have already been queried. Thus, it can be safely retrieved from the `HttpSessionState` object and placed in a page-level variable that other methods in the page will utilize. If this is the first request, the data is queried from the data store using the `GetTitles` method of a data access class, the `DataSet` saved in session state. In either case, the `DataSet` is then bound to the `DataGrid` control to display the data.

> **Tip**
>
> As with classic ASP tracking, session state requires overhead, so if a particular page won't be accessing the `Session` object, you should set the `EnableSessionState` attribute of the `Page` directive at the top of the HTML to `False`. You can also turn off session state for the entire site by setting the mode attribute of the `sessionState` element to `Off` in the configuration file Web.config.

In ASP, it wasn't recommended to store data in the `Session` object because its implementation had two significant weaknesses:

- The 120-bit `SessionID` used to identify the session was always stored as a cookie on the browser. Therefore, if the security policy of a user's employer didn't allow cookies, the `Session` object couldn't be populated.

- The data associated with the session and accessed through the `SessionID` was stored in process on the Web server that initiated the session. As a result, the session data couldn't be shared in a Web farm scenario in which multiple Web servers are processing requests from multiple clients. Although programmatic techniques and system software such as the Windows 2000 Network Load Balancing (NLB) service can be configured to force a client to access the same Web server for each request (referred to as *sticky IP*), the overhead and possible imbalance that server affinity creates reduces scalability.

Fortunately, the ASP.NET session implementation addresses both of these weaknesses.

By default, sessions in ASP.NET are configured in the same way as classic ASP; that is, an in-memory cookie is sent to the browser that contains the `SessionID`; the session data itself is stored in the memory of the server that initiated the session, and the session timeout is set to 20 minutes. However, the manner and storage attributes for session data can also be configured in the Web.config file within the ASP.NET application. For example, to use cookieless sessions, in which ASP.NET no longer sends a cookie but includes the SessionID in the query string of each request, you simply set the cookieless attribute of the sessionState tag to true as follows:

```
<sessionState mode="InProc" cookieless="true" timeout="20" />
```

When the page is processed, it then extracts the SessionID from the query string and associates the user request with the appropriate session. In this way, cookies are not required.

Using a cookieless session has no impact on where the session data is stored, only on how it is accessed. However, ASP.NET includes two options for storing the session data outside the Web server.

SQL Server Storage

The first option is to store the session data in a SQL Server database. This can be done by setting the mode attribute of the sessionState element in Web.config to "SqlServer". When this is set, the ASP.NET runtime stores session data in a SQL Server database called ASPState on the SQL Server pointed at by the sqlConnectionString attribute. This attribute should contain the data source and security credentials necessary to log on to the server like so:

```
<sessionState mode="SQLServer"
    sqlConnectionString="server=ssosa;uid=aspSession;pwd=@#r6t;
    trusted_connection=yes;pooling=true"
    cookieless="false"
    timeout="20" />
```

When configured, the application should run identically to when the session data is stored in-process on the Web server. However, keep in mind that all the objects in the session's collection will be serialized at the end of each Web request and transported over the network and saved in the SQL Server database. On each request, the data is read from the database and deserialized into the appropriate objects. This implies that all objects saved in the Session object's collections must be able to be serialized and deserialized by being marked with the Serializable attribute, or additionally derived from MarshalByValueComponent, or have implemented the ISerializable interface.

Obviously, storing session state in the database is a tradeoff between scalability and reliability over performance in the following ways:

- Session data stored in SQL Server increases the amount of network traffic and database connections generated by the application.

- Session data decoupled from the Web server can be easily shared across servers in a Web farm, thereby increasing scalability.

- Session data stored on a separate machine isn't lost when the application crashes or is restarted.

- Session data stored separately from the Web server doesn't impact the memory requirements of the Web server as does in-process storage.

16

If none of the previous considerations are relevant to your application, use the in-process setting because it performs better.

State Server

NEW TERM   In addition to storing session data in a SQL Server, ASP.NET also provides for storing data in a separate in-memory cache controlled by a Windows service. The service is called the **ASP.NET State service** (aspnet_state.exe) and can be run on either the same machine as the Web server or a separate machine. To use the service, the mode attribute of the sessionState element in Web.config is set to "StateServer", and the stateConnectionString attribute must include the server and port used to connect to the service like so:

```
<sessionState mode="StateServer" stateConnectionString="tcpip=ssosa:42424"
    cookieless="false" timeout="20" />
```

In this case, the state service is running on a machine called "ssosa" at the port 42424, which is the default. The port can be configured at the server by modifying the Port value in the aspnet_state registry key under the HKLM\SYSTEM\CurrentControlSet\Services.

Obviously, using the state service has the same advantage of process isolation and sharability across a Web farm. However, if the state service is stopped, all session data is lost. In other words, the state service doesn't persistently store the data as does SQL Server; it simply holds it in memory.

View State

The ASP.NET programming model supports the concept of view state where information about the state of a Web Form is embedded in the HTML page sent to the browser. This information is used by the ASP.NET runtime to populate the properties of the controls on the page and the page itself when the form is posted back to the server. The view state is represented in the hidden __VIEWSTATE control on the page in the browser and the ViewState property of the Page object.

To add custom information such as a `DataSet` to the `ViewState`, you can programmatically manipulate the underlying `StateBag` object exposed by the `ViewState` property. The `StateBag` class simply exposes a collection of `StateItem` objects by implementing the `ICollection`, `IDictionary`, and `IEnumerable` interfaces. You can add items to the `StateBag` of a page by calling the `Add` method and providing the key and the value as arguments. For example, as shown in Listing 16.8, you could use add a `DataSet` to the `ViewState` in the same way that you could use the `HttpSessionState` object.

LISTING 16.8   Using view state. This listing shows the `Load` event of a page using view state information.

```
Private Sub Page_Load(ByVal sender As System.Object, _
  ByVal e As System.EventArgs) Handles MyBase.Load

  If Not Page.IsPostBack Then
    ' Fill the DataSet with titles from a particular publisher
    dsTitles = compData.GetTitles(Me.Request.Form("PubCode"))
    Me.ViewState.Add("dsTitles") = dsTitles
  Else
    dsTitles = CType(Me.ViewState("dsTitles"),DataSet)
  End If

  ' Bind the Data
  DataGrid1.DataSource = dsTitles
  DataGrid1.DataBind()

End Sub
```

Using the view state in this way has two advantages over session state. Particularly, there is less overhead on the server because the objects aren't persisted anywhere and simply travel with the form. In addition, view state promotes information hiding because only this particular Web Form needs to see these values. However, the flip side is that an object stored in view state is accessible only in the particular page in which it's created. If the object must be accessible across pages, you'll need to use session state. Also, because view state is represented as a binary string embedded in the page sent to the browser, the larger the object you store in view state, the more bandwidth it takes to move the object back and forth between the browser and Web server. For this reason, you should consider using view state only if the `DataSet` or `DataTable` contains a limited number of rows.

Validating Controls

As with Windows Forms controls, you also need to be able to validate user input in a Web Form. To make this process simple, ASP.NET includes controls derived from `BaseValidator`, as shown in Table 16.1.

TABLE 16.1 Web Forms validation controls. The controls listed here all derive from BaseValidator.

Control	Description
CompareValidator	Used to compare the contents of the control with a constant or another control
CustomValidator	Used to validate the contents of the control based on custom logic
RangeValidator	Used to ensure that the control's value is between a lower and upper limit
RegularExpressionValidator	Used to validate a control based on a regular expression
RequiredFieldValidator	Used to ensure that the control has a value
ValidationSummary	Used to display the error messages from all the validation controls on the page

As shown in Table 16.1, the six validation controls handle everything from making sure that a control is populated to handling custom validation code running on the server. In total, these controls offer a level of functionality that must be custom coded in Windows Forms. Each instance of one of these controls, with the exception of the ValidationSummary control, can be used to validate one control on the form. To validate multiple controls, you need to add multiple instances of the validator controls to the page as well. After you do so, the HTML code in the page for a single control might look like the following code snippet:

```
<asp:RequiredFieldValidator id=LNameValidator
   ControlToValidate="txtLName" Display=Dynamic
   CssClass="body-copy" runat="server"
   ErrorMessage="Last Name is required" Text="*" >
</asp:RequiredFieldValidator>
```

In this case, the RequiredFieldValidator is used to make sure that the txtLName control on the form contains a value (as indicated by the ControlToValidate property). You might also use a RegularExpressionValidator control to make sure that an e-mail address is entered in the appropriate format, like so:

```
<asp:RegularExpressionValidator
  id="EmailAtValidator" runat="server"
  ErrorMessage="Email Address must contain @"
  ValidationExpression="(.)+(@)+(.)+"
  Display=Static Text="*" CssClass="body-copy"
  ControlToValidate="txtEmail">
</asp:RegularExpressionValidator>
```

Note | Of course, as with other controls, you can programmatically manipulate the properties of validation controls in the code for the page as well.

Here, the `RegularExpressionValidator` is used to ensure that the e-mail address contains an "@". Note that the `ValidationExpression` property is populated with a regular expression where the expression ensures that at least one character (.)+ precedes the "@" symbol (@) followed by at least one more character (.)+.

Note | In the case where a single control is the target of two validation controls, there is an order of precedence to how they are fired. As you might expect, the `RequiredFieldValidator` is fired first, followed by the `RegularExpressionValidator`.

Finally, you can also place a `ValidationSummmary` control on the page that enables you to display all the error messages in a central location. In this way, the messages can be grouped so that users don't have to scan the page searching for error messages. A `ValidationSummary` control on the page would be rendered as follows:

```
<asp:ValidationSummary id=ValidationSummary
    runat="server" ShowMessageBox=True CssClass="body-copy"
    DisplayMode= BulletList HeaderText="Errors occurred.">
</asp:ValidationSummary>
```

Note that the `DisplayMode` property is set to `BulletList` to indicate that the errors display in a list of bulleted items directly beneath the `HeaderText`. The `ShowMessageBox` property takes effect when the validation is done on the client and displays a message box with all the errors in addition to printing them to the validation summary control. In addition, error messages print out in red by default. This can be changed by setting the properties of the control (such as `ForeColor`) or using a Cascading Style Sheet (CSS). In this case, the `CSSClass` property is set to `"body-copy"`, which sets the font according to the style sheet linked in the `LINK` tag at the top of the page.

By default, the validation controls perform the validation on the client if the browser supports DHTML by rendering JavaScript code in the HTML page. This is the default so that server roundtrips are reduced and makes the application more responsive. To force validation to occur on the server for individual controls, you can set the `EnableClientScript` property of the control to `False`, whereas for the entire page, you can set the `ClientTarget` attribute of the `Page` directive to "downlevel".

> **Note**
>
> Validation can be disabled on the server by setting the `Enabled` property of the validation control to `False`. If validation must be disabled from client-side script, you can set the `Page_ValidationActive` global variable to `False`. This variable is included on pages that use client validation through a JavaScript file (`WebUIValidation.js`) included with the page.

16

You'll also notice in the previous code snippets that both the `ErrorMessage` and `Text` properties are set. Typically, you'd only set the `ErrorMessage` property, but because the page includes a `ValidationSummary` control, the `Text` property specifies the message that will be displayed at the location of the validation control, whereas the `ErrorMessage` is displayed in the `ValidationSummary` control. In this way, you can provide a visual cue to the user as to which fields were in error, much like the `ErrorProvider` control, and still group all the error messages in one place.

When the validation controls use client-side validation and all the validation passes, the form is posted back to the server. However, if the validation controls actually perform their validation on the server, the validation occurs before the server event that initiated the postback occurs. Rather than taking any special action (other than error reporting) when errors are encountered, the validation controls simply set the `IsValid` property of the individual controls and the `Page` object to `False`. As a result, code on the server must check for this value before proceeding. Not checking this property results in errors reported to the client but normal processing to otherwise continue.

Customizing Validation

Although the `RegularExpressionValidator` control is especially flexible, you have the option of customizing the validation process. You can accomplish this on the server by adding a `CustomValidator` control to the page and setting its `ControlToValidate` property to the appropriate control. Then, within the page class, you can create a method to handle the `ServerValidate` event of the control.

This method then performs the validation by referring to the value argument that contains the value of the control being validated. Returning `True` from this function means that the validation was successful. This technique can be used, for example, to dynamically validate the control against values read from a database.

An analogous technique can be used to perform custom validation on the client by populating the `ClientValidationFunction` property with the name of a client-side function to execute.

Summary

When building the presentation services tier of a multi-tier application, you need to be concerned with issues of data binding, navigation, and validation, among others. Today you learned the basics of how the objects exposed by ADO.NET can be used in both Windows Forms and Web Forms applications to display, edit, and validate data.

However, to get the data that the presentation services tier works with, you need to create classes in the data services tier. Tomorrow, you'll learn some strategies and techniques you can use to implement the data services tier.

Workshop

This workshop will help reinforce the concepts covered in today's lesson.

Quiz

1. What is the purpose of the `CurrencyManager` object on a Windows Form?

   The `CurrencyManager` object manages the position and state of a data source on a Windows Form. This is required because the data source itself has no concept of an internal cursor.

2. Are there any caveats to setting up data binding on a Windows Form?

   The biggest caveat is that you must make certain that the data source you specify when adding bindings to the `BindingCollection` object is the same for all controls. Using a different expression by, for example, specifying just the `DataSet` in one case and both the `DataSet` and `DataTable` in the other, will result in two `CurrencyManager` objects being created. The end result will be that the controls won't be synchronized when navigation occurs.

3. What are the assumptions you need to consider when using Web Forms data binding?

   Data binding in Web Forms assumes that most binding is read-only and so it does not support automatically updating a data source with data from the bound controls. In addition, it adheres to the stateless nature of the Web by not trying to manage the position of a data source as the `CurrencyManager` does in Windows Forms.

4. What are some techniques for minimizing the roundtrips to the data store when using data binding in Web Forms?

   In order to reduce the traffic to the database server when using binding in Web Forms, you can opt to store the data in session state (`HttpSessionState` object), view state, application state (`HttpApplicationState` object), or the `Cache` object.

Each has its advantages for particular scenarios, although session state is the most flexible. This is because session state enables you to cache data on a per-user basis that is available to all pages accessed by that user and can be stored externally to the Web server to support Web farm scenarios.

Exercise

Build a simple Windows Forms application that contains a `DataGrid` and controls for several of the columns in the `Titles` table in the ComputeBooks database. Ensure that as you scroll through the `DataGrid`, the values in the other controls track with the current row.

Answers for Day 16

Exercise Answer

One possible solution is to create a simple form that retrieves a `DataSet`, creates a `DataView`, and then binds the control to the `DataView` as shown in Listing 16.9 (note that the Web Form designer generated code is omitted).

LISTING 16.9 Binding to titles. This form binds a `DataView` created from a `DataSet` to both a `DataGrid` and other controls.

```
Imports System.Data.SqlClient

Public Class TitlesForm
  Inherits System.Windows.Forms.Form

  Protected dvTitles As DataView

  Private Sub TitlesForm_Load(ByVal sender As System.Object, _
    ByVal e As System.EventArgs) Handles MyBase.Load

    Dim con As New SqlConnection( _
      "server=ssosa;database=computebooks;trusted_connection=yes")
    Dim da As New SqlDataAdapter("usp_GetTitles", con)
    Dim dsTitles As New DataSet()

    da.SelectCommand.CommandType = CommandType.StoredProcedure

    da.MissingSchemaAction = MissingSchemaAction.AddWithKey
    Try
      da.Fill(dsTitles)
      dvTitles = New DataView(dsTitles.Tables(0))
      DataGrid1.DataSource = dvTitles
```

LISTING 16.9 continued

```
Catch sqlE As SqlException
  MsgBox(sqlE.Message)
End Try

' Set up bindings
txtISBN.DataBindings.Add("Text", dvTitles, "ISBN")
txtTitle.DataBindings.Add("Text", dvTitles, "Title")
txtDesc.DataBindings.Add("Text", dvTitles, "Description")
txtPrice.DataBindings.Add("Text", dvTitles, "Price")
txtAuthor.DataBindings.Add("Text", dvTitles, "Author")
dtPubDate.DataBindings.Add("Value", dvTitles, "PubDate")

AddHandler txtPrice.DataBindings(0).Format, AddressOf Me._formatCurrency
End Sub

Private Sub _formatCurrency(ByVal sender As Object, _
  ByVal e As ConvertEventArgs)
  If e.DesiredType Is GetType(String) Then
    e.Value = Format(e.Value, "currency")
  End If
End Sub

End Class
```

Figure 16.5 shows the resulting form.

FIGURE 16.5

Binding to titles. This form uses both simple and complex binding to display data from a DataView *object.*

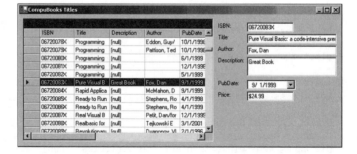

WEEK 3

DAY 17

ADO.NET in the Data Services Tier

As you learned yesterday, for your presentation services tier to be able to consume data, your data services tier needs to supply it. To that end, the data services tier is responsible for providing an interface through which both the presentation and business services tiers can interact. This approach abstracts the data access code from the other tiers and makes it possible to reuse the classes in other applications.

Today and tomorrow, you'll learn about designing the data access classes that live in the data services tier. You'll also learn how you can take advantage of implementation inheritance and other features of the .NET Framework to create a flexible and robust solution. Specifically, today you'll learn

- How to design a base class for your data services tier for both serviced and non-serviced components
- Strategies for incorporating custom exception handling and logging
- How to design data access classes
- How to abstract the creation of provider-specific objects
- How to use pure .NET classes

Using an Abstract Base Class

As we've discussed elsewhere in this book, the fact that the common language runtime and thus managed languages can use implementation inheritance enables you to take advantage of polymorphism and write code that is both reusable and generic. It comes as no surprise that you can utilize this feature when you build your data access classes.

In the following sections, you'll learn how to create a base class for both non-serviced and serviced components. These base classes will incorporate some commonly implemented features and will be reusable across projects.

Creating a Base Class

When designing a reusable base class, you first need to understand its benefits and think clearly about what kinds of services it should and should not provide.

Of course, the fundamental reason to create a base class is so that developers deriving from the class can increase their productivity by not having to reinvent the wheel in order to handle issues such as logging. At the same time, the base class can be used to ensure that core services such as connection management, logging, and exception handling are handled in a standard fashion across your organization. For that reason, a data access base class should implement only features that are common to all your data access classes. In other words, it should not assume that its descendants will always work with DataSet objects as opposed to data readers, or that the descendants will always be running from within a particular environment such as ASP.NET. Your goal should be to design the base class to be as generic as possible and yet to provide useful services.

To illustrate these concepts, consider the base class shown in Listing 17.1.

LISTING 17.1   A data access base class. This base class implements connection management, logging, and exception handling.

```
Option Strict On
Imports System.Data.SqlClient

Namespace ComputeBooks.Data
  Public MustInherit Class ComputeBooksDABase : Implements IDisposable

    Private _connect As String
    Private _daSwitch As BooleanSwitch
    Private _sqlCon As SqlConnection
    Private _disposed As Boolean

    Protected ReadOnly Property Disposed() As Boolean
      Get
```

LISTING 17.1   continued

```
      Return _disposed
    End Get
End Property

Protected ReadOnly Property SqlCon() As SqlConnection
    Get
       Return _sqlCon
    End Get
End Property

Protected ReadOnly Property SwitchEnabled() As Boolean
    Get
       Return _daSwitch.Enabled
    End Get
End Property

Public Property ConnectString() As String
    Get
       Return _connect
    End Get
    Set(ByVal Value As String)
      _connect = Value
      Me.SqlCon.ConnectionString = _connect
      Me.WriteTrace("ConnectString set to" & _connect)
    End Set
End Property

Public Sub New(ByVal connect As String)
  _initClass()
  Me.ConnectString = connect
  Try
     Me.SqlCon.ConnectionString = Me.ConnectString
  Catch e As Exception
     Me.ThrowComputeBookException("Could not set the connection string", e)
  End Try
End Sub

Public Sub New()
  _initClass()
End Sub

Private Sub _initClass()
 _sqlCon = New SqlConnection()
 _daSwitch = New BooleanSwitch("daSwitch", "Data Access")
  Me.WriteTrace("Instance created")
End Sub

Protected Sub WriteTrace(ByVal message As String)
   ' Write a message to the trace if the switch is enabled
```

LISTING 17.1 continued

```
      Trace.WriteLineIf(Me.SwitchEnabled, Now & ":" & message)
    End Sub

    Public Sub Dispose() Implements IDisposable.Dispose
      Dispose(True)
    End Sub

    Protected Sub Dispose(ByVal disposing As Boolean)
      If disposing Then
        ' Clean up SQL Connection
        If Me.SqlCon.State = ConnectionState.Open Then
          Me.SqlCon.Close()
        End If
        _sqlCon = Nothing
      End If

      Me.WriteTrace("Disposed")
      Trace.Flush()
    _disposed = True

      ' Make sure Finalize does not run
      GC.SuppressFinalize(Me)
    End Sub

    Protected Overrides Sub Finalize()
      Dispose(False)
    End Sub

    Protected Sub ThrowComputeBookException(ByVal message As String, _
      ByVal e As Exception)
      Dim newMine As New ComputeBookDAException(message, e)

      ' Trace the error
      Me.WriteTrace(message & "{" & e.Message & "}")

      ' Throw
      Throw newMine
    End Sub

  End Class

End Namespace
```

ANALYSIS As you can see in Listing 17.1, the ComputeBooksDABase class is placed in the ComputeBooks.Data namespace. The class follows the naming conventions suggested in the online documentation, where organization name is at the highest level followed by the functionality. In this case, this class would also likely be compiled into its own assembly so that other developers (perhaps even working in different languages) could reference it in their projects. The classes that developers would derive from the base class might then be placed in namespaces directly under the ComputeBooks.Data namespace, such as ComputeBooks.Data.OrderProcessing. Once again, this illustrates that the base class should be generic so that it can be reused across projects.

Note

> Alternatively, the base class could be compiled into a .NET module (using the command-line compiler) and then used in multi-file assemblies built with the Assembly Linker (AL.exe) command-line utility. However, it would be far easier to compile it into an assembly along with any other interfaces or classes that might be used by data access developers in your organization. With an assembly, you also have the option of placing it in the Global Assembly Cache (GAC) so that multiple applications on the same machine access the same version.

17

You'll notice that the class is also marked as MustInherit (abstract in C#) so that instances of it can't be created directly. This makes sense because the class provides only auxiliary services and therefore can't be used in a standalone mode. Because the class is abstract, the name has been appended with "Base" as is recommended in the design guidelines in the online documentation.

The class itself contains the Disposed, SqlCon, SwitchEnabled, and ConnectString properties, along with the Dispose, WriteTrace, and ThrowComputeBookException methods. The first three properties are read-only because they are created by the base class. They are also protected so that they can be seen only by a descendant of this class and are not available publicly. The ConnectString is specified either through the overloaded constructor or using the property. In total, the base class provides the following services:

- **Connection Management.** The private _initClass method creates a new SqlConnection object when an instance of the class is created and returns it through the protected SqlCon property. In addition, the connection string to use is exposed through the ConnectString property and can be set in the constructor. In this way, derived classes needn't worry about creating a connection object or associating it with the connection string. In addition, the class implements the IDisposable interface so that clients have the option (although they don't have to use it) of disposing of the SqlConnection object. The inclusion of both the private and public Dispose methods follows the pattern shown in the online documentation.

- **Tracing.** You'll notice that the class includes a private variable called _daSwitch that is instantiated as a BooleanSwitch object in the _initClass method. This object is used in conjunction with the SwitchEnabled property and protected WriteTrace method to provide a way for the base class and its descendants to conditionally write tracing information to a log. (We'll discuss this feature in more depth in the following section.)

- **Exception Handling.** In conjunction with a custom class called ComputeBookDAException, the base class handles wrapping exceptions that are caught into instances of the custom exception class and throws them back to the caller in the protected ThrowComputeBookException method. (We'll discuss ComputeBookDAException in more detail shortly.)

After a class inherits from this base class, it has access to all of the public and protected members.

Conditional Tracing

As you learned in the previous section, one of the base class's services is the use of conditional tracing. This is accomplished by using the Trace and BooleanSwitch classes from the System.Diagnostics namespace.

The Trace class is used to instrument your application to output diagnostic information so that developers and administrators can pinpoint performance problems or validate the input and output of methods. In addition, tracing is helpful for understanding what is happening in nonvisual code segments like those in the data services tier. The Trace class exposes Write, WriteIf, WriteLine, and WriteLineIf methods that can be used to write data to one or more listeners. You can see that the WriteTrace method of the ComputeBooksDABase class uses the WriteLineIf method.

NEW TERM **Listeners** are objects derived from TraceListener and are exposed through the Listeners property of both the Trace and Debug objects (these objects share the underlying TraceListenerCollection). By default, the only object in the collection is an instance of DefaultTraceListener that writes both the Trace and Debug output to the Output window within VS .NET. However, applications can add new listeners to the collection to redirect the output. In fact, TraceListener serves as the base class for the EventLogListener and TextWriterTraceListener classes, which write output to the event log and to a file or stream, respectively.

For example, an application can allow the Trace output from the ComputeBooksDABase class and its descendants to be logged to a file by adding a TextWriterTraceListener object to the collection as follows:

```
Trace.Listeners.Add(New TextWriterTraceListener("DataAccess.log"))
```

The constructor of `TextWriterTraceListener` also accepts `Stream` or `TextWriter` objects.

As you might expect, the extensibility of the .NET Framework also enables you to create your own listener by deriving from `TraceListener` and overriding its `Write` and `WriteLine` methods. This is especially useful if you want to standardize application tracing throughout your organization.

Note

> Developing a custom listener can also be a powerful technique because the overloaded `Write` and `WriteLine` methods of the `Debug` and `Trace` classes also support passing objects directly to the listener. In this way, you can write a listener that abstracts the trace processing of an object so that developers using your listener don't need to be concerned with passing specific data to the listener.

17

The second part of the conditional tracing technique shown in the base class is the use of the `BooleanSwitch` object. Basically, switch objects like `_daSwitch` in the `ComputeBooksDABase` class enable applications to control whether trace or debug output is displayed. In this case, you'll notice that the switch is instantiated in the `_initClass` method and is passed two values in the constructor. The first is the `DisplayName`; the second is the `Description`. The `DisplayName` property is the name associated with the switch throughout the application and used in the application's configuration file to turn the switch on and off. The `Description` is simply human-readable text.

To use the switch, the client application can include a `system.diagnostics` element with the application configuration file. For example, a client application that uses a descendant of `ComputeBooksDABase` might have the following section in its configuration file (Web.config for ASP.NET applications):

```xml
<?xml version="1.0"?>
<configuration>
 <system.diagnostics>
    <switches>
        <add name="daSwitch" value="1" />
    </switches>
    <trace autoflush="true" indentsize="4">
    </trace>
 </system.diagnostics>
</configuration>
```

Here, `daSwitch` is set to 1, which is on or enabled. By default, if the switch isn't found in the configuration file, its `Enabled` property will be set to `False`. In addition, the file here indicates that the `AutoFlush` property of the `Trace` object should be set to `True` so that data will automatically be flushed from the buffer to the underlying stream with each write.

Now you can see how the `WriteTrace` method works. It simply tests to the `Enabled` property of the switch object using the protected `SwitchEnabled` property and then writes the message passed to it to the trace listeners.

Custom Exceptions

The other service that base class encapsulates is the throwing of exceptions. The technique used here is for the base class to use a custom exception class particular to the ComputeBooks data services tier called `ComputeBooksDAException`, as shown in Listing 17.2.

LISTING 17.2 A custom exception. This class is used by the base class and its descendants to wrap exceptions.

```
Namespace ComputeBooks.Data

  <Serializable()> _
  Public Class ComputeBookDAException : Inherits ApplicationException

    Public Sub New(ByVal message As String)
      MyBase.New(message)
    End Sub

    Public Sub New(ByVal message As String, _
      ByVal originalException As Exception)
      MyBase.New(message, originalException)
    End Sub

    Protected Sub New(ByVal info As SerializationInfo, _
      ByVal context As StreamingContext)
      MyBase.New(info, context)
    End Sub

    ' Add custom members here
  End Class
End Namespace
```

ANALYSIS Like the base class, the `ComputeBooksDAException` class exists in the `ComputeBooks.Data` namespace, although it derives from `ApplicationException`. Because it inherits most of its functionality from `ApplicationException`, it simply needs to define constructors that, in this case, accept either a message or a message in conjunction with the original exception that was thrown.

> **Note**
>
> The class is marked with the `Serializable` attribute so that it can be serialized across application domains by the common language runtime in the event that this exception is raised in code running remotely. You'll note that the class also includes a protected constructor that assists in the serialization process.

The protected `ThrowComputeBookException` method then uses this class by creating a new instance of it and throwing it back to the caller. An example of how this technique is used can be seen in the constructor of `ComputeBooksDABase` that accepts the connect string. There, the code uses a `Try Catch` block to catch exceptions raised by setting the `ConnectionString` property of the `SqlConnection` object. If one is caught, it is encapsulated in a `ComputeBookDAException` and is thrown. In this way, clients can differentiate exceptions coming from the base class and its descendants from other classes using their own `Try Catch` logic.

Handling Serviced Components

The base class shown in Listing 17.1 works wonderfully when your data access classes don't rely on Component Services for distributed transactions, object pooling, and other services. For a class to use these services, it must inherit directly or indirectly from the `ServicedComponent` class in the `System.EnterpriseServices` namespace. Because the .NET Framework supports only single inheritance, classes derived from `ComputeBooksDABase`, as shown in Listing 17.1, can't use Component Services. As a result, if you know that your classes will use these services, you can create a second base class that mimics the first but that derives from `ServicedComponent`, as shown in Listing 17.3. Both classes can then be made available in the same assembly so that developers can choose which to derive from, depending on their requirements.

LISTING 17.3 Serviced component base class. This class can be used as the base class for serviced components.

```
Namespace ComputeBooks.Data
  <ClassInterface(ClassInterfaceType.AutoDual), _
    Transaction(TransactionOption.Supported), _
    EventTrackingEnabled(True), _
    ConstructionEnabled(Enabled:=True)> _
  Public MustInherit Class ComputeBooksDAServicedBase
    Inherits ServicedComponent

    Private _connect As String
    Private _daSwitch As BooleanSwitch
```

LISTING 17.3   continued

```
Private _sqlCon As SqlConnection

Public Sub New()
  _sqlCon = New SqlConnection()
  _daSwitch = New BooleanSwitch("daSwitch", "Data Access")
  ' Add a listener for the Event Log
  Trace.Listeners.Add(New EventLogTraceListener("ComputeBooksDA"))
End Sub

Protected ReadOnly Property SqlCon() As SqlConnection
  Get
    Return _sqlCon
  End Get
End Property

Public Property ConstructString() As String
  Set(ByVal Value As String)
    _connect = Value
  End Set
  Get
    Return _connect
  End Get
End Property

Protected ReadOnly Property SwitchEnabled() As Boolean
  Get
    Return _daSwitch.Enabled
  End Get
End Property

Protected NotOverridable Overrides Sub Construct(ByVal s As String)
  ' Implements object construction
  _connect = s
  Try
    _sqlCon = New SqlConnection(_connect)
  Catch e As Exception
    Me.ThrowComputeBookException("Connect string cannot be set", e)
  End Try
End Sub

Protected Overrides Function CanBePooled() As Boolean
  ' Default is that the objects will not be pooled
  Return False
End Function

Protected Overrides Sub Activate()
  WriteTrace("Activate")
End Sub
```

LISTING 17.3   continued

```vb
Protected Overrides Sub Deactivate()
  WriteTrace("Deactivate")
End Sub

Protected Overridable Sub WriteTrace(ByVal eventMessage As String)
  ' Writes the event to the Application log
  Dim objLog As EventLog

  Try
    Trace.WriteLineIf(Me.SwitchEnabled, _
      Now & ": " & eventMessage & vbCrLf & _createTraceString())
  Catch e As Exception
    ' Not important so skip it
  End Try
End Sub

Private Function _createTraceString() As String
  ' Used to write events to the application event log
  Dim traceMess As New StringBuilder()

  With traceMess
    .Append("Class: " & Me.GetType.ToString & vbCrLf)
    .Append("Construct String: " & _connect & vbCrLf)
    .Append("Activity:" & ContextUtil.ActivityId.ToString & vbCrLf)
    .Append("Context:" & ContextUtil.ContextId.ToString & vbCrLf)
    .Append("Transaction?" & ContextUtil.IsInTransaction.ToString & vbCrLf)
    .Append("Security?" & ContextUtil.IsSecurityEnabled.ToString & vbCrLf)
    If ContextUtil.IsInTransaction Then
      .Append("TransactionId:" & _
        ContextUtil.TransactionId.ToString & vbCrLf)
      .Append("Direct Caller:" & _
        SecurityCallContext.CurrentCall.DirectCaller.AccountName & vbCrLf)
      .Append("Original Caller:" & _
        SecurityCallContext.CurrentCall.OriginalCaller.AccountName)
    End If
  End With

  Return traceMess.ToString()
End Function

Protected Sub ThrowComputeBookException(ByVal message As String, _
  ByVal e As Exception)
  Dim newMine As New ComputeBookDAException(message, e)

  ' Trace the error
  WriteTrace(message & "{" & e.Message & "}")

  ' Throw
  Throw newMine
End Sub
```

17

LISTING 17.3   continued

```
End Class
End Namespace
```

ANALYSIS   You can see that the `ComputeBooksDAServicedBase` class is substantially the
same as the class shown in Listing 17.1, with the following changes:

- It inherits from `ServicedComponent` to give it access to the Component Services infrastructure.

- It includes attributes from the `System.EnterpriseServices` namespace to indicate that a dual COM interface is created when the class is placed in Component Services, that distributed transactions are supported, that statistical tracking is enabled, and that the object construction is enabled.

- It overrides the `Construct` method of `ServicedComponent` in order to catch the connection string that is specified in the Component Services Manager.

- Its constructor automatically creates an `EventLogTraceListener` so that trace output will also be redirected to the Application event log under the source ComputeBooksDA.

- The private `_createTraceString` method collects information about the serviced component through the `ContextUtil` and `CallContext` objects so that the `WriteTrace` method can output this information to the log.

In addition to these differences, you'll notice that the `ComputeBooksDAServicedBase` doesn't expose a parameterized constructor. It doesn't need to because the connection string will be fed to the object from the `Construct` method automatically. In any event, serviced components shouldn't expose parameterized constructors because Component Services doesn't know how to handle them.

It's also important to note that even though the base class specifies attributes such as `Transaction` as defaults, the derived class can and should override them by specifying the attribute as well. For example, the declaration of the following class overrides the transactional behavior because the component requires transactions rather than simply supporting them:

```
<ClassInterface(ClassInterfaceType.AutoDual), _
Transaction(TransactionOption.Required)> _
Public Class ComputeBooksStores : Inherits ComputeBooksDAServicedBase

  <AutoComplete()> _
  Public Sub DoSomething()
    ' Do my work
```

```
        MyBase.WriteTrace("Done doing my stuff")
    End Sub

End Class
```

> **Note**   For more information about using Component Services, see Chapter 9 of my Sams book *Building Distributed Applications with Visual Basic .NET*.

Designing Data Access Classes

After your base class has been created, you can move on to creating the actual data access classes that make up your data services tier. Once again, the purpose of the data access classes is to isolate the data access logic from the other tiers and provide a robust interface for manipulating the data in your application.

As you design and implement the classes, however, you'll run across several design issues that you must address. This section is designed to give you a feel for those issues and then show how you can abstract the .NET Data Provider used and implement a purely class-based approach in your data services tier, as mentioned on Day 15, "Using ADO.NET in a Multi-Tier Application."

Design Issues

There are several design issues that you'll want to address as you design your classes. These apply not only to data access classes, but also to other classes that you design for reuse.

> **Note**   For additional information on class design issues in .NET, see "Design Guidelines for Class Library Developers" in the online documentation. Microsoft released a tool on www.gotdotnet.com called Microsoft FxCop. This utility analyzes assemblies and provides information as to how well it conforms to the Microsoft design guidelines.

Data-Centric Versus Application-Centric

As you approach data access classes, one of your first decision points is whether to design your data access classes to be data-centric or application-centric. In other words, should the methods of the classes simply reflect how the data is stored in the data store, or should they reflect how the data is used in the application? Using the former approach results in a very granular approach because you create a class for each table in the ComputeBooks database and well-defined methods for each class, such as Get, Add, Delete, and Update. The latter approach typically results in fewer classes defined along functional boundaries, such as a WebData class used in ComputeBook's public Web site. This class might contain methods such as GetTitles that support the arguments typically used for displaying title information on the site. Of course, depending on the complexity you expect, you might also factor the methods into multiple application-specific classes along data-centric lines, such as Titles, Stores, and Orders.

Generally, I recommend using the application-centric approach because it offers the biggest bang for the buck. Using this approach, the classes are immediately able to be used productively and result in fewer lines of code in the presentation and business services tiers. Further, the ways in which the data needs to be accessed in multiple applications usually converge, and so using this approach often results in reusability as well. By contrast, using a data-centric approach results in you having to write more code in both the data services and other tiers. Remember that one of the goals of the data services tier is abstraction, so simply exposing each table as a class basically exposes the data model itself. However, it should be cautioned that using an application-centric approach doesn't mean that your data access classes perform business logic. Always keep in mind that the purpose of the data access classes is to select, insert, update, and delete data, not to apply business rules or processes.

> **Tip**
>
> I would also make the same recommendation at the stored procedure layer. Generally, you want to create application-specific stored procedures that access data as it needs to be manipulated in the application. This entails using WHERE, JOIN, and ORDER BY clauses liberally and returning only the columns required for the application-specific functionality. For this reason, if multiple applications are going to access the same database, you should consider using an additional application-specific prefix in your naming conventions for stored procedures.

Naming Conventions and Constructors

After you've decided on an approach, you need to apply solid coding practices to the design. Two of the primary issues you'll need to consider are using naming conventions and constructors.

Naming Conventions

You've probably noticed that the capitalization conventions for classes, variables, data types, arguments, and so on are slightly different than those you might have used before. In fact, the .NET Framework classes use three different styles of capitalization:

- Pascal case
- Camel case
- Uppercase

NEW TERM **Pascal case** is the most prevalent and refers to identifiers with no spaces and where each individual word is capitalized. In .NET, you should use Pascal case to identify classes, enumerated types, events, public fields, interfaces, methods, namespaces, and properties. For example, the declaration of the ComputeBooksDABase class in Listing 17.1 uses Pascal case.

NEW TERM The second most prevalent convention is the use of **camel case.** Camel case refers to identifiers in which the first word in the identifier is left as lowercase whereas subsequent words are capitalized. In the .NET Framework, camel case is used for parameters and protected fields, so, for example, the constructor of the ComputeBookDAException class was defined as follows:

```
Public Sub New(ByVal message as String, ByVal originalException as Exception)
```

Note

Notice that the parameters use camel casing, whereas the names of the method and the types use Pascal casing.

NEW TERM **Uppercase** is reserved only for identifiers that consist of two or fewer letters. As a result, you'll typically see uppercase used for namespaces such as System.IO and System.Web.UI. Keep in mind as well that different languages handle capitalization differently, so you don't want to create code that requires case sensitivity. In other words, if you are writing a class in C# (which is case sensitive), you shouldn't create both ReadXml and readXml methods because clients using VB .NET (which is case sensitive) wouldn't be able to differentiate between the two.

What Happened to Hungarian Notation?

VB .NET developers will note that in VB and VBScript, parameters and variables often had a two- or three-letter prefix that denoted the data type. Some also had a prefix that denoted the scope. For example, str was used for strings and int was used for integers, whereas m was used for modules level and l was used for local. This Hungarian notation was informative but resulted in long variable and parameter names. For the most part, Hungarian notation is no longer used in .NET. Instead, the identifier, especially if it is visible externally, should be in camel case and simply describe the meaning of the variable or parameter. The only prefix that you'll typically see is an underscore to denote that a field or method is private to a class.

Namespaces should also use Pascal case, as in the `ComputeBooks.Data` namespace we discussed earlier.

You should use consistent naming rules when naming your classes and interfaces. In the earlier example of the `ComputeBookDAException` class, the class name is a noun or noun phrase, uses Pascal casing, and is not prefixed with a "C" as you sometimes see (particularly in previous versions of VB). In addition, class names shouldn't use underscores and should avoid abbreviations where possible. In this case, the class name also contains a piece of its base class name to identify that `ComputeBookDAException` is a type of `Exception`. This can be useful as a general rule in order to assist developers using your class in getting an immediate feel for how your class might behave. However, it isn't a hard and fast rule.

Interfaces follow many of the same rules, such as the prohibition on underscores and abbreviations and the use of Pascal casing. However, interfaces should be prefixed with an "I" and can be named using an adjective phrase that describes the functionality exposed by the interface (instead of using a descriptive noun or noun phrase). For example, the .NET Framework contains the `ICloneable` interface, which is implemented by a whole host of classes, such as `String`, `Stack`, `Array`, `SortedList`, and `Delegate` among others. Here, "cloneable" is an adjective that describes the functionality that the class gains by implementing the interface. Class and interface names should also only differ by the "I" prefix when the class is the standard implementation of the interface. For example, the `ComputeBooksDABase` class might provide the standard implementation of the `IComputeBooksDABase` interface.

Constructors

NEW TERM A concept that might be new to some developers developing data access classes is the use of **constructors** that can be parameterized and overloaded to allow parameters to be passed into the instance of a class during its initialization. There are several guidelines that you should be aware of, however, when defining constructors on your classes.

First, make sure that you limit the amount of work done in the constructor. Typically, a constructor should only capture the parameters passed to it and initialize private data within the instance. By performing lots of other work, you'll cause the class to appear sluggish and perhaps do extra work for nothing because the user of the class might never call another method on it. Rather, you should defer the work until the user of the class calls the specific feature. Additionally, the parameters you pass into a constructor should be viewed as shortcuts for setting properties on the class after the class has been created using an empty constructor. Thus, the following two C# code snippets should be semantically equivalent:

```
Stores s = new Stores();
s.Switch = mySwitch;
s.ConnectString = "server=ssosa;database=Quilogy;trusted_connection=yes";

Stores s = new Stores(
  "server=ssosa;database=Quilogy;trusted_connection=yes", mySwitch);
```

Note

> Note as well that the order the properties are set in the first snippet and the order they are exposed in the constructor in the second snippet shouldn't matter. In other words, all properties in a class should be able to be set in any order.

17

Second, in cases in which the constructor is overloaded to include different signatures, you should use a consistent ordering and naming pattern for the parameters. The typical approach is to provide an increasing number of parameters in order to allow the user of the class to provide more detailed information if required. In the previous example, the Stores class might provide the following three constructors:

```
Public Class Stores
  Public Sub New()
    ' implementation
  End Sub

  Public Sub New(ByVal connect As String)
    ' implementation
  End Sub

  Public Sub New(ByVal connect As String, ByVal trace As Switch)
    ' implementation
  End Sub
End Class
```

NEW TERM   In this case, the user can pass in more detailed information by using the second constructor and passing in a class derived from System.Diagnostics.Switch to capture trace output. Along these same lines, C# includes an interesting syntax that enables you to easily allow one constructor to call another using what is referred to as an **initializer list**. This is useful because it allows a default constructor (the one with no arguments), for example, to call one of the more specific constructors using default parameters. If the Stores class were rewritten in C#, the default constructor could call one of the other constructors automatically, as follows:

```
public Class Stores
{
  public Stores() : this("server=ssosa")
```

```
  {
    // implementation
  }

  public Stores(String connect)
  {
    // implementation
  }

  public Stores(String connect, Switch trace)
  {
    // implementation
  }
}
```

For special purposes, you can also create constructors that aren't public. Creating a protected constructor allows derived classes to pass specific information to the base class that it needs to operate while creating an empty private constructor in a class if you don't want instances of the class to be created. The latter technique is useful if the class exposes only Shared (static in C#) methods and so shouldn't be able to be instantiated. Keep in mind that if you don't create a constructor for a class, both C# and VB .NET will create a default constructor that accepts no arguments. However, after you create a constructor that accepts arguments, the compiler doesn't create the empty constructor.

Finally, constructors must also be considered when you create derived classes. For example, it's often necessary to pass information obtained in a parameterized constructor into the base class. This is the case, for example, when a class derived from Exception accepts a message in its constructor, as the ComputeBookDAException class does in Listing 17.2. At first glance, this might seem difficult because you would think that a base class must be initialized before its descendant classes. However, both VB .NET and C# include specific syntax that enables you to pass information from a derived constructor to its base class. In VB .NET, this is done by calling the New method of the MyBase object in the first line of the constructor, passing it the arguments it needs, as shown in Listing 17.2. In C#, the constructor declaration uses the base keyword like so:

```
public ComputeBookDAException(String message) : base(message)
{
  // other initialization here
}
```

In both cases, the base class is initialized using the message parameter passed to the constructor.

Overloaded and Private Methods

Finally, the design of your data access classes should take advantage of the ability to overload methods. This technique, which allows a single method to expose multiple signatures so that developers can choose which signature to call based on their needs, is especially effective in the methods used to query a data store. For example, consider the Books class shown in Listing 17.4.

LISTING 17.4 Data access class. This class takes advantage of overloaded and private methods to allow querying on the `Titles` table.

```
Option Strict On

Imports System.Data.SqlClient
Imports System.Data

Namespace ComputeBooks.Data

  Public Class Books : Inherits ComputeBooksDABase

    Public Sub New(ByVal connect As String)
      MyBase.New(connect)
    End Sub

    Public Sub New()
      MyBase.New()
    End Sub

    Public Overloads Function GetTitles() As DataSet
      _checkDisposed()
      Return _getTitles(Nothing, Nothing, Nothing, Nothing, Nothing)
    End Function

    Public Overloads Function GetTitles(ByVal isbn As String) As DataSet
      _checkDisposed()

      ' Validate
      If isbn Is Nothing OrElse isbn.Length = 0 Then
        Throw New ArgumentNullException("isbn", "Cannot be null or empty")
        Return Nothing
      End If
      Return _getTitles(Nothing, Nothing, isbn, Nothing, Nothing)
    End Function

    Public Overloads Function GetTitles(ByVal params() As Object) As DataSet
      _checkDisposed()

      ' Validate
      If params.Length <> 5 Then
        Throw New ArgumentException("Must pass in an array of 5 values")
        Return Nothing
      End If
```

LISTING 17.4   continued

```vb
    Dim author, isbn, title As String
    Dim pubdate As Date
    Dim catId As Guid

    Try
      author = CType(params(0), String)
      title = CType(params(1), String)
      isbn = CType(params(2), String)
      pubdate = CType(params(4), Date)
      catId = CType(params(3), Guid)
    Catch e As Exception
      Throw New ArgumentException("Arguments are not of the correct type")
    End Try


    Return _getTitles(author, title, isbn, pubdate, catId)
End Function

Private Function _getTitles(ByVal author As String, ByVal title As String, _
  ByVal isbn As String, ByVal lowPubDate As Date, _
  ByVal catID As Guid) As DataSet
  Dim da As New SqlDataAdapter("usp_GetTitles", MyBase.SqlCon)
  Dim titleDs As New DataSet()

  da.SelectCommand.CommandType = CommandType.StoredProcedure
  Try
    If Not isbn Is Nothing AndAlso isbn.Length > 0 Then
      da.SelectCommand.Parameters.Add(New SqlParameter("@isbn", _
        SqlDbType.NVarChar, 10))
      da.SelectCommand.Parameters(0).Value = isbn
    Else
      If Not title Is Nothing AndAlso title.Length > 0 Then
        da.SelectCommand.Parameters.Add(New SqlParameter("@title", _
          SqlDbType.NVarChar, 100))
        da.SelectCommand.Parameters(0).Value = title
      End If
      If Not author Is Nothing AndAlso author.Length > 0 Then
        da.SelectCommand.Parameters.Add(New SqlParameter("@author", _
          SqlDbType.NVarChar, 250))
        da.SelectCommand.Parameters(0).Value = author
      End If
      If lowPubDate.Equals(Nothing) Then
        da.SelectCommand.Parameters.Add(New SqlParameter("@pubDate", _
          SqlDbType.DateTime))
        da.SelectCommand.Parameters(0).Value = lowPubDate
      End If
      If Not catID.Equals(Guid.Empty) Then
        da.SelectCommand.Parameters.Add(New SqlParameter("@catId", _
          SqlDbType.UniqueIdentifier))
        da.SelectCommand.Parameters(0).Value = catID
```

LISTING 17.4 continued

```
        End If
      End If

      da.Fill(titleDs)
      Return titleDs
    Catch e As SqlException
      da = Nothing
      titleDs = Nothing
      Call MyBase.ThrowComputeBookException("GetTitles Failed", e)
    Finally
      If Not MyBase.SqlCon Is Nothing Then MyBase.SqlCon.Close()
    End Try
  End Function

    ' Other methods here

  Private Sub _checkDisposed()
    If MyBase.Disposed Then
      Throw New ObjectDisposedException("Books has been disposed")
    End If
  End Sub

  End Class

End Namespace
```

ANALYSIS You'll notice in Listing 17.4 that the Books class exists in the ComputeBooks.Data namespace and inherits from ComputeBooksDABase. After exposing both a parameterized and empty constructor, it exposes three signatures for the GetTitles method using the Overloads keyword.

Note The Overloads keyword isn't required in VB as long as none of the method signatures uses it. However, I recommend using it because it makes explicit your intention. In C#, there is no equivalent keyword.

You'll notice that methods allow the caller to specify no arguments, only the ISBN, or an array of optional parameters. In all three cases, the public method ultimately calls the private _getTitles method that accepts each argument individually. Obviously, implementing the logic of the GetTitles method once in a private method makes it easier to maintain and extend. However, before the private method is called, the public method is responsible for validating the arguments. For example, the signature that accepts the

ISBN ensures that a valid value is passed in and, if not, throws the
ArgumentNullException. In the case of the method that accepts the array of objects, it
checks to ensure that the array contains the correct number of objects and then parses the
array into the local variables passed to the private method.

The private _getTitles method is then responsible for creating the SqlDataAdapter
object and populating its Parameters collection. Note that the parameters are added to
the collection only if the values are valid. In this way, the method can effectively support
optional parameters. Note also that the usp_GetTitles stored procedure is where the
work of creating the SELECT statement to retrieve the data is performed. In this way, only
one stored procedure is needed to query the Titles table in different ways. After the
parameters are populated, the DataSet is filled and returned.

 Note

> The usp_GetTitles stored procedure defaults the parameters to NULL and
> then builds a SELECT statement based on the parameters that are actually
> passed. The statement is then executed using the SQL Server sp_executesql
> system stored procedure.

Using this technique also has the advantage of being maintainable because the signature
that exposes the array of objects can obviously be extended to query using different or an
extended set of parameters without affecting the public interface exposed to callers.

To call the GetTitles method, a client can then instantiate the Books class and then call
either of the three versions of the GetTitles method. This is shown in the following
snippet:

```
Books b = new Books(_connect);
DataSet ds = new DataSet();

ds = b.GetTitles();  // returns all titles
ds = b.GetTitles("06720001X");  //returns one ISBN
ds = b.GetTitles(new Object[]
  {"Fox, Dan", null, null, null, null });  // returns books authored by me
```

Abstracting Providers

As you learned last week, one of the decisions you must make when designing an application is which .NET Data Provider to use because ADO.NET supports both specific and
generic providers. Which provider you choose depends on a variety of factors, including
the functionality and performance of the provider in addition to the likelihood of your
switching data stores in the future. In fact, many independent software vendors (ISVs)
developing packaged applications will need to make this decision very early in their use
of ADO.NET.

You'll notice that both the `ComputeBooksDABase` and `Books` classes assume that they will always access SQL Server because they are hardcoded to use the objects in the `System.Data.SqlClient` namespace. In the event that ComputeBooks moved to an Oracle solution in the future, these classes would have to be rewritten to use either the OleDb provider or a specific Oracle provider that might be available by then. To make these classes more generic, one solution, of course, would be to simply use the OleDb provider because it can be used to access either SQL Server or Oracle based on the OLE DB provider in use. Although this would result in a single code base, you would lose the performance and functionality gains of a specific provider like SqlClient. A second option is to develop multiple versions of each class and then compile various versions of the application using command line switches. This might appeal to ISVs that need to support multiple data stores but require the performance of specific providers.

However, a more elegant solution is to design your classes with an additional layer of abstraction using the abstract factory design pattern. Using this pattern, both the base class and the data access class can rely on a factory class to create the objects of the appropriate type based on configuration settings. The `ProviderFactory` class that uses this approach is shown in Listing 17.5.

17

LISTING 17.5   Abstracting providers. This class abstracts the creation of provider-specific objects and uses interfaces to return the objects.

```
Namespace ComputeBooks.Data

  Public Enum ProviderType
    SqlClient = 0
    OLEDB = 1
  End Enum

  Public Class ProviderFactory

    Sub New(ByVal provider As ProviderType)
      _pType = provider
    End Sub

    Sub New()
    End Sub

    Private _pType As ProviderType = ProviderType.SqlClient
    Private _pTypeSet As Boolean = False

    Public Property Provider() As ProviderType
      Get
        Return _pType
      End Get
```

LISTING 17.5 continued

```
        Set(ByVal Value As ProviderType)
          If _pTypeSet Then
            Throw New ReadOnlyException("Provider already set to " & _
              pType.ToString)
          Else
            _pType = Value
            _pTypeSet = True
          End If
        End Set
      End Property

      Public Function CreateDataAdapter(ByVal commandText As String, _
        ByVal connection As IDbConnection) As IDataAdapter
        Try
          Select Case _pType
            Case ProviderType.SqlClient
              Return New SqlDataAdapter(commandText, _
                CType(connection, SqlConnection))
            Case ProviderType.OLEDB
              Return New OleDbDataAdapter(commandText, _
                CType(connection, OleDbConnection))
          End Select
        Catch e As Exception
          Throw New ComputeBookDAException( _
            "Could not create IDbDataAdapter object", e)
        End Try
      End Function

      Public Overloads Function CreateParameter(ByVal paramName As String, _
        ByVal paramType As Object) As IDataParameter
        Try
          Select Case _pType
            Case ProviderType.SqlClient
              Return New SqlParameter(paramName, paramType)
            Case ProviderType.OLEDB
              Return New OleDbParameter(paramName, paramType)
          End Select
        Catch e As Exception
          Throw New ComputeBookDAException( _
            "Could not create IDataParameter object", e)
        End Try
      End Function

      Public Overloads Function CreateParameter(ByVal paramName As String, _
        ByVal paramType As Object, ByVal size As Integer) As IDataParameter
        Try
          Select Case _pType
            Case ProviderType.SqlClient
```

LISTING 17.5 continued

```
            Return New SqlParameter(paramName, _
              CType(paramType, SqlDbType), size)
          Case ProviderType.OLEDB
            Return New OleDbParameter(paramName, _
              CType(paramType, OleDbType), size)
        End Select
      Catch e As Exception
        Throw New ComputeBookDAException( _
          "Could not create IDataParameter object", e)
      End Try
    End Function

    Public Function CreateConnection(ByVal connect As String) As IDbConnection
      Try
        Select Case _pType
          Case ProviderType.SqlClient
            Return New SqlConnection(connect)
          Case ProviderType.OLEDB
            Return New OleDbConnection(connect)
        End Select
      Catch e As Exception
        Throw New ComputeBookDAException( _
          "Could not create IDbConnection object", e)
      End Try
    End Function

    Public Function CreateCommand(ByVal cmdText As String, _
      ByVal connection As IDbConnection) As IDbCommand
      Try
        Select Case _pType
          Case ProviderType.SqlClient
            Return New SqlCommand(cmdText, CType(connection, SqlConnection))
          Case ProviderType.OLEDB
            Return New OleDbCommand(cmdText, _
              CType(connection, OleDbConnection))
        End Select
      Catch e As Exception
        Throw New ComputeBookDAException("Could not create IDbCommand object", e)
      End Try
    End Function

  End Class
End Namespace
```

17

ANALYSIS The ProviderFactory class simply exposes a property called Provider, which can be passed in the constructor and which specifies the provider that is to be used using the `ProviderType` enumerated type (which, in this case, supports the SqlClient and OleDb providers). The class then includes a series of `Create` methods that create the appropriate data adapter, parameter, connection, and command objects for the provider using a simple `Select Case` statement. Note that the `CreateParameter` method is overloaded so that the size can also be specified.

 Note

> A more generic technique to implement a provider factory could easily be implemented by using a configuration file that enumerated the supported providers. Then the `Activator` class in the `System` namespace could be used to dynamically create instances of the appropriate classes. We'll look at this technique tomorrow.

In all cases, the factory methods accept parameters and return values using the interfaces that both providers support and that we discussed on Day 8, "Understanding .NET Data Providers."

After the `ProviderFactory` is in place, classes such as `Books` can create an instance of the class in their constructors, passing in the appropriate provider, typically found in a configuration file, like so:

```
Public Sub New(ByVal connect As String, ByVal provider As ProviderType)
   MyBase.New()
   _pf = New ProviderFactory(provider)
   MyBase.Con = _pf.CreateConnection(connect)
End Sub
```

In this case, the variable _pf refers to a private data member that references an instance of the `ProviderFactory` class. Note that the constructor of the class has been augmented to support passing in the provider as well as the connection string. In addition, the base class has also been modified so that the protected `Con` property (of type `IDbConnection`) can be set using the `CreateConnection` method.

Note

> If your base class needs to rely on the `ProviderFactory` as well, you might instead simply declare a private variable of `ProviderFactory` in the base class and expose it as a protected property.

Methods within the data access classes such as _getTitles can then be rewritten to use the instance of the `ProviderFactory` class as shown in Listing 17.6.

LISTING 17.6   Using the `ProviderFactory` class. This method uses the `ProviderFactory` to create the appropriate objects based on the provider.

```vb
Private Function _getTitles(ByVal author As String, ByVal title As String, _
 ByVal isbn As String, ByVal lowPubDate As Date, _
 ByVal catID As Guid) As DataSet
 Dim da As IDbDataAdapter
 Dim titleDs As New DataSet()

 da = _pf.CreateDataAdapter("usp_GetTitles", MyBase.Con)

 da.SelectCommand.CommandType = CommandType.StoredProcedure
 Try
   If Not isbn Is Nothing AndAlso isbn.Length > 0 Then
     da.SelectCommand.Parameters.Add(_pf.CreateParameter("@isbn", _
       DbType.String, 10))
     da.SelectCommand.Parameters(0).Value = isbn
   Else
     If Not title Is Nothing AndAlso title.Length > 0 Then
       da.SelectCommand.Parameters.Add(_pf.CreateParameter("@title", _
         DbType.String, 100))
       da.SelectCommand.Parameters(0).Value = title
     End If
     If Not author Is Nothing AndAlso author.Length > 0 Then
       da.SelectCommand.Parameters.Add(_pf.CreateParameter("@author", _
         DbType.String, 250))
       da.SelectCommand.Parameters(0).Value = author
     End If
     If lowPubDate.Equals(Nothing) Then
       da.SelectCommand.Parameters.Add(_pf.CreateParameter("@pubDate", _
         DbType.DateTime))
       da.SelectCommand.Parameters(0).Value = lowPubDate
     End If
     If Not catID.Equals(Guid.Empty) Then
       da.SelectCommand.Parameters.Add(_pf.CreateParameter("@catId", _
         DbType.GUID))
       da.SelectCommand.Parameters(0).Value = catID
     End If
   End If

   da.Fill(titleDs)
   Return titleDs
 Catch e As Exception
   da = Nothing
   titleDs = Nothing
   Call MyBase.ThrowComputeBookException("GetTitles Failed", e)
 Finally
   If Not MyBase.Con Is Nothing Then MyBase.Con.Close()
 End Try
End Function
```

17

The point to note in Listing 17.6 is that the method doesn't use any of the SqlClient-specific objects (or enumerations), so it can be executed using either provider.

Returning Custom Objects

The final issue to consider when designing data access classes is how the data will be returned. As you learned on Day 15, your choices include exposing DataSet objects, data readers, or custom objects. Although the first two options are simplified by the fact that ADO.NET supports them natively, the third option is attractive because it provides a pure object-based interface to the data for clients rather than through the abstraction of DataSet or data reader. As you'll see, however, this approach also results in you having to write more code to populate the classes and manipulate their data.

As an example, consider the case in which ComputeBooks wants to expose its customer data using custom classes. To begin, you would write a Customer class that exposed the properties of the customer. In addition, you could factor properties that have their own properties such as Address into separate classes as shown in Listing 17.7.

LISTING 17.7 Data as an object. This listing shows the Customer and Address classes used to represent a customer.

```
<Serializable()> _
Public Class Customer

  Private _custId As Guid
  Private _fName As String
  Private _lName As String
  Private _emailAddress As String

  <XmlElement()> _
  Public Address As Address

  Public Sub New(ByVal values() As Object)
    'Array of values
    If values.Length = 8 Then
      Me.CustomerID = values(0)
      Me.FName = values(1)
      Me.LName = values(2)
      Me.EmailAddress = values(7)

      Me.Address = New Address()
      With Me.Address
        .Street = values(3)
        .City = values(4)
        .StateProv = values(5)
        .PostalCode = values(6)
      End With
```

LISTING 17.7   continued

```
   Else
     Throw New ComputeBookDAException( _
       "The array passed into the Customer was invalid")
   End If
   End Sub

Public Sub New()
End Sub

<XmlAttributeAttribute("ID")> _
Public Property CustomerID() As System.Guid
  Get
    Return _custId
  End Get
  Set(ByVal Value As System.Guid)
    _custId = Value
  End Set
End Property

<XmlElement()> _
Public Property FName() As String
  Get
    Return _fName
  End Get
  Set(ByVal Value As String)
    _fName = Value
  End Set
End Property

<XmlElement()> _
Public Property LName() As String
  Get
    Return _lName
  End Get
  Set(ByVal Value As String)
    _lName = Value
  End Set
End Property

<XmlElement()> _
Public Property EmailAddress() As String
  Get
    Return _emailAddress
  End Get
  Set(ByVal Value As String)
    _emailAddress = Value
  End Set
End Property
```

17

LISTING 17.7   continued

```vb
End Class


<Serializable()> _
Public Class Address

  Private _address As String
  Private _city As String
  Private _stateProv As String
  Private _postalCode As String
  Private _addType As AddressType

  Public Enum AddressType
    Home = 0
    Business = 1
  End Enum

  <XmlAttributeAttribute()> _
  Public Property Type() As AddressType
    Get
      Return _addType
    End Get
    Set(ByVal Value As AddressType)
      _addType = Value
    End Set
  End Property

  <XmlElement()> _
  Public Property Street() As String
    Get
      Return _address
    End Get
    Set(ByVal Value As String)
      _address = Value
    End Set
  End Property

  <XmlElement()> _
  Public Property City() As String
    Get
      Return _city
    End Get
    Set(ByVal Value As String)
      _city = Value
    End Set
  End Property

  <XmlElement()> _
  Public Property StateProv() As String
```

LISTING 17.7 continued

```
    Get
      Return _stateProv
    End Get
    Set(ByVal Value As String)
      _stateProv = Value
    End Set
  End Property

  <XmlElement()> _
  Public Property PostalCode() As String
    Get
      Return _postalCode
    End Get
    Set(ByVal Value As String)
      _postalCode = Value
    End Set
  End Property

End Class
```

ANALYSIS   Although much of Listing 17.7 is straightforward, the interesting aspect is that the class is marked with the `System.Xml.Serialization.SerializableAttribute`. This attribute ensures that the common language runtime can serialize an instance of this class. This is necessary if the object is passed between application domains or serialized to XML using the `XmlSerializer` class, for example, if you wanted to save the object to disk. In addition, each property is marked with an attribute that specifies how the property is to be represented when serialized (in this case, either an element, attribute, or array, although you could also specify other XML types or ignore the property altogether).

Tip

If you already have an XSD document that describes your data, you can alternatively use the XSD.exe command-line utility to auto-generate these skeleton classes for you.

To represent multiple customers, you could create a strongly typed collection class to hold them as shown in Listing 17.8.

LISTING 17.8   Creating a collection. This class holds a collection of Customer objects and is derived from CollectionBase.

```
Public Class CustomersCollection : Inherits CollectionBase
  ' Stores a collection of customers

  Public Sub Add(ByVal c As Customer)
    Me.InnerList.Add(c)
  End Sub

  Default Public ReadOnly Property Item( _
    ByVal i As Integer) As Customer
    Get
      Return Me.InnerList(i)
    End Get
  End Property

End Class
```

In this case, the CustomersCollection class inherits from CollectionBase and simply holds an ArrayList that contains the Customer objects. Because this class supports the IList and IEnumerable interfaces, it can be bound to controls in both Windows and Web Forms user interfaces, as you learned yesterday. This class can then be used to return a collection of customers in a data access class like so:

```
Public Class Customers : Inherits ComputeBooksDABase

  <XmlArray()> _
  Public Function GetCustomers() As CustomersCollection
    ' implementation
  End Function

  ' Other members
End Class
```

After this infrastructure has been coded, you have to write some code that loads the persisted state of the object to an instance of your class. For example, your data access class could expose a GetCustomer method like that shown in Listing 17.9 to create an instance of the Customer object and return it to the client.

LISTING 17.9   Populating an object. Behind the scenes, you can use an ADO.NET data reader to populate your objects.

```
Public Function GetCustomer( _
  ByVal emailAddress As String) As Customer

  ' Go get a customer
  Dim cm As IDbCommand
```

LISTING 17.9   continued

```
    Dim parm As IDataParameter
    Dim dr As IDataReader
    Dim cust As Customer
    Dim values(7) As Object

    cm = pf.CreateCommand("usp_GetCustomers", _
      MyBase.Con)
    cm.CommandType = CommandType.StoredProcedure
    parm = pf.CreateParameter("@emailAddress", DbType.String)
    parm.Value = emailAddress
    cm.Parameters.Add(parm)

    Try
      MyBase.Con.Open()
      dr = cm.ExecuteReader(CommandBehavior.CloseConnection)
      dr.Read()
      dr.GetValues(values)
      _cleanValues(values)
      cust = New Customer(values)   ' Create a new Customer
    Catch Ex As Exception
      MyBase.ThrowComputeBookException("Could not get customer " & _
        emailAddress, Ex)
      Return Nothing
    Finally
      dr.Close()
    End Try

    Return cust

End Function
```

ANALYSIS   In Listing 17.9, the ProviderFactory from Listing 17.5 is used to create the command object to read the customer information from a stored procedure. The GetValues method then reads the entire row into an array and passes it to a private method that performs cleanup, such as trimming the string values and converting the null columns (DBNull.Value) to Nothing. The array is then passed to the constructor of the Customer object shown in Listing 17.7 and the new customer is returned from the method. Of course, you could also extend this code to retrieve more than one customer and populate the CustomerCollection. You would also need to provide your own implementation to save changes to the customer back to the data store.

Summary

When you design your data services tier, it's important to take advantage of the features of the .NET Framework to create flexible and effective classes. Today, you learned how

17

you can use features such as implementation inheritance, overloaded methods, interface-based programming, and serialization in your data access classes.

However, even if you follow the recommendations and techniques discussed today, you'll still end up writing quite a bit of repetitive ADO.NET code in your data access classes. Tomorrow, you'll learn how to take the abstractions discussed today one step further and implement a data factory class.

Workshop

This workshop will help reinforce the concepts covered in today's lesson.

Quiz

1. What is the purpose of creating a base class for your data services tier?

   Because there is some functionality that will be common across data access classes, both within a particular application and within an organization, it makes sense to implement that functionality once and then reuse it across all your classes. By factoring the common code into an abstract base class, you or other developers can take advantage of implementation inheritance in .NET to reuse core code that handles the common features, such as connections, logging, and exception handling.

2. Why would you need to create a separate base class for classes that will use Component Services?

   For a object to utilize the services of Component Services, such as distributed transactions, object pooling, and just-in-time activation, the class must ultimately be derived from the ServicedComponent class in the System.EnterpriseServices namespace. Because .NET supports only inheritance from a single base class, your base class needs to inherit from ServicedComponent.

3. What are some considerations you should be aware of as you design data classes?

   The most fundamental decision regards the granularity and design methods themselves. Typically, your classes will encapsulate more functionality if they are application-centric rather than data-centric. The former approach entails creating methods that map to the functionality of your application rather than mapping only to the data itself. Other considerations include using naming conventions and constructors and taking advantage of overloading in your classes.

4. Why might you use a provider factory class in your data services tier?

   A provider factory class can be used to offload the creation of provider-specific objects into a separate class that your data access classes can rely on. This allows the decision as to which provider to use to be delayed until runtime. This works by programming to the interfaces that all providers support rather than the concrete classes themselves.

Exercise

Augment the Books class shown in Listing 17.4 to add a GetReviews method that retrieves the reviews associated with a particular ISBN using the usp_GetReviews stored procedure and the ProviderFactory class shown in Listing 17.5.

Answers for Day 17

Exercise Answer

As with the GetTitles method, one possible solution is to create a method that uses the CreateDataAdapter and CreateParameter methods of the ProviderFactory class to create the appropriate objects and fill a DataSet, as shown in the following code:

```
Public Function GetReviews(ByVal isbn As String) As DataSet

  Dim da As IDbDataAdapter
  Dim reviewDs As New DataSet()

  da = _pf.CreateDataAdapter("usp_GetReviews", MyBase.Con)
  da.SelectCommand.CommandType = CommandType.StoredProcedure

  ' Validate
  If isbn Is Nothing OrElse isbn.Length = 0 Then
    Throw New ArgumentNullException("isbn", "Cannot be null or empty")
    Return Nothing
  End If

  Try
    da.SelectCommand.Parameters.Add( _
      _pf.CreateParameter("@isbn", DbType.String))
    da.SelectCommand.Parameters(0).Value = isbn
    da.Fill(reviewDs)
    Return reviewDs
  Catch e As Exception
    da = Nothing
    reviewDs = Nothing
    Call MyBase.ThrowComputeBookException("GetReviews Failed on ISBN " & isbn,
e)
  Finally
    If Not MyBase.Con Is Nothing Then MyBase.Con.Close()
  End Try
End Function
```

17

DAY **18**

Building a Data Factory

Yesterday, you learned how .NET features such as inheritance can be used to create classes in the data services tier of a multi-tier application. Along the way you saw examples of both the direct and abstracted providers approaches to using .NET Data Providers. The former approach entails declaring provider-specific objects in your methods and coding directly to them, whereas the latter approach allows for the use of a `ProviderFactory` class that abstracts the creation of provider-specific objects. However, there is also a third approach that you can use, known as the internal data factory. This approach is more complicated and will be the focus of today's lesson.

Specifically, today you'll learn

- The purpose and benefits of creating a data factory
- Another technique for abstracting the .NET Data Provider
- How to abstract statements executed against a data store
- How to increase performance by using a cache

Creating a Data Factory

 Simply put, a **data factory** is a class that exposes methods and properties that abstract not only the provider used, but also common operations such as the instantiation and population of connection, command, and parameter objects. In this way, the data factory abstracts as much of the ADO.NET code as possible from the rest of the application.

> **Note**
>
> MSDN recently published an article that described a data factory for SQL Server called a "Data Access Application Block." The primary difference between that approach and the one described today is that the Data Access Application Block is SQL Server–specific and is therefore neither provider nor database independent.

Obviously, this approach has several benefits, foremost among them being the reduction in the amount of code that you have to write and the ability to dynamically decide which provider to use. However, in addition to those benefits, the data factory can be designed to include second-level benefits such as

- **Database Independence**. Not only is it possible to abstract the provider by using interface-based programming, but a data factory can also abstract all the database-specific syntax from your application by introducing the concept of "statements" that map to particular database-specific SQL statements.

- **Caching**. After the data factory has created a particular command object and its parameters based on a logical statement, the factory can then cache it, thereby allowing it to be reused. In this way, performance is increased because the data factory never has to create the same command object twice.

To illustrate the functionality that the data factory provides to your data access classes, Table 18.1 includes a description of each of its public methods and properties and their purposes. The remainder of today will be devoted to looking at a couple of key aspects of the factory, including how the provider and statement are abstracted and how caching is implemented.

> **Tip**
>
> Because the entire data factory class is more than 1,000 lines of code, all the code can't be shown. To get the entire class, download the code files associated with this book on the Sams Web site at www.samspublishing.com.

TABLE 18.1 Public Members of the Data Factory Class

Signature	Description
Properties	
CacheFilePath	Property that specifies the path where the statement files can be found
Connection	Property that returns the connection object
Provider	Property that specifies the provider to use
UseCache	Property that specifies whether to cache any new statements and whether to use those already in the cache
Methods	
BeginTransaction	Starts a transaction and returns it
CreateDataAdapter	Creates and returns a data adapter based on the statements passed to it
CreateSqlFiles	Overloaded; shared method that creates XML statement files asynchronously for all stored procedures in a SQL Server database
CreateSqlFile	Shared method that creates an XML statement file for a particular SQL Server stored procedure
ExecuteDataReader	Overloaded; returns a data reader based on the statement passed to it and optionally can use transactions and command behaviors
ExecuteNonQuery	Overloaded; executes a statement and optionally uses a transaction and returns a return value and output parameters
ExecuteScalar	Overloaded; executes a statement and returns the value. Optionally returns the return value and uses a transaction
ExecuteSqlXmlReader	Executes a statement that uses the FOR XML functionality of SQL Server; will throw an exception if the instance isn't using SqlClient
GetDataSet	Overloaded; returns a DataSet based on the statement and optionally uses a transaction
GetDataTable	Overloaded; returns a DataTable based on the statement and optionally uses a transaction
GetProviders	Shared method that returns an array containing the intrinsically supported providers
GetXsltResults	Transforms the results from the statement using the given stylesheet
RemoveStatement	Shared method that removes a particular statement from the internal cache
SyncDataSet	Synchronizes the given DataSet using the given data adapter
Events	
SqlFilesCreated	Event raised when the asynchronous CreateSqlFiles method completes

18

The data factory class itself is written in VB. Because it will be used by the entire
ComputeBooks organization, it is placed in the ComputeBooks.Data namespace. The
class is also sealed (marked as NotInheritable) and imports several namespaces in
addition to those that are defaulted for all VB projects. Listing 18.1 shows the resulting
declaration of the class.

LISTING **18.1**   The DataFactory class. This class is used internally in data access classes to
abstract much of the ADO.NET code that must be written.

```
Option Strict On

Imports System.Collections.Specialized
Imports System.Xml
Imports System.Xml.Xsl
Imports System.IO
Imports System.Data.SqlClient
Imports System.Data.OleDb
Imports System.Reflection
Imports System.Data.Common

Namespace ComputeBooks.Data
  Public NotInheritable Class DataFactory
      ' Public and private members
  End Class
End Namespace
```

Abstracting the Provider

As with the ProviderFactory class discussed yesterday, one of the main jobs of the data
factory is to abstract the provider. However, the DataFactory class does this using a different technique.

The basic approach used is that when an instance of the DataFactory is created, it is
passed the connection string and optionally the provider in the constructor (the provider
may also be set using the Provider property). This triggers the _createProviderTypes
private method that creates five Type objects for the particular provider specified. These
Type objects represent the connection, command, data reader, parameter, and data
adapter, and are used to dynamically instantiate the provider-specific types when needed.
In fact, the method then also creates an instance of the connection object to be exposed
through the Connection property.

The interesting aspect of _createProviderTypes, however, is that if the Provider property isn't set to "SqlClient" or "OleDb," it will look for an XML file called
DataFactory.config and read other provider information it contains. For example, if the

DataFactory were going to use a custom provider created by ComputeBooks, the DataFactory.config file would look as shown in Listing 18.2.

LISTING 18.2 Configuring the `DataFactory` class. This file can be used to specify additional providers that the class supports.

```xml
<?xml version="1.0" encoding="utf-8" ?>
<DataFactory>
  <Provider name="Cbks" assembly="ComputeBooksData.dll">
    <Connection type="ComputeBooks.Data.CbksConnection" />
    <Command type="ComputeBooks.Data.CbksCommand" />
    <Parameter type="ComputeBooks.Data.CbksParameter" />
    <DataAdapter type="ComputeBooks.Data.CbksDataAdapter" />
    <DataReader type="ComputeBooks.Data.CbksDataReader" />
  </Provider>
</DataFactory>
```

Listing 18.3 shows the complete `_createProviderTypes` method.

LISTING 18.3 Creating provider types. This private method creates the provider-specific `Type` objects used by the class.

```vb
Private Sub _createProviderTypes()
    ' Provider and connection string are set so instantiate the connection object
    ' May need to read from the XML file

    Dim xmlConfig As New XmlDocument()
    Dim provNodes As XmlNodeList
    Dim prov As XmlNode
    Dim provAssembly As [Assembly]

    Select Case Me.Provider
      Case "SqlClient"
        _conType = GetType(SqlConnection)
        _comType = GetType(SqlCommand)
        _drType = GetType(SqlDataReader)
        _daType = GetType(SqlDataAdapter)
        _parmType = GetType(SqlParameter)
        _paramtypes = _sqlParamTypes
      Case "OleDb"
        _conType = GetType(OleDbConnection)
        _comType = GetType(OleDbCommand)
        _drType = GetType(OleDbDataReader)
        _daType = GetType(OleDbDataAdapter)
        _parmType = GetType(OleDbParameter)
        _paramtypes = _oledbParamTypes
      Case Else
```

18

LISTING **18.3**   continued

```vb
        _paramtypes = _otherParamtypes
        ' Load a provider dynamically
        Try
          xmlConfig.Load("DataFactory.config")  ' Relative path
          provNodes = xmlConfig.GetElementsByTagName("Provider")

          For Each prov In provNodes
            If prov.Attributes("name").Value = Me.Provider Then
              ' Load the assembly
              _provAssembly = prov.Attributes("assembly").Value
              provAssembly = [Assembly].LoadFrom(_provAssembly)

              ' Load the data provider types
              If Not prov.SelectSingleNode("Connection") Is Nothing Then
                _sconType = prov.SelectSingleNode( _
                    "Connection").Attributes("type").Value
                _conType = provAssembly.GetType(_sconType, True, True)
              End If
              If Not prov.SelectSingleNode("Command") Is Nothing Then
                _scomType = prov.SelectSingleNode( _
                    "Command").Attributes("type").Value
                _comType = provAssembly.GetType(_scomType, True, True)
              End If
              If Not prov.SelectSingleNode("DataAdapter") Is Nothing Then
                _sdaType = prov.SelectSingleNode( _
                    "DataAdapter").Attributes("type").Value
                _daType = provAssembly.GetType(_sdaType, True, True)
              End If
              If Not prov.SelectSingleNode("DataReader") Is Nothing Then
                _sdrType = prov.SelectSingleNode( _
                    "DataReader").Attributes("type").Value
                _drType = provAssembly.GetType(_sdrType, True, True)
              End If
              If Not prov.SelectSingleNode("Parameter") Is Nothing Then
                _sparmType = prov.SelectSingleNode( _
                    "Parameter").Attributes("type").Value
                _parmType = provAssembly.GetType(_sparmType, True, True)
              End If
            End If
          Next
        Catch e As Exception
          _throwException( _
            "Could not load the provider, check the DataFactory.config file", e)
        End Try
    End Select

    ' Create an instance of the connection object
    Try
      If Not _conType Is Nothing Then
```

LISTING 18.3 continued

```
      _connection = CType(Activator.CreateInstance(_conType, _
         False), IDbConnection)
      _connection.ConnectionString = _connect
    End If
  Catch e As Exception
    _throwException("Could not create connection object.", e)
  End Try
End Sub
```

ANALYSIS You'll first note in Listing 18.3 that a simple Select Case statement is used if the provider is set to either "SqlClient" or "OleDb." If so, the GetType method is used to simply return the types and store them in private Type variables. However, in the Case Else block, an XmlDocument object is used to load the DataFactory.config file into memory where each Provider element is traversed to see whether it matches the Provider property. If so, the shared LoadFrom method of the System.Reflection.Assembly class is invoked to load the assembly that contains the provider by creating an Assembly object.

 Note You'll notice in Listing 18.3 that the Assembly class is referenced using brackets [] both in the declaration and when calling the shared method. This is required in VB because Assembly is also a reserved keyword.

Next, each of the five Type objects is populated by navigating to the appropriate XmlNode in the document and using the GetType method of the Assembly object. If the DataFactory.config file is in error, the private _throwException method is called. As you probably guessed, the variables such as _conType and _sconType are declared at the class level as Type and String objects, respectively.

After the types have been specified, the connection object is created and its connection string is set using the shared CreateInstance method of the System.Reflection.Activator class. Note that the connection object is cast to the IDbConnection interface using the CType method because even though the actual object is of type SqlConnection, for example, the connection will be referenced by the interface. This is the technique that is used throughout the data factory class to dynamically create provider objects.

Handling Data Types

You've probably also noticed in Listing 18.3 that the _paramTypes variable is populated for each provider. For example, if SqlClient is the provider, the variable is set to

18

_sqlParamTypes. If OleDb is the provider, the variable is set to _oledbParamTypes, and if there is a custom provider, the variable is set to _otherParamTypes. Each of these three variables refers to shared Hashtable objects that contain the names of data types and the values they correspond to in the SqlDbType, OleDbType, and DbType enumerations, respectively. All four of the variables are declared at the class level as follows:

```
Private Shared _sqlParamTypes As New Hashtable()
Private Shared _oledbParamTypes As New Hashtable()
Private Shared _otherParamtypes As New Hashtable()
Private _paramtypes As Hashtable
```

The Hashtable objects themselves are populated in the shared constructor of the class, a small snippet of which is shown in Listing 18.4.

LISTING 18.4   Referencing data types. The shared constructor populates the Hashtable objects that map the names of data types to the values in the enumerations.

```
Shared Sub New()
  ' Setup the types used by the providers
  _sqlParamTypes.Add("bigint", SqlDbType.BigInt)
  _sqlParamTypes.Add("bit", SqlDbType.Bit)
  _sqlParamTypes.Add("varchar", SqlDbType.VarChar)
  _sqlParamTypes.Add("char", SqlDbType.Char)
  _sqlParamTypes.Add("string", SqlDbType.NVarChar)
  _sqlParamTypes.Add("integer", SqlDbType.Int)
  ' [Others omitted]

  ' OleDb types
  _oledbParamTypes.Add("BigInt", OleDbType.BigInt)
  _oledbParamTypes.Add("Boolean", OleDbType.Boolean)
  _oledbParamTypes.Add("BSTR", OleDbType.BSTR)
  _oledbParamTypes.Add("string", OleDbType.VarWChar)
  _oledbParamTypes.Add("int", OleDbType.Integer)
  _oledbParamTypes.Add("long", OleDbType.BigInt)
  ' [Others omitted]

  ' Other provider types
  _otherParamtypes.Add("string", DbType.String)
  _otherParamtypes.Add("integer", DbType.Int32)
  _otherParamtypes.Add("short", DbType.UInt16)
  _otherParamtypes.Add("boolean", DbType.Boolean)
  _otherParamtypes.Add("date", DbType.Date)
  ' [Others omitted]
End Sub
```

The purpose of _paramTypes and of the Hashtable objects to which it refers is two-fold. First, it allows the DataFactory class to associate the appropriate data types with parameter objects, and second, it allows database-independent statement files to be written. We'll discuss these files later.

Abstracting the Statement

The creation of the provider Type objects and the connection object occur when an instance of the DataFactory class is created. When one of its methods, such as GetDataSet, is invoked, the class must then use the types to execute the method.

NEW TERM However, in addition to abstracting the provider, the DataFactory class also abstracts the SQL that's executed against the provider using the concept of statements. A **statement** is simply the definition of the SQL and the set of parameters that need to be executed. In this way, a statement is analogous to a command object, but isn't provider or database specific.

By abstracting the statement and the specification of parameters, the methods in the DataFactory class—and in the data access classes that use it—needn't be concerned with database specifics. The mechanisms used to achieve this independence are statement files formatted as XML used to encapsulate each specific statement executed by your application.

For example, a method in a data access class written in C# that needs to return all the books written by a particular author could be coded as follows:

```
DataFactory df  = new DataFactory(_connect, "SqlClient");
df.CacheFilePath = new DirectoryInfo(".");

HybridDictionary parms = new HybridDictionary();
parms.Add("author", "Fox, Dan");
DataSet ds  = new DataSet();
ds = df.GetDataSet("GetTitles", parms);
```

In this small code snippet, a new instance of the DataFactory class is created and is passed both a connection string and the hardcoded value of "SqlClient" specifying that SQL Server will be used.

> **Note** Obviously, your classes could also read the provider value from a configuration file, as was done with the connection string as shown on Day 9, "Using Connections and Transactions."

18

The CacheFilePath property is then set, which specifies the directory in which to search for statement files (in this case, the default directory). The GetDataSet method is then passed a HybridDictionary, which contains the parameters as name-value pairs along with the string "GetTitles", which is the name of the statement. Internally, the DataFactory class translates the "GetTitles" string into the command object it represents by reading its information from a statement file.

>
>
> The HybridDictionary class can be found in the System.Collections.Specialized namespace and is interesting because when the collection is small, it stores its item in a ListDictionary. As the number of items grows, it switches to using a Hashtable. As a result, this class is useful when you don't know ahead of time how many elements the collection will contain.

Because this process is the meat of the DataFactory class, we'll take each aspect of statements in turn, including parsing the statement file, using the statement cache, and creating statement files.

Parsing the Statement File

As mentioned previously, the statement is abstracted into a statement file that specifies the SQL and parameters needed to execute the statement. Listing 18.5 shows an example of a statement file for the GetTitles statement.

LISTING 18.5   A statement file. This file abstracts the calling of the usp_GetTitles stored procedure in a SQL Server database.

```xml
<?xml version="1.0" encoding="utf-8" ?>
<DataFactory>
    <Statement name="GetTitles" type="StoredProcedure">
        <Sql>usp_GetTitles</Sql>
        <Parameters>
          <Param name="author" SqlName="@author" type="string"
          maxLength="30" direction="Input" />
          <Param name="title" SqlName="@title" type="string"
          maxLength="100" direction="Input" />
        </Parameters>
    </Statement>
</DataFactory>
```

ANALYSIS   Although the file is straightforward, note that the Sql element specifies the database-specific SQL syntax to use and can therefore also contain inline SQL statements such as the following:

```
<Sql>SELECT * FROM Titles WHERE author = @author</Sql>
```

After the GetDataSet method is invoked as in the earlier code snippet, the DataFactory ultimately calls its private _getStatement method, which returns an IDbCommand object with its parameters and connection fully specified. Figure 18.1 shows the process flow for this method.

FIGURE 18.1

Returning a statement. This diagram shows the process flow of the _getStatement method that either pulls a statement out of the cache or creates it dynamically.

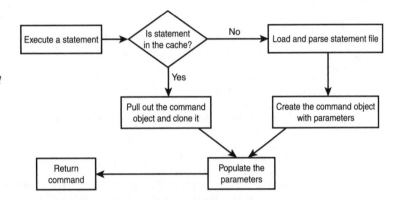

As you can see from Figure 18.1, the _getStatement method initially determines whether the statement has already been executed and therefore is in shared cache. If so, and if the UseCache property is set to True, the statement is pulled out of the cache and processed, as you'll see in the next section.

However, if the statement is not in the cache, as would happen the very first time the "GetTitles" statement is executed, the method must load and parse the statement file and create the command and parameter objects. It does this by invoking a private _getStatementFromFile method that looks in the path specified by CacheFilePath for a file with the name *statement*.config. If the file is found, it is loaded and parsed using an XmlTextReader as shown in Listing 18.6.

LISTING 18.6   Parsing the statement file. This method loads and parses the statement file.

```
Private Function _getStatementFromFile(ByVal statement As String) As Statement
    Dim found As Boolean
    Dim s As statement
    Dim xlr As XmlTextReader
    Dim fileName, temp As String

    ' Get the file name
    fileName = Me.CacheFilePath.FullName & "\" & statement & ".config"
```

LISTING 18.6   continued

```
If Not File.Exists(fileName) Then
  _throwException("File for statement " & statement & _
    " does not exist.", Nothing)
Else
  xlr = New XmlTextReader(fileName)
End If

Try
  xlr.WhitespaceHandling = WhitespaceHandling.None
  xlr.MoveToContent()

  Do While xlr.Read()
    Select Case xlr.Name
      Case "Statement"
        If xlr.GetAttribute("name") = statement Then
          ' Found it
          found = True
          s = New statement()
          s.Parms = New ArrayList()
          s.CommandType = CType(System.Enum.Parse(s.CommandType.GetType, _
            xlr.GetAttribute("type"), True), CommandType)
          xlr.Read()
          s.SQL = xlr.ReadElementString("Sql")
          s.Name = statement
        End If
      Case "Param"
        If found Then
          Dim p As New Parm()
          p.Name = xlr.GetAttribute("name")
          p.SQLName = xlr.GetAttribute("SqlName")
          p.Type = xlr.GetAttribute("type")
          temp = xlr.GetAttribute("maxLength")
          If Not temp Is Nothing Then p.maxLength = CInt(temp)
          temp = Nothing
          temp = xlr.GetAttribute("SourceColumn")
          If Not temp Is Nothing Then p.SourceColumn = temp
          p.Direction = CType(System.Enum.Parse(p.Direction.GetType, _
            xlr.GetAttribute("direction"), True), ParameterDirection)
          s.Parms.Add(p)
        End If
    End Select
  Loop

  If _daSwitch.Enabled Then
    Trace.WriteLine("Successfully read " & fileName)
  End If
  Return s    ' success
```

LISTING 18.6   continued

```
    Catch e As Exception
      _throwException("Could not parse " & fileName, e)
    Finally
      xlr.Close()
    End Try
  End Function
```

ANALYSIS In Listing 18.6, the method first builds the file path and determines whether the file exists using the `System.IO.File` class. If so, it loads the file using the `XmlTextReader` object and parses it using a `Do Loop` and the `Read` method. The `Select Case` statement then looks for `Statement` and `Param` elements in the statement file, which are then parsed and loaded into `Statement` and `Parm` structures. The structures are declared as `Friend` within the assembly that contains the `DataFactory` class as follows:

```
Friend Structure Statement
  Public Name As String
  Public SQL As String
  Public CommandType As CommandType
  Public Parms As ArrayList
  Public Command As IDbCommand
End Structure

Friend Structure Parm
  Public Name As String
  Public SQLName As String
  Public Type As String
  Public Direction As ParameterDirection
  Public maxLength As Integer
  Public SourceColumn As String
 End Structure
```

As you might expect, the `Parms` field of the structure holds an `ArrayList` used to contain instances of the `Parm` structure. After the structures are populated, the `Statement` structure s is returned from the method. The `Command` field of the `Statement` structure is used to reference the fully instantiated command object with its parameters.

Note   Just as in the base classes we discussed yesterday, the `DataFactory` classes uses a `BooleanSwitch` to control tracing output so that you can generate a log file.

18

Using the Statement Cache

To minimize the number of times the DataFactory class needs to access the file system, and to avoid having to create command and parameter objects repeatedly, the class stores statements that have already been accessed in a shared Hashtable.

As shown in Figure 18.1, the _getStatement method first checks the cache to see whether the statement has already been loaded. It does this by checking a Hashtable referred to with the _procs variable. Just as with the Hashtable objects used to store the data types for each provider, the _procs variable points to a Hashtable that is provider specific. This is required because multiple instances of the DataFactory using different providers might be used in the same application. This is implemented by declaring _procs and a synchronized Hashtable at the class level like so:

```
Private Shared _provCache As Hashtable = Hashtable.Synchronized(New Hashtable())
Private _procs As Hashtable
```

 Note   The Hashtable class contains a shared Synchronized method that automatically creates a thread-safe wrapper for the Hashtable class. This means that multiple threads can add to the Hashtable concurrently.

Then, when the Provider property is set, the _provCache Hashtable is inspected to see whether a Hashtable already exists for the provider. If not, a new synchronized Hashtable is created and added to _provCache. Listing 18.7 shows the definition of the Provider property.

LISTING 18.7   Setting the provider. The Set block of the Provider property creates or references the provider-specific Hashtable.

```
Public Property Provider() As String
  ' Sets up the provider to use
  Get
    Return _provider
  End Get
  Set(ByVal Value As String)
    ' See if there is a cache for this provider
    If _provCache.ContainsKey(Value) Then
      _procs = CType(_provCache(Value), Hashtable)
    Else
      _provCache.Add(Value, Hashtable.Synchronized(New Hashtable()))
      _procs = CType(_provCache(Value), Hashtable)
    End If
    _provider = Value
```

LISTING 18.7 continued

```
        _createProviderTypes()
    End Set
End Property
```

ANALYSIS As you can see in Listing 18.7, the provider cache is first checked with the ContainsKey method to see whether a Hashtable exists in its collection for the provider (specified by Value). If so, the _procs variable simply references it; if not, a new Hashtable is created and added to _provCache. In either case, the _createProviderTypes method is then executed to create the provider-specific Type objects, as shown in Listing 18.3.

The _getStatement method in Listing 18.8 then uses the _procs variable and the _getStatementFromFile method to implement the algorithm shown in Figure 18.1.

LISTING 18.8 Creating and caching a statement. This method implements the process flow shown in Figure 18.1.

```
Private Function _getStatement(ByVal statement As String, _
 ByVal parms As HybridDictionary, ByVal setParmValue As Boolean) As IDbCommand
 Dim s As statement
 Dim com, newCom As IDbCommand
 Dim p As Parm
 Dim newParm As IDbDataParameter

 ' See if its in the cache
 If Not Me.UseCache OrElse _procs.ContainsKey(statement) Then
   If _daSwitch.Enabled Then
     Trace.WriteLine("Cache hit for " & statement)
   End If
   ' Pull it out of the cache
   s = CType(_procs.Item(statement), statement)
   newCom = CType(_cloneObject(s.Command), IDbCommand)
 Else
   s = _getStatementFromFile(statement)
   ' Build the command, add the parameters
   com = CType(Activator.CreateInstance(_comType, False), IDbCommand)
   com.CommandText = s.SQL
   com.CommandType = s.CommandType

   ' Now add the parameters
   For Each p In s.Parms
     Dim args(1) As Object
     args(0) = p.SQLName
     ' Get the type
     If _paramtypes.ContainsKey(p.Type) Then
```

18

LISTING 18.8   continued

```
      args(1) = _paramtypes(p.Type)
  Else
    _throwException("Invalid type in statement " & statement, Nothing)
  End If

  ' Create the parameter object
  newParm = CType(Activator.CreateInstance(_parmType, args), _
  IDbDataParameter)
  ' Set its properties
  newParm.Direction = p.Direction
  If Not p.SourceColumn Is Nothing Then
     newParm.SourceColumn = p.SourceColumn
  End If
  If p.maxLength > 0 Then newParm.Size = p.maxLength
  newParm.Value = DBNull.Value
  ' Add it to the collection
  com.Parameters.Add(newParm)
Next

s.Command = com

' Add it to the cache
If Me.UseCache Then
  _procs.Add(statement, s)
  ' Clone the object that was just created
  newCom = CType(_cloneObject(com), IDbCommand)
  If _daSwitch.Enabled Then
    Trace.WriteLine("Added " & statement & " to cache.")
  End If
Else
  newCom = com
End If

End If

' Populate the parameters
For Each p In s.Parms
  If setParmValue AndAlso parms.Contains(p.Name) Then
    CType(newCom.Parameters(p.SQLName), IDataParameter).Value = _
    parms.Item(p.Name)
  End If
Next

' Return the command with the populated parameters
newCom.Connection = _connection
Return newCom

End Function
```

The _getStatement method first checks the cache (_procs) for the statement, and if it finds the statement, it extracts the Command field and passes it to the private _cloneObject method to make a copy of the command object.

 Note

> The _cloneObject method simply casts for the ICloneable interface and, if it exists, uses its Clone method to create a copy of the object. This works for both SqlCommand and OleDbCommand objects because they both support the interface and perform *deep copies* (copies that also copy the object's collections, such as the parameters collection). In order for custom providers to be used with the DataFactory, therefore, their command objects would need to do likewise.

This must be done so that multiple instances of the DataFactory running on multiple threads won't be competing to work with the same command object. This is especially the case because each command object must have its parameter values set differently each time a method is called.

If the statement isn't found in the cache, the appropriate command object is created using the CreateInstance method of the Activator class. Its CommandText and CommandType properties are then set to the values in the Statement structure. Next, the parameters are created by traversing the Parms ArrayList of the Statement structure. The interesting aspect of this code is that when the parameter object is created with the CreateInstance method, it is passed an array (args) as the second argument. This array is mapped to the constructor of the class, for example OleDbParameter, and contains the name of the parameter and its data type. Note that the parameter type is retrieved from the _paramtypes Hashtable we discussed earlier.

After the parameter object is created, its Direction, SourceColumn, Size, and Value properties are all set and the parameter is added to the collection. The new command object is then referenced in the Command field of the Statement structure.

Note

> As you can tell from this code, although some providers such as SqlClient don't require you to create all the parameter objects if you don't use them, the DataFactory does in fact create all the parameter objects defined in the statement file regardless of whether they will ultimately be called. If the parameters have default values in the stored procedure, a client needn't populate its HybridDictionary object with values for all the parameters.

18

If the cache is in use, the statement is added to the cache for future use and a new command is created that will actually be used during this execution.

For this particular execution, then, the parameter objects need to be populated with values. This is accomplished by traversing the Parms ArrayList and determining whether the HybridDictionary passed into the method from the client (that contains author = "Fox, Dan" for example) contains parameters of the same name. If so, the Value property is populated by retrieving the value from the parameter. This technique was used so that clients needn't add the parameters to the HybridDictionary in any particular order and needn't provide values for all the parameters.

Finally, the command object is associated with the private connection object and is returned. At this point, a fully populated command object with the appropriate parameter values has been created. It can then be used to execute the command through the ExecuteScalar or ExecuteDataReader method, or to populate a DataSet, DataTable, or data reader.

Creating Statement Files

Of course, using statement files implies that someone or something must create a statement file for each stored procedure or SQL statement executed against the data store. In particularly large applications, this can be a daunting task.

To automate the process, the DataFactory exposes shared CreateSqlFile and CreateSqlFiles methods, which create a file for a single SQL Server stored procedure and for all the stored procedures in a database, respectively. Both methods are overloaded and end up calling the private _createSqlFile and _createSqlFiles methods.

Most of the work is accomplished in the _createSqlFile method, which is passed the SqlConnection object, the name of the stored procedure, the directory to create the file in, and a flag indicating whether to populate the SourceColumn attribute. The method relies on the sp_procedure_params_rowset system stored procedure, and uses a SqlDataReader to read the procedure metadata returned and an XmlTextWriter object to write out the statement file, as shown in Listing 18.9.

LISTING 18.9   Creating statement files. This method creates a statement file for a single stored procedure.

```
Private Shared Sub _createSqlFile(ByVal con As SqlConnection, _
  ByVal procName As String, ByVal cacheDir As DirectoryInfo, _
  ByVal defaultSourceColumn As Boolean)
  ' Writes the file for a stored procedure in SQL Server 2000
```

LISTING 18.9 continued

```
Dim com As New SqlCommand("sp_procedure_params_rowset", con)
Dim dr As SqlDataReader
Dim statement As String
Dim fs As FileStream
Dim xlr As XmlTextWriter
Dim closeOnFinish As CommandBehavior = CommandBehavior.Default

com.CommandType = CommandType.StoredProcedure
com.Parameters.Add("@procedure_name", procName)

' Take off the prefix if one exists
If Left(procName, Len(ProcPrefix)) = ProcPrefix Then
  statement = Mid(procName, 5)
Else
  statement = procName
End If

Dim fileName As String = cacheDir.FullName & "\" & statement & ".config"

Try
  If con.State = ConnectionState.Closed Then
    closeOnFinish = CommandBehavior.CloseConnection
    con.Open()
  End If

  dr = com.ExecuteReader(closeOnFinish)

  ' Open the file
  If File.Exists(fileName) Then
    File.Delete(fileName)
  End If

  fs = New FileStream(fileName, FileMode.CreateNew)
  xlr = New XmlTextWriter(fs, Text.Encoding.Default)
  xlr.Indentation = 2
  xlr.Formatting = Formatting.Indented
  xlr.WriteStartDocument()
  xlr.WriteComment("Generated by the DataFactory at " & _
  Now.ToLongDateString())
  xlr.WriteStartElement("DataFactory")
  xlr.WriteStartElement("Statement")
  xlr.WriteAttributeString("name", statement)
  xlr.WriteAttributeString("type", "StoredProcedure")
  xlr.WriteElementString("Sql", procName)
  xlr.WriteStartElement("Parameters")

  Do While dr.Read
    xlr.WriteStartElement("Param")
    xlr.WriteAttributeString("name", Mid(dr("PARAMETER_NAME").ToString(), 2))
```

18

LISTING 18.9 continued

```
        xlr.WriteAttributeString("SqlName", dr("PARAMETER_NAME").ToString())
        xlr.WriteAttributeString("type", dr("TYPE_NAME").ToString())
        If defaultSourceColumn Then
          xlr.WriteAttributeString("SourceColumn", _
            Mid(dr("PARAMETER_NAME").ToString(), 2))
        End If
        If Not IsDBNull(dr("CHARACTER_MAXIMUM_LENGTH")) Then
          xlr.WriteAttributeString("maxLength", _
            dr("CHARACTER_MAXIMUM_LENGTH").ToString)
        End If
        Select Case dr("PARAMETER_TYPE")
          Case 4
            xlr.WriteAttributeString("direction", "ReturnValue")
          Case 1
            xlr.WriteAttributeString("direction", "Input")
          Case 2
            xlr.WriteAttributeString("direction", "InputOutput")
          Case 3
            xlr.WriteAttributeString("direction", "Output")
        End Select
        xlr.WriteEndElement() ' Param
      Loop
      xlr.WriteEndDocument()

  Catch e As Exception
    Throw New Exception("Could not create XML for " & procName, e)
  Finally
    If Not dr Is Nothing Then dr.Close()
    If Not xlr Is Nothing Then xlr.Flush()
    If Not fs Is Nothing Then fs.Close()
  End Try

End Sub
```

ANALYSIS You'll notice after setting up the call to the stored procedure, the method uses the shared field `ProcPrefix` to remove any naming convention that the procedure might use to create a more generic statement and therefore file name. Although it can be changed, by default `ProcPrefix` is set to "usp_"—a common naming convention for user-defined SQL Server stored procedures.

The remainder of the method simply executes the stored procedure and traverses the results while using the methods of the `XmlTextWriter` to write out the statement file.

A client could then call one of the overloaded signatures like so:

```
DataFactory.CreateSqlFile(connect, "usp_GetSchedule", _
  new DirectoryInfo("C:\\ComputeBooks"),true);
```

This would result in the file GetSchedule.config being created in the ComputeBooks directory.

One of the most interesting aspects of these shared methods, however, is that the CreateSqlFiles method operates asynchronously so that the statement files can be created on a separate thread. This is accomplished using an asynchronous delegate declared at the class level like so:

```
Private Delegate Sub WriteSqlFiles(ByVal connect As String, _
  ByVal cachedir As DirectoryInfo, _
  ByVal defaultSourceColumn As Boolean)
```

The CreateSqlFiles method can then use the delegate to execute the _createSqlFiles method on a background thread like so:

```
Public Shared Sub CreateSqlFiles(ByVal connect As String, _
  ByVal cacheDir As DirectoryInfo)
  ' Create files for each of the stored procs in
  ' the database on a separate thread

  Dim async As New AsyncCallback(AddressOf _createSqlCallback)
  Dim createFiles As New WriteSqlFiles(AddressOf _createSqlFiles)
  createFiles.BeginInvoke(connect, cacheDir, False, async, Nothing)

  ' Now this thread is free
End Sub
```

Here, the _createSqlCallback method will be called when the _createSqlFiles method completes on the background thread. This _createSqlCallback method simply calls the EndInvoke delegate and raises the SqlFilesCreated event.

Note For more information on using asynchronous delegates, see the "Asynchronous Design Pattern Overview" topic in the online documentation or my articles on .NET patterns on InformIT.com.

Using ASP.NET Caching

Although not shown today, the DataFactory class can also be used to take advantage of ASP.NET caching to enable the site to be dynamically updateable. If the DataFactory class were used from an ASP.NET application, items associated with each statement could be added to the System.Web.Caching.Cache object using its Add or Insert methods. When items are added to the cache, they can be associated with a file dependency (CacheDependency object) so that when the file changes, the item is automatically removed from the cache. When this happens, your ASP.NET application can be notified using the CacheItemRemovedCallback delegate. It can

> then call the Remove method of the DataFactory instance to remove the item from the DataFactory's cache as well. In this way, an administrator can re-create statement files using an administrative Web page that calls the shared methods discussed in this section. The application will automatically use the new versions of the files the next time the statement is executed.

Using the DataFactory

Now that you've seen how the DataFactory class is implemented internally, a look at several of the public methods it exposes will illustrate how the implementation is used. First, consider the ExecuteScalar method, which exposes three signatures that include the statement, parameters, and optionally an Integer passed in by reference to catch the return value, and a transaction object to associate with the command. All three public methods ultimately call the private _executeScalar method shown in Listing 18.10.

LISTING **18.10** Implementing the DataFactory. This private method is called by the public ExecuteScalar methods.

```
Private Function _executeScalar(ByVal statement As String, _
  ByVal parms As HybridDictionary, ByRef returnVal As Integer, _
  ByVal transaction As IDbTransaction) As Object
  ' Return a single value using ExecuteScalar

  Dim com As IDbCommand
  Dim val As Object
  Dim leaveOpen As Boolean = False

  ' Get the command
  com = _getStatement(statement, parms, True)
  If Not transaction Is Nothing Then
    com.Transaction = transaction
  End If

  Try
    If com.Connection.State = ConnectionState.Closed Then
      com.Connection.Open()
    Else
      leaveOpen = True
    End If
    val = com.ExecuteScalar()
    Dim p As IDataParameter
    For Each p In com.Parameters
      If p.Direction = ParameterDirection.ReturnValue Then
        returnVal = CInt(p.Value)
        Exit For
```

LISTING 18.10 continued

```
      End If
    Next
    Return val
  Catch e As Exception
    _throwException( _
        "Failed to execute ExecuteScalar method for statement " & statement, e)
  Finally
    If Not leaveOpen Then com.Connection.Close()
  End Try

End Function
```

ANALYSIS As you can see in Listing 18.10, the method relies on the private `_getStatement` method to return an `IDbCommand` object with fully populated parameters. The command object is then associated with a transaction if one is passed to the method. Because the connection object might already be open (for example, if a transaction is active), the method then checks to see whether the connection needs to be opened. After calling the `ExecuteScalar` method and capturing the returned value, the parameters are traversed to catch the return value. Finally, the value returned from `ExecuteScalar` is returned to the caller and the connection is closed if necessary.

In another example, the `_getDataSet` method shown in Listing 18.11 is called by the public `GetDataSet` methods. Unlike the `_executeScalar` method, the retrieval of the command object is wrapped into the private `_setupDataAdapter` method that dynamically creates the data adapter and populates its `SelectCommand` with the command object returned in the statement. After the data adapter is created, the `DataSet` is filled and its `ExtendedProperties` collection is populated with metadata that your data access classes might be able to use.

LISTING 18.11 Returning a `DataSet`. This private method is used by the public `GetDataSet` methods.

```
Private Function _getDataSet(ByVal statement As String, _
  ByVal parms As HybridDictionary, _
  ByVal transaction As IDbTransaction) As DataSet
  ' Returns a DataSet given the statement

  Dim da As IDataAdapter
  Dim ds As New DataSet()

  da = _setupDataAdapter(statement, parms, transaction)
```

LISTING 18.11   continued

```
Try
  ' Fill and return
  da.MissingMappingAction = MissingMappingAction.Passthrough
  da.MissingSchemaAction = MissingSchemaAction.AddWithKey
  da.Fill(ds)
  ds.DataSetName = statement
  ds.ExtendedProperties.Add("Creator", "DataFactory class")
  ds.ExtendedProperties.Add("TimeCreated", Now.ToShortTimeString)
  ds.ExtendedProperties.Add("Statement", statement)
  ds.ExtendedProperties.Add("Parameters", parms)
  Return ds
Catch e As Exception
  _throwException("Could not fill DataSet", e)
End Try

End Function
```

By using these public methods, the methods of a data access class such as the
_getTitles method shown yesterday in Listing 17.4 can be simplified as shown in
Listing 18.12.

LISTING 18.12   Using the DataFactory. This method uses the DataFactory to retrieve
titles.

```
Private Function _getTitles(ByVal author As String, ByVal title As String, _
  ByVal isbn As String, ByVal lowPubDate As Date, _
  ByVal catID As Guid) As DataSet

  Dim parms As New HybridDictionary()

  Try
    If Not isbn Is Nothing AndAlso isbn.Length > 0 Then
      parms.Add("isbn", isbn)
    Else
      If Not title Is Nothing AndAlso title.Length > 0 Then
        parms.Add("titles", title)
      End If
      If Not author Is Nothing AndAlso author.Length > 0 Then
        parms.Add("author", author)
      End If
      If lowPubDate.Equals(Nothing) Then
        parms.Add("lowPubDate", lowPubDate)
      End If
      If Not catID.Equals(Guid.Empty) Then
        parms.Add("catID", catID)
      End If
    End If
```

LISTING 18.12   continued

```
      Return _df.GetDataSet("GetTitles", parms)
   Catch e As DataFactoryException
     Call MyBase.ThrowComputeBookException("GetTitles Failed", e)
   End Try
End Function
```

Note that the _df variable is a class-level private variable that references an instance of
the DataFactory class created in the constructor of the Books class. The key differences
to note between Listing 18.12 and the original method in Listing 17.4 are as follows:

- When using the DataFactory, the method doesn't need to create or call any
  provider-specific objects. This is provider independence.

- When using the DataFactory, the method doesn't need to know which stored procedure is executed to return the data nor the actual names of the parameters
  exposed by the procedure. This is database independence.

- When using the DataFactory, the number of lines of code in the method was
  reduced by 35%.

Measuring Performance

The obvious issue with using a data factory approach like the one presented today is the
cost of creating type objects for the provider dynamically and reading the statement files
from the file system. Keep in mind that the performance hit incurred when creating the
provider types happens only when the DataFactory is instantiated. Further, reading a
particular statement file should occur only once in the entire application, which will have
a negligible effect on performance.

In fact, in tests conducted with Microsoft Application Center Test (ACT) on a sample
ASP.NET application using the DataFactory, it was discovered that after the application
was running, the performance was actually slightly better using the DataFactory than
when not using it. Performance could further be enhanced by caching the provider-
specific type objects in a shared data structure as well. This would be especially effective
if the DataFactory used the ODBC or custom .NET Data Provider because the
DataFactory.config file wouldn't need to be parsed.

Summary

By creating an internal data factory, you can not only reduce the amount of code you
have to write in your data access classes, but also allow them to be provider and database
independent, while maintaining performance and even increasing it with the use of

caching. You can use the approach discussed today as a template for building your own data factory, or download the code from the Sams Web site.

Before you design your data access classes, you need to think about how they'll be used. Nowhere is this more important than in the implementation of XML Web Services. Tomorrow, you'll learn how ADO.NET can be used effectively in the XML Web Services you design.

Workshop

This workshop will help reinforce the concepts covered in today's lesson.

Quiz

1. What are the benefits of creating a data factory class?

   Using a data factory can have several benefits, including reducing the amount of code you have to write in your data access classes, abstracting the provider used, abstracting database-specific syntax, and caching command objects for reuse.

2. What method can you use to dynamically load assemblies and create objects based on their type information?

   In the System.Reflection namespace, the Assembly class exposes shared LoadFrom, Load, and LoadWithPartialName methods to load an assembly into memory, whereas the Activator class exposes a shared CreateInstance method to create instances of a type at runtime.

3. How can database independence be achieved in a data factory?

   To make the data factory database independent, you must not only abstract the provider objects used but also the SQL syntax used to execute statements against the data store. The DataFactory class shown today uses XML files, called statement files, in which the database-specific SQL syntax remains.

Exercise

Write a simple method that uses the DataFactory to update the Description column of a particular ISBN and then deletes the ISBN in the context of a single local transaction.

Answers for Day 18

Exercise Answer

One possible solution to the exercise in C# is as follows:

18

```
virtual void UpdTitles(string isbn, string desc)
{
    // Create the DataFactory
    DataFactory e = new DataFactory(_connect,"SqlClient");

    // Start a transaction
    IDbTransaction trans = e.BeginTransaction(IsolationLevel.ReadCommitted);

    // Setup the parameters
    HybridDictionary parms = new HybridDictionary();
    parms.Add("isbn", isbn);
    parms.Add("desc", desc);

    try
    {
        int retval = 0;
        int rows = e.ExecuteNonQuery("UpdateTitle", parms,ref retval,trans);
        Console.WriteLine(rows); //should be 1
        parms.Remove("desc");
        rows = e.ExecuteNonQuery("DeleteTitle", parms, ref retval, trans);
        Console.WriteLine(rows); //should be 1
        // success so commit the transaction
        trans.Commit();
    }
    catch (DataFactoryException ex)
    {
        // Error so rollback
        trans.Rollback();
        Console.WriteLine(ex.Message);
        Console.WriteLine(ex.InnerException.Message);
    }
}
```

The statement files for UpdateTitle and DeleteTitle can then be written as follows:

```
<?xml version="1.0" encoding="utf-8" ?>
<DataFactory>
    <Statement name="UpdateTitle" type="Text">
        <Sql>UPDATE Titles SET Description=@desc WHERE isbn = @isbn</Sql>
        <Parameters>
            <Param name="isbn" SqlName="@isbn" type="string"
              maxLength="10" direction="Input" />
            <Param name="desc" SqlName="@desc" type="string"
              maxLength="250" direction="Input" />
        </Parameters>
    </Statement>
</DataFactory>

<?xml version="1.0" encoding="utf-8" ?>
<DataFactory>
    <Statement name="DeleteTitle" type="Text">
```

```
          <Sql>DELETE FROM Titles WHERE ISBN=@isbn</Sql>
          <Parameters>
              <Param name="isbn" SqlName="@isbn" type="string"
                maxLength="10" direction="Input" />
              <Param name="returnVal" SqlName="@RETURN_VALUE" type="integer"
                maxLength="4" direction="ReturnValue" />
          </Parameters>
      </Statement>
  </DataFactory>
```

DAY **19**

ADO.NET and XML Web Services

As you learned on Day 1, "ADO.NET in Perspective," one of the design goals of ADO.NET was to efficiently support the multi-tier programming model that has been widely adopted in the industry in the last several years. To that end, you've learned how you can use the DataSet object to cache data returned from a data store, and then pass it between tiers of a distributed application by taking advantage of the serialization done behind the scenes by the common language runtime. Although this works great when the tiers are located on a single machine or a set of machines within a single data center, it also supports intranet and Internet scenarios in which the tiers are distributed across an organization or exist in entirely different organizations. In these cases, the glue that binds the tiers is XML Web Services. As you'll learn today, ADO.NET—because of its support for XML—integrates nicely with an XML Web Services model.

Specifically, today you'll learn

- How DataSet objects can be exposed through an XML Web Service
- How DataSet objects are consumed by an XML Web Service client
- How to update data through an XML Web Service using ADO.NET

Exposing Data Through a Web Service

To expose data retrieved using ADO.NET with an XML Web Service, you can rely on the deep integration of Web services standards with the .NET Framework and VS .NET. This integration, coupled with the XML integration already present in ADO.NET, enables developers to expose ADO.NET through a Web service as simply as exposing it through any data access class.

The remainder of this section will provide a short overview of XML Web Services technology, followed by the steps you need to implement to use Web services with ADO.NET.

XML Web Services Technology

 Simply put, an XML Web Service provides a programmatic interface to the Web using standard XML grammars. The most notable of these interfaces are **SOAP** (Simple Object Access Protocol), which is used to specify the message format, and **WSDL** (Web Services Description Language, usually pronounced "wizz-dul"), which is used to describe the Web service. Both of these are controlled by the World Wide Web Consortium (W3C). For example, the .NET Framework supports the SOAP 1.1 specification, which you can find at http://www.w3.org/TR/2000/NOTE-SOAP-20000508/.

> **Note**
>
> For a more complete discussion of Web service protocols, see Chapter 11 of my book *Building Distributed Applications with Visual Basic .NET* (published by Sams) and the SOAP and WSDL specifications on the W3C Web site at www.w3c.org.

These standard protocols, along with HTTP, of course, provide a remote procedure call–like (RPC) communication model that is message based. Further, the ubiquity of HTTP and the wide adoption of XML and SOAP in the industry make the availability of Web services to any device and platform a reality. In this way, Web services eliminate many of the religious wars of the late 1990s over object technologies (such as COM/DCOM versus CORBA versus RMI) by providing an industry standard way of exposing functionality and consuming it. This approach means that a Web service is conceptually similar to a middle-tier component that exposes its methods as a "black box." However, Web services don't rely on proprietary component architectures—instead, they use Internet standards that make them platform and language independent. These Web services then become the building blocks for application development as developers incorporate them into their applications to provide essential features.

In the long run, the low bar for entry and reliance on industry standards will free developers from having to use any specific language or toolset to create software that interoperates. For example, in the past, developers on the Windows platform built COM components and COM clients that could interoperate with each other using DCOM. However, this interoperation rarely, if ever, went beyond the developer's organization because of the limitations of DCOM and the absence of COM on any but the Windows platform. One of the key aspects of a Web service is that it abstracts the implementation of the application logic from the means used to communicate with it so that consumers of Web Services need only know where the service is located and the signatures of its methods. In this way, you can think of a Web service as simply another interface, albeit a programmatic one, to components you build with VB .NET.

In the short term, using a development tool that abstracts much of the heavy lifting required to build Web services, such as VS .NET, enables developers to remain highly productive and build Web services within their language of choice. With VS .NET, Microsoft is betting that as developers begin to adopt the Web service model, it will become the fundamental way in which devices (not just PCs, but also phones, PDAs, and a host of other Internet-enabled hardware) communicate. In addition, it will become as routine for applications to expose and consume Web services as it is today for applications to reuse components.

Building the Data Access Method

Because a Web service can be thought of as simply another interface to your data, you should strive to adhere to the multi-tier architecture discussed previously this week. In other words, you should create a data services tier that your Web services wrap to expose their data rather than writing data access code directly in the Web service itself. Taking this approach not only provides the layer of abstraction that makes maintenance and extensibility simpler, but also allows the data services code to be reused in ASP.NET pages as well.

19

For example, ComputeBooks might want to create a Web service that other public sites can call to retrieve a list of the top-selling books on the ComputeBooks site. This relationship is mutually beneficial. For example, a site that provides technical information for software developers is able to provide its users with information about what books (and therefore technologies) are currently hot, whereas ComputeBooks sees increased Web traffic resulting from the clickthroughs from the site using the Web service. Further, it's obvious that this information would also be useful to provide on ComputeBooks' own public site so that users browsing for books could see which books are popular. By abstracting the code required to retrieve the top-selling books into a method of a data access class (that returns a `DataSet` for example), it could be reused in both the Web service and ASP.NET page.

As a result, ComputeBooks first creates or adds a method to an existing data access class that queries the database to return the books. This class relies on a version of the ComputeBooksDABase class we discussed on Day 17, "ADO.NET in the Data Services Tier," that also incorporates support for the DataFactory class you learned about yesterday. Listing 19.1 shows the class definition and the TopSellers method.

LISTING 19.1 Exposing top sellers. This class and method exposes the top five best-selling books for a specified time period.

```
Imports ComputeBooks.Data
Imports System.Collections.Specialized

Public Class WebData : Inherits ComputeBooksDABase

    Public Sub New(ByVal connect As String, ByVal provider As String)
      MyBase.New(connect, provider)
    End Sub

    Public Function TopSellers(ByVal daysOut As Short) As DataSet

      Dim ds As New DataSet("Catalog")
      Dim parms As New HybridDictionary()

      parms.Add("daysOut", daysOut)

      Try
        ds = MyBase.Factory.GetDataSet("Top5Sellers", parms)
        ds.Tables(0).TableName = "TopSellers"
        ds.Namespace = "www.computebooks.com"
        ds.Prefix = "cbks"
        Return ds
      Catch e As Exception
        MyBase.ThrowComputeBookException("TopSellers operation failed", e)
      End Try

    End Function
End Class
```

ANALYSIS In Listing 19.1, the WebData class includes a parameterized constructor that allows clients to pass in both the connection string and the provider to use. The base classes' constructor uses this information to initialize the instance of the DataFactory class that it uses internally.

You'll also notice that because the ComputeBooksDABase class exposes the DataFactory class as a protected property called Factory, it can be accessed in the TopSellers method using the MyBase (base in C#) keyword. The GetDataSet method is then called and passed the statement name "Top5Sellers". "Top5Sellers" encapsulates the stored procedure usp_Top5Sellers, which takes as its only parameter the number of days in the past to consider. For example, passing 30 into the TopSellers method, and thus into the stored procedure, returns the top five best-selling books over the past 30 days.

You'll also notice that the TableName property of the DataTable is populated to ensure that the XML is returned with the proper element names, along with Namespace and Prefix properties of the DataSet.

When the data services tier contains the method that the Web service will call, ComputeBooks can create the Web service to expose the data.

Building the Web Service

Within VS .NET, Web services are exposed in an ASP.NET Web Application or Web Service project as .asmx files. After opening or creating a project, you can click on the File menu or the project in the Solution Explorer and choose the Add New Item menu. This will invoke the Add New Item dialog from which you can choose Web Service to add the .asmx file with its associated code file to the project.

The methods of the Web service must be placed into a class (typically inherited from System.Web.Services.WebService) that is defined in the associated code file.

> **Note**   Although not required, by inheriting from WebService, the Web service class has access to the HTTP context information that includes the Session and Application state objects provided by ASP.NET.

19

New Term   The default behavior is for VS .NET to create a **code-behind file** that has the same name as the .asmx file with the appropriate language extension (.cs or .vb). What makes this programming model really productive is the fact that the methods themselves are simply defined just as any other method in a class would be, with the exception that the method is marked with the WebMethod attribute from the System.Web.Services namespace. This attribute indicates that this method should be exposed through the Web service. In this way, the HTTP handler for the .asmx file does all the work by encapsulating the code required to listen for requests, parsing them, invoking the proper method, and sending results. The end result is that developers needn't work directly with SOAP or WSDL.

For example, ComputeBooks could create a Web service in C# called Catalog that exposes the GetTopSellers method. This is shown in Listing 19.2 (minus the Web services designer-generated code).

LISTING 19.2   Creating the Web service method. This listing shows the code for the Web service that exposes the method used to return the top-selling books.

```csharp
using System;
using System.Collections;
using System.ComponentModel;
using System.Data;
using System.Diagnostics;
using System.Web;
using System.Web.Services;
using ComputeBooks.Data;
using System.Configuration;

namespace ComputeBooks.Web
{
    /// <summary>
    /// ComputeBooks Catalog web service
    /// </summary>
    [WebService(Namespace="www.computebooks.com/catalog",
    Description="ComputeBook's Catalog Web Service",
    Name="ComputeBooksCatalog")]
    public class Catalog : System.Web.Services.WebService
    {
      public Catalog()
      {
        InitializeComponent();
      }

      [WebMethod(Description="Retrieves the 5 top selling books",
        EnableSession=false)]
      public DataSet GetTopSellers(short daysOut)
      {
          DataSet books;

          // Read the configuration information
          string connect =
            ConfigurationSettings.AppSettings["SqlConnect"].ToString();
          string provider =
            ConfigurationSettings.AppSettings["Provider"].ToString();

          // Instantiate the data access class and call the method
          WebData data = new WebData(connect,provider);
          books = data.TopSellers(daysOut);
          return books;
      }
    }
}
```

ANALYSIS What you should notice in Listing 19.2 is that the entire Web service is encapsulated in the `Catalog` class within the `ComputeBooks.Web` namespace. The only method it exposes through the service (the only one with the `WebMethod` attribute) is `GetTopSellers`. This method accepts the number of days in the past for which to base the calculation and passes this value to the `TopSellers` method of the data access class shown in Listing 19.1. However, before calling the method, the Web service is responsible for retrieving the connection string and .NET Data Provider to use. In this case, those values are specified in the Web.config file within the `appSettings` element like so:

```
<?xml version="1.0" encoding="utf-8" ?>
<configuration>
  <appSettings>
    <add key="SQLConnect" value="data source=ssosa;
    initial catalog=ComputeBooks;user id=user;pooling=true" />
    <add key="Provider" value="SqlClient" />
  </appSettings>
</configuration>
```

These values are then passed to the constructor of the `WebData` class and subsequently to the `DataFactory` class before calling the `TopSellers` method. When the `DataTable` has been retrieved, it is simply returned from the Web service.

You'll also notice that the `Description` property is specified in both the `WebMethod` and `WebService` attributes to include the description of the Web service and the method to display to a user using the test harness page created by VS .NET. The `WebService` attribute also includes an explicit namespace declaration that will apply to all XML elements that directly pertain the Web service. In addition, the `WebMethod` attribute includes the `EnableSession` property that explicitly specifies that this method doesn't require the use of ASP.NET session state.

Note All Web service methods do automatically have access to the `Application` object and therefore ASP.NET application state. However, to gain access to session state, the method must have the `EnableSession` property set to `true`.

After the Web service has been compiled, it can be navigated to and tested simply by calling the Catalog.asmx file, as shown in Figure 19.1.

FIGURE 19.1

Testing a Web service. This screenshot shows the test harness page dynamically created by ASP.NET that can be used to test the Web service. The window in the foreground is the result of testing the Web service using the Invoke button.

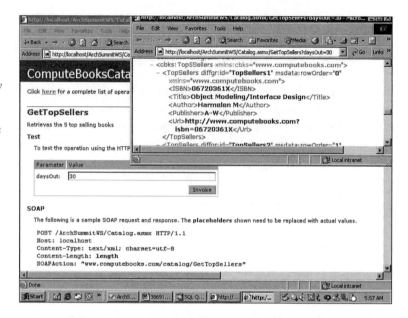

You'll notice in Figure 19.1 that the test harness page shows the method, its description, and the arguments it exposes. After entering 30 in the daysOut parameter and pressing the Invoke button, the XML document in the foreground is produced. The interesting aspect of this document is that it contains the XSD schema along with the DataSet serialized to a DiffGram. In this way, the caller of the Web service automatically has the information necessary to validate and use the XML.

Note

NEW TERM Actually, SOAP defines two ways that a Web service method, referred to as an **operation**, can be encoded in a request or response. The example here assumes the employment of document-style encoding (discussed in Section 5 of the SOAP specification) in which an XSD schema in the WSDL document is used to describe both the request and response. When using the document style, you can also specify how the parameters are to be encoded by explicitly using the SoapDocumentService attribute. Alternatively, you can use the SoapRpcMethod attribute on the Web method to specify the RPC encoding style in which parameters and return values are simply encoded using their names. However, if you use the RPC style, the Web service can't return objects such as the DataSet because no XSD schema will be generated. If you try to do so, an exception will be thrown.

Consuming Data in a Web Service

After the Web service has been built and exposed on the Web server, a client will typically call it by building a SOAP message and sending it to the server. However, Web services created by VS .NET by default also can be called using an HTTP-GET or POST. In this way, clients that don't support SOAP can still invoke the Web service. For example, a client can issue the following HTTP-GET to call the `GetTopSellers` method of the Catalog Web service:

```
GET /Catalog.asmx/GetTopSellers?daysOut=value HTTP/1.1
Host: www.computebooks.com
```

The result will be an XML document that includes the schema of the `DataSet` along with the serialized DiffGram encoded as follows:

```
HTTP/1.1 200 OK
Content-Type: text/xml; charset=utf-8
Content-Length: length
<?xml version="1.0" encoding="utf-8"?>
<DataSet xmlns="www.computebooks.com/catalog">
  <schema xmlns="http://www.w3.org/2001/XMLSchema">schema</schema>xml</DataSet>
```

However, clients that support SOAP can build a SOAP message and expect a SOAP message in return, like those shown in Listing 19.3.

LISTING 19.3   Calling the Web service. This listing shows the SOAP request and response messages that can be used with the Catalog Web service.

```
Request:
POST /Catalog.asmx HTTP/1.1
Host: www.computebooks.com
Content-Type: text/xml; charset=utf-8
Content-Length: length
SOAPAction: "www.computebooks.com/catalog/GetTopSellers"

<?xml version="1.0" encoding="utf-8"?>
 <soap:Envelope xmlns:xsi="http://www.w3.org/2001/XMLSchema-instance"
   xmlns:xsd="http://www.w3.org/2001/XMLSchema"
   xmlns:soap="http://schemas.xmlsoap.org/soap/envelope/">
   <soap:Body>
     <GetTopSellers xmlns="www.computebooks.com/catalog">
       <daysOut>short</daysOut>
     </GetTopSellers>
   </soap:Body>
</soap:Envelope>

Response:
HTTP/1.1 200 OK
```

19

LISTING 19.3   continued

```
Content-Type: text/xml; charset=utf-8
Content-Length: length

<?xml version="1.0" encoding="utf-8"?>
  <soap:Envelope xmlns:xsi="http://www.w3.org/2001/XMLSchema-instance"
     xmlns:xsd="http://www.w3.org/2001/XMLSchema"
     xmlns:soap="http://schemas.xmlsoap.org/soap/envelope/">
  <soap:Body>
    <GetTopSellersResponse xmlns="www.computebooks.com/catalog">
      <GetTopSellersResult>
        <xsd:schema>schema</xsd:schema>xml</GetTopSellersResult>
    </GetTopSellersResponse>
  </soap:Body>
</soap:Envelope>
```

ANALYSIS   You'll notice in Listing 19.3 that because document-style encoding is used in the Web service, the response message includes the XSD schema of the `DataSet` as well as the XML itself in the `GetTopSellersResult` element.

As a result, any client on any platform that can use HTTP, build the appropriate SOAP request message, and parse the SOAP response is able to call the Web service and use the data returned in the `DataSet`. From the ADO.NET perspective, the great thing about this architecture is that you have to work with only one type of object, the `DataSet`, to handle your data both internally in your data services tier and externally when you expose your data through a Web service. This simplifies the programming model and extends the reach of your applications beyond the Windows platform.

Using VS .NET

Although clients can certainly use HTTP-GET or POST or build the SOAP request message themselves, for a client using VS .NET, support is built into IDE to allow both discovery and referencing of Web services to take place. For example, assume that a fictional company called Cold Rooster Consulting wants to incorporate the ComputeBooks Catalog Web service into its Internet site to allow its customers to view the top-selling books. If the site is built with VS .NET in any of the .NET languages, Cold Rooster can do this by clicking on Add Web Reference from the context menu associated with the project in the Solution Explorer window. The resulting dialog contains an address bar that enables the developer to enter the URL of the Catalog Web service. By entering the address of the .asmx file or the .asmx file appended with the query string ?WSDL, the service will be located and the right Available References window populated, as shown in Figure 19.2.

FIGURE 19.2

Referencing a Web service. This dialog in VS .NET enables the developer to specify the end point of the Web service or search for it using UDDI.

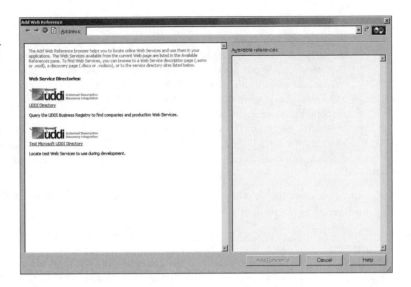

NEW TERM If the developer doesn't know the URL of the Web service or wants to search for other Web services, he or she can click on the Microsoft UDDI link in the window on the left. The developer can then navigate to the **UDDI** registry to search for various Web services using the HTML interface.

What Is UDDI?

UDDI (Universal Description, Discovery and Integration) is an industry initiative with more than 250 participating companies. Located at www.uddi.org, UDDI aims to integrate business services over the Internet by promoting a common protocol to publish and connect to Web services using directories. A Web service directory or registry allows businesses to publish their Web services in a searchable database. The UDDI specification calls for four types of information to be published in the registry, including business information, service information, binding information, and specifications for services. Both Microsoft and IBM host production UDDI directories that use the same protocols and are replicated, so either can be used to find a Web service.

The Add Web References dialog includes an automatic link to the Microsoft UDDI directory. In addition, developers can download the UDDI SDK from the same site. Features of the SDK include .NET classes that enable you to programmatically search the registry and host a lightweight registry of your own for internal use. Windows .NET Server, which is scheduled to ship in 2002, will contain a UDDI server that can be used behind the firewall to create a directory just for your organization.

19

The promise of a global directory coupled with WSDL means that development tools and custom code can be written to automatically find and use Web services without human interaction. For example, UDDI could be used to automatically locate an equivalent public Web service by searching for Web services that use the same definition (referred to as a **tModel** in UDDI) if the preferred Web Service isn't responding. In addition, developers can use UDDI to query for the new end point of a Web service if the call to a Web service fails because the provider of the service has changed the URL.

In either case, the developer can then click on the Add Reference button to add a Web reference to the project.

Note
Web references and the ability to call Web services can be added to any type of VS .NET project, including Windows Services, Windows Forms, console applications, and even other Web Service projects.

The result is a Web References folder in the Solution Explorer that contains a reference to the Web service. By default, the reference is named according to the Web Server contacted, although it can be changed by right-clicking on the reference and selecting Rename. You might want to rename it if the Web service may be accessed dynamically from other servers.

When the Web reference is added, VS .NET downloads the WSDL contract into the Web References folder and reverse-engineers it to build a client proxy class that can be used to invoke the Web service from within the application.

The proxy class will have the same name as the Web service—in this case, `ComputeBooksCatalog` —and exist in a namespace of the same name as the Web reference. The client proxy class enables the developer to work with the Web service as if it were any other managed class. In addition, and of particular interest to ADO.NET developers, if the Web service returns any strongly typed `DataSet` objects, the XSD schema for those `DataSets` are downloaded, and typed `DataSets` (as we discussed on Day 6, "Building Strongly Typed `DataSet` Classes") are generated for each. This is possible because the WSDL contract contains an `import` element with a `location` attribute that references a URL, allowing VS .NET to retrieve the schema of the `DataSet` using the following query string:

```
http://server/webService.asmx?schema=DataSetName
```

In this way, developers can programmatically work with the XML returned as if it were a typed `DataSet` rather than having to parse it using XML or having to use the generic `DataSet` object. In the case of the Catalog Web service, the `GetTopSellers` method simply returns a generic `DataSet` object, so no additional schema can be downloaded because the Web service doesn't know ahead of time what the schema of the `DataSet` will look like.

> **Note**
> Obviously, developers using Web services sometimes will need to update the reference if the publisher of the service changes it. By right-clicking on the Web reference and selecting Update Web Reference, the WSDL again will be downloaded and the client proxy class will be regenerated.

The code for the client proxy class doesn't appear in the Solution Explorer (except for in the Class view, which in this case shows the `ComputeBooksCatalog` class). However, you can view the class (and modify it if you're careful) by clicking on Show All Files in the Solution Explorer or looking in the project folder.

Although beyond the scope of this book, the client proxy class exposes methods for each Web method exposed by the Web service (such as `GetTopSellers`). In addition, it is derived from the `SoapHttpClientProtocol` class in the `System.Web.Services.Protocols` namespace, which contains methods and properties that enable finer-grained control of communication with the Web service such as `Url`, `Timeout`, and `Proxy`.

> **Note**
> In addition to the synchronous versions of the methods exposed by the Web service, the client proxy class also exposes begin and end methods for each method (for example, `BeginGetTopSellers` and `EndGetTopSellers`). These methods can be used to call the Web service asynchronously using asynchronous delegates. In this way, you can call the Web service on a separate thread to enable the user to continue working. For more information on asynchronous delegates, see the online documentation.

Because VS .NET does so much work for the developer, actually calling the Web service is trivial. All the developer needs to do is to create an instance of the proxy class and then call the method, as would be done with any other component.

NEW TERM However, in ASP.NET, one of the particularly effective strategies you can use to encapsulate the call to a Web service involves using a **Web User Control**.

19

Simply put, a Web User Control is an ASP.NET page with an .ascx extension that can be embedded in regular ASP.NET pages or other Web User controls. This architecture provides a great deal of flexibility because it enables developers to create controls that abstract specific functionality to be included on multiple pages. Using controls also enables developers to collaborate on a single Web site more easily by allowing individual user controls to be separately developed and then associated on a single page. Web User Controls can also be designed graphically in the VS .NET IDE in the same way as ASP.NET pages.

A Web User Control is added to an ASP.NET site by right-clicking on the project in the Solution Explorer and choosing Add Web User Control. In the code-behind file for the control, the class that is created is derived from the `UserControl` class in the `System.Web.UI` namespace. This class is ultimately derived from the `System.Web.UI.Control` class from which the `Page` class is also derived. As a result, the way that you code a Web User Control is basically the same as the way you code a regular ASP.NET page. For example, you can place code in the `Load` event of the control to initialize any child controls contained on the control. Listing 19.4 shows the code for the TopBooks Web User Control (minus the designer generated code) that Cold Rooster Consulting might use to encapsulate the call to the ComputeBooks Catalog Web service.

LISTING 19.4   Using a Web User Control. This is the code for the TopBooks.ascx.cs file that Cold Rooster Consulting uses to display the returned data from the Catalog Web service.

```
namespace ColdRooster
{
        using System;
        using System.Data;
        using System.Drawing;
        using System.Web;
        using System.Web.UI.WebControls;
        using System.Web.UI.HtmlControls;
        using ColdRooster.computebooks;

         /// <summary>
         /// TopBooks User Control
         /// </summary>
        public abstract class TopBooks : System.Web.UI.UserControl
        {
         protected System.Web.UI.HtmlControls.HtmlGenericControl lblMessage;
         protected System.Web.UI.WebControls.DataList dlBooks;

         private void Page_Load(object sender, System.EventArgs e)
         {
            // Put user code to initialize the page here
```

LISTING 19.4   continued

```
                    // Call the Catalog web service
                    ComputeBooksCatalog cat = new ComputeBooksCatalog();
                    cat.Timeout = 5000; //timeout to 5 seconds
                    DataSet ds = new DataSet();

                    try
                    {
                      ds = cat.GetTopSellers(30);

                       // bind to the DataList
                      dlBooks.DataSource = ds.Tables[0];
                      dlBooks.DataBind();
                    }
                    catch (Exception ex)
                    {
                      // cannot get the books, not a critical error
                      this.Visible = false;
                      logError(ex);
                    }
               }

            private void logError(Exception e)
            {
               // write this to a log for later inspection
            }
          }
      }
```

ANALYSIS   The interesting aspect of Listing 19.4 is, of course, the call to the Catalog Web
service itself in the Page_Load method. You'll notice that because a Web reference exists after the namespace is imported near the beginning of the page, the method
simply needs to instantiate a new ComputeBooksCatalog object before calling its
GetTopSellers method. However, before doing so, it uses the Timeout property of the
proxy class to timeout the call to the method if the response time exceeds five seconds.
In this way, the page will be assured to load relatively quickly even if the Web service
doesn't respond. If it doesn't, the control's Visible property is set to false so that the
control doesn't display at all and the exception is logged for later inspection.

After the DataSet object is returned from the GetTopSellers method, it's bound to a
DataList control by setting the DataSource property to the first table in the collection
and calling the DataBind method.

When the DataBind method is called, the DataTable is bound to the items in the
DataList control as shown in Listing 19.5.

19

LISTING 19.5   Data binding in a Web User Control. This listing shows the entire text of the TopBooks.ascx file that binds the results of the Web service to a `DataList` control.

```
<%@ Control Language="c#" AutoEventWireup="false" Codebehind="TopBooks.ascx.cs"
  Inherits="ColdRooster.TopBooks"
  TargetSchema="http://schemas.microsoft.com/intellisense/ie5"%>
<%@ OutputCache Duration="43200" VaryByParam="none" %>
<LINK rel="stylesheet" type="text/css"
  href="http://www.coldrooster.com/customer.css">
<b class="bookList">Most Populate Computer Books</b>
<br>
<span id="lblMessage" runat="server" class="bookList">
 <asp:DataList id=dlBooks runat="server" CssClass="bookList">
   <ItemTemplate >
     <a href='<%# DataBinder.Eval(Container.DataItem , "Url") %>'
       target=_blank>
        <%# DataBinder.Eval(Container.DataItem , "Title") %></a><br>
   </ItemTemplate>
 </asp:DataList>
Brought to you by <a href="http://www.computebooks.com">ComputeBooks</a>
</span>
```

ANALYSIS   You'll notice in Listing 19.5 that the HTML contained in a Web User Control needn't contain the HTML and BODY tags that you would find in a typical ASP.NET page. This is the case because the control will be embedded at runtime in the context of an existing page. In this case, the control simply contains a SPAN element that primarily includes a DataList ASP.NET Server Control.

As discussed on Day 16, "ADO.NET in the Presentation Services Tier," DataList controls can use data binding to bind to DataSet, DataReader, and DataView objects in ADO.NET. In this case, the DataBinder object is used to bind the Url and Title columns in the DataTable so that a simple list of hyperlinks is generated. Each link enables the user to navigate directly to the ComputeBooks public site in a separate browser window to view information about the book.

NEW TERM   Perhaps the most interesting aspect of Listing 19.5, however, is the use of **ASP.NET page output caching**. You'll notice that near the top of the page the OutputCache directive is specified and its Duration and VaryByParam attributes are set. This directive instructs ASP.NET to cache the output of the user control for 12 hours (43,200 seconds) and to do so regardless of any query string attached to the HTTP request. This has the effect of caching the call to the Web service so that it is called only twice per day regardless of the user. Obviously, this decreases the dependency on the Web service and makes the page more responsive.

To use the TopBooks user control, a page simply needs to include a `Register` directive that tells the page where to find the control and a tag that places the control into the page. For example, the Cold Rooster Consulting home page would include the following `Register` directive:

```
<%@ Register TagPrefix="Cbks" TagName="TopBooks" Src="TopBooks.ascx"%>
```

Then, within the body of the page, the following tag could be inserted to place the control:

```
<cbks:TopBooks id="TopBooks" runat="server" />
```

The result is that when the page is processed, so, too, will the user control, and its output will be streamed into the page at the appropriate position as shown in Figure 19.3.

FIGURE 19.3

Web service results. This screen shot shows the Cold Rooster Consulting home page with the TopBooks user control showing the results from the Catalog Web service.

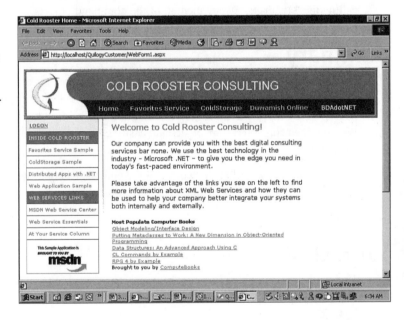

19

Updating Data Through a Web Service

From the ground already covered today, it should be fairly obvious that updating data with a Web service is basically the reverse of the process just shown. To update data, the Web service can expose a method that accepts a `DataSet` object as a parameter. When invoked, this method can use the standard technique of passing the `DataSet` or a particular `DataTable` to the `Update` method of a data adapter and then checking for errors as we discussed on Day 12, "Using Data Adapters." More typically, the method of the Web service will simply pass the `DataSet` to a method in the data services tier that will actually perform the update.

Alternatively, of course, a method in a Web service or in the data services tier could simply accept more granular parameters and then populate parameter objects directly before calling the `ExecuteNonQuery` method of the command object.

Summary

One of the primary design goals of ADO.NET was to make it effective for use in disconnected Web-based applications. Nowhere is this more evident or appropriate than in the world of XML Web Services, where ADO.NET can be used to both return data through a Web service using a `DataSet` object and easily consume the data when using VS .NET as the client.

As we approach the end of the week and the end of this book, we'll look at a few final issues starting tomorrow by examining performance optimization and interoperating with ADO.

Workshop

This workshop will help reinforce the concepts covered in today's lesson.

Quiz

1. Why is SOAP important?

   SOAP provides a standard XML grammar that a client and server can agree on to exchange XML messages so that the client can invoke operations on the server. It is both language and platform independent and has wide reach because of the ubiquity of HTTP and XML.

2. How should you architect the methods of your Web service?

   You can think of a Web service as simply an extension of the presentation services tier, albeit a programmatic rather than a graphical one, so it should be designed to utilize your data services tier. In this way, you get the benefit of code reuse and abstraction, which, combined with the simple programming model provided by ASP.NET, makes implementing a Web service fairly simple.

3. How does VS .NET allow a Web service to be called?

   When adding a Web reference to the ASP.NET project, VS .NET downloads the WSDL document from the Web service and creates a proxy class in the project that can be used to call the methods of the Web service as if they were exposed in any other managed class. The proxy class also supports asynchronous execution of the methods and can be used to dynamically change the end point of the Web service through the Url property.

4. What techniques can you use for consuming a Web service in an ASP.NET application?

   One particularly effective technique for calling a Web service from an ASP.NET page is to encapsulate the code to call it in a Web User Control. Using this approach, the data from the Web service can be reused on several pages. More importantly, you can take advantage of ASP.NET page output caching. By using output caching, you can decrease the number of calls to the Web service because the output from the first call can be cached. You can also set the duration the output will be saved in the cache as well as whether the cache will contain multiple copies for different browsers or query strings.

Exercise

Write a method that would extend the Catalog Web service by allowing a client to retrieve all the details for a particular book.

19

Answers for Day 19

Exercise Answer

One possible solution to the exercise is as follows.

First, to provide the Web service with the appropriate methods, the data services tier would need to be extended to support it. This means that the WebData class shown in Listing 19.1 would need to include a method such as TitleInfo that gets the information for a particular ISBN like so:

```
Public Function TitleInfo(ByVal isbn As String) As DataSet

    Dim ds As New DataSet("Titles")
    Dim dt As DataTable
```

```
    Dim parms As New HybridDictionary()

    parms.Add("isbn", isbn)

    Try
      ds = MyBase.Factory.GetDataSet("GetTitles", parms)
      ds.Tables(0).TableName = "Title"
      ds.Namespace = "www.computebooks.com"
      ds.Prefix = "cbks"
      Return ds
    Catch e As Exception
      MyBase.ThrowComputeBookException("TitleInfo operation failed", e)
    End Try

End Function
```

Note that this method relies on the DataFactory class exposed through its base class and a GetTitles.config file would need to exist on the Web server. Next, the Web service would simply expose a GetBook method that would call the method in the WebData class as follows:

```
[WebMethod(Description="Retrieves all the information for a particular ISBN",
  EnableSession=false)]
public DataSet GetBook(string isbn)
{
    DataSet books;

    // Read the configuration information
    string connect = ConfigurationSettings.AppSettings["SqlConnect"].ToString();
    string provider = ConfigurationSettings.AppSettings["Provider"].ToString();

    // Instantiate the data access class and call the method
    WebData data = new WebData(connect,provider,
      new DirectoryInfo(this.Server.MapPath("bin")));
    books = data.TitleInfo(isbn);
    return books;
}
```

DAY **20**

Performance and Interoperation

It almost goes without saying that even if you learn every aspect of the ADO.NET object model and use your knowledge to develop reusable and maintainable code, users won't accept your application if it doesn't perform well. Further, there will be times when your ADO.NET code must interoperate with ADO—for example when you need to call data access classes already in production written in VB 6.0.

As a result, today's short lesson will focus on getting the best performance possible out of your ADO.NET code and interoperating with ADO. To those ends, today you'll learn

- The top techniques you can use to increase performance of your ADO.NET applications
- How to read ADO `Recordset` data using a `DataSet`

Performance and Scalability Optimizations

If your organization is like most others, the ADO.NET applications you'll develop will get their data from a relational database, such as SQL Server or Oracle. As a result, the performance and scalability of your applications depends not only on the efficiency of code you write, but also (and more importantly) on the techniques you employ to actually retrieve and maintain the data. This section details those techniques enumerated in several categories, starting with those you can apply closest to the data and moving outward to the managed code.

Query Techniques

This set of techniques can be applied to the actual statements executed against the data store and can be used to increase the raw performance of an application.

Ask for the Appropriate Rows

Probably the most immediate way you can increase the performance of your applications is to ask for only the data that's absolutely required. Many applications spend a lot of time querying for data that the user will never see, but that "needs" to be available in case the user wants to scroll to it. Constantly retrieving hundreds or thousands of rows not only puts undue strain on the database server that needs to fulfill the request, but also consumes unnecessary network bandwidth and resources on the middle-tier component or Web server that must, for example, populate the DataSet and store it in memory. Generally speaking, most applications never need to query more than 50 rows at a time.

> **Note**   The techniques we discussed on Day 3, "Working with DataSets," for filtering DataSet objects using a DataView and the Select and Find methods should then be applied to these smaller and more appropriate result sets.

As a result, you should employ WHERE clauses in almost all your SELECT statements and return only enough rows to satisfy the immediate need of the user. You can then requery the database if and only if the user requires more data. As we discussed on Day 16, "ADO.NET in the Presentation Services Tier," in ASP.NET applications, you can take advantage of the custom paging behavior of the DataGrid control to execute statements that return only the relevant data for the particular page.

A second point that should be stressed is that you should remember that applications typically perform better when they ask for summarized data directly from the database server rather than retrieving all the detail rows and then summarizing them on the middle-tier server or client machine. Not only is the database server optimized for just these kinds of operations, but retrieving summarized data also decreases both the network bandwidth required and the resource requirements on the middle tier or client.

Ask for the Appropriate Columns

As a corollary to the previous technique, you should also ask for only the columns that the application requires. In other words, use specific column lists in your SELECT statements rather than simply using SELECT *. This not only makes your code easier to read because it's more explicit, but also ensures that the database server needn't go to the extra work of retrieving columns that will never be displayed or manipulated.

NEW TERM This technique is particularly important when your database server supports BLOB or long text columns that might be stored in separate data structures from the rest of the row. Asking for those columns when they're not needed simply wastes CPU cycles on the database server as the data is found and retrieved. Further, some database servers such as SQL Server support **covered queries** that can greatly increase performance. In a covered query, the database server needn't access the actual rows in the table on the disk if the query asks for only data found in the index the server is using to satisfy the query. And so, coupled with the appropriate use of indexes, asking for only those columns that are required can shorten the amount of time the database needs to fulfill the query.

Perform Joins on the Server

One of the things that relational database engines are particularly efficient at is joining tables together based on foreign key relationships. This is the case because in a normalized database, joins will often be required to display a complete logical record that is stored in multiple tables.

However, as you learned on Day 4, "DataSet Internals," in ADO.NET, you also have the ability to retrieve multiple sets of data and place each of them in a DataTable within a DataSet. Then you can use DataRelation objects to relate the tables in order to traverse the relationships programmatically, or show the relationship graphically in controls such as the Windows Forms DataGrid.

Although it's possible to use DataSet objects in this way, you should do so only when the data needs to be displayed in a master/detail relationship or is retrieved from multiple data sources and combined in the same DataSet. For most applications, it will be more efficient and simpler to join the related tables on the server using a JOIN or WHERE clause, and then read the joined result set directly into a DataSet or through a data reader. This is the case because the database server can use indexes on the server to join the related rows quickly, multiple result sets needn't be returned to the client, and only one result set need be loaded or traversed.

20

Note

> Of course, if you're going to update the data through a `DataSet`, the insert, update, and delete commands for the data adapter, along with their `SourceColumn` properties, need to be aware of which columns will be used to update which tables.

Database Techniques

This second set of techniques applies to higher-level design issues you can apply to the database itself. These are in addition to the database design issues we discussed on Day 13, "Working with SQL Server."

Make Sure That Indexes Are Employed

Many times during the development and testing phases of a project, developers and testers will use small data sets for their application. Although this is convenient and often necessary due to hardware limitations, it can mask performance problems that appear only when the application is put into production. Chief among these problems is the time it takes the database server to retrieve or update rows in larger tables.

NEW TERM   For a database server to efficiently access data in large tables, it relies on separate data structures (indexes) that are easily navigated and that typically point to the actual data in the rows. Without an appropriate index for a particular query, the server resorts to examining each row in the table. This is referred to as a **table scan**. Obviously, in tables with hundreds of thousands or millions of rows, table scans will be extremely slow, even on the best hardware available.

 Note

> **NEW TERM**   As we discussed on Day 13, SQL Server allows you to create both **clustered** and **nonclustered** indexes. The latter is a separate data structure that points to the row data, whereas the former actually organizes the entire table on the disk into one big index. Clustered indexes are appropriate when you typically access a particular table in ranges (such as when the BETWEEN clause is used) or when the results are typically ordered using an ORDER BY clause.

As a result, even if everything else in your application is as efficient as possible, not using indexes will ruin its performance because the time your application spends waiting for data far exceeds any other single task.

To make sure that your queries and statements use indexes, follow the suggestions we discussed on Day 13. These included tips on determining which columns to index, along with the tools provided by the database server, such as the Index Tuning Wizard and the SET SHOWPLAN ON statement in SQL Server.

Use Stored Procedures

As outlined on Day 13, employing stored procedures or other constructs that encapsulate SQL statements usually increases performance. This is because the procedures are pre-compiled on the server, result in less network traffic, and make it easier to create the appropriate indexes for your applications. Even if you don't use stored procedures, using standardized SQL statements and sp_executesql stored procedure in SQL Server also increases performance by allowing SQL Server to reuse statements saved in its cache.

Favor Output Parameters over DataSet Objects

On Day 10, "Using Commands," you learned how to catch both return values and output parameters from stored procedures. Because output parameters can typically use any data type supported by the database server, and also because you can have multiple output parameters for a single stored procedure, they can be used to return a single value or a related set of values to a client.

Although the code required to use output parameters is slightly more complex on both the client and the server, using them instead of returning a single row result set in a DataSet results in better performance. This is the case because the server needn't create a result set and the overhead of populating a DataSet object is eliminated. However, in SQL Server, using output parameters performs almost identically to using the ExecuteScalar method of the command object to retrieve a single value or to retrieve a single row with a data reader. However, this might not be the case with all database servers, so performing a few tests is warranted.

Tip

> Remember that you can pass the SingleRow value of the CommandBehavior enumeration to the ExecuteReader method of the command object. .NET Data Providers can then use this information to optimize retrieval of the data. The OleDb provider does this by using the IRow rather than the IRowset interface to bind the data.

20

Managed Code Techniques

The final set of techniques applies to the managed code you write and can be used to optimize performance on the middle-tier server.

Use Data Readers

As documented in the article "Performance Comparison: Data Access Techniques" published on the MSDN Web site, data readers typically offer the highest throughput (measured in requests per second) and lowest response time. In fact, the more rows that are returned, the greater the advantage (almost doubling the throughput) the data reader has. Data readers also lessen the resource load on the middle-tier server because the values aren't stored in memory as with a DataSet. As a result, in applications in which the data access code lives in the same application domain as the client code that uses it, you should consider returning data readers through the data services tier to allow clients to stream through data quickly.

 Tip

> Keep in mind that if you return a data reader, you should pass the CloseConnection value of the CommandBehavior enumeration to the ExecuteReader method to allow the client to close the connection automatically when the data reader is closed.

However, using data readers efficiently implies that you close them as quickly as possible in order to release connections back to the pool. This is because they tie up database connections while they're being processed.

Use Narrow Providers Where Possible

Because narrow providers like SqlClient can use native protocols to communicate with their data stores, they'll likely provide the fastest access to the data store. This can increase both performance (because individual clients will experience better response times) and scalability (applications will scale because resources such as connections are released more quickly). In fact, much of the impetus for creating the ProviderFactory and DataFactory classes on Days 17, "ADO.NET in the Data Services Tier," and 18, "Building a Data Factory," resulted from the desire to use a single code base and employ narrow providers rather than resort to using a broad provider such as OleDb.

Focusing only on the provider when writing managed code stands in sharp contrast to the past, when the only way to achieve better performance was to use a lower-level language and interfaces like C++ with the OLE DB COM interfaces instead of the combination of VB 6.0 and ADO 2.x. Because all managed code, regardless of language, ultimately compiles to intermediate language and is JIT compiled, there are no performance differences between the languages themselves. The interchangeable use of VB and C# in this book attests to that fact.

Minimize the Number of Round Trips

One of the problems developers unknowingly and often ran into when using ADO 2.x was that it was easy to incur extra round trips to the database server by inadvertently opening server-side cursors. In fact, in many cases, the client code would execute a stored procedure against the database server for each and every row returned to the client. Obviously, this situation hurts both scalability and performance because the time required to retrieve even small result sets is multiplied by the latency of the network and connections are being used longer than is necessary.

Because ADO.NET doesn't expose a server-side data access model, this particular problem is avoided. However, the same rule applies to the explicit code you write as well. In other words, you should always strive to minimize the number of times you request data from the data store because the time it takes to make a round trip to the data store is typically among the highest-cost operations your applications will perform. In addition, it decreases scalability by using more resources on the database server. One way to avoid incurring extra round trips is to take advantage of various caching techniques on the middle-tier server or client machine. At the same time, this must be balanced against consuming an undue amount of resources on the middle-tier by, for example, creating large DataSet objects and storing them in session state. Usually, only careful testing will reveal the proper balance for a particular application.

> **Note**
>
> The need to minimize round trips is one of the reasons (along with the fact that command builders don't use stored procedures) I recommend you don't use command builders such as the OleDbCommandBuilder. When the Update method of the data adapter is called, command builders must make a round trip to the data store to discover the schema information of the base table so that it can create the insert, update, and delete commands.

Always Use Connection Pooling

One of the best ways to increase scalability (although not performance) of an application is to make sure to take advantage of connection pooling. As we discussed on Day 10, both the SqlClient and OleDb providers allow connections to be stored and retrieved from a pool. This increases scalability because the expensive operation of constantly creating new connection objects is avoided. Although dependent on the design of the application, you would typically expect an application that used connection pooling to consume only one database connection for every five or more concurrent users.

20

> To monitor the number of connections both in and out of the pools for SqlClient, you can use the Performance Monitor utility found in the Administrative Tools group and select the counters under the .NET CLR Data performance object.

Keep in mind that for connection pooling to work, the connection string you use for your application must be identical and that all connections must be made with the same security credentials. Connection pooling is explicitly turned on for both SqlClient and OleDb, although it can be disabled by setting the Pooling attribute to false in the SqlClient connection string and the OLE_DB_SERVICES to –2 in the OleDb connection string.

Take Advantage of ASP.NET Caching

For ASP.NET applications, one of the most effective ways to increase the responsiveness and scalability of an application is to take advantage of its caching engine. In an ASP.NET application, you can take advantage of the cache using page and fragment caching as well as manipulating the cache directly.

Both page and fragment caching can be implemented using the OutputCache page directive in a Web form or user control in order to cache the output for the entire page or merely the portion rendered by the user control. This is the technique used in Listing 19.5, and, as you might imagine, is most useful when the page or control is built using an expensive database query.

> Although not used in Listing 19.5, the VaryByParam attribute of the directive is particularly useful for page and user control content generated from database queries because queries typically accept parameters. In addition, the directive supports VaryByHeader and VaryByCustom attributes to support caching for particular HTTP headers, browser types, and even custom information you specify.

If you need to have more granular control of the elements in the cache, you can manipulate the cache programmatically using the System.Web.Caching.Cache object exposed through the Cache property of the HttpContext object. Using this property, you can add objects—such as DataGrid controls and DataSet objects—to the cache. You even have the capability through the Add method or overloads on the Insert method to age-out its items, invoke a callback method when an item is removed, and create dependencies between items.

For example, to add a `DataGrid` control called `dgTitles` to the cache and then pull it from the cache if it is already populated, you could use the following snippet of C# code in the `Load` event of the page:

```csharp
if (this.Context.Cache["dgTitles"] == null)
{
   // populate the grid
   this.Context.Cache.Insert("dgTitles",dgTitles,null);
}
else
{
   dgTitles = this.Context.Cache["dgTitles"];
}
```

> **Note**
>
> Keep in mind that the ASP.NET cache is not tied to a particular user as is the session object. As a result, you would need to append user-specific information to the key name if you want to store user-specific data.

Use Multithreading for Long Queries

Although ADO.NET doesn't support multithreaded operations natively, it's relatively simple to add multithreading to an application that uses ADO.NET. This is particularly effective for Windows Forms–based applications when you know that you'll have long-running queries that can be completed while the user performs some other useful work.

In the .NET Framework, there are two primary means of doing work on multiple threads: using the `Thread` class and using asynchronous delegates.

Using the `Thread` Class

The `Thread` class can be found in the `System.Threading` namespace and enables you to spawn and control threads explicitly. For example, if you want to execute a method called `GetTitles` on a background thread, you could use the following code snippet:

```csharp
Thread tTitles = new Thread(new ThreadStart(this.GetTitles));
tTitles.Name = "TitlesQuery";
tTitles.Priority = ThreadPriority.BelowNormal;
tTitles.Start();
//Foreground thread is free
```

In this case, an instance of the `ThreadStart` delegate that points to the `GetTitles` method is passed to the constructor of the `Thread` object `tTitles`. The object can then have its properties, such as `Name` and `Priority`, set before invoking the `Start` method.

20

The Name property allows the thread's name to show up in the Debug Location toolbar in the VS .NET IDE when in debug mode, whereas the Priority property requests that the operating system run the thread at one of five priorities set using the ThreadPriority enumeration.

Note | In VB, you would use the AddressOf keyword to point to the GetTitles method in the constructor of Thread so that you wouldn't have to create the ThreadStart delegate explicitly.

After the Start method is invoked, the foreground thread is free to continue other work. Because the thread can still be referenced with the tTitles variable, however, it can be manipulated using its Suspend, Resume, Abort, Interrupt, and Join methods. The Join method is particularly interesting because it blocks the foreground thread until the other thread completes or a specified amount of time has elapsed. In this way, you can synchronize the activities of the foreground and background threads.

Using Delegates

The second technique for doing work on multiple threads is built into the .NET Framework and uses delegates to handle thread management and underlying infrastructure. This asynchronous delegate pattern is found throughout the .NET Framework.

The interesting aspect of this model is that it's client driven. This means that clients determine whether to call a method synchronously or asynchronously, either using methods provided by the server class (the class doing the work) or through an asynchronous delegate. For example, classes in the .NET Framework—such as FileStream and the proxy class generated by VS .NET for calling a Web service—provide Begin and End methods in addition to the standard methods that provide the functionality. These methods can be used to start and finish an asynchronous call. In the case of FileStream, this means that it supports both BeginRead and BeginWrite methods that can be used asynchronously, in addition to Read and Write methods that are used synchronously. Typical examples of where Begin and End methods already exist in the framework include network IO, remoting, and messaging.

However, if the class you want to call doesn't support Begin and End methods, you can still call one of its methods asynchronously by simply creating and invoking a delegate. This would be the case when you simply want to call a method like GetTitles of a data access class asynchronously. To do so, you can use the BeginInvoke and EndInvoke methods exposed by the delegate to call the method asynchronously.

Whether you're using server classes that expose Begin and End methods or calling a method asynchronously through a delegate, the pattern is basically the same.

First, the caller creates a delegate of type AsyncCallback that will point to the method that will be called when the asynchronous operations finish. This provides notification that the thread has completed its work. For example, if you want to call the GetTitles method asynchronously, you could be notified using a method called GetTitlesCallback like so:

```
AsyncCallback cb = new AsyncCallback(this.GetTitlesDone);
```

Next, the client code invokes the asynchronous operation and passes it the delegate either through the Begin method exposed by the server class or the BeginInvoke method if you're working with a class that doesn't expose them. If the data access class that contains the GetTitles method doesn't support the Begin and End methods, you would use a delegate as shown in the following code snippet:

```
//declared at the class level
public delegate void GetTitlesAsync(string publisher);

//in a method
GetTitlesAsync dgetTitles = new GetTitlesAsync(this.GetTitles);
dgetTitles.BeginInvoke("Sams",cb,null);
```

Note that the delegate is declared at the class level of the client code and can specify arguments passed to the method.

> **Note**
>
> Passing an argument to the delegate points out a key difference between using delegates and using threads explicitly. It's more difficult to pass arguments to an explicit thread because the ThreadStart delegate can only point to methods that don't take arguments. As a result, you'd have to resort to using thread local storage (TLS) to pass the thread values—a topic beyond the scope of this book. For more information, see Chapter 12 of my book *Building Distributed Applications with Visual Basic .NET*, published by Sams.

20

The delegate is then instantiated in the calling code and executed using the BeginInvoke method of the delegate. Note that the arguments to the GetTitles method, in this case "Sams," are passed first. They are followed by the AsyncCallback object and a state object that can be populated with any other state information you want to pass to the method. At this point, the thread that called BeginInvoke will be free to perform other operations as the execution of the GetTitles method continues on a separate thread managed by the common language runtime.

Finally, when the operation completes, the GetTitlesDone method will be called through the delegate, as shown in Listing 20.1.

LISTING 20.1   Using a callback. This method is called by the asynchronous delegate when the operation completes.

```
public void GetTitlesDone(IAsyncResult ar)
{
    // Extract the delegate from the AsyncResult.
    AsyncResult result = (AsyncResult)ar;
    GetTitlesAsync gt = (GetTitlesAsync)result.AsyncDelegate;

    // End the operation
    gt.EndInvoke(ar);

    //Switch back to main thread before updating UI
    MethodInvoker mi = new MethodInvoker(Form1.UpdateUI);
}
```

ANALYSIS   In Listing 20.1, you'll notice that the GetTitlesDone method must accept one parameter of type IAsyncResult. The IAsyncResult interface exposes several methods that can be called to determine whether the operation completed asynchronously, to retrieve the state passed to the Begin method, and even to poll or wait for the completion of the operation. In this case, the ar object is cast to an AsyncResult object from the System.Runtime.Remoting.Messaging namespace. The AsyncResult object then exposes the delegate that originally started the operation in its AsyncDelegate property. By casting to the GetTitlesAsync delegate, it can be retrieved and its EndInvoke method called to signal the completion of the operation. If the GetTitles method returns a value or used arguments passed by reference, they could be retrieved through the EndInvoke method as well.

After the operation is complete, control can be returned to the foreground thread. In a Windows Forms application, you might first want to update the user interface by calling a custom method such as UpdateUI on the form. To do so, you can use the MethodInvoker delegate of the Windows.Forms namespace as shown in Listing 20.1.

Although the pattern shown here is the one you'll most often use with asynchronous operations, the Begin methods can be called without the AsyncCallback delegate by passing in a null value (Nothing in VB .NET). In this case, you'll need to poll for the completion of the operation using the IsCompleted method of the IAsyncResult interface returned from the BeginInvoke method, simply call the EndInvoke method (which will block the current thread until the operation completes), or use the WaitHandle returned from the AsyncWaitHandle property of the IAsyncResult interface to wait for completion. In the first and third cases, you'll then need to explicitly call the End method.

Caution

> No matter which technique you use, you should be careful not to introduce locking contention into your application. In other words, ideally, each thread should access only objects and data private to it. If that can't be avoided, you can use the `Monitor` class in the `System.Threading` namespace to provide synchronized access to objects.

Interoperating with ADO

Interoperation with existing code is always important when you move to a new development platform or language, and moving to ADO.NET is no exception. In fact, many organizations will have an extensive set of COM components already developed and that may be deployed using Microsoft Transaction Server (MTS) or Component Services (COM+). In these cases, it certainly makes sense to reuse that existing code base, at least initially, rather than rewriting it all in ADO.NET. In that way, you can concentrate on implementing only the most cost-effective parts of your managed code.

To that end, ADO.NET supports integration with ADO `Recordset` objects through the `OleDbDataAdapter` object.

Reading ADO `Recordset` Data

As we discussed on Day 1, the `DataSet` object can in many respects be thought of as analogous to the disconnected `Recordset` object of ADO 2.x. As a result, it makes sense that you should be able to read an ADO `Recordset` into a `DataSet` object using a data adapter.

Although the `SqlDataAdapter` doesn't support it, the `OleDbDataAdapter` includes two overloaded signatures in its `Fill` method that accept ADO `Recordset` objects as the second parameter. Using this method, you can pass a `DataSet` to be populated into the `Fill` method along with a `Recordset`. The rules for filling the `DataSet` are the same as those discussed on Day 12, "Using Data Adapters."

20

NEW TERM However, the mechanism that makes accessing `Recordset` objects almost trivial is the **COM Interop** functionality of the .NET Framework. Simply put, COM Interop allows COM components to be called from managed code, and vice versa, by creating wrappers through which the calls pass. These wrappers, referred to as the **runtime callable wrapper (RCW)** for .NET to COM calls and the **COM callable wrapper (CCW)** for COM to .NET calls, abstract the differences between COM and .NET including reference counting versus garbage collection, COM types versus the Common Type System, type libraries versus metadata, and so forth.

> **Note**   For a list of how the ADO.NET types map to the ADO types, see the "ADO
> Type Mapping to a .NET Framework Type" topic in the online documenta-
> tion.

RCW Details

At runtime, the common language runtime creates one RCW for each COM object that
caches all references to the object from managed code. In this way, the RCW can manage
the lifetime of the COM object by dereferencing it at the appropriate time. As a result,
all calls to the COM object pass through the RCW, which is responsible for marshalling
data between the two and making sure that the appropriate interfaces are called on the
COM object. The RCW consumes the COM interfaces and therefore hides them from a
managed client. However, it retains all other custom interfaces implemented by the component and adds them to the metadata. When it does so, it exposes all members of all
implemented interfaces as a part of the managed class. In this way, a client doesn't have
to, but certainly may, cast to the appropriate interfaces before making a call to one of its
methods.

The RCW also is responsible for managing when the COM object's reference count is
decremented. The default behavior is to simply wait until the RCW is garbage collected
and to call the COM object's `Release` method at that time. Of course, when the reference
count reaches 0, the COM object deallocates itself.

For more information, see Chapter 9 of my book *Building Distributed Applications with
Visual Basic .NET*, published by Sams.

Before the component can be called by the runtime using the RCW, you must first import
it as a managed type using a metadata assembly. The easiest way to do this is to use the
Add References dialog in VS .NET. For example, assume that ComputeBooks has an
existing COM-based DLL written in VB 6.0 that exposes a `GetTitles` method that
returns a disconnected `Recordset` object. From inside a VS .NET project, you can right-
click on Add References and invoke the Add Reference dialog shown in Figure 20.1.

NEW TERM   Notice that the COM tab is activated and shows the COM components registered
on the local machine. When the `ComputeBooksData` component is selected, a
managed type is created in an **interop assembly** (or **metadata assembly**) generated in
the `obj` directory of the project called Interop.*component*, where *component* in this case
is ComputeBooksData.dll.

FIGURE 20.1

Adding a reference. This dialog enables you to add a reference to an existing COM component.

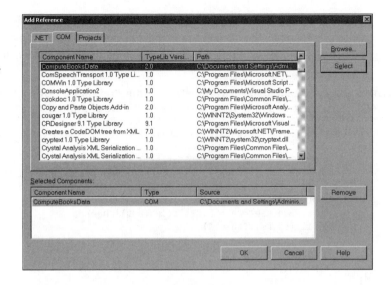

FIGURE 20.1

Adding a reference. This dialog enables you to add a reference to an existing COM component.

> **Note**
>
> You can alternatively import the COM component as a managed type using the Type Library Importer (tlbimp.exe) command-line utility or programmatically through the `System.Runtime.InteropServices.TypeLibConverter` class.

NEW TERM In addition to adding a reference to the `ComputeBooksData` component, the Add References dialog also automatically adds a reference to the **primary interop assembly (PIA)** for ADO 2.7 called ADODB. The PIA is a strongly named metadata assembly that is placed in the GAC and through which all clients will gain access to the COM component. You can think of PIAs as the "authorized" way to gain access to a COM component. Microsoft ships several PIAs (including the one for ADO) that are installed with the .NET Framework.

> **Tip**
>
> Behind the scenes, the CLSID key in the registry for the COM component can be updated with an assembly value that points to the PIA. In this way, when you select a registered COM component from the Add References dialog, VS .NET will attempt to load the PIA if it exists and, if not, prompt you to create the metadata assembly. You can create your own PIAs for COM components in your organizations using this technique as well.

20

At this point, the COM component can be called as if it were implemented in managed code. For example, the method in Listing 20.2 could be used to instantiate the COM component. It calls its `GetTitles` method to bind the resulting data to a grid control.

LISTING 20.2   Reading `Recordset` data. This method calls a COM component to retrieve an ADO `Recordset` and bind its results to a grid control using a `DataSet` object.

```
private void BindTitles(string publisher)
{
    DataSet ds = new DataSet("Titles");
    ComputeBooksData.QueryClass o = new ComputeBooksData.QueryClass();

    OleDbDataAdapter da = new OleDbDataAdapter();
    ADODB.Recordset rs = o.GetTitles(publisher);
    da.Fill(ds,rs,"Table1");

    dgTitles.DataSource = ds;
    rs.Close();
}
```

ANALYSIS   In Listing 20.2, you'll notice that the interop assembly is referenced as `ComputeBooksData.QueryClass`, where `ComputeBooks` is the name of the namespace (translated from the name of the DLL) and `QueryClass` is the name of the class. After instantiating the `OleDbDataAdapter`, the `Recordset` is retrieved into `rs` by calling the `GetTitles` method and passing it the publisher name passed into the method.

After the `Recordset` has been retrieved, it's copied into the `DataSet` using the overloaded `Fill` method, with the third argument specifying the name of the `DataTable` to populate. The `DataSet` is then bound to the `DataGrid` using the `DataSource` property.

Note   This operation is a one-way operation. In other words, when the `Recordset` is retrieved, it is read-only, so you would then need to use the `OleDbDataAdapter` or explicit commands to update the data that was retrieved.

Summary

Creating high-performance, scalable, and interoperable applications are key elements in creating applications that are accepted by users and that work with code already written and deployed.

By adhering to the query, database, and managed code techniques and using COM Interop with ADO as you learned today, you can create applications that perform well, are scalable, and that interoperate with your existing ADO components.

Tomorrow, on the final day, you'll learn about some possible future directions that ADO.NET might take in addition to summarizing some of the key information to take away from your exploration of ADO.NET.

Workshop

This workshop will help reinforce the concepts covered in today's lesson.

Quiz

1. What are two query techniques that you can use to maximize performance of your applications?

   Two rules you should always keep in mind are to ask for only the columns you will work with and, more importantly, to ask for only the rows that will be displayed. Not doing so results in extra work for the server as well as consumption of extra resources on the client or middle-tier machine.

2. Why might you not want to use command builders exposed by .NET Data Providers?

   Although command builders are convenient from the perspective of generating insert, update, and delete commands for a data adapter, they incur an extra round trip to the database server. Although the round trip happens only once, command builders also don't use stored procedures, which not only provide better performance but also abstract the database schema and can be secured.

3. What are two techniques for implementing multithreading in a .NET application?

   The .NET Framework provides the classes of the `System.Threading` namespace in addition to asynchronous delegates to create multithreaded applications. Asynchronous delegates are used throughout the Framework and are more elegant because they allow arguments to be passed into the thread and don't force you to manipulate threads directly.

4. Why might you need to use COM Interop?

   COM Interop enables you to call COM components from managed code and managed components from COM code. The former scenario is more frequent because organizations typically have existing COM components deployed that encapsulate well-tested business logic and data access code. Using COM Interop with the `OleDbDataAdapter` enables you to retrieve ADO `Recordset` objects and use them to populate `DataSet` objects.

20

Exercise

Create a console application that uses the asynchronous delegate pattern to call one of its private methods on a separate thread.

Answers for Day 20

Exercise Answer

One possible solution to the exercise follows. By using breakpoints and noting the results in the command window, you should be able to understand how the asynchronous delegate pattern works.

```
using System;
using System.Threading;
using System.Runtime.Remoting.Messaging;

namespace AsyncTest
{
        /// <summary>
        /// Summary description for Class1.
        /// </summary>
        class Class1
        {
         /// <summary>
         /// The main entry point for the application.
         /// </summary>
         private delegate int AsyncOp(string arg1);

         [STAThread]
         static void Main(string[] args)
         {
         // Show the current thread
          Console.WriteLine("Started on " + Thread.CurrentThread.GetHashCode());

           // Setup the callback
          AsyncCallback cb = new AsyncCallback(AsyncMethodDone);

           //Call the method asynchronously
          AsyncOp d = new AsyncOp(AsyncMethod);
          d.BeginInvoke("some data",cb,null);

          Console.ReadLine();
         }

         static private int AsyncMethod(string arg1)
         {
            // do the operation here, like get ADO.NET data
```

```
    // perhaps returning the number of rows
    return 5;
}

static private void AsyncMethodDone(IAsyncResult ar)
{
    // Show the current thread
    Console.WriteLine("Ended on " + Thread.CurrentThread.GetHashCode());

    // Extract the delegate from the AsyncResult.
    AsyncResult result = (AsyncResult)ar;
    AsyncOp d = (AsyncOp)result.AsyncDelegate;

    // End the operation and catch the return value
    int i = d.EndInvoke(ar);

    // Write out the return value
    Console.WriteLine("Resulting in " + i);
  }
}
}
```

20

Day 21

Futures and Wrap Up

Over the last 20 days, you've learned the ins and outs of ADO.NET and how it can be used to create high-performance, scalable, and distributed applications. However, that's not the end of the story. As with all things, change is inevitable, and in future releases of Microsoft products, including SQL Server and VS .NET, you'll see ADO.NET evolve so that it's easier to use and more integrated with other Microsoft products.

Today, in this final lesson, you'll learn about two of the directions Microsoft is taking with ADO.NET to extend its reach to the database server and to make it easier to access data in an object-oriented way.

To those ends, today you'll learn

- How ADO.NET will be extended in the next release of Microsoft SQL Server codenamed Yukon
- How ADO.NET might be extended in the next release of VS .NET through a technology called ObjectSpaces

Programming SQL Server .NET

 As mentioned on Day 1, in its initial release, ADO.NET splits the two main programming models encapsulated in the ADO Recordset object into two objects. The DataSet is analogous, although more powerful, than a disconnected Recordset, whereas the data reader is analogous to using a firehose cursor to provide forward-only, read-only, connected access to data. However, the ADO Recordset was also used to access data that remained on the database server through dynamic, server-side cursors. Late last year, Microsoft revealed how server-side data access is to be restored—and indeed greatly expanded—in ADO.NET when the next release of SQL Server code, named **Yukon,** (and probably called SQL Server .NET) is released in 2003.

> **Caution**
>
> Keep in mind that the details discussed here might change as the release of Yukon approaches. This discussion is intended only to give you an idea of what you might expect in the future.

To understand how server-side access will be implemented, the following sections discuss the benefits of allowing server-side access and a quick look at how it might be implemented.

Hosting the Common Language Runtime

The extent to which ADO.NET and the server-side programming model will be integrated is made manifest by the fact that Yukon will actually host the common language runtime in the database server process. This will allow code written in .NET assemblies to be stored in and executed by the database server, which will provide the following advantages:

- **Use of Any .NET Language**. Because the CLR will run in-process in Yukon, any .NET language can be used to write stored procedures, functions, triggers, and types. This frees developers from the restriction of only using Transact-SQL for server-side logic. Although T-SQL is functional, it's also obviously a fairly limited programming language.

- **Unified Programming Model**. By allowing managed code to run on the server, the programming model now used by ADO.NET developers can be extended to the server. In fact, Yukon will implement a server-side .NET Data Provider that will allow ADO.NET developers to leverage their current knowledge when writing server-side code.

- **Tool Leverage**. Because the code running in Yukon is simply managed code, you'll be able to leverage the same tools that you use today to build, debug, and manage ADO.NET applications. For example, VS .NET will be extended to create projects for Yukon and the debugger will be enhanced to allow integrated debugging in which you can step from client to server code across languages and across both managed and T-SQL code.

- **Performance**. Because the server-side .NET Data Provider will be hosted in the same process as the database engine, it won't have to use tabular data stream (TDS) to communicate with the server. Instead, it will have direct access to the server's data structures, offering it the highest performance possible. In addition, the provider will be integrated with Yukon's threading model, and Yukon will integrate with the managed garbage collector so as to efficiently use server resources. In fact, in preliminary tests, the compiled nature of managed code running on Yukon indicated that it would be much faster for complex expressions than the equivalent T-SQL expressions.

Accessing Data

As mentioned in the previous section, with Yukon, a server-side .NET Data Provider will be shipped that implements the ADO.NET programming model for writing code that lives on the server. That provider will likely contain the `System.Data.SqlServer` namespace.

From within a VS .NET project, you can then reference the `SqlServer` namespace and write functions, stored procedures, triggers, and types as methods exposed in a managed class. Those methods will make heavy use of the existing `System.Data.SqlTypes` namespace as the types for parameters passed to the methods and return values.

 Note

The types in the `SqlTypes` namespace have the major advantage of mapping directly to SQL Server types, of course, but also handle NULL values as expected for SQL Server, which decreases the amount of code you need to write.

For example, you could write a function to calculate the revenue generated for a particular book, as shown in Listing 21.1.

LISTING 21.1 Creating a function. This listing shows how you might create a function in Yukon using managed code.

```
using System.Data.SqlServer;
using System.Data.SqlTypes;
```

21

LISTING 21.1 continued

```
public class Books {
  public static SqlMoney RevByBook( string isbn )
  {
    SqlCommand cmd = SqlContext.GetCommand( );
    cmd.CommandText = "SELECT SUM(Quantity * UnitPrice) AS Revenue " +
    "FROM OrderDetails WHERE ISBN = @isbn";

    SqlParameter param = cmd.Parameters.Add("@isbn",
        SqlDbType.NVarChar, 10);
    param.Value = isbn;
    SqlMoney amount = cmd.ExecuteScalar( );
    return amount;
  }
}
```

ANALYSIS As you can see from Listing 21.1, the Books class simply contains the RevByBook method that accepts an ISBN and returns the amount of revenue generated using the SqlMoney type from the SqlTypes namespace.

Because the SqlServer namespace implements the common ADO.NET provider programming model, its SqlCommand object supports the CommandText and ExecuteScalar methods and exposes a set of SqlParameter objects associated with the command. Note that the command is generated using a static method of the SqlContext object that exposes information about the current context in which the code is executing, such as the connection information.

After the assembly is compiled, it can be saved in the database using a set of extensions for T-SQL. For example, the CREATE ASSEMBLY statement can be used to load the assembly into the server and register its contents like so:

```
CREATE ASSEMBLY CbksServer FROM '\\server1\sql\cbksserver.dll'
        WITH PERMISSION_SET = SAFE
        WITH AUTOREGISTER
```

In this case, the assembly is loaded into the server and referenced as CbksServer. The PERMISSION SET attribute specifies which of the code access security (CAS) permission sets to associate with the assembly. It is thought that assemblies will be able to be assigned SAFE, EXTERNAL_ACCESS, or UNRESTRICTRED permission sets, where SAFE allows only data access and computation, EXTERNAL_ACCESS allows calls to other managed code, and UNRESTRICTRED allows unmanaged and other managed code to be called similarly to extended stored procedures today. As you might expect, only a system administrator will be able to place assemblies in the third category.

It's important to remember that once the assembly has been created, as in the previous snippet, the actual bits for the assembly are stored inside the database server, so the path to the original assembly needn't be saved. This allows the server to fully manage the assembly, for example, so that it will be a part of database backups and restores.

The AUTOREGISTER attribute can be used to automatically register specific methods in the assembly as stored procedures, functions, triggers, or types using attributes in the SqlServer namespace. If the attributes are not present, you must then use the extensions to the T-SQL CREATE FUNCTION, CREATE PROCEDURE, CREATE TRIGGER, and CREATE TYPE statements. For example, the CREATE FUNCTION statement could then be written as follows:

```
CREATE FUNCTION RevByBook (@isbn nchar(10)) RETURNS money
EXTERNAL NAME 'CbksServer:Books.RevByBook'
DETERMINISTIC
RETURNS NULL ON NULL INPUT
```

As you can see, the RevByBook function accepts the same ISBN and returns the money SQL Server data type. The function is then mapped to the RevByBook method of the Books class in the "CbksServer" assembly.

There will be some restrictions on how the managed methods can be defined in order to map to specific SQL Server objects. For example, functions must be static and deterministic although stored procedures will be able to contain data definition language (DDL) and return result sets directly to clients.

To assist in the development of managed code for the server, you'll likely see two major improvements when Yukon ships:

- **SQL Server Work Bench**. This management tool, which will ship with Yukon, can be thought of as a code-management subset of VS .NET that makes deployment and versioning of assemblies and managing projects in the database easier. For example, it will contain a way to deploy assemblies to multiple servers.

- **Extensions to VS .NET**. VS .NET will also be extended with new project types that make it easier to create "server assemblies" that integrate T-SQL and managed code. These templates will ensure that the projects fit the requirements for deployment in Yukon. For example, by making sure that the code is verifiable and can be used with the predefined permission sets mentioned previously.

21

As a whole, this deep level of integration with Yukon will both enable you to leverage your ADO.NET skills on the server side and make your applications more responsive and maintainable.

Using ObjectSpaces

NEW TERM Also last fall, Microsoft revealed preliminary plans for tighter integration of object orientation with ADO.NET through a technical preview referred to as the **Microsoft ObjectSpaces framework**. This framework consists of a set of classes and interfaces grouped in a namespace (Microsoft.ObjectSpaces) that provides an object-oriented mapping layer to access data and might be shipped with a future release of VS .NET. This framework builds on the classes of ADO.NET and those in the System.Xml namespace to provide access to both XML data sources and relational data sources. Figure 21.1 shows the high-level architecture of the ObjectSpaces framework.

FIGURE 21.1

The Microsoft ObjectSpaces architecture adapted from the SDK documentation.

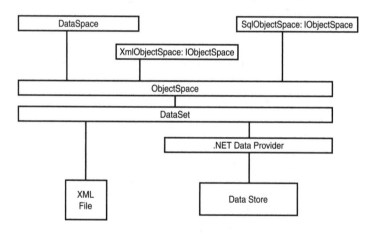

> **Caution**
>
> Just as with the discussion of Yukon, the ObjectSpaces framework is highly preliminary and should be used only as an idea of what you might see in a future release of VS .NET.

Note that ObjectSpaces provides three primary ways of abstracting data: through the DataSpace, the XmlObjectSpace, or the SqlObjectSpace classes. All three of these classes are derived from ObjectSpace and all read and write their data to an underlying DataSet that is eventually synchronized with a persistent store, such as an XML file or a database using a .NET Data Provider.

The primary difference between the DataSpace and both the XmlObjectSpace and the SqlObjectSpace is that the DataSpace has no inherent persistent store and can simply be created from any existing DataSet. The other two objects implement the IObjectSpace interface, so they can be used polymorphically so that client code needn't be concerned with whether the data resides in XML or in a relational database. In all three cases, the actual data always resides in a DataSet and is simply mapped into and out of the object dynamically by the ObjectSpace object.

To get a feel for how ObjectSpaces work, the following sections will show a simple example of providing object-oriented access to the ComputeBooks Customers table in SQL Server 2000.

Note

For a longer treatment of ObjectSpaces and how it compares architecturally with Enterprise Java Beans (EJB), see my two-part series on the subject on www.informit.com. Note that the example used here is the same as that discussed in the article.

Creating the Persistent Class

NEW TERM   The first task in exposing data using ObjectSpaces is to define the interface of the entity or object you wish to expose. In the ObjectSpaces Framework, defining the object is accomplished by creating a single **persistent class**. The persistent class is actually an abstract class (defined with MustInherit in VB or abstract in C#) that defines the properties, fields, methods, and events used by the client. Listing 21.2 shows the persistent class for the Customer object written in VB.

LISTING 21.2   A persistent Customer class. This class is used as the base class to allow the ObjectSpaces framework to represent a customer.

```
Namespace ComputeBooks.Data
  Public MustInherit Class CustomerOS

    Public MustOverride ReadOnly Property Id() As Integer
    Public MustOverride Property FName() As String
    Public MustOverride Property LName() As String
    Public MustOverride Property Address() As String
    Public MustOverride Property City() As String
    Protected MustOverride Property _stateProv() As String
    Public MustOverride Property PostalCode() As String
    Public MustOverride Property EmailAddress() As String

    <AliasAttribute("_stateProv")> _
```

21

LISTING 21.2   continued

```vb
        Public Property StateProv() As String
          Get
            Return _stateProv
          End Get
          Set(ByVal Value As String)
            If Len(Trim(Value)) <> 2 Then
              Throw New ArgumentException("State must be 2 characters")
            Else
              _stateProv = Trim(Value)
            End If
          End Set
        End Property

        Public ReadOnly Property Name() As String
          Get
            Return Trim(Me.FName) & " " & Trim(Me.LName)
          End Get
        End Property

        Public Sub OnCreate() 'can accept arguments
          ' called at object creation
        End Sub

        Public Sub OnMaterialize()
          ' called the first time an object is retrieved from the data store
        End Sub

        Public Sub OnDelete()
          ' called when the object is deleted from the ObjectSpace
        End Sub

      End Class
    End Namespace
```

ANALYSIS   At runtime, the ObjectSpaces framework creates a derived class from the persistent class and maps the data from the DataSet into and out of the members of the class. In addition, you'll notice that you can provide your own properties and methods, such as Name in Listing 21.2, that can be calculated from other members or perform other business functions.

Two of the interesting features of the persistent class are that you can insert business logic into the Get and Set blocks of a property, and you can reference remote methods to abstract business logic. The former feature is illustrated in the StateProv property that aliases the abstract _stateProv property by including the AliasAttribute and includes logic to validate the property as it is populated in the Set block. The latter feature is beyond the scope of this book, but entails creating an abstract method in the persistent class and then referencing the remote method in the XML mapping file discussed later.

Another interesting feature of the persistent class is that it supports the OnCreate, OnMaterialize, and OnDelete methods called by the ObjectSpaces framework when the object is created, populated from the data store, and removed, respectively. Although not shown in Listing 21.2, the OnCreate method is particularly useful for passing arguments to the class as it is instantiated and can be used, for example, to assign a client-generated primary key value to the object.

Although not shown in Listing 21.2, the persistent class can also include attributes that identify the primary key field and that link persistent classes in a parent-child relationship. In that way, when the ObjectSpaces framework instantiates an object of type Customer; for example, the client would be able to traverse the Orders for that customer as well, assuming you created a persistent class for Orders.

Creating the Mapping Files

After the persistent class is complete, you can create an XML mapping file and source file that define how columns in a database map to the properties of the persistent class and the data store connection information for that class, respectively.

 Note

> As an alternative to simply creating the mapping file by hand, the ObjectSpaces framework will likely ship with a graphical tool that can be accessed by right-clicking on the project in VS .NET and selecting the template item under Add New Item.

Listing 21.3 shows the simple mapping file for the Customer persistent class.

LISTING 21.3 XML mapping file. This file is used by the ObjectSpaces framework to map database tables and columns to the persistent class.

```
<map xmlns="http://www.microsoft.com/ObjectSpaces-v1">
  <type name="Customer" dataSource="Customers" source="ComputeBooks">
    <uniqueKey name="Id" mappedBy="autoIncrement" dataSource="CustomerId"/>
    <property name="FName" dataSource="FName"/>
    <property name="LName" dataSource="LName"/>
    <property name="Address" dataSource="Address"/>
    <property name="City" dataSource="City"/>
    <property name="_stateProv" dataSource="StateProv"/>
    <property name="PostalCode" dataSource="PostalCode"/>
    <property name="EmailAddress" dataSource="EmailAddress"/>
  </type>
</map>
```

21

ANALYSIS   You'll notice from Listing 21.3 that the type element is used to reference the persistent class in addition to specifying the name of the table (dataSource) and the connection (source) to use to get to the table. Each property element maps a property of the persistent class (name) to the name of a column in the table (dataSource). In addition, here the primary key is identified using the uniqueKey element and mapping it to the CustomerId column in the table. The mappedBy attribute indicates that the column is generated automatically by the data source for use with IDENTITY columns in SQL Server and sequences in Oracle. Because the Id property is generated from the data In addition to creating the mapping file, you also provide a connection file as shown here:

```
<sources xmlns="http://www.microsoft.com/ObjectSpaces-v1">
  <source name="ComputeBooks" adapter="sql"
   connection="Data Source=ssosa; Integrated Security=SSPI;
Database=ComputeBooks"/>
</sources>
```

The connection file simply identifies the connection (source) referenced in the mapping file in addition to the .NET Data Provider to use (sql or oledb) and the connection string to pass to the database server. By putting the connection information in an XML file, you can abstract it from the client code as well.

Querying the Customer

After the mapping and connection files are in place, the client can write code against the persistent class using the XmlObjectSpace or SqlObjectSpace classes. For example, to query a single customer, you could write the following code:

```
Dim os As New SqlObjectSpace("connect.xml", "map.xml")
Dim myCustomer As Customer
Dim strName As String

myCustomer = CType(os.GetObject(GetType(Customer), "Id = 1"), Customer)
strName = myCustomer.Name
```

NEW TERM   First, the SqlObjectSpace object is instantiated and passed the connection and mapping files shown previously. SqlObjectSpace is used because the data exists in a relational database. Next, the myCustomer object is populated using the GetObject method of SqlObjectSpace inherited from the IObjectSpace interface. You'll notice that the string "Id = 1" is passed as the second argument. This syntax is referred to as **OPath**, a derivative of XPath, which Microsoft developed specifically for the ObjectSpaces framework. Behind the scenes, the ObjectSpaces framework uses the combination of the OPath query and the mapping and connect files to connect to the database and formulate a SELECT statement to retrieve the customer identified with the CustomerID of 1. The result is then mapped into the myCustomer object, where the properties such as Name are then available.

In addition, through the `GetObjects` method of the `IObjectSpace` interface, you can automatically query multiple objects like so:

```
For Each myCustomer In os.GetObjects(GetType(Customer), "City = 'Richmond'")
  Console.WriteLine(vbCrLf & "Customer Id: " & myCustomer.Id & _
      vbCrLf & "Name: " & myCustomer.Name & _
      vbCrLf & "City: " & myCustomer.City & _
      vbCrLf & "PostalCode: " & myCustomer.PostalCode & vbCrLf)
Next
```

Once again, the framework formulates the correct `SELECT` statement based on the OPath query and configuration files.

Because both the `XmlObjectSpace` and `SqlObjectSpace` classes inherit the `IObjectSpace` interface, you can also program against either one polymorphically by simply referencing a variable of type `IObjectSpace` and using the `CreateObjectSpace` method of the `ObjectSpaceFactory` class like so:

```
Dim os As IObjectSpace = ObjectSpaceFactory.CreateObjectSpace("customer.xml")
```

In this case, customer.xml is a file that specifies the `ObjectSpace` object to use and the arguments to pass to its constructor as shown in the following code snippet. Here the `type` attribute points to the `SqlObjectSpace` object that will be used, whereas the `arg` elements point to the mapping files discussed previously.

```
<objectspace type="Microsoft.ObjectSpaces.SqlObjectSpace"
  xmlns="http://www.microsoft.com/ObjectSpaces-v1">
    <arg>connect.xml</arg>
    <arg>map.xml</arg>
</objectspace>
```

Updating the Customer

Of course, you can also create new rows in a database using ObjectSpaces. This is done using the `CreateObject` method of the `IObjectSpace` interface. The code in Listing 21.4 creates a new customer and populates its properties before calling the `Update` method to persist the object in the data store.

LISTING 21.4   Creating a new customer. This listing creates a new customer using the `CreateObject` method and saves it using the `UpdateAll` method.

```
myCustomer = CType(os.CreateObject(GetType(Customer)), Customer)

With myCustomer
    .FName = "Beth"
    .LName = "Fox"
    .Address = "21508 W44th"
```

21

LISTING 21.4 continued

```
        .City = "Overland Park"
        .StateProv = "MO"
        .PostalCode = "33221"
        .EmailAddress = "bethafox@foxden.com"
    End With

    Try
      ' Save Changes
      os.Update(myCustomer)
    Catch ex As UpdateException
      ' Handle error
    End Try

    Console.WriteLine("New ID = " & myCustomer.Id)
```

 ANALYSIS You'll notice from Listing 21.4 that the Update method is passed the new customer. The framework then proceeds to generate an INSERT or UPDATE SQL statement as appropriate and execute it on the data source. If the update succeeds, the framework automatically populates the new Id generated from the database.

If multiple customers are modified or added, the UpdateAll method can be used instead and can accept different arguments specified in the UpdateBehavior enumeration. For example, specifying the ThrowAtFirstError value will throw an exception as soon as the first error is returned from the data source. The IObjectSpace interface also supports Resync and ResyncAll methods that can be used to synchronize one or more objects from the data store to the client.

Note Although persistence managed by the ObjectSpaces Framework doesn't directly support stored procedures in the technical preview version, look for it to do so at least with the SQL Server .NET Data Provider in future releases.

The example shown today allows the ObjectSpaces Framework to handle the persistence to the data source automatically. However, when the data is more complex or comes from heterogeneous sources, you can opt to perform the persistence yourself.

This is accomplished by creating a class derived from the ObjectCustomizer abstract class and implementing methods such as CreateRow, GetRow, GetRows, InsertRows, UpdateRows, DeleteRows, GetChildRows, and GetParentRow. The class is then referenced in the type element of the mapping file so that the framework can instantiate it and call its methods when appropriate.

Summary and Final Thoughts

Even though ADO.NET was very recently released, you can see that things will continue to change as new server products such as SQL Server and subsequent versions of VS .NET are released. In both cases, however, a solid foundation in ADO.NET will make it easier to adjust to the changes because they incorporate many of same concepts and programming elements.

Over the last 21 days, you've journeyed through the depths of ADO.NET and have come to a fuller understanding of its goals, features, limitations, and promise for developing applications using VS .NET and the .NET Framework. Along the way, I hope I've also been able to share some ideas and techniques for applying ADO.NET in your applications.

I used the famous quote, "It is a capital mistake to theorize before one has data," from Sherlock Holmes in the Introduction. Now that you have the tools to obtain the data, you can build great applications to help your users theorize on the data to solve their business problems.

Workshop

This workshop will help reinforce the concepts covered in today's lesson.

Quiz

1. How will Yukon affect ADO.NET development?

   Yukon, the next release of SQL Server, will add extensions to ADO.NET that make server-side data access available. For example, it is likely that a namespace called `System.Data.SqlServer` will contain objects that enable you to open and manipulate server-side cursors. In addition, you'll be able to write stored procedures using managed code.

2. What are the benefits of hosting the common language runtime in SQL Server?

   Hosting the common language runtime in SQL Server will allow managed code to be used for server-side objects such as stored procedures, triggers, functions, and types. This means that those objects can be written in any of the more than 25 .NET languages, both the programming model and the developer tools can be leveraged, and performance can be increased.

3. What is the primary benefit of the ObjectSpaces Framework?

   ObjectSpaces abstracts the .NET Data Provider and database syntax from the client application while providing object-based access to the data. In that respect, it

21

combines some of the features we discussed in the `DataFactory` class on Day 18, "Building a Data Factory," with the approach of using custom classes we discussed on Day 17, "ADO.NET in the Data Services Tier."

4. How does ObjectSpaces accomplish its "objectification" of data?

   ObjectSpaces relies on what is called a persistent class that is marked as `MustInherit` (base in C#) and uses this class to create derived objects at runtime. The provider and database independence are achieved through the use of mapping files and the `SqlObjectSpace` and `XmlObjectSpace` classes.

Exercise

Your only exercise for today is to go out and create great ADO.NET applications.

WEEK 3

In Review

I hope that you've enjoyed the last three weeks and the time you've spent with ADO.NET! The last week focused on the design and implementation of multi-tier applications by focusing on each of the tiers, ranging from a high-level design view to the low-level implementation.

Among the key takeaways from this week should be that ADO.NET can be used to create high-performance distributed applications at least in part because of its ability to use data binding in Windows Forms and Web Forms applications, the ability to create an abstracted data services tier, and its ability to be used from within XML Web Services. You should also now understand the various techniques you can use and the reasons you might want to abstract the .NET Data Provider you intend to use in your applications.

Finally, this week should have reminded you that learning ADO.NET is time well spent because ADO.NET will play a big part in future directions on both the server and client side.

Now, you really should take a break, and it can even be a long one.

15

16

17

18

19

20

21

INDEX

Symbols

* (asterisk), wildcard character, 64
[ ] (brackets), Assembly class, 491
... (ellipsis) button, 35
( ) (parentheses), 64
% (percent sign), wildcard character, 64
# (pound sign), 64
; (semicolon), 219-220
' (single quotation mark), 64
<%# %> tags, data binding expressions, 433
_ (underscore), prefixes, 463

A

Abort method, threads, 542
abstract base classes
    conditional tracing, 454-456
    connection management, 453
    creating, 450-454
    custom exceptions, 456-457
    exception handling, 454
    tracing, 454
abstract factory patterns, 414
abstracted providers in data services tier, 414
abstracting
    data with ObjectSpaces framework, 558-559
    data providers, 470-476, 488-493
    statements, 493-505

abstractions, stored procedures, 247, 347
AcceptChanges method, 60
    DataRow class, 88
    DataSet class, 56
    DataTable class, 83
    rows, 114
    table rows, 126
AcceptChangesDuringFill property, data adapters, 195
accepting connection strings, code, 228
AcceptRejectRule property, 102
Access, 8
accessing
    data, 32, 44, 353-358, 363
    Excel, 370
    ODBC data sources, 362-370
    XML (eXtensible Markup Language) documents, 374

G

How can we make this index more useful? Email us at indexes@samspublishing.com

Y-Z

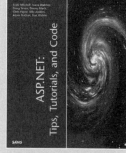